Newman's
BIRDS
OF SOUTHERN AFRICA

Newman's BIRDS OF SOUTHERN AFRICA

by Kenneth Newman

Illustrated by the author

To Ursula, Vanessa, Nicholas and Pamela

Struik Publishers (Pty) Ltd
(a member of The Struik New Holland Publishing Group (Pty) Ltd)
Cornelis Struik House
80 McKenzie Street
Cape Town 8001

Reg. No.: 1954/000965/07

First published in 1983 by Macmillan South Africa (Publishers) (Pty) Ltd
Published by Southern Book Publishers (Pty) Ltd in 1988
Published by Struik Publishers (Pty) Ltd in 2000

First Struik softcover edition 2000
ISBN: 1 86872 494 8
3 5 7 9 10 8 6 4 2

First Struik hardcover edition 2000
ISBN: 1 86872 493 X
1 3 5 7 9 10 8 6 4 2

First Struik pvc edition 2000
ISBN: 1 86872 492 1
1 3 5 7 9 10 8 6 4 2

Cover design by Alix Gracie
Concept design by Alix Gracie
Typesetting by Gerhardt van Rooyen
Set in 7/9 pt Akzidenz Grotesk

Edited and proofread by Marina Pearson
Illustrated by Ken Newman

Reproduction by Hirt & Carter Cape (Pty) Ltd
Printed and bound by NBD, Drukkery Street, Goodwood, Western Cape

Contents

Acknowledgements

This, the seventh edition of *Newman's Birds of Southern Africa* was originally planned to accommodate updated bird distribution maps based on that magnificent 1997 publication *The Atlas of Southern African Birds*, produced by the Avian Demography Unit at the University of Cape Town and published under the banner of BirdLife South Africa. While the new maps remain the major purpose of this revision it was while working with the Atlas that I discovered also a wealth of new information relating to bird distributions in southern Africa, their sub-speciations, habitats and movements. I felt unashamedly compelled to plunder this previously unpublished data for the benefit of the fieldguide. In the event one thing led to another and, since it became inevitable that the entire text would need resetting, my publisher decided to also give the book a new look with the emphasis on even greater user-friendliness.

I am greatly indebted to Prof. L.G. Underhill, James Harrison and their team of editors, namely D.G. Allan, M. Herremans, A.J. Tree, V. Parker and C.J. Brown, for collectively compiling the results of the 1987-92 atlasing fieldwork, involving as it did millions of records from six southern African countries. Without their enthusiasm and dedication towards the publication of the Atlas much of the data now freely available to the birding public may have remained unpublished for many more years.

I am also indebted to SAPPI Limited, for that organisation's continuing support and supply of Dukuza Fine Art Paper on which the book was printed.

These acknowledgements would be far from complete without mention of the expertise and input of Louise Grantham, Publishing Director of Southern Book Publishers (Pty) Limited. Louise's own interest in birds, coupled with her experience in natural history book publishing and her apparently inexhaustible enthusiasm for new books, has made my work on this edition (and others) a pleasure.

Kenneth Newman

Sponsor's foreword

Sappi has been associated with the Kenneth Newman bird book for the last three years. During this period we were astounded by the exponential growth of the birding fraternity in Southern Africa.

When we heard that Ken was planning an update of the popular Green Edition and that he was going to incorporate the latest information contained in the *Atlas of Southern African Birds*, we had no hesitation in supporting this new expanded edition. We are committed to increasing the awareness of all of our people of the importance and sensitivity of our environment and this new edition of *Newman's Birds of Southern Africa* will play an important role in creating that awareness.

As a significant landowner in this region, Sappi takes care in the way we manage our landholdings. Sappi supports the work of various nature conservation agencies in an effort to promote an understanding and appreciation of the richness and diversity of our environment. In addition, the company remains committed to a number of environmental sponsorships closely related to our business as we recognise the need to provide opportunities for future generations to grow in an environment of knowledge and expertise.

In line with this commitment we are therefore proud to once again be associated with *Newman's Birds of Southern Africa*. We wish you many hours of enjoyment in your garden or in the wild, improving your knowledge of our feathered friends.

Eugene van As

Executive Chairman

SAPPI Limited

Colour coding index

Ocean, Offshore and Subantarctic Birds

Inland Waterbirds

Ducks, Wading Birds and Shorebirds

Terrestrial Birds

Raptors

Sandgrouse, Doves, Parrots, Louries, Cuckoos, Coucals and Trogon

Owls and Nightjars

Aerial Feeders, Mousebirds, Hole Nesters and Honeyguides

Insect-eaters – Larks to Robins

Insect-eaters – Warblers to Starlings

Oxpeckers and Nectar Feeders

Seed-eaters

The birds of southern Africa

This fieldguide covers the whole of the southern African subregion as well as the subantarctic region adjacent to the continent.

Southern Africa is generally accepted as being that part of Africa lying south of the Zambezi-Okavango-Cunene rivers, or approximately 17°S. It embraces several national states and a diversity of geophysical regions ranging from tropical coasts to the most arid desert, and its bird fauna is correspondingly diverse. As might be expected, the birds show strong affinities with the avifauna of the rest of Africa south of the Sahara Desert (the Afrotropical region). The great majority of birds found in the subregion therefore also occur north of its limits.

ENDEMIC SPECIES

Of special interest, however, are the endemics: those species found in southern Africa and nowhere else. There are 95 endemics in the region and 72 near-endemics (species whose distribution extends just beyond southern Africa).

Southern African endemics

Apalis, Chirinda
Batis, Cape
Blackcap, Bush
Boubou, Southern
Bulbul, Cape
Bustard, Stanley's
Buzzard, Forest
Buzzard, Jackal
Canary, Black-eared
Canary, Black-headed
Canary, Forest
Canary, Protea
Chat, Ant-eating
Chat, Buff-streaked
Chat, Karoo
Chat, Mountain
Chat, Sickle-winged
Cormorant, Bank
Cormorant, Cape
Cormorant, Crowned
Courser, Burchell's
Crane, Blue
Eremomela, Karoo
Finchlark, Black-eared
Flycatcher, Fairy
Flycatcher, Fiscal
Francolin, Cape
Francolin, Grey-wing
Gannet, Cape
Grassbird
Gull, Hartlaub's
Harrier, Black
Ibis, Bald
Korhaan, Black
Korhaan, Blue
Korhaan, Karoo
Korhaan, White-bellied
Korhaan, White-winged
Lark, Barlow's
Lark, Botha's
Lark, Dune
Lark, Karoo
Lark, Melodious
Lark, Red
Lark, Rudd's
Lark, Sclater's
Lark, Short-clawed
Lark, Thick-billed
Longclaw, Orange-throated
Mousebird, White-backed
Oystercatcher, African Black
Penguin, Jackass
Pipit, Rock
Pipit, Yellow-breasted
Prinia, Karoo
Prinia, Saffron
Robin, Brown
Robin, Chorister
Robin, Karoo
Robin, White-throated
Rock Thrush, Cape
Rock Thrush, Sentinel
Rockjumper, Cape
Rockjumper, Orange-breasted

Shelduck, South African
Shoveller, Cape
Siskin, Cape
Siskin, Drakensberg
Starling, Pied
Sugarbird, Cape
Sugarbird, Gurney's
Sunbird, Greater Double-collared
Sunbird, Lesser Double-collared
Sunbird, Neergaard's
Sunbird, Orange-breasted
Swallow, Black Saw-wing
Swallow, South African Cliff
Tchagra, Southern
Tit, Cape Penduline
Tit, Southern Grey
Titbabbler, Layard's
Twinspot, Pink-throated
Vulture, Cape
Warbler, Barratt's
Warbler, Brier
Warbler, Cinnamon-breasted
Warbler, Knysna
Warbler, Namaqua
Warbler, Rufous-eared
Warbler, Victorin's
Weaver, Cape
Weaver, Sociable
White-eye, Cape
Woodpecker, Ground
Woodpecker, Knysna

Southern African near-endemics

Apalis, Rudd's
Babbler, Bare-cheeked
Babbler, Pied
Barbet, Pied
Batis, Pririt
Batis, Woodwards'
Bokmakierie
Boubou, Crimson-breasted
Bulbul, Red-eyed
Bunting, Cape
Bunting, Lark-like
Bush Shrike, Olive
Bustard, Ludwig's
Canary, Lemon-breasted
Canary, White-throated
Canary, Yellow
Chat, Herero
Chat, Tractrac
Cisticola, Cloud
Cisticola, Grey-backed
Coucal, Burchell's
Finch, Red-headed
Finch, Scaly-feathered
Finchlark, Grey-backed
Flycatcher, Chat
Flycatcher, Marico
Francolin, Hartlaub's
Francolin, Natal
Francolin, Red-billed
Francolin, Swainson's
Goshawk, Pale Chanting
Hornbill, Bradfield's
Hornbill, Monteiro's
Hornbill, Southern Yellow-billed
Korhaan, Red-crested
Korhaan, Rüppell's
Lark, Clapper
Lark, Gray's
Lark, Long-billed
Lark, Monotonous
Lark, Pink-billed
Lark, Sabota
Lark, Spike-heeled
Lark, Stark's
Lovebird, Rosy-faced
Parrot, Rüppell's
Prinia, Black-chested
Robin, Kalahari
Rock Thrush, Short-toed
Rockrunner
Sandgrouse, Burchell's
Sandgrouse, Double-banded
Sandgrouse, Namaqua
Shrike, White-crowned
Shrike, White-tailed
Sparrow, Cape
Starling, Burchell's Glossy
Starling, Cape Glossy
Starling, Long-tailed Glossy
Starling, Pale-winged
Sunbird, Dusky
Swallow, Greater Striped
Swift, Bradfield's
Tern, Damara
Tit, Ashy
Tit, Carp's Black
Tit, Southern Black
Titbabbler
Warbler, Barred
Waxbill, Swee
Waxbill, Violet-eared
Whydah, Shaft-tailed

INTRODUCED SPECIES

Many birds have been introduced into southern Africa in past years, but only eight species survive today. They are:

- Chukar Partridge
- Feral Pigeon
- Rose-ringed Parakeet
- (Indian) House Crow
- Indian Myna
- European Starling
- (European) House Sparrow
- Chaffinch

SEABIRDS

In addition to the wide variety of landbirds, the southern African coasts are visited by numerous pelagic seabirds, many of which breed on islands in the southern oceans. These seabirds, ranging in size from the diminutive storm petrels to the enormous albatrosses, are often very difficult to identify. Not only are many identified only by small details of plumage or flight pattern, but, in addition, they are normally glimpsed from the pitching deck of a ship or from wind-blasted and rain-lashed shores as they mount upwards briefly from a wave trough before descending again out of sight. Such are the difficulties of getting to grips with seabird identities that for many years little interest was shown in them by the average land-based birdwatcher. Even so, the birds of the northern seas have always been better known than those of the southern oceans through their more frequent contact with land. Since the 1960s, a gradual change has come about because of a new interest by leading nations of the world in the southern islands and in Antarctica itself. Permanent stations have been established for, among other things, weather monitoring. Teams of scientists are permanently or temporarily stationed in these inhospitable regions for the purpose of studying the ocean and its resources. As an example, the Percy FitzPatrick Institute of African Ornithology in Cape Town has for many years been studying seabird life in the seas adjacent to southern Africa. A succession of its researchers has been based on Marion Island, from where periodic visits are made to other islands as far afield as the Tristan da Cunha group, and much has been learned about the population dynamics, feeding ecologies and breeding biologies of some ocean birds. Stemming from this new interest in the southern seabirds, and the increased need for a specific guide to those found in southern African seas, the entire region south to the pack ice has been included in this fieldguide. Not only does it embrace all seabirds known to reach the shores of southern Africa, but also those that will be seen on or in the vicinity of the Tristan group (Tristan, Nightingale and Inaccessible islands), Gough, Bouvet, Marion and Prince Edward islands: a total of 19 additional species including some landbirds.

South Africa has recently extended its territorial waters to 200 nautical miles offshore in order to better protect its fisheries from foreign exploiters. This has led to an increase in sightings of ocean birds that now qualify for inclusion in the southern African species list. These ocean birds, most of which are unlikely to be seen by shorebound birders, are included in the Recent Vagrants section of the fieldguide from p. 444 onwards.

Identifying birds

With the array of birds that can be seen in southern Africa (over 900 species), identifying the bird you have seen can be extremely challenging. To make this process easier you need the right equipment, you need to use the equipment you have correctly and you need to make sure that you notice the features of the bird and its environment that will lead to an accurate identification.

WHAT DO YOU NEED TO IDENTIFY BIRDS?

Binoculars

Binoculars are an essential part of a birdwatcher's equipment; hardly any bird can be properly studied without them. Many good makes are available and 7 x 30, 8 x 35 or 10 x 40 are recommended. The first figure indicates the magnification and the second the field of view.

Generally speaking, the greater the diameter of the front, or objective, lens in proportion to the rear lens, or eyepiece, the more light is gathered and transmitted, and so the brighter the image. Many people also use a telescope to study distant, difficult-to-identify species.

Fieldguides and handbooks

A fieldguide is the next essential part of the birdwatcher's equipment. The fieldguide concept originated in the late 1930s in response to the need for portability coupled with ease of reference. First was the now famous series by Roger Tory Peterson, covering the birds of the United States of America. Later the idea caught on in Britain, Europe and elsewhere. For the serious birdwatcher a fieldguide is only a supplement to a more comprehensive and informative bird handbook, the latter usually being too bulky and cumbersome for normal fieldwork. The main purpose of a fieldguide is to help the observer identify a species speedily from an illustration and a brief description of plumage and song. More comprehensive information about the bird may then be sought at leisure from the appropriate handbook. Leading handbooks of the birds

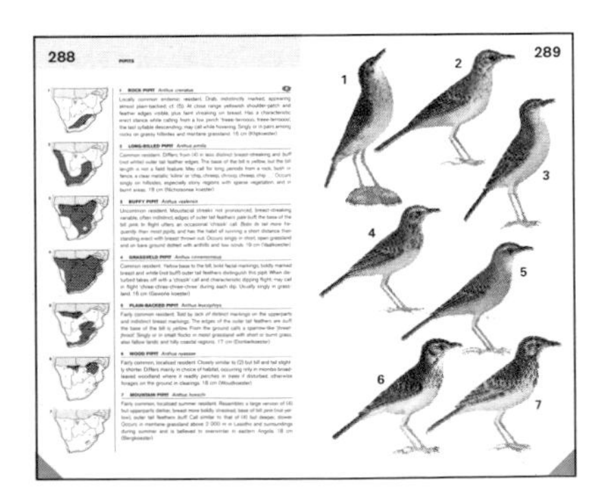
288

289

1
2
3
4
5
6
7

of the southern African subregion are the multi-volume *Birds of Africa* by the late Leslie Brown *et al.* and *Roberts' Birds of Southern Africa* by Gordon Lindsay Maclean, based on the original edition by the late Austin Roberts. In designing *Newman's Birds of Southern Africa* our first consideration has always been to make species identification in the field as simple as possible. Read pages 1–18 for detailed guidance on using this guide in a quick and easy identification process.

Bird-call tapes or compact discs

When learning the songs and calls of birds the use of either bird-call tapes or CDs can help tremendously. A wide range of tapes and CDs is available and many are linked to this fieldguide.

WHAT TO LOOK FOR WHEN YOU SEE A BIRD

It is a good idea to be aware of what you should look out for when you see a bird you wish to identify. The following six rules will help; try to memorise them. With practice they will come to mind automatically when you look at a new bird and will help you to remember its important features. If possible write what you have seen in a notebook at the time of sighting.

1. What is the bird's relative size?

Compare the bird with common ones that are well known to you. Is it larger or smaller than a sparrow? If larger, is it larger or smaller than a city pigeon? If larger, is it larger or smaller than a guineafowl?

14–15 cm

33 cm

53–58 cm

2. What is the bird's bill shape and colour?

The shape of a bird's bill is a guide to what it eats and therefore to the kind of bird it is. Is its bill short, stout and conical like that of a sparrow, or is it small and slender, long and slender, long and curved, powerful and hooked, etc.? What colour is its bill? Many birds have blackish bills but some bills are brightly coloured.

Insect-eater

Flower-prober

3. What length and colour are its legs?

Does the bird have unusually long legs, such as are found in many that wade in water or walk in long grass, or short legs as seen in swallows and swifts? Are its legs a distinctive colour?

4. What plumage colours or markings strike you?

If the bird has bold markings on its head, wings, body or tail these should be noted, as should any bright colours. Many birds have white wing-bars or tail-bars, others have distinct eyebrows, breast-bands, etc.

5. In what habitat do you see the bird?

Is it in the garden, in water, in grassland, bushveld or forest? The habitat in which the bird is seen is another important clue to the kind of bird it is (see description of habitats on page 10).

6. What is the bird doing?

Is it walking, hopping, wading or swimming? Does it peck at the ground, feed in the air, probe in the mud or feed in a tree? Try to detail its behaviour as closely as possible.

Often the details of a bird's structure, plumage or behaviour are soon forgotten and the observer may spend much time trying to recall them. If these six points are remembered or noted at the time of the observation, an analysis can be made when the bird has flown away.

How to use Newman's Birds of Southern Africa

Once you have noted down the answers to the six questions about the bird you have seen it is time to consult the fieldguide. Follow the five steps below to reach a verdict on which bird you have seen. The steps are explained in more detail in the next few pages.

Step 2

Using the running head at the top of the page, decide which page or group of pages you should be looking at.

Step 5

Read the text to pick up additional information and confirm the identification.

Step 3

Look at the pictures of the birds and decide which looks most like the bird you have seen.

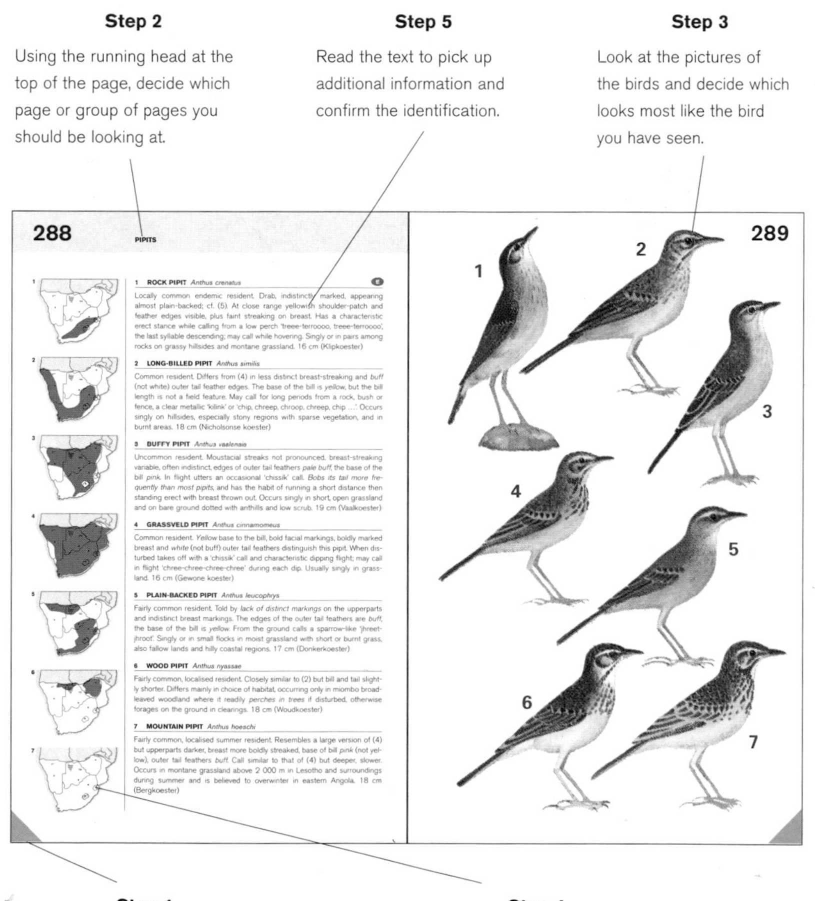

288 PIPITS

1 ROCK PIPIT *Anthus crenatus*

Locally common endemic resident. Drab, indistinctly marked, appearing almost plain-backed; cf. (5). At close range yellowish shoulder-patch and feather edges visible, plus faint streaking on breast. Has a characteristic erect stance while calling from a low perch 'treee-terroooo, treee-terroooo', the last syllable descending; may call while hovering. Singly or in pairs among rocks on grassy hillsides and montane grassland. 16 cm (Klipkoester)

2 LONG-BILLED PIPIT *Anthus similis*

Common resident. Differs from (4) in less distinct breast-streaking and *buff* (not white) outer tail feather edges. The base of the bill is *yellow*, but the bill length is not a field feature. May call for long periods from a rock, bush or fence, a clear metallic 'kilink' or 'chip, chreep, chroop, chreep, chip ...'. Occurs singly on hillsides, especially stony regions with sparse vegetation, and in burnt areas. 18 cm (Nicholsonse koester)

3 BUFFY PIPIT *Anthus vaalensis*

Uncommon resident. Moustacial streaks not pronounced, breast-streaking variable, often indistinct, edges of outer tail feathers *pale buff*, the base of the bill *pink*. In flight utters an occasional 'chissik' call. *Bobs its tail more frequently than most pipits*, and has the habit of running a short distance then standing erect with breast thrown out. Occurs singly in short, open grassland and on bare ground dotted with anthills and low scrub. 19 cm (Vaalkoester)

4 GRASSVELD PIPIT *Anthus cinnamomeus*

Common resident. *Yellow* base to the bill, bold facial markings, boldly marked breast and *white* (not buff) outer tail feathers distinguish this pipit. When disturbed takes off with a 'chissik' call and characteristic dipping flight; may call in flight 'chree-chree-chree-chree' during each dip. Usually singly in grassland. 16 cm (Gewone koester)

5 PLAIN-BACKED PIPIT *Anthus leucophrys*

Fairly common resident. Told by *lack of distinct markings* on the upperparts and indistinct breast markings. The edges of the outer tail feathers are *buff*, the base of the bill is *yellow*. From the ground calls a sparrow-like 'jhreet-jhroot'. Singly or in small flocks in moist grassland with short or burnt grass, also fallow lands and hilly coastal regions. 17 cm (Donkerkoester)

6 WOOD PIPIT *Anthus nyassae*

Fairly common, localised resident. Closely similar to (2) but bill and tail slightly shorter. Differs mainly in choice of habitat, occurring only in miombo broadleaved woodland where it readily *perches in trees* if disturbed, otherwise forages on the ground in clearings. 18 cm (Woudkoester)

7 MOUNTAIN PIPIT *Anthus hoeschi*

Fairly common, localised summer resident. Resembles a large version of (4) but upperparts darker, breast more boldly streaked, base of bill *pink* (not yellow), outer tail feathers *buff*. Call similar to that of (4) but deeper, slower. Occurs in montane grassland above 2 000 m in Lesotho and surroundings during summer and is believed to overwinter in eastern Angola. 18 cm (Bergkoester)

289

Step 1

Using the colour-coding, identify which section of the book you are most likely to find the bird in.

Step 4

Check the distribution map for the bird you have selected and see whether the bird occurs in the area, and whether it is present all year round or only some of the year.

WHICH GROUP DOES THE BIRD BELONG TO? (STEPS 1 AND 2)

The colour coding in the fieldguide has been designed to divide the bird species into 12 groups that are obviously different from one another. If you can place the bird you have seen into one of the 12 groups you immediately limit the number of species you need to consider in determining its identity. The groups are as follows:

2

Ocean, Offshore and Subantarctic Birds

Habitat is your best clue to placing birds in this group. The exceptions are some of the gulls, the African Skimmer and some of the terns which are also seen on inland waters.

Inland Waterbirds

Habitat is the defining feature once again (also see the next group).

Ducks, Wading Birds and Shorebirds

These birds are also found on inland and coastal waters and the shorebirds generally have long legs adapted for feeding in shallow water or on the shoreline.

Terrestrial Birds

These include the long-legged birds that inhabit dry land.

Raptors

Birds of prey all have bills and talons adapted for killing and eating meat.

Sandgrouse, Doves, Parrots, Louries, Cuckoos, Coucals and Trogon

This group is similar in general shape and jizz.

Owls and Nightjars

Very distinctive nocturnal birds. Most have distinctive calls also.

Aerial Feeders, Mousebirds, Hole Nesters and Honeyguides

A diverse group – species which catch their prey in flight, the distinctive mousebirds, the hole-nesting species (barbets, hornbills and hoopoes) and the honeyguides.

Insect-eaters – Larks to Robins

This group of slender-billed insect-eating birds have similarities of shape and behaviour.

Insect-eaters – Warblers to Starlings

This group contains more insect-eating species which can be recognised from their jizz.

Oxpeckers and Nectar Feeders

This is a small group of specialised feeders. The oxpeckers have very distinctive behaviour and the other species all feed on nectar.

Seed-eaters

The seed-eaters are distinguished by their strong, conical bills.

Once you have located the right group of birds the heading at the top of the page will tell you which family group (or groups) is dealt with on each page. Use this to find the page that probably features the bird you have seen.

COLOUR PLATES (STEP 3)

Use the colour illustrations to find the bird that looks most like what you have seen (watch out for colour variations). The birds have been painted, so far as is possible, in such a way as to reveal their characteristic shapes, colours, markings and stance, or 'jizz' as it is known in birding parlance. Where several species on a plate closely resemble each other, they are all drawn in a similar stance to facilitate direct comparison. All the main figures on a plate are in approximate proportion to each other and, wherever possible, all birds in a family are drawn to the same proportions whether on the same plate or not. In a few cases it has been necessary to depict larger birds of a family to a smaller scale than the others on the same plate, and in such cases they are clearly separated by a solid black line. Secondary figures showing birds in flight or performing some other characteristic action are not drawn to the same proportions as the main figures.

Symbols used on the colour illustrations

♂	denotes MALE
♀	denotes FEMALE
J	denotes an immature bird
Br	denotes breeding plumage
N-Br	denotes non-breeding plumage

It is customary in bird books to present species in strict taxonomic order, that is to say, in the order used by the national checklist. This usually means that one starts with the ostrich and the grebes, continues with seabirds, herons, ducks, etc., and finishes with canaries and buntings. In this fieldguide this order of presentation has been applied with elasticity. Because its basic purpose is to help with bird identification, and in the knowledge that many users may not be familiar with the various bird families and their characteristics, some species that have a visual resemblance to birds of another family have been illustrated with those they most closely resemble.

DISTRIBUTION MAPS (STEP 4)

Each bird description is accompanied by a small distribution map showing the areas in which it is likely to be found. These species ranges are rough guides only, based on present-day knowledge of the bird's occurrence.

Maps with a dark-coloured distribution indicate that the species is present in the distribution area throughout the year. Maps with a pale distribution indicate that there is a seasonal variation to the species distribution (in most cases the bird is only present in the summer months). A map which has dark and pale areas indicates that in part of its range the bird is present all year and in part of its range it is only present for some of the year.

Coloured areas represent the normal range, coloured spots show known local ranges of isolated populations, and open circles indicate where a species has been recorded but is not regular. In certain cases, notably among the waterbirds, areas of pale colours have been added to indicate temporary range extensions that occur under favourable weather conditions.

Because birds are highly mobile creatures, they frequently appear in the most unlikely places and one should be ever watchful for species occurring beyond the range shown on the maps. Comparison with the master maps (p. 6) will provide an accurate key to the locations shown on the distribution maps or in the text.

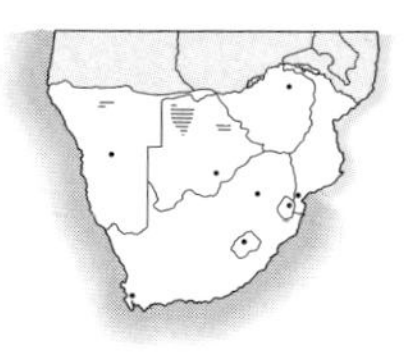

Ocean distribution
The broad band indicates a bird of the open seas, rarely seen from land.

Coastal distribution
The narrow band indicates a bird found along the coast.

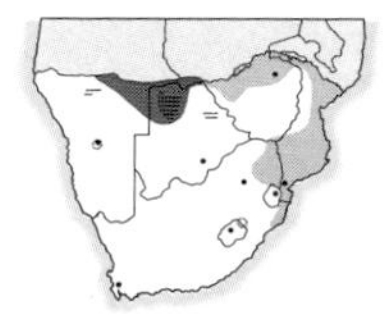

Resident and visitor
The dark area indicates that a bird is present all year; the pale area indicates where it ranges for part of the year.

Spots and circles
The coloured spots indicate the known ranges of isolated populations; the open circles indicate where a bird has been recorded but is not regular. Uncertain distribution is indicated by a question mark.

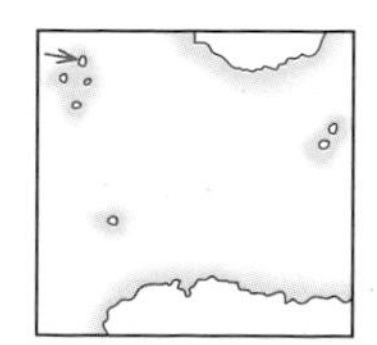

Subantarctic region
The arrows indicate on which island a bird is found. Other distribution indications are as for southern Africa.

6

SOUTHERN AFRICAN SUBREGION

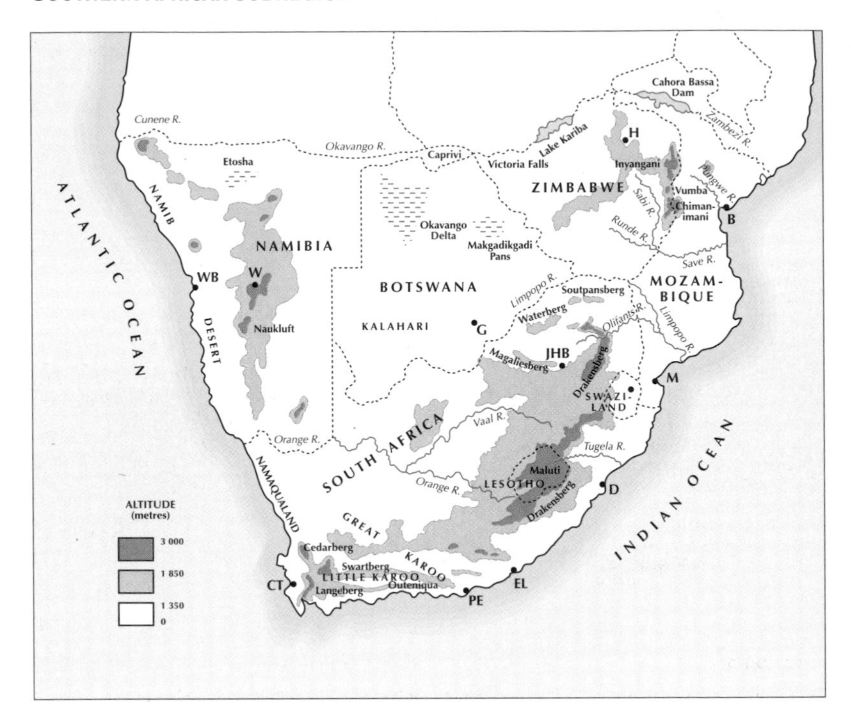

SUBANTARCTIC REGION

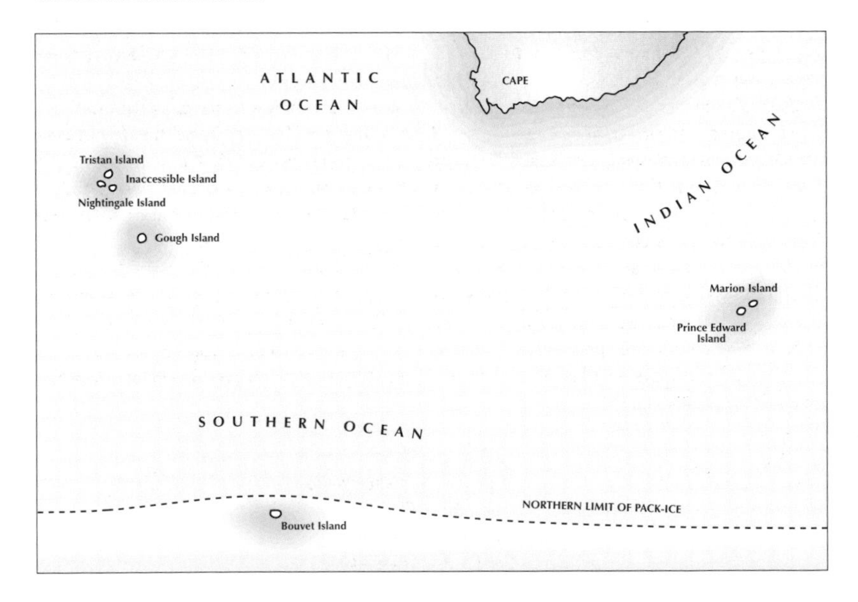

SPECIES DESCRIPTIONS (STEP 5)

The final step is to read the text about the bird you think you have identified to see whether the behaviour, call and habitat match those of the bird you have seen. The species descriptions have several components.

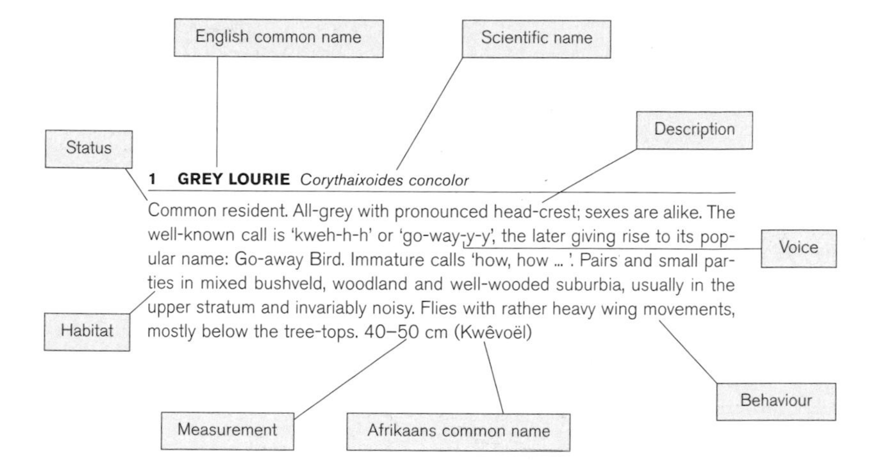

Bird names

In the descriptive text for each species, on the page facing the illustration of that species, the bird's common English name is given first in bold letters. In some cases a second common English name in wide use is also given. Immediately following the common name is the scientific name by which the species is known throughout the world regardless of language. This appears in italic and consists of the bird's genus and species, in that order. The Afrikaans common name is given in brackets at the end of the text.

Scientific names call for some explanation for the benefit of those unaccustomed to them. The accepted common names of species tend to vary from country to country. Therefore, based on the international system of scientific nomenclature originated in the 18th century by the Swedish naturalist, Carl Linnaeus, all animals (and this includes birds) have been placed in clear groups or taxa, using names based on Latin or ancient Greek, which obviates any risk of confusion. No two birds can have the same binomial (two-part) scientific name. First, all animal life is placed in classes, and birds belong to the class Aves, mammals to the class Mammalia, insects to Insecta, and so on. These classes are then divided into major groups known as orders. The orders are subdivided into families, the families into genera (genus is the singular), and the genera into one or more species. A species can further be divided into races or subspecies.

When the above system of scientific nomenclature is applied to the common House Sparrow, its credentials look like this:

Class:	Aves
Order:	Passeriformes
Family:	Ploceidae
Genus:	*Passer*
Species:	*domesticus*

Status of the species

Following the bird's names in the descriptive text is a brief statement of its known status. This is an attempt to give the reader an idea of the bird's relative abundance, whether it is rare, common, etc., and whether it is a seasonal visitor, a resident or a vagrant. Note that the term 'common', for instance, relates to the bird's frequency within its preferred or normal habitat, and not to the entire region.

Terms used to indicate bird status and abundance

Vagrant:	not normally seen in southern Africa
Very rare:	recorded 5 times or less in any 5-year period
Rare:	recorded 10 times or less in any year in suitable habitat
Uncommon:	recorded 30 times or less a month in suitable habitat
Fairly common:	recorded 1–10 times a day in suitable habitat
Common:	recorded 10–50 times a day in suitable habitat
Very common:	recorded 50–100 times a day in suitable habitat
Abundant:	recorded 100 times or more a day in suitable habitat
Seasonal:	seen at certain times of the year only
Winter:	April–August
Summer:	September–March
Localised:	seen only in restricted areas of suitable habitat
Resident:	breeds in southern Africa
Visitor:	non-breeding (Palaearctic or intra-Africa migrant)

Voice

After the description is a rendition of the bird's call or song, written as closely as possible to the sound heard. If it cannot be written, a general description is given of the type of song uttered. The transcription of birdsong into words is no easy matter, and no two people hear it or describe it in quite the same way. These descriptions should, therefore, be regarded as approximations only, and reference to one of the popular bird-call tapes is recommended.

'zik-zik-zik . . . zayzayzayzayzay'

Description of the species

This is a brief description of the bird, enlarging on what is shown in the illustration and, where possible, comparing it with other species with similar plumage. It is important to be familiar with certain terms used to describe a bird's anatomy. These are clearly indicated in the illustrations opposite.

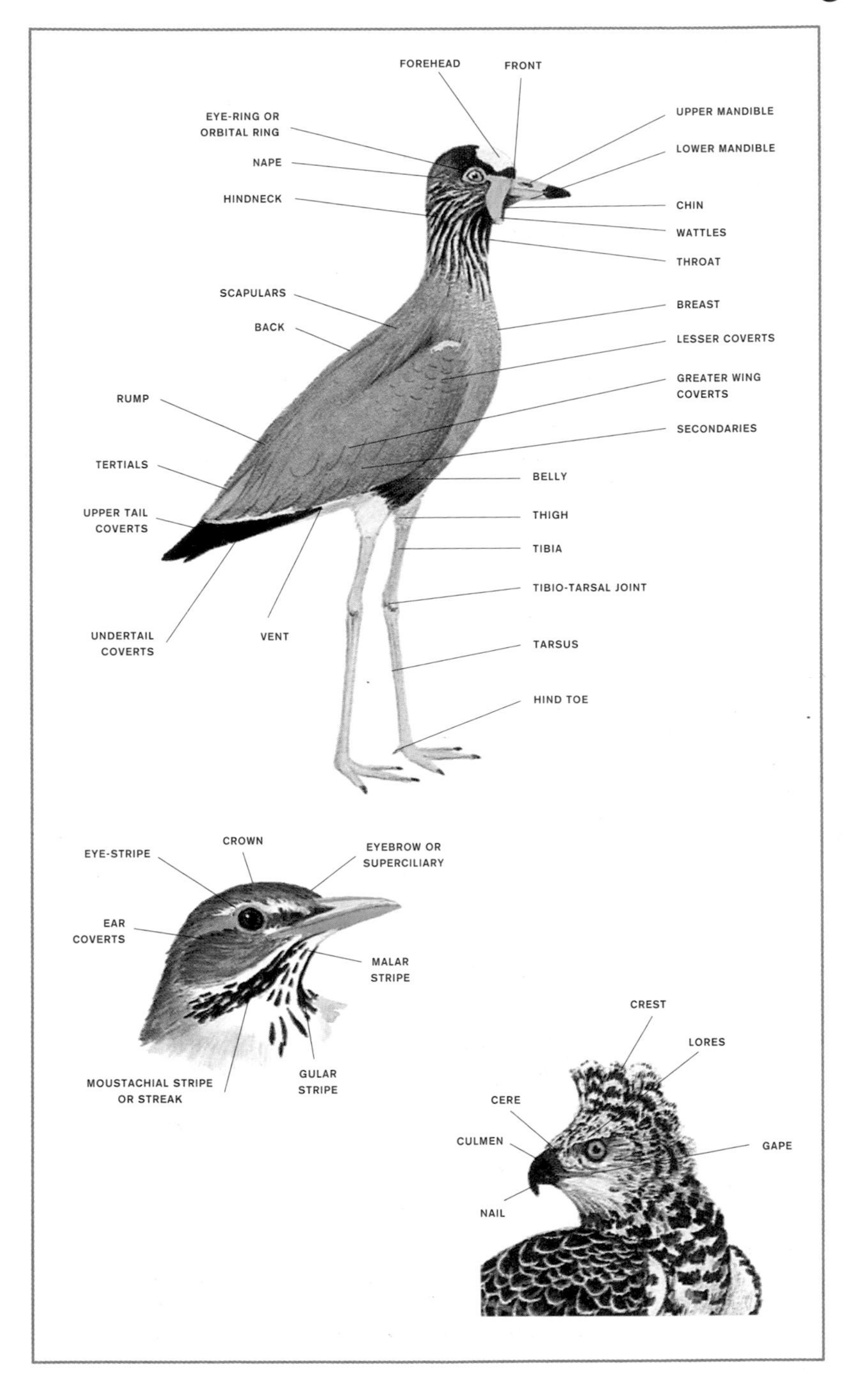
FOREHEAD
FRONT
EYE-RING OR ORBITAL RING
NAPE
HINDNECK
UPPER MANDIBLE
LOWER MANDIBLE
CHIN
WATTLES
THROAT
SCAPULARS
BACK
BREAST
LESSER COVERTS
RUMP
GREATER WING COVERTS
SECONDARIES
TERTIALS
BELLY
UPPER TAIL COVERTS
THIGH
TIBIA
TIBIO-TARSAL JOINT
UNDERTAIL COVERTS
VENT
TARSUS
HIND TOE
EYE-STRIPE
CROWN
EYEBROW OR SUPERCILIARY
EAR COVERTS
MALAR STRIPE
MOUSTACHIAL STRIPE OR STREAK
GULAR STRIPE
CREST
LORES
CERE
CULMEN
GAPE
NAIL

Bird habitats

The bird's usual habitat is described next and provides a vital clue to its usual haunts. All birds have a preferred habitat with often a specialised niche within that habitat, and many will disappear entirely if their habitat is destroyed or degraded, because they are unable to adapt to different living conditions. Thus, in order to see many bird species it is necessary to know and seek their preferred habitat, often a very restricted area or one difficult of access. There are several major habitat types in southern Africa.

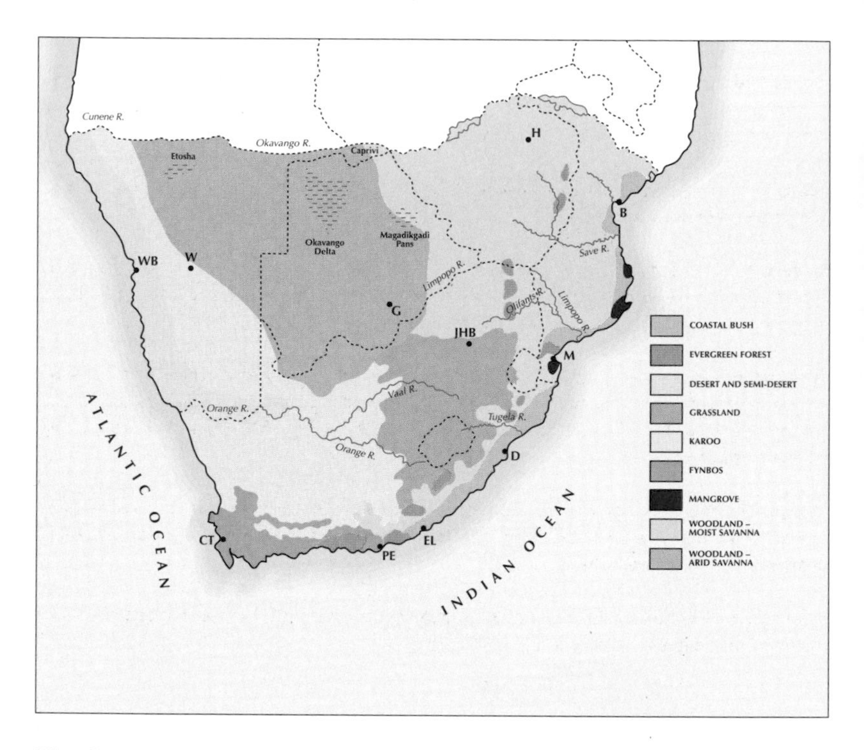

Woodland: The moist and arid savanna of southern Africa together make up its richest bird habitat. This variable habitat, covering about three-quarters of the region and supporting most of its bird species, can be further divided into areas known as bushveld, woodland, savanna, mopaneveld and miombo. Bushveld is a somewhat loose term applied to the woody veld found over much of the far north-eastern areas of southern Africa. It is comprised of various types of deciduous, small-tree woodland and mixed bush varieties and may include such diverse vegetation as scrub mopane, mixed thorn and broad-leaved bushes and even small patches of pure thornbush. The presence of all these bush types is dictated by variations in soil types, so that one sees frequent changes, each type intergrading with another. Woodland is made up of broad-leaved trees, usually deciduous, with wider spacing than is found in bushveld, so that their canopies do not touch.

Coastal bush: This consists of dense evergreen vegetation with thick undergrowth and some tall trees. It grows on sandy soils in a narrow strip along the east and south coasts and shares many characteristics and bird species with evergreen forest.

Forest: Throughout Africa indigenous forests are being increasingly cut back for fringe agriculture, or the trees felled for charcoal production. These evergreen, animal-rich regions have taken millions of years to reach their present-day climax, and are irreplaceable. As they disappear the birds that depend on them, and much other animal life besides, disappear too. Pockets of riverine evergreen forest occur in the midst of many other, more arid, habitats. Alien plantations of eucalyptus or pine trees should not be confused with indigenous evergreen forests.

Fynbos: A mixed succulent scrub occurring around the southern coast. Fynbos is home to many small bird species including several endemics.

Grassland: Grassland refers to the wide expanses of southern Africa where the ground cover consists of grasses but where trees are sparse or absent. Much of the central, higher-altitude areas of the region are comprised of grassland.

Karoo: The semi-arid south-central and west-central areas are stony with low, flat-topped koppies and sparse scrub vegetation.

Desert: The bird population of the great Namib Desert with its fringing semi-desert zone may at first appear impoverished, however in reality this desert supports a varied and highly interesting avifauna with many specialised endemic species.

Wetlands: The inland waters of southern Africa, including rivers, streams, dams, pans, estuaries, marshes and floodlands, are one of the most vulnerable habitat types. They are all too frequently drained or filled for industrial development or agriculture. Wetlands are very productive for the birdwatcher.

Mangrove: Mangroves are a threatened habitat confined to isolated pockets on the north-east and east coasts. These specialised communities of estuarine and intertidal fauna and flora are dominated by mangrove trees.

Coastline: The southern African coastline stretches for over 5 000 km and supports a wide variety of resident and migrant bird populations.

Mature woodland in the Zambezi River Valley

Stunted mopane savanna

Miombo broad-leaved woodland

Urban woodland

Mixed *Combretum/Burkea* woodland

Mature thorn savanna, a woodland habitat on Kalahari sands

Thornveld, a woodland habitat

Bushveld, a common mixed woodland habitat

Coastal bush

Evergreen forest

Evergreen forest interior

Riverine forest

Dune forest, an evergreen forest habitat surrounding a coastal lagoon

Commercial plantation

Fynbos

Fynbos

M. W. Fraser

Montane grassland

Karoo

Semi-desert in central Botswana

Dune desert (foreground) and stony desert intersected by riverine forest

The Okavango Delta, a wetland habitat

Floodlands, a wetland habitat

A pan, a temporary wetland habitat

Mangrove, an east-coastal wetland habitat

Peter Newman

A river estuary, a coastal wetland habitat

Peter Newman

Intertidal zone of a coastal habitat

Behaviour

Where relevant there is a description of the typical behaviour of the species, which is often a useful guide to its identity. Many species that closely resemble another can be accurately identified by small traits of behaviour, such as wing flicking, tail wagging or display procedure.

Measurement

Size is often difficult to gauge but the measurements are useful for comparison. It is a good idea to remember the size of three common birds and then to use that as a yardstick when looking at the sizes in the book: a House Sparrow is 14–15 cm, a Feral Pigeon is 33 cm and a Helmeted Guineafowl is 53–8 cm.

The measurements given represent those of a dead bird lying flat on a table, neither stretched nor compressed. If the bird has long legs which project beyond the tail, these are included in the total measurement. In a few cases only, where a species has seasonally long tail-plumes, the total measurement without and with the tail is given. The reason for measurements being taken in this way is that it is not practicable to measure a bird while it is standing, perched or swimming because various species hold themselves in different ways at different times. A long-necked bird may hold its head and neck outstretched or tucked in, some birds have a hunched posture while others of similar size may habitually stand erect.

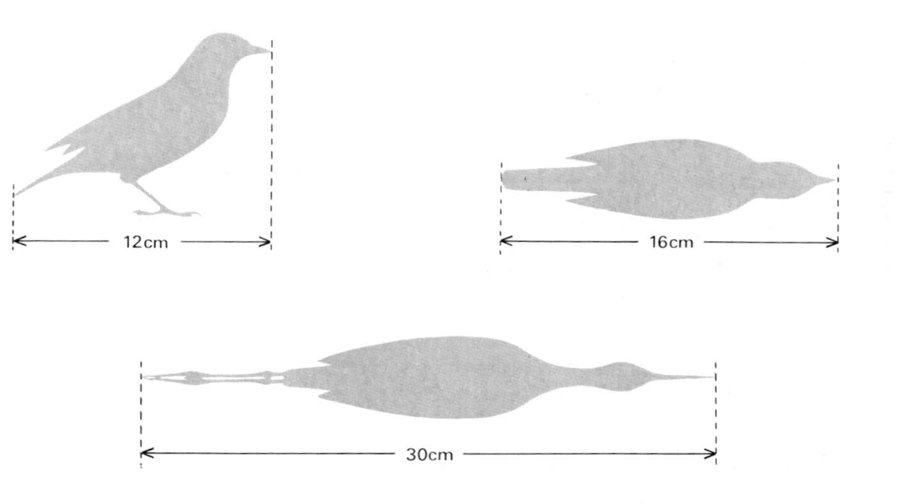

EXTRALIMITAL SUBANTARCTIC BIRDS

(This section does not include vagrant birds to the region.)

CORMORANTS

Family PHALACROCORACIDAE. Web-footed, long-necked, hook-billed, fish-eating waterbirds, which hunt their prey under water and surface to swallow it. Swim with body partially submerged and habitually stand out of water with wings spread to dry. Silent birds. See also p. 64.

1

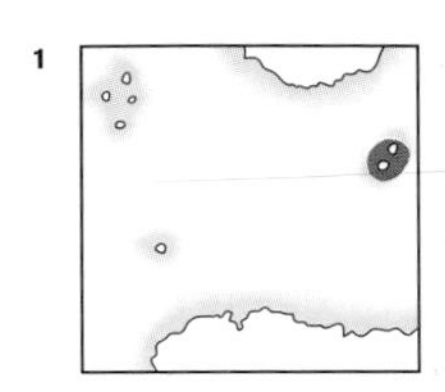

1 IMPERIAL CORMORANT *Phalacrocorax atriceps*

Common resident on Marion Island. The only cormorant in that region. Gregarious; breeds in small colonies on rocky headlands and low cliffs. 61 cm (Keiserduiker)

PENGUINS

Family SPHENISCIDAE. Flightless marine birds of the southern oceans. Characterised by stocky build, flipper-like wings, short legs and, on land, an erect stance. They dive to considerable depths in pursuit of fish. On the surface they swim with most of the body submerged, head held high. See also p. 28.

2

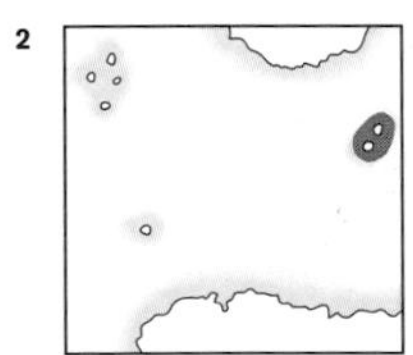

2 GENTOO PENGUIN *Pygoscelis papua*

Common. Bright red bill and orange feet and triangular, white ear-patches diagnostic. Immature resembles adult but has a duller bill and grey-mottled throat. Occurs in small breeding colonies on Marion and Prince Edward islands. Unlike other penguins shows fear of humans and makes off when approached. 76 cm (Witoorpikkewyn)

3

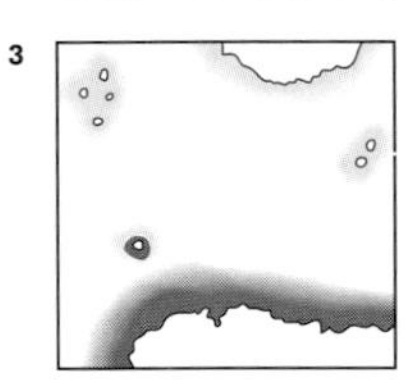

3 CHIN-STRAP PENGUIN *Pygoscelis antarctica*

Common. Thin black line across throat diagnostic for adult and immature. Found with (4) in small groups in pack ice. Very common breeder on Bouvet Island; vagrant to Marion Island. 76 cm (Bandkeelpikkewyn)

4

4 ADELIE PENGUIN *Pygoscelis adeliae*

Common. Identified by short stubby bill, black head and white eye-rings. At long range immature resembles (3) but has the black of the face extending below the eyes. Most often seen in small groups in the pack ice, resting out of water or 'porpoising' at speed through the water. 71 cm (Adeliepikkewyn)

5

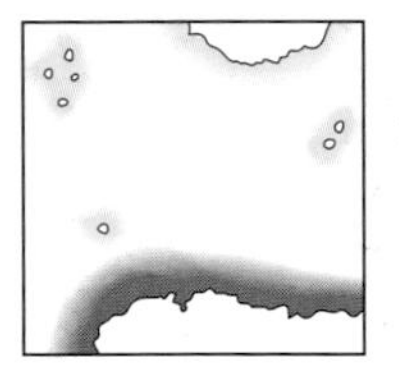

5 EMPEROR PENGUIN *Aptenodytes forsteri*

Uncommon. Largest penguin in the world. Distinguished from smaller King Penguin (p. 28) by pale yellow, not orange, patches on sides of head and shorter, more decurved bill. Confined to the ice shelf and pack ice within the Antarctic; rarely seen at sea. Mostly found singly or in small groups. 112 cm (Keiserpikkewyn)

N-Br
1
Br
2
3
5
4
J

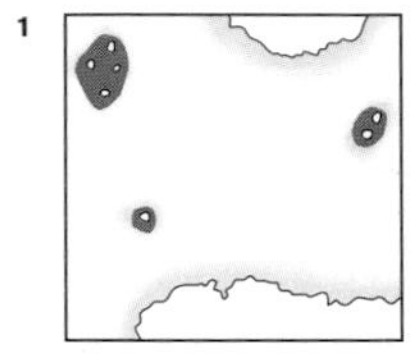

1

2

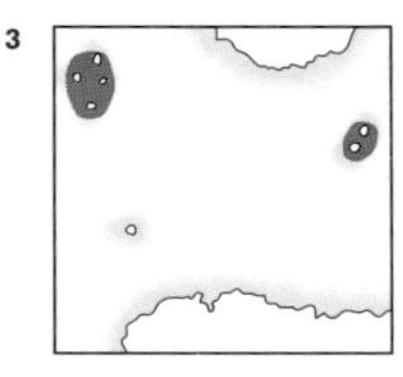

3

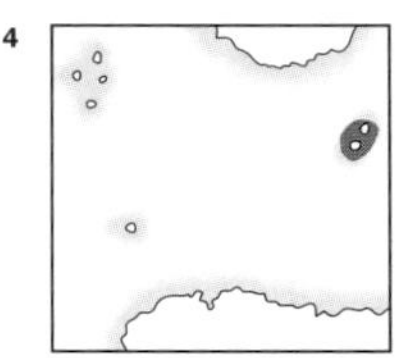

4

STORM PETRELS

Family OCEANITIDAE. Swallow-sized petrels of generally dark appearance, some with white rumps, underbodies or underwings, all with long, delicate legs. Fly with fluttering batlike action, erratic bounding action or with more direct, swallow-like flight. Many feed from the water's surface with feet pattering in the sea, and appear to walk on the water while remaining airborne with raised wings. Specific identification difficult except at close range See also p. 46.

1 GREY-BACKED STORM PETREL *Garrodia nereis*

Uncommon in offshore waters at Gough, Marion and Prince Edward islands. Dark head and flight feathers contrast with ash-grey back and rump. The only storm petrel in the region with uniformly grey back and rump; cf. (2). Usually solitary at sea. Flight swallow-like, hovering buoyantly when feeding and skipping from side to side low over the water. 17 cm (Grysrugstormswael)

2 WHITE-FACED STORM PETREL *Pelagodroma marina*

Common offshore at Tristan group. The only storm petrel in the region with white throat and breast and distinctive head markings. Rump pale grey (not white as in most other storm petrels) and contrasting with dark back. Legs very long and projecting beyond tail. Occurs in small groups of 2-4 which fly in ships' bow waves, and has a peculiar, fast swinging action as it skips and trails its long legs through the waves. 21 cm (Witwangstormswael)

DIVING PETRELS

Family PELECANOIDIDAE. Very small, short-necked, short-winged and short-tailed seabirds of the southern hemisphere. They fly close to the water's surface with rapid wing beats, bouncing off the waves like flying fish or plunging through them with no perceptible change of wing beat or speed. When settled on the water, they float high like grebes (p. 96) and take off after a short run across the surface.

3 COMMON DIVING PETREL *Pelecanoides urinatrix*

Common resident on Tristan group, Marion and Prince Edward islands. At sea indistinguishable from (4), differing mainly in bill shape and size; see illustrations. Otherwise seen as small, black and white birds with fast direct flight on short, whirring wings. Singly or in small groups around islands. 20 cm (Gewone duikstormvoël)

4 SOUTH GEORGIAN DIVING PETREL *Pelecanoides georgicus*

Common resident on Marion and Prince Edward islands; cf. (3) and bill illustrations. At sea behaviour identical to (3). On land breeds at higher elevations than (3) on islands, usually on non-vegetated cinder cones, where their small rat-like tunnels bury deep into the scoria. 19 cm (Kleinduikstormvoël)

23
1
2
3
4

TERNS

Family LARIDAE. Smaller than gulls, with more slender proportions; most species have forked tails. They plunge-dive for fish. See also pp. 54-61.

1

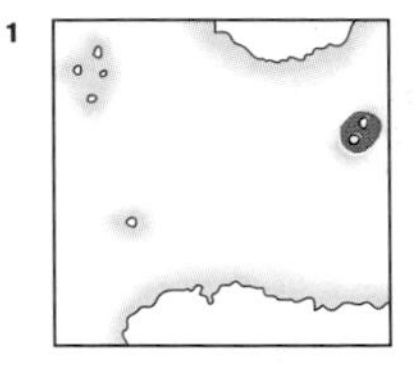

1 KERGUELEN TERN *Sterna virgata*

Resident on Marion and Prince Edward islands. Differs from Arctic Tern (p. 58) in darker grey colour, grey tail, grey underwings and shorter, thinner bill. Immature much darker and more heavily barred than immature Antarctic Tern (p. 58). Flight buoyant, reminiscent of a marsh tern (p. 60). Regularly feeds on insects taken from the ground on open grassy plains. 31 cm (Kerguelen-sterretjie)

PETRELS

Family PROCELLARIIDAE. Pelagic birds ranging in size from the tiny prions (15 cm) to the giant petrels and small albatrosses. See also pp. 34-41.

2

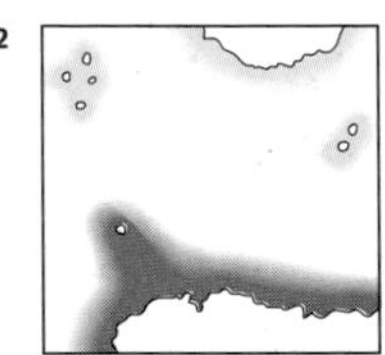

2 SNOW PETREL *Pagodroma nivea*

Common on pack ice and adjacent seas. Unmistakable, all-white bird. Flight rapid over sea and ice. More agile on land than other petrels. Sometimes runs over pack ice in the manner of a shorebird. Breeds on Bouvet Island. 34 cm (Witstormvoël)

SHEATHBILLS

Family CHIONIDIDAE. White, pigeon-like, scavenging birds of the southern islands and ice floes. Fly laboriously and reluctantly but can swim.

3

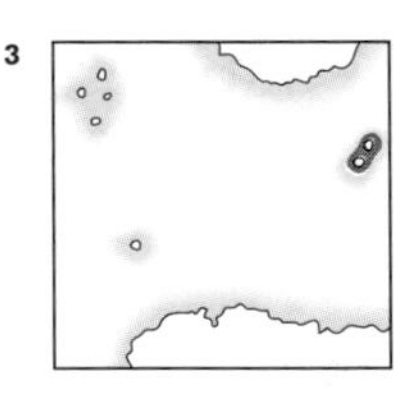

3 LESSER SHEATHBILL *Chionis minor*

Common resident on Marion and Prince Edward islands. Unmistakable, plump white bird with black bill and facial skin and pink legs. Usually in pairs or small groups which frequent penguin rookeries and grassy coastal plains feeding on penguin corpses, eggs and regurgitated food which they obtain by disturbing penguins feeding their young. 38 cm (Kleinpeddie)

SNOWY SHEATHBILL (Amerikaanse peddie) see p. 444.

RAILS

Family RALLIDAE. Smallish, long-legged, large-footed mainly terrestrial or water-associated birds. See also pp. 96-105.

4

4 GOUGH MOORHEN *Gallinula nesiotes*

Common on Gough Island; introduced to Tristan Island in recent years following past extirpation. Very similar to Moorhen (p. 98) but has red (not yellow) legs. Most frequent on the coastal plateau but more often heard than seen as it is very secretive and keeps within thick tangles of tree fern and bracken to avoid predation by skuas (p. 50). Wings very small but can flap for a short distance when disturbed. 27 cm (Gough-eilandwaterhoender)

5

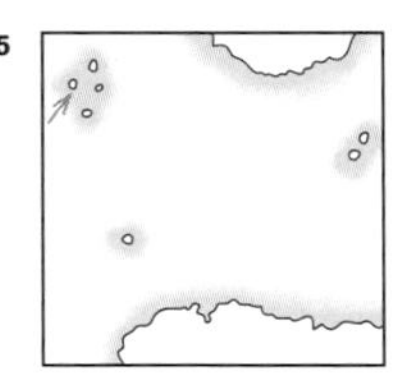

5 INACCESSIBLE ISLAND RAIL *Atlantisia rogersi*

Occurs on Inaccessible Island only, where common. Unmistakable, the only small rail on the island. Very vocal, the call 'pseep' heard all over the island. Individuals frequently glimpsed as they race, rodent-like, between tussock clumps. Inquisitive, coming into open areas to inspect unusual objects. 17 cm (Inaccessible-eilandriethaan)

Br
1
N-Br
2
3
4
5

1

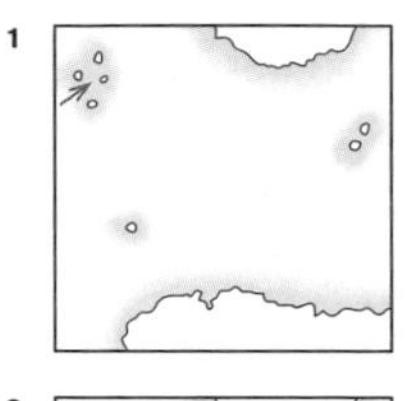

2

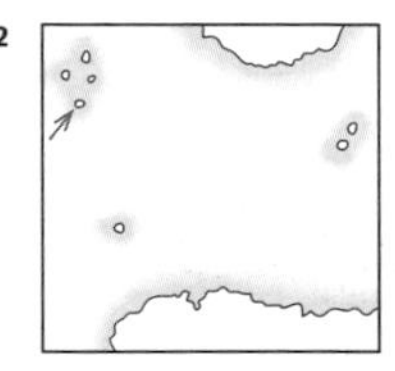

3

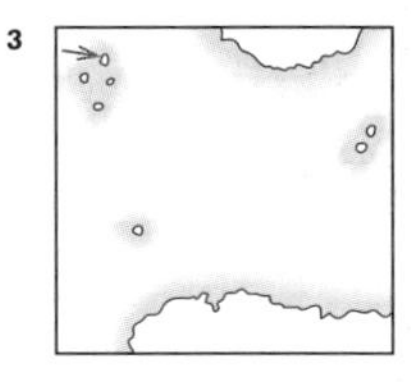

4

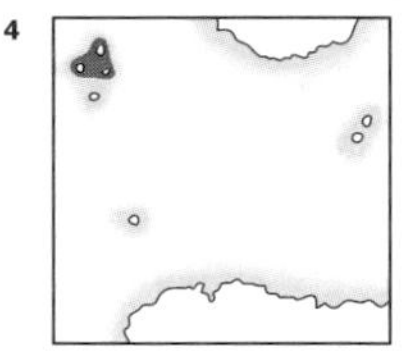

BUNTINGS

Family FRINGILLIDAE. The so-called buntings of the Tristan group and Gough Island differ from mainland buntings (p. 442) in several ways, being more closely allied to the Fringillidae of South America.

1 TRISTAN BUNTING *Nesospiza acunhae*

Common resident; confined to Inaccessible and Nightingale islands. Distinguished from (3) by smaller, thinner bill. The song is a melodious twittering or chirping 'chickory-chikky', followed by a wheezy 'tweeyer'. Birds on Inaccessible Island have larger bills, are more buffy on the breast and have a greater variety of higher-pitched calls than those on Nightingale Island. Pairs or small flocks forage on the ground or clamber over *Phylica* bushes in search of insects. 16 cm (Tristanstreepkoppie)

2 GOUGH BUNTING *Rowettia goughensis*

Common resident on Gough Island. Sexes markedly different but the only bunting on the island. Immature resembles female but is more richly coloured (orange-buff). Has a penetrating 'tissik' call note and utters a soft 'pseep' while feeding. Pairs and small groups throughout the island forage on the ground or clamber over tussocks and *Phylica* bushes. Inquisitive and unafraid of humans but dives for cover when a skua passes overhead. 16 cm (Goughstreepkoppie)

3 WILKINS' BUNTING *Nesospiza wilkinsi*

Common resident on Inaccessible and Nightingale islands. Occurs alongside (1) but is more heavily built and has a massive, thick bill used for cracking open hard *Phylica* nuts. The call of Nightingale Island birds is a clear 'tweet-twee-yeer, tweet-tweeyer'. Inaccessible Island birds have a similar but harsher call. Occurs mostly in the *Phylica* bush and tree-fern zone, less often in open grassy and tussock areas. 18 cm (Dikbekstreepkoppie)

THRUSHES

Family TURDIDAE. Largely terrestrial, insectivorous birds. The sexes are alike. See also p. 312.

4 TRISTAN THRUSH *Nesocichla eremita*

Common resident on Tristan, Inaccessible and Nightingale islands. Unmistakable, orange-brown thrush with heavy overlay of dark brown blotches, the wings showing much orange at rest and in flight. Immature has more orange spotting and streaking on the upperparts and smaller, more clearly defined spots on the underparts. Birds on Nightingale have a more streaky breast. The song is 'chissik, chissik, trrtkk, swee, swee, swee' or 'pseeooee, pseeooee, pseeooee, pseep-tee', sung from inside of canopy of *Phylica* bushes. Found in clearings in undergrowth where it hops about with typical thrush-like stance, turning over moss and leaf litter in search of food. Birds on Tristan Island are more secretive than those on Inaccessible and Nightingale islands. 22 cm (Tristanlyster)

27
1
♂
2
♀
3
4

BIRDS OF SOUTHERN AFRICA

PENGUINS

Family SPHENISCIDAE. Flightless marine birds of the southern oceans. Characterised by stocky build, flipper-like wings, short legs and, on land, an erect stance. Walk with a shuffling gait or, on rough terrain, a series of hops and slides in which the bill and stiff tail may be used as props. On snow and ice may lie prone, propelling themselves with their feet and flippers. In water the flippers are used in an oar-like action, and the feet as an aid to steering. They dive to considerable depths in pursuit of fish. On the surface they swim with most of the body submerged, head held high. Colours basically black and white. Sexes are alike.

1 ROCKHOPPER PENGUIN *Eudyptes chrysocome*

Vagrant. Distinguished by short, stubby red bill and pale yellow stripe from in front of the eye to the nape where it ends in a shaggy plume. Differs from (2) in *black forehead* and fairly stiff lateral head-plumes. Individuals, usually moulting birds, occasionally ashore on southern mainland coast (c. 50 records); otherwise not normally at sea in southern African waters. A summer breeder on Tristan group, Marion and Prince Edward islands. 61 cm (Geelkuifpikkewyn)

2 MACARONI PENGUIN *Eudyptes chrysolophus*

Rare vagrant. Distinguished from (1) by more robust bill plus orange-yellow eyebrows *which meet on the forehead;* the plumes loose and floppy. At sea distinguished from (1) with difficulty, but pale, fleshy sides of gape and white rump-spot diagnostic. Immature differs from immature of (1) in yellow stripe starting above eye (not in front of eye). At sea utters a harsh, nasal bark. A few individuals ashore on southern mainland coast; not known at sea in southern African waters. Summer breeder on Bouvet, Marion and Prince Edward islands. 71 cm (Macaronipikkewyn)

3 JACKASS PENGUIN *Spheniscus demersus* E

Very common to abundant endemic resident. Black and white facial pattern and white underparts with encircling black bar diagnostic; individuals sometimes with double bar as (a). Chick (b) and immature (c) as illustrated. The call is a donkey-like braying, heard mostly at night. Singly or in groups in coastal waters or large colonies on offshore islands; colonies and individuals occasionally on mainland beaches. 63 cm (Brilpikkewyn)

4 KING PENGUIN *Aptenodytes patagonicus*

Rare vagrant. Large size, long, pointed bill and bright orange ear-patches distinguish this from all other penguins in southern African waters; in Antarctic waters distinguished from larger Emperor Penguin (p. 20) by orange, not pale yellow, ear-patches. At sea utters a monosyllabic 'aark'. Rarely ashore on southern mainland coast. Breeds on Marion and Prince Edward islands. 94-100 cm (Koningpikkewyn)

1
2
a
3
c
4
b

ALBATROSSES

Family DIOMEDEIDAE. Huge, narrow-winged pelagic seabirds, occurring most frequently in southern African waters during the winter months. They glide close to the water's surface on motionless wings and are best identified by underwing patterns and bill colouring, immatures being different from adults. Many breed on southern ocean islands during summer.

1

1 ROYAL ALBATROSS *Diomedea epomophora*

Uncommon visitor. Race (a) distinguished by combination of dark upperwings (*not* extending across the back) and *no markings on head or tail.* Race (b) closely similar to (2) but differs in thick black leading edge of wing from carpal joint to wingtip. At close range black eyelids and black cutting edge to bill diagnostic. Immature initially has dark upperwing and *white leading edge*, which progressively extends *backwards* until upperwing is almost entirely white as (2). Recorded occasionally in south-western offshore waters. 120 cm (Koningmalmok)

2

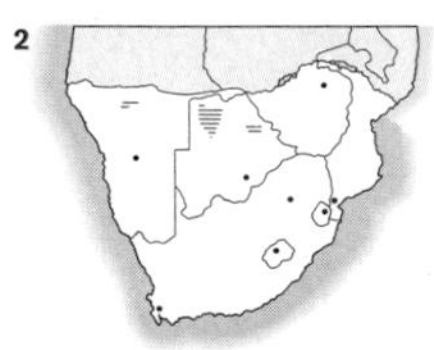

2 WANDERING ALBATROSS *Diomedea exulans*

Uncommon visitor. Adults of the white form (a) almost indistinguishable from adults of race (b) of the previous species, except at close range. Immature of all races initially has all-dark upperwing and body except for white face; belly then whitens as (c), becoming progressively paler, while upperwings whiten *from centre outwards* as (b); cf. (1) which whitens from leading edge. Stage (b) most commonly encountered. All waters, but sparse. Breeds Prince Edward, Gough, Marion and Inaccessible islands. 120 cm (Grootmalmok)

3

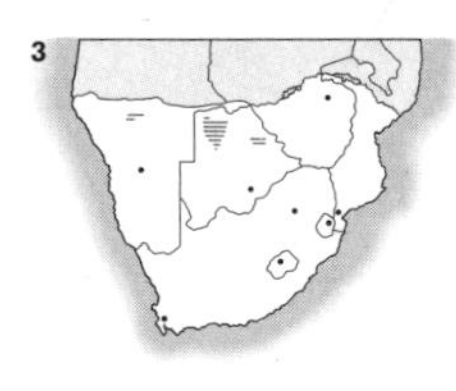

3 SHY ALBATROSS *Diomedea cauta*

Common winter, uncommon summer visitor. Largest black-backed albatross, approaching size of (1) and (2), but upperwings paler than other dark-winged species, underwings with *very narrow black borders* at all ages. Adult has greyish cheeks, white crown. Immature has varying amounts of grey on head, neck and breast, plus grey bill with black tip; cf. smaller immature Black-browed Albatross (overleaf) which has similar bill but dark underwing. All waters. 95 cm (Bloubekmalmok)

4

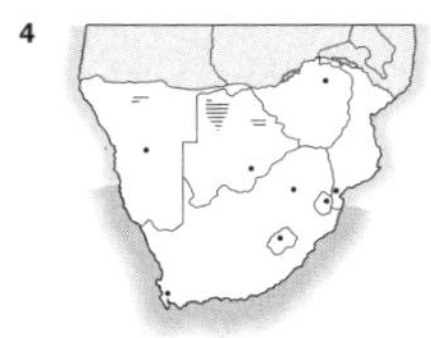

4 GREY-HEADED ALBATROSS *Diomedea chrysostoma*

Rare winter visitor. Grey head plus black bill with yellow ridges to upper and lower mandibles diagnostic. Immature has *all-dark underwings* and darker grey head but, through wear, head sometimes appears as pale as in immature Black-browed Albatross (overleaf), then all-dark bill is diagnostic; cf. also Yellow-nosed Albatross (overleaf). Sparse in all waters. Breeds on Prince Edward and Marion islands. 80-90 cm (Gryskopmalmok)

1 a b Jb

2 a a a b b c

3 J J

4 J

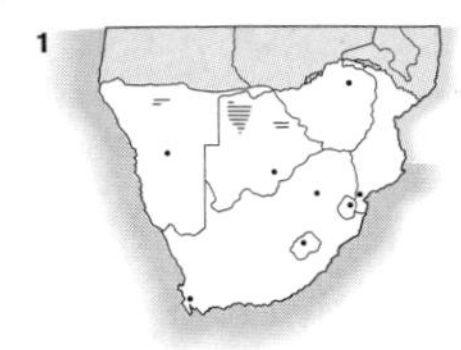

1 BLACK-BROWED ALBATROSS *Diomedea melanophris*

Common summer visitor; all year in southern offshore waters. All-yellow, pink-tipped bill diagnostic of adult. Immature has grey bill with dark tip and varying amounts of grey on head and sides of neck, sometimes forming a collar. Underwing initially all-dark, becoming paler centrally with age; cf. immature Grey-headed Albatross (previous page), which also has dark underwing but all-dark bill and smoky-grey head; cf. also immature of (2) plus Shy Albatross (previous page), both of which have predominantly white underwings with black borders. Most common albatross in southern offshore waters. 80-95 cm (Swartrugmalmok)

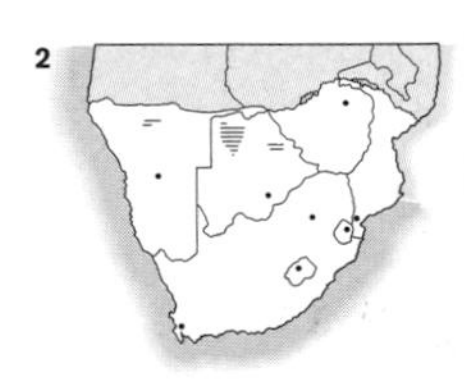

2 YELLOW-NOSED ALBATROSS *Diomedea chlororhynchos*

Common winter visitor to east coast, uncommon on west coast. Smallest, most slender albatross, race (a) with all-white head, race (b) (Tristan birds) with grey head; bill in both races black with yellow upper ridge. Race (b) distinguished from Grey-headed Albatross (previous page) by narrower black borders to underwings and yellow on bill confined to the upper mandible. Immature has same underwing pattern as adult but has *all-white head and black bill.* Summer breeder on Tristan group and Prince Edward Island. 75-81 cm (Geelneusmalmok)

LAYSAN ALBATROSS (Laysanmalmok) see p. 444.

3 DARK-MANTLED SOOTY ALBATROSS *Phoebetria fusca*

Rare visitor. All-dark, slender albatross with narrow wings and long, wedge-shaped tail. Differs from (4) in *uniformly dark back,* rarely showing contrast with upperwings except in very worn plumage but never as pale as (4). At close range pale yellow stripe on bill diagnostic. Immature of this and (4) difficult to identify at sea, but this species shows a *pale buffy collar* with grey not extending to lower back. Summer breeder on Tristan group, Marion and Prince Edward islands. Rare in southern offshore waters. 86 cm (Bruinmalmok)

4 LIGHT-MANTLED SOOTY ALBATROSS *Phoebetria palpebrata*

Rare vagrant. Adult differs from (3) in ash-grey mantle and body contrasting sharply with dark head, wings and tail. At close range pale blue stripe on bill diagnostic. Immature has all-pale back, slightly mottled, and pale underbody. Summer breeder on Bouvet, Marion and Prince Edward islands. Very rare in southern offshore waters. 86 cm (Swartkopmalmok)

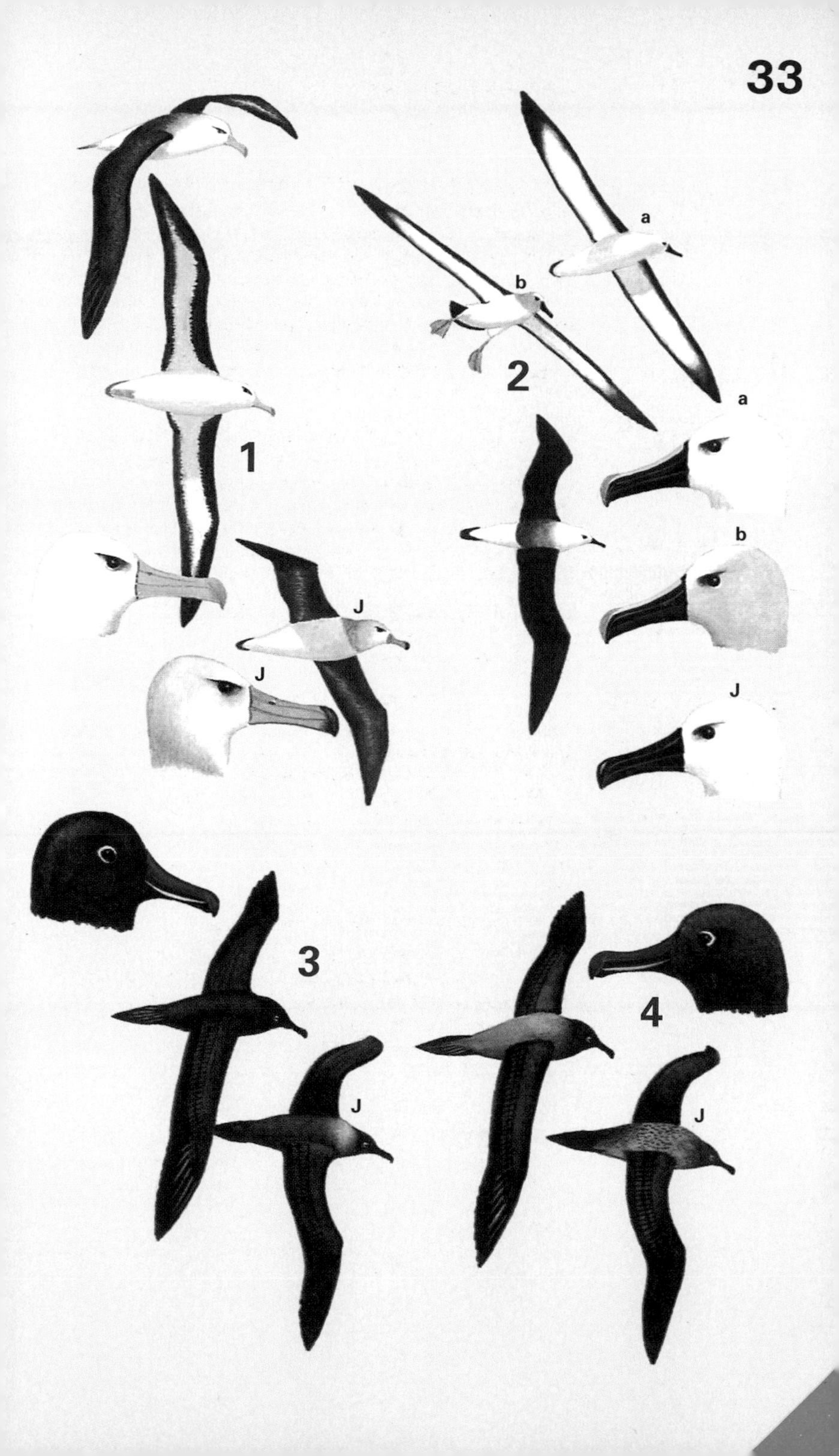
1
2
a
b
J
3
4

1

2
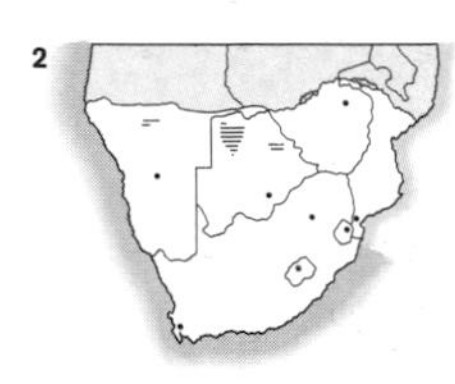
3
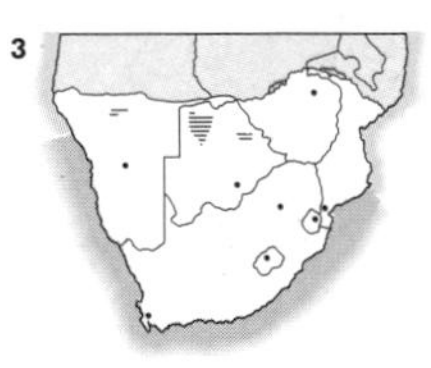
4

5
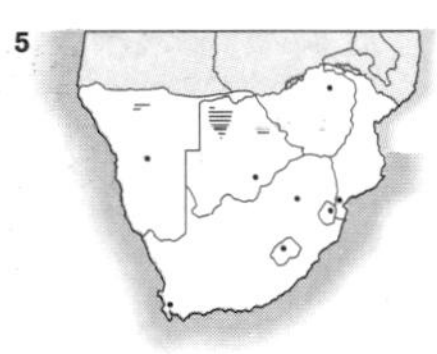

PETRELS, FULMARS, SHEARWATERS AND PRIONS

Family PROCELLARIIDAE. A large and varied group of long-winged pelagic birds, ranging in size from the small prions (14-20 cm) to the giant petrels, which approach the size of a small albatross. They are characterised by a single nasal tube (enclosing both nostrils which open obliquely or vertically) surmounting the upper mandible, drab plumage colours and a typically stiff-winged mode of flight. All breed on islands in the subantarctic and visit southern African offshore waters mainly during the winter months, when they may be seen foraging for offal around fishing trawlers.

1 NORTHERN GIANT PETREL *Macronectes halli*

Common all-year visitor. This and (2) distinguished from the sooty albatrosses (previous page) by massive pale bill, thinner wings, bulkier bodies and a humpbacked appearance in flight. This species is difficult to tell from (2) unless bill colour seen: *fleshy yellow with a dark tip.* Adult has some white around the face but never as extensive as in (2). Immature identifiable only at close range by bill colour. Congregates around seal islands on the west coast. Breeds on Marion and Prince Edward islands. 75-90 cm (Grootnellie)

2 SOUTHERN GIANT PETREL *Macronectes giganteus*

Common all-year visitor. Two morphs: (a) normal with extensive area of white or speckled-white on head extending to upper breast: more extensive than in (1); (b) entirely white except for a few scattered black feathers. Bill pale flesh with greenish tip. Immature: cf. (1). Singly or in small numbers, especially around trawlers. Breeds on Gough, Bouvet (?), Marion and Prince Edward islands. 75-90 cm (Reusenellie)

3 WHITE-CHINNED PETREL *Procellaria aequinoctialis*

Common all-year visitor. Differs from all other dark petrels, except (1) and (2), by much larger size, darker colour and greenish-yellow bill; the white chin is small (absent in the immature). Gregarious in large numbers around trawlers; a common offshore petrel. A summer breeder on Marion Island and the Tristan group of islands. 58 cm (Bassiaan)

4 SPECTACLED PETREL *Procellaria conspicillata*

Rare, non-breeding visitor. Closely similar to the previous species but smaller and told by extensive white markings on the head, while lacking the white throat. Breeds on Inaccessible Island in the Tristan group and, when not breeding, disperses mostly westwards to the waters of southern Brazil: very infrequent off the coat of Namibia. An endangered species. 51 cm (Brilstormvoël)

5 GREAT-WINGED PETREL *Pterodroma macroptera*

Uncommon all-year visitor. Characterised by long, thin wings held at sharp angle at the carpal joint. Differs from similar-sized Sooty Shearwater (p. 44) in *dark underwings,* from (3) by smaller size and *short black bill.* Singly at sea, moving with dashing, twisting flight, often towering high above the water. Winter breeder on Tristan group, Marion and Prince Edward islands. 42 cm (Langvlerkstormvoël)

35
1
a
a
2
b
J
3
5
4

1
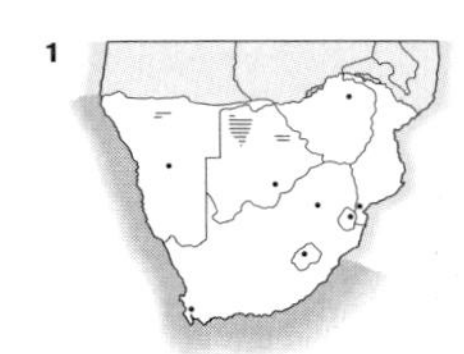

1 ANTARCTIC FULMAR *Fulmarus glacialoides*

Rare winter visitor. Identified by pale grey upperparts with white patches at the base of the primaries. Underparts white except for grey trailing edge to wings (cf. Snow Petrel, p. 24, which is entirely white). Occurs singly, most often around trawlers. Breeds on Bouvet Island. 46 cm (Silwerstormvoël)

2

2 ANTARCTIC PETREL *Thalassoica antarctica*

Rare vagrant. Resembles Pintado Petrel (overleaf) but is larger, lacks white patches and checkering on the upperwings; has instead broad white area on trailing edge of upperwings. From below is white with brown head, bold brown leading edge to wings and tail narrowly tipped brown. General appearance browner than Pintado Petrel. Common in the pack ice, gathering in large flocks and resting on icebergs and ice floes, often in company with Snow Petrels (p. 24). Vagrant to Marion Island and southern offshore waters. 43 cm (Antarktiese stormvoël)

3
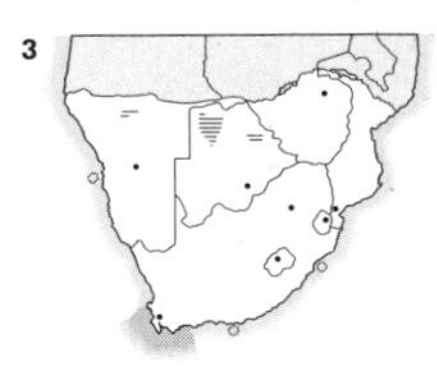

3 ATLANTIC PETREL *Pterodroma incerta*

Rare winter visitor. Essentially an all-dark-brown petrel with white lower breast and belly (in worn plumage throat and breast can appear mottled), upperparts uniformly dark brown. Superficially resembles Soft-plumaged Petrel (overleaf) but is larger and lacks the white throat and breast-band of that species; also Grey Petrel (p. 42) but is much darker above and has a short black bill (not slender pale bill). Solitary at sea but gathers in rafts off islands of Tristan group where it breeds in summer. 43 cm (Bruinvlerkstormvoël)

4

4 WHITE-HEADED PETREL *Pterodroma lessonii*

Rare winter visitor. Snow-white head with dark eye-patches, entirely white underbody and tail and dark underwings render this species unmistakable. The upperparts are grey-brown with a conspicuous, dark open M across the back and wings. Solitary at sea and *avoids foraging at trawlers.* 45 cm (Witkopstormvoël)

1
2
3
4

1
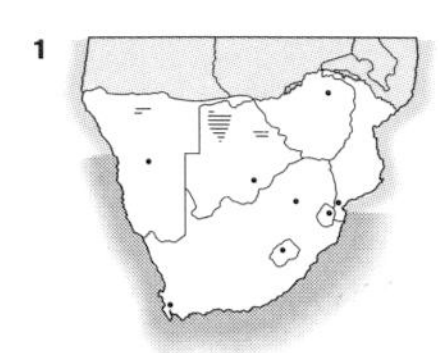

2
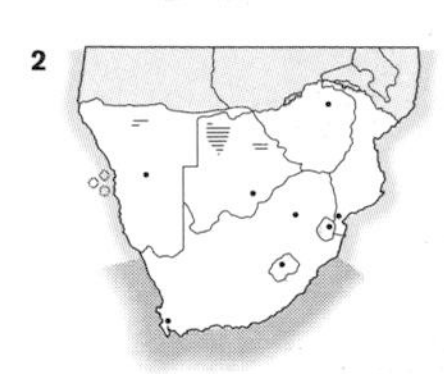

3
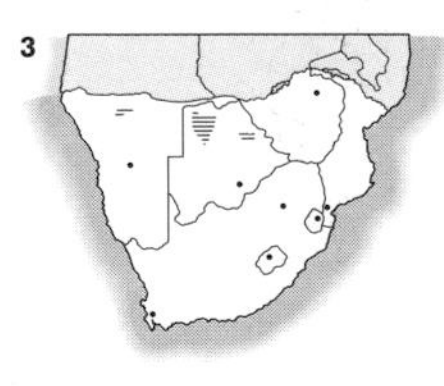

4

1 SOFT-PLUMAGED PETREL *Pterodroma mollis*

Uncommon winter visitor. Resembles Atlantic Petrel (previous page) but is smaller, has *dusky breast-band* on entirely white underparts from *throat to tail.* Faint shadow of open M pattern across upperwings and back. Rare dark phase (b) differs from larger Great-winged Petrel (p. 34) in less uniform, slightly mottled underparts, and from (2) in these features plus less grey appearance. At sea occurs singly or in pairs; does *not* scavenge around trawlers. Summer breeder on Gough, Marion and Prince Edward islands. 32 cm (Donsveerstomvoël)

2 KERGUELEN PETREL *Lugensa brevirostris*

Rare offshore visitor occasionally wrecked in large numbers on eastern coast. Very similar in shape and outline to Great-winged Petrel (p. 34) but is *much smaller* and grey, not dark brown. The head appears unusually large. The underwings have a thin, pale leading edge from body to carpal joint, noticeable at close range. Differs from the dark phase of (1) in greyer coloration and more uniform underparts. Flies very fast with rapid wing beats interspersed with long glides over the waves, then towers high above the sea, *much higher than any other petrel.* Summer breeder on Tristan group, Marion and Prince Edward islands. 36 cm (Kerguelense stormvoël)

3 PINTADO PETREL *Daption capense*

Abundant winter visitor. An unmistakable pied petrel with two white patches on each upperwing and a checkered pattern on back and rump. Underparts white with dark brown borders to wings (bolder on the leading edge) and tailtip; cf. Antarctic Petrel (previous page). Occurs singly or in vast flocks which attend trawlers; regularly seen from shore in stormy weather. Breeds on Bouvet Island. 36 cm (Seeduifstormvoël)

4 BULWER'S PETREL *Bulweria bulwerii*

Rare vagrant. Prion-sized, all-dark-brown petrel with long wings and long, wedge-shaped tail which appears pointed. Pale diagonal wing-bar on upperwings seen only at close range. No similar-sized, all-dark petrel occurs in the southern African region; cf. prions (overleaf). Flight action prion-like but much more erratic, staying closer to wave surface. Seen rarely in south-western offshore waters. 26-8 cm (Bulwerse stormvoël)

5 ANTARCTIC PRION *Pachyptila vittata desolata*

Included for size comparison. See overleaf. (Duifwalvisvoël)

a
b
1
a
2
3
4
5

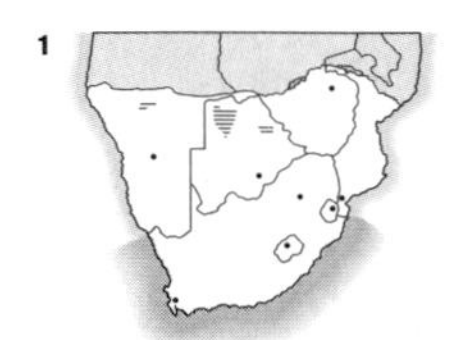

1 BLUE PETREL *Halobaena caerulea*

Offshore winter visitor. Occasionally blown ashore in large numbers. A small blue-grey petrel resembling a prion (see below) but larger and with dark markings on the crown, nape and sides of breast, and a square-cut, *white-tipped tail.* Open M pattern across upperwings and back fainter than in prions. Often seen in company with flocks of prions. Breeds on Marion and Prince Edward islands. 30 cm (Bloustormvoël)

PRIONS

Small blue-grey petrels that breed on islands in the subantarctic and disperse throughout the southern seas when not breeding. They are erratic, non-breeding visitors to our shores and have such closely similar plumage patterns as to be specifically almost indistinguishable at sea. All have a dark open M pattern across their upperwings and mantle, their tails wedge-shaped and dark-tipped; cf. (2). Prions fly fast and erratically, twisting from side to side and alternately revealing their white underparts and dark upperparts. They are occasionally blown ashore and wrecked, large numbers of corpses then littering beaches. In the hand specific identification is possible by examination of bill shape and size; see illustrations. The three species and three subspecies at present all have separate common names, but the taxonomy of the group is complex and future reclassifications are possible.

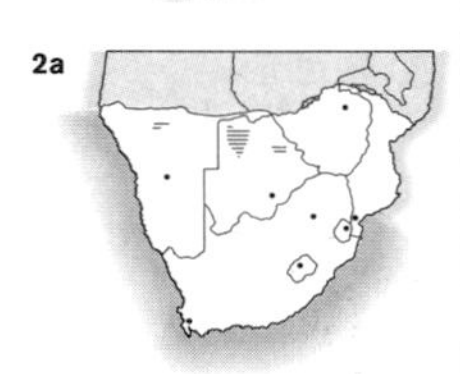

2a BROAD-BILLED PRION *Pachyptila vittata*

Uncommon visitor, mostly to the west coast. In the hand its black, extremely broad and flattened bill is diagnostic; its body is bulky and the tail is only slightly tipped black. Birds visiting our shores probably breed on Gough Island or the Tristan group. 30 cm (Breëbekwalvisvoël)

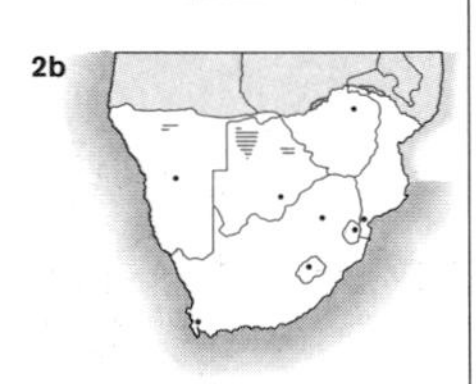

2b ANTARCTIC or DOVE PRION *Prachyptila v. desolata*

Uncommon visitor, mostly in winter. This is the smallest and most abundant race of the previous species, its bill smaller and lighter in colour. Breeds on various subantarctic islands. 27 cm (Antarktiese walvisvoël)

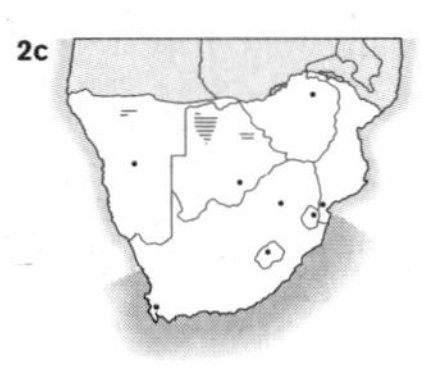

2c SALVIN'S or MEDIUM-BILLED PRION *Pachyptila v. salvini*

Very uncommon visitor, mostly to the east coast. A race of (2a) which is smaller than that species but larger than (2b). It breeds on islands in the subantarctic and in the Indian Ocean. 28-30 cm (Salvinse walvisvoël)

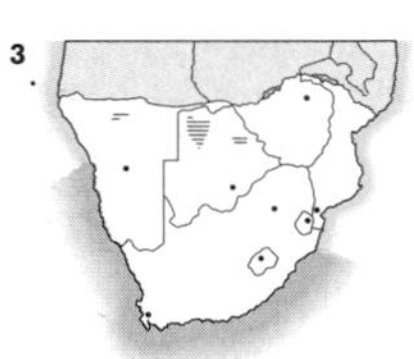

3 SLENDER-BILLED PRION *Pachyptila belcheri*

Irregular, winter-visiting vagrant to our shores but occasionally irrupting in large numbers. Stranded individuals have been recorded on Western Cape and Indian Ocean coasts. Breeds on southern islands on the Indian Ocean and is generally paler in colour than other prions in our region. 27 cm (Dunbekwalvisvoël)

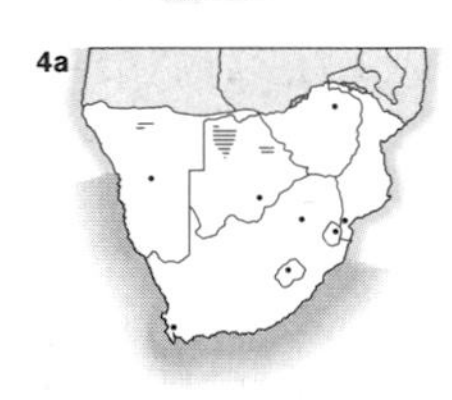

4a FAIRY PRION *Pachyptila turtur*

Rare visitor June-November, with strandings on all coasts. Breeds in summer on subantarctic islands. Small and pale in colour, especially about the head. 23-25 cm (Swartstertwalvisvoël)

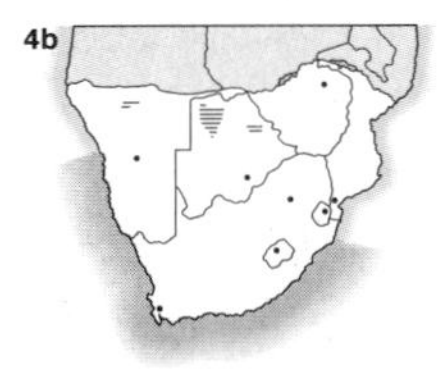

4b FULMAR PRION *Pachyptila t. crassirostris*

Rare race of (4a). Distinguishable only by its wider and deeper bill. 24 cm (Fulmarwalvisvoël)

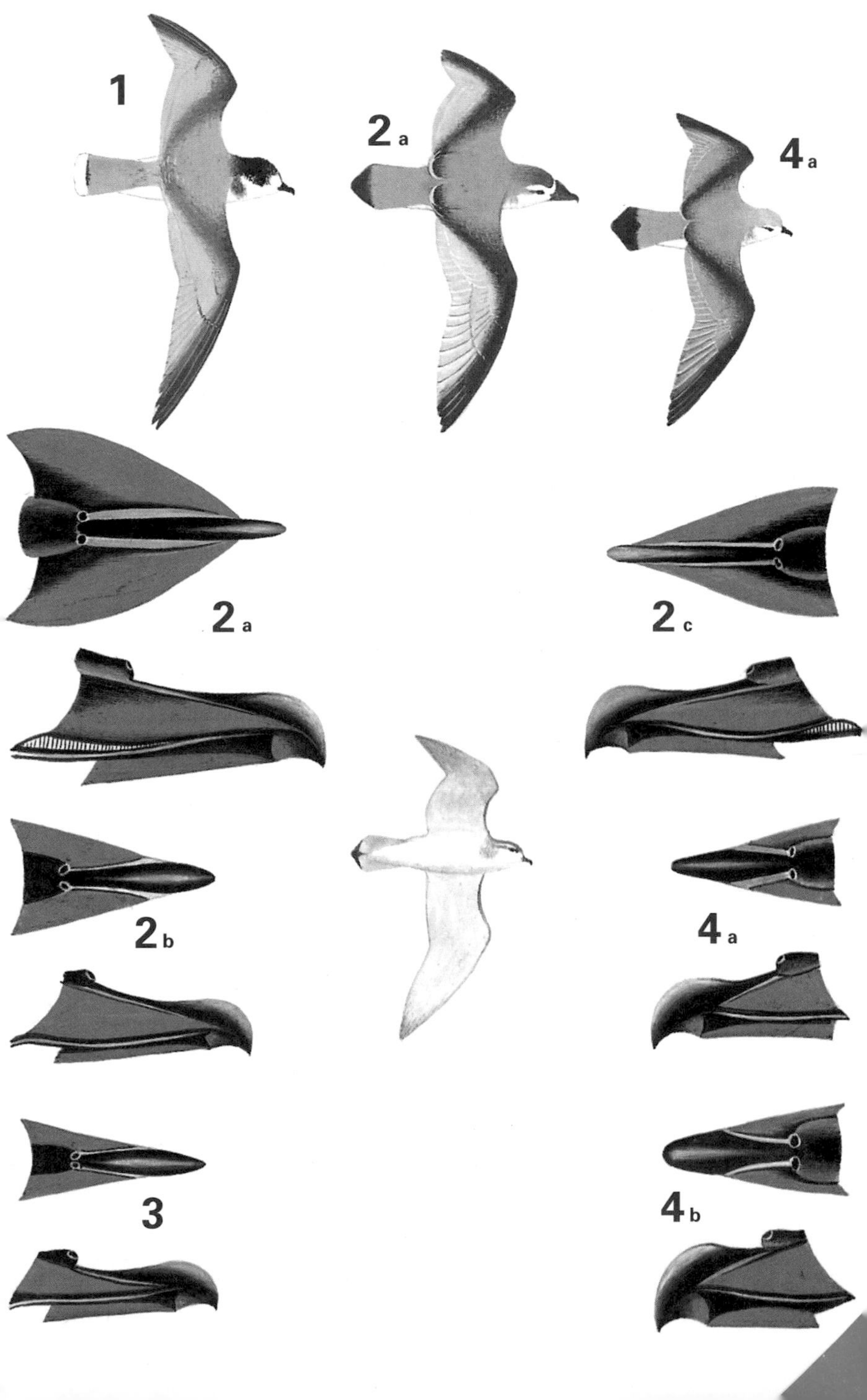
1
2a
4a
2a
2c
2b
4a
3
4b

1

1 GREY PETREL *Procellaria cinerea*

Rare visitor to south-western offshore waters. A large grey and white petrel which resembles (3) but differs in conspicuous dark underwings and undertail. Flight action stiff with shallow wing beats on straight, ridged wings. Solitary at sea and rarely scavenges around trawlers. Winter breeder on Tristan group, Marion and Prince Edward islands. 48 cm (Pediunker)

SHEARWATERS

Differ from other petrels in having long, thin bills and, with a few notable exceptions, short, rounded tails. The smaller species fly with short bursts of rapid wing-flapping alternating with long, stiff-winged banking glides low over the water.

2
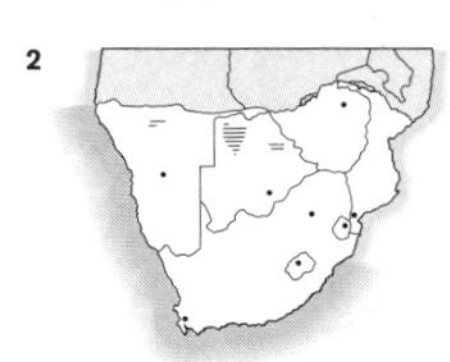

2 GREAT SHEARWATER *Puffinus gravis*

Common visitor. Similar in size to (3), from which it differs in darker upperparts, distinctive black cap, white collar and dark smudges on belly. At close range white on rump and dark bill may be seen. Usually in small flocks, but large rafts gather on feeding grounds in western offshore waters. Summer breeder on Tristan group. 45-50 cm (Grootpylstormvoël)

3
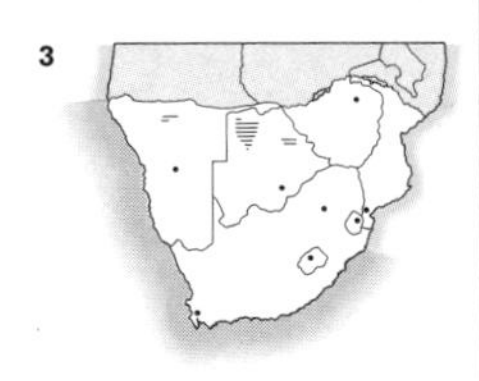

3 CORY'S SHEARWATER *Calonectris diomedea*

Common summer visitor. Ash-brown upperparts, lack of any capped appearance and yellow bill distinguish it from (2). The flight is also slower and more laboured. In worn plumage can show a white rump. Gregarious in small numbers and regularly seen from the shore. 46 cm (Geelbekpylstormvoël)

4

4 MANX SHEARWATER *Puffinus puffinus*

Rare summer visitor. The second smallest shearwater in the region. All blackish above, underbody and underwings white extending almost to the wingtips. Distinguished from Little and Audubon's Shearwaters (overleaf) by larger size, more extensive black on the head extending below the eyes and white undertail coverts. Flight action less fluttering than either Little or Audubon's Shearwater, with longer glides between wing beats. Occurs singly in flocks of Sooty Shearwaters (overleaf). 35-7 cm (Swartbekpylstormvoël)

1
2
3
4

1

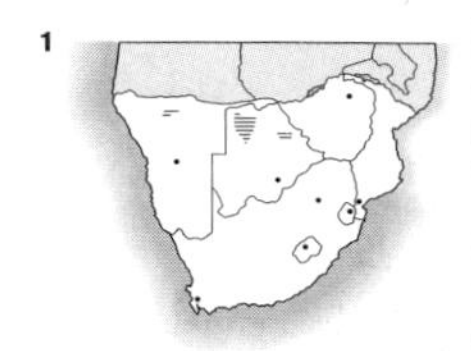

1 SOOTY SHEARWATER *Puffinus griseus*

Abundant all-year visitor. A sooty-brown shearwater with *conspicuous pale areas on the underwings,* this separating it from all other dark petrels in the region. Feeds in mixed flocks of Cape Gannets (p. 48) and Cape Cormorants (p. 64), sometimes in thousands. Often seen close inshore. Less commonly forages around deep-sea trawlers. 46-53 cm (Malbaatjie)

2

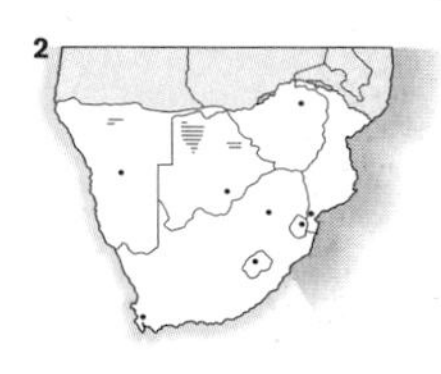

2 WEDGE-TAILED SHEARWATER *Puffinus pacificus*

Vagrant to east coast. Closely resembles (3) but differs in smaller size and *dark bill.* Tail wedge-shaped (not rounded) and appears pointed when not spread. Wings broad at the base and held slightly bowed, not straight and stiff as (1). Rare pale morph not recorded in our region. Singly or in small groups. Fewer than 10 records. 42 cm (Keilstertpylstormvoël)

3

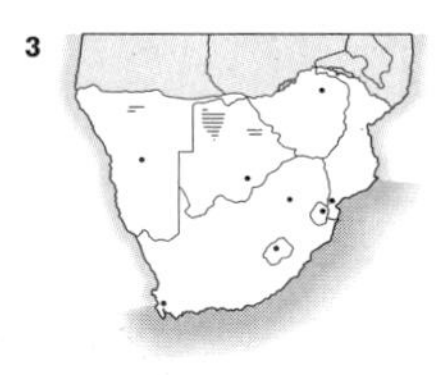

3 FLESH-FOOTED SHEARWATER *Puffinus carneipes*

Rare winter visitor to east coast. Larger than (1) and differs in dark underwings. Smaller than White-chinned Petrel (p. 34), the bill pink with a dark tip (not pale green). Differs from (2) in larger size, narrower, longer wings and rounded (not pointed) tail. Flesh-coloured legs and feet when extended appear as a pale vent at long range. Accompanies foraging flocks of Cape Gannets (p. 48) in Agulhas current. 45 cm (Bruinpylstormvoël)

4

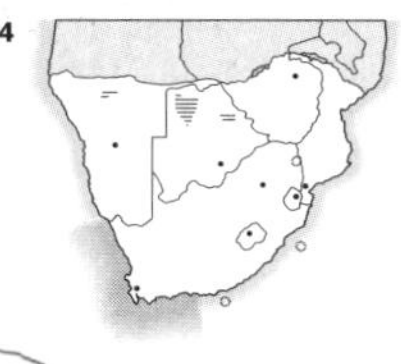

4 LITTLE SHEARWATER *Puffinus assimilis*

Rare visitor, chiefly to south-western coast in summer. A very small, black and white shearwater which flies with rapid wing beats interspersed with short glides. Much smaller size, white face (a) and flight action separate it from Manx Shearwater (previous page). Race (b) has dark grey upperparts; cf. (5). Occurs singly with (1) and occasionally at trawlers. 28 cm (Kleinpylstormvoël)

5

5 AUDUBON'S SHEARWATER *Puffinus lherminieri*

Rare vagrant to east coast. Similar in size to (4) and with similar flight action, but differs in dark brown upperparts (not black) and dark undertail. Race (b) of (4) has dark grey upperparts which can appear brown; dark undertail is therefore the best character for identifying Audubon's Shearwater. No inshore sightings but occurs in the Mozambique channel. 30 cm (Swartkroonpylstormvoël)

6 A **storm petrel** is included for comparison of size with shearwaters. See overleaf.

1
2
3
4
5
6
a
a
a
b
b

1

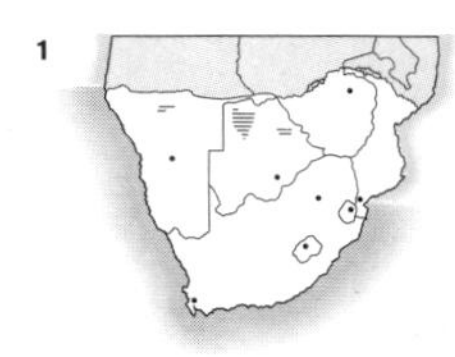

2

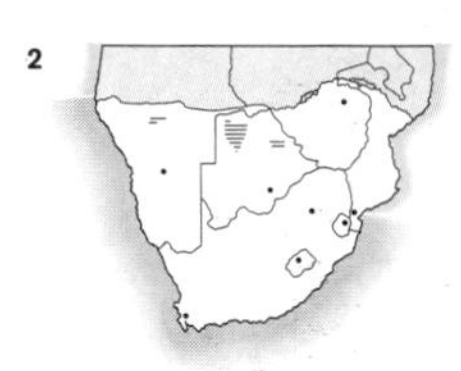

3

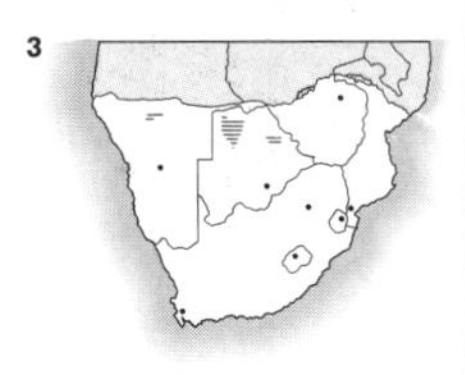

4

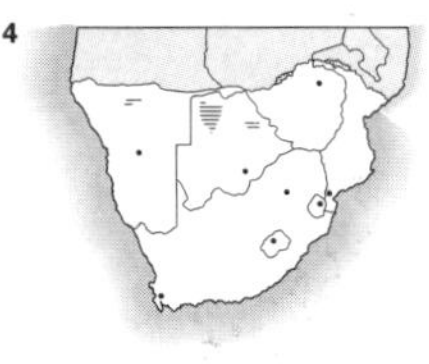

5

STORM PETRELS

Family OCEANITIDAE. Swallow-sized petrels of generally dark appearance, some with white rumps, underbodies or underwings, all with long, delicate legs. Fly with fluttering bat-like action, erratic bounding action or more direct, swallow-like flight. Many feed from the water's surface with feet pattering in the sea and appear to walk on the water while remaining airborne with raised wings. Specific identification difficult except at close range. See previous page for size comparison with shearwaters. See also p. 22 for subantarctic storm petrels.

1 EUROPEAN STORM PETREL *Hydrobates pelagicus*

Common summer visitor. The smallest seabird in the region. Identified from (3) by more pointed wings, white stripe on underwing and legs that do not project beyond the tail in flight. Flight bat-like, direct. Occasionally patters water with feet. Occurs in large flocks and is frequently beach-wrecked. 14-18 cm (Swartpootstormswael)

2 LEACH'S STORM PETREL *Oceanodroma leucorhoa*

Uncommon summer visitor. Differs from (1) and (3) in slightly larger size, longer wings, more slender appearance and, at close range, forked tail. Flight erratic, bounding over the waves and sometimes flying like a small shearwater. Unlike other storm petrels *does not patter feet on water.* Occasionally seen in small flocks, but usually solitary at sea. 22 cm (Swaelstertstormswael)

3 WILSON'S STORM PETREL *Oceanites oceanicus*

Common all-year visitor and rare resident. Best identified by rounded wings, uniformly dark underwing pattern and long, spindly legs projecting well beyond a square tail. Has yellow-webbed feet but almost impossible to see at sea. Flight action more swallow-like, not bat-like as (1). A small population breeds on off-shore Cape islands. 16-19 cm (Geelpootstormswael)

4 BLACK-BELLIED STORM PETREL *Fregetta tropica*

Uncommon winter visitor. Larger than (3), differing in white underwings and *white belly with black stripe down the centre* which broadens on the vent and encompasses entire undertail coverts. Differs from Grey-backed Storm Petrel (p. 22) in larger size and white rump. Habitually flies in front of or alongside ships and has a bounding flight action, occasionally bouncing off waves on its breast; cf. (5). Solitary at sea. Summer breeder on southern ocean islands. 20 cm (Swartstreepstormswael)

5 WHITE-BELLIED STORM PETREL *Fregetta grallaria*

Uncommon winter visitor. Difficult to tell from (4) unless seen at close range but has *entirely white belly, the white extending onto the undertail coverts.* Mantle and wing coverts tipped grey, giving paler-backed appearance than (4). Habitually flies in front of or alongside ships with bounding flight, occasionally bouncing off waves on its breast; cf. (4). Solitary at sea. Occurs from southern Namibia to the east coast but is most common in the south, February-March. 20 cm (Witpensstormswael)

MATSUDAIRA'S STORM PETREL (Matsudairase stormswael) see p. 444.

1
2
3
4
5

1

2
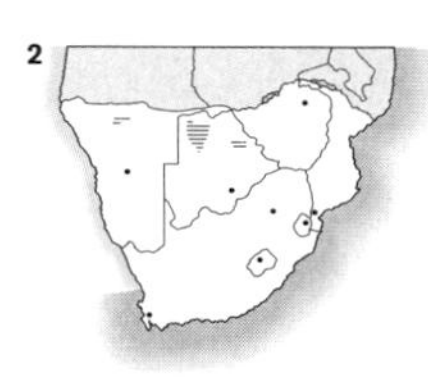

3

4
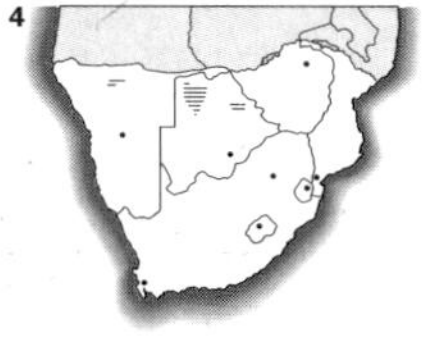

5

TROPICBIRDS

Family PHAETHONTIDAE. Tern-like seabirds with the two central tail feathers elongated into streamers, lacking in immatures. Usually seen singly. The flight is fluttering interspersed with long glides. Catch fish by plunge-diving from a height of 12-16 m above the sea. Their normal distribution is pantropical.

1 WHITE-TAILED TROPICBIRD *Phaethon lepturus*

Uncommon visitor. Distinguished from (2) by yellow bill, white tail streamers and black marks on the upperwings. Immature has blacker wingtips than immature of (2). Indian Ocean waters, occasional on the east coast; infrequent on the west coast. 40 cm (excluding tail streamers). (Witpylstert)

2 RED-TAILED TROPICBIRD *Phaethon rubricauda*

Uncommon visitor. Distinguished by red bill and red tail streamers. Plumage almost entirely white or flushed pink when breeding. Immature has a distinctive black bar through the eye; the bill initially black, later becoming yellow, then orange. Indian Ocean waters, occasional on the east coast. 46 cm (excluding tail streamers). (Rooipylstert)

3 RED-BILLED TROPICBIRD *Phaethon aethereus*

Rare vagrant. Adults are told by the red bill and white tail streamers. Underparts white, upperparts well-barred, resembling those of immatures of other tropicbirds on this page but the red bill is diagnostic. Immature has a dull yellow bill and no tail streamers plus a black eye-stripe that extends to its nape. Recorded off the west coast and Cape peninsula. 50 cm (excluding tail-streamers). (Rooibekpylstert)

BOOBIES AND GANNETS

Family SULIDAE. Large, robust seabirds with long, thick necks and straight, conical bills. The smaller boobies have a tropical distribution, gannets a temperate one. All catch fish by mostly plunge-diving from about 20 m above the sea. Flight stiff-winged with powerful, fairly rapid wing beats, head and neck stretched forward.

BROWN BOOBY (Bruinmalgas) see page 444.

4 CAPE GANNET *Morus capensis* E

Common to locally abundant endemic resident. Unmistakable, large black and white seabird with yellow head and hindneck. At close range distinctive black lines on the bill and face plus a *long black line* down the centre of the throat are visible. The tail is normally black, but rare individuals have white outer tail feathers. Immature all-dark initially, heavily spotted and freckled all over, the body, head and neck becoming white in that sequence, finally wings (at about two years). Singly or in straggling flocks offshore, large aggregations over fish shoals. Individuals plunge-dive repeatedly. Roosts at night colonially on offshore islands or at sea. 84-94 cm (Witmalgas)

5 AUSTRALIAN GANNET *Morus serrator*

Rare vagrant to southern African coastal waters. Almost identical to (4) but has much shorter central throat stripe (see illustration) and white outer tail feathers. 84-92 cm (Australiese malgas)

49
J
1
2
J
3
4
4
5
J

SKUAS, GULLS AND TERNS

Family LARIDAE. Skuas are robust, predominantly brown, predatory seabirds with characteristic white flashes at the base of their primary feathers, wedge-shaped tails with the two central feathers elongated, and dark bills and feet. Immatures all very similar with heavily barred bodies. Gulls and terns described on following pages.

1

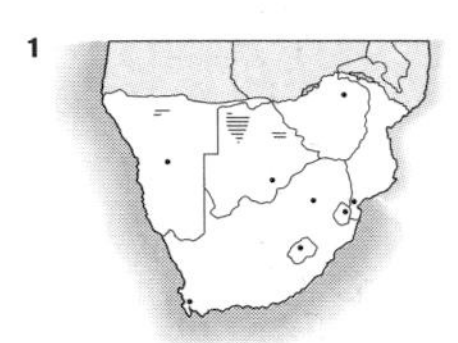

1 ARCTIC SKUA *Stercorarius parasiticus*

Common summer visitor. Larger than Hartlaub's Gull (overleaf). Plumage very variable between pale (a) and dark (b) morph birds. Differs from (3) in smaller size, narrower-based wings and more agile flight. In adults of both colour morphs pointed central tail feathers project 3-4 cm beyond tailtip. A falcon-like species which chases small gulls and terns. Occurs close inshore, singly or in small groups. 46 cm (Arktiese roofmeeu)

2

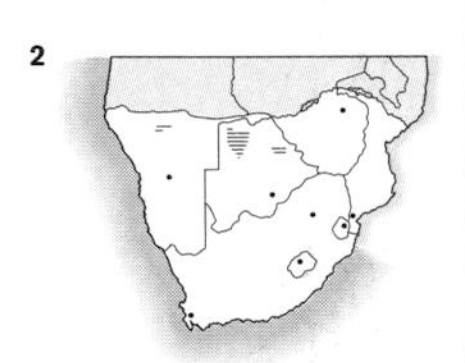

2 LONG-TAILED SKUA *Stercorarius longicaudus*

Uncommon summer visitor. Adults in summer unmistakable with pale, grey-brown upperparts, dark trailing edge to upperwings and long, pointed tail projections. A rare dark morph also occurs. Adults and immatures in winter lack tail projections and may be difficult to distinguish from (1) but are more slender, tern-like in flight. Less parasitic than other skuas and regularly scavenge at trawlers in Cape waters. 54 cm (Langstertroofmeeu)

3

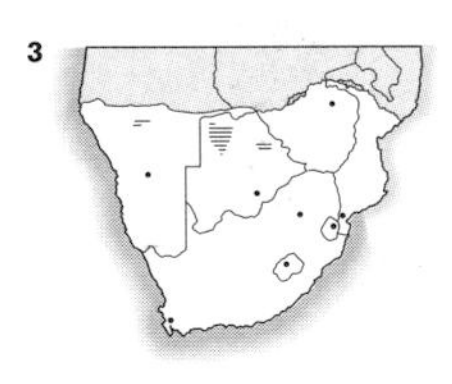

3 POMARINE SKUA *Stercorarius pomarinus*

Uncommon summer visitor. Pale (a) and dark (b) morphs occur. Larger than (1), approaching size of Kelp Gull (p. 54). Broader wings, bulkier body and longer-tailed appearance also help to distinguish it from (1). In breeding plumage central tail feathers project 4-8 cm beyond tail and are blunt and twisted. Usually in pairs or small groups which chase gulls and terns. 50 cm (Knopstertroofmeeu)

4

4 SOUTH POLAR SKUA *Catharacta maccormicki*

Rare vagrant. Pale morph told by its whitish head, golden nape and pale body contrasting with dark brown upperparts; the rare dark morph and immatures are difficult to distinguish from (5) but are smaller, more compact and with smaller bills and heads. Occurs singly at sea and chases Cape Gannets (previous page) at trawlers. Common in pack-ice and on ice-shelf. 52 cm (Suidpoolroofmeeu)

5

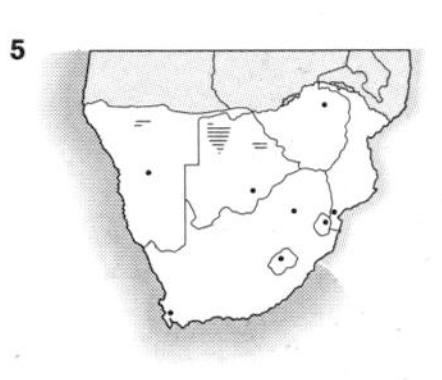

5 SUBANTARCTIC SKUA *Catharacta antarctica*

Common all-year visitor. Superficially like immature Kelp Gull (p. 54) but larger and darker, with conspicuous white flashes at base of primaries. Distinguished from all small skuas by bulky, broad-winged appearance and short, wedge-shaped tail; cf. (4). Usually singly at sea but gathers in flocks at trawlers. 58 cm (Bruinroofmeeu)

a
1
a
b
2
b
3
a
4
5

GULLS

A well-known group of scavenging shore- and seabirds, most with white underparts and grey or black upperparts. Their tails are rounded or shallowly forked, their bills and feet yellowish or reddish. Gulls do not dive into the water, but pluck offal or refuse from the surface or from land. Flocks utter loud screaming sounds when feeding.

1 HARTLAUB'S GULL *Larus hartlaubii* E

Common to abundant endemic resident. Slightly smaller than (5); in breeding plumage differs in having faint traces of a grey hood, *dark eyes* and deeper red bill and legs; at other times head is entirely white. Immature also has all-white head; bill and legs are dark brown; only a few spots show on tailtip. Individuals and flocks scavenge in coastal regions. The common small gull of the west coast, sometimes breeding on beachfront rooftops. 38 cm (Hartlaubse meeu)

2 FRANKLIN'S GULL *Larus pipixcan*

Rare summer vagrant. Breeding adult has all-black head with white eyelids; rosy flush on breast. Grey wings with a white bar across the wing separating the grey from a black wingtip are diagnostic. Non-breeding adult's head is grizzled black and white. Immature has a dark mantle and wings, white underparts and rump, broad black tip to tail and dark smudges on nape. Singly or in company with other gulls. 33 cm (Franklinse meeu)

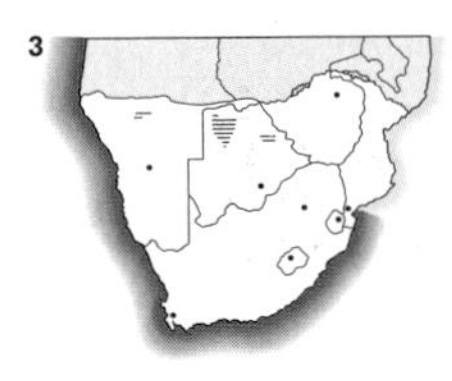

3 SABINE'S GULL *Larus sabini*

Common summer visitor. The only small gull in our region with all-black forewings and forked tail. Smaller than (1) and very tern-like in flight. In breeding plumage has whole head dark grey and, at close range, black bill with yellow tip. Non-breeding adult and immature lack dark grey head, but have a dark patch on nape and hindneck. Singly or in very large flocks at sea, rarely ashore. 33 cm (Mikstertmeeu)

4 BLACK-HEADED GULL *Larus ridibundus*

Rare vagrant. Dark chocolate-brown head of breeding adult unmistakable. Otherwise differs from (1) and (5) in smaller size, shorter, thinner bill, much greater expanse of white on forewing and white underwing. In non-breeding plumage head is all-white with black spot behind eye. Singly, often in company with (5). 35-8 cm (Swartkopmeeu)

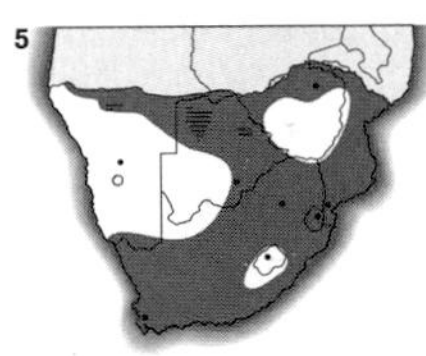

5 GREY-HEADED GULL *Larus cirrocephalus*

Common to abundant resident. Breeding adult has all-grey hood, pale yellow eyes and bright red bill and legs; non-breeding adult has a grey smudge on the ear coverts only; cf. (1). Immature has the frontal half of the head pale grey with a darker ear-patch which extends over the crown, plus a dark bill; see illustration. A gull of our inland waters (where it breeds) and coasts. 42 cm (Gryskopmeeu)

6 BLACK-LEGGED KITTIWAKE *Rissa tridactyla*

Rare vagrant. *Yellow bill* and grey upperwing with small black tip diagnostic of adult. Immature very similar to (3) but larger, lacks the forked tail and has a dark bar across hindneck, plus conspicuous open M pattern across upperwings. Solitary at sea or in company with (3). 41 cm (Swartpootbrandervoël)

Br
Br
N-Br
1
J
Br
2
N-Br
J
N-Br
Br
3
Br
N-Br
4
Br
Br
Br
5
J
J
J
6
Br

1 KELP GULL *Larus dominicanus*

Very common resident. Adult has dark eyes and whitish-yellow feet; cf. (2). Immature initially mottled dark brown all over with paler barred rump (could be mistaken for a skua, p. 50, but lacks white patches at bases of primaries); with age becomes paler, going through mottled brown and white stages with dark brown legs. Singly or in small groups scavenging along coasts, especially harbours, rarely inland. 60 cm (Swartrugmeeu)

2 LESSER BLACK-BACKED GULL *Larus fuscus*

Uncommon visitor. Very similar to (1) but smaller and more slender, with wings projecting well beyond tail at rest, bill less robust, thinner and more slender, *eyes pale straw in colour* (not dark), legs and feet bright chrome-yellow. Immature has similar plumage sequence to (1) but is generally paler, with same slender shape as adult and flesh-coloured (not dark brown) legs and feet. Singly or in small groups at river estuaries and inland waters. 53-6 cm (Kleinswartrugmeeu)

HERRING GULL (Haringmeeu) see p. 444.

SKIMMERS

Family RYNCHOPIDAE. Tern-like birds with specialised bills and feeding behaviour. Three species worldwide.

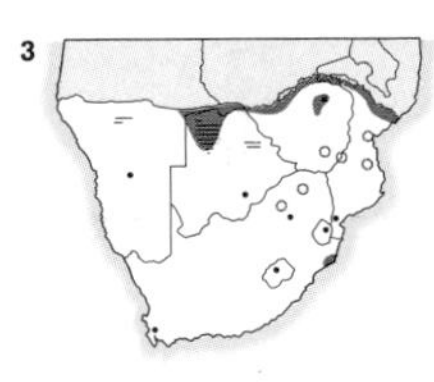

3 AFRICAN SKIMMER *Rynchops flavirostris*

Fairly common, localised resident. A brown and white tern-like bird with distinctive bill structure; this and feeding action diagnostic. Immature has streaked forehead, buff-edged feathers on upperparts and blackish bill with red base. Feeds by flying low over the water's surface with the long lower mandible immersed in a skimming action. Rests on sandbanks. Small flocks on large, permanent rivers, lakes and lagoons. 38 cm (Waterploeër)

TERNS

Differ from gulls in more agile flight, more slender proportions and, in most species, deeply forked tails. The majority feed at sea, plunge-diving for fish, a few (the marsh terns) feed mainly on insects caught in dipping flight or plucked from the surface of inland ponds, lakes and rivers. Bills and feet red, yellow or black.

4 ROYAL TERN *Sterna maxima*

Rare vagrant to northern Namibian waters. Differs from very similar Swift Tern (overleaf) in black cap extending to bill in breeding plumage and orange (not yellow) bill; in non-breeding plumage told by almost white head, orange bill and paler grey upperparts. Usually solitary, sometimes in company with Swift Terns. 48-50 cm (Koningsterretjie)

5 CASPIAN TERN *Hydroprogne caspia*

Common resident. Largest tern in our region. Massive red bill and overall size render it unmistakable. In pairs or small parties at coastal lagoons and large inland waters. 52 cm (Reusesterretjie)

Ja
1
Jb
1
2
J
3
N-Br
Br
4
N-Br
Br
5

1 LITTLE TERN *Sterna albifrons*

Non-breeding summer visitor. This and Damara Tern (overleaf) are the smallest terns in our region. In breeding plumage distinguished from Damara Tern by well-defined white forehead, yellow legs and black-tipped yellow bill; in non-breeding and immature plumage by shorter black bill and darker grey back; in flight by dark leading edge of wings which contrasts with pale secondaries. Has very fast wing beats and frequently hovers when feeding. Small flocks mostly on the east coast. 24 cm (Kleinsterretjie)

2 BLACK-NAPED TERN *Sterna sumatrana*

Rare vagrant. Intermediate in size between (1) and Common Tern (overleaf). A small, very pale tern with diagnostic black line running from eyes and broadening to form a black patch on nape. First primary feather noticeably black in flight. Immature resembles (1) but is larger, has longer, slightly decurved bill and pink flush on breast if seen at close range. Associates with (1) and Common Terns on KwaZulu-Natal coast. 33 cm (Swartkroonsterretjie)

3 GULL-BILLED TERN *Gelochelidon nilotica*

Rare vagrant. Similar in size to (4) but differs in having a thick, stubby, black bill unlike that of any other tern. At rest reveals unusually long legs and stands higher than other terns. Occurs mostly over inland waters and feeds like a marsh tern (p. 60), often pursuing insects. 38 cm (Oostelike sterretjie)

4 SANDWICH TERN *Sterna sandvicensis*

Common summer visitor. Much larger than Common Tern (overleaf), its back paler than other similar-sized terns. Differs from (3) in much slimmer appearance and long, thin bill, *black with a yellow tip.* Occurs in small groups along the coast; feeds just offshore and rests on beaches. 40 cm (Grootsterretjie)

5 LESSER CRESTED TERN *Sterna bengalensis*

Common summer visitor. Similar in size to (4) but has darker back and *orange bill.* Differs from (6) in smaller size and orange bill, from much larger Royal Tern (previous page) in size and darker grey back. Feeds in small numbers over estuaries and open sea. 40 cm (Kuifkopsterretjie)

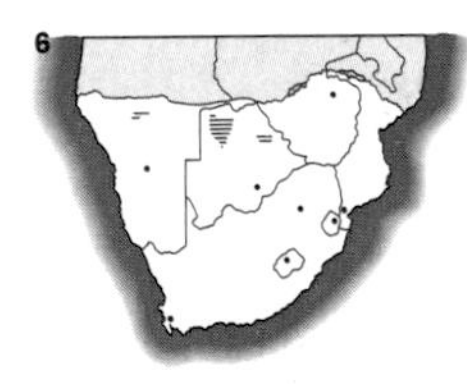

6 SWIFT TERN *Sterna bergii*

Common resident. Intermediate in size between Caspian Tern (previous page) and (4). Bill colour *yellow,* not orange as in (5) and Royal Tern (previous page). Immature has heavily barred back and tail, pale yellow bill and sometimes yellow legs. Occurs in small groups in coastal waters. Roosts on beaches and estuaries. 50 cm (Geelbeksterretjie)

1
Br
N-Br
N-Br
Br
2
Br
J
Br
J
Br
3
N-Br
Br
Br
4
N-Br
Br
Br
5
N-Br
Br
6
Br
N-Br
Br

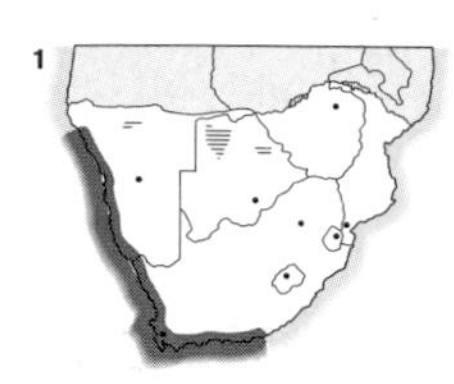

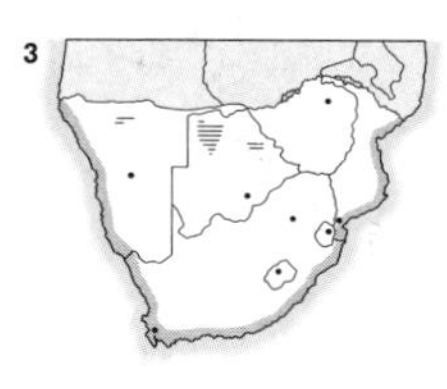

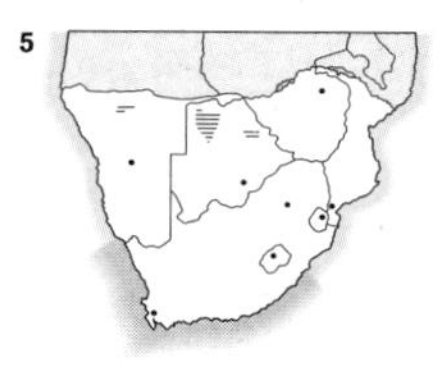

1 DAMARA TERN *Sterna balaenarum* NE

Uncommon, near endemic resident. Small size and all-black cap diagnostic of breeding plumage. At other times differs from Little Tern (previous page) in longer, slightly decurved bill, paler grey back and dumpier body shape. In flight the leading edge of wings not as dark as in Little Tern; at long range appears almost white. Small groups on southern and west coast, feeding offshore and in bays and estuaries. 23 cm (Damarasterretjie)

2 WHITE-CHEEKED TERN *Sterna repressa*

Rare vagrant. In breeding plumage almost identical to (5), differing in back, rump and tail being uniformly dark grey. Also difficult to tell from (3) but is slightly smaller, much darker, uniformly grey above and with much grey on underparts. Flies like a marsh tern (overleaf). Occurs singly in roosts of (3). 33 cm (Witwangsterretjie)

3 COMMON TERN *Sterna hirundo*

Abundant summer visitor. Distinguished from (4) and (5) by longer bill and, at rest, noticeably longer legs; in flight in non-breeding plumage by grey rump and tail, not white as in (4) and (5), and by inner primaries *only* being translucent. Note black tip to red bill in breeding plumage. Occurs in thousands offshore, roosting in estuaries and on beaches. 35 cm (Gewone sterretjie)

4 ARCTIC TERN *Sterna paradisaea*

Common summer visitor. Differs from (3) in very short legs and shorter, thinner bill. In flight in non-breeding plumage grey back contrasts with white rump and tail while *all primaries appear translucent,* and differs from (3) in much whiter appearance, thinner bill and more buoyant flight. Frequents roosts of (3) on beaches and estuaries. 35 cm (Arktiese sterretjie)

5 ANTARCTIC TERN *Sterna vittata*

Common winter visitor. Breeding plumage unmistakable: overall dark grey with long, white cheek-stripe and black cap. Differs from rare (2) in white (not grey) rump and tail and from (6) in darker grey colour, plumper body and thicker, more robust bill. Non-breeding plumage retains much of the grey underparts; bill remains dark red with black at tip and along ridges. Immature heavily barred buff on mantle. Roosts on rocky shorelines and sandy beaches. Feeds far out at sea. Breeds on Tristan group, Marion and Prince Edward islands. 38 cm (Grysborssterretjie)

6 ROSEATE TERN *Sterna dougallii*

Uncommon resident. Differs from all other small terns in much paler back and red bill with dark tip. In breeding plumage breast is suffused with pink but looks white at a distance. Tail streamers very long in this species. Singly or in small groups at coast; found in roosts of (3). 38 cm (Rooiborssterretjie)

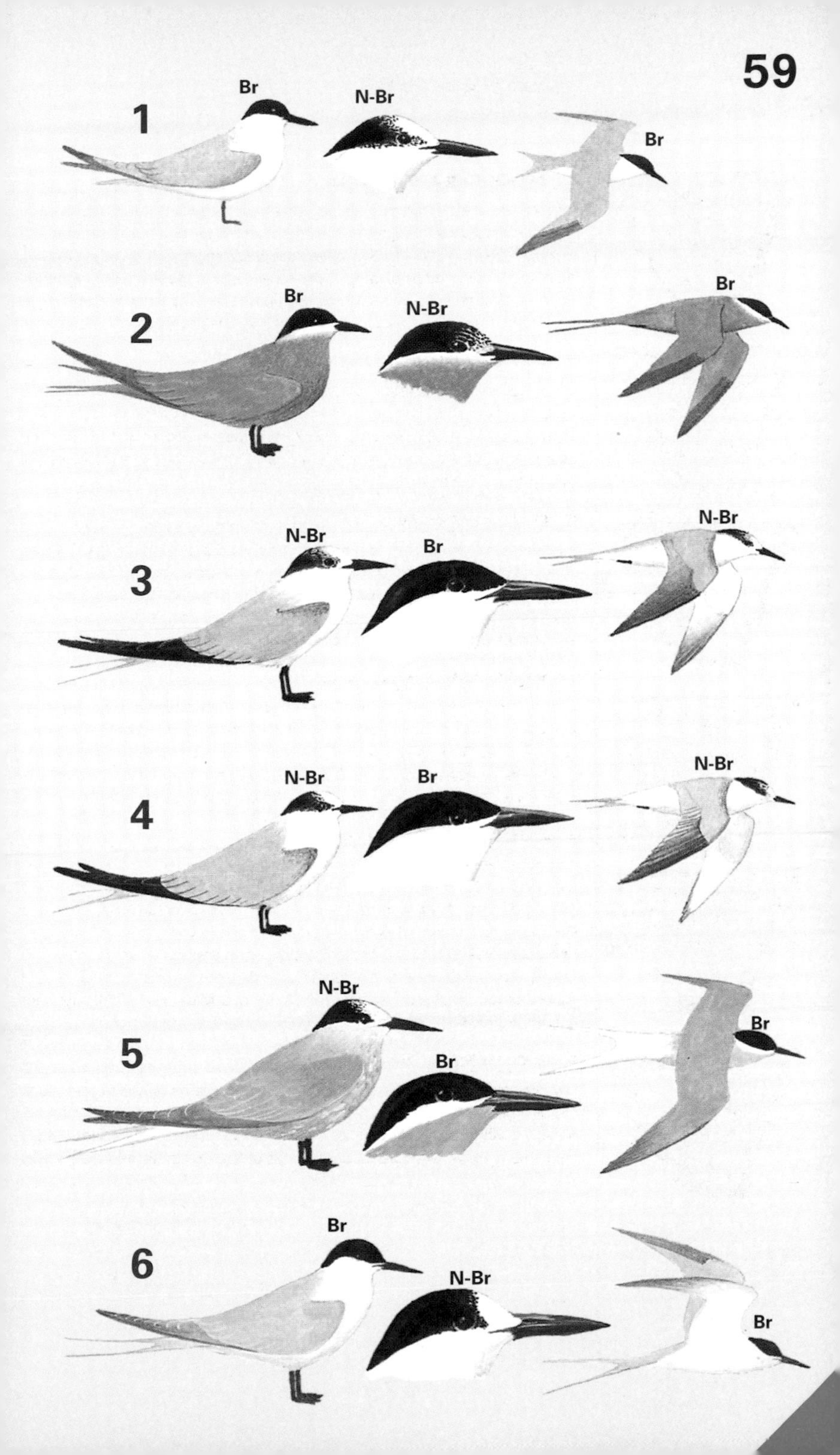

1
Br
N-Br
Br
2
Br
N-Br
Br
3
N-Br
Br
N-Br
4
N-Br
Br
N-Br
5
N-Br
Br
Br
6
Br
N-Br
Br

1 SOOTY TERN *Sterna fuscata*

Uncommon visitor. Very similar to (2) but has dark brown (not grey-brown) back and small triangular white forehead-patch with no white stripe over the eyes. Immature is sooty-brown above and below with buff speckling on back, pale vent and white outer tail feathers. The call is a harsh 'wekawek'. Normally seen only in small numbers after cyclonic weather in the Indian Ocean. 42 cm (Roetsterretjie)

2 BRIDLED TERN *Sterna anaethetus*

Rare vagrant. Slightly smaller than (1), differing in grey-brown back and white on forehead being narrower, extending as white eyebrow-stripe above and behind eyes. Immature is white below, upperparts barred buff, not speckled as in (1). Occurs on east coast with (1) after cyclones. 38 cm (Brilsterretjie)

3 COMMON NODDY *Anous stolidus*

Rare vagrant. Main differences between this species and (4) are size, bill length and extent of white on crown; see head illustrations. Occurs singly, from Mozambique to south-western Cape. Is normally mobbed by Hartlaub's Gulls (p. 52), which mistake it for a skua. 41 cm (Grootbruinsterretjie)

4 LESSER NODDY *Anous tenuirostris*

Rare vagrant. Differs from (3) in size, bill length and extent of white on crown; see head illustrations. Immature very similar to adult but has whiter forehead. Occurs on east coast in roosts of Common Terns (previous page) after cyclones. 36 cm (Kleinbruinsterretjie)

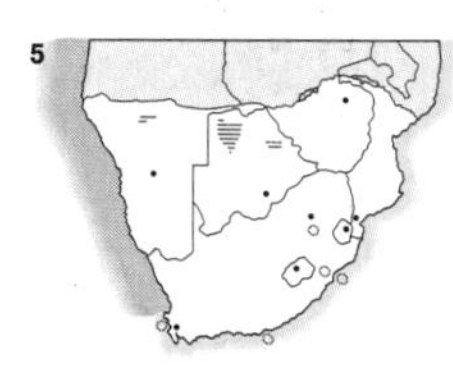

5 BLACK TERN *Chlidonias niger*

Uncommon summer visitor. In non-breeding plumage differs from other marsh terns in slightly smaller size, generally much darker appearance, the rump and tail being uniform with back, more extensive black on head and diagnostic black smudges on sides of breast. Rarely seen inland over fresh water; occurs on coast alongside Common Terns (previous page) and feeds at sea. 23 cm (Swartsterretjie)

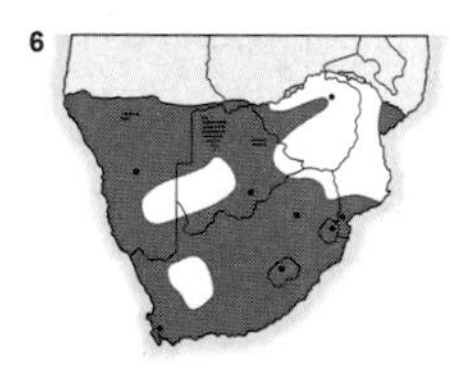

6 WHISKERED TERN *Chlidonias hybridus*

Uncommon resident. In breeding plumage differs from White-cheeked Tern (previous page) in short tail with a shallow fork and white vent; from Antarctic Tern (previous page) in short grey (not white) tail. In non-breeding plumage differs from other marsh terns in less extensive black on head, thicker, heavier bill and less buoyant flight. Occurs on freshwater pans and lakes where it sometimes breeds. 23 cm (Witbaardsterretjie)

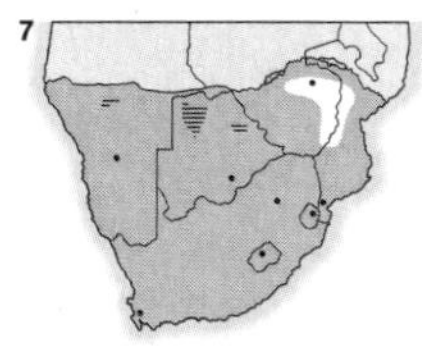

7 WHITE-WINGED TERN *Chlidonias leucopterus*

Common summer visitor. Unmistakable in breeding plumage. In non-breeding plumage differs from (5) in paler head, grey rump, the tail being paler than the back and lack of dark smudges on sides of breast. Occurs over fresh water, sometimes in large numbers. 23 cm (Witvlerksterretjie)

1

2

3

4

Br

5

N-Br

N-Br

Br

6

Br

N-Br

Br

7

Br

N-Br

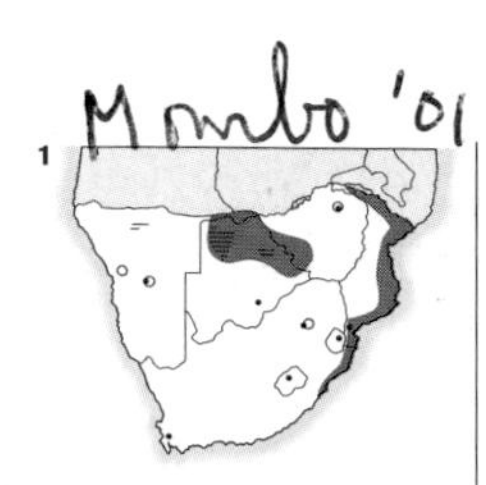

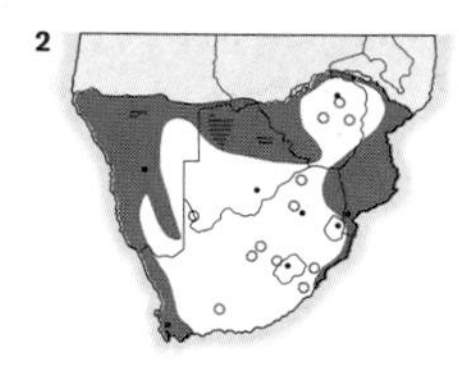

PELICANS

Family PELECANIDAE. Huge, white waterbirds with large bodies, short legs with webbed feet, long necks, long bills and a naked distensible pouch beneath the lower mandible. They catch fish by gathering in flocks and driving the shoals into shallow water where they scoop the fish up in their bill-pouches. Walk awkwardly but soar effortlessly, sometimes to great heights.

1 PINK-BACKED PELICAN *Pelecanus rufescens*

Uncommon, localised resident. Adult in non-breeding plumage has grey upperparts and a greyish-white head and underparts, the bill pale yellow with a pink tip, legs buffy-yellow. In flight told from (2) by greyish underwing and *dark grey* (not black) flight feathers. Adult in breeding condition has the bill pouch rich yellow surmounted by a pink edge to the upper mandible, the legs and feet rich orange-yellow; at close range pinkish feathers can be seen on the back. Immature has a rust-brown head, neck and upperparts, white underparts, and pale yellow bill and pouch; see illustrations. Breeding populations occur in KwaZulu-Natal and northern Botswana; a vagrant elsewhere. 135 cm (Kleinpelikaan)

2 EASTERN WHITE PELICAN *Pelecanus onocrotalus*

Common, localised resident. Adult in non-breeding plumage told from (1) by larger size and all-white appearance; the bill is pale yellow and pink, the pouch yellow, legs yellow. In flight the underwings are white contrasting with *black* flight feathers. Adult in breeding plumage has a pink flush to the body and a yellow patch on the upper breast; the upper mandible remains pink and grey and the pouch yellow, but the legs and feet turn pink. Immature has head and neck dusky in various degrees (darkest when young), dark brown wings and tail, the underparts yellowish as illustrated. Occurs in flocks on coastal islands (including artificial guano islands), estuaries, bays, lagoons and occasionally on large dams; locally common in the vicinity of Cape Town, Walvis Bay and Swakopmund in Namibia and in northern Botswana. 180 cm (Witpelikaan)

1
J
N-Br
Br
Br
2
J
N-Br

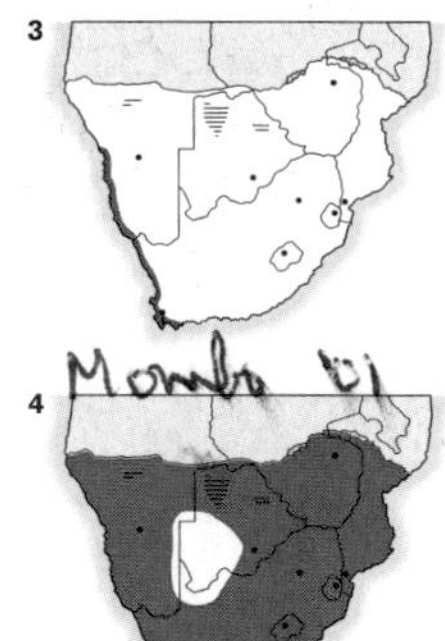

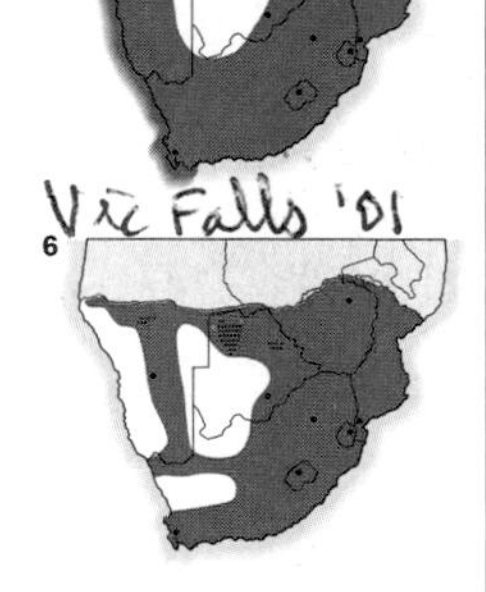

CORMORANTS

Family PHALACROCORACIDAE. Waterbirds with webbed feet, long necks and hooked bills. They eat fish and frogs, which they hunt under water; they surface to swallow their prey. Swim with body partially submerged and habitually stand out of water with wings outspread to dry. Distribution of (1-3) marine, (4-6) mainly fresh water. Silent birds.

1 CAPE CORMORANT *Phalacrocorax capensis* E

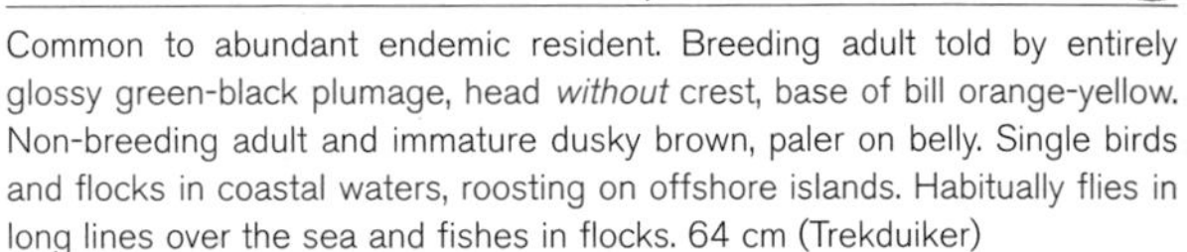

Common to abundant endemic resident. Breeding adult told by entirely glossy green-black plumage, head *without* crest, base of bill orange-yellow. Non-breeding adult and immature dusky brown, paler on belly. Single birds and flocks in coastal waters, roosting on offshore islands. Habitually flies in long lines over the sea and fishes in flocks. 64 cm (Trekduiker)

2 BANK CORMORANT *Phalacrocorax neglectus* E

Common endemic resident. Told by heavy-bodied appearance, crested head and a white rump when breeding; wings dark brown, rest black with bronze sheen. Immature duller black. Single birds or small groups in coastal waters, especially standing on small islands and offshore rocks. 75 cm (Bankduiker)

3 CROWNED CORMORANT *Phalacrocorax coronatus* E

Fairly common endemic resident. A marine cormorant told from (4) by an overall *blacker appearance,* permanent crest all year and shorter tail. Immature is brown. Singly or in small groups on rocky coastlines and coastal islands, occasionally lagoons. 54 cm (Kuifkopduiker)

4 REED CORMORANT *Phalacrocorax africanus*

Common resident. Adults with all-black bodies (male with small crest on forehead) and grey-brown speckled wings; female illustrated is a sub-adult, at which stage it is able to breed. Both sexes have yellow to reddish facial skin and ruby-red eyes, the bill yellow. The brownish immature has off-white (never pure white) underparts, upper breast more buffy. Singly or in groups on any inland water. Occasionally at the coast; cf. (2). 60 cm (Rietduiker)

5 WHITE-BREASTED CORMORANT *Phalacrocorax carbo*

Common or localised resident. Identified by large size, white throat and breast or, in immature, entirely white underparts, *much whiter* than immature of (4). Adult has green eyes, pale grey bill with a darker culmen and yellow facial skin. Singly or in groups on coastal rocks, islands and estuaries, plus large inland waters. 90 cm (Witborsduiker)

DARTERS

Family ANHINGIDAE. Slender-necked, straight-billed diving birds.

6 DARTER *Anhinga melanogaster*

Common resident. Told from cormorants by longer, thinner neck with a characteristic kink, straight (not hooked) bill, more rufous colouring and generally slender appearance. Male is blacker than female and has long silvery-beige plumes on the mantle when breeding, the bill grey. Female generally browner, the bill creamy-white. Immature similar to female as illustrated, head and neck markings indistinct. Swims with only the head and neck above water and perches with outstretched wings after swimming. Singly or in small groups on large inland waters. 79 cm (Slanghalsvoël)

65
1
J
2
3
4
♂
♀
J
5
J
6
J

HERONS

Family ARDEIDAE. Water-associated birds with long bills and necks and long legs. Egrets are also part of the heron family. When breeding, many species have long, filamentous plumes on their backs or lower breast, or on both, while others have more or less permanent long plumes on their napes. In flight their heads are tucked into their shoulders, thus differing from storks, ibises and cranes. They seldom soar. Many herons are solitary in habit and secretive, others are gregarious and much in evidence. Most perch in trees and nest in trees or reeds, or even on the ground. All have harsh, squawking voices heard mostly when flushed. The four comparative silhouettes on the page opposite represent A: Dwarf Bittern (1); B: Squacco Heron (p. 68); C: Little Egret (p. 72); D: Grey Heron (p. 74).

1

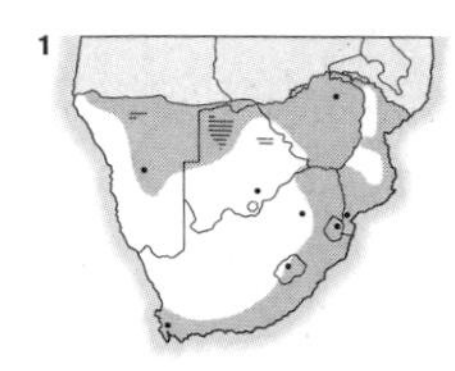

1 DWARF BITTERN *Ixobrychus sturmii*

Uncommon summer resident and visitor. Adult unmistakable with slate-grey upperparts and heavily streaked underparts but looks all-dark at a distance; orange-yellow legs and feet hang down in flight. Immature has rufous underparts and rufous-tipped feathers to the upperparts, differing from other immature small herons in this and orange-yellow legs. The flight is direct and pigeon-like. Usually solitary (sometimes breeds in loose colonies) and largely crepuscular or nocturnal. Frequents well-wooded rivers and bushes or thickets standing in floodwaters. When disturbed may adopt a sky-pointing posture; see illustration. Perches in a tree when flushed. Nomadic. 25 cm (Dwergrietreier)

2

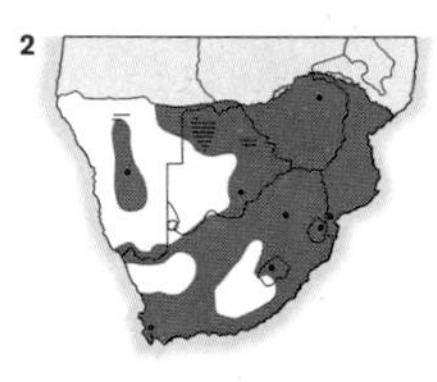

2 LITTLE BITTERN *Ixobrychus minutus*

Uncommon resident and visitor. Bold markings of male unmistakable; female recognised by buffy neck and black cap. Immature differs from that of (1) mainly in paler, less rufous underparts and olive (not orange-yellow) legs; from immature of (3) in tawny (not dark) folded wings. Solitary or scattered in reed-beds or sedges. A diurnal species. Difficult to flush, sky-pointing to avoid detection. Nomadic. 26 cm (Woudapie)

3

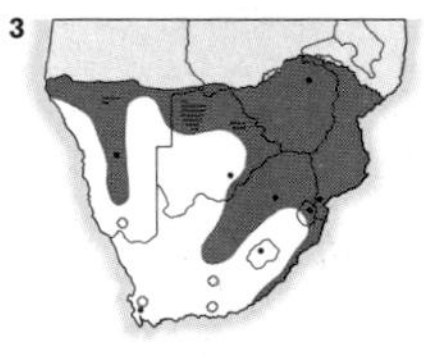

3 GREEN-BACKED HERON *Butorides striatus*

Common resident. In the field its upperparts appear grey-green, the feathers all clearly edged creamy, sides of neck and flanks grey, cap black; takes off with yellow feet prominent. Immature identified by dark upperparts with *whitish spots on folded wings;* cf. immature of (1) and (2). A common small heron, usually singly on well-wooded rivers, large dams, pans and estuaries or lagoons with mangroves. Active by day, hunting from a low branch or dead tree in water or on shoreline. Perches in a tree when flushed. 41 cm (Groenrugreier)

4

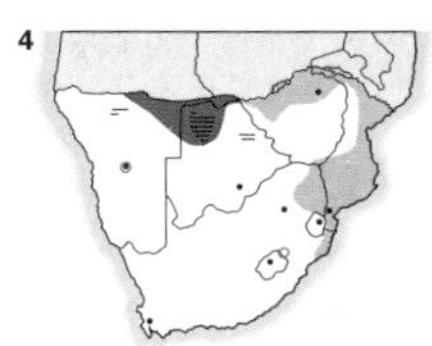

4 RUFOUS-BELLIED HERON *Butorides rufiventris*

Uncommon summer resident and visitor, endemic to southern and central Africa. A robust, all-dark heron. Non-breeding adult has pale yellow bill (upper mandible grey), facial skin and legs. When breeding the bill, facial skin and legs become coral-pink as illustrated. Immature has buff-edged feathers on the upperparts. Nomadic, solitary and secretive on secluded waters with ample fringing and surface vegetation. When flushed perches in a tree or drops into dense vegetation. 58 cm (Rooipensreier)

67
A
B
C
D
J
1
♀
J
♂
2
3
J
Br
4
N-Br

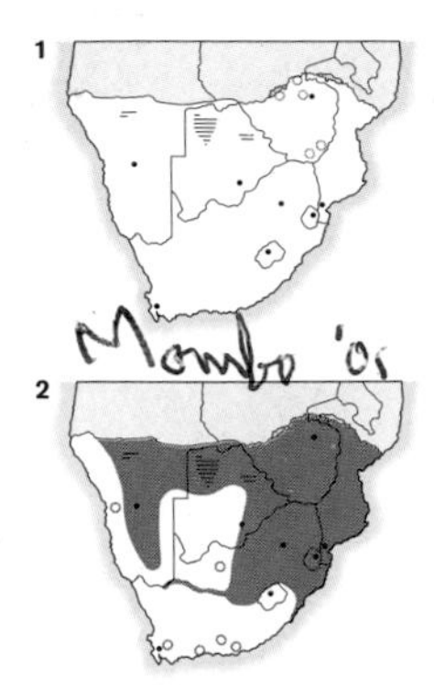

1 MADAGASCAR SQUACCO HERON *Ardeola idae*

Rare winter vagrant. Occurs only in non-breeding plumage, differing from (2) in much darker brown upperparts, neck streaks broader and bolder; in flight these contrast strongly with white wings. Bill greenish with black tip and culmen. Recorded occasionally in eastern Zimbabwe, possibly more frequent in Mozambique; regular in east Africa. 47 cm (Malgassiese ralreier)

2 SQUACCO HERON *Ardeola ralloides*

Fairly common to very common resident. In non-breeding plumage differs from (1) in paler, less contrasting upperparts, the bill yellowish with blackish culmen. Legs normally pale yellow but pinkish-red for a few days when breeding. In flight looks like a white egret unless upperparts visible. Solitary at lakes, lagoons, marshes, sewage ponds and streams. 43 cm (Ralreier)

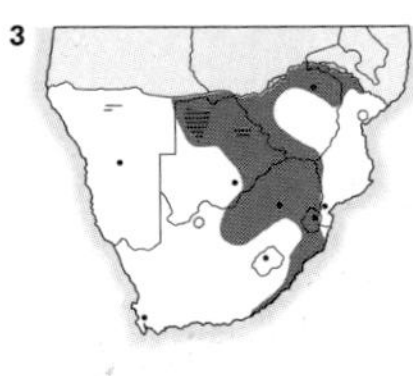

3 BLACK EGRET *Egretta ardesiaca*

Uncommon to locally common resident. Differs from (4) in more robust proportions, uniform overall colouring and dark legs with *bright yellow feet.* Has unique habit of forming a canopy with its wings when fishing. Single birds or groups, sometimes large flocks, at the fringes of lagoons, floodpans and dams, less often on rivers. Nomadic. 66 cm (Swartreier)

4 SLATY EGRET *Egretta vinaceigula*

Uncommon, localised resident. In proportions like a slate-grey Little Egret (p. 72). Distinguished from (3) by *yellow lower legs* and feet and, at close range, buff foreneck plus yellow eyes and facial skin. Plumes on the nape sometimes absent. Seen mostly singly in shallow, well-vegetated floodpans and river backwaters of the Okavango Delta, Linyanti and Chobe River regions of northern Botswana; a vagrant elsewhere. 60 cm (Rooikeelreier)

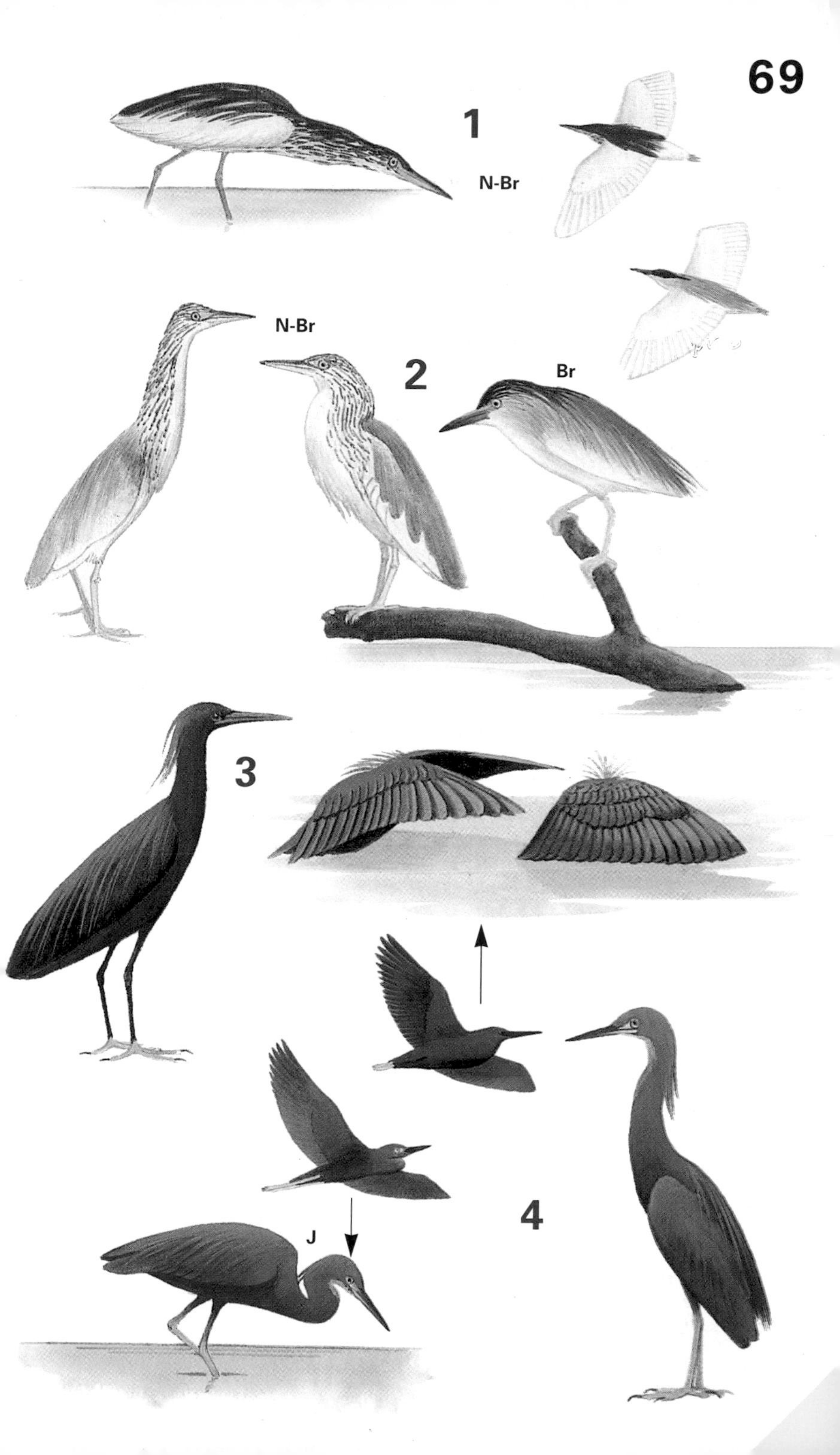
1
N-Br
N-Br
2
Br
3
4
J

1

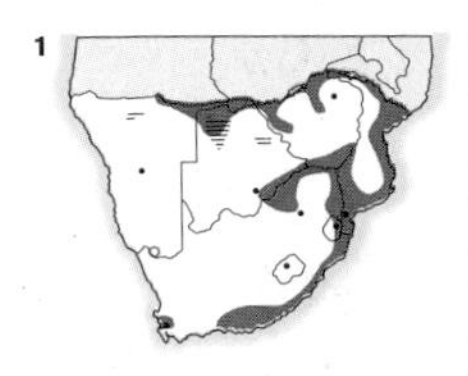

1 WHITE-BACKED NIGHT HERON *Gorsachius leuconotus*

Uncommon resident. Black hood, yellow facial markings and legs plus rufous plumage diagnostic. White back-plumes are present at all ages. When alarmed into flight utters a toad-like 'kraak'. Singly or in pairs, sparsely distributed on quiet rivers and dams where secretive, hiding by day in dense waterside vegetation and emerging only at night. Most frequent on the panhandle of the Okavango River in northern Botswana. 53 cm (Witrugnagreier)

2

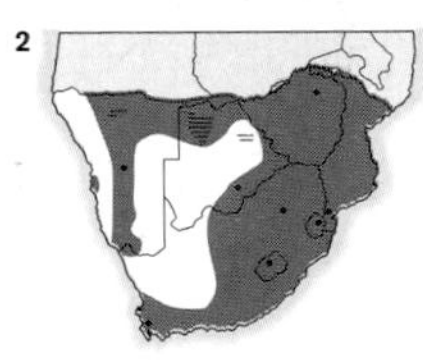

2 BLACK-CROWNED NIGHT HERON *Nycticorax nycticorax*

Common resident and visitor. Adult has characteristic black cap and back contrasting with white and grey wings and underparts; nape-plumes may be absent. Immature differs from adult of (3) in being smaller, with orange eyes and white spots to the tips of the feathers on the upperparts. Single birds, pairs or groups occur on river backwaters, dams and lagoons, roosting by day in trees or waterside vegetation. Some roosts may harbour up to 18 birds each day. It emerges late afternoon in preparation for nocturnal hunting. Nomadic when not breeding. 56 cm (Gewone nagreier)

3

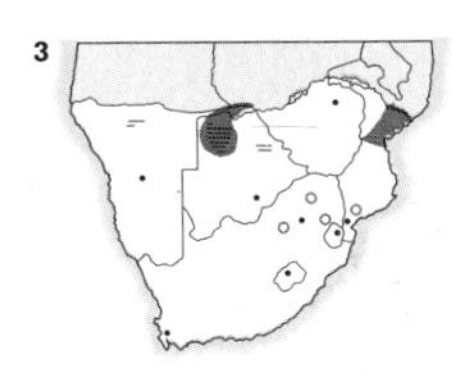

3 BITTERN *Botaurus stellaris*

Rare resident. Similar to immature of (2) but a much larger bird with a more thickset appearance, more heavily streaked overall, with black cap and yellow or red-brown eyes. In flight has a much greater wingspan than (2) and the entire foot protrudes beyond the tail. Normal take-off call is 'squark', otherwise utters a booming call day or night during the breeding season (summer). Solitary and highly secretive in seasonal floodplains, permanent marshes and streams in grassland; where it remains mostly concealed in reed-beds and similar dense, emergent vegetation. When alarmed adopts an upright, sky-pointing stance. Is not easily flushed. 64 cm (Grootrietreier)

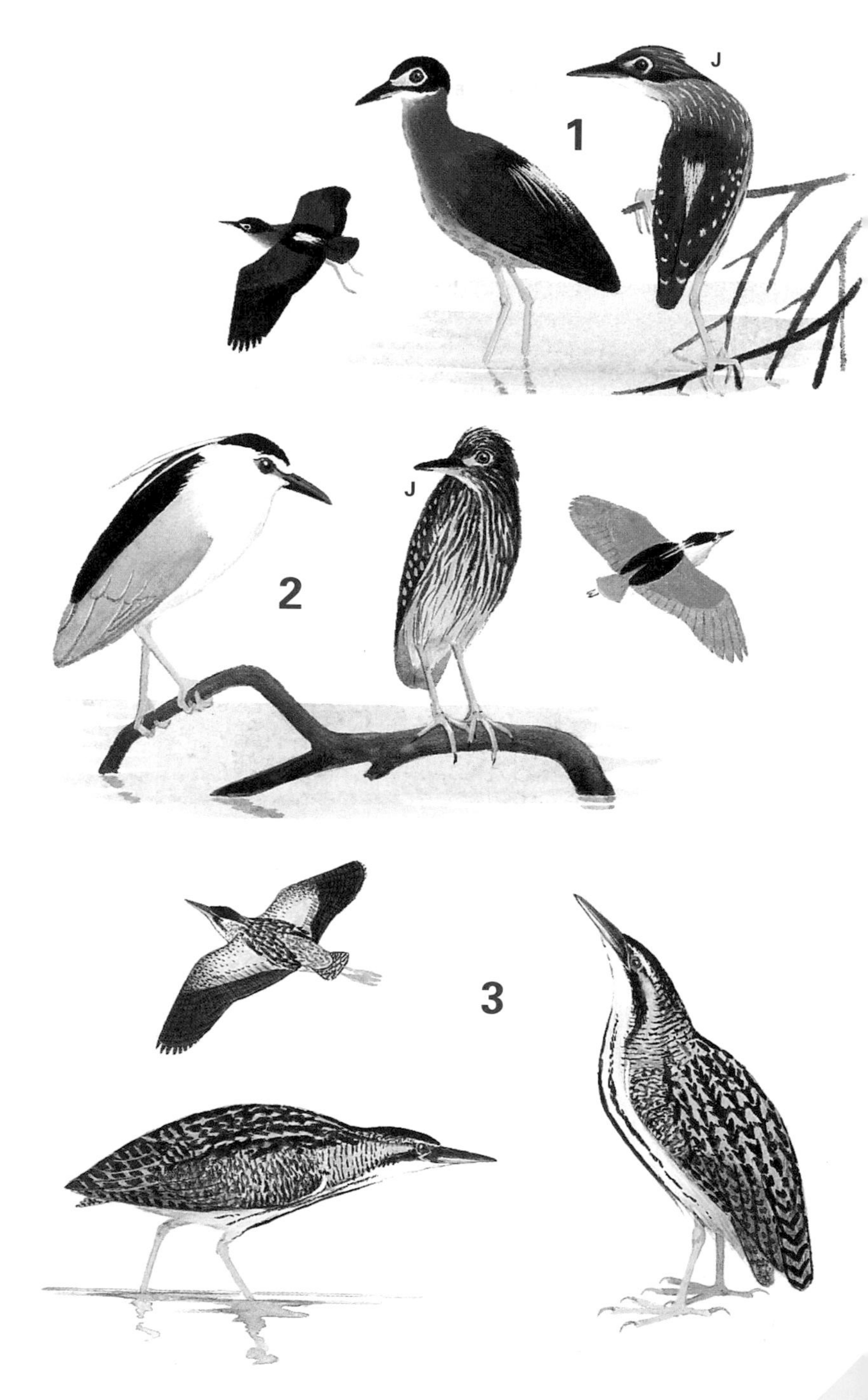
J
1
2
J
3

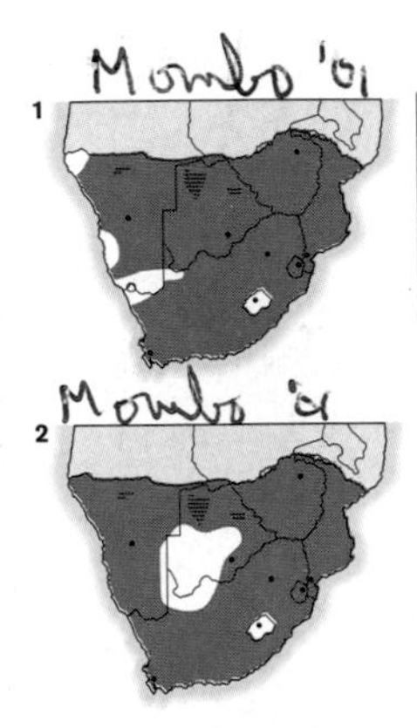

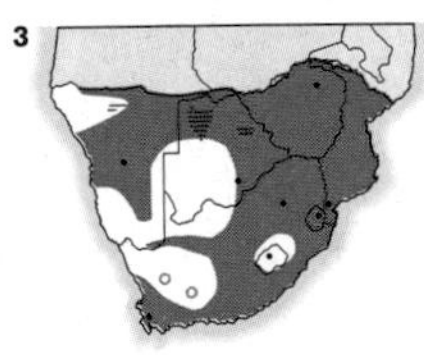

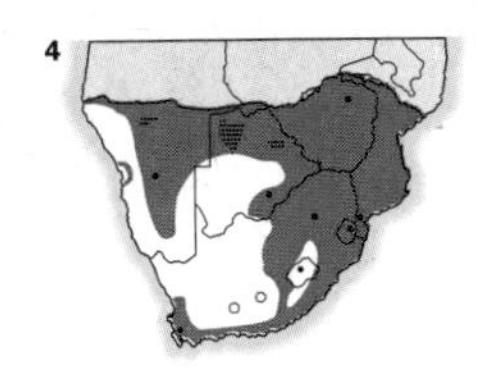

1 **CATTLE EGRET** *Bubulcus ibis*

Very common resident and partial migrant. Buff feathers present on breeding adult October-March only. Bill short, yellow or coral, legs the same, feet dusky. Immature differs from (2) in smaller size, shorter, thicker neck and *black feet.* Flocks, large and small, attend grazing cattle or wild animals in reserves. They fly to and from regular roosts mornings and evenings. Large numbers breed in reeds or in trees over water. Most common in summer when resident birds are augmented by an influx from central Africa. 54 cm (Vee-reier)

2 **LITTLE EGRET** *Egretta garzetta*

Fairly common resident. Larger, longer-necked, more slenderly proportioned than (1), bill and legs longer and black, *feet yellow.* Head-plumes, breast-plumes and back-plumes present only when breeding. Immature lacks plumes. Solitary on quiet inland waters, estuaries and coastal pools, always near water. Stands quietly in shallows or walks forward slowly, stealthily hunting. 64 cm (Kleinwitreier)

3 **YELLOW-BILLED or INTERMEDIATE EGRET** *Egretta intermedia*

Uncommon resident. Larger than (1) and (2), more heavily built, but smaller than (4). Plumes usually absent or reduced when not breeding. Bill and *upper legs normally yellow* (orange-red briefly when breeding), lower legs and feet blackish-green. The neck has the characteristic kink of the larger herons and, in profile, the long lower neck feathers tend to stick out; cf. (4). Often confused with (4) but can be told by the short gape which finishes *below the eye* (not behind it). Usually solitary on quiet, well-vegetated pans and floodlands. 68 cm (Geelbekwitreier)

4 **GREAT WHITE HERON** *Casmerodius albus*

Fairly common resident. Large, long-necked, long-legged egret with normally orange-yellow bill, therefore frequently misidentified as (3), but is much larger with *entirely black legs* and feet. The line of the gape extends *behind the eye;* cf. (3). For a few weeks when breeding the bill is black, often with a yellow base, and filamentous plumes are present on the back. Single birds are usually seen standing motionless in shallows of large rivers, dams, estuaries and floodpans. The species is dispersive and nomadic. 95 cm (Grootwitreier)

Br
N-Br
1
J
N-Br
2
Br
Br
3
N-Br
4

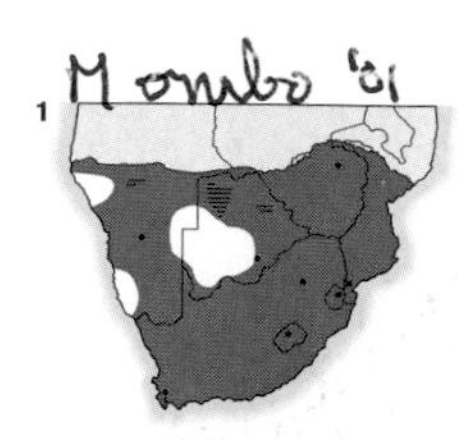

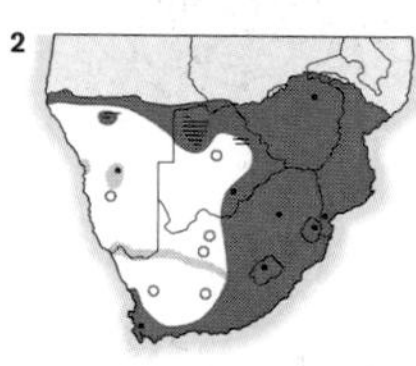

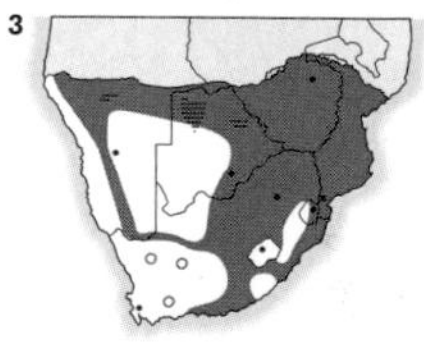

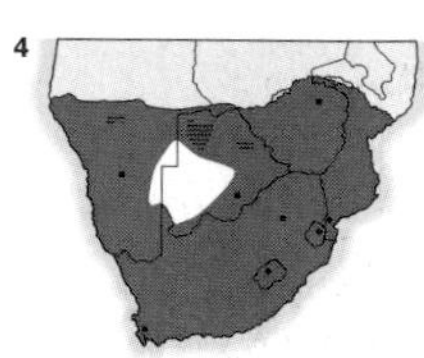

1 GREY HERON *Ardea cinerea*

Common resident. At rest adult differs from the Black-headed Heron (4) in the white crown above a broad black band that extends from forehead to nape; head and neck otherwise white; bill and legs yellow (reddish briefly when breeding). In flight shows *entirely grey underwings.* Immature is much paler than adult and immature of the Black-headed Heron, also differing in the yellow (not grey) bill and legs. Solitary, feeding in the shallows of quiet dams, pans, rivers, lagoons and estuaries; may sometimes forage in coastal rock pools. Stands motionless for long periods or creeps forward stealthily in a crouched attitude. 100 cm (Bloureier)

2 PURPLE HERON *Ardea purpurea*

Fairly common resident. Often confused with (3) but is much smaller, more slender; the neck is slender and snake-like, the bill thin. Immature less brightly coloured about the neck, markings less clearly defined. Solitary and secretive, preferring the shelter of reeds and other emergent vegetation fringing quiet dams, pans and marsh pools. May visit garden fish ponds. Nomadic. 89 cm (Rooireier)

3 GOLIATH HERON *Ardea goliath*

Uncommon resident. Larger than all other herons, more robustly proportioned, with slate-grey upperparts and rich rufous underparts. The heavy bill and long legs are slate-grey. Immature browner above, whitish streaked with brown below. Singly or in pairs on rivers, lakes, pans and estuaries. Hunts in deeper waters than most other herons, standing motionless for long periods or walking slowly. Flies with very slow wing beats. 140 cm (Reusereier)

4 BLACK-HEADED HERON *Ardea melanocephala*

Common resident. Differs from the superficially similar Grey Heron (1) in entirely black (or dark blue-grey) top to the head and back of the neck, plus slate-grey bill and legs; in flight told by *black and grey underwings.* Immature greyer than immature of the Grey Heron, bill and legs pale grey (not yellow). Singly or in scattered groups in grassland (especially pastures), grassy road verges, farmlands and marshes. *Seldom feeds in water* but roosts and breeds in trees or in reeds over water. 97 cm (Swartkopreier)

J
1
2
3
4
J

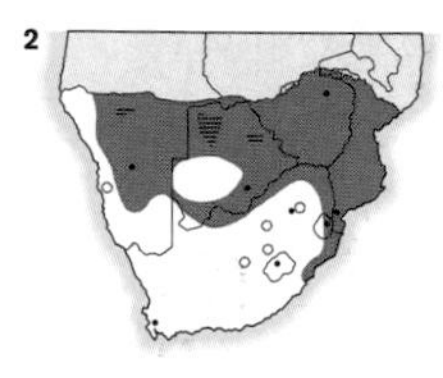

STORKS

Family CICONIIDAE. Large to very large long-legged and long-necked birds with straight, stout bills. Plumage mostly black and white or blackish, bills and legs whitish, reddish or dark. Storks walk with stately gait and frequently rest on the ground with the lower part of their legs stretched forward; see illustration of immature Marabou (2). In flight the neck is stretched out (unlike herons, which fly with the neck retracted) and the legs may trail down at a slight angle to the body. Most members of this family sometimes soar to great heights during the heat of the day, many are communal in habits and most frequent water or damp places to some extent. Food ranges from large insects, reptiles, frogs and other waterlife to carrion in one species. They have no voice except guttural sounds and hisses made at the nest, but bill-clapping is used as a greeting between pairs. The nests are large stick structures placed in trees or on rocks, cliffs or the ground, according to species.

1 SADDLE-BILLED STORK *Ephippiorhynchus senegalensis*

Uncommon resident. A large, strikingly coloured stork unlikely to be confused with any other either at rest or in flight. Immature has grey instead of black markings, the white areas mottled with black, bill dull, blackish. Singly or in pairs in the shallows of large rivers, lakes, dams, floodplains and marshes. 145 cm (Saalbekooievaar)

2 MARABOU STORK *Leptoptilos crumeniferus*

Uncommon to locally common visitor and resident. A huge, bare-headed, bare-necked stork with a distensible fleshy pouch on the lower foreneck. Unlike other storks flies with the neck tucked in. Immature, as illustrated, has a woolly covering to the head. Generally in groups of a few birds, sometimes larger flocks, frequently associating with vultures at animal carcasses and refuse dumps. Mostly found in wildlife sanctuaries where many congregate at kills or around camps. Groups also gather on river sandbanks to bathe and rest. Sometimes soars to great heights. Otherwise spends much time standing inactive or perched. 152 cm (Maraboe)

♀

♂

1

2

J

1
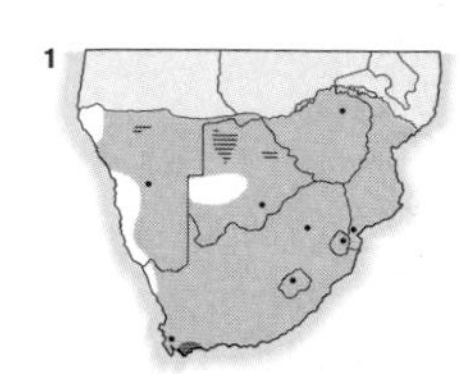

2
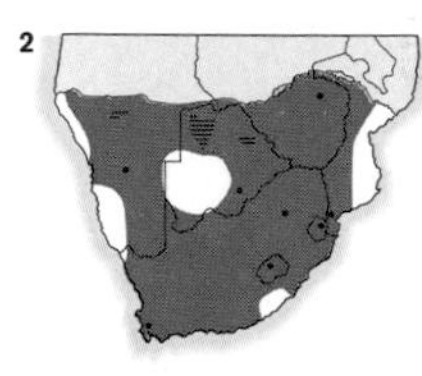

3
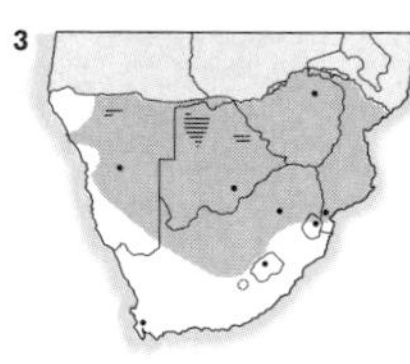

1 WHITE STORK *Ciconia ciconia*

Common summer visitor and resident. Unmistakable, large black and white stork with red bill and legs. Seen singly or in small groups. In summer large flocks feed in grassland, farmlands and bushveld, often mixing with Abdim's Storks (3). They tend to avoid large, permanent floodplains and marshes. Flocks often soar and travel at great heights on hot days. May suddenly appear in a district and remain a few days to feed, then depart, this behaviour especially linked to infestations of agricultural pests. Annual influxes vary from year to year. 117 cm (Witooievaar)

2 BLACK STORK *Ciconia nigra*

Uncommon resident. Similar to Abdim's Stork (3) but differing from it in larger size, red bill and longer, red legs. Immature has a yellowish-green bill and legs, and duller black plumage. Occurs *singly or in pairs* but groups sometimes gather to roost in trees at night. Frequents cliffs and gorges when breeding, otherwise forages on rivers, dams and estuaries. 122 cm (Grootswartooievaar)

3 ABDIM'S STORK *Ciconia abdimii*

Common non-breeding summer visitor. Smaller, shorter-legged than the Black Stork (2), the bill tawny, face blue and legs pink with red joints and feet. In flight this species and the Black Stork are difficult to tell apart unless seen at close range, but Abdim's Stork *usually occurs in flocks,* sometimes in hundreds. Feeds in grassland, agricultural lands and bushveld, often mixing with White Storks (1). Flocks soar to great heights when moving and, like White Storks, move about in response to insect outbreaks. 76 cm (Kleinswartooievaar)

1

2

3

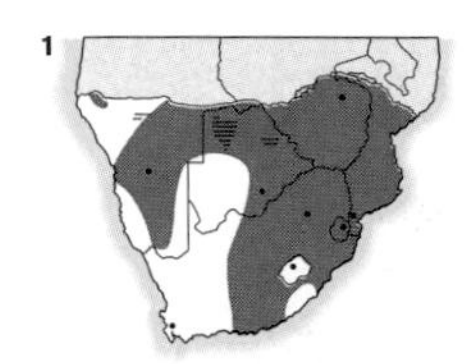

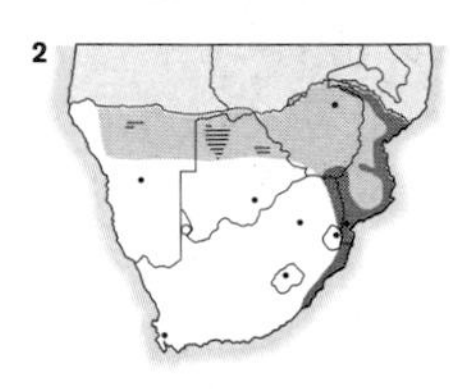

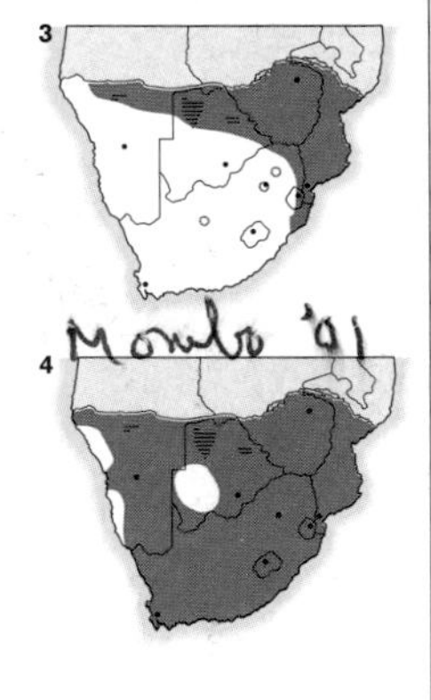

1 YELLOW-BILLED STORK *Mycteria ibis*

Fairly common to locally common resident and visitor. Told by white plumage, yellow bill and red face, forehead and legs; the white plumage has a pink tinge when breeding. Immature has greyish plumage; the bill is grey with a yellow base and the red on the head is lacking; see illustration. Small groups or large flocks occur on floodpans, large rivers, lakes and estuaries, usually near woodlands. Feeds by wading and probing with the bill partly open beneath the water while constantly moving. 97 cm (Nimmersat)

2 WOOLLY-NECKED STORK *Ciconia episcopus*

Sparse resident and common summer visitor. Identified by woolly white neck and head with black face; undertail coverts *project beyond the tail.* Immature similar but duller, the bill horn-coloured. Usually singly but large influxes during summer at floodplains, pans and rivers in well-wooded regions of northern Botswana and the Zambezi Valley in Zimbabwe. 86 cm (Wolnekooievaar)

3 OPEN-BILLED STORK *Anastomus lamelligerus*

Uncommon to locally common resident and visitor. A small stork appearing all-black with a tawny bill. At close range the gap between the mandibles is visible; this is lacking in the immature. Singly or in flocks at large rivers, floodlands and pans in wooded regions. Feeds on freshwater mussels and snails caught while wading. Rests at the waterside or perches in trees. Nomadic; flocks on the move soar to great heights. It breeds opportunistically when water levels are suitable, building nests colonially in trees in floodlands. 94 cm (Oopbekooievaar)

HAMERKOP

Family SCOPIDAE. A long-legged freshwater bird, widespread in Africa south of the Sahara and having no close relatives.

4 HAMERKOP *Scopus umbretta*

Common resident. A small, dull brown waterbird with a large, backward projecting crest and heavy, conical black bill; sexes are alike, immature similar. In flight sometimes utters a nasal 'wek … wek … wek …'; at rest may repeatedly utter a wavering, high-pitched 'wek-wek-warrrrk'. Singly, sometimes in groups when feeding, at almost any freshwater locality and at estuaries. Feeds in the shallows, shuffling its feet to disturb frogs and fish. At deeper waters of large lakes may hover briefly before swooping down to seize fish near the surface. Builds huge, domed nests in waterside trees (see illustration) or on cliffs. 56 cm (Hamerkop)

81
1J
1
2
3
4

1

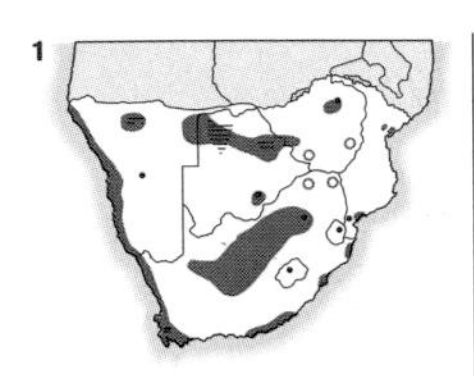

2

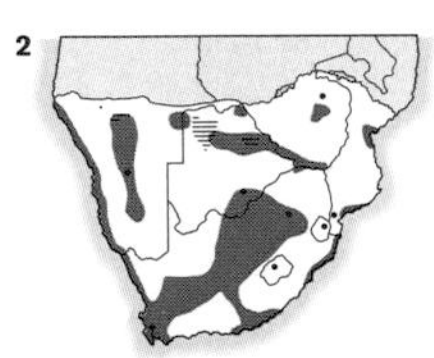

3

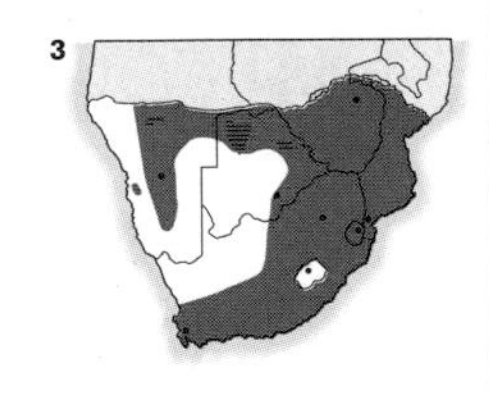

FLAMINGOES

Family PHOENICOPTERIDAE. Occur in flocks of many thousands or singly. The two species may be found together. They prefer shallow saline pans, dams and estuaries, as well as sheltered coastal bays, but are nomadic and remain in one place only for as long as conditions are suitable. Over most of the region they are infrequently seen. Both species have a honking call which, in flocks, sounds like babbling. Immatures are grey-brown with a bill pattern similar to that of adults.

1 LESSER FLAMINGO *Phoeniconaias minor*

Locally abundant resident and visitor. Its regular haunts are indicated on the map in solid red but it may occur temporarily anywhere within the shaded area. Distinguished by evenly coloured *dark maroon bill* which looks black at a distance. This species is pinker, more evenly coloured than the Greater Flamingo. In flight the wing coverts are mottled with dark red. 102 cm (Kleinflamink)

2 GREATER FLAMINGO *Phoenicopterus ruber*

Locally abundant resident and visitor. Its regular haunts are indicated on the map in solid red but it may occur temporarily anywhere within the shaded area. Distinguished by *pink bill with black tip.* In company with the Lesser Flamingo it appears taller and whiter. In flight the wing coverts are a uniform scarlet. 140 cm (Grootflamink)

IBISES AND SPOONBILLS

Family PLATALEIDAE. Fairly large waterbirds with longish legs. Ibises have decurved bills, spoonbills have spatulate bills. All but the Hadeda Ibis are silent.

3 AFRICAN SPOONBILL *Platalea alba*

Fairly common resident. Distinguished from other white waterbirds by pink legs and pink, spoon-shaped bill. Immature has wings and head streaked brown. Singly or in groups on seasonal pans, floodplains, dams, lagoons and rivers. It feeds by moving its partially open bill in a sideways action below water. It breeds colonially in reed-beds or in trees. Nomadic when not breeding. 91 cm (Lepelaar)

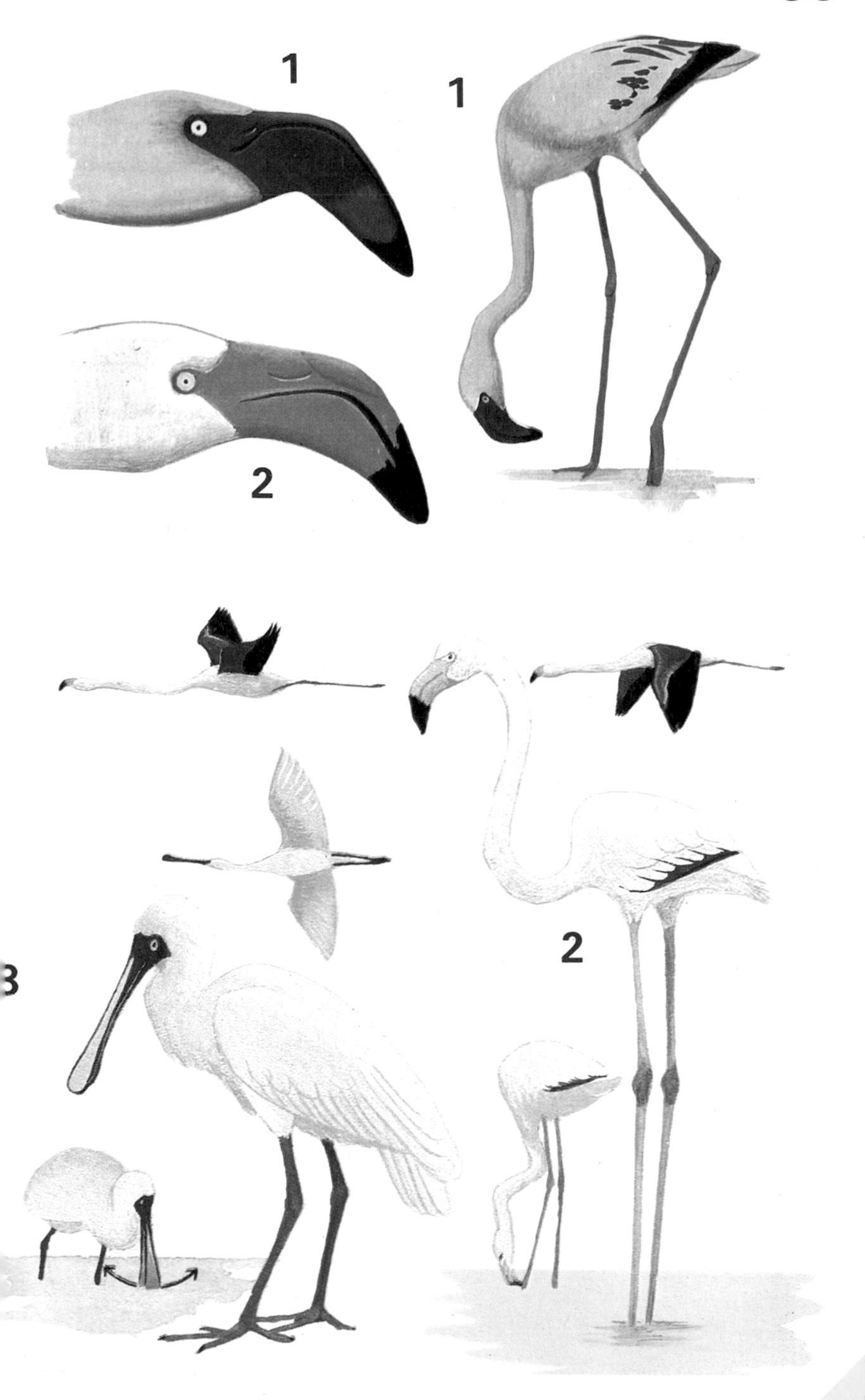
1
1
2
2
3

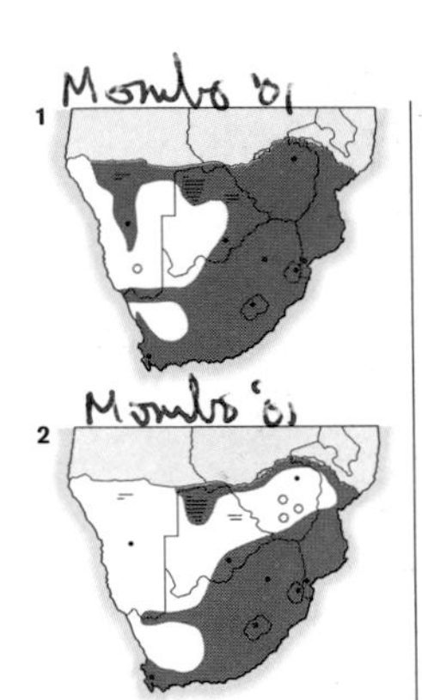

1 SACRED IBIS *Threskiornis aethiopicus*

Common resident. The decurved black bill and black head, neck and legs contrast with otherwise white plumage. In the immature the black head and neck are speckled white, front of the neck white; see illustration. Groups or flocks forage in marshy ground, dams, on shorelines, agricultural lands, rubbish dumps and in breeding colonies of other large birds. Migratory to some degree within Africa; in southern Africa is most common in summer. 89 cm (Skoorsteenveër)

2 HADEDA IBIS *Bostrychia hagedash*

Common resident. Identified by heavy body with fairly short legs, decurved bill and iridescent pink shoulder plus white cheek-stripe. In flight shows heavy, broad wings. Immature is dull, fluffy-headed. Very noisy, especially early morning and evening; when perched or in flight utters a raucous 'HA! ha-a-a … ha-ha-a-a …'. Often several call in unison. Usually two to six or more feed on damp ground, near water or in vleis, plantations, agricultural lands, playing fields and suburban gardens. Roosts in tall trees and flies to and from feeding grounds early and late in the day. 76 cm (Hadeda)

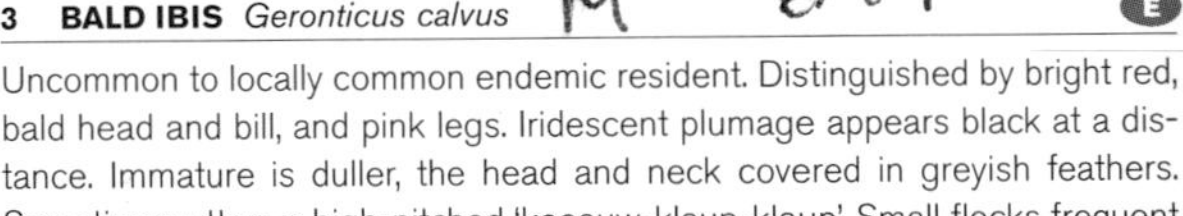

3 BALD IBIS *Geronticus calvus* E

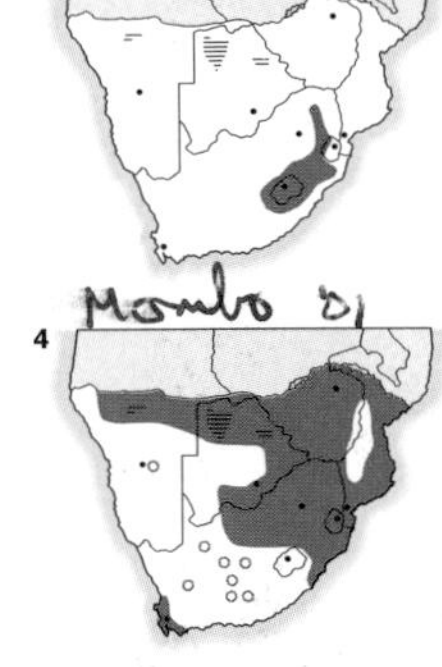

Uncommon to locally common endemic resident. Distinguished by bright red, bald head and bill, and pink legs. Iridescent plumage appears black at a distance. Immature is duller, the head and neck covered in greyish feathers. Sometimes utters a high-pitched 'keeauw-klaup-klaup'. Small flocks frequent montane grassland in the eastern high-rainfall region, breeding and roosting on cliffs. Feeds singly or in groups in grassland, agricultural lands and burnt veld. 79 cm (Kalkoenibis)

4 GLOSSY IBIS *Plegadis falcinellus*

Locally common resident and visitor. More slender and lighter-bodied than other ibises. Bronze-brown with iridescent green wings when breeding; at other times the head and neck are flecked with white; see illustrations. Immature is a paler brown, the throat whitish. Single birds or small flocks frequent grasslands, farmlands, vleis, pans, sewage works and lake shores. 71 cm (Glansibis)

FINFOOTS

Family HELIORNITHIDAE. Three species worldwide; one in Africa. Resemble ducks and cormorants but are unrelated to either.

5 AFRICAN FINFOOT *Podica senegalensis*

Uncommon resident. Differs from ducks and cormorants in bright orange-red bill and legs. Has no characteristic call. Singly or in pairs on quiet, tree-fringed rivers where it swims quietly beneath the overhanging branches. Swims with much of the body submerged, head and neck stretched forward with each foot-stroke. Shy and retiring. If disturbed, flies low across the water paddling with its feet, making a distinctive splashing sound. Seldom flies. Roosts at night on a low, overhanging branch. 63 cm (Watertrapper)

1

J

2

3

4

N-Br

Br

5

♀

♂

♂

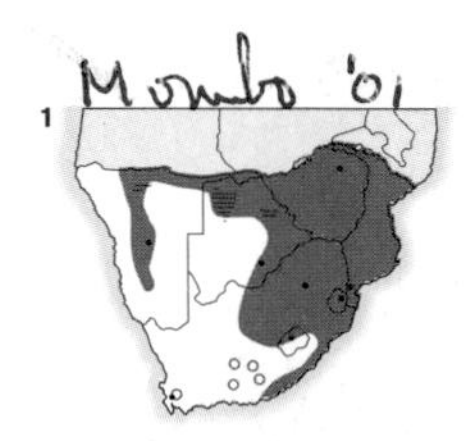

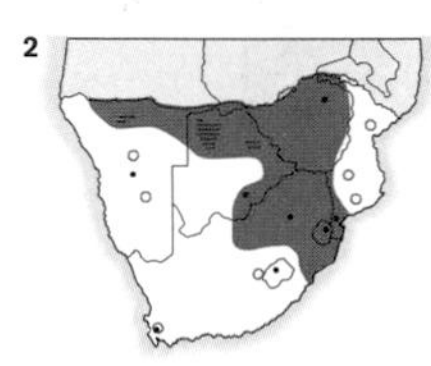

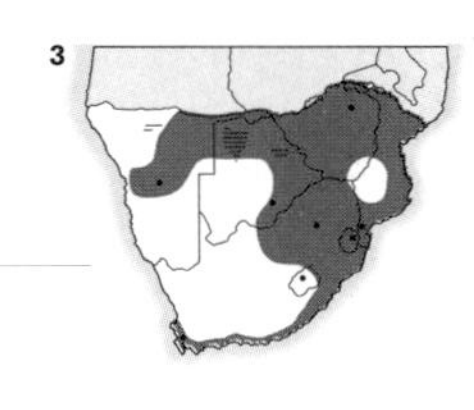

GEESE AND DUCKS

Family ANATIDAE. Most of our ducks are either migratory to some extent or locally nomadic, their movements being dictated by food, rainfall and breeding requirements. Many show marked plumage differences between the sexes (sexual dimorphism). Ducks and geese undergo a flightless 4-8 week period each year when they moult all their flight feathers at once.

The large Spur-winged and Egyptian Geese (p. 88) differ from geese of the northern hemisphere in having longer bills and legs, the Pygmy Goose (p. 88) being our only representative of the 'true' geese.

Ducks of the genus *Dendrocygna* or whistling ducks, which include the White-faced and Fulvous Ducks on this page, differ from those of other genera in having close-set legs placed well back on the body which enables them to stand erect and walk without waddling. In addition they show no sexual dimorphism and have whistling voices. In contrast ducks of the genus *Anas*, often referred to as 'dabbling ducks', have widely spaced legs placed centrally on the body which causes them to stand with the body horizontally and to walk with a waddle. They are further typified by quacking voices.

1 WHITE-FACED DUCK *Dendrocygna viduata*

Common resident. Distinguished from female South African Shelduck (overleaf) by black head and neck, darker plumage and *erect stance*. Immature has the face smudged brown. The call is a loud, shrill 'swee-swee-sweeoo', often by many birds in a flying flock. Flocks, often large, occur on large rivers, lakes, dams, estuaries, floodplains and sewage ponds, especially where there is surface and emergent vegetation. Spends much of the day resting on shorelines or sandbanks. It is locally nomadic and also makes long-range movements northwards in winter. 48 cm (Nonnetjie-eend)

2 FULVOUS DUCK *Dendrocygna bicolor*

Fairly common resident. Cream-coloured flank-feathers on golden-brown plumage diagnostic. Immature resembles adult. Less vocal than the White-faced Duck, it repeats two resonant notes 'tsoo-ee'. In pairs or small flocks on a variety of quiet waters, often with the previous species. Spends much time swimming during the day. Is nomadic when not breeding. 46 cm (Fluiteend)

3 WHITE-BACKED DUCK *Thalassornis leuconotus*

Uncommon resident. White back visible only in flight. Best told while swimming by the pale spot at the base of the bill, sharply tapering bill with deep base and a humped back sloping down to the submerged tail. Immature resembles adult. Utters a soft whistle 'cur-wee'. In pairs or small groups on secluded pans, lagoons and dams with ample surface and emergent vegetation. Seldom seen out of water. Dives readily. Nomadic when not breeding. 43 cm (Witrugeend)

1
2
3
1
2
3

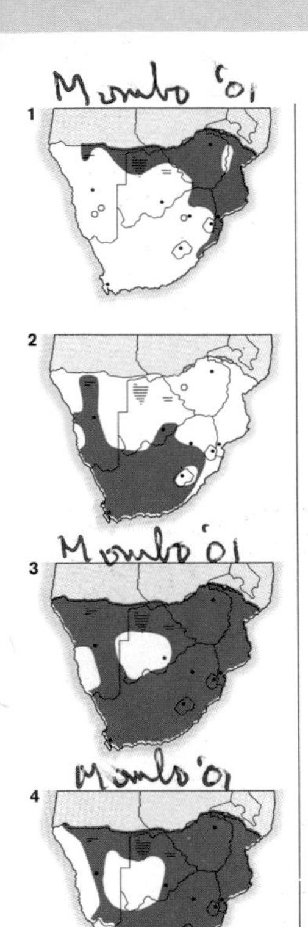

1 PYGMY GOOSE *Nettapus auritus*

Locally common resident. Identified by small size, dark green upperparts and short, yellow bill. Immature resembles female. Male utters a soft twittering whistle 'choo-choo' or 'pee-wee' and a repeated, subdued 'tsu-tswi … tsu-tswi …'; female a weak quack and a twittering whistle. Pairs or groups on quiet, sheltered pans, dams and pools with clear water and water lilies. When alert, remains motionless among the surface vegetation and is difficult to detect. Dives readily and perches in trees. 33 cm (Dwerggans)

2 SOUTH AFRICAN SHELDUCK *Tadorna cana* E

Common endemic resident. A long-bodied duck with horizontal stance. Female differs from White-faced Duck (previous page) in grey (not black) head and neck. In flight both sexes differ from the Egyptian Goose (3) in richer rufous body colouring and grey head plus white face in female. Immature is duller than adult. Female initially has white circles around the eyes, these extending over the face with maturity. Male utters a deep 'hoogh', 'how' or 'honk', the female alternating with a harsher 'hark'; females hiss while accompanying immatures. Courting pairs are noisy and aggressive. Pairs or flocks frequent brackish pans, dams and lakes, and large deep waters especially when in wing-moult, then diving if pursued. May also be seen away from water when breeding. Nomadic when not breeding. 64 cm (Kopereend)

3 EGYPTIAN GOOSE *Alopochen aegyptiacus*

Abundant resident. Distinguished from (2) by long neck, long pink legs and pink bill plus rufous eye-patches. Immature is duller. Very noisy in social interactions; male utters a husky wheezing sound, female a harsh, nasal, high-pitched 'hur-hur-hur-hur'. Both sexes extend the head and neck when calling. Pairs occupy small waters or sections of rivers, but large numbers often gather on deep waters to moult their wing feathers or on sandbanks when large rivers are in spate. Often flies in the evening to communal grazing grounds. 71 cm (Kolgans)

4 SPUR-WINGED GOOSE *Plectropterus gambensis*

Common resident. Very large size and glossy black plumage diagnostic. Mature male has a fleshy caruncle on the forehead and a variable amount of white on the face and underparts, least in southern populations. In flight the prominent white forewings separate this species from Knob-billed Duck (p. 94). Immature is brown, showing little or no white. Not very vocal; male utters a soft, high-pitched 'cherwit' in flight, either sex a four-syllable 'chi-chi-chi-chi'. Occurs in flocks in a variety of wetlands, especially favouring floodplains. Readily perches in dead trees. They fly in V-formations or staggered lines. Very large numbers may gather on deep waters during the winter wing-moult, diving if pursued. 102 cm (Wildemakou)

♂ 1 ♀
♂
♀

♀ 2 ♂
♀

3

♀
J
♂ 4

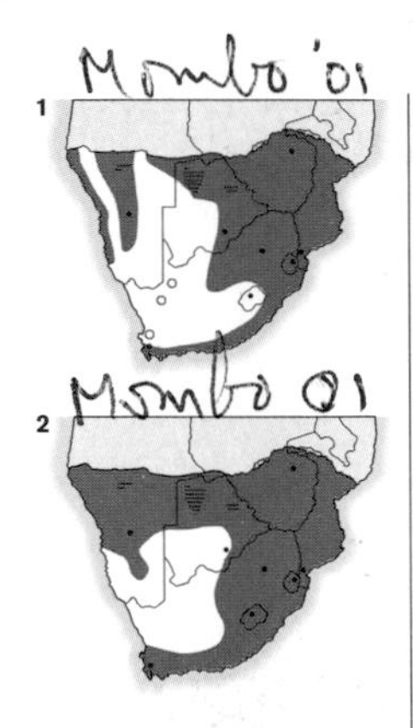

1 HOTTENTOT TEAL *Anas hottentota*

Common resident. Differs from the next species in very small size, grey-blue (not red) bill and absence of any speckling on the rear part of the body. When swimming the flank feathers usually overlap the wing to form a zigzag dividing line. Normally silent. Pairs and groups frequent shallow freshwater marshes, pans and dams, especially sewage ponds. Spends much of day resting out of water. 35 cm (Gevlekte eend)

2 RED-BILLED TEAL *Anas erythrorhyncha*

Very common resident. Larger than the previous species, differing in pinkish-red bill and completely spotted body. In flight shows a creamy speculum. The few sounds made by this species are soft, audible only at close range. Frequently in large flocks on lakes, floodplains, dams and sewage ponds; smaller numbers during the rainy season when there are widespread long-distance dispersals. 48 cm (Rooibekeend)

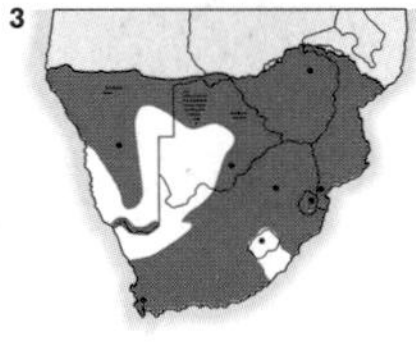

3 SOUTHERN POCHARD *Netta erythrophthalma*

Common resident. Male differs from the Maccoa Duck in darker colouring with uniform head and back, longer neck and more elegant proportions. Female told from female of that species by *whitish crescent on sides of head* plus white throat and bill-base. In flight the whitish speculum extends the full width of the wing. It has no distinctive call. Pairs or flocks occur on deep fresh water. Regular long-distance migrations have been recorded from as far afield as Kenya. 51 cm (Bruineend)

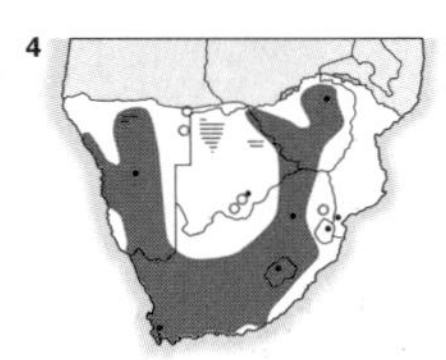

4 MACCOA DUCK *Oxyura maccoa*

Uncommon, nomadic resident. A small, squat species with a thick bill-base. Breeding male unmistakable. Female and male in non-breeding plumage differ from female of the Southern Pochard (3) in *horizontal facial stripes* and squat appearance. Generally silent. Occurs on dams and lakes with extensive fringing reed-beds, usually more females than males. Seldom seen out of water during the day. Swims low in the water with tail trailing, the tip submerged, or with tail stiffly erect. In courtship the male often swims with head and neck stretched forward, the neck inflated and the bill in the water making bubbles, tail erect. Both sexes dive frequently. The species is nomadic during spring and summer. 46 cm (Bloubekeend)

1
2
3
♀
♂
♀
♂
4
♀
♂
♂
♀

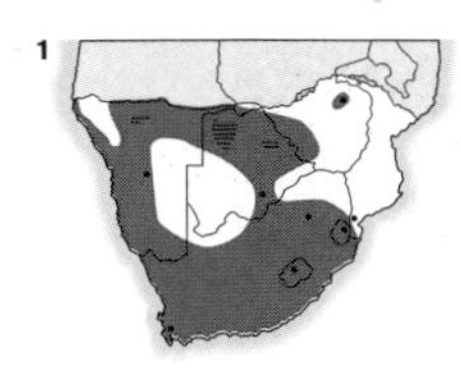

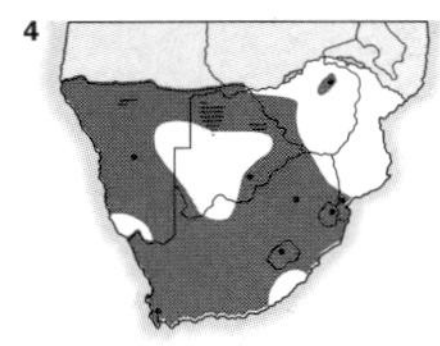

1 CAPE SHOVELLER *Anas smithii*

Common endemic resident. A dull, brownish duck identified by large, black, spatulate bill and yellow-orange legs; cf. (2). In flight shows a dark green speculum and pale blue forewings. Immature is duller. Normally silent but male sometimes utters an explosive 'rrar' or a series of quiet, hoarse 'cawick' sounds with rising inflection, sometimes interspersed with a fast, rattling 'rarararara'; female may utter a series of notes with downward inflection, a rippling chatter 'chachachachacha' or a persistent quacking. Pairs or flocks in shallows of tidal estuaries, lagoons and sewage ponds; indifferent to large, open waters. Most common in the south-western Cape and south-eastern region of southern Africa, moving mostly between the two regions. 53 cm (Kaapse slopeend)

2 NORTHERN SHOVELLER *Anas clypeata*

Very rare visitor. Male most likely to occur in non-breeding plumage as illustrated; then differs from the previous species in larger, pale buff (not black) bill and paler overall appearance. Single birds and pairs occur occasionally in widely separated localities, mostly July-December. Males in breeding plumage are probably escapees from private wildfowl collections. 51 cm (Europese slopeend)

3 GARGANEY *Anas querquedula*

Very rare visitor. Male most likely to occur in non-breeding plumage which resembles that of the female. A small, brownish duck with distinct streaks *above and below the eyes;* differs from female Maccoa Duck (previous page) in this and a more slender bill. Sits low in the water when swimming. Occurs occasionally December-March in Zimbabwe, Botswana and northern South Africa. 38 cm (Somereend)

4 CAPE TEAL *Anas capensis*

Common resident. A small, pale duck with pink, upturned bill; looks almost white at a distance. In flight shows a predominantly white speculum with a dark green central patch. Immature resembles adult. Usually silent. In flocks – large flocks when in wing-moult – on coastal lagoons, salt pans, sewage ponds and tidal mud flats. Has a preference for brackish waters and soda lakes. Long-distance movements have been recorded within southern Africa. 46 cm (Teeleend)

♂
♂
♀
1
♀
♂
♂
N-Br ♂
♀
2
♀
N-Br ♂
♀
♂
3
♀
♀
4

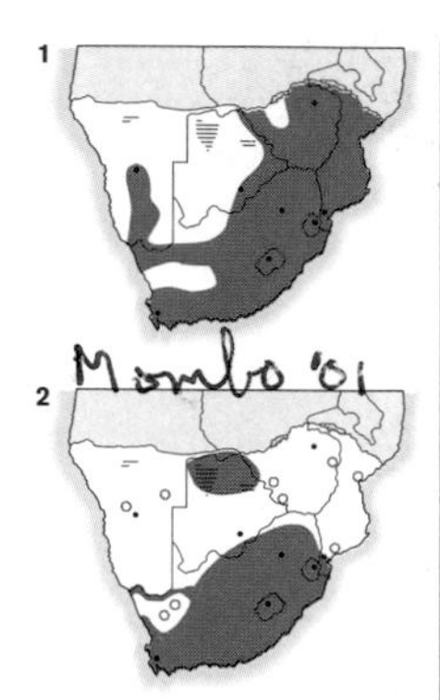

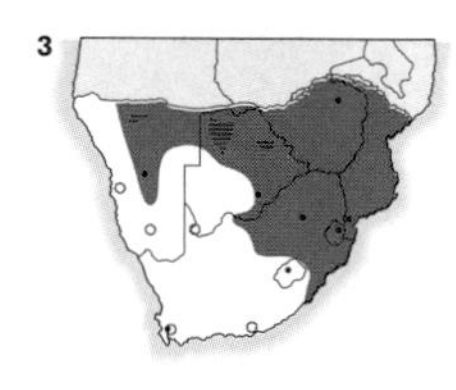

1 AFRICAN BLACK DUCK *Anas sparsa*

Uncommon resident. Characterised by dark grey-brown plumage with bold white spots on wings and back, speculum green with white border. Immature browner, spots buffy, belly barred white. When swimming appears short-necked, long-bodied. Mostly calls when pairs are flying; female utters a persistent, loud quacking, male an almost imperceptible 'weep … weep … weep …'. During the daytime pairs inhabit streams and rivers with stony bottoms (often in well-wooded valleys), moving to larger, open waters at sunset to roost. 51-4 cm (Swarteend)

2 YELLOW-BILLED DUCK *Anas undulata*

Very common resident. Bright yellow bill with black central patch diagnostic. Feathers are brown but edged with white, broadly on flanks and underparts, giving ashy appearance; head and neck dusky. In flight shows iridescent green speculum. Immature has feathers edged buffy, underparts more heavily spotted. No distinctive calls but on taking off female utters loud, evenly spaced quacks. Pairs and flocks on various open waters: estuaries, lakes, dams, flooded lands, pans and slow-running rivers with pools. In the dry season large numbers often congregate on open waters, dispersing widely during rains. 53-8 cm (Geelbekeend)

3 KNOB-BILLED DUCK *Sarkidiornis melanotos*

Uncommon to locally common resident. Male (much larger than female) distinguished by glossy dark blue upperparts, white underparts, the head and neck well speckled black (washed yellow when breeding) and a large fleshy caruncle on forehead and bill. Female duller and lacking caruncle. Immature quite different from adult; see illustrations. In first year (a) has dark brown upperparts and pale buff underparts plus distinct eye-stripe; sub-adult (b) is more like female but underparts orange-buff, with heavier spotting on head and neck. Mostly silent. Flocks, often large in the dry season, frequent marshes, temporary bushveld pans, floodplains and estuaries. Often perches in dead trees. 64-79 cm (Knobbeleend)

PINTAIL (Pylsterteend) see p. 452.

1

2

♂

♀

3

♂ Br

♂ N-Br

3

a

b

1
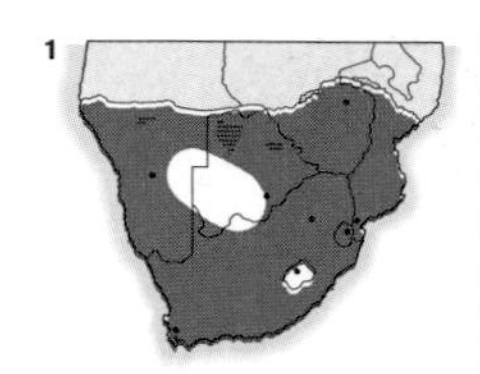
2
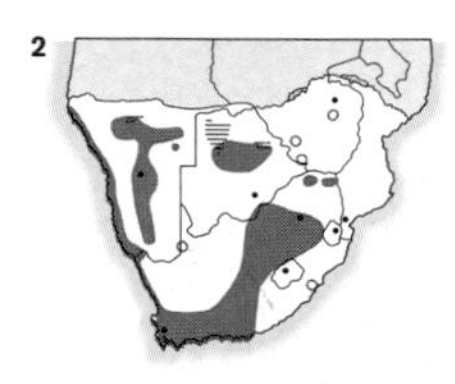
3

4
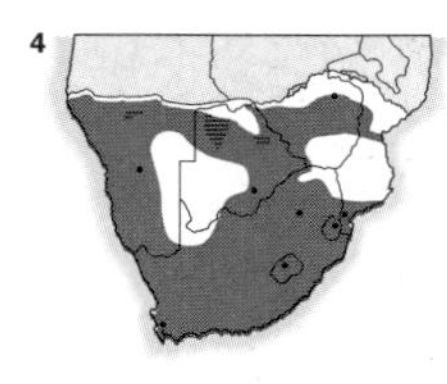

GREBES

Family PODICIPEDIDAE. Small to fairly large, almost tailless waterbirds. Feed beneath the surface by diving, remaining submerged 20-50 seconds. Seldom seen on land but fly long distances at night to new waters. Breeding and non-breeding plumages differ. Small chicks are striped on the upperparts, the head stripes remaining until nearly fully grown. Ride on parents' backs when small.

1 DABCHICK *Tachybaptus ruficollis*

Common resident. Smaller than any duck. Rufous neck and creamy spot at base of bill diagnostic of breeding bird, at other times differs from (2) in dull (not white) underparts and dark eyes. The call is a descending, laughing trill. Single birds or loose groups occur on inland waters, seldom large rivers. Dives frequently and skitters across the water when chasing rivals. 20 cm (Kleindobbertjie)

2 BLACK-NECKED GREBE *Podiceps nigricollis*

Locally common resident. Larger than (1), the black plumage and golden flanks and ear coverts of adult in breeding plumage unmistakable; when not breeding has a white throat and foreneck. *The eyes are red at all times.* Utters a quiet 'poo-eep' and a rapid chattering. Small groups on quiet saline waters or densely packed flocks in sheltered bays on the southern and west coast. When preening habitually exposes its white belly by rolling to one side on the water. Highly nomadic. 28 cm (Swartnekdobbertjie)

3 GREAT CRESTED GREBE *Podiceps cristatus*

Uncommon resident. Unmistakable. In non-breeding plumage differs from (2) in white head with cap only black, darker ruby-red eyes, larger bill and larger overall size. Normally silent. Pairs occur on large inland waters bordered by low, emergent vegetation. On water, when preening, habitually exposes its white underparts like (2). 50 cm (Kuifkopdobbertjie)

COOTS, GALLINULES, MOORHENS, CRAKES AND RAILS

Family RALLIDAE. Small to fairly large, long-legged, large-footed, mainly freshwater-associated birds. A few species inhabit grassland, vleis or lush forest undergrowth. Most water-associated species habitually flick their tails to reveal white undertail coverts. Coots and moorhens are blackish with brightly coloured forehead shields and bills; gallinules have blue-green plumages; crakes and rails have mostly cryptic colouring; the minute flufftails or pygmy crakes with marked sexual dimorphism.

4 RED-KNOBBED COOT *Fulica cristata*

Very common resident. The only all-black waterbird with white frontal shield and bill; legs and lobed feet grey. Immature is ash-brown, no white shield. Normal call 'clukuk' or 'crornk'. Singly or many on open inland waters with reed-beds. Swims, occasionally dives, or walks at edges of reed-beds or on shoreline, occasionally further afield in marshlands. Habitually stands on floating nest mounds. Frequently pursues other coots in noisy overwater chases. 43 cm (Bleshoender)

1
Br
N-Br
2
N-Br
Br
Br
3
N-Br
4

1 

2 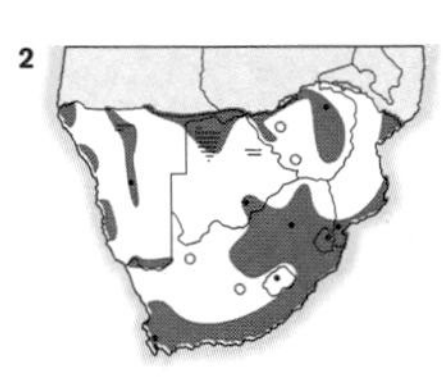

3 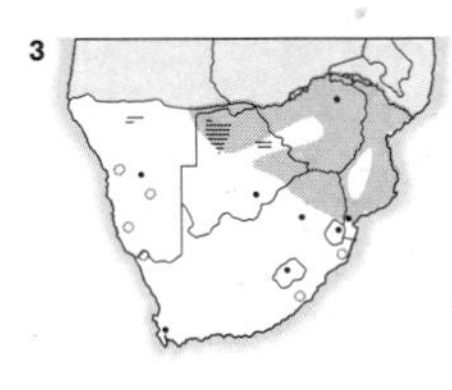

4 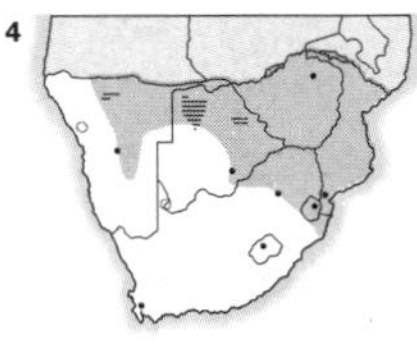

5 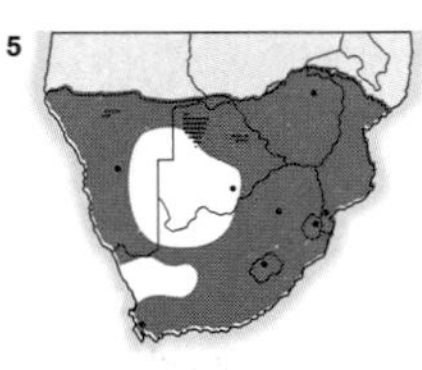

1 AMERICAN PURPLE GALLINULE *Porphyrula martinica*

Vagrant. Adult differs from (2) in small size, *pale blue* frontal shield, yellow-tipped bill and *pale yellow legs.* Most arrivals are immatures as illustrated, mainly dull khaki-brown with a greenish flush on the back and wings, belly dull blue. At least 20 records for the south-western coast. 33 cm (Amerikaanse koningriethaan)

2 PURPLE GALLINULE *Porphyrio porphyrio*

Common resident. Larger than (1), differing in *red* frontal shield and bill plus *pink legs.* Immature is duller, brownish with red-brown legs. Has a deep, explosive bubbling call plus various shrieks and groans. Singly or in pairs in marshes and the vegetation surrounding inland waters, especially sewage ponds. Walks about on mud flats and reed-bed fringes, sometimes clambering about tangled reeds. Can swim and is not secretive. 46 cm (Grootkoningriethaan)

3 LESSER GALLINULE *Porphyrula alleni*

Uncommon and irregular late summer resident. Small, large-footed waterbird with green upperparts, dark blue body, neck and head, and red bill and legs. The frontal shield is variable in colour: dull apple-green to bluish. Immature as illustrated; cf. immature of (4). The call is a series of rapidly delivered clicks 'dik-dik-dik-dik ...' or a melodious, rolling 'purrrrr-pur-pur-pur' during courtship. A shy bird; occurs singly or in pairs on secluded ponds with dense fringing vegetation where it climbs about tangled reeds, walks on water lilies or swims. 25 cm (Kleinkoningriethaan)

4 LESSER MOORHEN *Gallinula angulata*

Uncommon summer resident. Small, blackish waterbird differing from (5) in smaller size and yellow bill (only culmen and frontal shield red as illustrated). The legs are greenish or red-brown. Immature much duller; see illustration. The call is three to five rapid hoots 'tu-tu-tu- ...'. Singly or in pairs on shallow ponds with surface and fringing vegetation, vleis and flooded grassland, but erratic and secretive. 23 cm (Kleinwaterhoender)

5 MOORHEN *Gallinula chloropus*

Common resident. Larger than (4), with bright red bill and frontal shield, tip of bill and legs yellow, flank feathers white. Immature is browner. The call is a high-pitched, descending 'kr-rrrrk'. Frequents dams, pans and quiet rivers with fringing reed-beds, singly or in pairs. Swims more in open water than (4) but also feeds out of water in vleis and marshlands. 30-36 cm (Waterhoender)

J
1
2
♂ Br
J
3
4
4 J
5

FLUFFTAILS

Family RALLIDAE. Smallest of the crakes. Highly secretive and difficult to flush, but once airborne fly a short distance with legs dangling before dropping back into cover; can seldom be flushed a second time. Calls are usually the only indication of a species' presence.

1

1 WHITE-WINGED FLUFFTAIL *Sarothrura ayresi*

Uncommon, localised resident. Identified by white wing-patches when flushed. The call is a soft, deep 'woop, woop, woop, woop, woop …', often several birds calling simultaneously. Occurs in high-lying marshes in southern Africa but known from only a few scattered localities. 14 cm (Witvlerkvleikuiken)

2

2 STRIPED FLUFFTAIL *Sarothrura affinis*

Rare, localised resident. Male has chestnut head *and* tail; female probably indistinguishable from female of Buff-spotted Flufftail (overleaf). The call is loud and distinctive, a drawn-out 'huuuuuuuuuuuuuuu'. Frequents rank vegetation bordering forests and woodland in montane grassland. 15 cm (Gestreepte vleikuiken)

3

3 STREAKY-BREASTED FLUFFTAIL *Sarothrura boehmi*

Rare summer resident. Best identified by call, a deep and rapid 'booooo' at about two-second intervals and repeated about 12 times; also a high-pitched 'bee' about 12 times with no appreciable pause. Occurs in vleis, flooded grassland and grass bordering lakes and swamps, most records from eastern Zimbabwe. 15 cm (Streepborsvleikuiken)

4
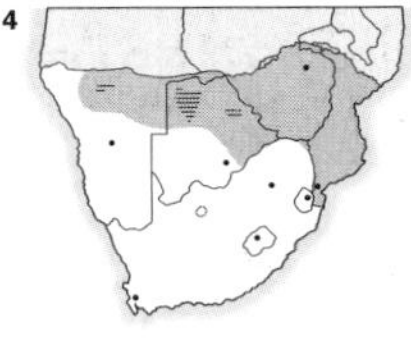

4 SPOTTED CRAKE *Porzana porzana*

Uncommon summer visitor. Differs from African Crake (overleaf) in generally paler colouring, less boldly barred flanks and yellow bill with red base, and from (5) in more spotted, less streaked appearance plus yellow bill. The call is a series of whip-like notes 'hwitt-hwitt-hwitt', seldom heard in southern Africa. Occurs in dense vegetation in shallow water, occasionally in fringing vegetation around pans in dry regions. 24 cm (Gevlekte riethaan)

5

5 STRIPED CRAKE *Aenigmatolimnas marginalis*

Uncommon summer visitor. Differs from (4) in more streaky, less spotted upperparts, paler underparts and thicker, darker bill. The call (heard at night) is a constant ticking like a wristwatch 'tak-tak-tak-tak-tak …'. Found in flooded grassland and small pools. Secretive and shy. Occasionally breeds in southern Africa in years of good rainfall. 24 cm (Gestreepte riethaan)

1

♂ ♀ ♂

2

♂ ♀ ♂

3

♂ ♂ ♀

4

5

♂ ♂ ♀

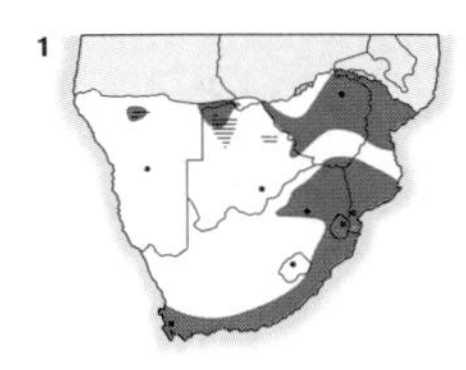

1 RED-CHESTED FLUFFTAIL *Sarothrura rufa*

Fairly common resident. Very similar to the next species, but reddish colouring of male extends onto its mantle and lower breast. Female is much darker but paler on chest and throat. The normal call is a much-repeated 'ooo-ooo-ooo-ooo-dueh-dueh-dueh …', but also utters a quail-like 'ick-kick-kick-kick …' and a loud, rapid squeaking 'dui-dui-dui …' up to 40 or more times, fading off at the end. Calls mainly at night and on dull days. A secretive bird of marshes, damp valleys and vleis where it remains concealed in dense vegetation. 15-17 cm (Rooiborsvleikuiken)

2 BUFF-SPOTTED FLUFFTAIL *Sarothrura elegans*

Fairly common resident. Male told from the previous species by less extensive reddish colouring and spotted, not streaked, plumage. Female is paler and uniform. The call is a long, drawn-out and mournful 'wooooooooooo-eeeeeeeee' like the sound of a tuning fork, rising at the end. Frequents the moister areas of evergreen forests, overgrown wastelands and long grass, occasionally in well-wooded suburban gardens, but very secretive. 17 cm (Gevlekte vleikuiken)

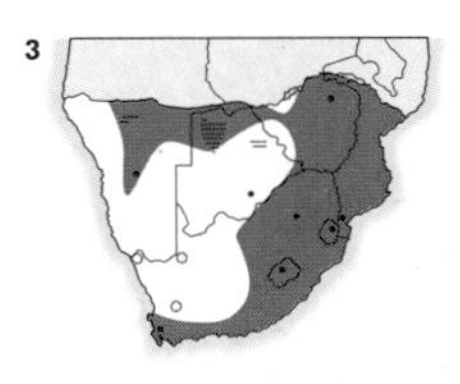

3 BAILLON'S CRAKE *Porzana pusilla*

Uncommon resident and visitor. Male illustrated. Female has whitish throat and central breast. Utters a low, piping 'quick-quick'. Highly secretive, inhabiting marshes, lush waterside vegetation and flooded grassland. Sometimes emerges into the open but dives into cover again at the least disturbance. 18 cm (Kleinriethaan)

4 CORNCRAKE *Crex crex*

Uncommon summer visitor. A short-billed, tawny crake with blackish upperparts, barred flanks and chestnut wing coverts. Silent in southern Africa. Found in lucerne, rank grass, fallow fields and airfields, sometimes near streams. When flushed flies off with legs dangling, the chestnut wings conspicuous. 37 cm (Kwartelkoning)

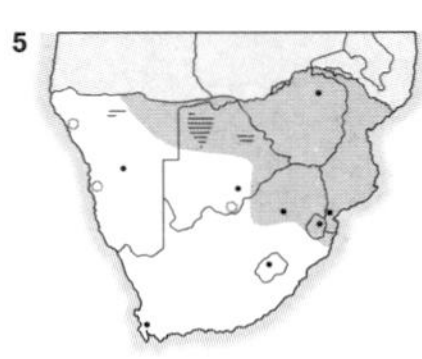

5 AFRICAN CRAKE *Crex egregia*

Uncommon summer visitor. Heavily mottled upperparts and boldly barred underparts distinctive. Utters a high-pitched chittering trill of eight or nine notes. Found in grassland, vleis and thickets. Secretive but will emerge to visit rain puddles on roads. It flushes readily. 20-23 cm (Afrikaanse riethaan)

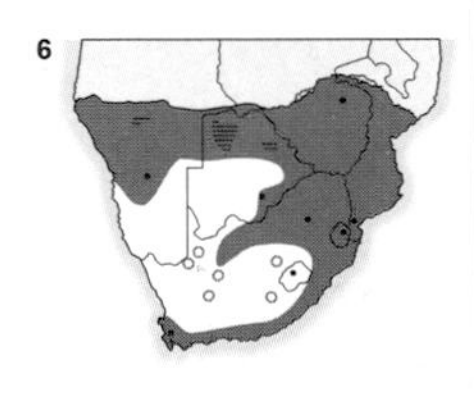

6 BLACK CRAKE *Amaurornis flavirostris*

Common resident. The call is an explosive, harsh 'rr-rr-rr' ending in a resonant croak; also various clucking sounds. Single birds or scattered individuals at the waterside on quiet rivers, lakes, dams and floodpans, or walking on floating vegetation. It is not secretive. 20-23 cm (Swartriethaan)

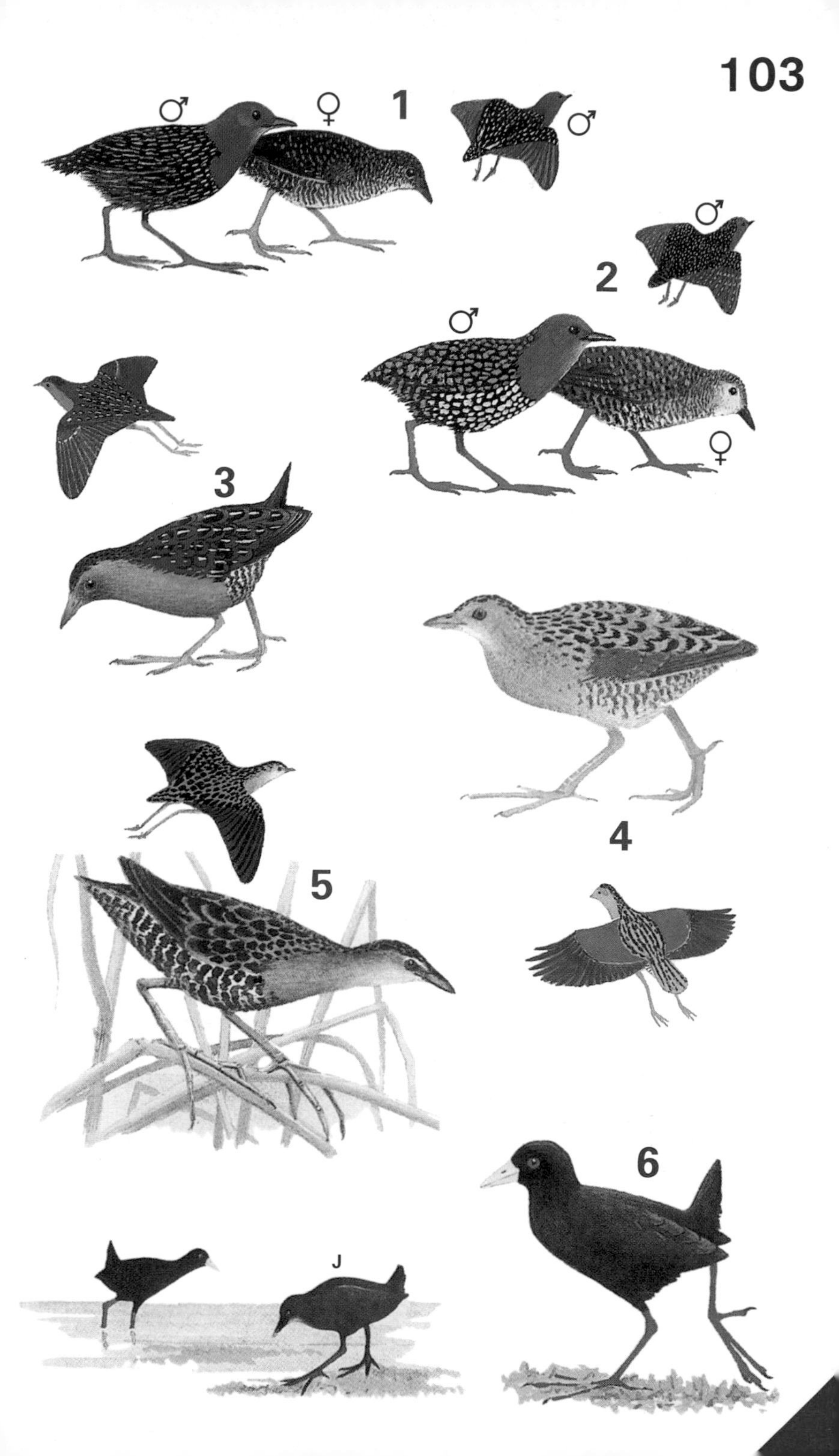
1
♂
♀
♂
2
♂
♂
♀
3
4
5
6
J

1

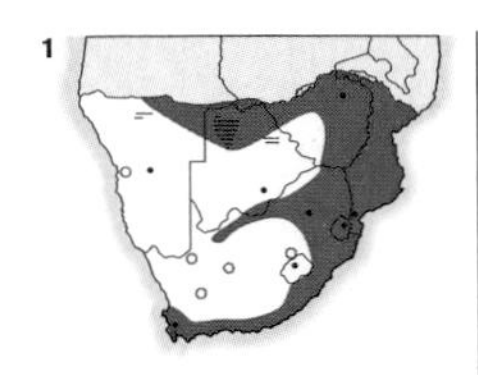

1 AFRICAN RAIL *Rallus caerulescens*

Fairly common resident. Identified by long red bill and legs, brown upperparts and striped underparts. Immature is sooty-brown, white of throat extending to central breast, flanks barred rufous. The call is a shrill, trilling rattle 'creeea-crak-crak-crak ...'. A shy, skulking bird of reed-beds and thick swamp vegetation, only occasionally emerging at pool fringes. Moves with stealth and speed, flicking its tail continuously. 36 cm (Grootriethaan)

2

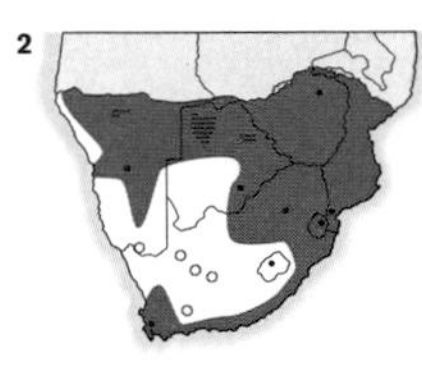

PAINTED SNIPES

Family ROSTRATULIDAE. Not related to true snipes. More colourful.

2 PAINTED SNIPE *Rostratula benghalensis*

Uncommon nomadic resident. Immature resembles male. Not a vocal species. Pairs and groups are found on muddy shorelines of dams, pans and swamp pools, usually where reeds or other waterside vegetation offers immediate refuge. When walking frequently bobs its hindquarters up and down. Shy and retiring. 28-32 cm (Goudsnip)

3

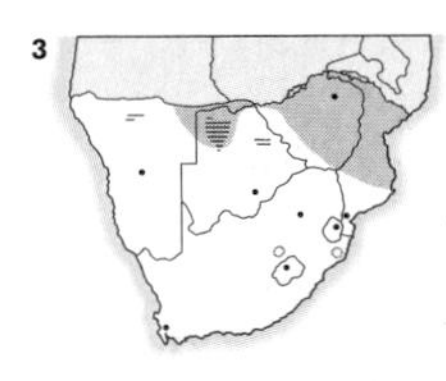

PLOVERS, SNIPES AND ALLIES

Families CHARADRIIDAE (plovers and turnstones) and **SCOLOPACIDAE** (sandpipers, snipes and allies). Terrestrial and waterside birds. Large plovers are long-legged and stand erect; small plovers hold their bodies horizontally, postures hunched. Sandpipers, often called shorebirds or waders, are plover-like migrants breeding in the northern hemisphere (when males assume richly coloured plumage) and migrating south in drab non-breeding plumage. Illustrations show these shorebirds in non-breeding plumage unless otherwise indicated.

3 GREAT SNIPE *Gallinago media*

Rare summer visitor. Differs from (4) in shorter bill, spotted upperwing coverts and more heavily streaked underparts plus flight behaviour. Silent in Africa. Flushes reluctantly but then rises silently and *flies straight* before dropping down again. Singly in marshy localities. Sparsely distributed. 35 cm (Dubbelsnip)

4

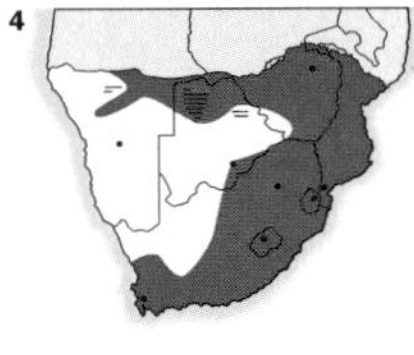

4 AFRICAN or ETHIOPIAN SNIPE *Gallinago nigripennis*

Common resident. Differs from (3) in whiter underparts and no white in tail. When flushed takes off with a 'chuck' call and *zigzags at low level* before resettling. In breeding season flies high, then zooms down steeply with fanned tail feathers vibrating to make a soft whinnying sound known as drumming. Singly or in pairs in marshy localities. 32 cm (Afrikaanse snip)

5

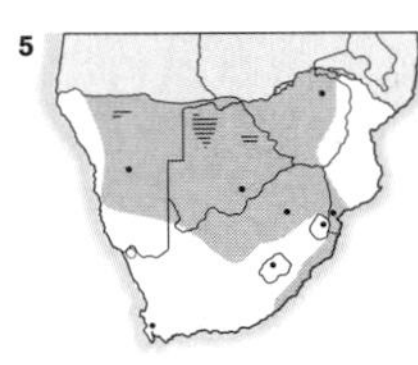

5 CASPIAN PLOVER *Charadrius asiaticus*

Fairly common summer visitor. The male illustrated is in breeding plumage (often seen February to March). Female in breeding plumage may have rufous breast-band incomplete, the dark lower edge always absent. Immature resembles non-breeding adult, but the breast-band may be confined to a patch on either side; then differing from Sand Plover (overleaf) in whiter underparts and *quite different habitat*. The call is a shrill 'ku-wit', loudest at night, softer and more piping by day. Flocks on plains with short grass and burnt areas, often in the semi-arid region of north-central Botswana and northern Namibia. Habitually runs rather than flies. 21-3 cm (Asiatiese strandkiewiet)

1
♀
♂
2
3
4
N-Br
5
♂ Br

1 MONGOLIAN PLOVER *Charadrius mongolus*

Rare summer visitor. Differs from (2) in less heavy bill, shorter legs and the lack of any clear mark between bill and eye. Utters 'chitic, chitic' on take-off and, occasionally, a short soft trill. Singly or in small groups mostly on east coast tidal flats from Mozambique to KwaZulu-Natal 20 cm (Mongoolse strandkiewiet)

2 SAND PLOVER *Charadrius leschenaultii*

Rare summer visitor. Differs from (1) in much heavier bill, longer legs and larger size; cf. also immature of (6) which is smaller and has a white collar. Flight call is a short 'drrit'; also utters a trill 'chirrirrip', longer than in (1). Singly or in small groups on tidal mud flats, especially east coast estuaries and lagoons. 22 cm (Grootstrandkiewiet)

3 CHESTNUT-BANDED PLOVER *Charadrius pallidus*

Common resident. Female lacks the black forecrown and lores. Utters a soft 'chuck' on take-off. Singly, in pairs and scattered flocks on salt pans, coastal lagoons and sand flats, less frequently singly or in pairs inland at pans, gravel pits, dams and banks of large rivers. Inland records widespread but irregular. 15 cm (Rooibandstrandkiewiet)

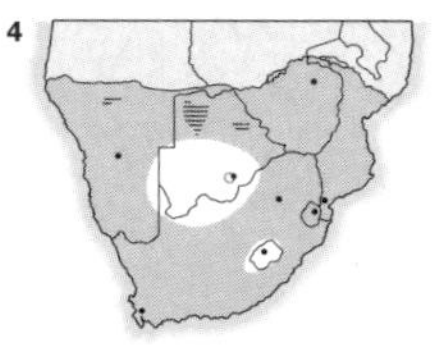

4 RINGED PLOVER *Charadrius hiaticula*

Uncommon summer visitor. Single bold black breast-band extending around neck diagnostic. In flight it differs from the next species in distinct white wing-bar. The call is 'coo-eep' or 'too-li'. Singly or in small parties, often with the next species, on shorelines of coastal lagoons, estuaries and inland waters. 18 cm (Ringnekstrandkiewiet)

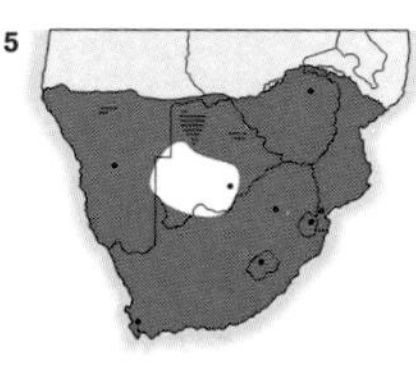

5 THREE-BANDED PLOVER *Charadrius tricollaris*

Common resident. Identified by double black breast-bands, one on either side of white band encircling neck; cf. (4). Immature has the upper band brown and incomplete, the lower band flecked white, the head uniformly brown. The call is 'wick-wick' or 'tiuu-it, tiuu-it'. Singly, in pairs or small parties on shores and shallows of almost any inland water. 18 cm (Driebandstrandkiewiet)

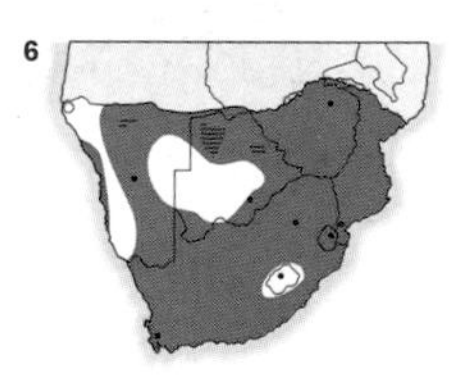

6 KITTLITZ'S PLOVER *Charadrius pecuarius*

Common and widespread resident. Distinguished by black mask and forecrown, white *band encircling back of neck* and yellow-buff breast. Immature lacks the black mask and forecrown and the yellow breast; is distinguished from the similar Mongolian Plover (1) mainly by white collar, darker upperparts and habitat. In-flight call of adult is 'tip-peep'; also utters a trilling 'trittritritritritrit'. Usually found in small parties at the edges of inland waters, coastal estuaries, open ground and airfields. 16 cm (Geelborsstrandkiewiet)

KENTISH PLOVER (Bleekstrandkiewiet) see p. 446.

1
N-Br
2
N-Br
♂
3
♀
J
4
5
6
6 J

1

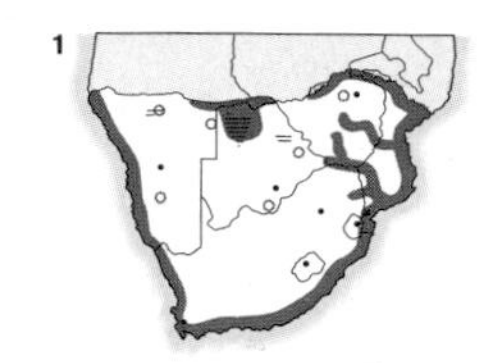

2

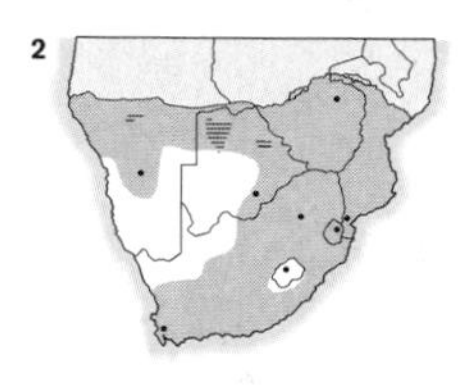

3

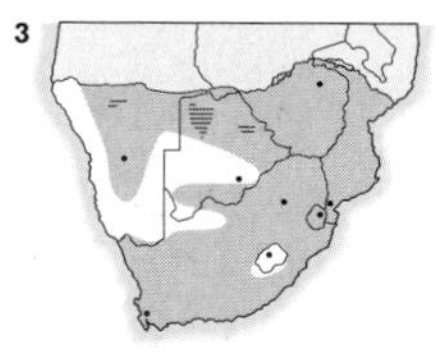

4

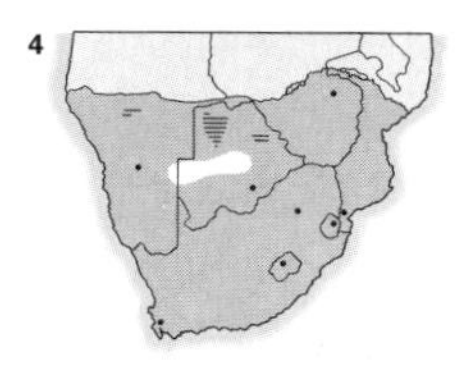

1 WHITE-FRONTED PLOVER *Charadrius marginatus*

Common resident. The sand-coloured race (a), occurring in the western Cape and on the east coast, differs from the rare Mongolian Plover (previous page) in much smaller size, dark line on lores (between bill and eye) plus more slender bill and white collar. Immature resembles female. The west coast race (b) is greyer, less yellow on the breast. Utters a soft 'wit' or 'twirit' in flight. Singly or in pairs on sandy seashores; also on some inland lakes and large rivers with sandbanks, e.g. the Zambezi, Limpopo and Olifants. At the coast it feeds on wet sand close to receding waves, running rapidly or flying away low as the next wave advances. 18 cm (Vaalstrandkiewiet)

2 MARSH SANDPIPER *Tringa stagnatilis*

Common summer visitor. Clear white underparts diagnostic. Differs from the Greenshank (3) in smaller size, straight, slender bill and yellowish legs. In flight shows white back and rump as (3) but its feet protrude further. When put to flight calls a soft rapid 'tjuu-tjuu-tjuu'. Singly or in small groups on coastal lagoons and estuaries or inland waters. Feeds by probing in shallows. 23 cm (Moerasruiter)

3 GREENSHANK *Tringa nebularia*

Common summer visitor, a few all year. Has clear white underparts as the Marsh Sandpiper (2) but is larger, with more robust, slightly upturned bill and green-grey legs. In flight it also shows extensive white back and rump, its feet *slightly* protruding. On take-off calls a loud *triple* 'tew-tew-tew'. Usually singly on coastal or inland waters. Shy and difficult to approach. When flushed *towers up and utters its triple call* before flying off some distance. 32 cm (Groenpootruiter)

4 RUFF *Philomachus pugnax*

Abundant summer visitor. Male much larger than the female (the reeve). Characterised by short, straight bill with slightly bulbous tip, featureless face, except for a small white patch at the base of the bill, and *boldly scaled or mottled upperparts* caused by pale edges to dark feathers, legs orange in adult, grey-green in immature. Male breeding plumage variable; may be seen in spring or autumn with black, white or rufous neck. In flight it shows *white oval patches on sides of dark tail.* Birds in a flock may call 'chit' in a twittering chorus. Singly, in groups or large flocks in shallows of coastal and inland waters, flooded fields and farmlands. Takes flight in dense flocks. 24-30 cm (Kemphaan)

1
♀
♂
♂
2 N-Br
3
N-Br
♂ J
Br
4
Br
Br
4
♀
N-Br

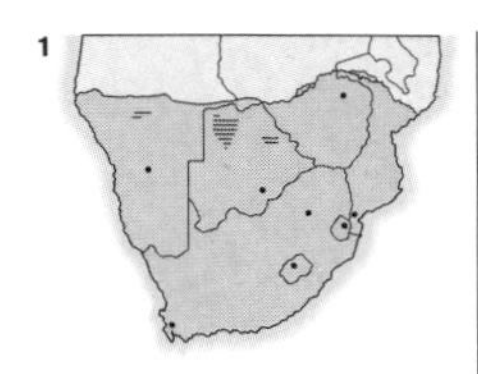

1 **LITTLE STINT** *Calidris minuta*

Common summer visitor, a few all year. Differs from the next species in slightly longer, more slender bill and more heavily *blotched* upperparts *(dark feather centres)*; well-worn plumage may appear paler, so bill shape is the best guide. Utters a sharp 'chit' or rapid 'chitchitchit ...'. Singly at coastal estuaries and lagoons plus various inland waters. Feeds on shorelines and in shallows with hunched, head-down posture. 14 cm (Kleinstrandloper)

2 **RED-NECKED STINT** *Calidris ruficollis*

Rare summer visitor. Told from the previous only with care; bill slightly shorter, more robust and less tapered; upperparts paler, feathers more grey with *dark central shafts,* not blotches; general appearance longer but with shorter legs than (1). Breeding plumage diagnostic with rufous head, neck and breast. Voice a weak, short 'chit'. Singly on coastal estuaries and lagoons, especially along the east coast. 15 cm (Rooinekstrandloper)

3 **BROAD-BILLED SANDPIPER** *Limicola falcinellus*

Rare summer visitor. Identified by fairly long bill with a flattened, *decurved tip,* streaked head and short legs. In breeding plumage shows additional stripes on mantle, these and head-stripes giving snipe-like flight pattern. Call is a soft trill. Singly on coastal estuaries, quiet bays, lagoons and pans, rarely inland. 17 cm (Breëbekstrandloper)

PHALAROPES

Long-legged oceanic 'sandpipers'. Swim buoyantly like small gulls and, with the exception of (6), feed from the surface with pirouetting action. Occasionally on inland waters, otherwise well offshore in Atlantic waters. Female breeding plumages brighter than those of males, non-breeding plumages identical.

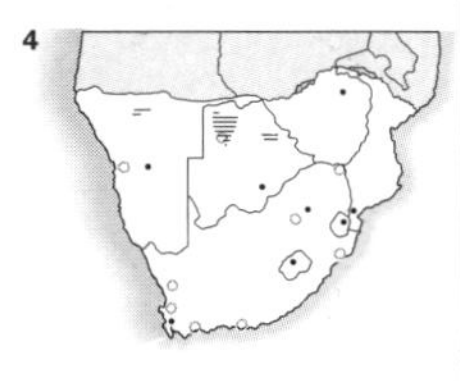

4 **RED-NECKED PHALAROPE** *Phalaropus lobatus*

Rare summer visitor. In non-breeding plumage identified by thin bill (about same length as head) and *dark grey* upperparts; may have dark cap. In breeding plumage told by rufous band from ear coverts to upper breast. Flocks at sea or singly on coastal lagoons and shallow ponds. 17 cm (Rooihalsfraiingpoot)

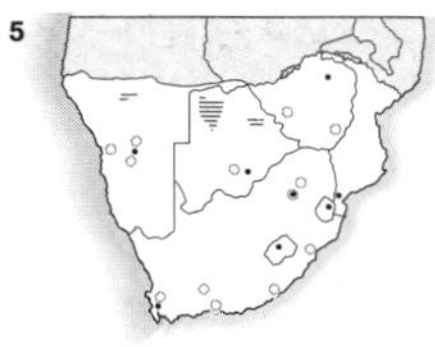

5 **GREY PHALAROPE** *Phalaropus fulicaria*

Fairly common summer visitor. In non-breeding plumage identified by short, fairly robust bill with (usually) yellow base; pale *uniform* upperparts. In breeding plumage told by *rufous underparts.* Flocks at sea or singly on deep inland waters. 20 cm (Grysfraiingpoot)

6 **WILSON'S PHALAROPE** *Phalaropus tricolor*

Summer vagrant. Identified in non-breeding plumage by long, needle-like bill, *lack* of eye-patch, *straw-coloured* legs, no wing-bar. In breeding plumage has *black* legs, black eye-patch extending to upper neck, rufous patch from lateral neck to mantle and white underparts. Singly on shallow inshore waters. May feed by *wading in shallows,* running about on partially flexed legs while lunging rapidly from side to side with bill. If swimming stabs rapidly at surface, occasionally spinning. 22-4 cm (Bontfraiingpoot)

All migrant shorebirds in non-breeding plumage unless otherwise indicated.

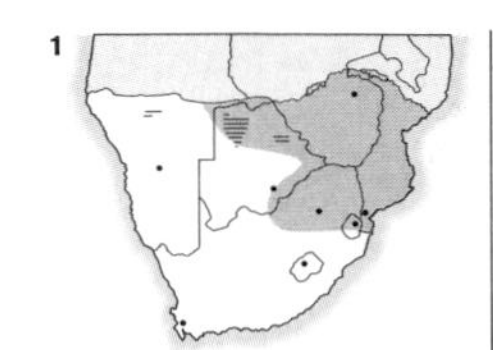

1

1 GREEN SANDPIPER *Tringa ochropus*

Uncommon summer visitor. Differs from the Wood Sandpiper (4) in darker, less obviously spotted upperparts and longer bill; in flight has larger white rump, barred tail and *dark underwing coverts.* When flushed towers up, uttering a loud, shrill 'weet-a-weet', then makes off with erratic, snipe-like flight. Solitary on small, quiet streams and grassy ponds. 23 cm (Witgatruiter)

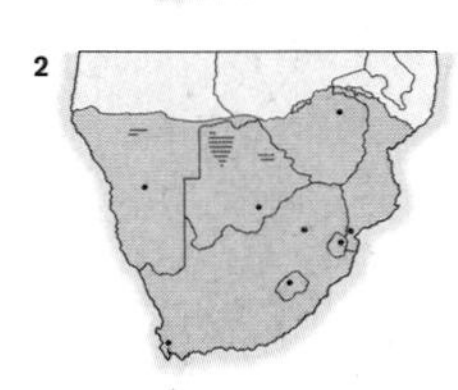

2

2 COMMON SANDPIPER *Actitis hypoleucos*

Common summer visitor, a few all year. Has diagnostic white pectoral region *showing above the folded wing,* medium-short, robust bill and habit of *frequently bobbing its hindquarters.* In flight shows no white rump but faint wing-bar and white outer tail feathers. When flushed makes off, uttering a shrill 'twee-wee-wee'; flies low with stiff, downward-bowed wings, flapping with sporadic flicking action below the horizontal. Singly on shores of rivers, lakes, dams, estuaries and rocky coasts. 20 cm (Gewone ruiter)

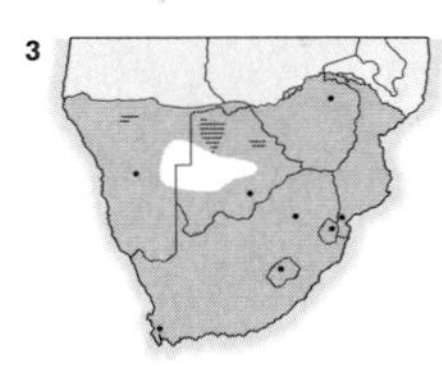

3

3 CURLEW SANDPIPER *Calidris ferruginea*

Abundant summer visitor. The most common small shorebird with a decurved bill. Differs from very similar but *rare* Dunlin (p. 116) in gently tapering bill and, in flight, *broad white rump;* from *rare* Broad-billed Sandpiper (previous page) in evenly decurved bill (not curved at the tip only), longer legs, less contrasting upperparts and broad white rump. Calls 'chiet-chiet' in flight and 'tchirrrr' when standing; often very vocal when chasing each other. Occurs in small flocks at inland pans and dams (especially sewage ponds) and in very large flocks at coastal lagoons, estuaries and west coast bays. 19 cm (Krombekstrandloper)

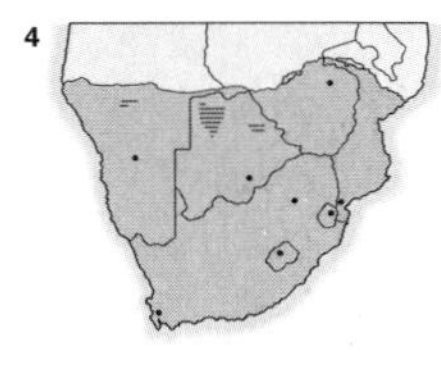

4

4 WOOD SANDPIPER *Tringa glareola*

Common summer visitor, some all year. Has well-spotted upperparts, broad, distinct eyebrow, short, straight bill and fairly long legs. In flight shows white underwing coverts, differing mainly in this and bill length from the Green Sandpiper (1); feet protrude beyond tail. When flushed towers up and calls a flat, triple 'chiff-iff-iff'; also has a high-pitched alarm call 'tchi-tchi-tchi-tchi-tchi'. Singly or in small groups on most shallow inland waters, flooded grassland and coastal estuaries. 20 cm (Bosruiter)

All migrant shorebirds in non-breeding plumage unless otherwise indicated.

1

1 **PECTORAL SANDPIPER** *Calidris melanotos*

Rare summer visitor. Differs from Ruff (p. 108) in smaller size, shorter yellow legs and well-streaked buffy breast terminating in a sharp line and contrasting with pure white underparts; full breeding plumage is slightly more rufous. In flight shows no clear wing-bars but snipe-like streaks on back. Usual call is 'kreek' or 'prritt', one or more times. Takes off with erratic snipe-like action, then flies straight. Singly on coastal estuaries and inland at sewage works and in moist grassland, often mixing with other shorebirds. 20-23 cm (Geelpootstrandloper)

2

2 **SANDERLING** *Calidris alba*

Common summer visitor. A small shorebird of very white appearance with dark shoulder-patch and short, thick bill; larger and paler than any stint (p. 110). When flushed calls a liquid 'blt-blt'. Flocks, large or small, mostly on open seashores, characteristically running along the water's edge at speed and feeding where the waves have receded. Feeds in a hunched, head-down posture, probing wet sand hurriedly, continuously. Flight is low and direct, white wing-bars conspicuous. 19 cm (Drietoonstrandloper)

3

3 **TEREK SANDPIPER** *Xenus cinereus*

Common summer visitor. Distinguished by long upcurved bill, short, orange-yellow legs and pale grey-brown upperparts with a dark shoulder. In flight the white secondaries and grey rump are diagnostic. Breeding plumage similar. Calls 'tur-lip' or 'turr-loo-tew'. Singly or in flocks on coastal estuaries and lagoons, occasionally on inland waters. Bobs its rear up and down like Common Sandpiper (previous page). When feeding moves about rapidly, sometimes running at speed between bouts of deep probing with its bill. 23-5 cm (Terekruiter)

4

4 **KNOT** *Calidris canutus*

Common summer visitor. Differs from other short-billed shorebirds by plump-bodied appearance; frequently assumes semi-breeding plumage before departure in autumn. In flight the wings appear long and pointed, the white wing-bars conspicuous. Calls 'knut', sometimes in a series; a flock may utter a more liquid 'whit-wit'. Flocks at coastal lagoons, estuaries and rocky shores, especially along the west coast; individuals rarely inland. Feeds with a slow forward movement while probing mud several times between steps. Flocks fly in dense packs, twisting and turning at speed. 25 cm (Knoet)

5

5 **RUDDY TURNSTONE** *Arenaria interpres*

Common summer visitor. Characterised by long body, hunched, head-in-shoulders appearance and horizontal stance plus striking plumage pattern; all stages between full breeding and non-breeding plumages occur. Flight or contact call 'kuiti-kuiti-kuiti' or 'tuck-a-tuck', in mild alarm given about five times, then tails off to 'ti-tititi'. Flocks of five to 20 frequent coastal mud flats and shorelines, especially rocky shores; occasionally on inland waters. Feeds by turning over small stones, shells, caked mud and debris. If flushed flies off low, revealing extensive white back and wing-bars. 22 cm (Steenloper)

All migrant shorebirds in non-breeding plumage unless otherwise indicated.

VERY RARE VAGRANT SHOREBIRDS

The species on this plate have, at best, been seen a few times only in southern Africa.

1

1 LONG-TOED STINT *Calidris subminuta*

Fractionally smaller than Little Stint (p. 110) from which it is best distinguished by greenish-yellow (not black) legs and richer, darker brown upperparts streaked with pale buff. Differs from (2) in richly marked (not uniform) upperparts. Adopts characteristic stance, stretching its neck and standing very upright. 13-15 cm (Langtoonstrandloper)

2

2 TEMMINCK'S STINT *Calidris temminckii*

Very similar to Little Stint (p. 110) but has yellowish (not black) legs and feet and fairly uniform, unmarked grey upperparts. In flight the outer tail feathers are white, not grey as in Little Stint. 13-15 cm (Temminckse strandloper)

3

3 BAIRD'S SANDPIPER *Calidris bairdii*

Larger than Little Stint (p. 110) but smaller than Curlew Sandpiper (p. 112). Has characteristic upperparts, appearing very scaled. Overall body shape slender, streamlined, wingtips projecting well beyond tail. Head shape diagnostic, appearing squarish like a shorebird of the genus *Tringa* rather than a stint. 14-16 cm (Bairdse strandloper)

4

4 WHITE-RUMPED SANDPIPER *Calidris fuscicollis*

Similar in shape and size to Baird's Sandpiper (3) but has longer, very slightly decurved bill and lacks the scaled upperparts. Told from Curlew Sandpiper (p. 112) which also has a white rump by much smaller size and shorter bill. 15-17 cm (Witrugstrandloper)

5

5 DUNLIN *Calidris alpina*

Can be confused with Curlew Sandpiper (p. 112) but is smaller and has a dark (not white) rump, shorter, less decurved bill and browner, more marked upperparts. 15-22 cm (Bontstrandloper)

6

6 BUFF-BREASTED SANDPIPER *Tryngites subruficollis*

Looks like a richly coloured, diminutive Ruff (p. 108). The short, straight bill and small, rounded head, combined with the lack of wing-bars or white oval patches on the sides of the tail, should rule out confusion with Ruff. 18-19 cm (Taanborsstrandloper)

7

7 LESSER YELLOWLEGS *Tringa flavipes*

Could be confused only with Wood Sandpiper (p. 112) from which it differs in always having bright lemon-yellow legs. Larger, longer-legged and much more slender than Wood Sandpiper. 23-25 cm (Kleingeelpootruiter)

GREATER YELLOWLEGS (Grootgeelpootruiter) see p. 446.

All migrant shorebirds in non-breeding plumage unless otherwise indicated.

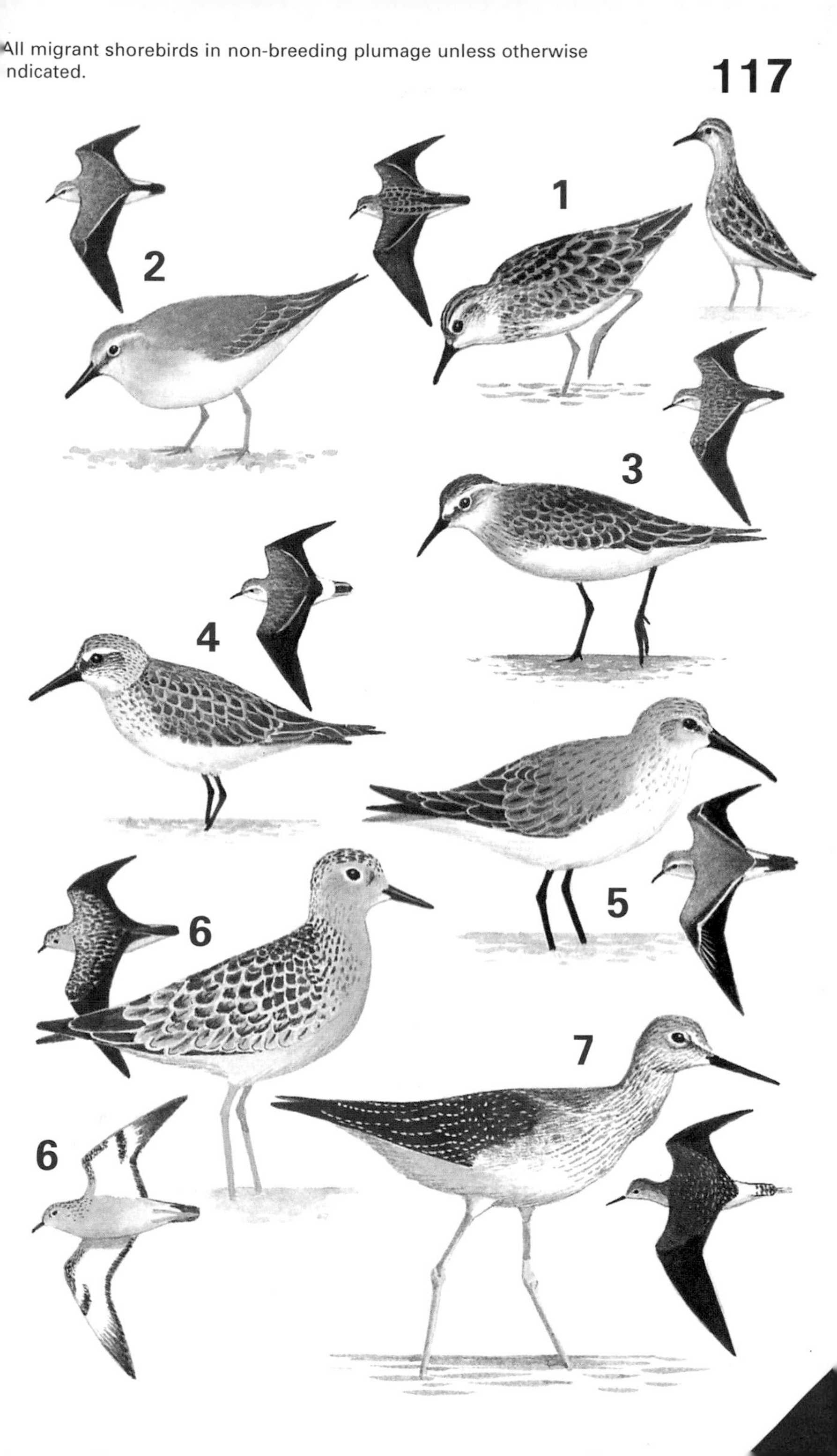

1 REDSHANK *Tringa totanus*

Rare summer visitor. Differs from (2) in less lanky, browner appearance; from most other shorebirds in red or orange legs and reddish base to moderately long, straight bill; from orange-legged Ruff (p. 108) in plain upperparts and bill shape. In flight the only shorebird with white triangular patches on the wings, plus white back, rump and tail, the latter faintly barred. Calls 'teu-he-he' on take-off. Flight erratic with jerky, deliberate wing beats, feet slightly protruding beyond the tail. Usually singly, often with other shorebirds, on coastal mud flats, estuaries, lagoons and inland waters. 25 cm (Rooipootruiter)

2 SPOTTED REDSHANK *Tringa erythropus*

Rare summer vagrant. Lankier and more gracefully proportioned than (1), bill and legs longer; overall appearance greyish with usually some spotting on the upperparts; whitish underparts. Posture fairly erect. In flight shows no wing-bar and has white oval patch on back; feet protrude more than in (1). The call is a deep 'cheewit'. May occur at either inland or coastal waters. 30 cm (Gevlekte rooipootruiter)

3 BLACK-TAILED GODWIT *Limosa limosa*

Rare summer visitor. Despite *straight bill and longer legs* is not easily distinguished from (4) at rest, but head, neck and breast are of uniform tone, *not* streaked. In flight the broad black tail-band and prominent white upperwing-bars are distinctive. When flying may call a loud 'wicka-wicka-wicka'. Usually singly, mostly at inland waters but a few coastal records. 40-50 cm (Swartstertgriet)

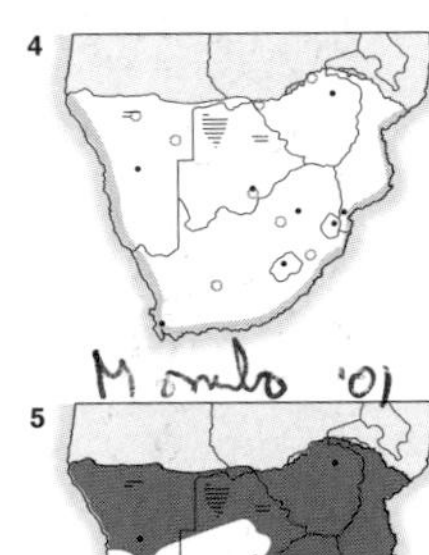

4 BAR-TAILED GODWIT *Limosa lapponica*

Fairly common summer visitor. Stockier appearance with shorter legs than (3); bill long (longest in females) and gently *upcurved* (not straight); head, neck and breast more obviously streaked. In flight the tail shows numerous light bars at close range, the wings lack bars. The call is a deep 'god-whit'. Singly or in flocks (sometimes several hundreds) on tidal mud flats and sheltered bays; occasionally on inland waters. 36-9 cm (Bandstertgriet)

HUDSONIAN GODWIT (Amerikaanse griet) see p. 446.

5 AFRICAN JACANA *Actophilornis africanus*

Common resident. Immature has a *black* stripe through the eye and *black* crown; cf. (6). The call, uttered while standing or flying, is 'kyowrrr'. Individuals or scattered groups walk on floating vegetation on lily-covered pans, dams and river backwaters. Frequently chases others in short dashes or in low flight while calling loudly. 40 cm (Grootlangtoon)

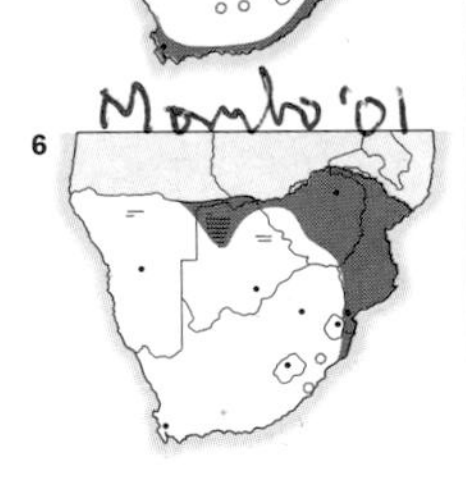

6 LESSER JACANA *Microparra capensis*

Uncommon, localised resident. Very much smaller than (5): sparrow-sized minus feet. Differs from immature of (5) in pale feather edges to brown upperparts giving scaled effect; central mantle and back deep bronze-brown, forehead brown, *crown and eye-stripe chestnut,* underparts white. Immature has a dark crown, the nape golden-chestnut. Silent except for an occasional 'kruk'. Occurs on lily-covered ponds, dams and river backwaters. 20 cm (Dwerglangtoon)

1
N-Br
Br
2
N-Br
Br
3
N-Br
4
♀
N-Br
Br
Br
5
J
6

1

2

3

4

5

GOLDEN PLOVERS

Previously known as the Lesser Golden Plover, with two races, but now given full specific status as American Golden Plover and Pacific Golden Plover. Rare vagrants that reach our shores in non-breeding plumage when their specific identity can be problematical. They differ from the similar Grey Plover (3) in its non-breeding plumage in having dull grey (not black) 'armpits', fairly long upper legs and golden-spangled upperparts plus more elegant proportions and an upright stance.

1 AMERICAN GOLDEN PLOVER *Pluvialis dominica*

Appears slightly more robust than (2) and differs also in having a *clear white eyebrow that becomes wider posteriorly*, a darker crown plus a dull greyish breast with white (not yellow) mottling, the belly drab (not white). Its upperparts are dull grey-brown with all feathers edged buff-yellow. In flight it differs from the Grey Plover (3) in having a dark rump and plain grey underwings; its feet do not protrude beyond its tail. The call is a melodious 'tu-ee' or 'tee-tew'. Few substantiated records for southern Africa, all of single birds January-April in coastal regions. (Elsewhere this species is also known to frequent inland grasslands.) 24-8 cm (Amerikaanse goue strandkiewiet)

2 PACIFIC GOLDEN PLOVER *Pluvialis fulva*

Slightly smaller, less robust than (1), the eyebrow and head with a yellow wash, rest of upperparts grey-brown spotted golden-yellow; greyish throat, neck and breast feathers edged yellow, belly pure white. In flight from above the wings show a barely visible white wing-bar, the rump is dark and *its feet protrude beyond its tail*; the underwings are grey. The call is the same as that of (1) plus a repeated 'chu-leek' or 'too-lick'. Records for southern Africa exceed those of (1). 23-6 cm (Oosterse goue strandkiewiet)

3 GREY PLOVER *Pluvialis squatarola*

Common summer visitor, a few all year. Non-breeding plumage (a) resembles (1) but this species is more chunky with *greyish* overall appearance. Larger size, short, stout bill and fairly long legs distinguish this from other smaller shorebirds. In flight shows black 'armpits'. Both partial breeding plumage (b) and full breeding plumage occur in spring and autumn. Has a far-carrying whistle 'tlui-tlui' or 'pee-u-wee'. Singly or in flocks on tidal flats and secluded seashores; occasionally inland. 28-30 cm (Grysstrandkiewiet)

4 LESSER BLACK-WINGED PLOVER *Vanellus lugubris*

Uncommon resident. Closely resembles (5) but upperparts *olive-brown* (not warm brown), the white forehead *forward* of the eye, the dark lower breast-band usually narrow, legs dark brown. See illustrations for upper and underwing flight patterns. The call is a piping 'thi-wit'. Small parties in dry grassland and open woodland. 23 cm (Kleinswartvlerkkiewiet)

5 BLACK-WINGED PLOVER *Vanellus melanopterus*

Fairly common visitor and resident. Differs from (4) in white forehead extending to *above* the eye, a bright red eye-ring, a broad dark band on the lower breast and dark red legs. See illustrations for upper and underwing flight patterns. The normal call is a harsh 'tlu-wit', the alarm call a shrill 'che-che-che-cherek', rising to a scream when highly agitated. Usually in flocks in hilly grassland, on golf courses and playing fields where grass is short. 29 cm (Grootswartvlerkkiewiet)

121
2
1
a
b
Br
3
4
5

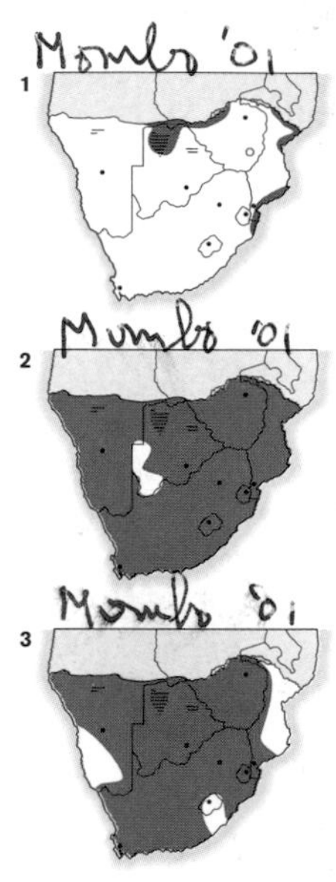

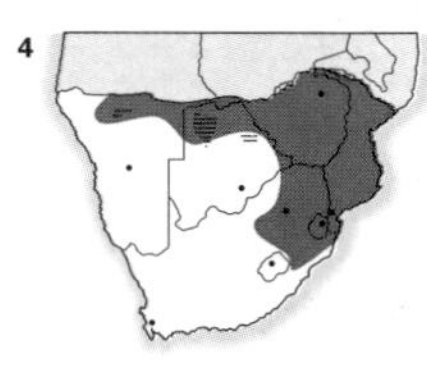

1 **LONG-TOED PLOVER** *Vanellus crassirostris*

Uncommon, localised resident. Distinguished by white frontal half of head, neck and upper breast contrasting with black nape, rear neck and breast-band, plus very long toes. In flight reveals predominantly white wings; cf. (5). The call is 'wheet' and, in flight, a clicking 'kick-k-k-kick-k-k-k'. Pairs or groups on quiet sections of large rivers (especially the Zambezi) and their backwaters, lakes, floodpans and floodplains where it feeds by walking on floating vegetation. 30 cm (Witvlerkkiewiet) Mombo 6/01

2 **BLACKSMITH PLOVER** *Vanellus armatus*

Very common resident. A pied plover with *grey wings and mantle.* Immature, as illustrated, has the basic plumage pattern of adults but in tones of speckled brown. The call is a metallic 'klink, klink, klink …' repeated loudly and continuously when disturbed. Pairs and scattered individuals frequent the shores of a wide variety of inland waters, marshy ground, flooded fields and other moist places. 30 cm (Bontkiewiet) Mombo 6/01

3 **CROWNED PLOVER** *Vanellus coronatus*

Very common resident. Distinguished by white circle surrounding a black cap, plus mainly red bill and red legs; eyes usually pale yellow, sometimes dark brown. At times very noisy, calling 'kie-weeet' on the ground or a repeated 'kree-kree-kreeip-kreeip …' in flight, day or night. Pairs and groups are found on dry open ground where the grass is short or burnt, especially on airfields; also in lightly wooded country. They often fly about in small groups at some height calling repeatedly. 30 cm (Kroonkiewiet) Mombo 6/01

4 **WATTLED PLOVER** *Vanellus senegallus*

Common resident. Bright yellow bill, wattles and legs distinguish this plover from all but (5), from which it differs in shorter wattles, white patch *only* on forecrown, a streaked neck, lack of white bar on the folded wing and *brown breast and underparts* except for the belly. The call is a shrill 'kwep-kwep-kwep-kwep', speeding up with increased agitation. Pairs and small groups frequent grassy waterside localities, riverbanks, dam walls, fringes of sewage ponds and vleis. 35 cm (Lelkiewiet)

5 **WHITE-CROWNED PLOVER** *Vanellus albiceps*

Uncommon, localised resident. Distinguished from (4) by longer wattles (longer than the bill), a broad white band (dark-edged in males) extending from the bill over the crown, *entirely* white underparts and a black wing bordered with white above. In flight the wings appear mainly white; cf. (1). A noisy species, the call a sharp 'peep, peep-peep, peep …' uttered at rapid speed if the bird is flushed. Pairs and groups frequent the shores and sandbanks of large perennial rivers. 30 cm (Witkopkiewiet)

1
J
2
3
4
5

1 EUROPEAN OYSTERCATCHER *Haematopus ostralegus*

Rare visitor. Fairly large, pied shorebird with orange bill and pink legs. Usually occurs in southern Africa as non-breeding or immature, the latter with dark tip to bill. In breeding plumage lacks white throat. The call is a shrill 'kleeep' and a shorter 'pic, pic'. Singly or in small groups on sandy coastlines, river mouths and lagoons. Sometimes in company with the larger African Black Oystercatcher (2). 43 cm (Bonttobie)

2 AFRICAN BLACK OYSTERCATCHER *Haematopus moquini* 

Common endemic resident. The only entirely black shorebird with red bill, eye and legs. Immature is browner. Normal call 'klee-weep, klee-weep'; alarm call a sharp 'ki-kik-kiks'. Singly or in small groups on rocky coastlines, estuaries and coastal lagoons. Is most common on the Cape and Namibian coastlines. 51 cm (Swarttobie)

3 WHIMBREL *Numenius phaeopus*

Common summer visitor, a few all year. Differs from (4) in markedly smaller size, shorter decurved bill (about two and a half times length of head) and dark cap with pale central line; see illustration. In flight shows extensive white back and rump. Call is a twittering 'peep-eep-eep-eep-ee'. Singly or in small groups on coastal lagoons, rocky shorelines, estuary and harbour mud flats; less frequently on inland waters. 43 cm (Kleinwulp)

4 CURLEW *Numenius arquata*

Uncommon summer visitor. Much larger than (3) with enormously long, decurved bill. Shows no distinctive pattern on crown. In flight shows similar large white area on back and rump to (3) but generally paler overall appearance. Utters various calls, including 'cur-lew' or 'coorwe-coorwe' and 'quee-quee-quee'. Groups, up to about 50 to 60, on coastal shorelines (especially southern and western coasts), estuaries, coastal lagoons, tidal rivers and harbours. A vagrant to inland waters. 59 cm (Grootwulp)

Br
1
N-Br
2
3
4

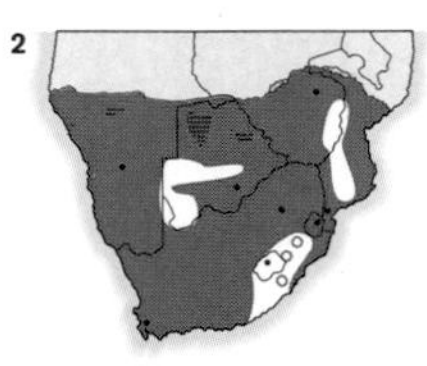

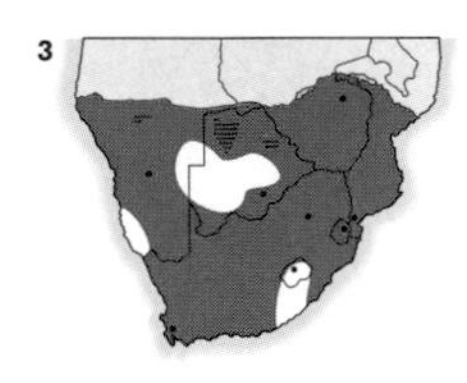

CRAB PLOVER

Family DROMADIDAE. The Crab Plover is a monotypic species confined to the east coast from the Red Sea to northern Mozambique; a vagrant further south.

1 CRAB PLOVER *Dromas ardeola*

Rare visitor. Long-legged, mainly white shorebird; immature browner as illustrated. Differs from other similar black and white birds in *heavy, thick bill.* Flies stiff-winged, the legs protruding well beyond the tail. Utters a harsh 'crook' or 'cheeruk' when flushed. Occurs in small flocks (up to about 30) on east coast mud flats at coastal lagoons and estuaries, often in association with mangroves. Most frequent in Mozambique. 38 cm (Krapvreter)

AVOCETS AND STILTS

Family RECURVIROSTRIDAE. Elegant, long-legged, long-billed, black and white wading birds, avocets with upturned bills, stilts with straight bills. Both species have a Eurasian distribution.

2 AVOCET *Recurvirostra avosetta*

Common resident. Thin, upturned bill diagnostic. Immature dark brown where adult is black. Calls a liquid 'kluut', several birds sometimes calling together. Flocks, varying from a few individuals to hundreds, in shallow waters of inland lakes, dams and pans (especially sewage ponds) and at coastal lagoons and estuaries. Feeds by wading, the immersed bill being swept from side to side while the bird walks slowly forward, or while swimming. Nomadic when not breeding and irregular in many regions. 43 cm (Bontelsie)

3 BLACK-WINGED STILT *Himantopus himantopus*

Common resident. Black and white plumage and long red legs conspicuous both at rest and in flight. Adult may have a dusky crown to the head, while immature is even duskier about the head as illustrated. The call, often given in flight, is a loud 'kik-kik-kik-kik-kik'or 'kyik'. Individuals, pairs or flocks at inland pans, dams and vleis, especially sewage ponds, plus coastal lagoons and estuaries. Wades in the shallows with the legs well immersed while feeding on the surface. 38 cm (Rooipootelsie)

1

J

2

3

J

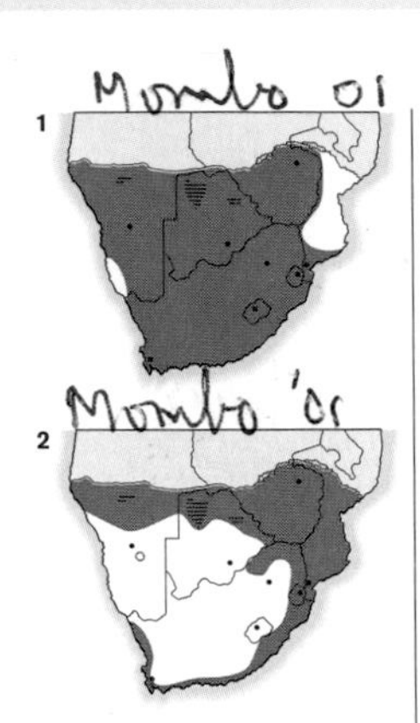

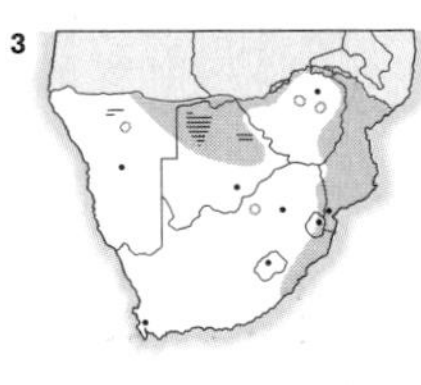

DIKKOPS

Family BURHINIDAE. Plover-like birds with large heads and eyes, long legs, feet without a hind claw and tawny colouring. Normally walk with short, mincing steps. Nocturnal and crepuscular, spending the daytime resting in some concealed position. Sexes are alike, immatures resemble adults.

1 SPOTTED DIKKOP *Burhinus capensis*

Common resident. Distinguished from (2) by heavily spotted upperparts, no wing-bar and by habitat preference. Most vocal on moonlit nights, flying about restlessly and calling a shrill, eerie 'chwee-chwee, chwee-chwee, chwee, chwee, chwee, tiu-tiu-tiu …', trailing off at the end. Pairs frequent dry rocky ground with short grass, open fields and open areas within woodland; frequently in little developed urban areas. Rests by day under bushes or among rocks, running off with lowered head if disturbed. 44 cm (Dikkop)

2 WATER DIKKOP *Burhinus vermiculatus*

Common resident. Distinguished from (1) by distinct *grey wing-bar,* edged black, plus habitat. Calls at night and at dusk, a piping, melancholy 'whee-wheeoo-wheeoo'. Singly or in small groups on the banks of large rivers or lakes where there is fringing vegetation. Lies up during the day in reeds or beneath overhanging bushes, becoming active at dusk. 40 cm (Waterdikkop)

PRATINCOLES AND COURSERS

Family GLAREOLIDAE. Pratincoles are migratory and nomadic birds with very short legs in relation to body-length. At rest or in their elegant, often erratic flight they resemble terns. Feed mostly in the air in flocks. Their calls are of a 'kip-kip-kip …' nature. The related coursers are more plover-like with erect stance, but unlike plovers lack a hind toe; they are terrestrial feeders. Sexes are alike in both groups.

3 RED-WINGED PRATINCOLE *Glareola pratincola*

Locally common summer resident. Differs from (4) in *rufous underwing coverts and white-tipped secondaries;* see flight illustration. Flocks occur on floodlands, estuaries and lakesides, occasionally on farmlands. At times flocks rise in great, wheeling columns and perform remarkable aerial manoeuvres. When settling, habitually stands briefly with wings raised. 25 cm (Rooivlerksprinkaanvoël)

4 BLACK-WINGED PRATINCOLE *Glareola nordmanni*

Locally common summer visitor. Differs from (3) in entirely blackish underwings, less red on the gape and slightly more extensive yellow-buff colouring on the lower breast. Flocks on floodlands, estuaries, lakesides and farmlands. Behaviour as the previous species. 25 cm (Swartvlerksprinkaanvoël)

5 ROCK PRATINCOLE *Glareola nuchalis*

Common, localised resident. Smaller than (3) and (4), has no throat-patch, outer tail feathers are only slightly elongated; narrow white collar and red legs diagnostic. Flocks on large rivers and lakes, especially near boulder-strewn rapids. Perches on rocks protruding from the water and feeds by hawking over the water. 18 cm (Withalssprinkaanvoël)

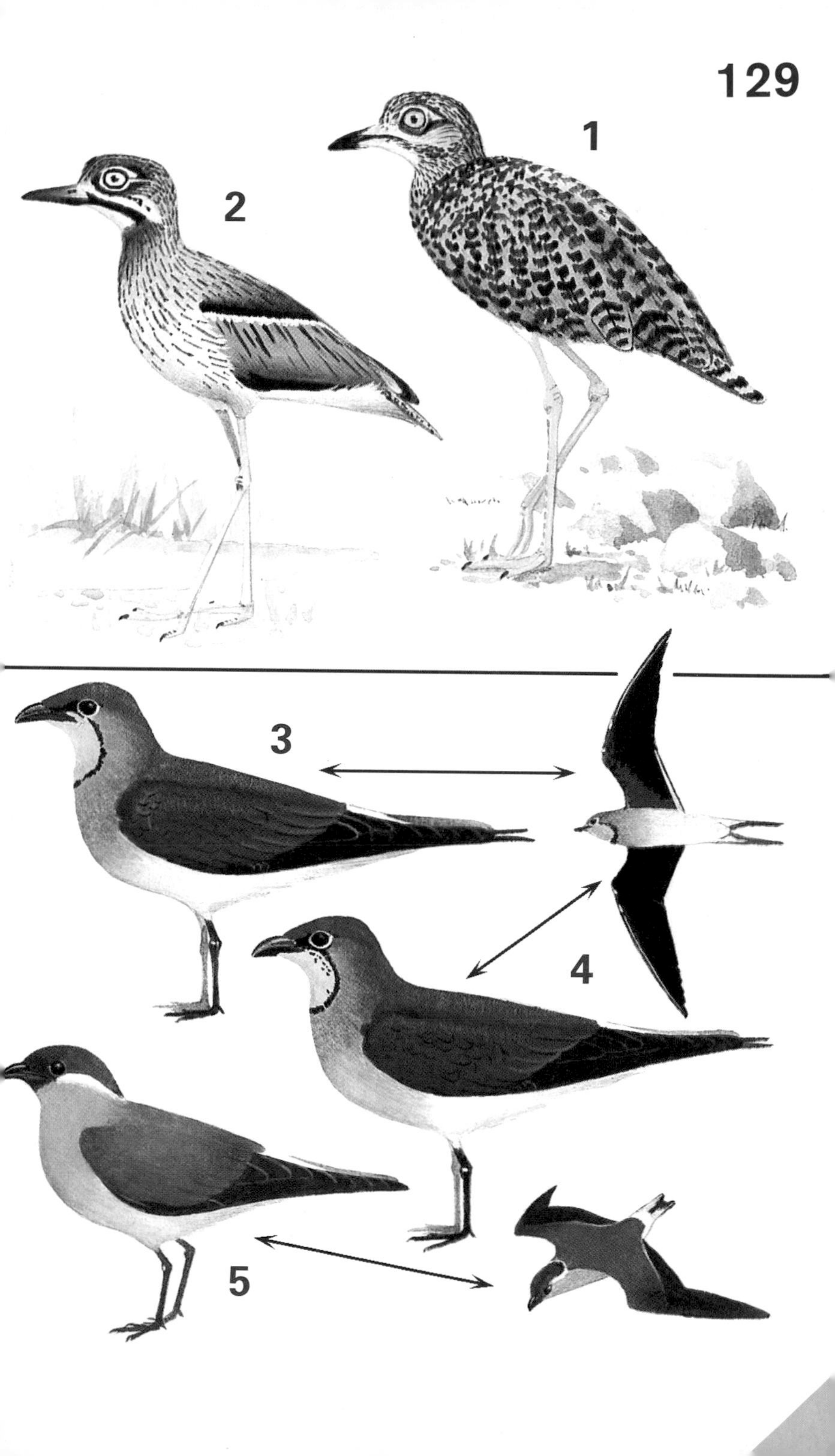
1
2
3
4
5

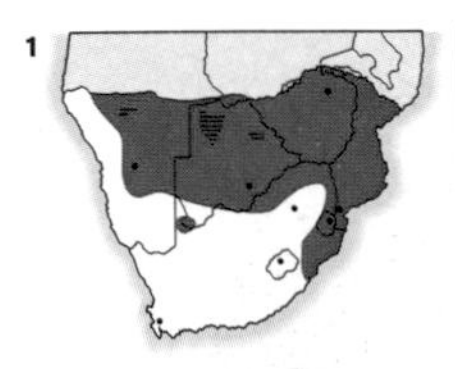

1 BRONZE-WINGED COURSER *Rhinoptilus chalcopterus*

Uncommon visitor and resident. Larger than other coursers; has *red legs* and distinctive head markings, these less clearly defined in the immature. At night calls a shrill 'ji-ku-it' or a plaintive 'groraag'. A nocturnal species of well-wooded regions, especially favouring mopane woodland. Roosts by day beneath a bush and feeds at night in open areas and on roads. 25 cm (Bronsvlerkdrawwertjie)

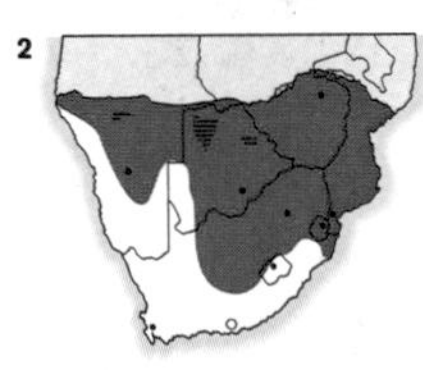

2 TEMMINCK'S COURSER *Cursorius temminckii*

Fairly common resident. A small, white-legged, *rufous-capped* courser; cf. (3). Immature is speckled buff on upperparts and crown. May call a sharp 'err-err-err' in flight. Pairs and small groups on freshly burnt or well-grazed grassland and airfields. Stands with erect stance, then runs rapidly forward before stooping briefly to feed; occasionally bobs its head and tail. Nomadic. 20 cm (Trekdrawwertjie)

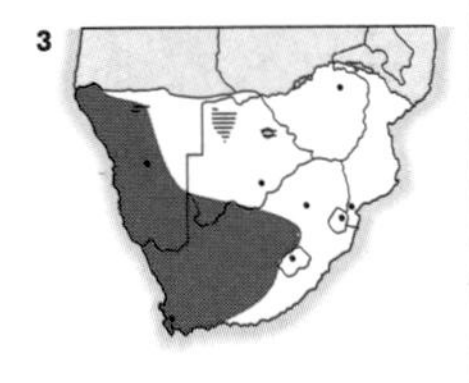

3 BURCHELL'S COURSER *Cursorius rufus* E

Uncommon endemic resident. Differs from (2) mainly in *grey hindcrown* and the extent of its white belly. Immature is mottled on upperparts. A quiet species; may call 'kok-kok-kwich'. Habitat and habits very similar to (2). Small groups in short grassland. Bobs its head and hindquarters more than (2) and jerks its body backwards and forwards or sideways. Nomadic. 23 cm (Bloukopdrawwertjie)

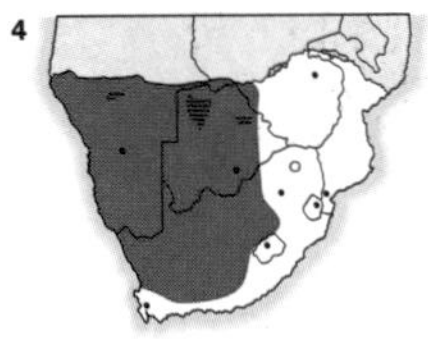

4 DOUBLE-BANDED COURSER *Smutsornis africanus*

Common resident. A distinctive, pale courser with two black bands encircling the lower neck and upper breast. Immature is similar. Normally silent but may call 'pee-wee' if put to flight; also calls 'chik-kee, chik-kee, chik-kee-kee-kee-kee' while flying at night. In pairs or scattered groups in arid grassland or semi-desert, fringes of dry pans and barren, stony flats. Active day and night and seemingly indifferent to hot conditions. Runs rather than flies. Nomadic. 22 cm (Dubbelbanddrawwertjie)

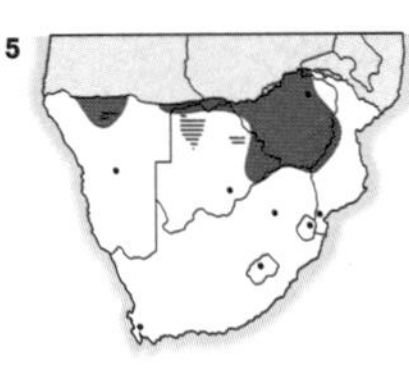

5 THREE-BANDED COURSER *Rhinoptilus cinctus*

Uncommon visitor and resident. Darker than (4) with bold head markings and bands spanning the upper breast (not encircling the neck). Immature has lower band poorly defined. It is mainly nocturnal, and calls mostly at night, 'chick-a-chuck-a-chuck-a-chuck'. Singly or in pairs in well-grassed woodland and thornveld of the drier regions. When approached it freezes, usually with its back to the observer. 28 cm (Driebanddrawwertjie)

2
1
3
4
5

BUSTARDS AND KORHAANS

Family OTIDIDAE. Large, long-legged, long-necked terrestrial birds, cryptically coloured, with short tails and feet having three forward-facing toes. Most have elaborate courtship displays involving plumage transformations, flights or unusual calls.

1

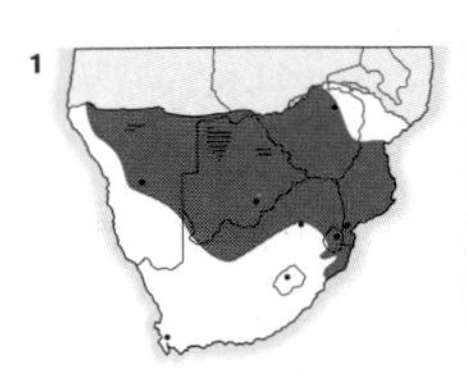

1 RED-CRESTED KORHAAN *Eupodotis ruficrista* NE

Common, near endemic resident. Told from other small korhaans by creamy-white V marks on the upperparts; has shorter legs and shorter neck than Black-bellied Korhaan (p. 136). Female has a broad white band across the lower breast, reduced in the male to a small patch on either side of breast. Red crest of courting male, raised when the crown, breast and neck feathers are also raised, is seldom seen and is *not* a field feature. Territorial call of male starts with a series of clicks increasing in speed and changing into a series of shrill, piercing whistles 'phee-phee-phee-phee ...' repeated up to 10 or more times. Courting pairs perform a duet, a rapid 'wuk-wuk-wuk-wuk ...' rising in volume and frequency to 'wuka-wuka-wuka-wuka ...' before the male switches to the whistling call. In aerial display the male flies up steeply to about 20 m and then tumbles as though shot, almost to the ground. Singly or in pairs in bushveld. 53 cm (Boskorhaan)

2

2 WHITE-BELLIED KORHAAN *Eupodotis cafra* 

Uncommon endemic resident. A small, distinctive korhaan, male with dark cap and throat plus blue-grey front of neck. The call, heard morning and evening, is 'takwarat' repeated several times at decreasing volume; this is sometimes preceded by several 'throat-clearing' sounds thus: 'aaa-aaa-aaa-takwarat-takwarat-takwarat ...'. If flushed calls 'kuk-pa-wow' as it flies off. Pairs and small parties in tall grassland, farmlands and occasionally thornveld. 53 cm (Witpenskorhaan)

3

3 BLACK KORHAAN *Eupodotis afra* 

Common endemic resident. On the ground indistinguishable from (4), to which it is closely related, but in flight from above both sexes differ from (4) in having *entirely black primary wing feathers*. The male is unmistakable; female told from other female korhaans by pink bill with a pale tip, this feature also present in the immature. The male calls a raucous 'krra-a-a-aak wet-de-wet-de-wet-de...' in flight or from a slightly elevated position on the ground. It frequents Karoo scrub and coastal dunes. 53 cm (Swartkorhaan)

4

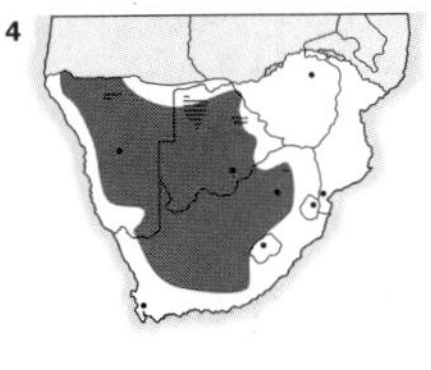

4 WHITE-WINGED BLACK KORHAAN *Eupodotis afraoides* E

Common endemic resident. On the ground indistinguishable from (3). In flight both sexes show *extensive white on their otherwise black primaries*. In all other respects, including voice, this species is a duplicate of (3). It frequents dry, open grassland, arid scrublands and Kalahari sandveld. 53 cm (Witvlerk-korhaan)

5

5 BLUE KORHAAN *Eupodotis caerulescens* 

Common endemic resident. The only korhaan with entirely blue-grey neck and underparts. Male calls mostly early morning 'kakow, kakow, kakow ...', and several birds may call in unison; the flight call is a deep-throated 'knock-me-down ...'. Pairs and small groups frequent highveld grassland and irrigated lands. 50-58 cm (Bloukorhaan)

1
♂
♀
♀
2
♀
♂
3
♂
3 & 4
♀
4
5
♂
♀
♂

1
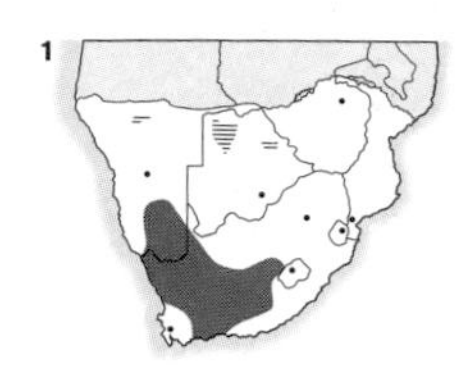

1 **KAROO KORHAAN** *Eupodotis vigorsii*

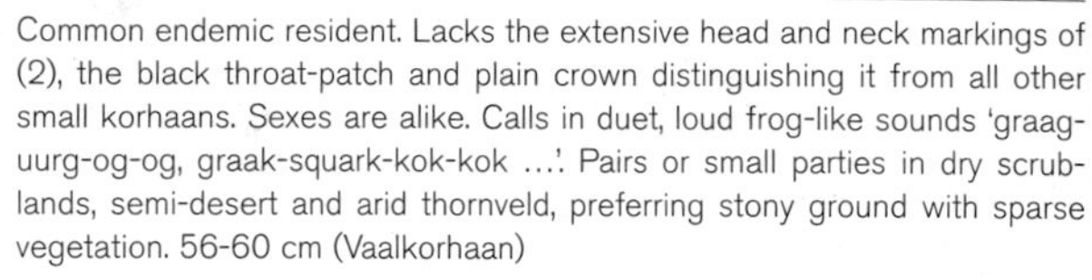

Common endemic resident. Lacks the extensive head and neck markings of (2), the black throat-patch and plain crown distinguishing it from all other small korhaans. Sexes are alike. Calls in duet, loud frog-like sounds 'graag-uurg-og-og, graak-squark-kok-kok ...'. Pairs or small parties in dry scrublands, semi-desert and arid thornveld, preferring stony ground with sparse vegetation. 56-60 cm (Vaalkorhaan)

2

2 **RÜPPELL'S KORHAAN** *Eupodotis rueppellii*

Common resident, near endemic to Namibia. Similar to (1) but has more extensive head and neck markings. Sexes are alike. Calls in duet, a deep, resonant 'waaa-a-re-e, waaa-a-re-e ...', first sound by the male, next three by the female, repeated in long sequences. Individuals also draw the head back and then thrust it forward, calling a deep 'augh'. Flight call is a rapid 'quark-quark-quark ...'. Pairs frequent very arid regions and stony desert plains in western Namibia. 56-60 cm (Woestynkorhaan)

3
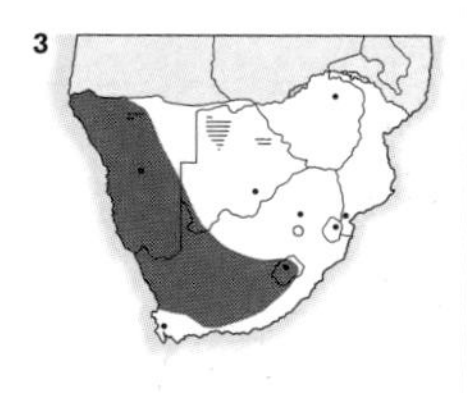

3 **LUDWIG'S BUSTARD** *Neotis ludwigii*

Fairly common, near endemic resident. Differs from (4) in brown (not black) cap and lack of large black and white areas on the folded wing. The call, heard during courtship, is a deep-voiced 'klop ... klop ... klop'. At this time (October-November) the male fluffs out its plumage and inflates its neck, revealing white underfeathers, while calling at about 10-second intervals. Solitary or in small groups in semi-arid Karoo and arid Namib plains. 75-90 cm (Ludwigse pou)

4

4 **STANLEY'S BUSTARD** *Neotis denhami stanleyi*

Uncommon, endemic resident. Larger than (3), and differing mainly in its *black cap* with white central parting plus black and white wing coverts and secondaries, which are visible as a large black patch on the folded wing. The breeding male has no grey on its neck. In northern Botswana and north-western Zimbabwe the closely similar race *Neotis d. jacksoni* occurs as a non-breeding visitor in open woodland. The present race *Neotis d. stanleyi* is normally silent. In courtship the male fluffs its plumage, erects its fanned tail revealing white undertail coverts, and inflates its neck. Pairs and small groups are found in hilly grassland, karoo and coastal grassland of KwaZulu-Natal. 86-110 cm (Veldpou)

1
2
4
3
♀
4
♂
♂

1
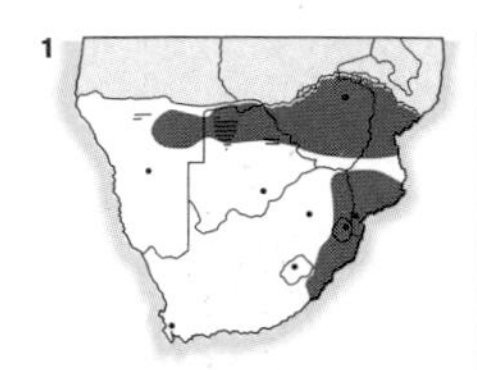

2
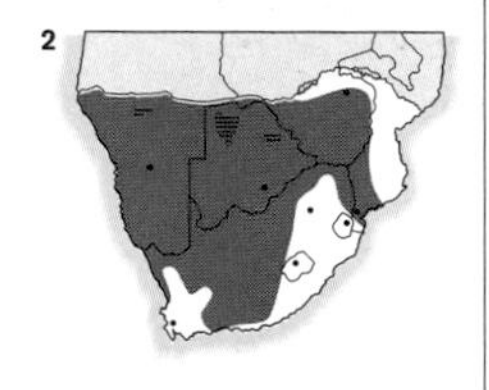

1 BLACK-BELLIED KORHAAN *Eupodotis melanogaster*

Common resident. Characterised by long legs (proportionately longer than any other korhaan); male in flight by *white upperwings.* Male has entirely black underparts, extending in a line up the front of the neck to the chin. Female has *white underparts.* Male calls while posturing as follows: first the head and neck are withdrawn and wings drooped (illustration 1); head and neck are fully stretched upwards while the bird utters a dull 'waak' or 'phwoe' (illustration 2); head is then lowered about halfway to the body and it utters a throaty grunt followed by a five-second pause; then it utters a sharp, whip-like sound 'ooor-whip'. During courtship the male performs an aerial display in which the white upperwings are strikingly presented; see flight illustration. The underwing is black except for a prominent white patch at the base of the primaries. Found singly or in pairs in rank, moist grassland. 58-65 cm (Langbeenkorhaan)

2 KORI BUSTARD *Ardeotis kori*

Common resident. Identified by huge size and crested head. Sexes are alike but male is about 20 per cent larger than female. Walks slowly with measured strides and flies reluctantly. In courtship the male calls a deep 'wum, wum, wum, wum, wummmmm'. Male also performs an elaborate courtship display: the throat-pouch is inflated and the frontal neck feathers splayed outwards revealing their white bases, the head with raised crest is drawn back, the wings are drooped and the tail deflected upwards and forwards to the neck with the white undertail coverts splayed outwards conspicuously; see illustration of male in partial display. Singly, in pairs or groups in open woodland, bushveld and semi-arid grasslands in the Karoo and Namibia. 135 cm (Gompou)

137
1
♀
♂
1
2
1
2

1

2

3

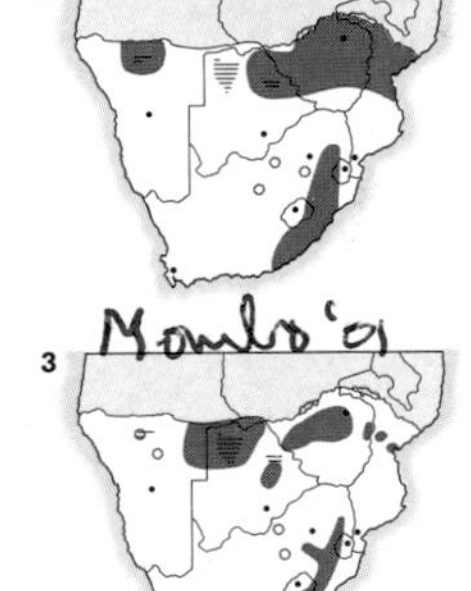

CRANES

Family GRUIDAE. Large, long-legged terrestrial birds, differing from storks in having short bills and being quite vocal. Like storks, they fly with heads and necks outstretched. They indulge in elaborate dancing displays with wings outstretched when courting, sometimes involving more than two birds. The South African populations of all three crane species have declined markedly in recent years.

1 BLUE CRANE *Anthropoides paradiseus*

Uncommon endemic resident, but threatened. Distinctive blue-grey, long-legged bird with bulbous head and long wing-plumes looking like a trailing tail. Immature lacks these plumes. The call is a loud, rattling, nasal 'kraaaarrk'. Occurs in pairs and flocks in Karoo, hilly grassland, moist valleys, farmlands and lakesides. Prefers fairly high altitudes and is nomadic when not breeding. 105 cm (Bloukraanvoël)

2 CROWNED CRANE *Balearica regulorum*

Fairly common resident, but threatened. Immature has less developed crest and wattles and looks browner. The call is a two-syllabled trumpeting, sounding like 'ma-hem'. Usually in flocks in grassland, farmlands, near vleis and other marshy regions, both in highlands and at the coast. Roosts on offshore islands, in reed-beds in river estuaries and in trees. Nomadic when not breeding. 105 cm (Mahem)

3 WATTLED CRANE *Bugeranus carunculatus*

Uncommon resident; endangered. A very large crane with distinctive wattles hanging either side of the chin. Immature lacks wattles. Seldom vocal but can utter a loud, drawn-out, bell-like 'horuk'. Pairs and small groups are sparsely distributed in vleis, swamplands, fringes of large lakes and high-altitude grassland. Is most frequent in northern wetlands of Botswana. Often wades in shallow water while feeding. Wary and difficult to approach. 120 cm (Lelkraanvoël)

Note: Whereas these cranes may be fairly common in some parts of southern Africa their numbers have become very reduced in the Republic of South Africa and the species should be regarded as endangered in this country.

1
2
3
3

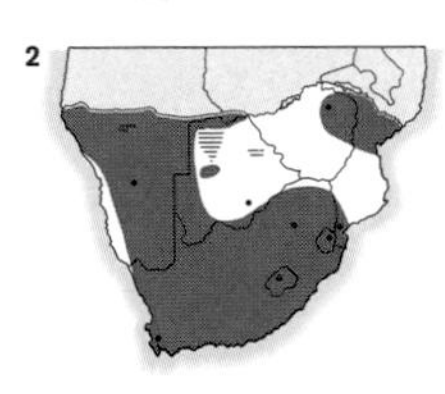

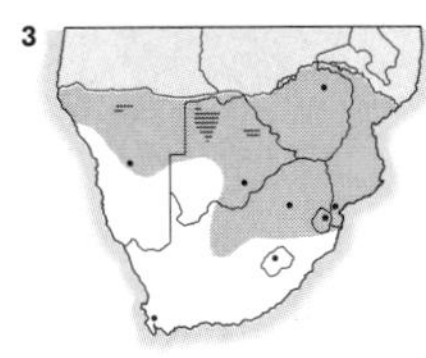

QUAILS AND FRANCOLINS

Family PHASIANIDAE. Terrestrial birds of mostly gregarious habits (quails excepted). Male francolins have leg-spurs (lacking in females) and crowing, ringing or cackling calls which are useful identification features. Immatures resemble adults but are duller. Quails are nomadic and irruptive, whereas francolins are more sedentary.

1 BLUE QUAIL *Coturnix adansonii*

Rare summer visitor to eastern Zimbabwe. Male told by dark overall colouring and large white throat-patch, female from other female quails by smaller size and *lack* of white eyebrow or throat-patch. The call is a piping, three-note, descending whistle, the first note much louder than the others. Pairs or small parties in moist grassland and vleis. Sparsely distributed at all times, its occurrence infrequent. A vagrant to areas outside of Zimbabwe. 15 cm (Bloukwartel)

2 COMMON QUAIL *Coturnix coturnix*

Common resident and visitor. Told by pale underparts in both sexes; in flight difficult to tell from (3). The call is a penetrating 'whit-WHIttit, whit-WHIttit …' uttered day or night when breeding; if flushed calls 'pree-pree-pree'. Usually flushes with reluctance. Pairs in bushveld, grassland, pastures and cultivated fields. 18 cm (Afrikaanse kwartel)

3 HARLEQUIN QUAIL *Coturnix delegorguei*

Uncommon to fairly common summer resident, a few all year. Male told by bold black markings on white throat and chestnut underparts. Female distinguished from female of (2) by dark 'necklace' across throat to ear coverts. The call is a loud 'wit, wit-wit, wit, wit-wit-it', similar-sounding to (2) but more metallic. Pairs and small coveys in rank grass, especially in damp regions within grassland and bushveld. Most frequent in Zimbabwe and northern Botswana. Nomadic, sometimes irrupting in great numbers locally, then suddenly disappearing again. 18 cm (Bontkwartel)

♂
1
♀
♂
2
♀
♂
3
♀

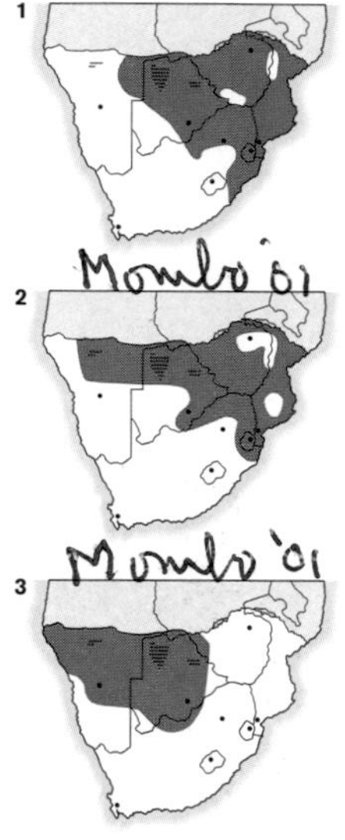

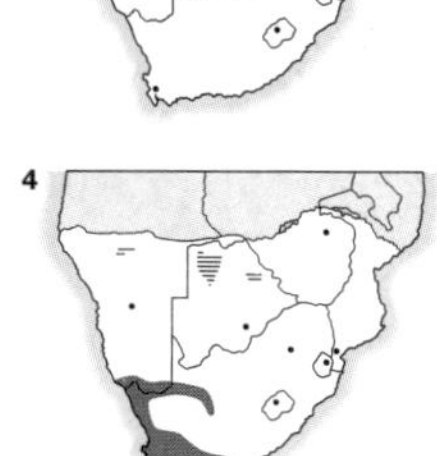

1 COQUI FRANCOLIN *Francolinus coqui*

Common resident. A small species. Male has tawny head and neck plus barred underparts. Female has white throat bordered black plus black eyebrow extending to the upper neck. The call is a piping 'ko-kwee, ko-kwee …' or 'be-quick, be-quick …' repeated continually; males also utter a loud, high-pitched crowing 'kek, KEKekekekekekekekekekek', the second note loudest and all others diminishing in volume. Habitually walks in a slow, stooped manner as the female illustrated, especially when crossing roads and other open spaces, and crouches motionless when alarmed. Pairs or small family groups frequent well-grassed bushveld and woodland. 28 cm (Swempie)

2 CRESTED FRANCOLIN *Francolinus sephaena*

Common resident. Identified by dark cap (the feathers of which are raised in alarm) over a prominent white eyebrow, red legs and the habit of holding the *tail raised like a Bantam chicken;* in flight black tail is conspicuous. Race (a) is widespread; race (b), previously known as Kirk's Francolin, differs in having no dark blotching on the upper breast and in streaked underparts and orange-yellow legs; this race is restricted to north of the Beira district and beyond the Zambezi. The call is a shrill 'kwerri-kwetchi, kwerri-kwetchi' sounding like 'beer and cognac, beer and cognac'. Pairs or small groups in bushveld, broad-leaved woodland, thickets near rivers and forest fringes, mostly keeping within cover. 32 cm (Bospatrys)

3 RED-BILLED FRANCOLIN *Francolinus adspersus* NE

Common, near endemic resident. Identified by red bill, yellow skin surrounding the eyes and *finely barred* underparts; cf. Natal Francolin (p. 146). Has a very loud, harsh, crowing call which increases to a frenzied cackling. Occurs in pairs and groups in Kalahari thornveld. Frequents low scrub and thickets, especially along rivers, but feeds on open ground. 30-38 cm (Rooibekfisant)

4 CAPE FRANCOLIN *Francolinus capensis* E

Common to abundant Cape endemic. A large, dark francolin, only the underparts prominently streaked white. Shows a blackish tail in flight. The call is a loud, high-pitched cackling 'kwek, kwek, kwek, kwekek-kwekek-kwekek-kwekek-kwekek-kek-kek-kek …', the sound rising and then decreasing in volume and fading at the end. Singly or in small coveys in fynbos, wooded kloofs and riverside scrub. 40-45 cm (Kaapse fisant)

♂ 1 ♀

a 2 b

3

4

1

2

3

4

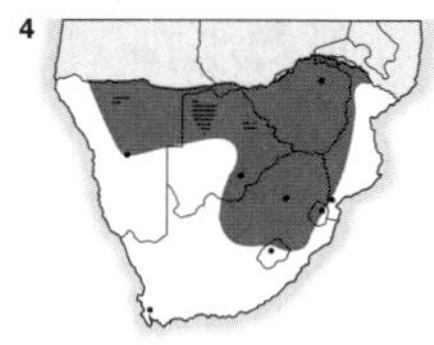

1 HARTLAUB'S FRANCOLIN *Francolinus hartlaubi*

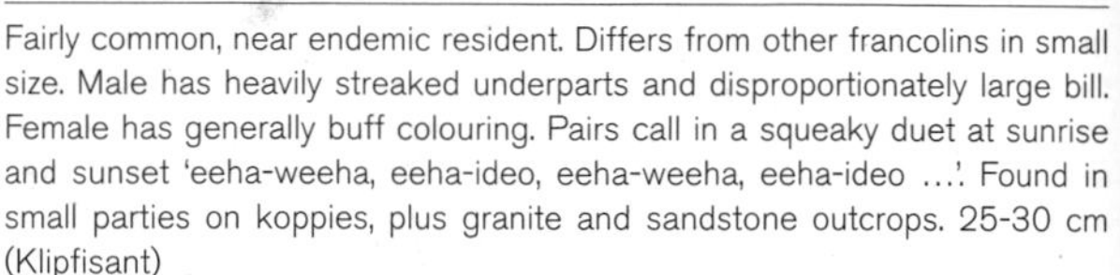

Fairly common, near endemic resident. Differs from other francolins in small size. Male has heavily streaked underparts and disproportionately large bill. Female has generally buff colouring. Pairs call in a squeaky duet at sunrise and sunset 'eeha-weeha, eeha-ideo, eeha-weeha, eeha-ideo …'. Found in small parties on koppies, plus granite and sandstone outcrops. 25-30 cm (Klipfisant)

2 GREY-WING FRANCOLIN *Francolinus africanus*

Common endemic resident. Predominantly grey, the *throat well spotted with black,* the underparts *closely barred black,* thus differing from all white-throated species (overleaf). Immature has more white about the throat and the barring of the underparts extends to the lower neck. The normal call is a squeaky 'kwe-kwe-kwe-kwe-skwekeeoo-skwekeeoo-skwekeeoo-keeoo-keeoo'. If flushed groups rise steeply into the air with much noise. Occurs in coveys of five to 10 on grassy hillsides, montane grassland and coastal flats. 31-3 cm (Bergpatrys)

3 RED-NECKED FRANCOLIN *Francolinus afer*

Common resident. At least six different plumage forms occur but *in all* the bill, facial mask, throat and legs are red: (a) in Swaziland and north-eastern South Africa; (b) in south-eastern coastal areas; (c) from eastern Zimbabwe to Beira district; (d) (the smallest) in Cunene River region, Namibia. There are also other intermediate forms between these. The call is a harsh crowing 'choorr, choorr, choorr, chwirr' fading at the end or, when flushed, 'choor-choor'. If pursued takes refuge in trees. Small groups occur in valley bush, forest fringes, coastal bush and fallow agricultural lands. 32-44 cm (Rooikeelfisant)

4 SWAINSON'S FRANCOLIN *Francolinus swainsonii*

Common, near endemic resident. The *only red-necked francolin with black legs and black bill,* the basic plumage colour uniform overall; cf. (3). Utters a harsh crowing 'krrraaak-krrraaak-krrraaak …' fading at the end. Male calls from a low branch or anthill. Singly or in small coveys in bushveld, woodland and fallow agricultural lands, usually not far from water. 34-9 cm (Bosveld-fisant)

♂
1
♀
2
a
c
d
3
b
4

1

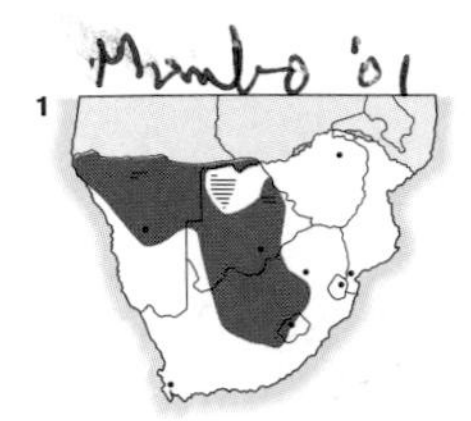

1 ORANGE RIVER FRANCOLIN *Francolinus levaillantoides*

Common resident. The palest form (a) occurs in central and northern Botswana and, with more deep red spotting on the underparts, also in Namibia; elsewhere is more rufous about the head and underparts, more liberally spotted deep red as (b) and (c). Distinguished from (3) by the red spotting of the underparts *extending up to the white throat* and lack of a black and white speckled patch on the upper breast. The call is 'pirrie-perrie, pirrie-perrie, pirrie-perrie ...'. Coveys of about 12 in dry regions with sparse vegetation, flat, dry grasslands or open woodland on sandy soils. 33-5 cm (Kalaharipatrys)

2

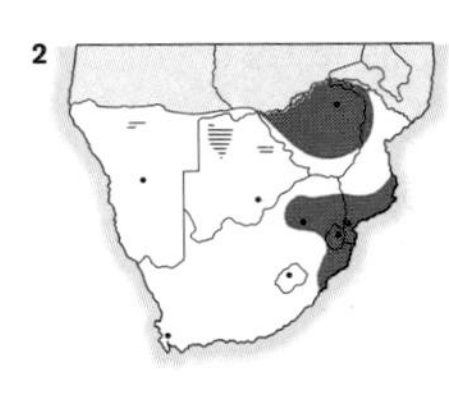

2 SHELLEY'S FRANCOLIN *Francolinus shelleyi*

Uncommon to locally common resident. Differs from Grey-wing Francolin (previous page) in *clear white throat with black surround,* clear white stripe through the eye and ear coverts, plus a large patch of deep red blotches on the upper breast, extending to the flanks. The call is a shrill, musical crowing sounding like 'I'll drink yer beer' repeated three or four times. Found in grassy woodland and grassland (montane grassland in eastern Zimbabwe), especially near rocky koppies. 33 cm (Laeveldpatrys)

3

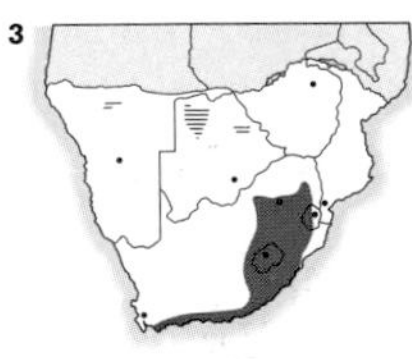

3 RED-WING FRANCOLIN *Francolinus levaillantii*

Uncommon resident. Differs from (1) in extensive ochre patch extending from the eye to the lower hindneck, and *large patch of black and white speckling on the upper breast.* The call is a high-pitched 'cherp-cherp-cherp-cherp-chirreechoo-chirreechoo-chirreechoo ...'. Favours grassland at all altitudes and grassy fynbos in the southern Cape. Usually in small coveys. 38-40 cm (Roolvlerkpatrys)

4

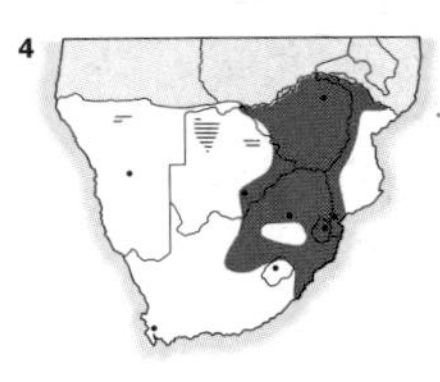

4 NATAL FRANCOLIN *Francolinus natalensis*

Common, near endemic resident. Identified by entirely *black and white barred underparts* (bolder bars than in Red-billed Francolin, p. 142), plus red legs and red bill with a yellow base. The call is a harsh 'kwali, KWALI, kwali'; when alarmed utters a raucous cackling. Parties of six to 10 favour granite koppies, riverine forests, wooded valleys and thornveld, generally in rocky situations and seldom far from water. 30-38 cm (Natalse fisant)

5

5 CHUKAR PARTRIDGE *Alectoris chukar*

An introduced species, feral on Robben Island. Has bold black barring on the flanks plus a black band encircling the foreparts from forehead to upper breast. Has a cackling call. It occurs in coveys of 5-15 birds in alien *Acacia* on the island. 33 cm (Asiatiese patrys)

a
b
1
c
2
3
4
5

1
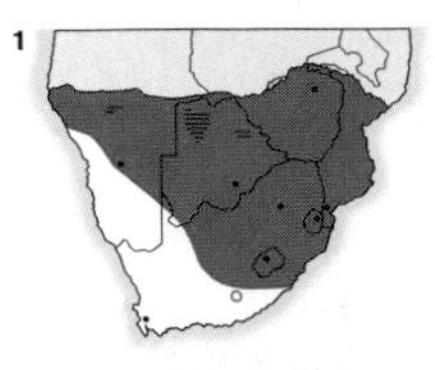

2

3
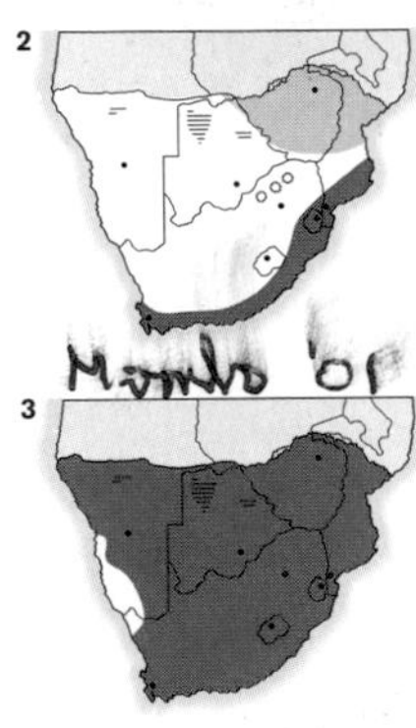

4
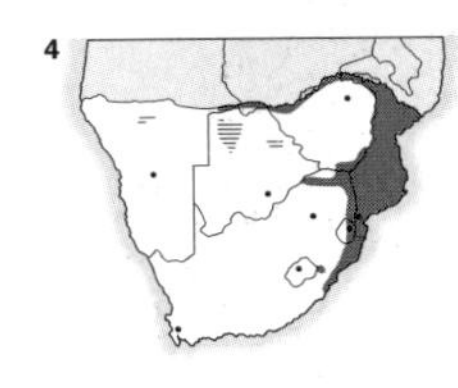

BUTTON QUAILS

Family TURNICIDAE. Very small terrestrial birds, superficially similar to true quails (p. 140) but lacking a hind toe. Colour patterns similar in both sexes but females are more richly coloured than males. Immatures are like males but spotted all over their breasts. They flush reluctantly, usually at one's feet, then fly low for a short distance before settling again.

1 KURRICHANE BUTTON QUAIL *Turnix sylvatica*

Common resident. Told from (2) by whitish sides to the head, cream-coloured eye and heart-shaped spots on the sides of the neck and breast. The call is a deep, resonant 'hoooo hoooo' made at two-second intervals by the female. Singly or in pairs in grassland with patches of tall grass, bush savanna, bushveld with good grass cover, cultivated and fallow farmlands. 14-15 cm (Bosveldkwarteltjie)

2 BLACK-RUMPED BUTTON QUAIL *Turnix hottentotta*

Sparse resident and summer visitor. Told from (1) by chestnut sides to the head and brown eye; in flight *by dark rump.* The call resembles that of (1) but is lower in pitch. Singly or in pairs in moist grassland and irrigated lands. Uncommon and irregular. 14-15 cm (Kaapse kwarteltjie)

GUINEAFOWLS

Family NUMIDIDAE. Differ from the related pheasants, partridges and francolins in having bare heads surmounted by casques or plumes, unfeathered necks in adults, predominantly grey plumages and lack of leg-spurs. Highly gregarious unless breeding.

3 HELMETED GUINEAFOWL *Numida meleagris*

Very common resident. Told by blue neck, red cap and horny casque on head. Chick (a) is buffy-brown, striped darker; juvenile (b) predominantly brown, darker on upperparts, head-stripes remaining until casque has started growing (cf. francolins, pp. 142-7); immature (c) resembles adult but has feathered neck, dark brown helmet and rudimentary casque. Normal adult call is a much-repeated 'ker-bek-ker-bek-ker-bek, krrrrrr ...'; female also utters a continual piping 't-phueet-t-phueet-t-phueet ...'. Flocks when not breeding, sometimes very large, in grassland, bushveld and farmlands. Goes to water regularly in the evenings. 53-8 cm (Gewone tarentaal)

4 CRESTED GUINEAFOWL *Guttera pucherani*

Locally common resident. Blacker than (3) with characteristic black head-plumes. Immature is barred chestnut, buff and black on the upperparts. Has a rattling alarm call; when breeding calls 'tick-tack, ticktack-tirr-tirr-tirr'. Flocks in lowland and riverine forests, lowveld broad-leaved woodland and thickets, coastal bush and dune forests. 50 cm (Kuifkoptarentaal)

1
♀
2
♀
3
c
b
a
4

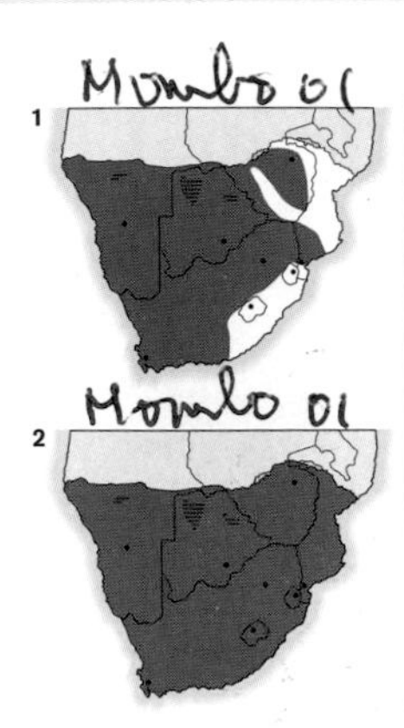

1 **OSTRICH** *Struthio camelus*

Family STRUTHIONIDAE. Common resident. Well-known, enormous, flightless bird. Immature is like a small, scruffy female and is usually accompanied by adults. Male utters a lion-like roar. Usually in pairs or groups, sometimes with many young birds present. The tail colour of adult males varies according to region, from whitish to grey or cinnamon-brown. Wild ostriches occur in isolated pockets throughout southern Africa, especially in the large nature reserves. Inhabits woodland and wooded grassland in the east and thornveld or grassland in the more arid western regions. About 2 m (Volstruis)

2 **SECRETARYBIRD** *Sagittarius serpentarius*

Family SAGITTARIIDAE. Common resident. Large, long-legged grey and black bird with long, loose black feathers projecting behind the head. Adult has orange face, immature yellow face. Normally silent but sometimes utters a frog-like croak. Usually in pairs walking through grassland, bushveld or savanna at all altitudes. Sometimes runs a short distance with spread wings and may also soar to a great height. Roosts on top of thorn trees. 125-50 cm (Sekretarisvoël)

1
♂
♀
2

1

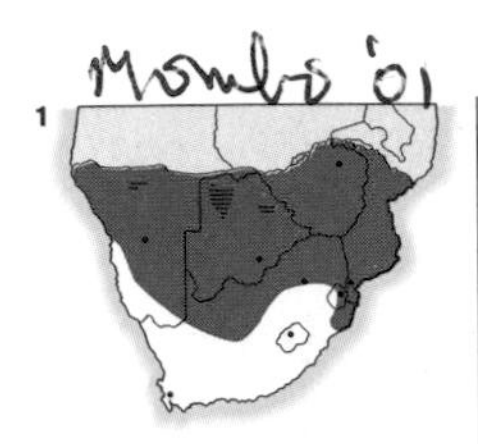

2

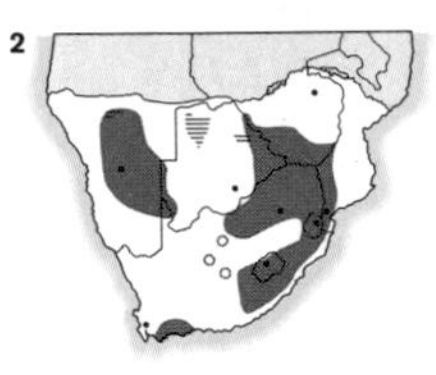

3

VULTURES, KITES, EAGLES, BUZZARDS, HAWKS, HARRIERS AND GYMNOGENE

Family ACCIPITRIDAE. Diurnal birds of prey (raptors) characterised by hooked bills suited to a mainly carnivorous diet. Each group hereafter described separately.

Vultures are typified by their large size, heavy, hooked bills, necks wholly or partially devoid of feathers (the exception being the aberrant Bearded Vulture) and, for birds of prey, relatively weak feet not suited to grasping prey. Vultures feed on carrion, soar with ease during much of the day and bathe in ponds and rivers. Normally silent, but hiss and squeal when squabbling over food.

1 WHITE-BACKED VULTURE *Gyps africanus*

Common resident. Adult difficult to distinguish from (2) unless the white back is seen, but at close range the eye is dark (not honey-coloured); old birds become very pale. Immature lacks the white rump but differs from immature of (2) in darker, less rufous plumage, black (not pink) skin on neck and lack of white collar feathers. A bushveld vulture, it normally outnumbers all others in this habitat and gathers regularly in considerable numbers at carrion. Otherwise in good weather soars all day at a great height. Roosts and nests in trees; cf. (2). 90-98 cm (Witrugaasvoël)

2 CAPE GRIFFON VULTURE *Gyps coprotheres* E

Common endemic resident. Similar to (1), but larger. Adult is very pale in colour and may have an almost white back; at close range the eye is honey-coloured. Immature more rufous, warmer brown than immature of (1), the neck pink with white feathers at the base. The common vulture of the central regions and ranging widely when not breeding. Often perches on pylons. Frequents high cliffs when breeding (May-October); colonies then comprise dozens or hundreds of birds, otherwise singly or in groups anywhere but rare in Zimbabwe and Mozambique. 105-15 cm (Kransaasvoël)

3 BEARDED VULTURE or LAMMERGEIER *Gypaetus barbatus*

Uncommon, localised resident. Differs from all other vultures in loosely feathered head and legs, the 'beard' visible in both adult and immature. Unlikely to be confused with any other bird of prey within its restricted range; in flight wedge-shaped tail diagnostic. Singly or in small numbers in the Drakensberg and Maluti mountains of the south-east, rarely further afield. Soars by day and roosts on inaccessible cliffs. South African population estimated at 204 pairs. 110 cm (Baardaasvoël)

Underwing:
Cape Griffon Vulture

Underwing:
White-backed Vulture

J
J
1
J
J
2
J
3

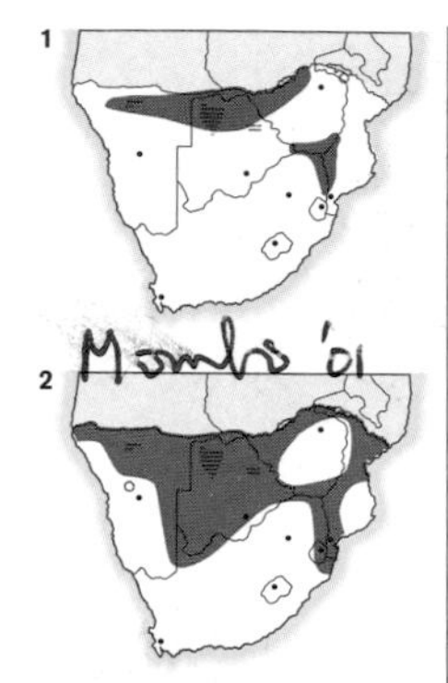

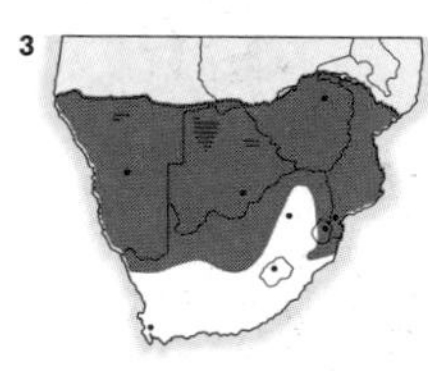

1 **HOODED VULTURE** *Necrosyrtes monachus*

Fairly common, localised resident. A small, slender-billed vulture. Adult has the white, downy feathers of the hindneck forming a hood over the head, plus white ruff, 'pants' and legs; cf. others on this page which all have heavy bills. See underwing flight patterns below. Immature is all-brown including downy head and neck, only the face pink; the rare Egyptian Vulture immature (overleaf) also has a slender bill but differs in having a well-feathered head. Occurs in small numbers in protected game areas, the Okavango region and the Zambezi Valley. Joins other vultures at carrion. Most frequently seen where mammalian predators occur. 70 cm (Monnikaasvoël)

2 **WHITE-HEADED VULTURE** *Trigonoceps occipitalis*

Uncommon resident. Distinguished by large size, adult with white head, neck and underparts, heavy red and blue bill plus pink face and legs. Female differs from male in having white inner secondary wing feathers visible both at rest and in flight; see below. Immature much browner on underparts, head feathers tawny. At carrion usually seen in pairs, greatly outnumbered by other vultures. 85 cm (Witkopaasvoël)

3 **LAPPET-FACED VULTURE** *Torgos tracheliotos*

Fairly common resident. A huge, massive-billed vulture. Adult has crimson head and neck, plus streaked underparts with white 'pants' which contrast with dark body and underwings in flight; see below. Immature has dark 'pants' and various amounts of white mottling on the mantle. The long feathers of its ruff can be raised to frame the head, as illustrated. Usually in pairs in bushveld or, in the arid west, thornveld and desert. A powerfully built vulture which dominates all others at food sources. 115 cm (Swartaasvoël)

Hooded Vulture from below

Adult

Immature

White-headed Vulture from below

Male

Female

Lappet-faced Vulture from below

Adult Immature

J

1

J

♀

J

2

3

J

1 **EGYPTIAN VULTURE** *Neophron percnopterus*

Rare visitor. Immature can be confused with immature of Hooded Vulture (previous page), but the head is fully feathered, not covered in woolly down. At all ages has a distinctly diamond-shaped tail in flight; cf. (2). Singly or in pairs, especially in nature reserves or scavenging in rural areas, but very infrequent. 64-71 cm (Egiptiese aasvoël)

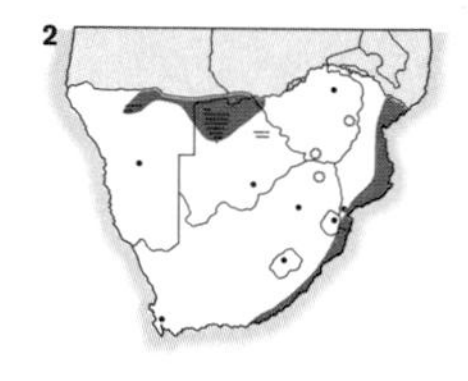

2 **PALM-NUT VULTURE** *Gypohierax angolensis*

Rare visitor and localised resident. Adult and immature differ from (1) in lack of loose feathers on the head, heavier, more aquiline bill and, in flight, squarish (not diamond-shaped) tail. Adult distinguished by entirely white head, neck and body, black wing feathers and tail; cf. African Fish Eagle (p. 168). Occurs singly or in pairs most regularly in Mozambique and further south along the east coast, plus northern Botswana and northern Namibia. A vagrant to other scattered northerly points, particularly immature birds. At the coast frequents stands of oil palms (on which it feeds and in which it breeds) or forages on beaches and the shores of lagoons and pans. Spends long periods each day perched, but, unlike other vultures, flies at any time regardless of thermals. 60 cm (Witaasvoël)

J
1
J
J
2
J

1
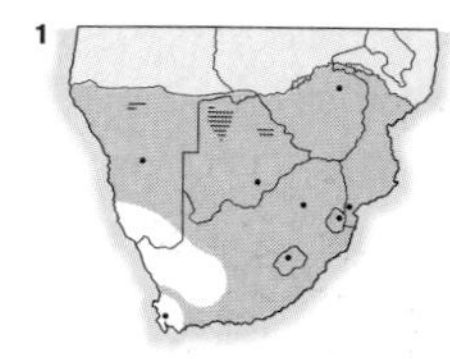

2
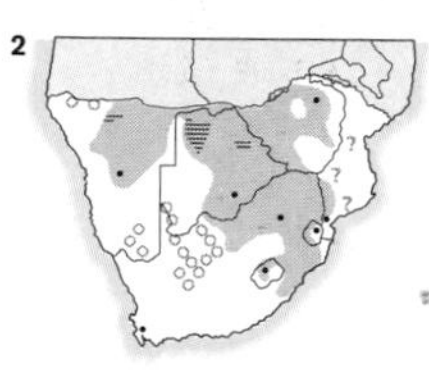

3

4

MILVUS KITES

Large, long-winged raptors with V-shaped tails. Spend much of the day flying in leisurely fashion at low height while scanning the ground, their tails constantly twisting as they manoeuvre. Feed by scavenging and also catch various small animals.

1 YELLOW-BILLED KITE *Milvus migrans parasitus*

Common summer visitor and resident. Distinguished from (2) by yellow bill, brown head and more deeply forked tail. Immature has a black bill (only the cere is yellow), but is distinguished from (2) by brown head and more rufous colouring on underparts. While flying sometimes calls 'kleeeuw', ending with a trill. Occurs anywhere, sometimes in large flocks at a food source, and mixes with the Black Kite. 55 cm (Geelbekwou)

2 BLACK KITE *Milvus migrans migrans*

Fairly common summer visitor. Distinguished from (1) by greyish head at all ages plus black bill (only the cere is yellow) and less deeply forked tail which appears square-cut when fanned. Immature is paler below with brown blotches. More often seen in flocks than (1), especially large numbers gathering at emergences of flying termites; otherwise behaviour as (1). 55 cm (Swartwou)

SNAKE EAGLES

Characterised by *unfeathered legs,* heads with loose feathers which give a round-headed appearance, plus large yellow eyes. Still-hunt by watching the ground from a perch, or hunt while flying.

3 WESTERN BANDED SNAKE EAGLE *Circaetus cinerascens*

Uncommon, localised resident. A small, robust, ash-brown eagle, distinguished from (4) at all ages by the single broad, dark tail-bar (a second bar is mostly obscured by the undertail coverts) and by indistinct barring on belly only. Immature is variable, at first mainly white about the head and underparts. Occurs in riverine forests and floodplains, still-hunting from a leafless branch in a tall tree. 55 cm (Enkelbandslangarend)

4 SOUTHERN BANDED SNAKE EAGLE *Circaetus fasciolatus*

Uncommon, localised resident. Distinguished from (3) at all ages by longer tail with two bars, adult also by well-barred underparts from lower breast to vent. Immature like that of (3) except for tail-bars. Occurs sparsely along the north-east coast, Mozambique and eastern Zimbabwe. Frequents open areas near exotic plantations, riverine and lowland forests. Still-hunts from a tree. 60 cm (Dubbelbandslangarend)

1
2
3
J
4
J

1

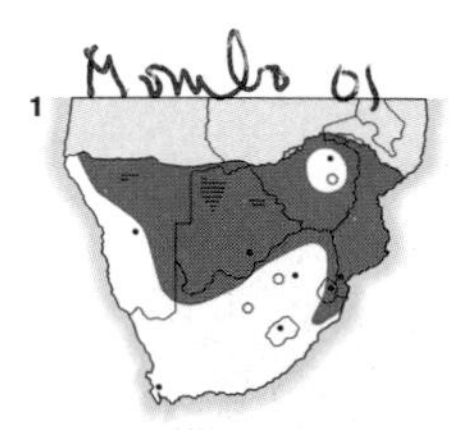

2

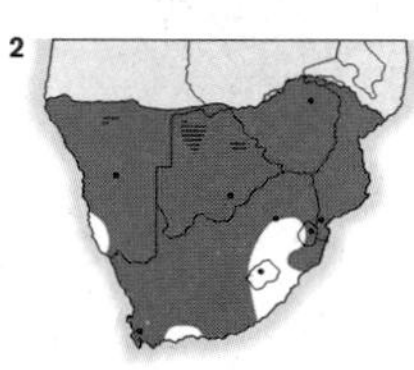

3

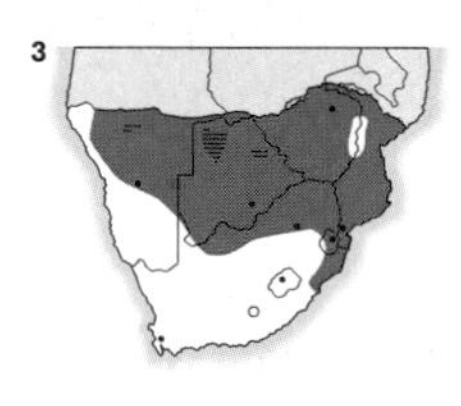

1 BATELEUR *Terathopius ecaudatus*

Fairly common, localised resident. A distinctive, bulky-looking black eagle with red facial skin and legs and tawny wing coverts, female with tawny secondaries as (a). The back is normally chestnut-brown, less often creamy white as (b). In flight appears almost tailless, long wings tapered, male with widest black trailing edge; see below. Immature has longer tail and progresses from uniformly dull brown with slaty face and legs (c) to brown mottling with purple face and legs (d). In flight may call a loud 'schaaaaaaaw'; while perched often calls 'kau-kau-kau-ko-aaagh'. Sometimes makes wing-claps while flying. Normally flies at low altitude over bushveld and woodland, using little wing-flapping but prolonged glides with a sideways rocking action as though balancing. This eagle is regarded as 'vulnerable' in South Africa. 55-70 cm (Berghaan)

2 BLACK-BREASTED SNAKE EAGLE *Circaetus pectoralis*

Fairly common resident. Adult differs from larger Martial Eagle (p. 168) in *bare legs,* unspotted underparts and, in flight, predominantly *white* (not dark) underwings. Immature starts as (a), then progress to stage (b), the head gradually darkening, underparts becoming clear. Usually singly in bushveld or grassland, occasionally perched, more often flying high and hovering; *the only eagle to hover regularly.* Snakes are taken into the air, killed and eaten in flight. Nomadic. 63-8 cm (Swartborsslangarend)

3 BROWN SNAKE EAGLE *Circaetus cinereus*

Common resident. Large brown eagle identified by whitish, unfeathered legs, large yellow eyes and erect stance. In flight dark body and underwing coverts contrast with silvery-white flight feathers; the tail has four clear, dark bands. Immature starts with similar plumage to adult but less dark (a), then progresses to mottled stage (b). At all ages the downy underfeathers are white, therefore even adult appears speckled when moulting. Singly in any woodland or coastal grassland. Still-hunts conspicuously from a bare branch or pylon, killing and eating large snakes on the ground or in a tree. Occasionally hovers. Nomadic. 71-6 cm (Bruinslangarend)

Bateleur from below

Adult male; Adult female

Sub-adult male; Immature female

Black-breasted Snake Eagle from below

Adult

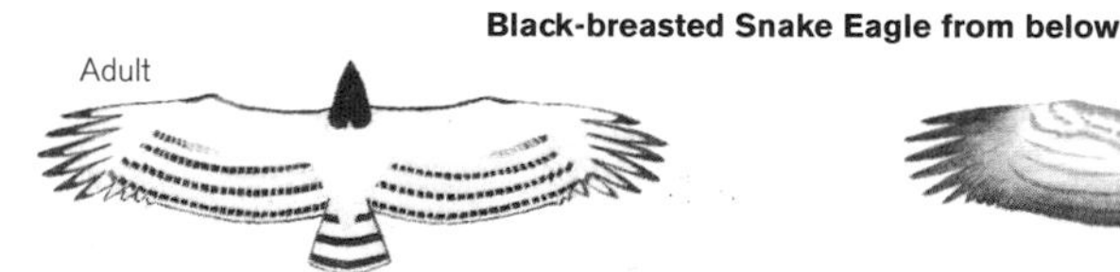

Immature

Brown Snake Eagle from below

Adult

Immature

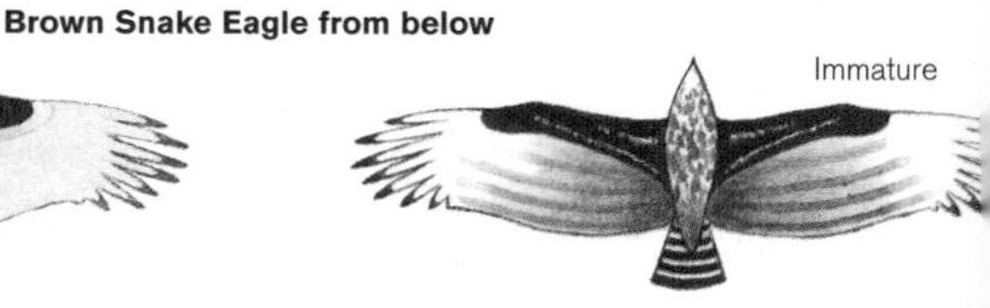

Jd

♀

1

a

b

♂

Jc

Jb

2

Ja

3

Jb

Ja

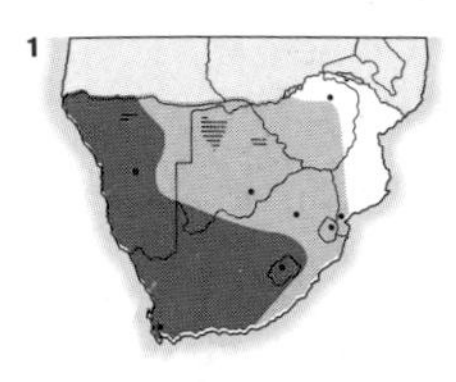
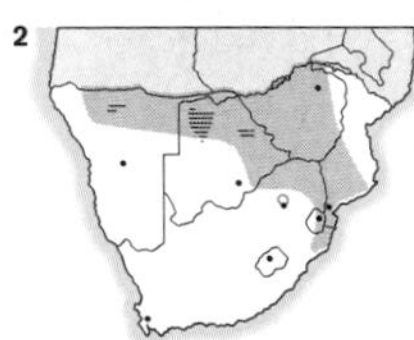
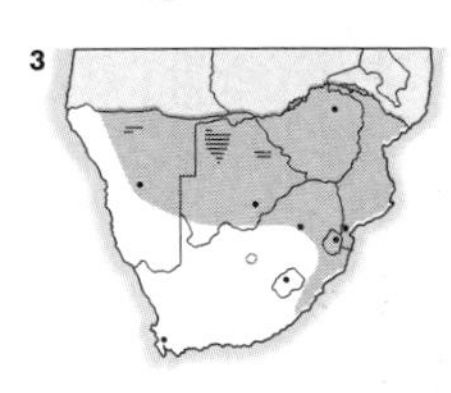

TRUE EAGLES

True eagles are distinguished from all other raptors by their *fully feathered legs.* Prey is killed either by impact or by crushing in powerful talons and the flesh is torn by the well-hooked bill. Most eagles hunt while flying, wheeling effortlessly in rising warm air, and are seldom seen perched during fair weather.

1 BOOTED EAGLE *Hieraaetus pennatus*

Fairly common resident and summer visitor. Occurs in two colour morphs, dark brown (a) and white or buffy (b), the latter most common. At rest buffy wing coverts show as a broad bar on the folded wing; *white shoulder-patch diagnostic.* In flight (see below) a translucent wedge shape is visible on the inner primaries. Upperwing pattern similar to *Milvus* kites (p. 158) but tail not forked. Immature similar to adult. Occurs mainly in the montane regions of western South Africa and Namibia, ranging more widely in summer, together with non-breeding visitors from the north as shown by the distribution map. 48-52 cm (Dwergarend)

2 LESSER SPOTTED EAGLE *Aquila pomarina*

Common summer visitor, November-March. Identified at rest by narrowly feathered 'stovepipe' legs, immature with white spots on the folded wings. In flight appears broad-winged, tail rounded; from above immature shows translucent patches at the base of the primaries, thin white edges to the coverts and a white crescent at the base of the tail; cf. larger Steppe Eagle (overleaf). Usually in well-wooded regions of the Kruger National Park, Moremi Wildlife Reserve and Chobe National Park where it often mixes with Steppe Eagle flocks at termite emergences. 65 cm (Gevlekte arend)

3 WAHLBERG'S EAGLE *Aquila wahlbergi*

Common summer resident, August-March. Occurs in several colour morphs shown as (a), (b) and (c); (a) probably most common. Dark-headed and white-headed individuals also occur; see (d) and (e). In flight shows fairly narrow, parallel wings and *square tail held mostly closed;* see below. Sometimes utters a whistling 'peeeeoo' in flight. A summer-breeding eagle and the most common brown eagle this time of year in bushveld, broad-leaved woodland and wooded valleys. 55-60 cm (Bruinarend)

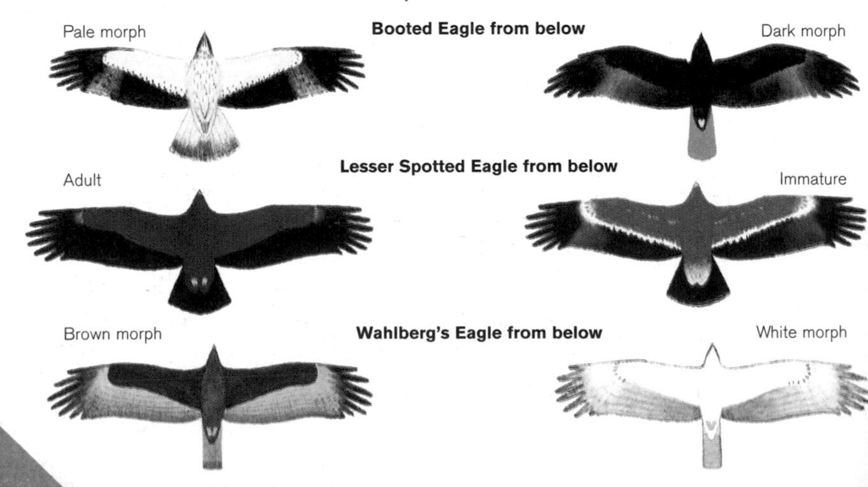

1
a
b
b
J
2
J
3
a
b
c
d
e
d
b

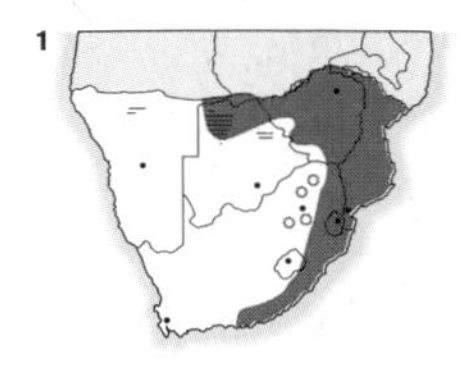

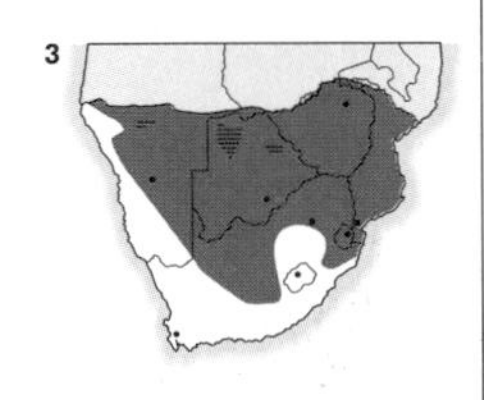

1 LONG-CRESTED EAGLE *Lophaetus occipitalis*

Fairly common resident. Long crest on head and wing pattern distinctive; the legs may be white or black and white. Sometimes calls in flight, a shrill 'weee-er' or 'peerr-wee' repeated. Usually singly in forest fringes, exotic plantations (especially *Eucalyptus*) and wooded valleys; prefers hilly, moist conditions. Soars mostly in the mornings and frequently perches prominently at roadsides. 53-8 cm (Langkuifarend)

2 STEPPE EAGLE *Aquila nipalensis*

Fairly common summer visitor. Adult is darker and plainer than the darkest Tawny Eagle (3); its prominent orange-yellow gape extends back to a point *level with the back of the eye;* slightly shorter in the race *A. n. orientalis* (but still larger than in the Tawny Eagle). A buffy patch is often present on the hindcrown. Immature very like (3) but has the longer gape; in flight shows much white in the wings (see below); cf. (3) and Lesser Spotted Eagle (previous page). Eats termites and is often seen consuming them on the ground, especially in the Kalahari. Also raids breeding colonies of queleas (pp. 402-5), feeding on eggs and nestlings. 75 cm (Steppe-arend)

3 TAWNY EAGLE *Aquila rapax*

Fairly common resident. Adult either tawny with or without dark brown mottling on the wings (a and b), or red-brown with dark mottling (c). Immature may be gingery-brown or pale as (d), then very similar to immature of (2). At all ages the gape does *not* extend beyond the *centre of the eye.* In flight shows no barring on the tail, little white in the wings and none on the upper tail coverts; see flight patterns below. Most frequent in wooded game areas where it perches conspicuously on the top of trees. 65-72 cm (Roofarend)

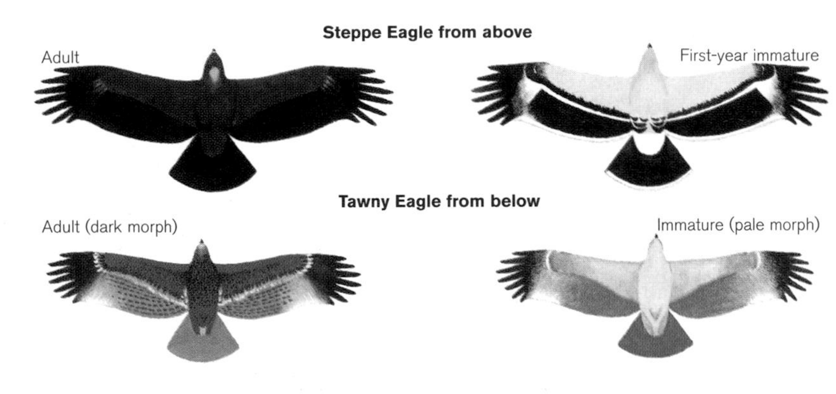

J
1
2
J
2
a
a
b
3
J
d
c

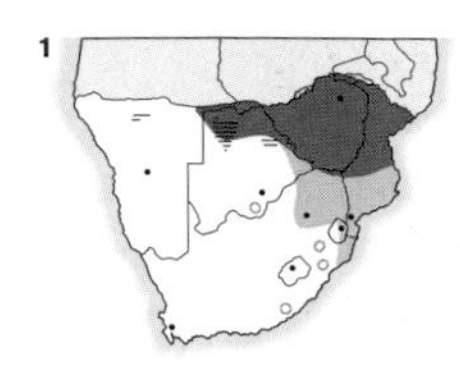

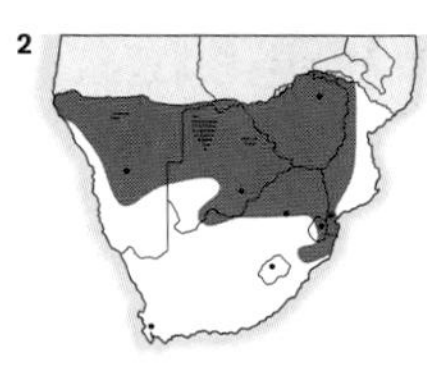

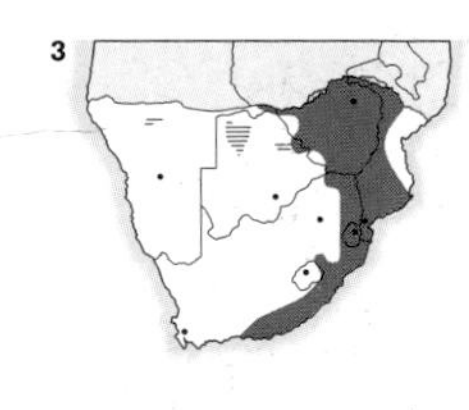

1 AYRES' EAGLE *Hieraaetus ayresii*

Uncommon resident and summer visitor. A small, rapacious eagle with white underparts either lightly spotted (a) or dark and heavily spotted (b). Forehead of adult may be white or dark, then appears as a cap extending to below the eyes. Leading edge of the wing frequently unspotted, then shows as a white shoulder-patch on the folded wing, underwings heavily barred as illustrated; immature much paler. Frequents well-wooded regions, wooded hillsides and *Eucalyptus* plantations, even in rural suburbia, but sparsely. A summer visitor in the south of its range. 46-55 cm (Kleinjagarend)

2 AFRICAN HAWK EAGLE *Hieraaetus spilogaster*

Fairly common resident. Superficially resembles (1) but is a medium-large eagle; female may be more heavily spotted than male. In flight underwing pattern diagnostic with characteristic white 'windows' at the base of the primaries and broad terminal tail-band. Immature is rufous on the head and underparts with varying amounts of dark streaking on the breast as illustrated; cf. immature Black Sparrowhawk (p. 180) which has *bare legs.* The call is a flute-like 'klu-klu-klukluee'. Usually in pairs in wooded savanna and well-wooded hillsides. Pairs soar conspicuously in the mornings, otherwise it perches within the canopy of a well-foliaged tree for much of the day. 60-65 cm (Grootjagarend)

3 CROWNED EAGLE *Stephanoaetus coronatus*

Fairly common resident. Large and powerful, its comparatively short wings adapted to manoeuvring at speed through forest trees. Adult is dark with crested head and heavily barred or blotched underparts; in flight barred underwings and tail plus rufous underwing coverts are diagnostic. Immature is initially white on the head and underparts (a), becoming progressively spotted and blotched (b). Pairs are very vocal within their territory, the male calling loudly during a daily undulating aerial display flight 'kewee-kewee-kewee ...', repeated about 20 times as the bird dives and rises; female's voice lower-pitched: 'koi koi koi ...'. Pairs have territories in evergreen forests, forested kloofs, dense riparian forests with large trees and well-wooded hillsides, often near water. 80-90 cm (Kroonarend)

Ayres' Eagle (immature) from below

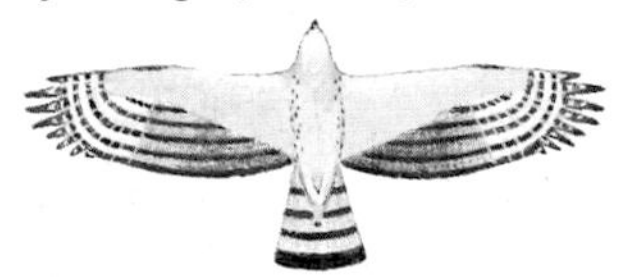

African Hawk Eagle (immature) from below

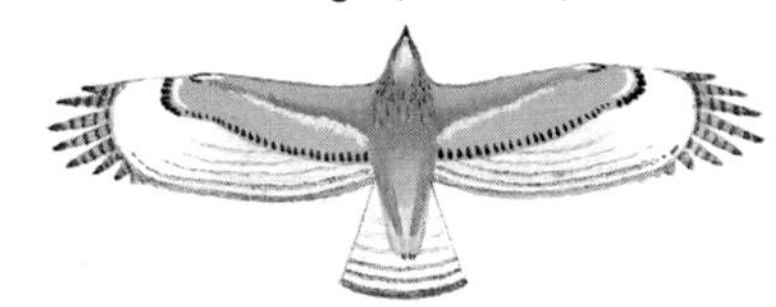

Crowned Eagle (immature) from below

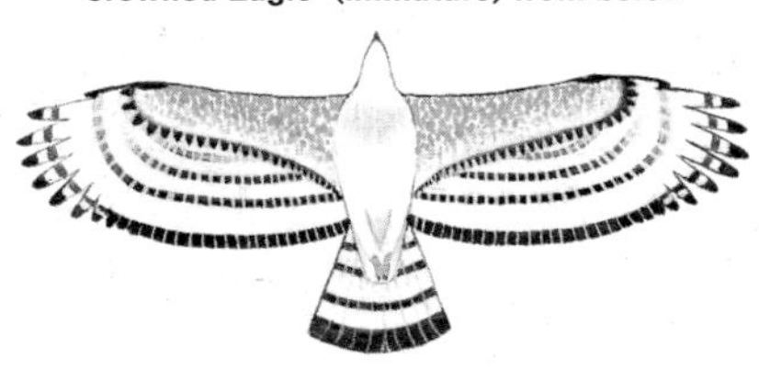

1
a
b
J
2
J
Ja
3
Jb

Vic. Falls + Mombo '01

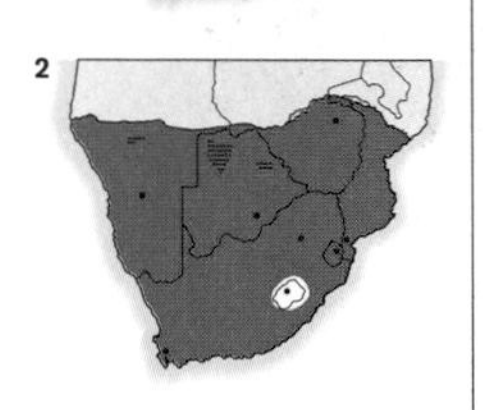

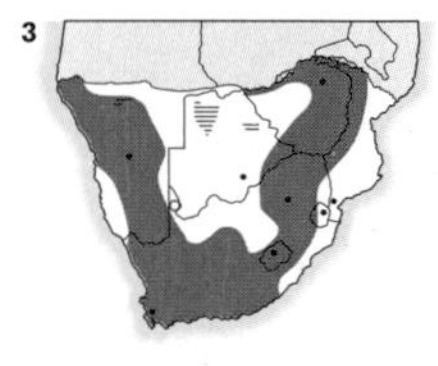

1 AFRICAN FISH EAGLE *Haliaeetus vocifer*

Fairly common resident. Well known and distinctive. Very young, free-flying birds (a) are easily mistaken for other brown eagles, but pale demarcation line of emergent white upper breast is usually detectable beneath the heavy brown markings; after one year the plumage pattern begins to resemble that of the adult although heavy brown streaks still remain on the white (b). The ringing, far-carrying call is 'weee-ah, hyo-hyo-hyo' or 'heee-ah, heeah-heeah', the male's voice more shrill than the female's. Calls while perched or in the air. Usually in pairs at large rivers, lakes, dams, estuaries and seashores in remoter regions; immatures occasionally on small ponds. Conspicuous and noisy, perching on exposed waterside trees or flying over the water. 63-73 cm (Visarend)

Mombo + Vic Falls 6/01

2 MARTIAL EAGLE *Polemaetus bellicosus*

Fairly common resident. Distinctive large, long-legged eagle, most similar to Black-breasted Snake Eagle (p. 160) but differing in spotted underparts and fully feathered legs; in flight by dark (not whitish) underwings. Immature as illustrated, differing from first-plumage Crowned Eagle (previous page) in brownish, not entirely white head. Calls a loud, ringing 'kloo-ee, kloo-ee …'. Singly in bushveld, woodland, thornveld, grassland and hill country. Hunts while flying or from a perch in a leafy tree. 78-83 cm (Breëkoparend)

3 BLACK or VERREAUX'S EAGLE *Aquila verreauxii*

Fairly common resident. Large black eagle with white V mark on the back. In flight has characteristic narrow-based wings with white flashes at the base of the primaries. Immature is mottled brown as illustrated, differing from Tawny Eagle (p. 164) in rufous crown and nape, plus pale legs heavily marked with dark brown. Usually silent. Pairs are found in mountains, rocky hills and gorges, usually perched on rocks or flying at no great height. 84 cm (Witkruisarend)

African Fish Eagle (immature) from below

Martial Eagle (immature) from below

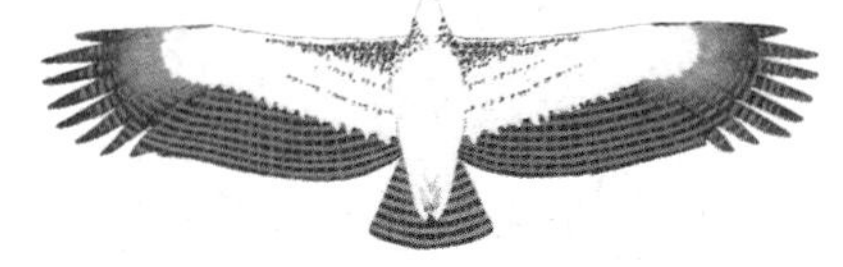

Black Eagle (immature) from below

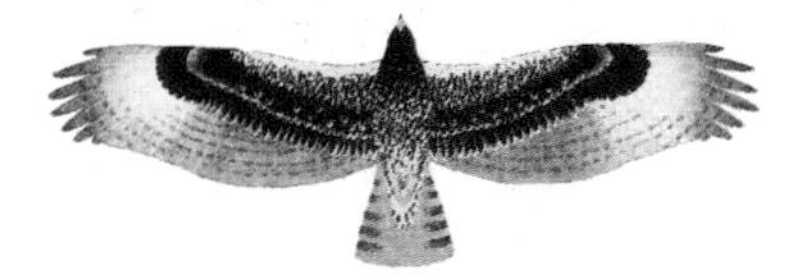

Jb
Ja
1
J
2
3
J

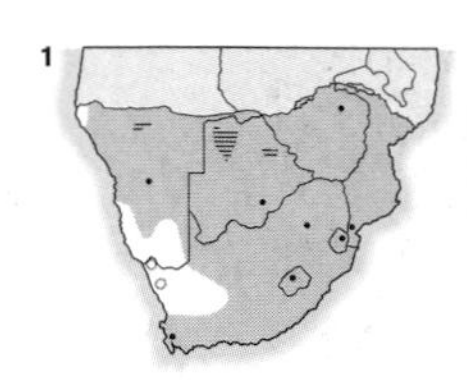

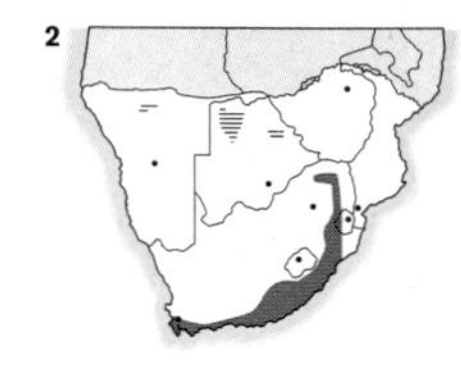

BUZZARDS

Large, soaring hawks about the size of a small eagle, of robust build with fairly large, rounded heads, bills aquiline but small, ceres large, lower legs unfeathered, wings moderately long and rounded, tails rounded when spread.

1 STEPPE BUZZARD *Buteo buteo vulpinus*

Very common summer visitor. Adults variable, most commonly as (a) but dark form (b) and russet form (c) are frequently seen while other variations also occur. Diagnostic feature common to all except the very dark form is a distinct pale *zone across the breast,* which divides the streaked or smudged upper breast from the banded underparts. In flight the spread tail appears pale cinnamon with a dark terminal band. Immature has entirely streaked or blotched underparts as illustrated, the eye paler. Much smaller than Brown Snake Eagle (p. 160) and lacks the large yellow eyes of that species. In flight sometimes calls 'kreeeeee', especially when two or more are flying together. This is the brown buzzard commonly seen on roadside posts in summer, or circling slowly overhead. Usually singly or two to three individuals in grassland and similar open situations, less often in wooded country, but flocks follow forested hills when migrating in October and early March. 45-50 cm (Bruinjakkalsvoël)

2 FOREST BUZZARD *Buteo trizonatus* 

Uncommon endemic resident. Similar to (1) but smaller; at all ages the underparts have drop-shaped brown blotches (not horizontal bands), densest in adults, with clear regions across the lower breast and underbelly. In flight from below wings appear whiter than in (1); tail has only indistinct terminal band. Immature has little spotting on underparts. The call, uttered in flight, is 'keeeo-oo'. Usually singly near montane plantations and forests or adjacent grassy plateaux, perching on the fringe of some open area. When disturbed flies easily through dense plantations. 45 cm (Bosjakkalsvoël)

LONG-LEGGED BUZZARD (Langbeenjakkalsvoël) see p. 454.

J
J
b
1
a
c
2
J

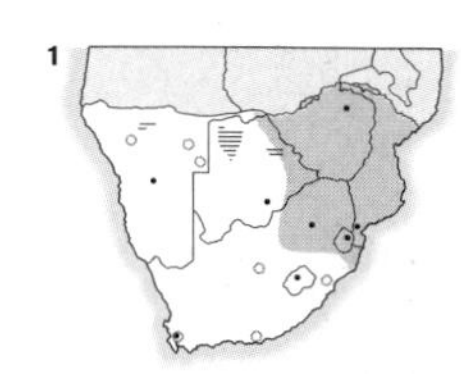

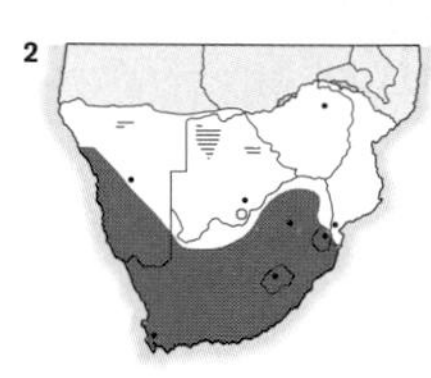

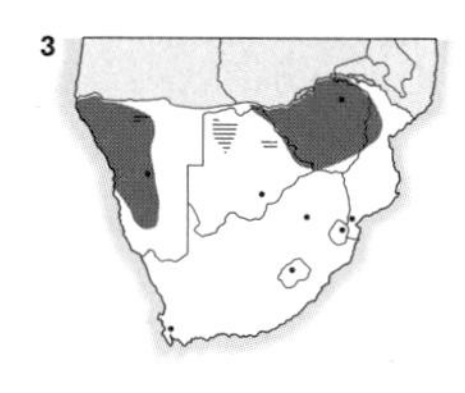

1 HONEY BUZZARD *Pernis apivorus*

Fairly common summer visitor. Slightly larger than Steppe Buzzard (previous page) but could be mistaken for it. Plumage very variable; (a) probably most common, while a dark morph (b) and paler morphs occur (see below). Appears smaller-headed than Steppe Buzzard, with longer tail and with *yellow or orange* (not brown) eyes. In flight the head protrudes well forward of the long wings; underwings have dark carpal patches, tail two dark central bands and one terminal band. Immature lacks distinct tail-bands, has brown eyes. Prefers wooded country and may walk about the ground in search of wasps' and bees' nests. 54-60 cm (Wespedief)

2 JACKAL BUZZARD *Buteo rufofuscus* E

Common endemic resident. Chestnut breast and tail of adult distinctive. Flight pattern shows rounded wings and wide, short tail. Occasionally occurs with breast blotchy-black, even all-white, then distinguished from (3) by dark (not white) underwing coverts. Immature is pale rufous, often much paler than illustrated, and shows no tail-bands. The call is a jackal-like, high-pitched 'kweh' or a mewing 'kip-kweeeu, kweeeu, kweeeu' while flying. Occurs in hilly or montane regions and adjacent grassland. Often perches on roadside posts. 44-53 cm (Rooiborsjakkalsvoël)

3 AUGUR BUZZARD *Buteo augur*

Common resident. Adult distinctive with almost entirely white underparts and reddish tail. Female often has dark throat as illustrated, otherwise size and proportions same as (2). In flight male is told from Black-breasted Snake Eagle (p. 160) by reddish tail and more rounded wings. Immature is similar to immature of (2) but lacks the rufous tail; the underwing coverts are slightly buffy, the secondaries and tail have light barring. Voice similar to that of (2). Prefers well-wooded hill country with rocky outcrops. 44-53 cm (Witborsjakkalsvoël)

Two pale morph Honey Buzzards from below in fast-glide posture

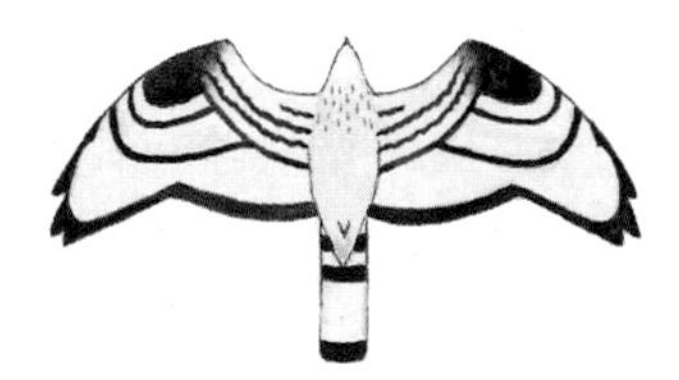

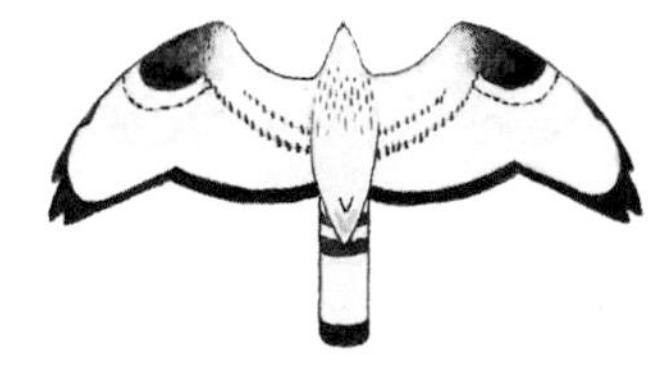

a
1
J
b
a
J
2
♂
♀
3
♂

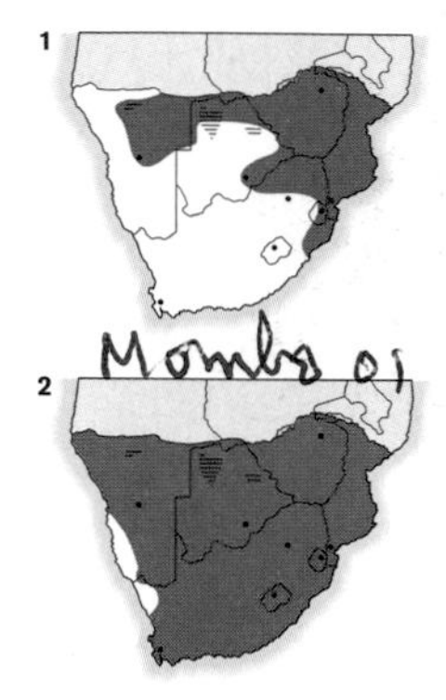

1 LIZARD BUZZARD *Kaupifalco monogrammicus*

Fairly common resident. A small, stocky grey hawk resembling an *Accipiter* (overleaf), but distinguished by diagnostic white throat with vertical black streak and two bold white tail-bands (sometimes only one present). Immature more buffy above and below, throat-streak less clear. The call is a whistling 'klioo-klu-klu-klu', uttered regularly while perched. Occurs in broad-leaved woodland, mixed bushveld and well-treed farmlands. Often perches partially concealed in the canopy of a tree. Nomadic. 35-7 cm (Akkedisvalk)

2 BLACK-SHOULDERED KITE *Elanus caeruleus*

Common resident. A distinctive small raptor with pure white underparts, grey upperparts, black carpal patches and ruby-red eyes. Graceful in flight, whitish with black wingtips; cf. much larger, summer-visiting Pallid Harrier (p. 182). Immature similar but more buffy about the head and underparts as illustrated. Normally silent, but may utter a weak 'weeet-weeet-weeet' when agitated. Singly or in pairs in grassland and lightly wooded country, including rural suburbia. Perches conspicuously on leafless trees, roadside posts or wires, often raising and lowering its tail while watching the ground. *In flight may hover* for periods of five to 20 seconds, and frequently hunts at dusk. Roosts communally in reed-beds or trees. Nomadic. 30 cm (Blouvalk)

GOSHAWKS AND SPARROWHAWKS

True hawks characterised by slender bodies, short, rounded wings, long tails, small sharp bills and long, bare, often slender legs and toes. Secretive, catch their prey (usually small birds) in a low, rapid aerial pursuit from the cover of a leafy tree. Females are larger than males.

3 RUFOUS-BREASTED SPARROWHAWK *Accipiter rufiventris*

Fairly common, localised resident of the southern and eastern regions. All-rufous, plain-bodied sparrowhawk. Could be mistaken for immature Ovambo Sparrowhawk (overleaf), but top of head and upperparts generally much darker. Singly in stands of exotic trees and forest patches in montane grassland. It often hunts over grassland by flying through cover, surprising small birds. 33-40 cm (Rooiborssperwer)

1
2
J
3
♂
♀ J

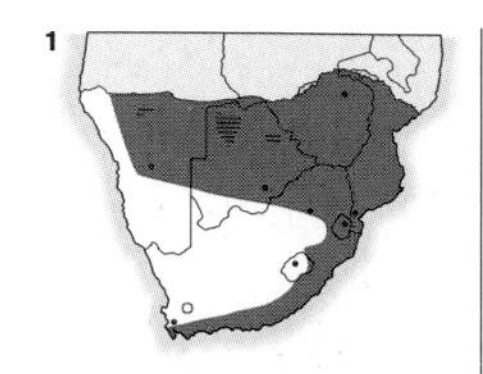

1 **LITTLE SPARROWHAWK** *Accipiter minullus*

Fairly common resident. Adult identified by very small size, yellow eyes and slender yellow legs and, in flight, two conspicuous white spots on the upper tail. Immature recognised by heavy spotting on the underparts. Call is a single-syllabled 'ki' rapidly repeated. Singly in densely wooded situations, forest fringes, riverine forests, woodland, wooded valleys and stands of exotic trees. Secretive. 23-5 cm (Kleinsperwer)

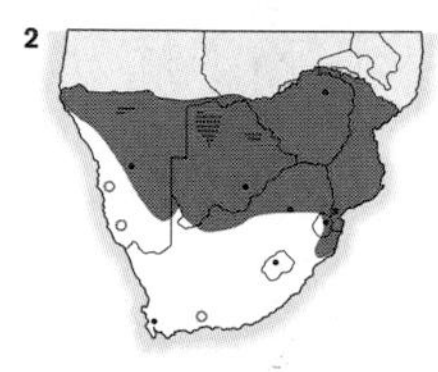

2 **LITTLE BANDED GOSHAWK or SHIKRA** *Accipiter badius*

Fairly common resident. Adult identified by rufous-banded underparts extending to the throat, red eyes and, in flight by plain grey upperparts, *lacking of any white on the rump* and upper tail. May sometimes show small white spots on the mantle. Immature differs from immature of (1) in eyes and legs being more orange-yellow, and broad reddish brown streaks and banding on the underparts; from immature of (3) in dark cap, lack of white rump, plus eye and leg colour. Call is a metallic, two-syllabled 'kli-vit' repeated, also a plaintive 'tee-uuu'. Singly in a wide range of woodland types, even in semi-arid regions. Less secretive than other small *Accipiter* hawks, frequently perching in the open, even on posts. It feeds mainly on reptiles. 30-34 cm (Gebande sperwer)

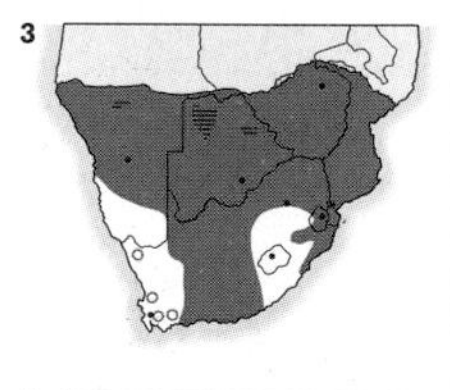

3 **GABAR GOSHAWK** *Micronisus gabar*

Fairly common resident. Normal adult (a) identified by grey throat and breast plus deep red eyes, red cere and legs and, in flight, by *broad, white rump-patch*. Less common melanistic form (b) has same colours of soft parts but lacks the white rump. Immature as illustrated, boldly blotched rufous all over head, neck and breast, eyes yellow, cere and legs coral. In flight shows white rump; cf. immature of (2). Call is a high-pitched, rapid piping 'pi-pi-pi-pi-pi ...'. Singly in open woodland, tree savanna and *Acacia*-dominated riparian bush. Hunts in low flight in more open country, otherwise from a perch within cover. 30-34 cm (Witkruissperwer)

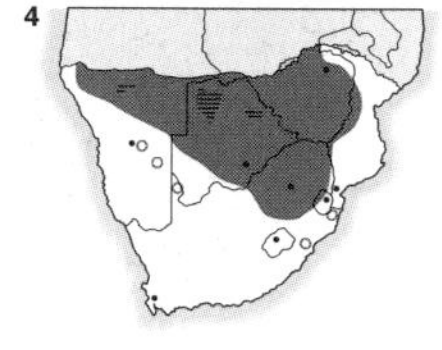

4 **OVAMBO SPARROWHAWK** *Accipiter ovampensis*

Fairly common resident. Adult identified by grey barring on underparts extending to throat, yellow, orange or red cere and yellow or orange-red legs. In flight shows pale central tail-feather shafts; small white rump-patch variable, often absent. Immature either pale (a) or rufous (b), the rufous form more common in Zimbabwe; lightly marked on underparts, cere and legs dull yellow or orange. A very rare melanistic form occurs. Call is a slowly repeated 'kiep, kiep, keip ...' rising in scale. Sparsely distributed in tall woodland or, on the highveld, in isolated stands of *Eucalyptus* or poplars (*Populus* spp.) where it is the most common small *Accipiter*. 33-40 cm (Ovambosperwer)

J
1
J
2
3
J
b
a
Ja
4

1
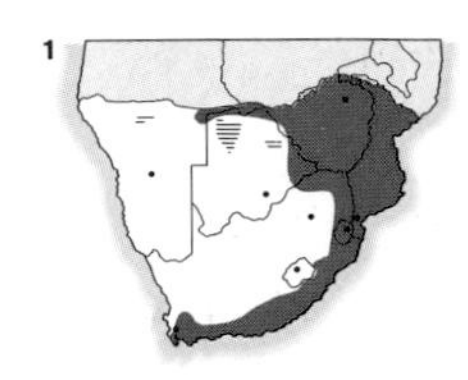

1 **AFRICAN GOSHAWK** *Accipiter tachiro*

Fairly common resident. A medium-sized goshawk (female much larger than male), upperparts slate-grey in male, dark brown in female, the underparts finely barred rufous; eyes and legs yellow, cere grey. Immature browner above, the underparts well spotted with black drop-shaped spots; cf. much smaller immature Little Sparrowhawk (previous page). Territorial male displays prominently in the mornings by flying high with bouts of fast wing beats followed by glides while calling 'krit' at two- or three-second intervals; may also utter the same call from cover while perched. Unobtrusive in montane, lowland and riparian forests, wooded valleys, exotic plantations and suburban fringes. Partially crepuscular. 36-40 cm (Afrikaanse sperwer)

2
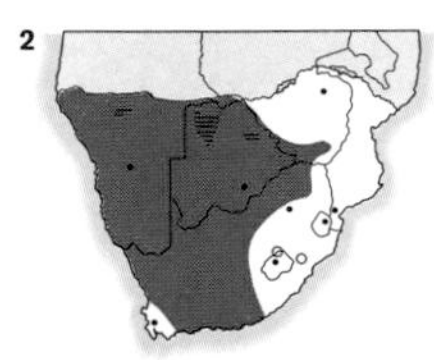

2 **PALE CHANTING GOSHAWK** *Melierax canorus*

Common, near endemic resident. Large, pale grey goshawk with coral-pink cere and legs. Difficult to tell from (3) when perched, except for slightly paler upperparts, but in flight shows much white on the upperwings plus a *white rump*. Immature of this and (3) very similar. In the breeding season adults call loudly and melodiously while perched, especially at dawn 'kleeeeuw, kleeeeuw, kleeeeuw, klu-klu-klu-klu'. Perches conspicuously with upright stance on the top of a thornbush or on a roadside post. Also forages on the ground in search of small prey, peering under rocks and logs. Seldom flies high; usually moves with low swoops from perch to perch. Occurs in arid thornveld, Karoo and Kalahari sandveld. South of the Limpopo River its range is mostly west of (3). 53-63 cm (Bleeksingvalk)

3
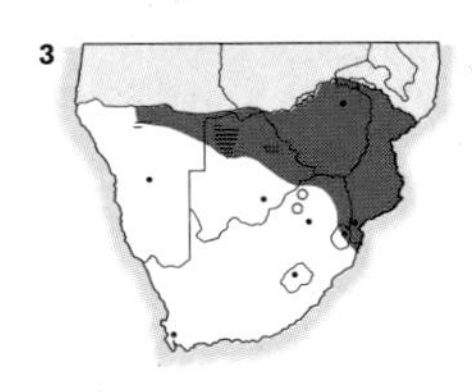

3 **DARK CHANTING GOSHAWK** *Melierax metabates*

Fairly common resident. Very similar to (2) but slightly darker grey. In flight the upperwings are more uniformly grey, the rump finely barred (not pure white); see illustration. Immature browner, the soft parts initially yellow, becoming orange or coral red while still in immature plumage. In the breeding season adults call from a perch for long periods 'phaleeoo-phwe-phwe-phwe-phwe …', the last sound often repeated up to 30 times. Frequents broad-leaved woodland and mixed bushveld; usually perches within the canopy on the top of a tree. South of the Limpopo River its range is mostly east of (2). 50-56 cm (Donkersingvalk)

1
J
2
3
J

1
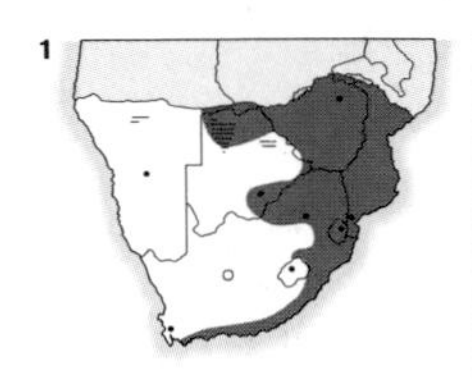

2
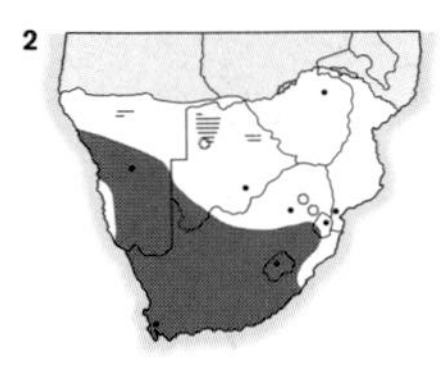

3

1 BLACK SPARROWHAWK *Accipiter melanoleucus*

Fairly common resident. Large black and white hawk, normally with white or partially white underparts (a), thighs and vent either speckled black and white or entirely black, eyes orange or red, cere and legs dull yellow. Melanistic form (b) has only throat white plus some white feathers on the flanks. Immature buffy below streaked with dark brown; may be more streaked than illustration; cf. immature African Hawk Eagle (p. 166) which is larger and has fully feathered legs. Usually silent but may call 'kew-kew-kew-kew-kew' near its nest. Singly or in pairs in well-developed riverine forests, tall woodland or, more commonly, *Eucalyptus* plantations. Though retiring and difficult to see, frequently breeds near human habitations. 46-58 cm (Swartsperwer)

HARRIERS

Long-winged, long-tailed, long-legged hawks, which inhabit grassland or marshes. Usually fly low with leisurely, buoyant flight, head bent downwards and legs dangling slightly, bouts of flapping alternating with glides. Settle on the ground or perch on posts, less often in trees. Silent birds.

2 BLACK HARRIER *Circus maurus*

Fairly common endemic resident. Adult appears entirely black when settled, but in flight shows striking white flight feathers, white rump and banded tail. Sexes are alike. Immature has pale buff underparts and heavily spotted upper breast; in flight shows white wing flashes and white rump. Singly or in pairs over fynbos, Karoo, grassland and croplands, occasionally hovering briefly before dropping to the ground. 48-53 cm (Witkruisvleivalk)

3 EUROPEAN MARSH HARRIER *Circus aeruginosus*

Uncommon summer visitor. At rest male told from African Marsh Harrier (overleaf) by paler head; in flight by much paler underwings plus grey upperwings and tail. Female much darker, almost black, with pale crown and leading edges to wings. Frequents marshlands and moist fields. 48-56 cm (Europese vleivalk)

J
a
1
J
b
2
J
J
♂
♀
3

1
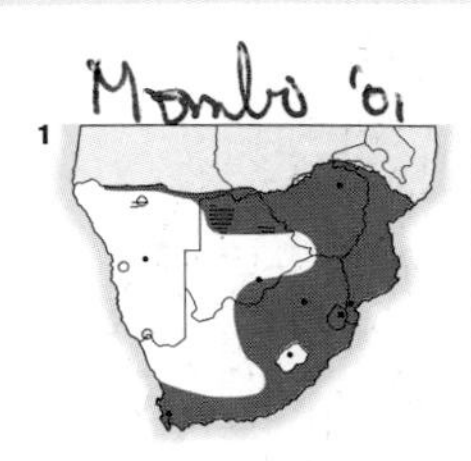

2
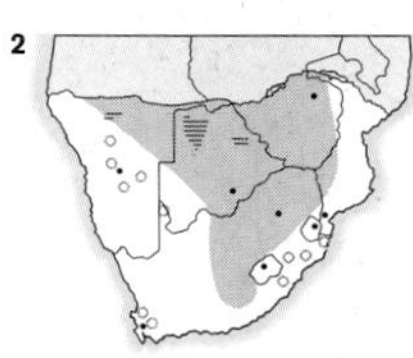

3
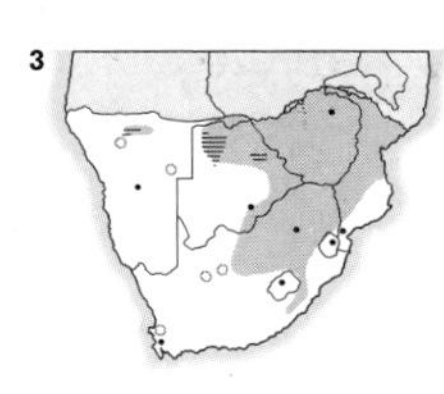

1 AFRICAN MARSH HARRIER *Circus ranivorus*

Common resident. Adult differs from the uncommon European Marsh Harrier (previous page) in darker, more richly coloured underparts, although old birds may become whiter about the head; also more richly coloured on underparts than female of (2) or (3), tail not obviously barred above. Immature has diagnostic pale breast-band. Usually singly, flying over marshland and reedbeds, occasionally over cultivated fields. Rests on the ground, sometimes on a fence post. 44-9 cm (Afrikaanse vleivalk)

2 PALLID HARRIER *Circus macrourus*

Uncommon summer visitor. Male differs from male of (3) in appearing *much whiter* in the field, wingtips with only narrow black sections, otherwise plain pale grey above, totally white below; cf. Black-shouldered Kite (p. 174). Female indistinguishable from female of (3) unless white collar is visible behind the dark ear coverts; *white rump* and clearly banded tail separate it from (1). Singly, flying low over lowland and montane grassland, often near the edge of woodland. Nomadic. 44-8 cm (Witborsvleivalk)

3 MONTAGU'S HARRIER *Circus pygargus*

Uncommon summer visitor. Male recognised by darker grey colouring than male of (2), this extending over the head, throat and breast; rest of underparts have brown streaks; in flight by *entirely* black wingtips, the upperwings with additional black bars along the centres, underwings with narrow black and rufous barring. Altogether less white than (2). Female hardly distinguishable from female of (2) except for the lack of any white markings behind the ear coverts; white rump and well-barred tail preclude confusion with (1). Singly, flying low over grassland or savanna, frequently in same areas as (2). Nomadic. 40-47 cm (Blouvleivalk)

1
J
J
J
♂
♂
2
♀
♀
♂
♂
♀
3

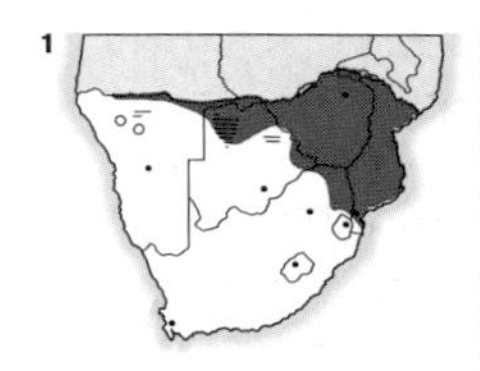

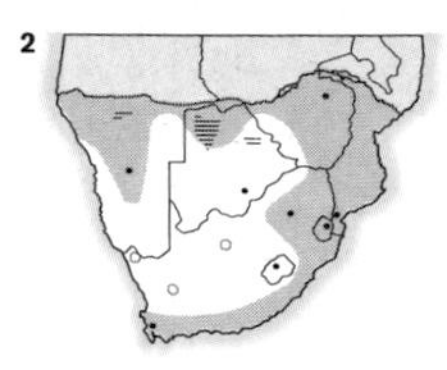

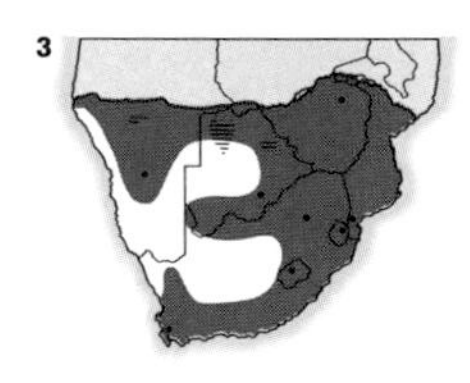

1 BAT HAWK *Macheiramphus alcinus*

Uncommon to sparse resident. A dark brown hawk with pale yellow eyes and white legs and feet. At close range dark centre line on a pale throat, two white spots on the back of the head and white eyelids diagnostic. In flight appears sharp-winged, the flight rapid. Immature has white underparts with dark streaking on the breast, a dark patch on the lower breast plus a variable amount of white spotting on the underwings. When displaying, adult may call a high-pitched 'kik-kik-kik-kik-keee'. By day roosts well concealed in a leafy tree, emerging to hunt bats and small birds only at dusk and into the night or, in dull weather, also in the early morning. Frequents riparian forests, evergreen forests and other heavily wooded regions, including the edges of exotic plantations. 45 cm (Vlermuisvalk)

2 OSPREY *Pandion haliaetus*

Family PANDIONIDAE. Uncommon summer visitor. Slightly crested head, masked appearance and white underparts identify this large hawk at rest, the breast-band often vestigial, strongest in immatures. In flight appears large-winged, small-headed; underwing has bold, dark carpal patch and dark central bar, tail is well banded. Normally silent. Spends much of the day perched over or near water on a post, branch or rock. Hunts over water, flying slowly with shallow, loose wing beats, occasionally hovering briefly; plunge-dives when catching fish. Singly at coastal bays, estuaries and lagoons or large inland waters. 55-63 cm (Visvalk)

3 GYMNOGENE or AFRICAN HARRIER-HAWK *Polyboroides typus*

Common resident. A large grey hawk with black flight feathers and black tail with a *bold white central band,* bare yellow face (flushes red when excited) and yellow legs. In flight appears broad-winged, white tail-band diagnostic; sometimes has dark carpal patches on the upperwings. Immature initially dark brown, later light brown and more mottled; see illustrations. In flight may utter a high-pitched whistle 'su-eeee-oo', especially near its nest, otherwise silent. Clambers about trees and rocks, inserting its long legs into cavities in search of bats, lizards and other small creatures, and raids weaver, swift and woodpecker nests to eat the nestlings. Occurs in a wide range of habitats from montane forests and plantations to woodland, bushveld or thornveld at lower levels, especially riparian forests and wooded valleys. 60-66 cm (Kaalwangvalk)

185
J
J
1
2
3
J
J
J

1
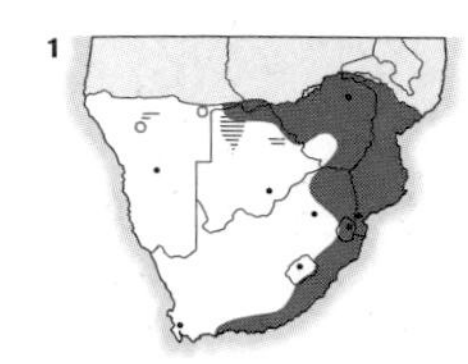

1 CUCKOO HAWK *Aviceda cuculoides*

Uncommon resident. Recognised by its grey, crested head, the grey extending to the neck and upper breast, plus boldly rufous-barred underparts. In flight appears harrier-like with long wings and tail, the flight action is buoyant and leisurely, wing beats slow with spells of gliding. Immature also has crested head, its white underparts with heart-shaped spots. Calls 'ticki-to-you' repeated slowly. Spends much time perched on a conspicuous vantage point but also makes occasional soaring flights. Usually singly near forest fringes, riparian forests, mixed woodland and plantations. 40 cm (Koekoekvalk)

FALCONS

Small raptors characterised by pointed wings and, usually, prominent 'sideburns'. Females are larger than males. Aerial hunters, typically seizing smaller birds in a rapid dive from above. Characteristic calls are high-pitched 'kek-kek-kek-kek' sounds, uttered when agitated. Kestrels are small falcons which eat insects caught in the air with their feet or small mammals and reptiles caught on the ground. Their flight is more leisurely than that of true falcons.

2
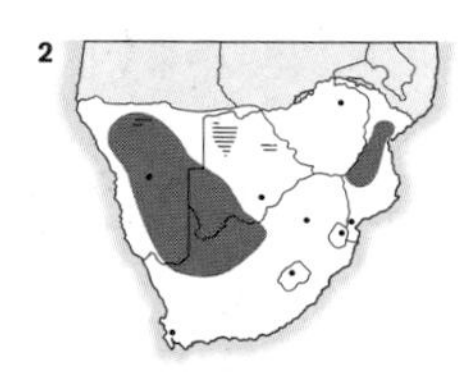

2 PYGMY FALCON *Polihierax semitorquatus*

Common resident. Identified by very small size and entirely white underparts, the female with a chestnut-brown back; in flight by speckled wings and white rump. A species of the dry west, less frequently in Mozambique. Pairs usually seen perched on thorn trees or baobabs, often close to the communal nests of the Sociable Weaver (p. 406) (or Red-billed Buffalo Weaver (p. 404) in Mozambique) with which it lives in close association. 19,5 cm (Dwergvalk)

3

3 TAITA FALCON *Falco fasciinucha*

Very rare, localised resident. A stocky, short-tailed falcon identified by unmarked rufous underparts plus white chin and throat; in flight by these features and rufous underwing coverts. Haunts rocky gorges and cliffs, especially along the Zambezi River. Flies strongly and at speed. May be seen trying to catch swifts or bats in the evening. 28 cm (Taitavalk)

4

4 SOOTY FALCON *Falco concolor*

Rare summer visitor. Adult all-grey with blackish face and pale yellow cere and legs, differing from Grey Kestrel (p. 190) in darker colour and long, pointed wings which extend beyond the tail when perched. Immature also *greyer* than similar small falcons, with grey spots on creamy underparts, *white hind-collar* and no rufous colouring. Occurs in eastern coastal forests, bush and stands of large, broad-leaved trees, being active mostly at dusk, otherwise perches most of day. 31 cm (Roetvalk)

5
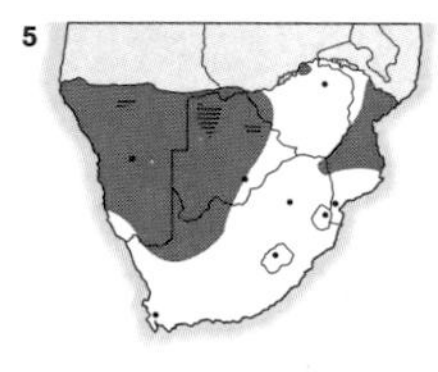

5 RED-NECKED FALCON *Falco chicquera*

Uncommon resident. Identified by rusty crown and nape plus well-barred appearance. Immature has dark crown and lightly barred underparts. Generally seen in palm savanna in the north and east and also with camelthorn trees in the west. Hunts other birds in short sallies from a tree. Sometimes hunts in collaboration with the Gabar Goshawk (p. 176) in the Kalahari. 30-36 cm (Rooinekvalk)

J
1
♂
2
♀
3
J
4
J
5

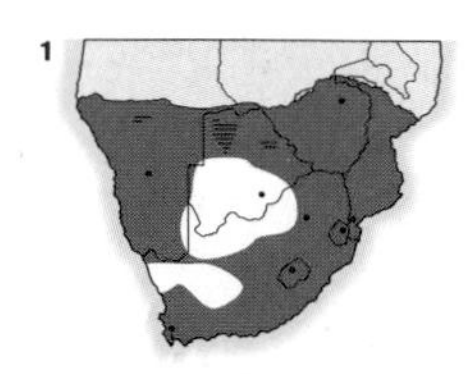

1 PEREGRINE FALCON *Falco peregrinus*

Uncommon resident and summer visitor. Resident birds (a) have closely barred underparts, visiting birds are whiter, lightly spotted (b); immatures lightly streaked. In flight appears sharper-winged than (2), though less so than (3). Usually near cliffs when breeding, otherwise anywhere, frequently in towns. Flies with rapid, shallow wing beats followed by a brief glide, but spends much of the day perched. Sparsely distributed. 34-8 cm (Swerfvalk)

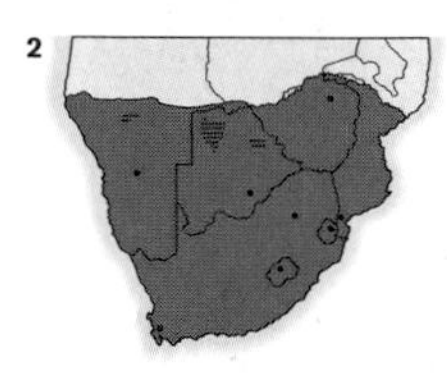

2 LANNER FALCON *Falco biarmicus*

Fairly common resident. The largest falcon in the region, identified at all ages by whitish or pale buff underparts and *russet crown.* In flight appears broader-winged than (1); the *tail is spread* much of the time. Immature has heavily streaked underparts; the russet crown is paler than in adult. Occurs in almost any habitat, most often near cliffs or in lightly wooded country, but also frequents tall buildings in some towns and stands of *Eucalyptus* trees. More frequently seen in flight than (1), progressing with bouts of fast wing-flapping followed by circling glides. 40-45 cm (Edelvalk)

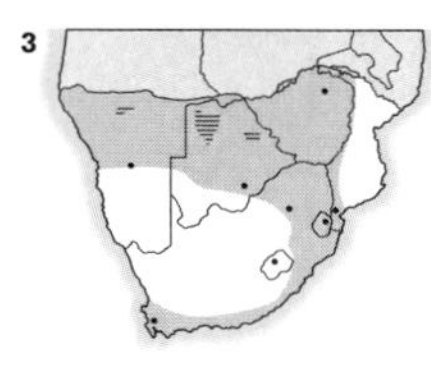

3 HOBBY FALCON *Falco subbuteo*

Uncommon summer visitor. A small falcon identified by heavily streaked body, adult with *rufous thighs and undertail coverts;* in flight by long pointed wings heavily marked on the undersides; see below. Singly or in small flocks in light woodland and town fringes. Hunts mostly at dusk, flying rapidly and with agility in pursuit of swallows and bats, or more leisurely with much gliding when catching flying termites, which are seized with the feet. 30-35 cm (Europese boomvalk)

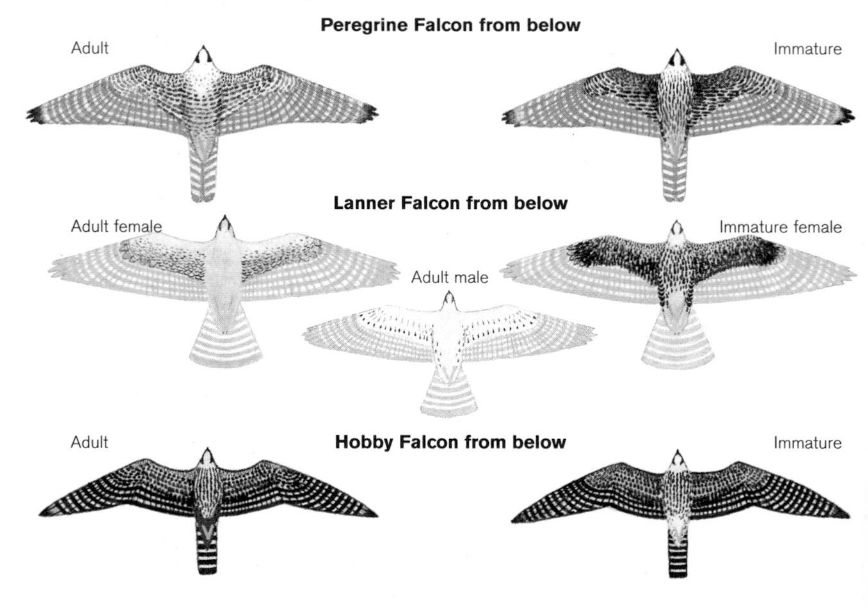

1
a
b
Ja
J
2
♂
♀
J
3

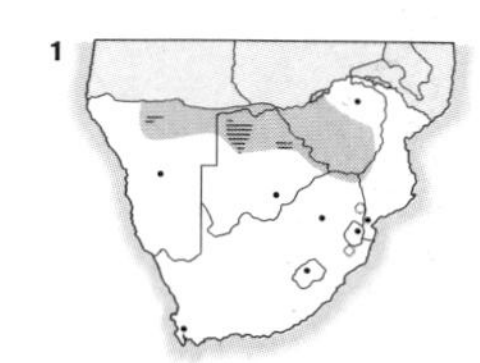

1 AFRICAN HOBBY FALCON *Falco cuvierii*

Rare summer visitor. The most rufous falcon in the region, differing from any rufous kestrel (overleaf) in its dark upperparts and behaviour. Likely to be seen singly in association with scattered palm trees on Kalahari sand and in broad-leaved woodland elsewhere, but sparsely distributed and irregular over much of its range. Flight shape and behaviour similar to visiting Hobby Falcon (previous page). 28-30 cm (Afrikaanse boomvalk)

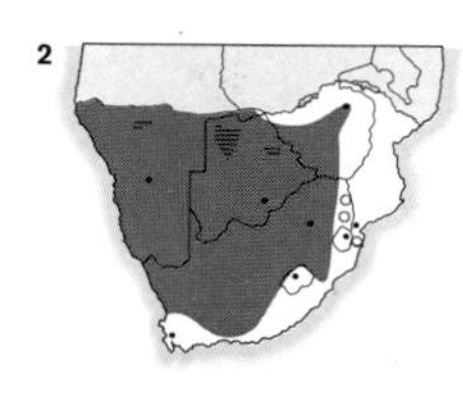

2 GREATER KESTREL *Falco rupicoloides*

Common resident. At rest told from Rock or Lesser Kestrel (overleaf) by entirely rufous plumage with blackish streaks, spots and bars all over, plus *whitish eyes,* and in flight by white underwings. Immature is closely similar but has dark eyes. Singly or in pairs in grassland or lightly wooded thornveld, especially in arid regions. Usually perches on top of a thorn tree or roadside post, sometimes hovers. 36 cm (Grootrooivalk)

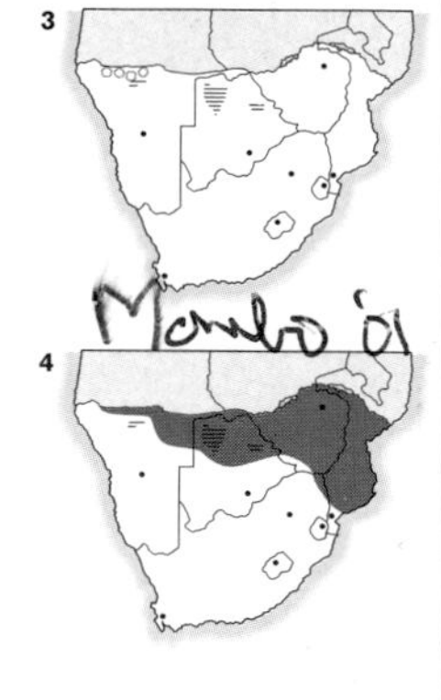

3 GREY KESTREL *Falco ardosiaceus*

Rare, localised resident. An all-grey kestrel with yellow soft parts, differing from Sooty Falcon (p. 186) mainly in stockier build and shorter wings which *do not reach the end of the tail when perched.* The immature's plumage has a brown wash but otherwise resembles the adult. Resident in arid north-western palm savanna and broad-leaved woodland, usually perched on tree or post from where it makes short, rapid, low flights to another perch or across open, grassy areas. Flight always fast and direct, *not* typical of a kestrel. Occurs sparsely. 30-33 cm (Donkergrysvalk)

4 DICKINSON'S KESTREL *Falco dickinsoni*

Uncommon, localised resident. Distinctive grey kestrel with almost white head and neck, very pale rump and yellow soft parts. Immature is slightly browner on its underparts. Occurs singly or in pairs in broad-leaved woodland, mixed bushveld and thornveld, especially in association with baobabs and palms in low-lying regions. Still-hunts from a tree perch, swooping to the ground to catch its prey. Capable of rapid flight but usually flies leisurely. 28-30 cm (Dickinsonse valk)

1
J
2
3
4

1
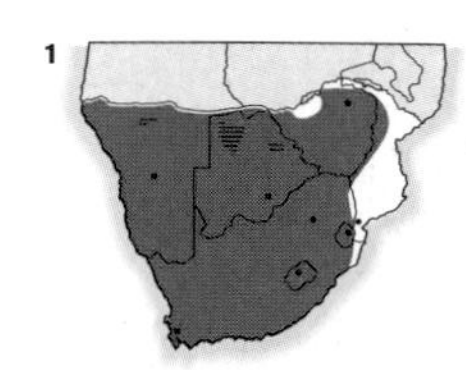

2
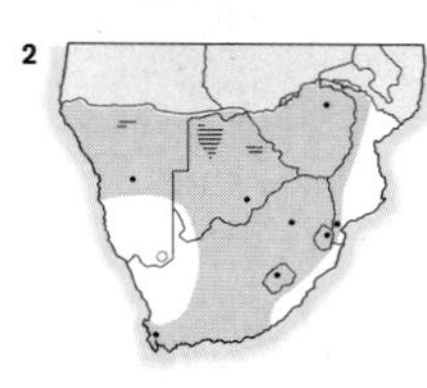

3

4
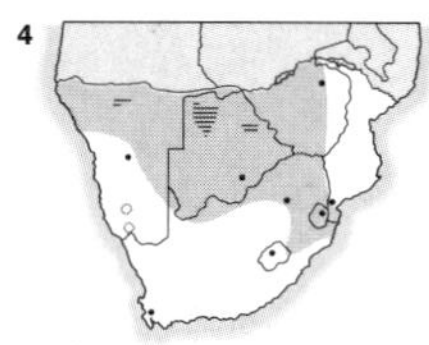

1 ROCK KESTREL or COMMON KESTREL *Falco tinnunculus*

Common resident. Female may or may not have grey head; sometimes like immature with head same colour as rest of plumage but heavily streaked dark brown (see illustration). Differs from (2) mainly in lack of contrast between upper- and underparts, plus behaviour. Singly or in pairs in hilly country and grassland. Perches on roadside posts or flies 5-20 m above ground, frequently turning into wind and *hovering;* cf. Black-shouldered Kite (p. 174), the only other small raptor that regularly hovers. Roosts on cliffs or in trees. 30-33 cm (Kransrooivalk)

2 LESSER KESTREL *Falco naumanni*

Uncommon to locally common summer visitor. Both sexes differ from (1) in paler underparts (male with more grey in the wings) and behaviour. Occurs in flocks, often hundreds in grassland and Karoo, perching on roadside posts, pylons, wires or bushes, or wheeling in leisurely flight. Flocks roost in tall trees (usually *Eucalyptus*), often in country towns. Its numbers have declined dramatically in recent years. A threatened species. 28-30 cm (Kleinrooivalk)

3 EASTERN RED-FOOTED or AMUR KESTREL *Falco amurensis*

Common summer visitor. A small kestrel, both sexes distinctive. Immature greyer, less rufous than immature of (4). Occurs in flocks, often large, and frequently mixing with (2) or (4), in grassland and farmlands. Usually perches on power lines, roadside posts or fences, frequently taking flight for brief sorties before resettling. Roosts in tall trees and is most commonly seen in the eastern regions. 28-30 cm (Oostelike rooipootvalk)

4 WESTERN RED-FOOTED KESTREL *Falco vespertinus*

Uncommon summer visitor. Adults distinctive. Immature more rufous than immature of (3). Occurs in flocks and often mixes with (3). Habitat and behaviour identical to (3) but distribution generally more westerly. 28-30 cm (Westelike rooipootvalk)

193
♂
J
♀
♀
♂
1
♂
♀
♀
♂
2
♂
♀
♂
J
3
♂
J
♀
♂
4

SANDGROUSE

Family PTEROCLIDIDAE. Pigeon-like birds with cryptic colouring, males more boldly patterned than females. Wings pointed, bills short, legs short with the front of the tarsus feathered to the toes. Their walk is shuffling but their flight swift and powerful, the birds often covering considerable distances daily to reach water where, at certain favoured pools, they gather in great flocks morning or evening. All inhabit arid western regions, the Double-banded Sandgrouse ranging to the east.

1
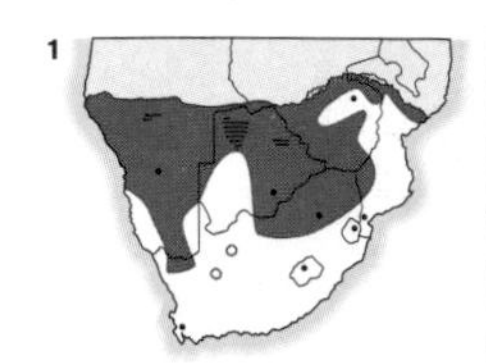

1 DOUBLE-BANDED SANDGROUSE *Pterocles bicinctus* NE

Common, near endemic resident. Male distinguished by black and white bars on forehead, both sexes by fine black barring on belly. Calls 'chuck-chuck'; flocks come to drink after sunset calling 'Don't *weep* so Charlie'. Pairs or flocks are widespread in bushveld and broad-leaved woodland, especially favouring mopane woodland. 25 cm (Dubbelbandsandpatrys)

2
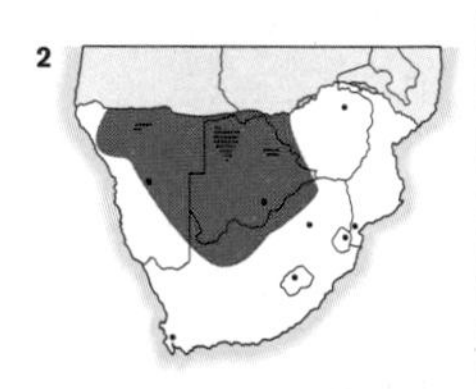

2 BURCHELL'S SANDGROUSE *Pterocles burchelli*

Common, near endemic resident. Both sexes told from other sandgrouse by ochre colouring and all-over, heavy white spotting, male with grey about face, ear coverts and throat, female with yellowish face and ochre barring on belly. If alarmed on the ground, utters a 'gug-gug-gug' sound but in flight calls 'chock-lit, chock-lit, chock-lit'. Normally in pairs but flocks at waterholes, in Kalahari sandveld. 25 cm (Gevlekte sandpatrys)

3
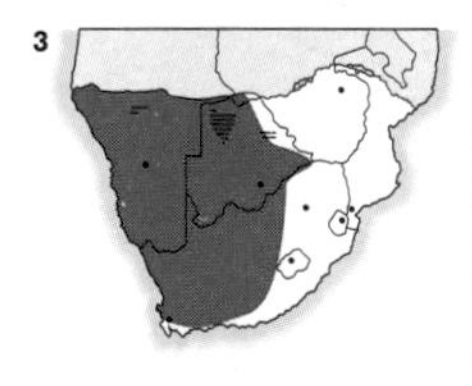

3 NAMAQUA SANDGROUSE *Pterocles namaqua*

Common, endemic resident. Best told from other sandgrouse by its long, pointed tail. Flight call 'kelkiewyn'. Pairs or flocks in sandy or stony deserts, Kalahari, Karoo, thornveld and grassland. Most abundant in the Karoo and Namibia. Frequently mixes with (2) at waterholes, drinking mainly in the mornings. 28 cm (Kelkiewyn)

4
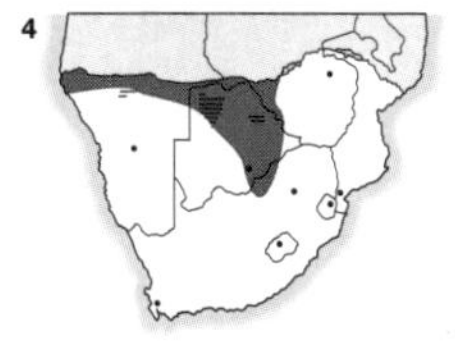

4 YELLOW-THROATED SANDGROUSE *Pterocles gutturalis*

Locally common resident and visitor. Larger than other sandgrouse; male has bold black gorget; both sexes have clear, pale yellow throats and ear coverts, blackish bellies and underwings. In flight calls a harsh 'tweet' or 'tweet-weet'; on arriving at a waterhole emits a hoarse 'golli, golli'. Mainly concentrated in northern Botswana but extending eastwards into Zimbabwe, south-east to as far as Rustenburg and westwards into northern Namibia. 30 cm (Geelkeel-sandpatrys)

1
2
3
4

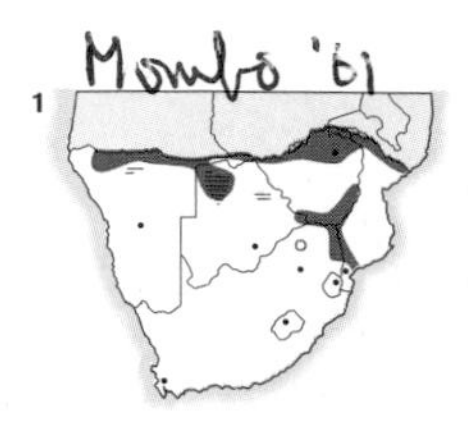

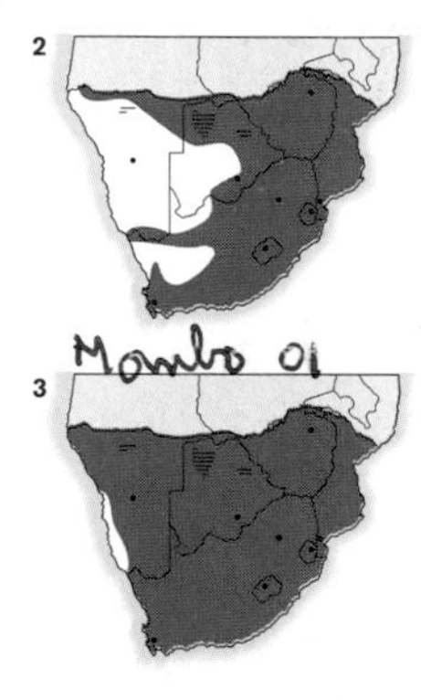

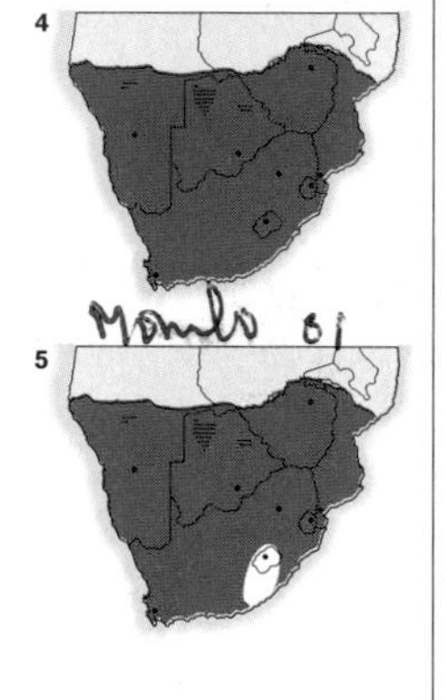

PIGEONS AND DOVES

Family COLUMBIDAE. A well-known group of birds. The distinction between pigeons and doves is ill-defined: larger species tend to be called pigeons, smaller ones doves. Immatures are dull versions of the adults. All except the fruit-eating pigeons feed on the ground.

1 AFRICAN MOURNING DOVE *Streptopelia decipiens*

Common resident. The only collared dove with a totally grey head plus *yellow eye* with red eye-ring. The call is distinctive, a soft 'kur-kurr' repeated once or twice; also a soft, descending 'kur-r-r-r-r-r-r'. Occurs in mixed woodland adjacent to large rivers. Has a highly localised distribution, but is common where it occurs. 30 cm (Rooioogtortelduif)

2 RED-EYED DOVE *Streptopelia semitorquata*

Common resident. Differs from (1) in having grey on top of the head only, *red eye* with a purple-pink eye-ring, the breast a deeper pink. The call is 'coo-coo, coo-*koo*-cuk-coo', the accent on the fourth syllable, likened to 'I am, a *red*-eyed dove'. Occurs in riverine forests, well-developed woodland, mixed bushveld, exotic plantations and suburbia. The largest of the ring-necked doves. 33-6 cm (Grootringduif)

3 CAPE TURTLE DOVE *Streptopelia capicola*

Very common, locally abundant resident. Colouring varies locally from very pallid to quite sooty-grey, but in all the head is uniform; has no eye-ring. In flight shows similar white outer tail feathers to (4), but mantle and wing coverts are greyish (not cinnamon). The call is a harsh 'work *harder,* work *harder* …' much repeated; also a snarling 'kerrr' on landing. One of the commonest, most widespread birds in the region, occurring in a wide range of habitats, frequently with (4), but present also in more arid regions. 28 cm (Gewone tortelduif)

(EUROPEAN) TURTLE DOVE (Europese tortelduif) see p. 446.

4 LAUGHING DOVE *Streptopelia senegalensis*

Very common, sometimes abundant resident. Has no black collar. Pinkish head and cinnamon breast with black spots plus rusty-coloured back diagnostic. In flight shows white outer tail feathers like (3), but mantle is rusty or cinnamon-coloured. The call is a soft 'coo-coo-*cuk*-coo-coo'. Widespread in a variety of habitats, often with (3), yet unaccountably absent from some regions. Common in suburbia. 25 cm (Rooiborsduifie)

5 NAMAQUA DOVE *Oena capensis*

Common resident. At all ages identified by long tail, male with black patch from forehead to breast. In flight combination of brown flight feathers and long tail diagnostic. The call is a seldom heard, explosive 'twoo-hoo'. Commonly seen in grassland, fallow fields, thornveld and eroded areas, particularly in dry regions. Perches on low bushes and fences; flies low at great speed. Nomadic; irregular visitor to southern and south-eastern coastal areas. 27 cm (Namakwaduifie)

1
2
3
4
♂
J
5
♀

1

2
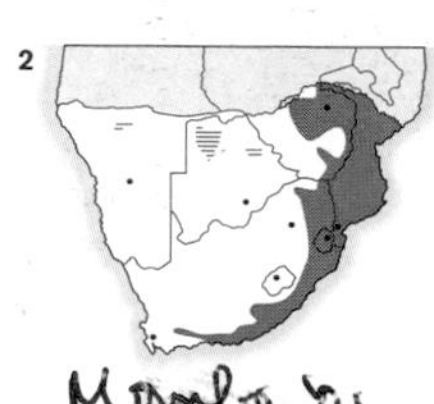

3
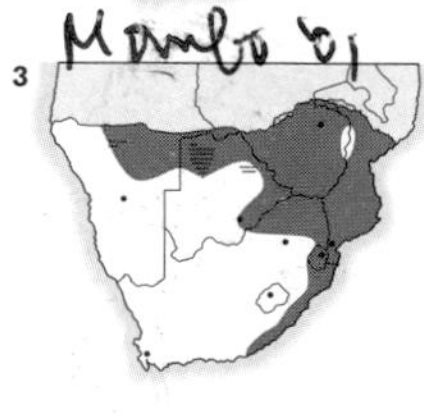

4
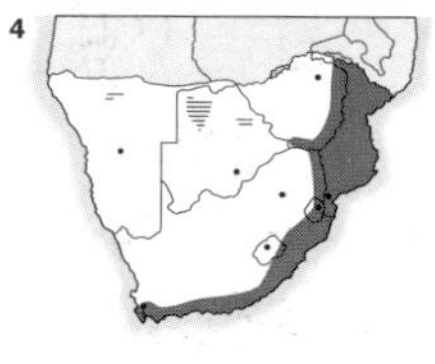

5
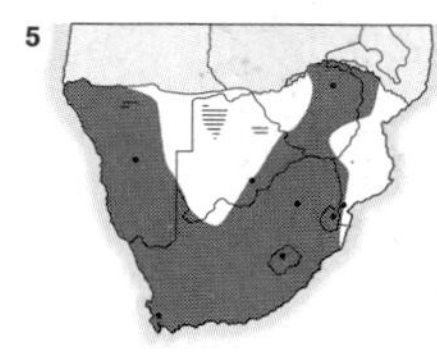

1 DELEGORGUE'S PIGEON *Columba delegorguei*

Rare resident. A dark pigeon. Male told by iridescent lower hindneck and mantle, showing purple-pink or green according to the fall of light, plus white feathering on mantle; female similar but head browner, no white on mantle. Call is a quiet, rasping 'uh-hoo' followed by a softer, deeper 'cuck-koo, coo-coo-coo-coo-coo' descending the scale. Sparsely distributed in coastal and eastern montane evergreen forests. Secretive, single birds or pairs remaining in the canopy, but highly mobile. Flocks sometimes gather to feed on ripe fruits. Most active early morning and late afternoon. 29 cm (Withalsbosduif)

2 TAMBOURINE DOVE *Turtur tympanistria*

Fairly common resident. White underparts unique and conspicuous. Call 'coo, coo, cu-cu-du-du-du-du', very similar to Emerald-spotted Dove (overleaf) but speeding up, not tailing off, and terminating abruptly. Singly or in pairs in coastal bush, montane and riverine forests. Shy and elusive. Perches in a low position or feeds on the ground. Makes off at great speed when disturbed. 23 cm (Witborsduifie)

3 GREEN PIGEON *Treron calva*

Common resident. Told by bright green colouring, yellow on wings and yellow leg feathers plus red base to bill and red legs. Call an explosive, high-pitched yet melodious bubbling, descending in pitch. Flocks frequent well-wooded regions, riverine forests and wooded hillsides where wild figs are fruiting. Difficult to locate from its habit of remaining still among the foliage, concealed by its cryptic colouring. When approached closely the flock explodes from the tree and flies off rapidly. 30 cm (Papegaaiduif)

4 CINNAMON DOVE *Aplopelia larvata*

Fairly common resident. Very shy and secretive, but its presence often revealed by its call, a soft, mournful 'hoo-oo' with rising inflection on the second syllable. Pairs inhabit the interior of evergreen forests and plantations, feeding on the ground. Usually seen only when flushed, then flies off rapidly dodging through the trees. 25-30 cm (Kaneelduifie)

5 ROCK PIGEON *Columba guinea*

Very common resident. Told by deep red, white-spotted upperparts, grey head and underparts plus red facial mask. Call is a loud and prolonged cooing 'cook, cook, cook, cook ...' rising to a crescendo, then falling. Flocks inhabit cliffs, mine shafts, road bridges, caves and buildings, often making lengthy daily flights to water or to feed in grain fields. 33 cm (Kransduif)

1
2
♂
♀
3
4
5

1 BLUE-SPOTTED DOVE *Turtur afer*

Uncommon, localised resident. Very similar to (2) but upperparts browner, wing-spots purple-blue and *bill red with yellow tip.* In flight both species show rufous wings and black back-bands; probably indistinguishable unless settled. Call like that of (2) or Tambourine Dove (previous page) but more abruptly terminated. Singly or in pairs on edges and in clearings of evergreen forests, in riverine forests and dense thickets. Occurs mostly in eastern Zimbabwe and the escarpment region of extreme north-east of South Africa. 22 cm (Blouvlekduifie)

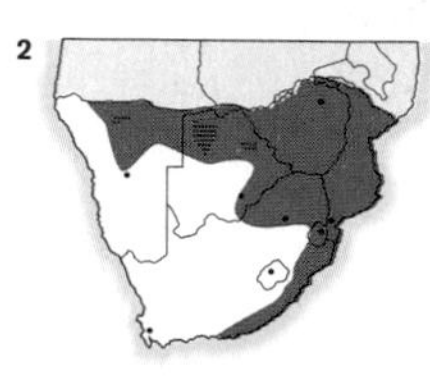

2 EMERALD-SPOTTED DOVE *Turtur chalcospilos*

Very common resident. Apart from green wing-spots, differs from (1) in all-dark, reddish bill and greyer upperparts. Typical wood dove flight pattern distinctive (see illustration) but not diagnostic. The well-known call is a soft, descending cooing 'du, du … du-du … du-du-dudu-du-du-du …' *tailing off at the end.* Occurs in woodland, bushveld, riparian forests and coastal bush. When flushed rises abruptly and makes off at speed. 20 cm (Groenvlekduifie)

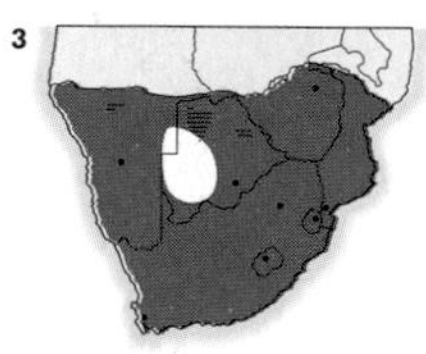

3 FERAL PIGEON (DOMESTIC or TOWN PIGEON) *Columba livia* 

Common to abundant resident. An introduced species. Very well known and highly variable in colour. A wild-living domestic breed descended from the Rock Dove of North Africa and Europe. Main colour forms shown, but many combinations also occur including pure white, white with dark head and dark grey with white head. Calls 'coo-roo-coo'. Mainly in larger towns where very tame. Dependent on human habitation but flocks may frequent cliffs, mine shafts and farmlands. 33 cm (Tuinduif)

4 RAMERON PIGEON *Columba arquatrix*

Fairly common resident. Yellow bill and feet conspicuous, even in flight; otherwise appears as a large, dark pigeon with pale head. Call is a deep bubbling 'crrooo, crooca, crooca, coooo'. Usually in small flocks where trees are fruiting, even entering suburban gardens. In montane regions roosts in evergreen forests or exotic plantations, flying considerable distances daily to food source. Often goes to roost early, sunning itself conspicuously on tree-tops in late afternoon. 40 cm (Geelbekbosduif)

1
2
3
4

1

2

3

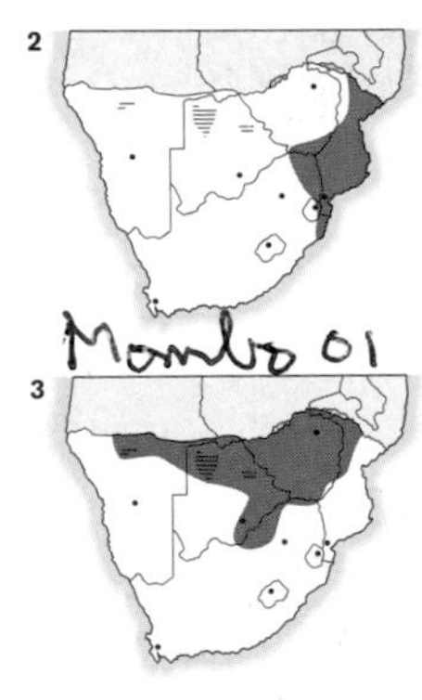

4

5

PARROTS AND LOVEBIRDS

Family PSITTACIDAE. A well-known group of gregarious birds with hooked bills. They use their feet and bills to clamber about trees. Parrots feed mainly in trees on fruits and kernels, the latter obtained by cracking the hard pericarps. Lovebirds feed on seeds, grain, berries and flowers, frequently foraging on the ground. All are highly social and utter shrill shrieks.

1 ROSE-RINGED PARAKEET *Psittacula krameri*

Fairly common, localised resident. An introduced Asian species. The only long-tailed, apple-green parrot in the region. Female has no neck-ring. Has established itself just north of Durban, less frequently further north. Small flocks of (presumably) aviary escapees also occur in the Johannesburg area. 40 cm (Ringnekpapegaai)

2 BROWN-HEADED PARROT *Poicephalus cryptoxanthus*

Common resident. A green parrot with brown head and yellow eyes; in flight shows an apple-green back and yellow underwing coverts. Immature is duller than adult. Small flocks occur in broad-leaved woodland, mixed bushveld and thornveld, feeding in large trees. 23 cm (Bruinkoppapegaai)

3 MEYER'S PARROT *Poicephalus meyeri*

Common resident. Differs from (2) in entirely grey-brown upperparts, head and breast; has a yellow bar on the forehead, yellow shoulders and some yellow on the underwing coverts. In flight shows *blue-green* back. Immature has no yellow on forehead and very little on the shoulders. Pairs and small flocks in broad-leaved and riverine woodland. This species and (2) hybridise where their ranges overlap. 23 cm (Bosveldpapegaai)

4 RÜPPELL'S PARROT *Poicephalus rueppellii*

Common, near endemic resident. Differs from (3) in grey head and, in female, blue back, belly and vent plus yellow shoulders; *male lacks the blue back.* Both sexes have yellow underwing coverts. Immature resembles female. Small flocks in arid woodland and thornveld. 23 cm (Bloupenspapegaai)

5 CAPE PARROT *Poicephalus robustus*

Uncommon, localised resident. Large, mostly green parrot occurring in two distinct forms: (a) the endemic race, with yellow-brown head and neck, occurs in a broken strip in the eastern interior, and (b) which extends north to Tanzania, with greyish head and neck. Both have orange leg feathers and shoulders but orange forehead is variable; this colour absent or vestigial in immature. In flight adult shows pale green back and rump. Occurs in pairs and small flocks in evergreen forests and mature woodland. Small flocks often fly long distances daily to reach fruiting trees, returning at night to favoured forest roosts. 35 cm (Grootpapegaai)

1 ♂
2
3
4 ♀
5
a
b

1

1 BLACK-CHEEKED LOVEBIRD *Agapornis nigrigenis*

Status uncertain; possible visitor from Zambia. The dark face distinguishes this lovebird. Old records exist for Victoria Falls and the Caprivi. It may still occur sparsely in those regions but no recent sightings recorded. Normally occurs in miombo woodland and river valleys. 13-14 cm (Swartwangparkiet)

2
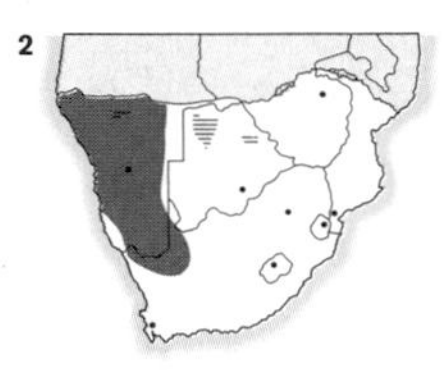

2 ROSY-FACED LOVEBIRD *Agapornis roseicollis* 

Locally common, near endemic resident. Differs from (3) in pale bill and bright *blue back and rump* (not green), which is especially visible in flight. Occurs in flocks in dry woodland, tree-lined rocky gorges and along tree-lined watercourses in the arid west. 17-18 cm (Rooiwangparkiet)

3

3 LILIAN'S LOVEBIRD *Agapornis lilianae*

Locally common resident. Differs from (2) in reddish bill and *green* (not blue) back and rump. Flocks occur in thornveld and broad-leaved woodland in the Zambezi River valley. 17-18 cm (Niassaparkiet)

TROGONS

Family TROGONIDAE. Among the world's most colourful birds, trogons are found in Africa, America and Asia. They have weak feet with two toes directed forward and two backward. The skin of trogons is delicate and easily torn, while the feathers drop out easily if the bird is handled. In museum specimens the red breast-colouring fades if exposed to light for long periods.

4
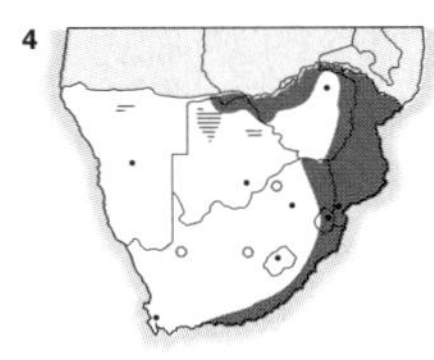

4 NARINA TROGON *Apaloderma narina*

Fairly common resident. The only forest bird with scarlet underparts and iridescent green upperparts. The bill is pale yellow; the head with turquoise-blue skin patches when breeding. The small illustration shows the male with inflated throat when calling. The immature resembles the female but with breast and shoulders lightly barred. Difficult to locate in its forest habitat since it often perches with its green back towards the observer. In the breeding season (October-December) it can be located by its call, a low 'hoot-hoot ... hoot-hoot ... hoot-hoot' repeated regularly and slowly. Usually in pairs in evergreen forests, or adjacent plantations (at high altitudes only in summer). Moves away from high-altitude haunts in winter at which time it may be encountered in lowland riverine forests and gardens. 29-34 cm (Bosloerie)

1
2
3
♂
♀
4
♂

1

2

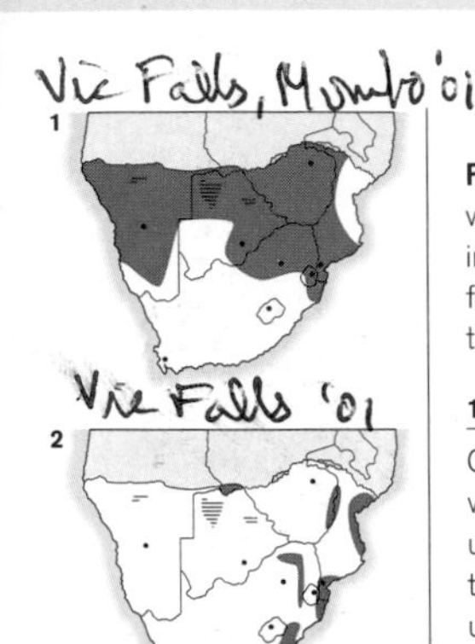

3

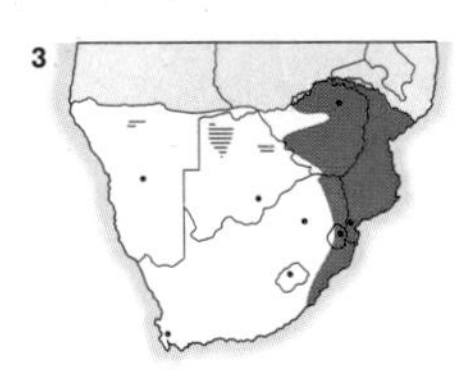

4

LOURIES or TURACOS

Family MUSOPHAGIDAE. Fruit-eating Afrotropical forest or bushveld birds with crested heads, fairly long tails and an agile springing action when jumping along branches. Most are beautifully coloured and have crimson primary feathers which are strikingly revealed in flight. Immatures are dull versions of the adults. Note: The family name 'Lourie' is used only in southern Africa.

1 GREY LOURIE *Corythaixoides concolor*

Common resident. All-grey with pronounced head-crest; sexes are alike. The well-known call is 'kweh-h-h' or 'go way-y-y', the latter giving rise to its popular name: Go-away Bird. Immature calls 'how, how …'. Pairs and small parties in mixed bushveld, woodland and well-wooded suburbia, usually in the upper stratum and invariably noisy. Flies with rather heavy wing movements, mostly below the tree-tops. 47-50 cm (Kwêvoël)

2 KNYSNA LOURIE *Tauraco corythaix*

Common, localised resident. At rest recognised by its matt-green body and crested head with white markings, the upper tail and folded wings being an iridescent greenish-blue while its eye-rings and bill are red. Its crimson flight feathers are revealed in flight. Within southern Africa three long-crested races of the species are recognised, and each has a discrete distribution. Reichnow's Lourie *T.c. reichenowi* occurs from St Lucia northwards, Livingstone's Lourie *T.c. livingstonii* in eastern Zimbabwe and Schalow's Lourie *T.c. schalowi* in northern Botswana and the Caprivi region of Namibia. The sexes are alike in all races; the immatures duller. The normal call is a slow 'kerk-kerk-kerk-kawk-kawk-kawk-kawk' and a high-pitched 'kek-kek-kek-kek' alarm call given as it flies away. Within its forest habitat it utters a hoarse 'breathing' sound 'hurr … hurr' when it detects the presence of human intruders. Usually in pairs or family groups in montane mistbelt forests and evergreen forests in lowland and coastal regions. Easily overlooked when feeding but strikingly obvious in flight. 47 cm (Knysnaloerie)

3 PURPLE-CRESTED LOURIE *Tauraco porphyreolophus*

Common resident. Differs from (2) in dark blue crest with a purple sheen, more blue on the folded wings and tail, ochre-washed breast and *black bill.* The call is a long sequence of notes, starting quietly and rising to a crescendo 'kerkerkerkerker-kok-kok-kok-kok-kok-kok …', the last sound repeated about 20 times, becoming more deliberate and spaced out. Also utters a jumbled series of 'kokokok …' sounds. Pairs occur in coastal forests, riparian forests in bushveld and in well-wooded valleys, usually preferring drier conditions than (2). Conspicuous only in flight. 47 cm (Bloukuifloerie)

4 ROSS'S LOURIE *Musophaga rossae*

Very rare vagrant from Zambia. Recorded once in the Okavango Delta, northern Botswana. 50 cm (Rooikuifloerie)

1
a
b
2
3
4

1
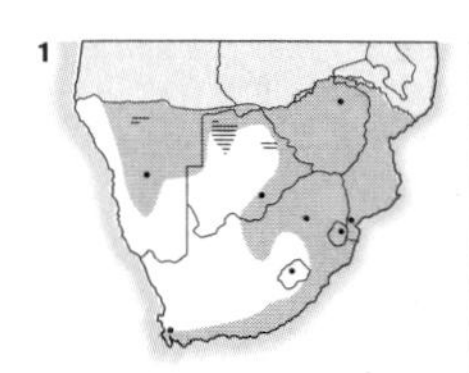
2
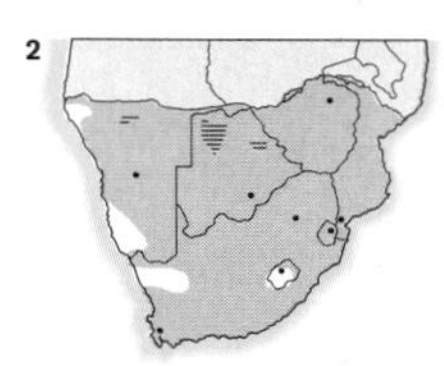
3
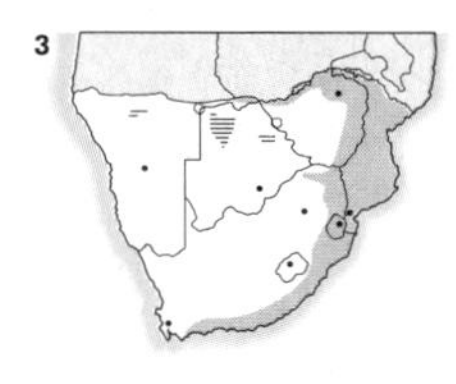
4
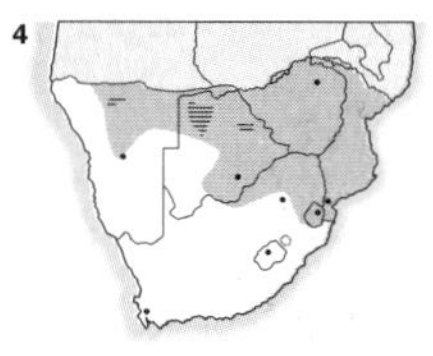
5
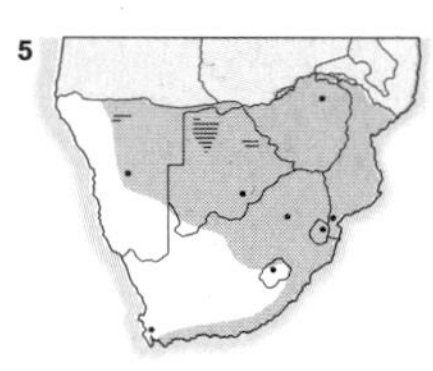

CUCKOOS AND COUCALS

Family CUCULIDAE. Cuckoos are brood parasites, laying their eggs in the nests of other birds, and the majority are absent from southern Africa during the period March-September. The related coucals are larger, more robust and mainly sedentary birds which build their own nests and rear young in the conventional manner.

1 KLAAS'S CUCKOO *Chrysococcyx klaas*

Common summer resident, some present all year. Male differs from (2) in having a white mark *behind the eye only* and no white wing markings; also *dark eyes, green bill* and white outer tail feathers. Female differs from female of (3) in the *white mark behind the eye* and less barring below. The call is a mournful 'hueet-jie' repeated five or six times. Usually singly in a variety of wooded habitats including well-wooded suburbia. Parasitises a wide range of insectivorous passerine birds. 17 cm (Meitjie)

2 DIEDERIK CUCKOO *Chrysococcyx caprius*

Common summer resident. Both sexes differ from male of (1) in having white marks *before and behind* the eyes, a white central stripe over the crown and *multiple white marks on the wings;* also red eyes and a black bill. Female is more coppery on the upperparts. Immature has a coral-red bill, blue eyes and spotted underparts; immature female mostly coppery above. Male calls a plaintive 'dee-dee-dee-deederik'; female calls 'deea-deea-DEEA'. Usually singly in a variety of wooded habitats including reed-beds and suburbia. Parasitises weavers, bishops and sparrows. 18,5 cm (Diederikkie)

3 EMERALD CUCKOO *Chrysococcyx cupreus*

Fairly common summer resident. Male identified by yellow belly; female from female of (1) by the absence of a white mark behind the eye, much bronzier upperparts and heavily barred underparts, plus dark eyes and bluish bill and feet. The call is a clear 'teeu-tu-tui' or 'Pretty, Geor-gie'. Occurs in the upper stratum of forests and valley bush. Parasitises forest robins, warblers and flycatchers. 20 cm (Mooimeisie)

4 STRIPED CUCKOO *Clamator levaillantii*

Fairly common summer resident. Differs from the white morph of (5) in larger size and *heavily streaked throat and breast.* Sexes are alike. The call is 'klew klew klew klew' followed by a long warbling 'chiriiririri ...' and other shrill warbling sounds. Occurs in pairs in woodland, riparian woodland and bushveld. Parasitises babblers. 38-40 cm (Gestreepte nuwejaarsvoël)

5 JACOBIN CUCKOO *Clamator jacobinus*

Common summer resident. Two colour morphs: (a) with clear white underparts and (b) totally black except for white wing-bar. Noisy and conspicuous, calling a shrill, flute-like 'kleeuw, pewp-pewp, kleeuw, pewp-pewp ...'. Pairs occur in woodland, riparian forests, valley bush and bushveld. Parasitises bulbuls and other small birds. 33-4 cm (Bontnuwejaarsvoël)

♂
1
♀
♂
2
♀
J
♀
4
3
♂
b
5
a

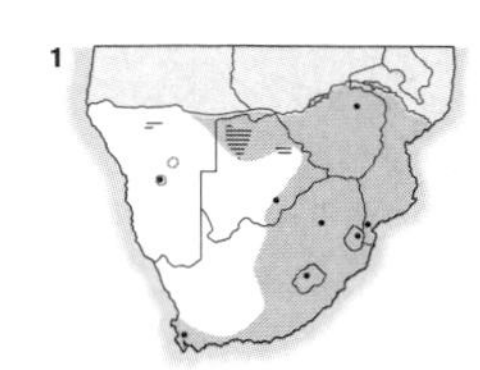

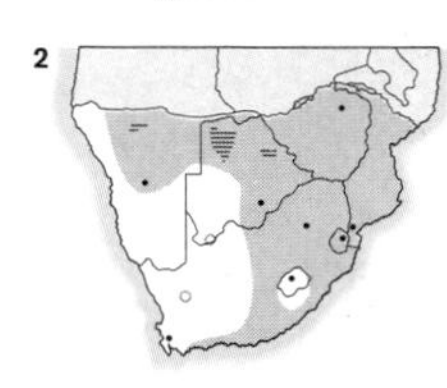

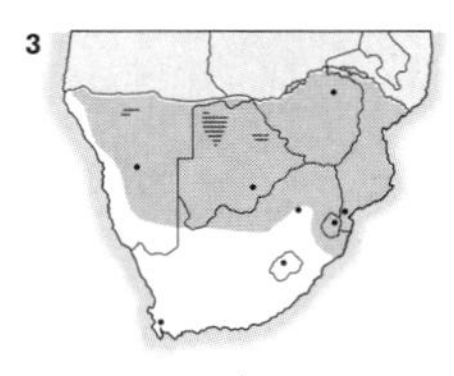

1 RED-CHESTED CUCKOO *Cuculus solitarius*

Common summer resident. Told from others on this page by the *broad* russet upper breast; recently fledged birds have the entire head and upperparts dark charcoal-grey, all feathers edged white as illustrated. The well-known call of the male resembles the Afrikaans name 'Piet-my-vrou', loud and frequently repeated; the female calls 'pik-pik-pik-pik'. Occurs in a variety of wooded habitats including exotic plantations and suburbia. Male calls from a high tree and often in flight when, in common with others on this page, it appears hawk-like; see small illustration. Parasitises mostly robins. 28 cm (Piet-my-vrou)

2 EUROPEAN CUCKOO *Cuculus canorus*

Uncommon, non-breeding summer visitor. Female (illustrated) told from (1) by generally much fainter russet collar extending obscurely onto the nape and ear coverts. Male lacks russet colouring and is *almost indistinguishable from (3);* the base of the bill *only* is normally greenish-yellow, but sometimes like (3); see bill illustrations. The undertail has white spots. In one race the upperparts, especially the head, are pale grey. Female may occur in a rare brown morph. Silent in Africa, occurring in any woodland. 30-33 cm (Europese koekoek)

3 AFRICAN CUCKOO *Cuculus gularis*

Fairly common summer resident. Scarcely differs from male of (2) but the undertail is barred (not spotted) while the basal half of the bill is *yellow* and more conspicuous; see bill illustrations. Told from (4) by larger size and paler grey upperparts. Immature well barred like that of (1) but with a paler head. Best identified by the male's call, a melancholy 'hoop-hoop' or 'coo-cuck'; female utters a loud 'pikpikpikpik'; cf. (1). Occurs in woodland and mixed bushveld. A known host is the Fork-tailed Drongo (p. 296). 32 cm (Afrikaanse koekoek)

4 LESSER CUCKOO *Cuculus poliocephalus*
MADAGASCAR LESSER CUCKOO *Cuculus rochii*

Rare, non-breeding visitors. Lesser Cuckoo visits January-April; Madagascar Lesser Cuckoo April-September. Small versions of (3). Almost indistinguishable from (2) and (3) apart from size, darker upperparts and head. Lesser Cuckoo probably does not call in Africa; Madagascar Lesser Cuckoo calls like (1) but deeper, a four-syllabled 'Piet-my-vrou-vrou'. Both have been recorded in riparian forests and broad-leaved woodland. 27 cm (Kleinkoekoek; Madagaskarkoekoek)

5 BARRED CUCKOO *Cercococcyx montanus*

Uncommon summer visitor and resident. Told by long tail plus brown and tawny colouring. Its call is distinctive, a much-repeated 'ree-reeoo ...', rising to a crescendo and then fading. An elusive, localised species, recorded only in riparian and broad-leaved forests in eastern Zimbabwe and the Zambezi River valley. A suspected host is the African Broadbill (p. 274). 33 cm (Langstertkoekoek)

J
1
♀
2
♂
3
4
5
2
3

1

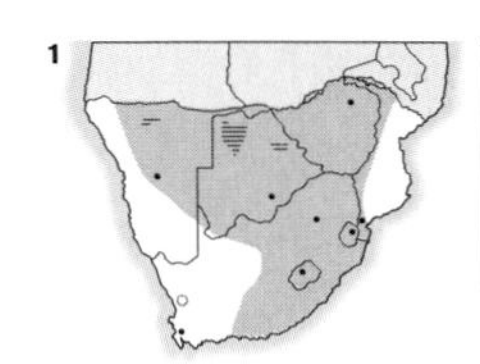

1 GREAT SPOTTED CUCKOO *Clamator glandarius*

Fairly common summer resident. A large cuckoo, distinguished by grey crested head, white-spotted upperparts and creamy-white underparts. Immature similar but the cap is black, crest less pronounced and the primary feathers chestnut-brown. The common call is a rasping, rapid 'keeow keeow keeow keeow ...' repeated in strophes of about eight. Occurs in woodland and savanna. Parasitises crows and starlings. 38-40 cm (Gevlekte koekoek)

2

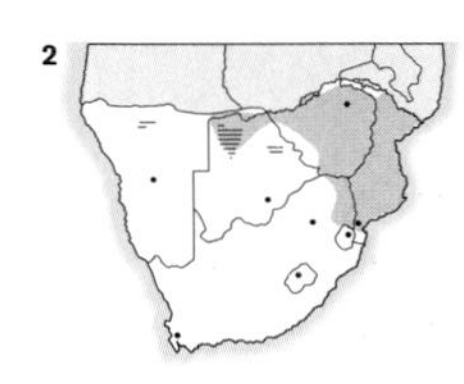

2 THICK-BILLED CUCKOO *Pachycoccyx audeberti*

Uncommon summer resident. Adult told by plain grey upperparts and entirely white underparts, plus heavy bill. Immature has a white head dappled grey on the crown plus broad white edges to the wing feathers. Has a loud querulous call 'chee cher cher' and a rippling 'Oui yes yes'. Usually singly in any woodland; a restless, elusive species. Known to parasitise Red-billed Helmet Shrikes (p. 380). 34 cm (Dikbekkoekoek)

3

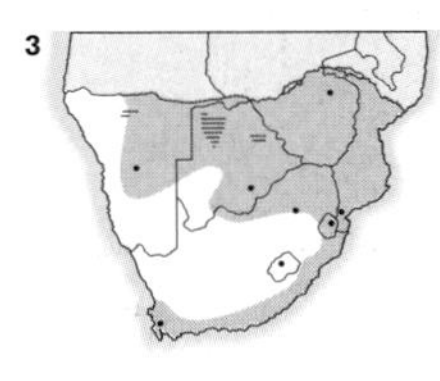

3 BLACK CUCKOO *Cuculus clamosus*

Common summer resident. Entirely black; immature more brown-black. Male utters a much-repeated, monotonous call 'whoo whoo whee', rising on the last syllable, likened to 'I'm so sick'; female has an excitable-sounding 'wind-up' call 'yowyowyowyowyowyow', reaching a crescendo and dying away. Usually singly in any well-wooded region, including suburbia. Perches in one place for long periods when calling. Parasitises boubou shrikes, including the Crimson-breasted Boubou (p. 374). 30 cm (Swartkoekoek)

4

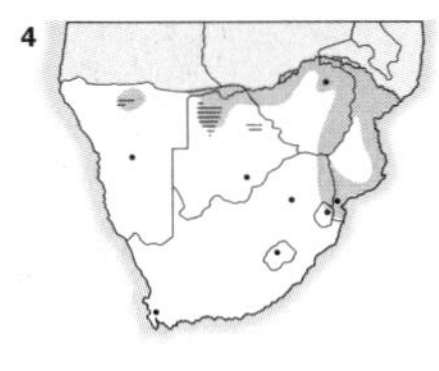

4 BLACK COUCAL *Centropus bengalensis*

Uncommon summer resident. Breeding adult distinctive as illustrated, female noticeably larger than male. Non-breeding adult similar to immature but darker above. The call, with the bird in a hunched, head-lowered stance, starts with a low 'ooom ooom ooom', then, with the head lifted, the bird utters a bubbling 'pop pop'. When excited also calls 'kwik kwik kwik'. Occurs singly or in pairs in the long, rank grass and associated bush thickets of marshes and flooded grassland. 32-7 cm (Swartvleiloerie)

5

5 GREEN COUCAL *Ceuthmochares aereus*

Fairly common localised resident. Large yellow bill and long green tail diagnostic. Immature is similar. Has several loud calls, 'tik tik tik tiktiktik ker ker ker kerkerkerker ...', speeding up towards the end, plus long drawn-out sounds 'phooeeep, phooeeep, phooeeep ...'. Occurs in thick vegetation in lowland and coastal forests; shy and secretive. 33 cm (Groenvleiloerie)

J
1
2
J
3
4
J
5

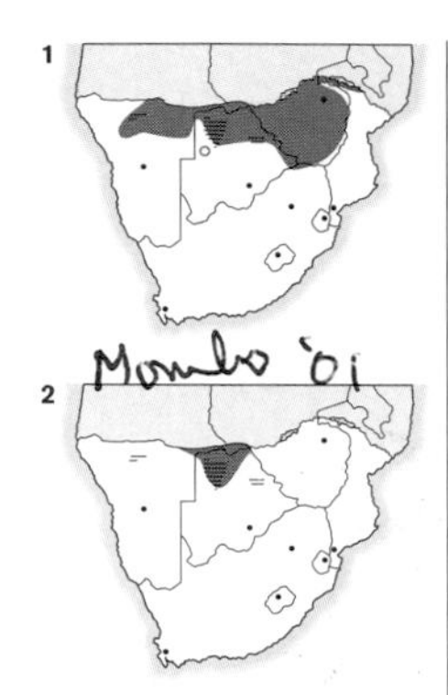

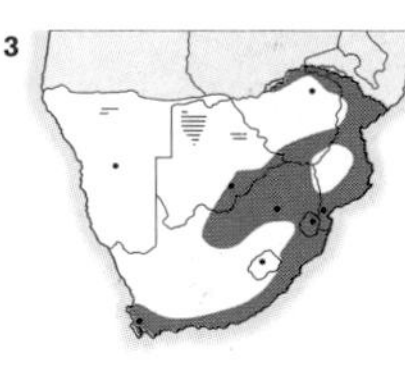

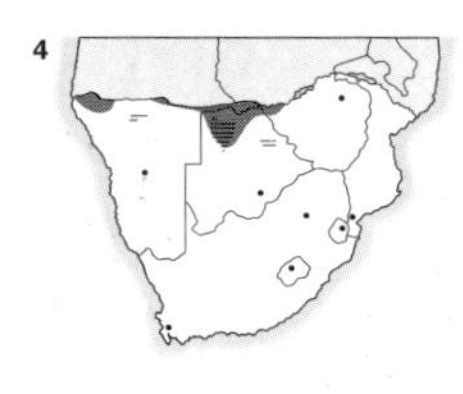

Note: The coucals on this page cannot be safely identified by their calls, which are nearly identical, a deep bubbling 'doo doo doo doo doo …' up to 20 times, descending then ascending, reminiscent of liquid pouring from a bottle. They also have harsh 'kurrr' alarm calls. Secretive, only occasionally perching conspicuously.

1 SENEGAL COUCAL *Centropus senegalensis*

Common resident. Distinguished from (2) with difficulty, but is smaller, has a less heavy bill and a shorter tail with green iridescence. Differs from (3) in having *unbarred upper tail coverts.* Immature is duller, upperparts barred black, upper tail coverts finely barred buff, thus very similar to immature of (3), but their ranges are mutually exclusive. Occurs singly or in pairs in dense riparian vegetation, reed-beds and thickets away from water. 41 cm (Senegalvleiloerie)

2 COPPERY-TAILED COUCAL *Centropus cupreicaudus*

Common resident. Larger than (1) and (3) with heavier bill, darker mantle, purple-black cap and longer tail *with a coppery sheen,* upper tail coverts indistinctly barred buff. Immature has the wing feather tips barred dark brown, tail feathers barred tawny. With experience can be told from other coucals by its deeper, richer call. Occurs in reed and papyrus beds plus riparian thickets in the Okavango Delta and Chobe River of northern Botswana, plus the western Zambezi River of Zimbabwe. 44-50 cm (Grootvleiloerie)

3 BURCHELL'S COUCAL *Centropus burchelli* NE

Common, near endemic resident. Adult larger than (1) with finely barred upper tail coverts, otherwise closely similar but their ranges do not overlap. Fledgling has a small whitish eyebrow, fine whitish streaking on the head (see illustration) and dark barring on the upperparts; eyes blue-grey, not crimson. Singly or in pairs in reeds, dense riparian and bushveld thickets, tall rank grass and well-wooded suburbia. Mostly secretive but will sometimes perch conspicuously. 44 cm (Gewone vleiloerie)

4 WHITE-BROWED COUCAL *Centropus superciliosus*

Common resident. Adult differs from (3) in having a white eyebrow and the head and nape well streaked with white, otherwise closely similar at all ages. Behaviour and habitat preferences as for (3). 44 cm (Witbrouvleiloerie)

1
2
4
3
J

OWLS

Families TYTONIDAE and STRIGIDAE. Nocturnal, erect-standing birds of prey characterised by large, rounded heads, large forward-facing eyes set in a flattened face and feathered legs (except for Pel's Fishing Owl). Some have feather adornments on their heads which resemble ears. Immatures are usually darker and fluffier than adults.

1

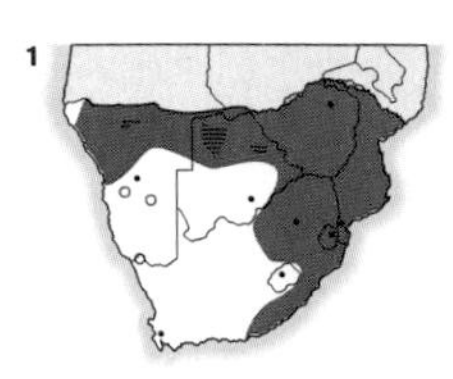

1 MARSH OWL *Asio capensis*

Common to uncommon resident. Medium-sized, dark brown owl with small 'ear' tufts; shows russet wings in flight. Sometimes calls 'kraak' in flight. Singly or in pairs in long grass on marshy ground, in vleis and near dams. Often active early mornings and late afternoons, flying low or perching on a fence post. When flushed from the grass during daytime flies in circles over the intruder before resettling. 36 cm (Vlei-uil)

2

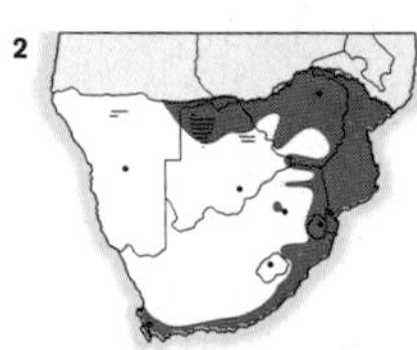

2 WOOD OWL *Strix woodfordii*

Fairly common, localised resident. Told by lack of 'ears', large, pale, spectacle-like eye-orbits and barred underparts. Immature has smaller eye-orbits and darker colouring. Male calls a rapid 'HU-hu, HU-hu-hu, hu-hu', female replies with a higher-pitched 'whoo'. Pairs and family groups in forests, well-developed riverine forests and exotic plantations. During the day roosts in large trees close to the trunks. 30-36 cm (Bosuil)

3

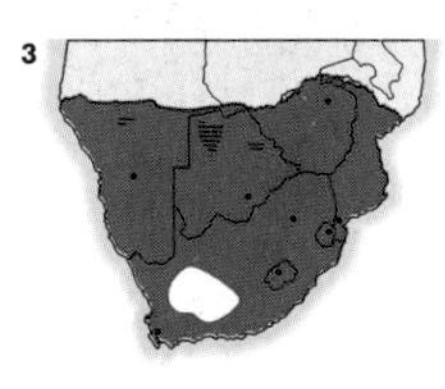

3 BARN OWL *Tyto alba*

Common resident. A pale, slimly built owl with heart-shaped facial disc and whitish underparts. Told from (4) by paler upperparts. The call is an eerie, wavering screech. Singly or in pairs in a variety of habitats, roosting and breeding in large trees, caves, buildings and Hamerkop nests (p. 80); common in suburbia. 30-33 cm (Nonnetjie-uil)

4

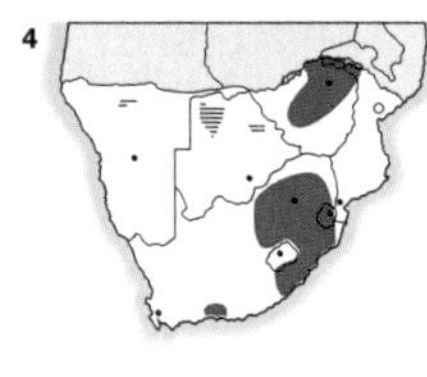

4 GRASS OWL *Tyto capensis*

Uncommon resident. Closely similar to (3) but distinguished by darker upperparts and different habitat. Hisses when disturbed; also utters a husky screech resembling that of (3). Singly or in pairs in moist grassland. When disturbed during the day flies directly away and resettles; cf. (1). 34-7 cm (Grasuil)

1
2
3
4

1

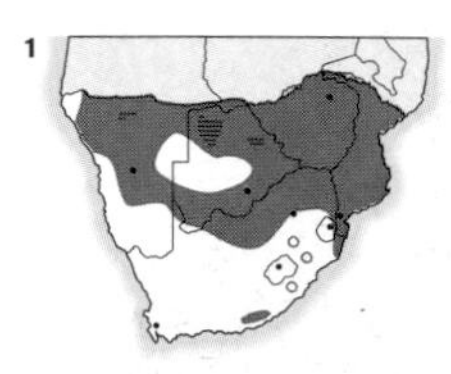

1 AFRICAN SCOPS OWL *Otus senegalensis*

Common resident. The plumage resembles tree-bark, the grey form (a) being commoner than the brown (b). The only very small owl with 'ear' tufts. Calls mostly at night, sometimes by day, a soft 'prrrrp' repeated at about 10-second intervals. Singly or in pairs in any woodland and mixed bushveld. By day perches in a tree, close to the trunk, where its cryptic colouring makes detection difficult. This camouflage is further enhanced by its habit of depressing its feathers to appear long and thin, and of raising its 'ear' tufts and half closing its eyes, creating the illusion of a tree stump; see (a). 15-18 cm (Skopsuil)

2

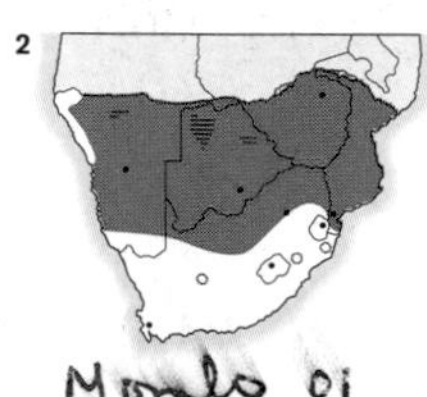

2 WHITE-FACED OWL *Otus leucotis*

Common resident. Largest of the small owls. Predominantly grey with *orange* eyes, a distinct *white facial disc with broad black outline* and 'ear' tufts. The call, heard only at night, is an explosive, bubbling 'b-b-b-b-b-bhooo' repeated. Singly or in pairs in woodland, riverine forests, mixed bushveld and thornveld, preferring the drier regions with large trees. 25-8 cm (Witwanguil)

3

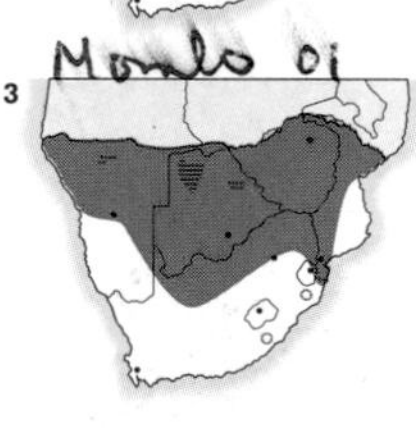

3 PEARL-SPOTTED OWL *Glaucidium perlatum*

Common resident. A very small 'earless' owl, upperparts brown with small white spots, underparts white, streaked with brown and with pearl-like spots. Has two black marks on its nape giving the impression of eyes. The call, often heard by day, is a series of ascending notes 'tee-tee-tee-tee-tee-tee-tee-tee ...' followed by a brief pause, then a series of descending notes 'teeew, teeew, tew, tew, tew, tew, tew ...'. Occurs in any woodland, including mopane, mixed bushveld and riverine forests. Is often seen by day and is frequently mobbed by other small birds. 15-18 cm (Witkoluil)

4

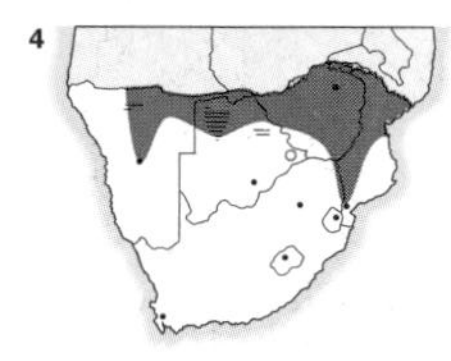

4 BARRED OWL *Glaucidium capense*

Common resident. Slightly larger than (3), the upperparts finely barred, the wings with a row of bold white spots reaching the shoulder, underparts white with brown spots arranged in rows. The call is an urgent 'kerrooo-kerrooo-krrooo-krrooo-krrooo-krrooo-krrooo ...' or 'krrooo-trrooo, krrooo-trrooo ...', either sequence repeated many times. Found mostly in well-developed riverine forests and large-tree woodland fringing lakes; also in mixed bushveld where it spends the day roosting in dense thickets. Less often seen by day than the previous species. 20 cm (Gebande uil)

1
a
b
2
3
4

1

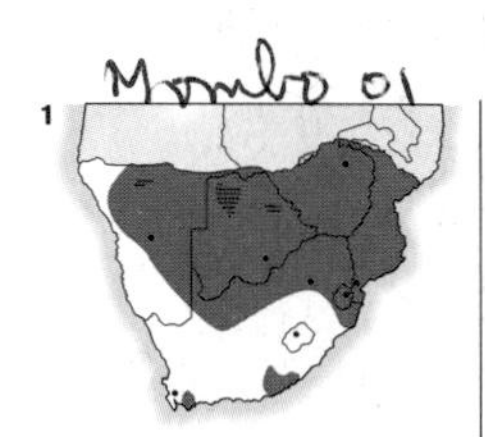

2

3

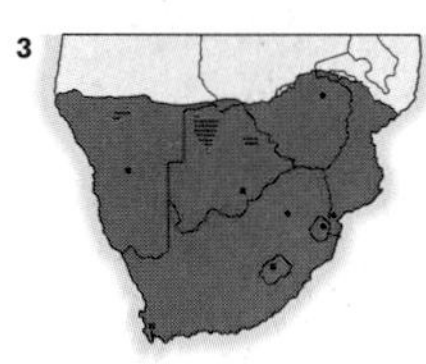

1 GIANT EAGLE OWL *Bubo lacteus*

Fairly common resident. A large grey owl; immature is browner. Told by *pink eyelids* and dark brown eyes at all ages. 'Ear' tufts not always raised. Voice is a series of deep grunts 'hu-hu-hu, hu-hu'; female and young utter a long-drawn-out whistle which may be repeated all night. Singly in large trees in bushveld and open savanna, especially along rivers and watercourses. 60-65 cm (Reuse-ooruil)

2 CAPE EAGLE OWL *Bubo capensis*

Uncommon resident. A large brownish owl of stocky proportions. Easily confused with (3) but differs in combination of larger size, orange-yellow eyes (orange in immature) and heavily blotched underparts with *bold* barring; feet and talons larger. Birds in Zimbabwe and Mozambique are larger than the southern race. Calls 'HU-hu-hu' or 'HU-hu', emphasis on the first syllable; alarm call 'wak-wak'. Pairs frequent valleys (in bush or grassland) with cliffs or rocks at the higher end, or grassland with rock outcrops and trees. 48-55 cm (Kaapse ooruil)

3 SPOTTED EAGLE OWL *Bubo africanus*

Very common resident. A fairly large, grey-brown owl, easily confused with (2) from which it differs in smaller size, pale yellow eyes, lightly blotched underparts with *fine barring,* and smaller feet and talons; see (a). A rufous form (b) with orange-yellow eyes also occurs, though less commonly; this told from (2) by fine barring on underparts. Male calls 'hu-hooo', female 'hu-hu-hooo', the sound rising on the second syllable. Usually in pairs in a wide range of habitats from bushveld to suburbia where it perches on buildings or feeds on lawns at night. Large exotic trees and rocky hillsides are also much favoured. 43-50 cm (Gevlekte ooruil)

1
2
3
a
b

1
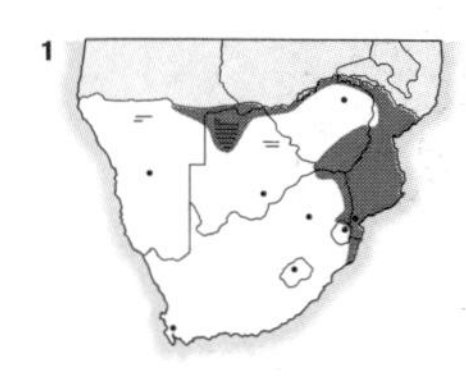

2
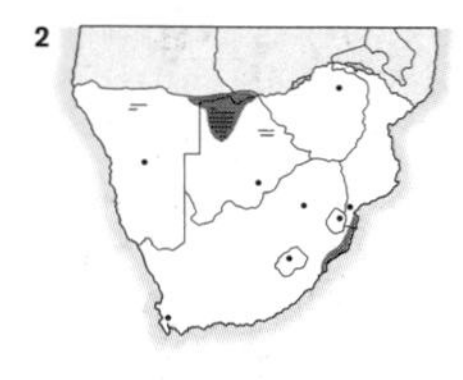

1 PEL'S FISHING OWL *Scotopelia peli*

Uncommon, localised resident. A very large, distinctive owl, differing from others in cinnamon underparts and rufous-brown upperparts. In repose the head has a flattish appearance with the slightest suggestion of 'ear' tufts. When excited the head feathers are fluffed out, giving the head a rounded appearance. Normal call is a deep, resonant 'oogh', the mate replying with a higher-pitched 'ooh'; also utters various other hoots, grunts and screeches. Pairs or single birds occur along large, slow-flowing and well-forested rivers. Strictly nocturnal; spends the day perched in the dense foliage of a large tree or creeper. When flushed flies a short distance and resettles in another tree from where it watches the intruder. Fishes in quiet pools or slow-running waters from a low perch, dropping feet first onto its prey. 63-5 cm (Visuil)

NIGHTJARS

Family CAPRIMULGIDAE. Nocturnal, insectivorous birds with soft, cryptically coloured plumage, short bills, wide gapes surrounded by stiff bristles, large eyes and short, weak legs. They hawk insects at night, lying up by day. If approached, may not flush until nearly trodden on; instead they close their eyes to narrow slits, thereby reducing the sun's reflection and so enhancing their camouflage. Habitually settle on country roads at night. All are so alike as to be nearly indistinguishable, but can be identified by characteristic calls; in the hand identified by wing and tail formulae, illustrated opposite and on pp. 225-7.

2 NATAL NIGHTJAR *Caprimulgus natalensis*

Rare, localised resident. The male has the entire outer web of the outermost tail feathers white and half the outer web of the second tail feather also white; wing-spots as illustrated. In the female the wing and tail markings are buff-coloured. From the ground calls a continuous 'chookchookchookchook ...' and a bubbling 'poipoipoipoipoipoi ....', both sequences less rapid than the call of the Mozambique Nightjar (overleaf). Occurs mainly in grassy, swampy and waterside locations in the eastern coastal belt and the Zambezi-Okavango area. 23 cm (Natalse naguil)

1

♂
2

1 PENNANT-WINGED NIGHTJAR *Macrodipteryx vexillaria*

Fairly common summer resident. Male with long wing-pennants unmistakable; female lacks any white in wings or tail. The call is a bat-like squeaking. Pairs occur in broad-leaved woodland and mixed bushveld, especially on hillsides in stony or sandy terrain. May be seen flying before nightfall. 25-8 cm (excluding male's wing streamers). (Wimpelvlerknaguil)

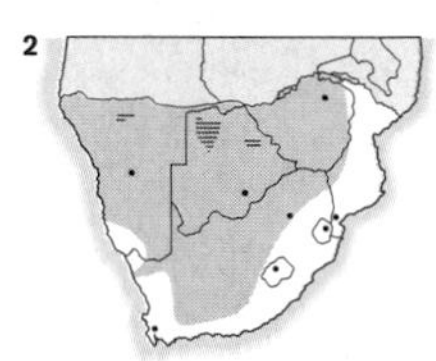

2 RUFOUS-CHEEKED NIGHTJAR *Caprimulgus rufigena*

Common summer resident. Identified by pale colouring and pale buff collar; see overleaf for full wing and tail formulae. Calls 'chwop, chwop, kewook-kwook' from ground or perch, and utters an even, sustained, purring sound like a small motor, with no variation. Occurs in dry woodland (especially protea woodland), thornveld and sparsely vegetated Kalahari sandveld, often on stony or gravelly ground. Rests beneath trees during the day, but if flushed may settle in a tree temporarily. 23-4 cm (Rooiwangnaguil)

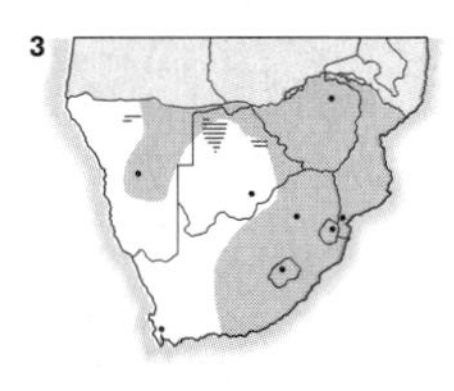

3 EUROPEAN NIGHTJAR *Caprimulgus europaeus*

Fairly common summer visitor. Identified by large size and dark colouring; see overleaf for full wing and tail formulae. Mostly silent in Africa but sometimes calls 'coo-ic' in flight and 'quick-quick-quick' from the ground. Occurs singly in woodland, riverine forests and plantations, preferring large trees where it roosts by day *lengthwise on a horizontal branch;* perches on branches more often than any resident nightjar. 25-8 cm (Europese naguil)

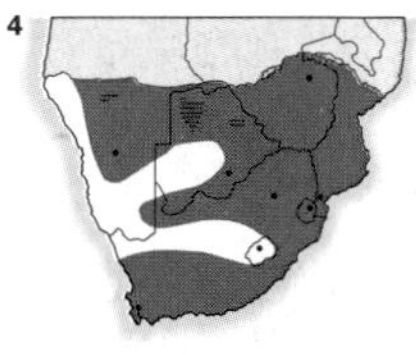

4 FIERY-NECKED NIGHTJAR *Caprimulgus pectoralis*

Common resident. Has extensive rufous colouring about the neck, head and upper breast; see overleaf for full wing and tail formulae. Has a characteristic descending, quavering call, resembling the words 'Good Lord, deliver us'. Occurs in any broad-leaved wooded region, often in well-wooded suburbia, especially in stands of exotic trees. Roosts on the ground by day. 23-5 cm (Afrikaanse naguil)

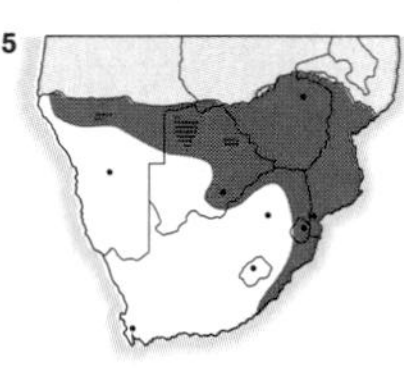

5 MOZAMBIOUE NIGHTJAR *Caprimulgus fossii*

Common resident. No distinctive colouring apart from wing and tail formulae; see overleaf. Utters a prolonged gurgling sound like an engine, which becomes louder or quieter with faster and slower frequency. Prefers open, sandy ground in woodland and savanna or near rivers and pans, plus coastal dunes. Roosts by day on the ground. 23-4 cm (Laeveldnaguil)

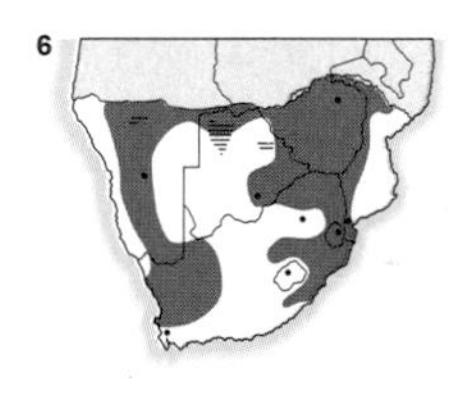

6 FRECKLED NIGHTJAR *Caprimulgus tristigma*

Common resident. Has *dark freckling* overall with few distinct markings, resembling weathered granite; see overleaf for full wing and tail formulae. The call is a high-pitched 'wheeoo-wheeoo' or 'cow-cow', at a distance like the yapping of a small dog. Associates with rocky koppies, escarpments and granite outcrops in woodland. By day roosts on shaded rocks, even on flat roofs in country districts. 27-8 cm (Donkernaguil)

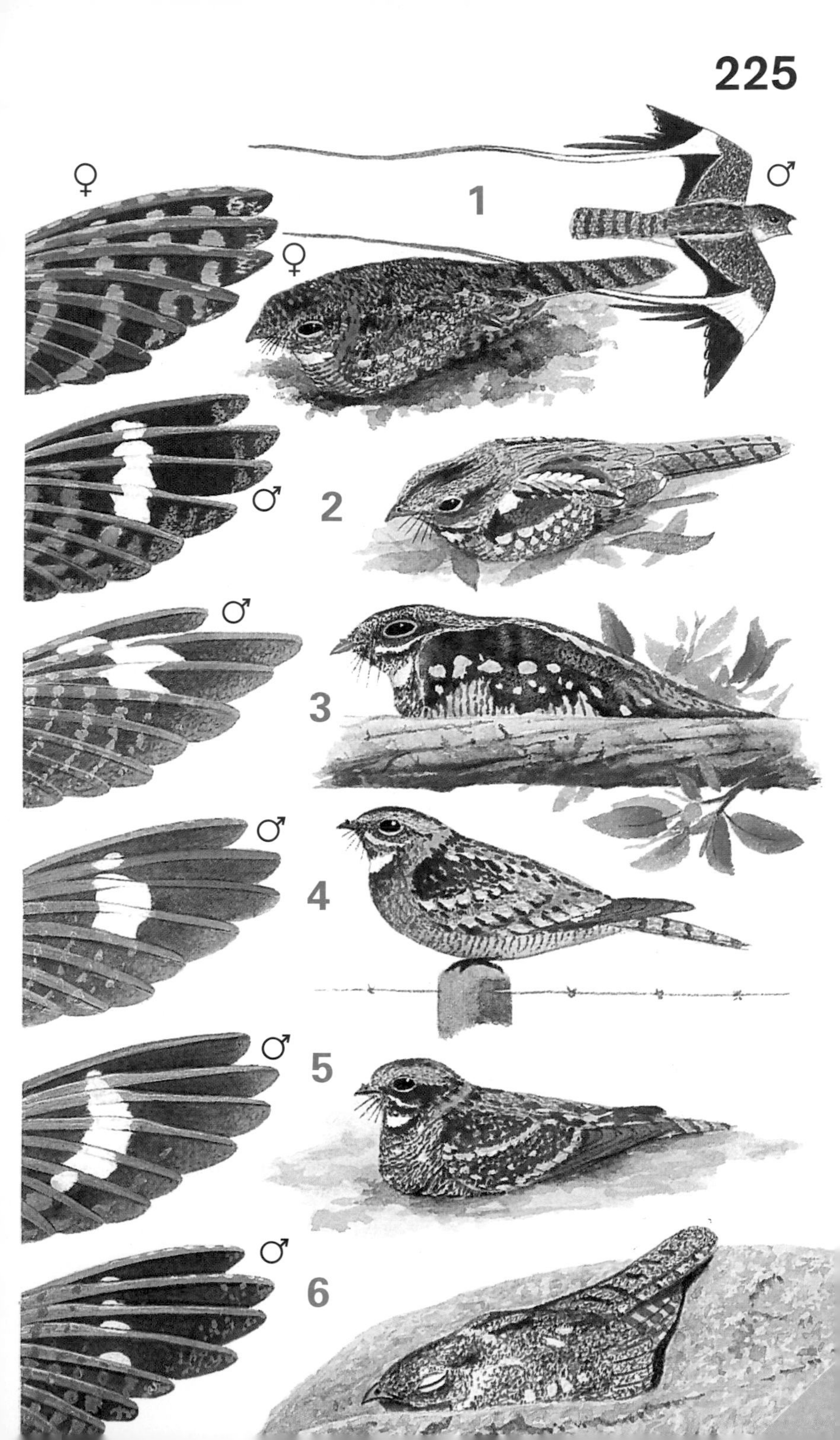

♀
1
♂
♀
2
♂
♂
3
♂
4
♂
5
♂
6

DIAGRAMMATIC ILLUSTRATIONS

These illustrations show the major wing feathers and outer tail feathers from above with the outer webs of each blackened for clarity. The position of the wing emarginations or 'kinks' in relation to the wing-spots, the format and colouring of the wing-spots (if present) plus the presence or

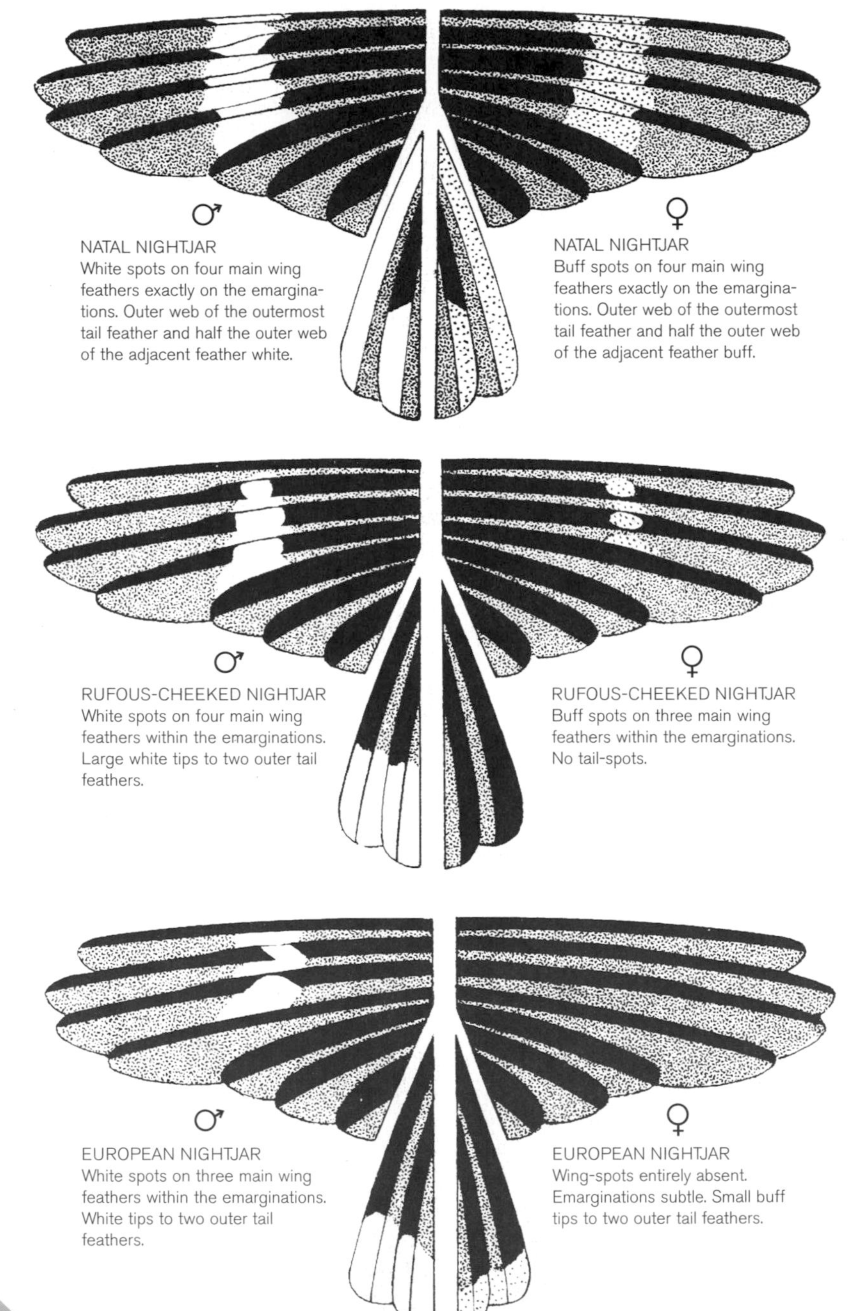

absence of bold tail markings are diagnostic for each species. The normal, irregular buff patterning present on nightjar feathers has been omitted. This diagram is intended to aid identification of nightjar road kills.

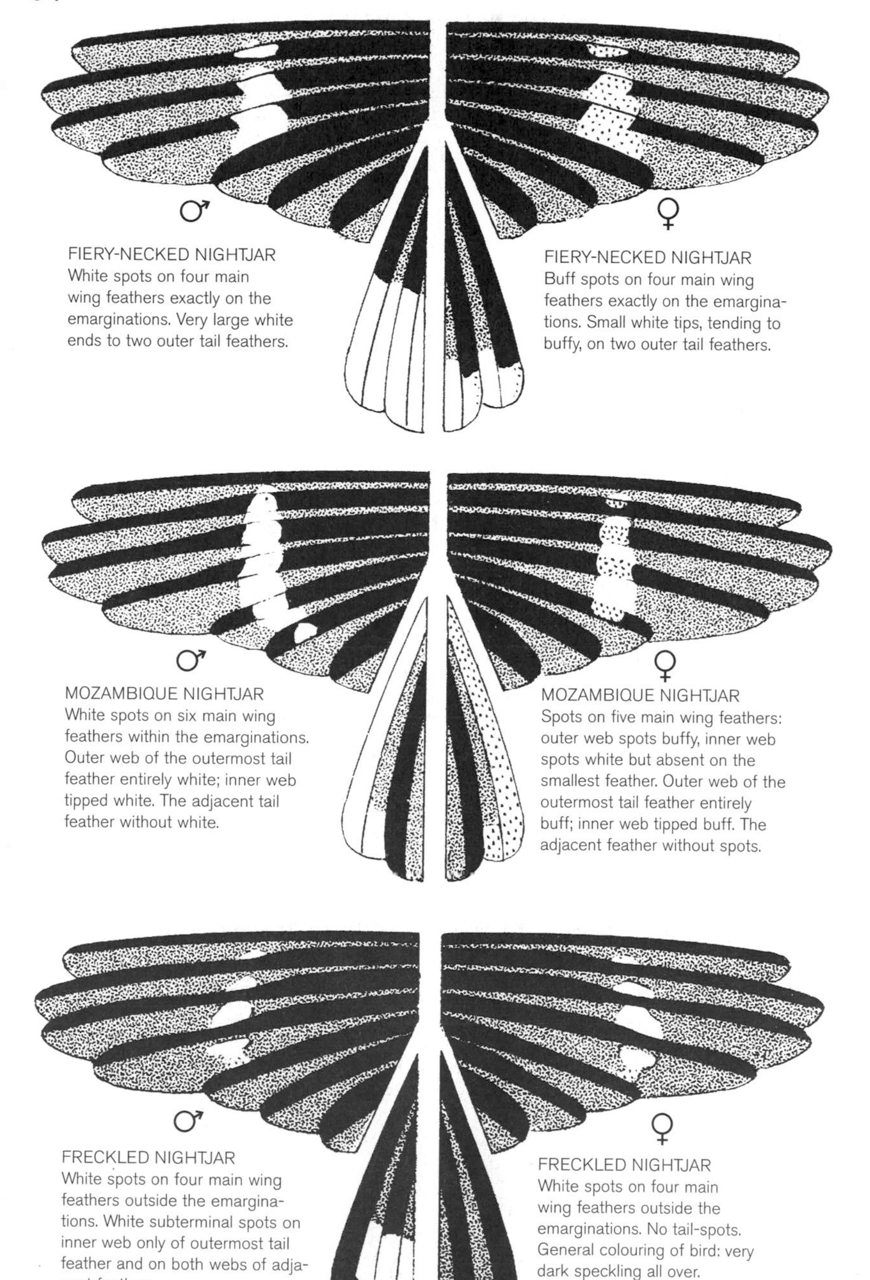

FIERY-NECKED NIGHTJAR
White spots on four main wing feathers exactly on the emarginations. Very large white ends to two outer tail feathers.

FIERY-NECKED NIGHTJAR
Buff spots on four main wing feathers exactly on the emarginations. Small white tips, tending to buffy, on two outer tail feathers.

MOZAMBIQUE NIGHTJAR
White spots on six main wing feathers within the emarginations. Outer web of the outermost tail feather entirely white; inner web tipped white. The adjacent tail feather without white.

MOZAMBIQUE NIGHTJAR
Spots on five main wing feathers: outer web spots buffy, inner web spots white but absent on the smallest feather. Outer web of the outermost tail feather entirely buff; inner web tipped buff. The adjacent feather without spots.

FRECKLED NIGHTJAR
White spots on four main wing feathers outside the emarginations. White subterminal spots on inner web only of outermost tail feather and on both webs of adjacent feather.

FRECKLED NIGHTJAR
White spots on four main wing feathers outside the emarginations. No tail-spots. General colouring of bird: very dark speckling all over.

1

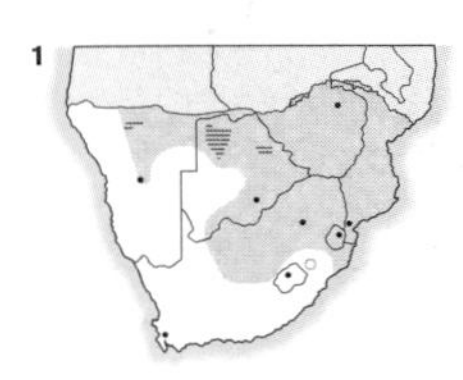

2

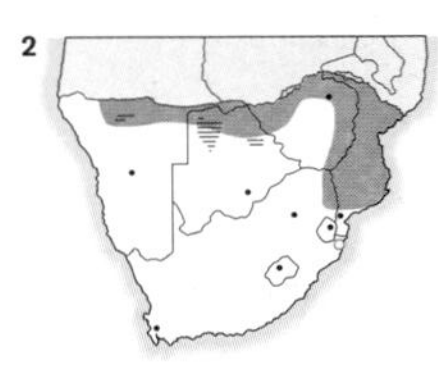

3

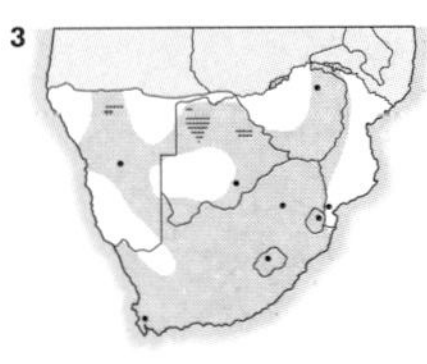

4

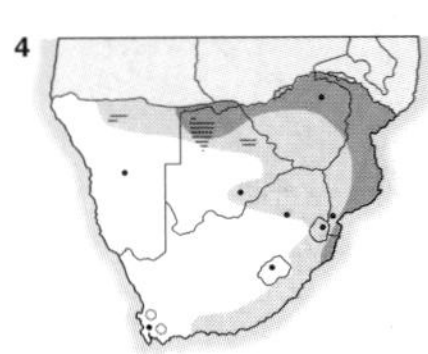

SWALLOWS AND MARTINS

Family HIRUNDINIDAE. Small, long-winged, aerial-feeding birds. Swallows have mostly glossy blue upperparts (some with rufous caps) and whitish, rufous or streaked underparts; the blackish saw-wing swallows (p. 234) are an exception. Saw-wing swallows have rough, saw-like leading edges to their primary feathers (not apparent in the field). The closely related martins are mostly brown above, white or brownish below and have square tails (most swallows have forked tails), except the House Martin which resembles a swallow. In all species immatures are duller than adults. They build nests with mud pellets or burrow tunnels in earth; they drink and bathe in flight by skimming the surface of still water, and perch to rest. See comparison between them and swifts on pp. 238-9.

1 RED-BREASTED SWALLOW *Hirundo semirufa*

Common summer resident. Identified by large size, *blue cap extending to below the eyes* and entirely orange-chestnut underparts. In flight differs from (2) in rufous (not white) underwing coverts and longer tail-shafts. Immature is duller above and much paler about the cheeks, chin and throat, the outer tail feathers shorter, but differs from (2) in having the dark cap extending below the eyes and onto the ear coverts. Adults utter a soft warbling. Pairs occur in summer near their nest sites: road culverts, low causeways (not over water) and antbear holes in open savanna and grassveld. Their flight is low and slow with much leisurely gliding. 24 cm (Rooiborsswael)

2 MOSQUE SWALLOW *Hirundo senegalensis*

Fairly common, localised resident. Told from (1) by white throat and upper breast; in flight by *white* underwing coverts and shorter tail-shafts. Utters a nasal, tin-trumpet-like 'harrrp', occasionally a guttural chuckling. Pairs and small flocks occur over large-tree woodland, mostly near water. Usually flies at some height, with bursts of fluttering flight followed by a glide. Frequently skims across dams and pans or perches in trees. 23 cm (Moskeeswael)

3 GREATER STRIPED SWALLOW *Hirundo cucullata* NE

Common, near endemic summer resident. Identified by chestnut cap, pale chestnut rump and *lightly streaked* underparts which appear almost white in flight; cf. (4). The call, uttered in flight, is a soft 'chissik'. In pairs when breeding, otherwise small flocks over open terrain, montane grassland, near culverts, rocky koppies and human habitation. Flies with much gliding and perches frequently on trees and wires. 20 cm (Grootstreepswael)

4 LESSER STRIPED SWALLOW *Hirundo abyssinica*

Common summer resident; some present all year. Differs from (3) in more heavily streaked underparts, appearing very dark in the field, and orange cap extending *over the ear coverts.* Flight call is a characteristic descending series of four notes 'eh-eh-eh-eh'. Pairs and small flocks near rivers, bridges, road culverts and buildings. Flies more actively than (3), with less gliding. Perches frequently on trees or wires. 16 cm (Kleinstreepswael)

1

2

3

4

1 BLUE SWALLOW *Hirundo atrocaerulea*

Rare, localised summer resident. Told by entirely glossy blue plumage and extended tail streamers, longest in males; saw-wing swallows (p. 234) are blacker and shorter-tailed. Has a wheezy, chittering call and a short, soft warbling song. Singly or in small parties in the vicinity of small streams in eastern montane grassland. An endangered species. 20-25 cm (Blouswael)

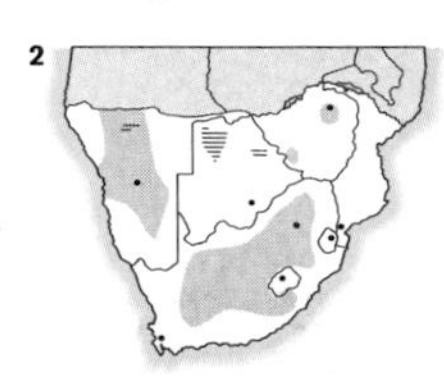

2 SOUTH AFRICAN CLIFF SWALLOW *Hirundo spilodera*

Common endemic summer resident. Square-tailed with mottled chin and throat; like European Swallow (overleaf) but with more robust appearance and pale throat. Immature is browner and duller above. Has a three- or four-syllable call 'chor-chor-chor-choor'. Flocks frequent the vicinity of their colonial breeding sites: cliffs, bridges, water towers and other buildings in dry grassland regions. 15 cm (Familieswael)

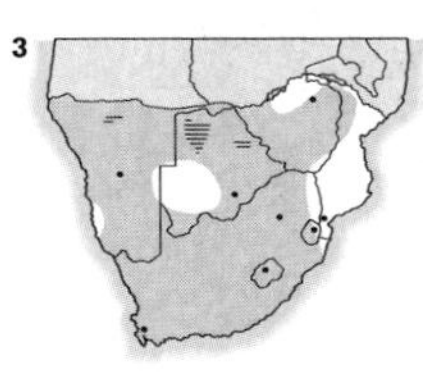

3 WHITE-THROATED SWALLOW *Hirundo albigularis*

Common summer resident; all year at low altitudes. Told from the European Swallow (overleaf) by clear white underparts with black breast-band. Utters a soft twittering and has a warbling song. In pairs near their nest site under a rock overhang, bridge, culvert, outbuilding or other artificial structure, usually near or over water. 17 cm (Witkeelswael)

4 RED-RUMPED SWALLOW *Hirundo daurica*

Told from other red-rumped swallows by tawny underparts and chestnut band across the nape. Utters a hoarse 'chirp' and subdued twittering. Frequents hilly districts and mixes with other swallows when feeding. A wanderer from Zambia and further north. 18 cm (Rooinekswael)

ANGOLA SWALLOW (Angolaswael) see p. 450.

♀
♂
1
2
3
4

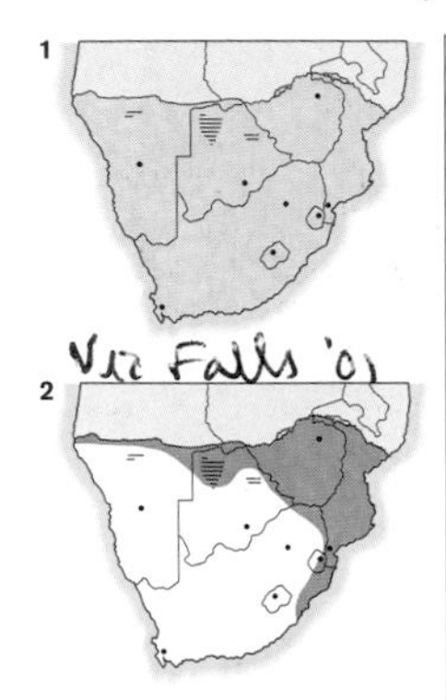

1 EUROPEAN SWALLOW *Hirundo rustica*

Abundant summer visitor. Told by dark chin and throat; moulting birds *often without rufous chin or long tail-shafts* (November-January); immatures common October-December. Flocks utter a soft twittering sound, especially when settled. Outnumbers all other swallows in summer, and mixes freely in flight with other swallows and with swifts over most habitats. Large flocks perch on telephone wires or in roads and very large flocks gather to roost in reedbeds. 18 cm (Europese swael)

2 WIRE-TAILED SWALLOW *Hirundo smithii*

Fairly common wetland resident. Told by *full* orange cap, entirely white underparts and *wire-like* tail streamers. The call is a twittering 'chirrik-weet' repeated from a perch and 'chit-chit' while flying. Pairs, sometimes small groups, are found near river bridges, dam walls, river gorges and buildings, seldom far from water. Perches on dead trees in water and on bridge rails; settles on the *road surface* of bridges and causeways. 13 cm (Draadstertswael)

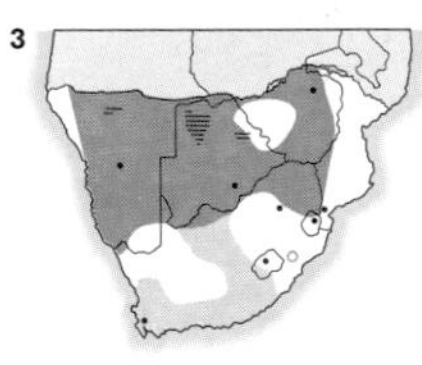

3 PEARL-BREASTED SWALLOW *Hirundo dimidiata*

Uncommon to fairly common resident and winter visitor. Identified by entirely blue upperparts including the head, entirely white underparts and lack of tail streamers. The call is a twittering 'chip-cheree-chip-chip'. Pairs frequent woodland and human settlements in summer; small flocks often in vleis in winter. Mostly in the drier regions but sparsely distributed throughout its range and present only in summer in many regions, especially the south. 14 cm (Pêrelborsswael)

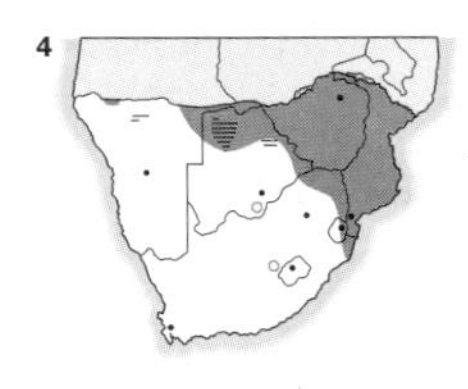

4 GREY-RUMPED SWALLOW *Pseudhirundo griseopyga*

Locally common resident. Grey-brown cap and pale grey rump are diagnostic, but cap not easily seen in flight and rump may appear almost white, then told from House Martin (p. 236) by more deeply forked tail and slender appearance. Utters a grating 'chaa' in flight. Usually in flocks in grassland within woodland, vleis, coastal plains and grassy riverbanks. Nests in ground burrows and may be seen flying in and out of these. It is often more common in the winter months. 14 cm (Gryskruisswael)

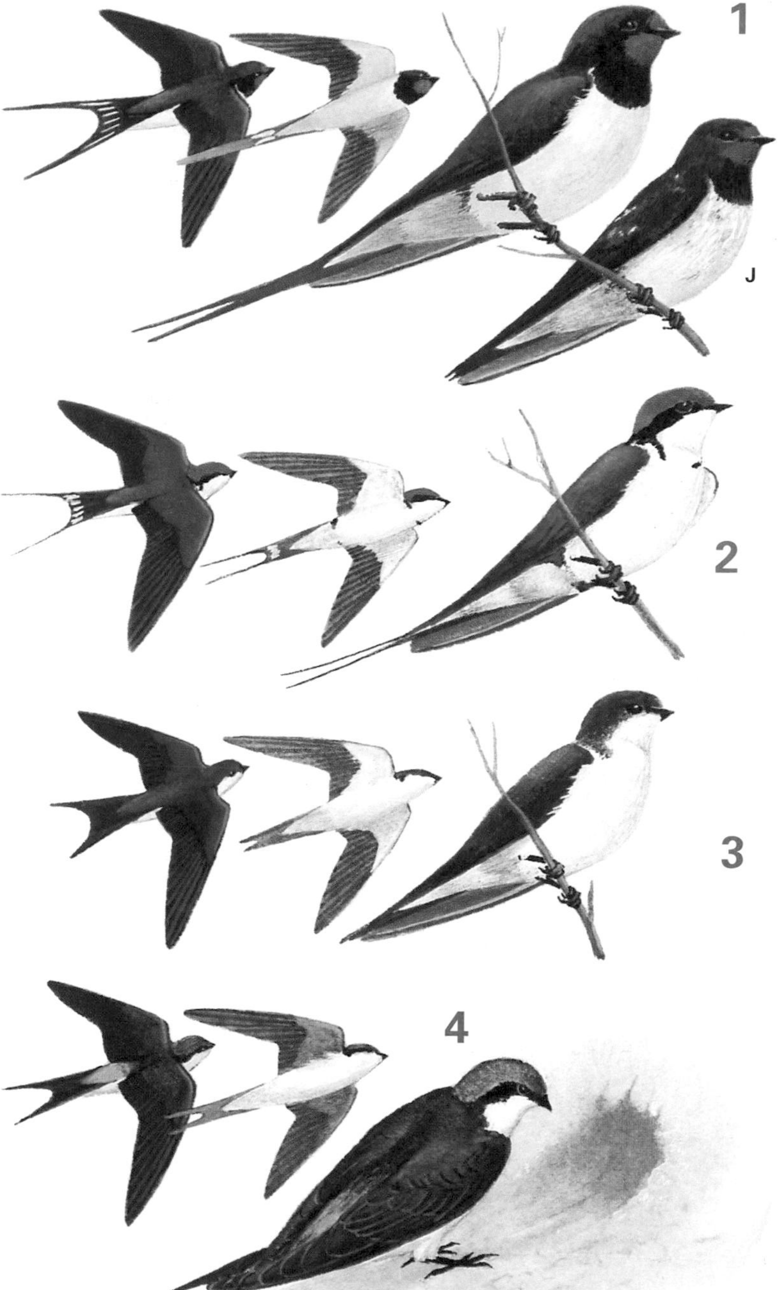

1

J

2

3

4

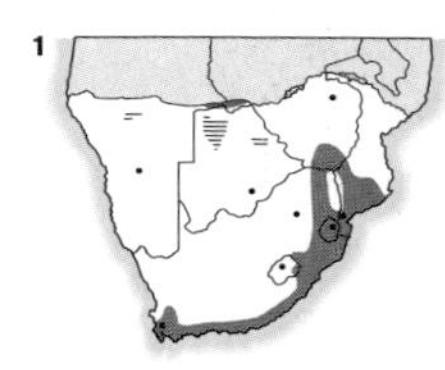

1 BLACK SAW-WING SWALLOW *Psalidoprocne holomelas*

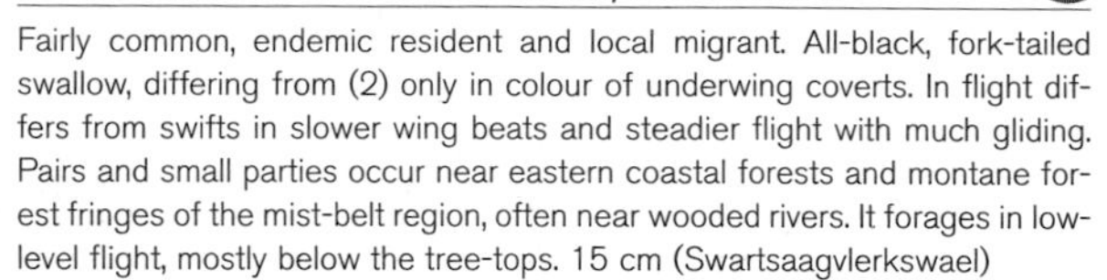

Fairly common, endemic resident and local migrant. All-black, fork-tailed swallow, differing from (2) only in colour of underwing coverts. In flight differs from swifts in slower wing beats and steadier flight with much gliding. Pairs and small parties occur near eastern coastal forests and montane forest fringes of the mist-belt region, often near wooded rivers. It forages in low-level flight, mostly below the tree-tops. 15 cm (Swartsaagvlerkswael)

2 EASTERN SAW-WING SWALLOW *Psalidoprocne orientalis*

Uncommon resident. Identical to (1) except for white or greyish underwing coverts, this feature also distinguishing it from any swift. Habits and habitat as for the Black Saw-wing Swallow (1). 15 cm (Tropiese saagvlerkswael)

WHITE-HEADED SAW-WING SWALLOW (Witkopsaagvlerkswael) see p. 450.

MARTINS

The name martin is loosely applied to certain species of swallow: generally, but not exclusively, those with brown plumage and square tails. Some martins build typical swallow-type mud nests, others breed in holes in banks.

3 (EUROPEAN) SAND MARTIN *Riparia riparia*

Uncommon to locally common summer visitor. A small martin differing from the larger Banded Martin (overleaf) in smaller size, all-dark underwings and lack of a white eyebrow. Flocks usually occur near large inland waters or river estuaries and other eastern coastal localities, but may occur anywhere with flocks of other swallows. 12 cm (Europese oewerswael)

4 MASCARENE MARTIN *Phedina borbonica*

Uncommon winter visitor. In flight differs from other martins in having streaked underparts and very dark upperparts; cf. martins overleaf. Small flocks occur occasionally over open woodland in Mozambique. An erratic visitor from Madagascar. 13 cm (Gestreepte kransswael)

1
2
3
4

1
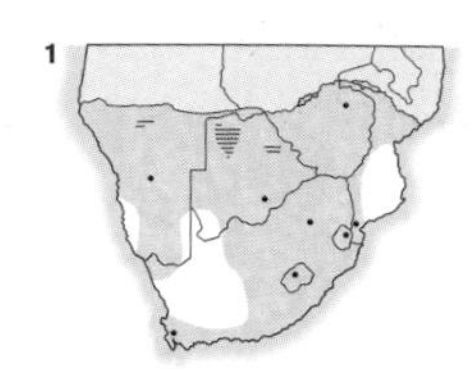

1 HOUSE MARTIN *Delichon urbica*

Common summer visitor. The only martin with blue upperparts, *white rump* and white underparts. Immature (with off-white rump) told from Grey-rumped Swallow (p. 232) by *blue cap* (not grey-brown) and only slightly forked tail. The call is a single 'chirrup'. Flocks occur anywhere, often associating with European Swallows (p. 232), from which it can be told in the air by smaller, more compact appearance, squarer tail and white rump. Flocks habitually forage at high altitudes. 14 cm (Huisswael)

2
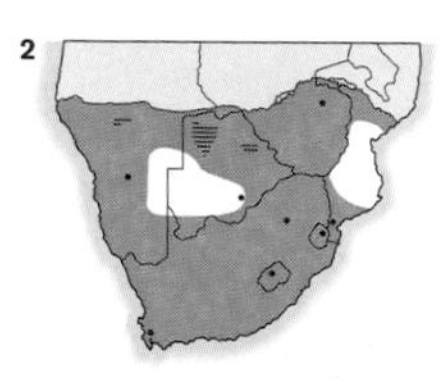

2 BROWN-THROATED MARTIN *Riparia paludicola*

Locally common resident. A small, almost entirely brown martin except for white belly; see (a). Sometimes occurs with entirely brown underparts (b); then told from (4) by lack of 'windows' in the tail and by more slender appearance. The call is a soft twittering. Flocks forage over rivers with sandy banks (in which it breeds), estuaries and other wetlands, roosting in reed-beds when not breeding. 13 cm (Afrikaanse oewerswael)

3
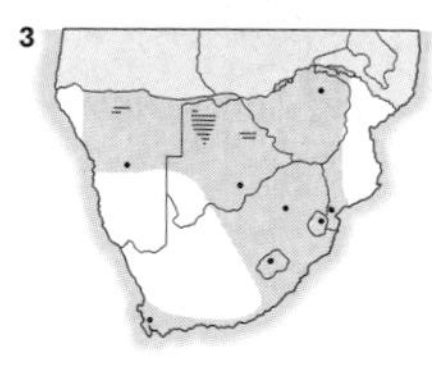

3 BANDED MARTIN *Riparia cincta*

Uncommon to locally common summer resident; occurs all year in northern Botswana and the Zululand coastal plains. Differs from Sand Martin (previous page) in broad breast-band, white eyebrow and square tail. Utters a melodious twittering while perched or flying. Flocks forage over grassland near water, breeding in riverbanks and termite mounds. The flight is slow and leisurely, the birds alighting frequently on a branch or fence to rest. 17 cm (Gebande oewerswael)

4
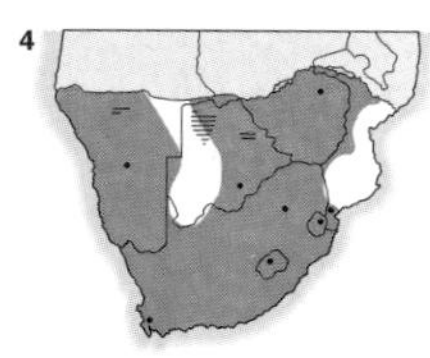

4 ROCK MARTIN *Hirundo fuligula*

Common resident. A stocky martin, told in flight by *broad wings and white 'windows'* in the fanned tail. Utters a melodious twitter. Pairs and small flocks frequent rocky cliffs, bridges, dam walls and tall buildings, often associating with other swallows and swifts. The flight is slow, with much gliding, twisting and turning. 15 cm (Kransswael)

1
J
2
a
b
3
4

SWALLOWS AND MARTINS

Swallows and martins can perch.

Swallows and martins have wider, comparatively more rounded wings than swifts.

Swallows are blue on their upperparts and white or orange, sometimes streaked or spotted, on their underparts.

Swallows may have orange caps, foreheads or throats, and buff or orange rumps.

Martins are brown, the underparts usually paler.

The House Martin is the exception, since it has the appearance of a swallow with a white rump.

Martins have squarish tails, many with white 'windows' in them, visible when the tail is fanned.

Swallows have forked tails, often with long streamers on the outer feathers; they frequently have 'windows' in the tail.

Swallows glide frequently between bouts of flapping flight.

COMPARED WITH SWIFTS

Swifts cannot perch.

The wings of a swift are slender and scimitar-like, and appear to sweep straight back from the body with little obvious bend at the carpal joint.

Swifts are dark grey-brown, blackish or ash-brown, and mostly appear all-dark in flight.

Swifts may have whitish throats and white rumps, but no bright colours.

Swifts may have square or forked tails; in our region only the Palm Swift has tail streamers.

Only the large Alpine Swift and the small Böhm's Spinetail have white on the belly.

Swifts sometimes fly with their wings steeply angled upwards while gliding.

Most swifts fly very rapidly with only brief gliding spells, and may flutter their wings briefly.

SWIFTS

Family APODIDAE. All-dark appearance, some with white markings. No sexual differences; immatures like adults. Entirely aerial in habits; they feed on airborne insects, never intentionally settling on the ground or a perch, only clinging to vertical surfaces or scrambling into crevices. Their calls are high-pitched screams. See previous page for comparison with swallows.

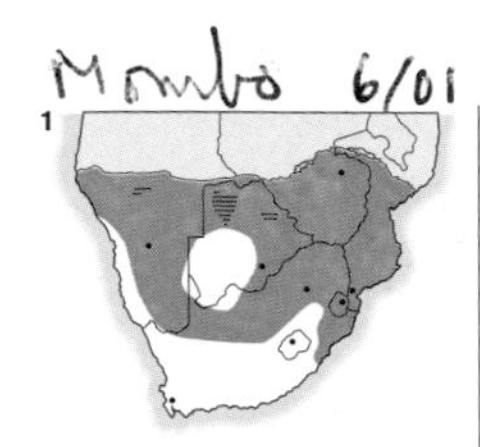

1 PALM SWIFT *Cypsiurus parvus*

Common resident. The most slender, long-tailed swift; entirely grey-brown. Usually in flocks, flying rapidly around tall palm trees where they roost and nest, less commonly under bridges and eaves of buildings. May mix with other swifts when feeding, but slim build diagnostic. 17 cm (Palmwindswael)

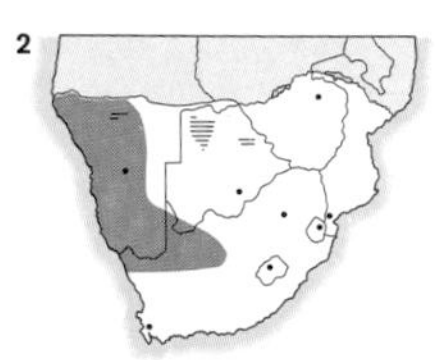

2 BRADFIELD'S SWIFT *Apus bradfieldi*

Common, near endemic resident. Similar to Eurasian and Black Swifts (overleaf) but body and underwing coverts paler, contrasting with the darker primaries and tail, these features apparent when seen flying in company with all-dark swifts. Flocks occur in the dry west, especially in the montane regions of Namibia, in summer, and in rocky gorges of the western Orange River; at other times singly or in small flocks away from mountains and gorges. 18 cm (Muiskleurwindswael)

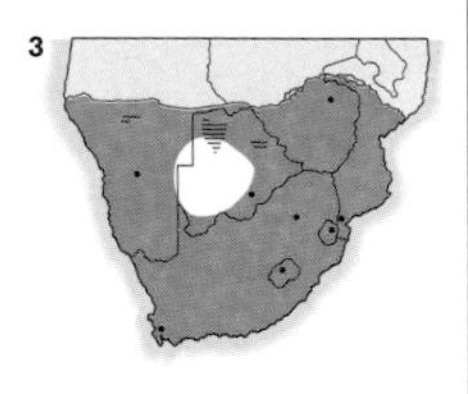

3 LITTLE SWIFT *Apus affinis*

Very common resident. Large white rump, which *curls around the sides of the body,* and square tail distinguish this species from all but the Mottled Spinetail (overleaf), from which it is told by *clear white throat.* Wings rather less pointed than other swifts. Often flies with its wings angled steeply upwards, tail fanned. A noisy species, flocks making a high-pitched screaming in flight. During the day feeds in flocks well away from its roosts and regularly mixes with other swifts or swallows. Very common in towns where it roosts and breeds under eaves and bridges, on silos and tall buildings. 14 cm (Kleinwindswael)

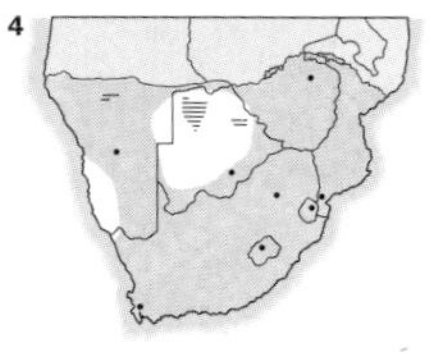

4 WHITE-RUMPED SWIFT *Apus caffer*

Very common summer resident. Most easily confused with (5), but has a slimmer build, more deeply forked tail and *thin white crescent on the rump* which does *not* extend over the sides of the body. Occurs in pairs anywhere except the most arid regions; common in suburbia, frequently occupying swallows' nests attached to buildings. 15 cm (Witkruiswindswael)

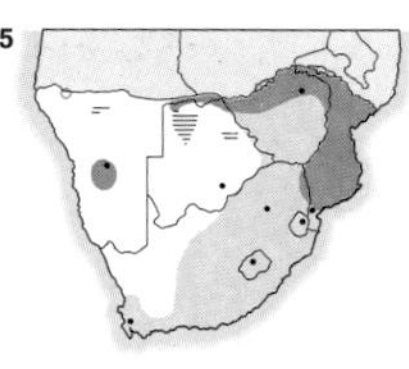

5 HORUS SWIFT *Apus horus*

Uncommon resident and summer visitor. Differs from (4) in stouter appearance, less deeply forked tail and large white rump-patch which extends to the sides of the body. Small flocks occur near riverbanks, sandbanks, quarries and cuttings where they breed and roost in holes in the banks; on the Zululand coast and Zambezi Valley in winter. 17 cm (Horuswindswael)

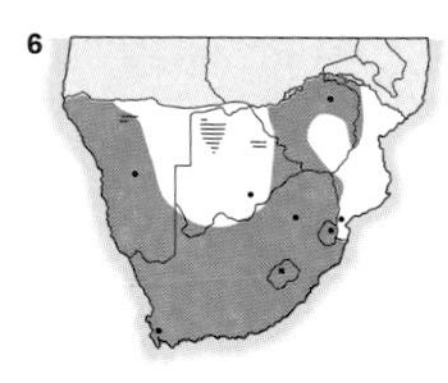

6 ALPINE SWIFT *Apus melba*

Common resident and summer visitor. Large size plus white throat and belly distinguish this from all other swifts. Seen mostly near high cliffs where it breeds and roosts, but also ranges far afield and at great height during the day. Flies with great power and speed, making an audible swishing sound. 22 cm (Witpenswindswael)

1
2
3
4
5
6

1 SCARCE SWIFT *Schoutedenapus myoptilus*

Rare, localised resident. Has no distinct markings. A light brown, fork-tailed swift, chin slightly paler than rest of its underparts. Groups and flocks occur near the rocky mountains and hills of eastern Zimbabwe above about 1 200 m, breeding and roosting in fissures in inaccessible cliffs. 17 cm (Skaarswindswael)

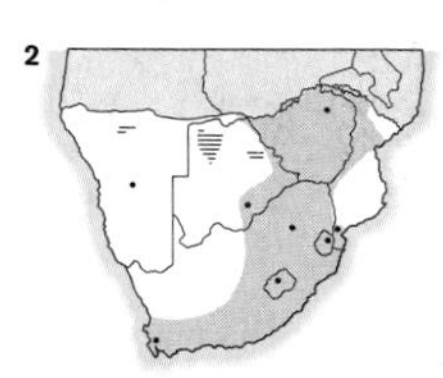

2 BLACK SWIFT *Apus barbatus*

Common summer resident. Fairly large, all-dark swift closely similar to the Eurasian Swift (3); identification very difficult but, from above, has marked contrast between paler inner secondaries and the dark back. From below its tail appears more deeply forked than in (3). Flocks are often seen flying in the vicinity of their roosts in mountain cliffs, especially in the late afternoon in summer. Unknown in Namibia, north-western Cape and Botswana (except for the extreme south-west). 19 cm (Swartwindswael)

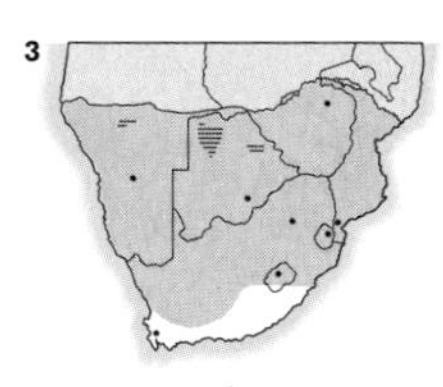

3 EURASIAN or EUROPEAN SWIFT *Apus apus*

Common summer visitor. All-blackish, differing from (2) in *uniform upperparts* (no contrast between inner secondaries and body); from below closely similar but tail less deeply forked; darker than Bradfield's Swift (previous page). In flight extremely difficult to separate from either Bradfield's Swift or Black Swift unless under optimum light conditions. Widespread in flocks November-February, always flying, often following thunderstorms; no known roosts. 18 cm (Europese windswael)

4 PALLID SWIFT *Apus pallidus*

Status uncertain. One specimen from Kuruman dated 1904. A pale swift with white throat and forked tail. Probably flies with flocks of other swifts and could be more regular than the single record suggests. 18 cm (Bruinwindswael)

5 MOTTLED SWIFT *Apus aequatorialis*

Fairly common, localised resident. A large, dark swift with mottled body and pale throat. Flocks occur near rocky cliffs in montane and hilly regions of Zimbabwe, breeding and roosting there during summer, ranging more widely at other times. Flies with great power and speed. 20 cm (Bontwindswael)

6 MOTTLED SPINETAIL *Telecanthura ussheri*

Uncommon, localised resident. A square-tailed, white-rumped swift similar to Little Swift (previous page), but with pale (not white) throat and upper breast and small white patches near the feet. Projecting tail-feather shafts not a field feature. Pairs and small parties frequent river valleys, broad-leaved woodland and forest fringes in the north-east, normally in association with baobab trees, breeding and roosting in tree cavities. Sparsely distributed. 14 cm (Gevlekte stekelstert)

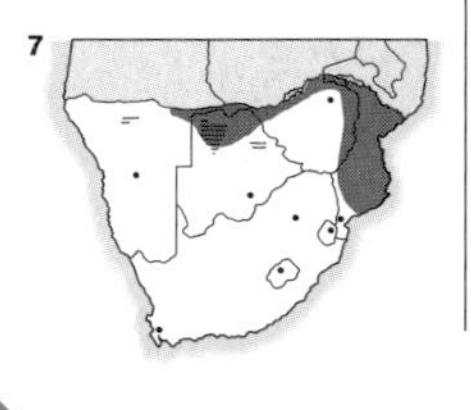

7 BÖHM'S SPINETAIL *Neafrapus boehmi*

Uncommon, localised resident. A small, distinctive swift with white underparts, white rump and *tailless* appearance. Pairs and small parties are found in dry broad-leaved woodland with baobab trees, usually near rivers and lowland valley forests. Flight is fluttering, bat-like and erratic. Breeds and roosts in hollow baobab trees and holes in the ground. 10 cm (Witpensstekelstert)

1
3
2
4
6
5
7

1

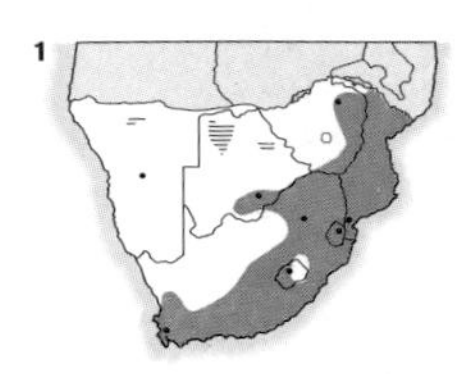

2

3

4

5

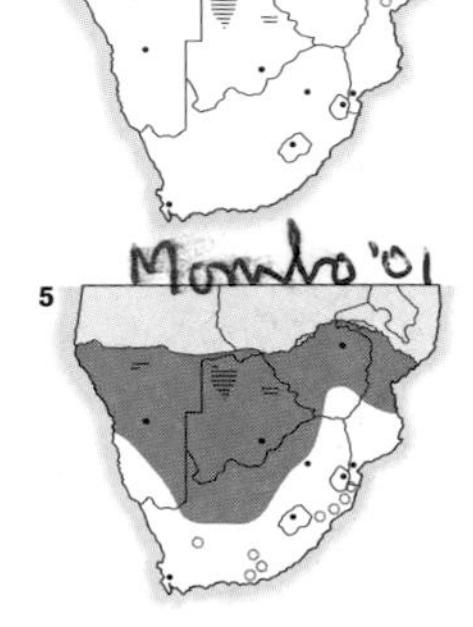

MOUSEBIRDS

Family COLIIDAE. Fruit-eating birds with crested heads, soft, hair-like plumage and long stiff tails. Usually in parties of about a dozen birds which maintain contact by call. When feeding they clamber, mouse-like, about bushes. Immatures resemble adults, but are duller, shorter-tailed.

1 SPECKLED MOUSEBIRD *Colius striatus*

Common resident. Identified by dull brown colouring and bill; black upper mandible, white lower mandible. The call is a rasping 'zwit-wit'. Flocks, which *fly in straggling groups,* frequent dense bush, scrub, forest fringes and suburbia in the moister regions. 30-35 cm (Gevlekte muisvoël)

2 WHITE-BACKED MOUSEBIRD *Colius colius* E

Common endemic resident. Identified by pale grey upperparts, buff underparts, white back (visible in flight only) and *whitish bill with black tip* to upper mandible. The call is 'zwee, wewit'. In flocks in thornveld, riverine bush and suburbia in the drier regions. 30-34 cm (Witkruismuisvoël)

3 RED-FACED MOUSEBIRD *Urocolius indicus*

Common resident. Identified by red facial mask. The call is a descending whistle 'tree-ree-ree', frequently repeated and uttered in flight as well as at rest. Flocks, which *fly in compact groups,* occur in thornveld, riverine forests and especially suburbia, favouring the moister regions. 32-4 cm (Rooiwangmuisvoël)

BEE-EATERS

Family MEROPIDAE. Highly coloured, aerial-feeding birds with long decurved bills, many with elongated tail feathers (absent in immatures). Most occur in flocks, catching flying insects while twisting and turning in graceful aerial manoeuvres or by hawking them from a perch in short aerial sallies, usually returning to the same branch or wire to eat their prey. Immatures are dull versions of the adults.

4 BÖHM'S BEE-EATER *Merops boehmi*

Uncommon, localised resident. Distinguished from the much larger Olive Bee-eater (overleaf) by rich *russet* cap (not dull olive-brown) and rich green colouring overall. The call is a chirping 'swee' plus a liquid trill. Small flocks occur near riverine forests, on the edges of dense thickets and in woodland clearings; sometimes hawks from a perch within the forest-fringe canopy. 21 cm (Roeskopbyvreter)

5 SWALLOW-TAILED BEE-EATER *Merops hirundineus*

Common resident. A small, fork-tailed bee-eater told from Little Bee-eater (overleaf) by bright blue collar and bluish underparts and tail. Immature lacks the yellow and blue throat, underparts pale apple green as illustrated. The call is a soft 'kwit kwit'. Flocks occur in a variety of woodland habitats, being especially common in the regions of Kalahari sands. Hawks from a perch, often near pans and dry riverbeds. Nomadic when not breeding. 20-22 cm (Swaelstertbyvreter)

Mombo 6/01

1
2
3
4
5
J

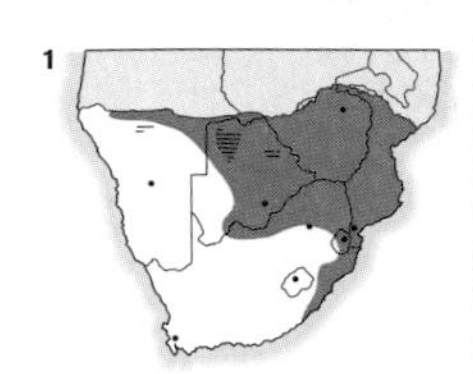

1 LITTLE BEE-EATER *Merops pusillus*

Common resident. Identified by small size, yellow throat, orange-buff underparts and squarish tail. Immature lacks the black collar and has pale green underparts. The call is a quiet 'chip, chip, trree-trree-trree'. In pairs or groups near rivers and in open areas in any woodland or thornveld, usually perching on some low branch or fence-strand from where they hawk. 17 cm (Kleinbyvreter)

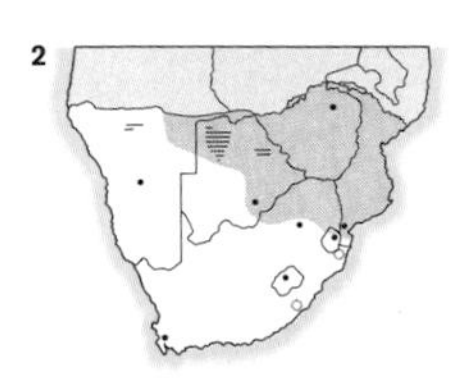

2 CARMINE BEE-EATER *Merops nubicoides*

Common summer resident and visitor. Immature has brown upperparts and pale cinnamon underparts with traces of pink. Individuals call a deep 'terk, terk'; flocks twitter. Flocks occur near large rivers, marshes, in woodland and mixed bushveld where they hawk from trees and from the ground. 33-8 cm (Rooiborsbyvreter)

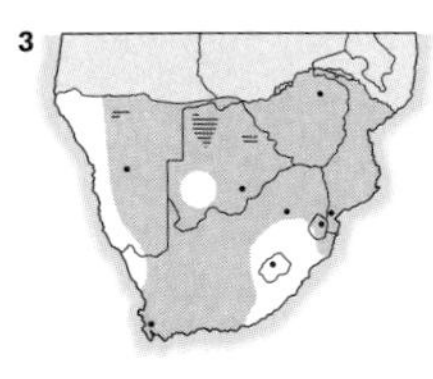

3 EUROPEAN or GOLDEN-BACKED BEE-EATER *Merops apiaster*

Common resident and summer visitor. Identified by golden-brown mantle, turquoise-blue forehead and underparts, plus yellow throat. The call in flight is diagnostic, a clear, liquid 'quilp' or 'kwirry'. Occurs in flocks anywhere, often mixing with other bee-eaters or perching on roadside telephone wires. Frequently flies at great height. 25-9 cm (Europese byvreter)

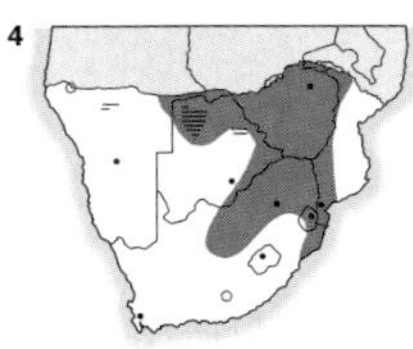

4 WHITE-FRONTED BEE-EATER *Merops bullockoides*

Common resident. Identified by white forehead and upper throat, plus red lower throat. The call is a querulous 'quirk' and other similar sounds. It occurs in flocks near rivers, often mixing with other bee-eaters. 22-4 cm (Rooikeelbyvreter)

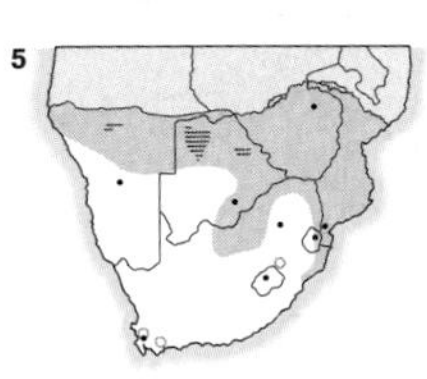

5 BLUE-CHEEKED BEE-EATER *Merops persicus*

Uncommon to locally common summer visitor. Distinguished from (6) by *pale blue forehead, eyebrows and cheeks,* plus yellow and brown throat and upper breast; a large bee-eater of generally green appearance. The short liquid call is 'prruik' or 'prree-oo, prree-oo'. Usually in small flocks near large rivers, floodpans, swamps and coastal grassland where it often hawks from a dead tree standing in water. 27-33 cm (Blouwangbyvreter)

6 OLIVE BEE-EATER *Merops superciliosus*

Uncommon summer visitor. Distinguished from (5) by *olive-brown cap,* all-brown throat and uniformly pale green underparts; from Böhm's Bee-eater (previous page) by large size, olive-brown (not russet) cap and paler green underparts. The call is similar to that of (5). Usually in small flocks in north-western Namibia, the Victoria Falls and Chobe River region and the middle Zambezi Valley, but far-ranging and may occur temporarily elsewhere. 29-33 cm (Olyfbyvreter)

WHITE-THROATED BEE-EATER (Witkeelbyvreter) see p. 450.

1
2
3
4
5
6

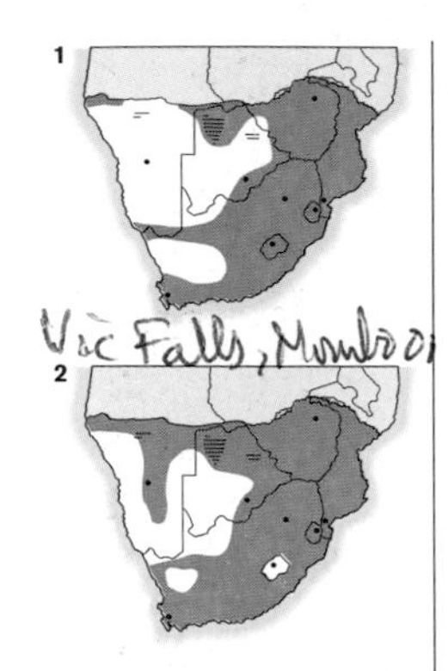

KINGFISHERS

Family HALCYONIDAE. Fish-eating or insect-eating birds with short legs and dagger-like bills. The fish-eating species plunge-dive for their food from a perch or, in some cases, after hovering. Fish are beaten into immobility before being swallowed. The insectivorous species hunt from a low branch, watching for and seizing insects on the ground. They breed in holes in banks or trees. Immatures resemble adults but are duller.

1 GIANT KINGFISHER *Ceryle maxima*

Common resident. Much larger than (2), the sexes differing as illustrated. The call is a raucous 'kek-kek-kek-kek-kek'. Singly or in pairs near wooded rivers, wooded dams and coastal lagoons. Perches on a branch, bridge or wire from where it watches the water; sometimes hovers briefly before plunge-diving. 43-6 cm (Reusevisvanger)

2 PIED KINGFISHER *Ceryle rudis*

Common resident. A large kingfisher but smaller than (1). Entirely black and white, the sexes differing as illustrated. The call is a high-pitched twittering, often by two or more birds at the same time. In pairs or small family parties inland on rivers, lakes, streams, dams and at coastal lagoons, estuaries and shoreline rock pools. Habitually hovers over water while fishing, then plunge-dives to seize prey. 28-9 cm (Bontvisvanger) Mombo 6/01

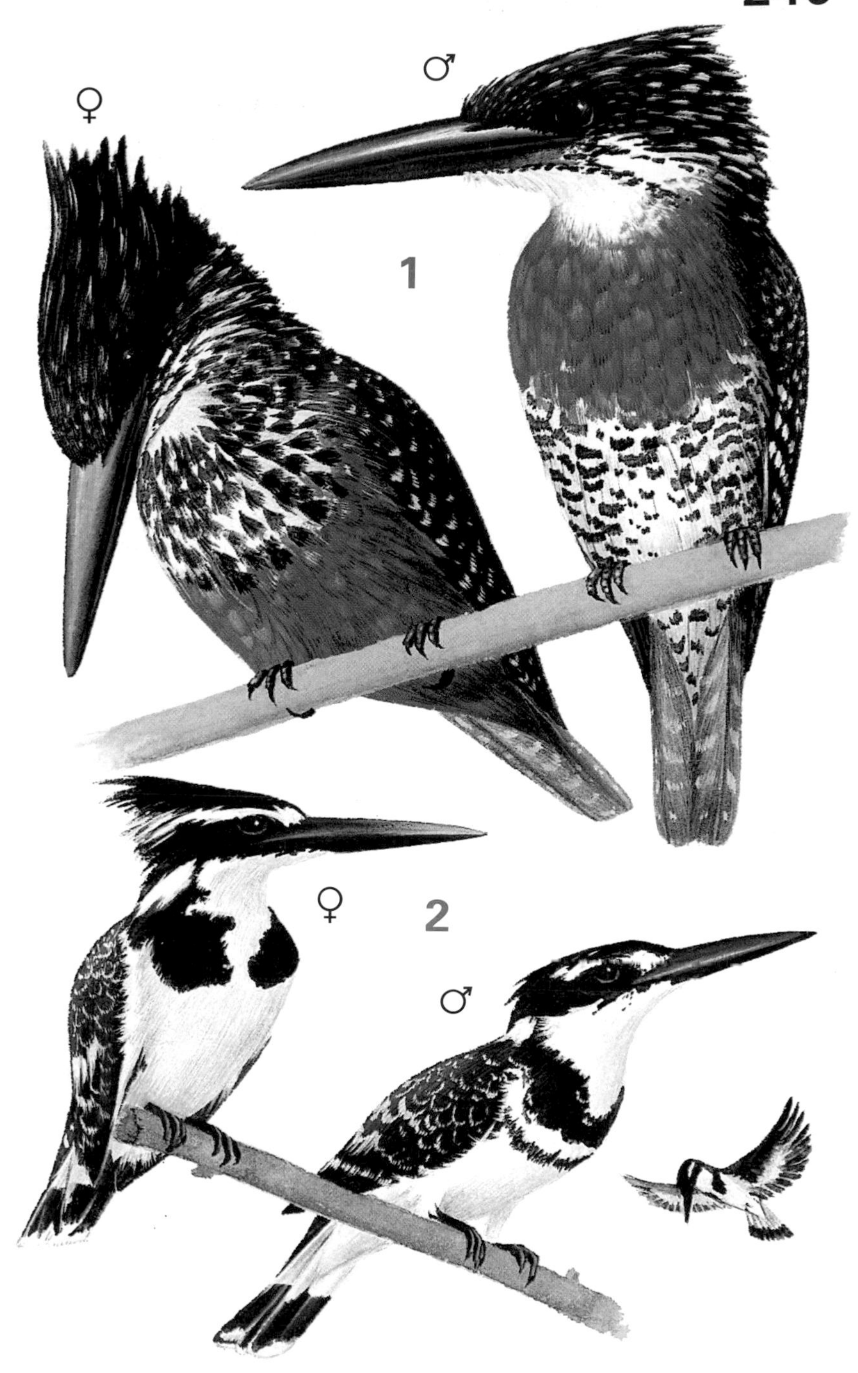
♀
♂
1
♀
2
♂

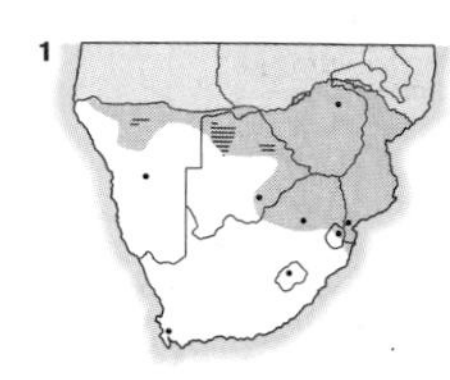

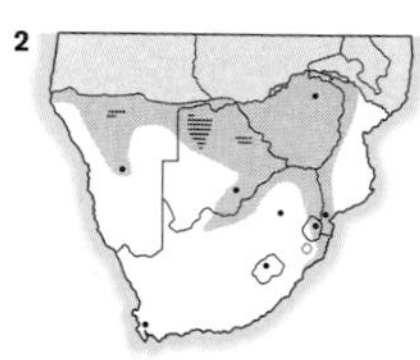

1 WOODLAND KINGFISHER *Halcyon senegalensis*

Common summer resident. Differs from (3) in having a red and black bill, whiter head and black patch from bill to ear coverts. Immature usually has *all-red bill,* sometimes with a black tip; then told from (3) by eye-stripe and blue (not grey) crown. Male calls continuously after arrival and until breeding is finished, a loud 'yimp-trrrrrrrrrrrrrrrrrrr', the last part drawn out and descending. Present October-April, occasionally later, in mixed bushveld and riverine or swamp-fringing woodland, singly or in pairs. Catches insects on the ground by still-hunting from a perch. Pairs greet each other with spread wings. 23-4 cm (Bosveldvisvanger)

2 GREY-HOODED or CHESTNUT-BELLIED KINGFISHER *Halcyon leucocephala*

Uncommon to locally common summer resident and visitor. Identified by grey head and mantle plus chestnut belly; cf. Brown-hooded Kingfisher (overleaf). Not very vocal, the call a weak, descending 'chi-chi-chi-chi'. An insectivorous kingfisher, found singly or in pairs in woodland or mixed bushveld September-April. Occasionally catches fish. 20 cm (Gryskopvisvanger)

3 MANGROVE KINGFISHER *Halcyon senegaloides*

Uncommon resident. Differs from the Woodland Kingfisher (1) in completely red bill and *greyish crown* and mantle. At the coast the call is a raucous 'tchit-tchoo, tcha-tcha-tcha-tch-tch-tch', ending in a trill and performed with raised wings; inland the call is a quieter 'cling-cling-cling-cling ...' with the bill pointed upwards. Singly or in pairs in mangroves at coastal estuaries, mainly during winter, or on major lowland rivers within 20 km of the coast, in bushveld during summer. Very sparsely distributed on the coast in the south, commoner in the Beira region; inland records few. 23-4 cm (Manglietvisvanger)

1
J
2
3

Vic Falls '01

Vic Falls 6/01

1
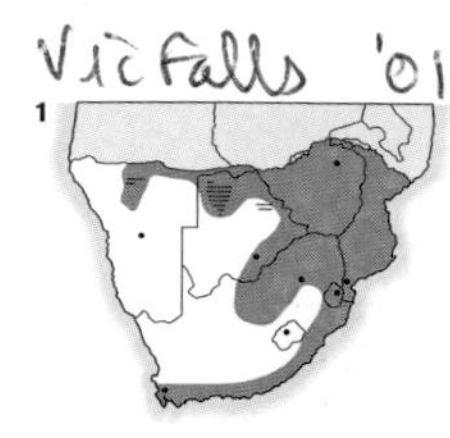

2
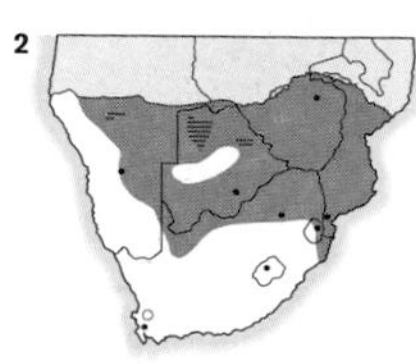

3
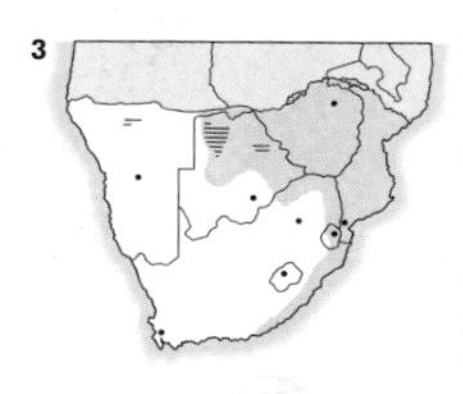

4
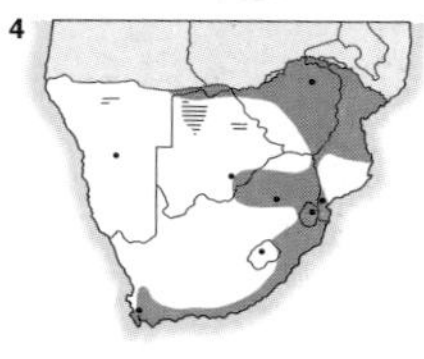

5
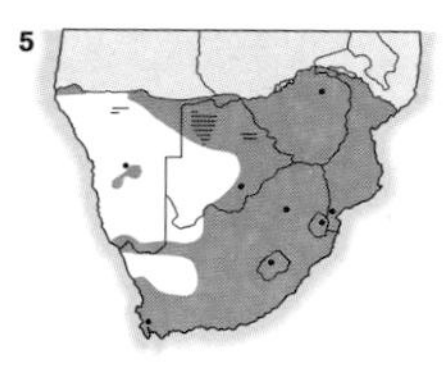

1 BROWN-HOODED KINGFISHER *Halcyon albiventris*

Common resident. Told from Grey-hooded Kingfisher (previous page) by larger size and streaked brown head, streaked buffy breast and flanks, female with brown (not black) wings and shoulders; from the Striped Kingfisher (2) also by larger size, larger, heavier bill, less obvious black eye-stripes and buffy underparts; in flight by *bright blue back and rump.* The call is a loud, *descending* 'kik-kik-kik-kik'. Usually singly in mixed bushveld, woodland, riverine forests, suburban parks and gardens. Still-hunts for insects from a low branch normally away from water, but will occasionally fish. 23-4 cm (Bruinkopvisvanger)

2 STRIPED KINGFISHER *Halcyon chelicuti*

Fairly common resident. A small, sombrely coloured kingfisher, distinguished from the Brown-hooded Kingfisher (1) by smaller size, streaked head, two-coloured bill, bold black eye-stripe extending to the nape and white collar encircling the neck. In flight shows blue upper tail coverts only; male has darker underwings than female. The call is 'tirrrrrr, deeeoo-deeeoo-deeeoo', by a pair calling in duet while performing a wing-opening display. Most often heard in the evening when several individuals may call from scattered points. Pairs in mixed bushveld and woodland, generally perched high on an outer branch far from water. 18-19 cm (Gestreepte visvanger)

3 PYGMY KINGFISHER *Ispidina picta*

Fairly common summer resident. Very similar to (5) but has mauve wash on ear coverts; crown colour is the same blue as rest of upperparts (not turquoise) and does not reach the eyes. Has no territorial call but utters a 'chip' sound in flight. Singly in a wide variety of wooded habitats from sea level to about 1 350 m, usually away from water. Still-hunts from a low perch, catching insects on the ground. Sparsely distributed. 13 cm (Dwergvisvanger)

4 HALF-COLLARED KINGFISHER *Alcedo semitorquata*

Uncommon resident. Identified by black bill, entirely bright blue upperparts and cinnamon lower breast and belly. Calls a shrill 'teep' or 'seek-seek'. Singly on small, heavily wooded inland waters and well-wooded estuaries. A fish-eater, perching low down over the water. Sparse. 20 cm (Blouvisvanger)

5 MALACHITE KINGFISHER *Alcedo cristata*

Common resident. Differs from (3) in having a *turquoise cap which reaches the eyes* and no mauve on the ear coverts. Immature has a black bill and duller plumage; see illustration and cf. (4). When flushed utters a shrill 'peep-peep'. Singly on almost any water with fringing vegetation, perching low down on a reed, branch or rock. 14 cm (Kuifkopvisvanger)

1
J
2
3
4
5
J

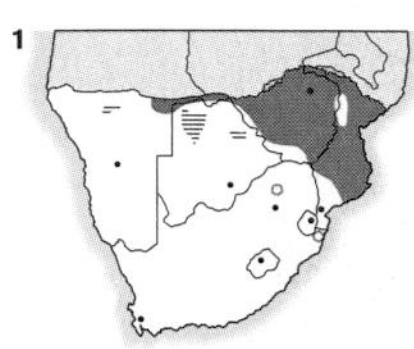

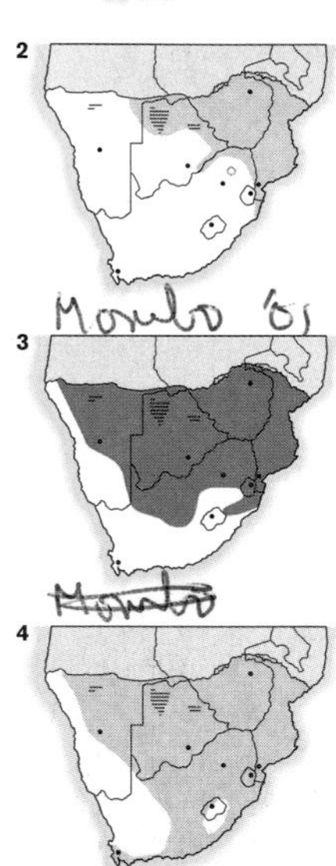

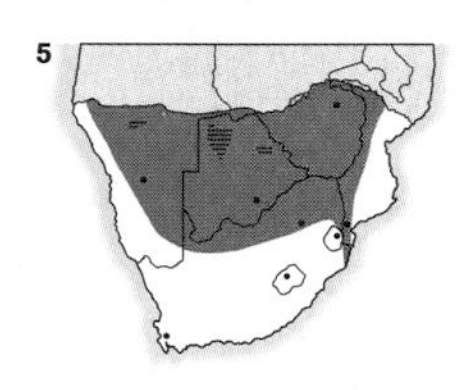

ROLLERS

Family CORACIIDAE. Colourful, heavy-billed birds with brilliant blue wing feathers and harsh, croaking voices. They spend much of the day still-hunting from a convenient perch, flying down to catch and eat large insects and other small prey on the ground. They breed in holes in trees (sometimes in holes in cliffs) and have active display flights, which involve violent aerial manoeuvres with much harsh calling.

1 RACKET-TAILED ROLLER *Coracias spatulata*

Uncommon visitor and resident. Identified by plain blue underparts and spatulate tips to the tail-shafts; cf. (3) and (4). Immature lacks elongated tail feathers and is more lilac on cheeks and sides of breast, but differs from immature of (4) in deep blue primary wing coverts (not greenish-blue) and generally browner upperparts. Has a high-pitched cackling call. Singly or in pairs in well-developed broad-leaved woodland. Sparse and irregular south of the Limpopo River. 36 cm (Knopsterttroupant)

2 BROAD-BILLED or CINNAMON ROLLER *Eurystomus glaucurus*

Fairly common summer resident. Cinnamon colour and yellow bill diagnostic. Immature has greenish-blue underparts and duller brown upperparts streaked black. Utters a harsh croaking and various cackling sounds. Singly, in pairs or scattered groups in well-developed riverine forests, broad-leaved woodland and the fringes of lowland forests. 27 cm (Geelbektroupant)

3 LILAC-BREASTED ROLLER *Coracias caudata*

Common resident. The only roller with lilac throat and breast and blue belly, vent and undertail. Tail-shafts are straight, not spatulate as in (1); often absent when moulting. Immature lacks tail-shafts and is duller, browner. Utters various harsh rattling sounds when displaying. Singly or in pairs in grassy regions within broad-leaved woodland and thornveld, preferring less densely wooded regions than (1); often numerous in stunted mopane woodland. A common roadside bird in some areas, perching on telephone wires. 36 cm (Gewone troupant)

4 EUROPEAN ROLLER *Coracias garrulus*

Fairly common summer visitor. Differs from (1) and (3) in lack of tail-shafts. Pale blue over entire head and underparts, rest of upperparts brown, but shows electric blue wings in flight. Mostly silent in southern Africa but sometimes utters a harsh 'rack-kack, kacker'. Singly, often many birds within sight of each other, in woodland, bushveld and even grassland where it perches on power lines. 30-31 cm (Europese troupant)

5 PURPLE ROLLER *Coracias naevia*

Fairly common resident. A large, heavily built roller with a square tail, upperparts olive-green, underparts deep reddish-brown heavily streaked white. Immature is duller. Utters various harsh cackling and cawing sounds and, when displaying, a continuous 'ka-raa-ka-raa-ka-raa ...' as it flies up. Usually singly in any woodland or thornveld. Perches fairly low down and is normally less active than other rollers. Has a rocking display flight in which the wings appear to beat independently, the bird calling as described above. Undergoes seasonal movements in some regions. 36-40 cm (Groottroupant)

1
2
3
4
5

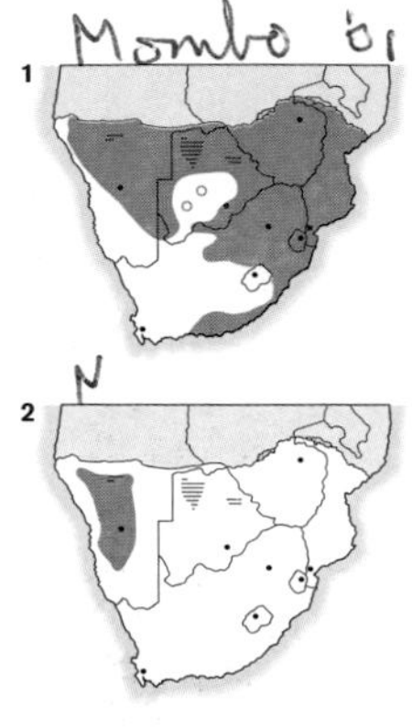

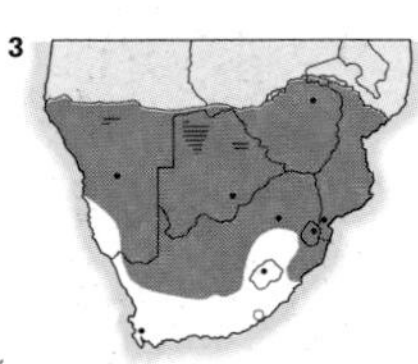

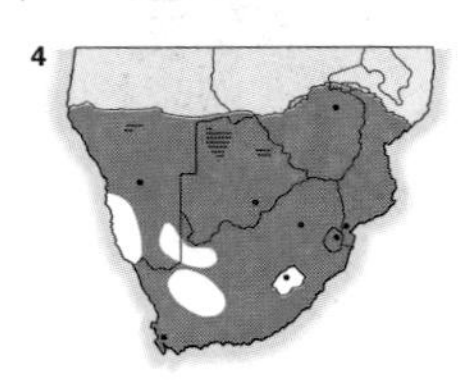

WOOD HOOPOES

Family PHOENICULIDAE. Glossy, dark blue-green birds with long graduated tails, long decurved bills and short legs. They clamber about tree trunks and branches probing with their bills in search of insects. Also investigate the nests of weavers and sparrows in their search for insects and may throw out eggs or small chicks while so doing. They nest in tree cavities.

1 RED-BILLED WOOD HOOPOE *Phoeniculus purpureus*

Common resident. Larger than (3) and with red (not black) bill and feet. Immature has a black bill, but less decurved than that of (3). The call is a high-pitched cackle started by one and taken up by others to produce a cacophony of hysterical cackling similar to but less mechanical-sounding than the call of the Arrow-marked Babbler (p. 310). Occurs in parties of three to eight in woodland or well-wooded suburbia. They fly from tree to tree in straggling procession, settling low down and working their way upwards before flying off to the next tree. 30-36 cm (Gewonekakelaar)

2 VIOLET WOOD HOOPOE *Phoeniculus damarensis*

Fairly common, localised resident. Larger than (1) and more violet-blue, even blackish about the head and mantle; see illustration. Similar in all other respects to (1) and mixing with the western race of that species in northern Namibia. 40-42 cm (Perskakelaar)

3 SCIMITAR-BILLED WOOD HOOPOE *Rhinopomastus cyanomelas*

Fairly common resident. Smaller than (1) and (2), the bill more decurved and black. Female and immature have a brownish throat and breast. Calls during summer 'pwep-pwep-pwep-pwep ...' repeated about 10 times at half-second intervals. Singly or in pairs in dry, well-developed broad-leaved woodland and thornveld. Feeds in large trees, clambering about the outer branches and twigs. Quieter, less conspicuous than (1). 24-8 cm (Swartbekkakelaar)

4 HOOPOE *Upupa epops*

Family UPUPIDAE. Common resident. The crest is normally held down, being raised when the bird is attentive or alarmed. Female and immature are duller than male. Has an undulating, butterfly-like flight, black and white wings then conspicuous. The call is 'hoop-hoop, hoop-hoop-hoop' frequently repeated (cf. call of African Cuckoo, p. 210); young birds being fed by adults call 'sweet, sweet'. Singly or in pairs in any open woodland, bushveld, parks and gardens. Walks about probing the ground with its bill. Seasonal fluctuations occur in some regions. 27 cm (Hoephoep)

1
2
3
4

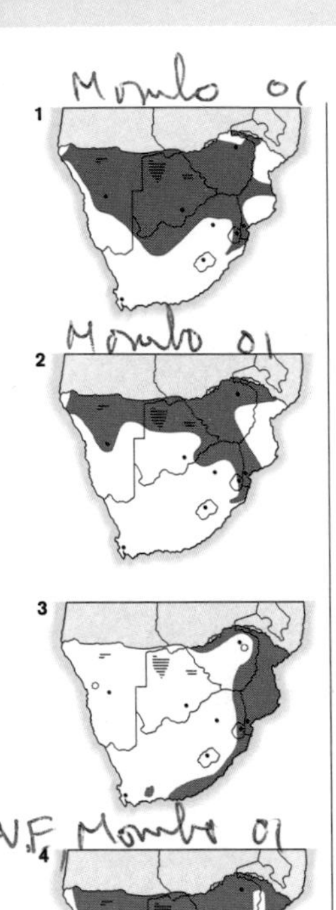

HORNBILLS

Family BUCEROTIDAE. Insectivorous and frugivorous birds with heavy-looking, decurved bills, sometimes with a horny casque on the upper mandible. Arboreal or terrestrial feeders, or both, they nest in holes in trees (among rocks in a few species) and, in most species, the female seals herself in during incubation. Their flight is heavy and undulating with periods of gliding.

1 SOUTHERN YELLOW-BILLED HORNBILL *Tockus leucomelas* 

Common, near endemic resident. Large yellow bill (smaller in female) separates this from all other hornbills. Immature has a duller yellow bill with a reddish base, then told from (2) by the large size of the bill. The call is 'wurk, wurk, wurk, wurk, wurk, wurk, wukwukak, wukwukak, wukak, wukak, wurk, wurk, wurk …', the sound working up to a crescendo then fading away. Often two birds call simultaneously with a wing-opening, head-bowing display. Pairs and small groups in dry bushveld, savanna woodland and thornveld. Feeds on the ground much of the time, also in fruiting trees. 48-60 cm (Geelbekneushoringvoël)

2 RED-BILLED HORNBILL *Tockus erythrorhynchus*

Common resident. Identified by combination of red bill and black and white checkered upperparts; cf. (3) which has plain brown upperparts. Immature has a shorter bill and buff spots on upperparts. The call is similar to that of (1) but is uttered more rapidly, 'wha, wha, wha, wha, wha, wha, kawacha, wacha, wacha, wacha, wacha, wacha …', also rising to a crescendo then fading. Pairs and small flocks frequent dry bushveld, broad-leaved woodland (particularly mopane) and thornveld, preferring drier conditions than (1), but often mixing with it. Forages mostly on open ground and probes actively with its bill. 42-50 cm (Rooibekneushoringvoël)

3 CROWNED HORNBILL *Tockus alboterminatus*

Fairly common resident. Differs from (2) in having a casque on the red bill and entirely dark brown upperparts. Immature has a more orange bill and buff-tipped feathers on the upperparts. The call is a series of melancholy, piping whistles. Singly or in pairs in riverine forest fringes, the canopy and fringes of lowland and coastal forests and well-wooded valleys. Feeds in the trees and roosts conspicuously on high, slender branches. 50-57 cm (Gekroonde neushoringvoël)

4 GREY HORNBILL *Tockus nasutus*

Common resident. The rather small, dark bill of the male is diagnostic; female has a smaller casque, that and the upper mandible creamy, the tip red; cf. Monteiro's and Bradfield's Hornbills (overleaf). Immature has a browner head and indistinct eyebrows; bill of young female is even more creamy. The call is a thin, piping, plaintive series of notes ascending then descending the scale, 'phe, phephee, pheephee, pheeoo, phew, pheeoo-pheeooo …'. Pairs and, in winter, flocks of up to about 30, in dry mixed bushveld, savanna and thornveld. Mainly arboreal. 43-8 cm (Grysneushoringvoël)

1
2
3
♂
4
♀

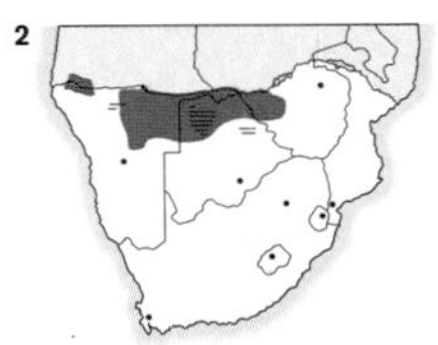

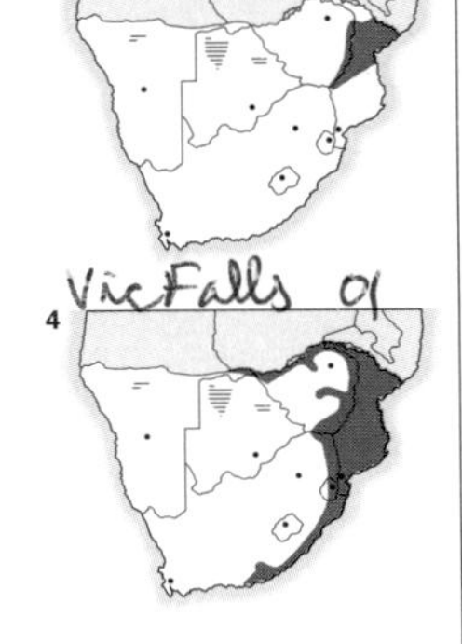

1 MONTEIRO'S HORNBILL *Tockus monteiri* 

Fairly common, near endemic resident. It differs from Bradfield's Hornbill (2) in having white spotting on the upper wing coverts, entirely white outer tail feathers and, when seen in flight, entirely white secondary wing feathers. In the female the facial skin and eye-rings are blue. The call when displaying is a hoarse 'tu-aack tu-aack' while its territorial call is 'kok kok kok kokok kokok kokok ...' rising in volume. Usually seen singly or in pairs in rocky regions (where it breeds) and in dry woodland in northern Namibia, feeding mostly on the ground. 54-8 cm (Monteirose neushoringvoël)

2 BRADFIELD'S HORNBILL *Tockus bradfieldi* 

Uncommon, near endemic resident. Distinguished from Monteiro's Hornbill (1) by entirely brown wings and its outer tail feathers having white tips only; from the Crowned Hornbill (previous page) by an orange (not red) bill which lacks a casque. The call is a series of piping whistles similar to that of the Crowned Hornbill, the call delivered with the bill pointing skywards. It can be found in a variety of habitats but most commonly in broad-leaved and mixed woodland on Kalahari sands in the dry north-western regions. 50-57 cm (Bradfieldse neushoringvoël)

3 SILVERY-CHEEKED HORNBILL *Bycanistes brevis*

Uncommon, localised resident. Identified by large size, pied colouring and heavy yellow bill with large casque. A noisy species, the most common sound a loud braying or growling 'quark-quark-quark'. In pairs or flocks in forests and well-developed riverine forests where trees are fruiting, feeding in the canopy. The wings make an audible soughing in flight. Vulnerable. 75-80 cm (Kuifkopboskraai)

4 TRUMPETER HORNBILL *Bycanistes bucinator*

Common lowland resident. Distinguished from (3) by smaller size, black (not yellow) bill and more white on the underparts. The characteristic call resembles the crying of a baby, a loud and far-carrying 'waaaa-aaa-aaa-aaa-aaaaaa' often uttered by several birds at once. Small flocks frequent well-developed riverine forests, lowland forests and moist woodland, feeding in the canopy of large fruiting trees. 58-65 cm (Gewone boskraai)

1
2
3
♂
♀
4

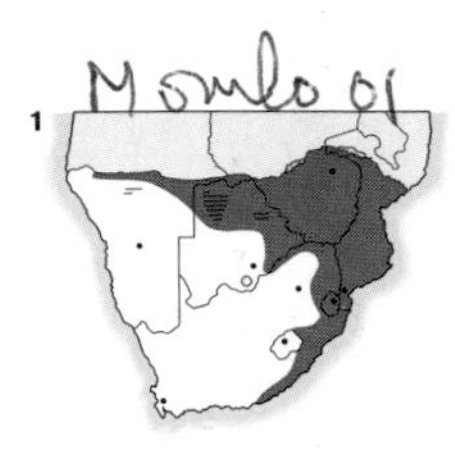

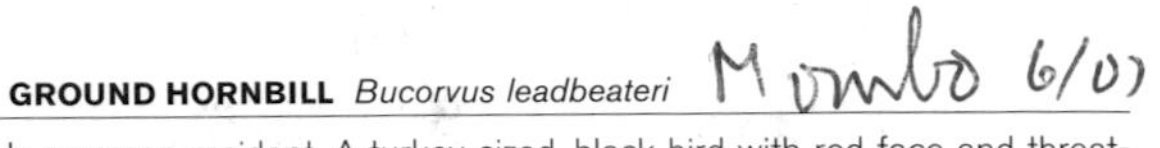

1 GROUND HORNBILL *Bucorvus leadbeateri*

Fairly common resident. A turkey-sized, black bird with red face and throat-pouch. Female has a blue central patch on the pouch. In flight shows white wing feathers. Immature has yellow facial skin and throat-pouch. The call is a deep booming, mostly heard at dawn 'oomph, oomph-oomph' frequently repeated. Usually in groups of four to 10 in bushveld, woodland and montane grassland. Mainly terrestrial, walking slowly in loose array in search of food. Takes off in low flight only if disturbed or when going to roost in a tree. Numbers have decreased in recent years. Vulnerable. 90 cm (Bromvoël)

BARBETS

Family CAPITONIDAE. Stout-billed, robust and often colourful relatives of the woodpeckers, with loud characteristic calls. They feed on fruits and insects and excavate nest-holes in trees. The smaller species are called tinker barbets from the likeness of their calls to the sound of a hammer on an anvil. Immatures are duller versions of the adults.

2 GREEN BARBET *Cryptolybia olivacea woodwardi*

Fairly common, very localised resident. Distinguished from Green Tinker Barbet (overleaf) by larger size plus black cap and yellow ear-patch, but their ranges are mutually exclusive. The call is a monotonous 'quop-quop-quop-quop ...'. Found only in the oNgoye Forest, Zululand and beyond our limits to the north. 17 cm (Groenhoutkapper)

3 WHYTE'S BARBET *Stactolaema whytii*

Fairly common, localised resident. Identified by brownish appearance, yellow forecrown and white wing feather edges. Utters a soft 'coo' at about one-second intervals. Small parties of about four birds are found in broad-leaved woodland in the vicinity of fig trees, and in suburbia in Zimbabwe. 18 cm (Geelbleshoutkapper)

4 WHITE-EARED BARBET *Stactolaema leucotis*

Common resident. Identified by pied appearance and prominent white ear-stripe. The common call is a loud 'trreee, trrreetrreetrreetrreetrree', which may be uttered by several birds simultaneously. Usually in noisy, conspicuous groups of two to six in coastal and lowland forest canopies and fringes, riverine forests and moist woodland where fig trees are fruiting. 17 cm (Witoorhoutkapper)

♀
♂
J
1

2
3
4

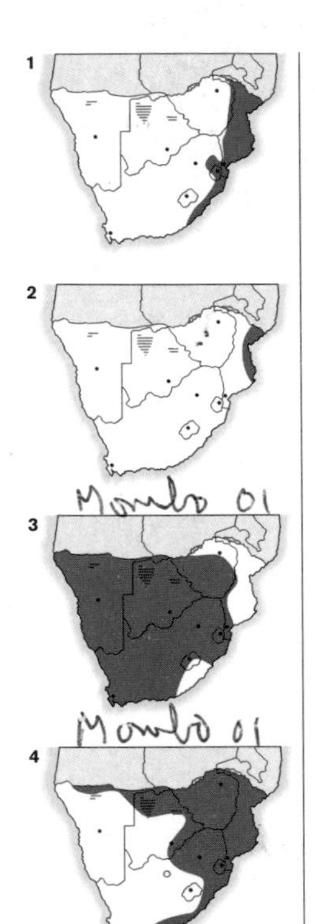

1 GOLDEN-RUMPED TINKER BARBET *Pogoniulus bilineatus*

Common resident. Told by its *black crown and back* plus white stripes on the sides of its head; the throat and upper breast are white shading to pale yellow on the belly while the folded wing shows bold yellow feather-edges. In flight its yellow rump is visible. The immature has yellow-tipped back feathers. The call is 'poop poop poop poop poop' usually in strophes of five or six; also a rapid, higher-pitched 'prrr-prrr-prrr'. An active, noisy species. Occurs in coastal and motane forests (mostly below 1 000 m) plus riverine forests. It frequents the canopy and midstratum singly or in pairs. 10 cm (Swartblestinker)

2 GREEN TINKER BARBET *Pogoniulus simplex*

Status unknown. A small, dull green bird with short heavy bill, pale yellow edges to wing feathers and golden rump. Calls 'pop-op-op-op-op-op', sometimes ending with a trill. A forest canopy species recorded once south of Beira. 10 cm (Groentinker)

3 PIED BARBET *Tricholaema leucomelas* NE

Common, near endemic resident. Differs from Red-fronted Tinker Barbet (overleaf) in larger size and white underparts (eastern race has yellow wash on flanks, no black streaks) and black bib of varying extent. Immature lacks the red forehead. The call is a loud nasal 'peh-peh', less frequently a hoopoe-like 'poop-poop'. Singly or in pairs in a wide range of dry woodland habitats. 17-18 cm (Bonthoutkapper)

4 BLACK-COLLARED BARBET *Lybius torquatus*

Common resident. The only local bird with bright red forehead, face and foreneck and heavy black bill; the tone of red varies regionally. Rarely, yellow replaces the red. Immature has red speckling on black. The call is a loud duet, starting with a whirring 'kerrr-kerrr-kerrr' and then becoming 'too-puddely-too-puddely-too-puddely-too-puddely …' about eight times, the calls usually accompanied by wing-quivering and swaying or bobbing. Also calls 'snaar'. Occurs in pairs or small groups in any broad-leaved woodland including well-wooded suburbia; in the drier regions is mostly restricted to riverine forests. 19-20 cm (Rooikophoutkapper)

5 CRESTED BARBET *Trachyphonus vaillantii*

Common resident. The degree of red scaling on the head is variable and less profuse in the female and immature. The male's call is a distinctive trilling like a muffled alarm clock 'trrrrrr …' which continues sometimes for long periods; louder, slower and of higher pitch when expressing agitation 'kekekekekek …'; female calls 'puta-puta-puta-puta …'. Singly or in pairs in well-wooded savanna, riverine forests and bushveld. Is attracted to fruit in suburban gardens. 23 cm (Kuifkophoutkapper)

1
2
3
4
5

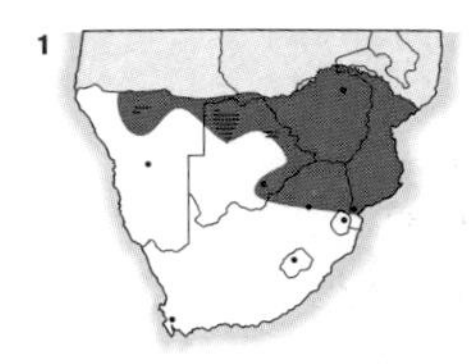
1

1 YELLOW-FRONTED TINKER BARBET *Pogoniulus chrysoconus*

Common resident. Forehead may be yellow or, in the highveld, orange, underparts very pale yellow; cf. (2). Immature has black forehead or traces of yellow. The call is a monotonous 'phoo-phoo-phoo-phoo-phoo ...' uttered for long periods on warm days. Also calls 'dit-dit-dit' in rapid morse-like strophes of three. Occurs in a variety of woodland habitats including riverine forests, mostly in the canopies of large trees. Is greatly attracted to mistletoe-type parasites of the genera *Viscum* and *Loranthus* and may be abundant when these are plentiful. 12 cm (Geelblestinker)

2

2 RED-FRONTED TINKER BARBET *Pogoniulus pusillus*

Common resident. Differs from (1) in *red* forehead and slightly yellower underparts. Immature has black forehead or traces of red. The call is a monotonous 'purp-purp-purp-purp-purp ...' repeated for long periods; also a high-pitched, rapid 'kew-kew-kew-kew ...'. Inhabits coastal and lowland forests, well-wooded riverbanks and valleys where it frequents the tree canopies. 10,5 cm (Rooiblestinker)

WOODPECKERS

Family PICIDAE. Small, robust birds with straight, pointed bills, stiff tails and zygodactylous feet in which the inner and outer toes are directed backward and the two central toes forward. They glean insects and their larvae from within crevices in trees and from beneath bark by tapping with their bills to loosen or chip the wood and inserting their long sticky tongues. While feeding, they use the tail as a prop. They normally occur in pairs and excavate holes in trees for nesting, these frequently being used in turn by other hole-nesting species. Many woodpeckers are very similar in appearance and are best identified by head and breast markings plus call. The aberrant Ground Woodpecker is entirely terrestrial and nests in holes in banks.

3

3 OLIVE WOODPECKER *Mesopicos griseocephalus*

Common resident. The only olive-green woodpecker in southern Africa. The call is a shrill 'chee-wit, chee-wit, chee-wit ...' or 'weer-dit weer-dit weerdit-dit' according to locality. In pairs in both lowland and montane forests and along adjacent forested streams. Feeds mostly in the mid- and upper strata amid moss- and lichen-encrusted branches. Pairs roost nightly in their nest-holes and, during inclement weather, will remain in the hole all day. 18-20 cm (Gryskopspeg)

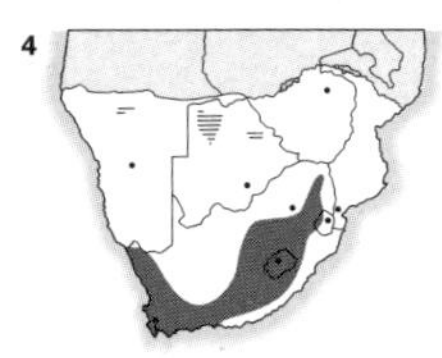
4

4 GROUND WOODPECKER *Geocolaptes olivaceus*

Common endemic resident. The only red-breasted woodpecker in southern Africa, but red colouring often less bold, less extensive than illustrated. Female lacks red moustachial streak. Immature is duller than adult, underparts with little red. Has a loud, harsh call 'kee-urrr, kee-urrr, kee-urrr'. Found in hilly, rock-strewn grassland, mountain slopes and dry gullies. Feeds entirely on the ground among rocks, singly or in small parties, often perching on a prominent rock. 26 cm (Grondspeg)

1
♂
2
3
♀
4

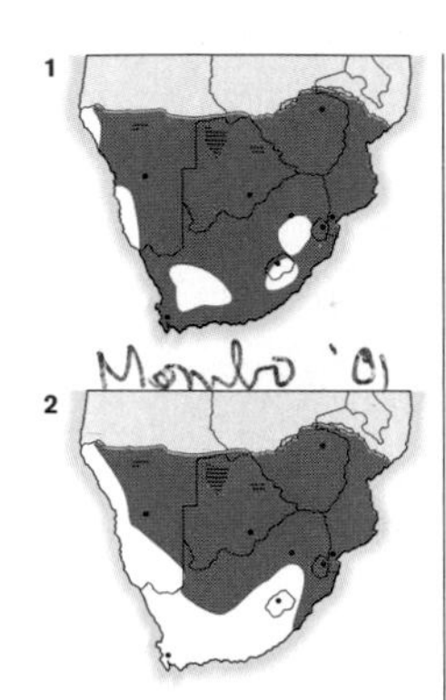

1 CARDINAL WOODPECKER *Dendropicos fuscescens*

Common resident. Identified by small size, *streaked* breast, black moustachial streak and brown forehead in both sexes, male with crimson crown, female with black crown. The call is a high-pitched, chittering 'kekekekekekekek'. In pairs in any broad-leaved woodland, thornveld or riverine bush, often in bird parties and frequently in quite small trees. Taps quietly. 14-16 cm (Kardinaalspeg)

2 GOLDEN-TAILED WOODPECKER *Campethera abingoni*

Common resident. Has streaks on breast but is larger than (1). Male has moustachial streak and entire crown red with black spots; in female these are black with white spots, only the nape being red. The call is a single nasal 'waaa'. Pairs occur in broad-leaved woodland, thornveld and bush fringing dry riverbeds. 20-23 cm (Goudstertspeg)

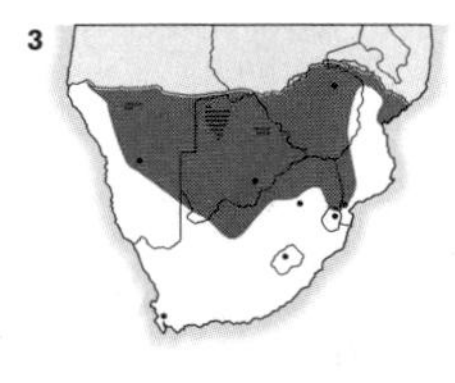

3 BENNETT'S WOODPECKER *Campethera bennettii*

Fairly common resident. A medium-sized woodpecker with spotted underparts (except in Namibia where unspotted). Male is identified by entirely red crown and moustachial streak, female by *brown facial and throat-patches.* The call is an excitable, high-pitched chattering, sometimes by two or three birds together 'whirrwhirrwhirrwhir-it-whir-it-whir-it-wrrrrrrrrr ...', often accompanied by wing-flapping. Usually in pairs or groups in broad-leaved woodland and thornveld, feeding mainly on the ground. 22-4 cm (Bennettse speg)

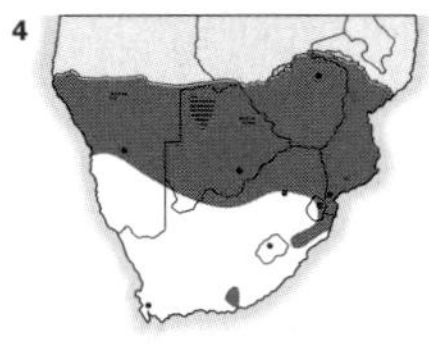

4 BEARDED WOODPECKER *Thripias namaquus*

Common resident. A large, long-billed species with *banded* underparts and a bold black moustachial streak and ear-patch. Male has only the top of the crown red. The call is a loud 'wickwickwick-wick-wick'. The male indulges in bouts of territorial drumming with its bill on a hollow branch; the drumming particularly loud and far-carrying 'trrrrrr-tap-tap-tap-tap-tap'. Singly in any tall woodland and riverine forest. 23-5 cm (Baardspeg)

1
♀
♂
2
♀
♂
3
♀
♂
4
♀
♂

1 LITTLE SPOTTED WOODPECKER *Campethera cailliautii*

Common, localised resident. Recognised by small size and lack of a moustachial streak in both sexes; cf. Cardinal Woodpecker (previous page). The call is a shrill 'hee' repeated about four times. Pairs are found in thick woodland and on the fringes of forests. Taps with a rapid action and feeds on ants. 16 cm (Gevlekte speg)

2 SPECKLE-THROATED WOODPECKER *Campethera scriptoricauda*

Uncommon, localised resident. Male has *unspotted throat;* female differs from female Golden-tailed Woodpecker (previous page) in spotted (not streaked) breast. Calls like Bennett's Woodpecker (previous page). In southern Africa recorded only in woodland between Beira and the Zambezi River in Mozambique. 19 cm (Tanzaniese speg)

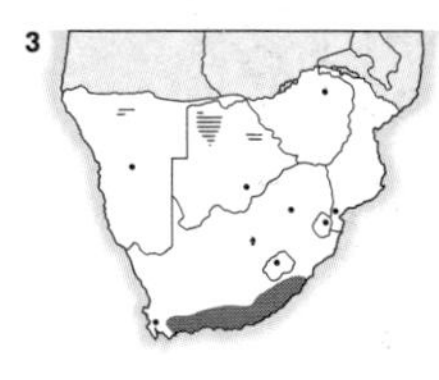

3 KNYSNA WOODPECKER *Campethera notata*

Fairly common, localised endemic resident. Both sexes have *well-spotted underparts* from chin to vent (except in north-easterly distribution where less spotted). Male has red moustachial streak with heavy black spots, like the forecrown. Female has no distinct moustachial streak. The call is 'keeek'. Pairs occur in coastal and valley bush, woodland and forest fringes. 20 cm (Knysnaspeg)

WRYNECKS

Family JYNGIDAE Although related to woodpeckers, wrynecks do not excavate nests but use natural tree cavities or the disused nests of barbets and woodpeckers. They feed on ants and termites.

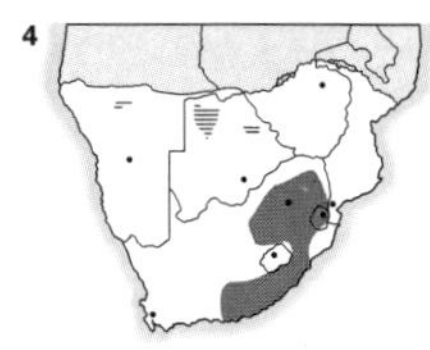

4 RED-THROATED WRYNECK *Jynx ruficollis*

Common, localised resident. Identified by rust-brown patch on throat and upper breast, plus brown-speckled upperparts with blackish broken line from crown to mantle. The call, frequently uttered, is a high-pitched 'kek-kek-kek-kek'. Singly or in pairs in various types of woodland and in suburbia, often in wattle trees (Australian *Acacia* spp.). Creeps about branches like a woodpecker, perches like a passerine or hops about the ground with its tail raised. 18 cm (Draaihals)

1 ♂ ♀

2 ♀ ♂

3 ♀ ♂

4

1

2
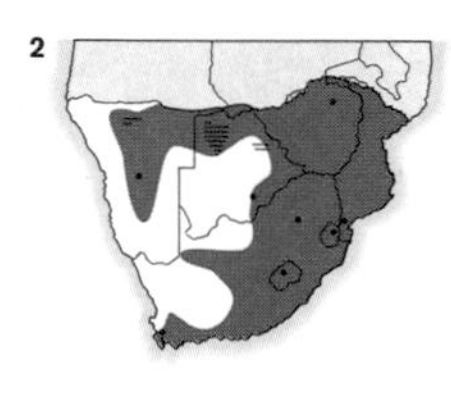

3

4
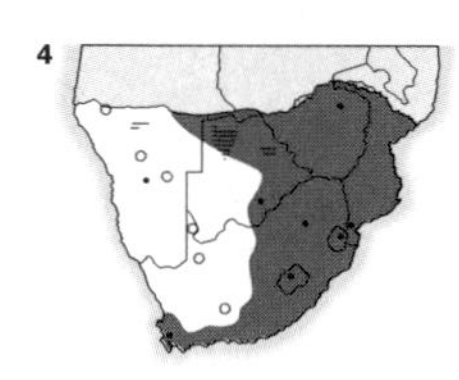

HONEYGUIDES

Family INDICATORIDAE. Small, inconspicuous birds which show *white outer tail feathers in flight.* Some species have distinctive calls and regular call-sites, others have weak, sibilant calls, which are seldom heard. Their food is mostly insects but a few species have developed the habit of leading people to wild bees' nests by continually chattering and fluttering conspicuously in the desired direction; when the bees' nest is broken open the honeyguide feeds on the wax and grubs. Like cuckoos they build no nests but parasitise various other small birds. Immatures are dull versions of the adults.

1 EASTERN HONEYGUIDE *Indicator meliphilus*

Uncommon, localised resident. Resembles (2) but has a stubbier bill and greener upperparts; the underparts have a yellow wash and faint streaking, especially on the throat. Utters a high-pitched whistle plus chattering notes. Occurs sparsely on forest fringes, degraded forest and in woodland, with records from eastern Zimbabwe and Mozambique. Is known to parasitise the White-eared Barbet (p. 262) and Golden-rumped Tinker Barbet (p. 264). 13 cm (Oostelike heuningwyser)

2 LESSER HONEYGUIDE *Indicator minor*

Common resident. Characterised by thick bill with a pale patch at the base and yellow edges to the wing feathers; told from (1) by duller appearance and lack of any streaking on the underparts. Uses a regular call-site from where it calls 'klew, klew, klew ...' in series of 30-40 calls at a time. Occurs singly in various wooded habitats including suburbia. 15 cm (Kleinheuningwyser)

3 SCALY-THROATED HONEYGUIDE *Indicator variegatus*

Fairly common resident. Told by streaky head and scaly breast, usually with yellow wash. Utters a high-pitched 'foyt-foyt-foyt' or, from a call-site, a ventriloquial and purring 'trrrrrrrr', *rising at the end.* A bird of forest fringes, riverine forests and valley bush, usually singly. Has been known to guide to bees' nests, otherwise hawks insects like a flycatcher. 19 cm (Gevlekte heuningwyser)

4 GREATER HONEYGUIDE *Indicator indicator*

Common resident. In both sexes the yellow shoulder-patch is frequently vestigial or absent and the dark throat of the male incomplete; thus adults often appear as nondescript, bulbul-sized birds. However, the *white outer tail feathers* are always present. Immature is distinctive, as illustrated. Male calls frequently and for long periods in summer from a regularly used call-site 'vic-terrr, vic-terrr ...', up to 11 times. Male performs a swooping display while making audible whirring sounds with its wings. Guides people to bees' nests, the call then a high-pitched chattering while the bird flutters in an agitated manner. Occurs singly in woodland, bushveld, exotic plantations and suburbia, but guiding mainly restricted to northern Boswana. 19-20 cm (Grootheuningwyser)

1
2
3
J
4
♀
4
♂

1 SLENDER-BILLED HONEYGUIDE *Prodotiscus zambesiae*

Fairly common resident. Differs from (2) in *greener upperparts* with yellow-edged flight feathers; the throat is dark, finely streaked with white. The call is a harsh repetitive 'skee-aa' while in undulating display flight over trees. Found singly in broad-leaved woodland, usually in the canopy. Parasitises mostly white-eyes. 11,5 cm (Dunbekheuningvoël)

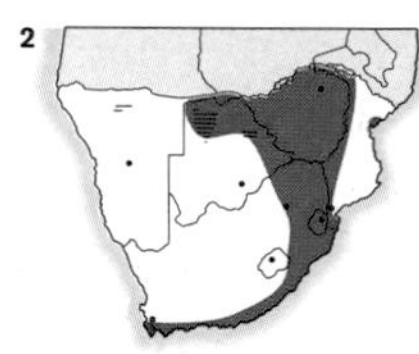

2 SHARP-BILLED HONEYGUIDE *Prodotiscus regulus*

Uncommon resident. Told from (1) by brown (not greenish) upperparts, white rump and white throat. Has a thin, tinkling call note resembling a weak version of the call of the Crested Barbet (p. 264) 'tirrrrrrrr ...', lasting about four seconds; also a sharp 'tseet' in aerial display. Usually perches high in a tree and *peers slowly from side to side while bobbing its head up and down* prior to calling. Catches insects on the ground or hawks them from a tree perch, then displaying the white rump and outer tail feathers. Occurs singly in open bushveld, plantations and suburbia. 13 cm (Skerpbekheuningvoël)

CREEPERS

Family SALPORNITHIDAE. Monospecific in Africa and India.

3 SPOTTED CREEPER *Salpornis spilonotus*

Uncommon, localised resident. Identified by decurved bill, heavily spotted appearance and behaviour. The call is a series of rapid sibilant notes 'sweepy-swip-swip-swip-swip' or 'keck-keck-keck ...' repeated five or six times. Clambers about the trunks and branches of trees like a woodpecker, working its way to the top before flying down at 45° to the base of the next tree. Singly or in pairs in broad-leaved woodland where it usually keeps out of sight behind the tree-trunk or branch. 15 cm (Boomkruiper)

BROADBILLS

Family EURYLAIMIDAE. One species in sub-Saharan Africa, 13 species in Asia.

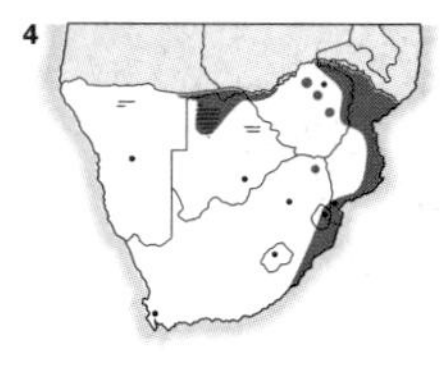

4 AFRICAN BROADBILL *Smithornis capensis*

Uncommon resident. Broad bill, dumpy appearance, black crown and heavily streaked underparts diagnostic. In display utters a frog-like 'purrrr-rupp'. Frequents forests, coastal bush and thickets where it perches low down and hawks insects like a flycatcher. When displaying makes a circular flight in the horizontal plane and reveals white feathers on its back. 14 cm (Breëbek)

PITTAS

Family PITTIDAE. Twenty-five species with a tropical distribution, of which one in southern Africa.

5 ANGOLA PITTA *Pitta angolensis*

Rare summer-breeding migrant. A brightly coloured, thrush-sized terrestrial bird with a short tail. Sexes are alike. Its call is a brief, frog-like 'quoip' as the bird flutters upwards a short distance and settles again on the same spot; several minutes may elapse between calls. Normally occurs in moist areas in forests, thickets and riverine forests where it scratches about in ground debris, only flying into trees to hide when alarmed. Remarkably inconspicuous within its preferred habitat. Moves in quick hops. Individuals are occasionally found well south of their normal distribution. 23 cm (Angolapitta)

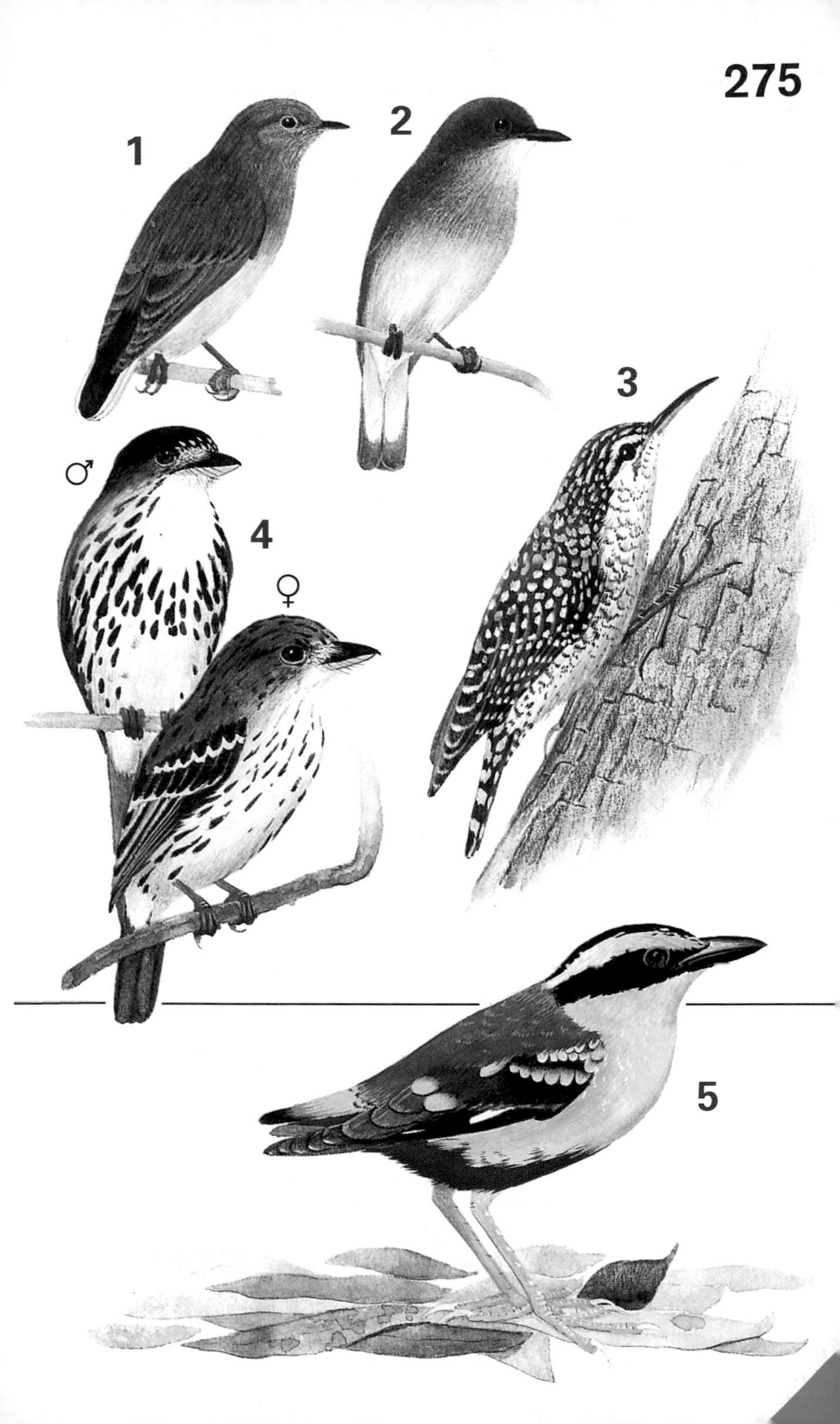
275
1
2
3
♂
4
♀
5

1

2

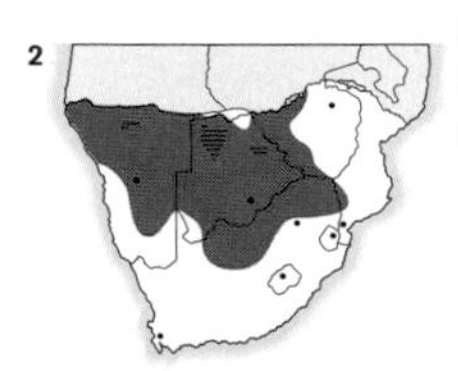

3

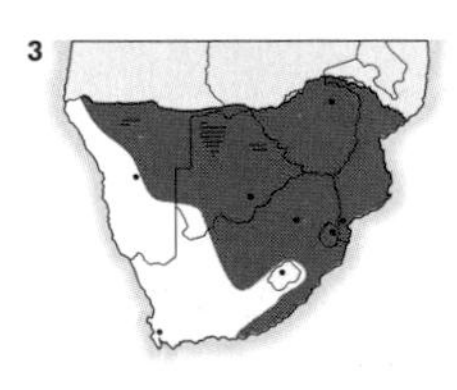

4

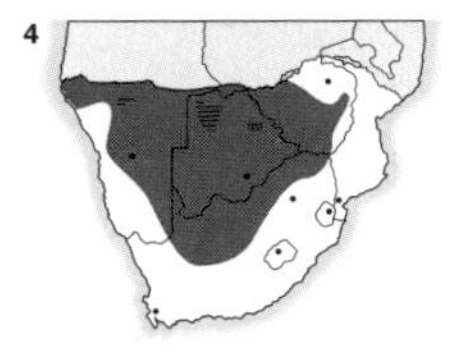

LARKS

Family ALAUDIDAE. Small, sombrely-coloured terrestrial birds with confusingly similar, nondescript plumage patterns consisting of greyish speckled upperparts and pale underparts, usually with some streaking or spotting on the breast. Many species show regional plumage variations, palest or greyest in the north or west. Immature birds resemble adults but are generally more speckled. Best identified by the male's call or song as well as behaviour and habitat. Their flight is usually of a dipping nature and is often of short duration.

1 MELODIOUS LARK *Mirafra cheniana*

Fairly common, endemic resident. Distinguished from (2) with difficulty, but white eyebrow more distinct, the well-streaked upperparts darker and the underparts more buffy, *contrasting with its white throat.* The heavy bill is short and conical. It utters a lively song, *mostly in high flight* (at which time rufous wing-patches are visible). The song continues for long periods and mimics the calls of other birds. It inhabits relatively dry grasslands dominated by rooigras *Themeda triandra*, grassy Karoo and sweet or mixed grasslands and pastures. 12 cm (Spotlewerik)

2 MONOTONOUS LARK *Mirafra passerina*

Common, near endemic resident. Best told from (1) by the lack of a distinct eyebrow and *white underparts.* In many regions it arrives in the summer rains and the male immediately starts calling, a monotonous and much-repeated 'corr-weeoooo' throughout the day and on moonlit nights. It calls from the ground, from a small bush or in flight. Singly or in closely scattered groups, several males often calling at the same time, in dry open mixed woodland with bare and stony patches and variable grass cover according to region. There is little overlap in the distributions of this species and (1). 14 cm (Bosveldlewerik)

3 RUFOUS-NAPED LARK *Mirafra africana*

Common resident. Distinguished by the rufous crown and wing-feather edges, typically with much rufous colouring above and below (a) or, in paler western birds (b), with white underparts faintly tinged buff and pale-edged feathers to the upperparts. The call, a good recognition feature, is a melancholy 'tseep-tseeooo', repeated at about eight second intervals. It also sings during an aerial cruise, especially at dusk, when it imitates other birds. Usually singly in open grassland, the male perching conspicuously on anthills, low bushes or posts when calling, *frequently shuffling the wings and raising the crest.* 18-19 cm (Rooineklewerik)

4 FAWN-COLOURED LARK *Mirafra africanoides*

Common resident. Best told by reddish-fawn (a) to distinctly fawn (b) colouring of upperparts (palest in the west) and white underparts. The white eyebrow is fairly distinctive while there is a *white stripe below the eye* visible at close quarters. The song, given from the top of a small tree, is a rapid and urgent 'te-e-e-tee-ree-tee-ree-chee' with variations; it also has a display flight and song. It feeds on open ground but flies to a tree-perch if disturbed. Usually singly, in pairs when breeding, in thornveld and the edges of woodland, *predominantly on Kalahari sand*, being most frequent in the dry west; localised in the east. 16 cm (Vaalbruinlewerik)

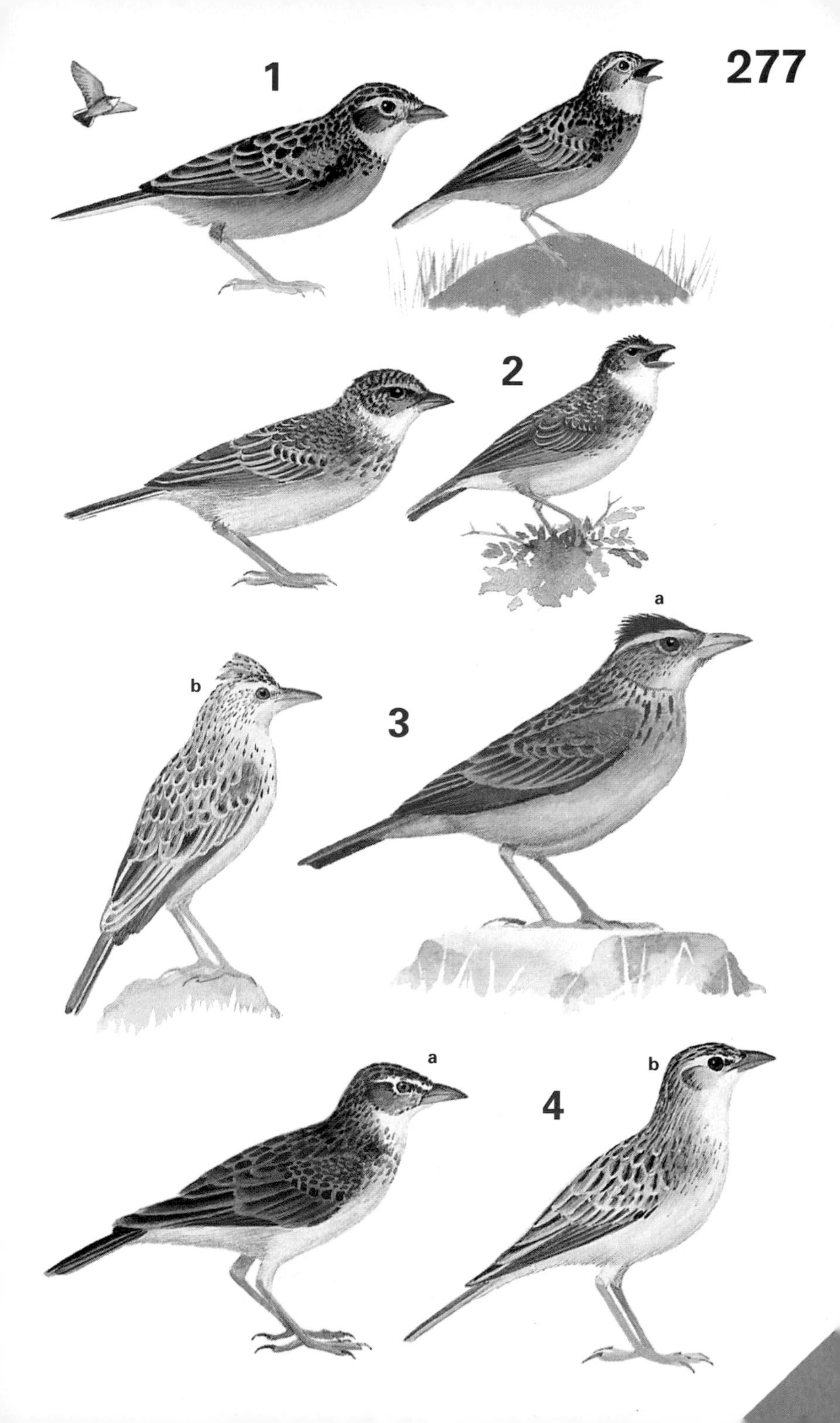

1
2
a
b
3
a
b
4

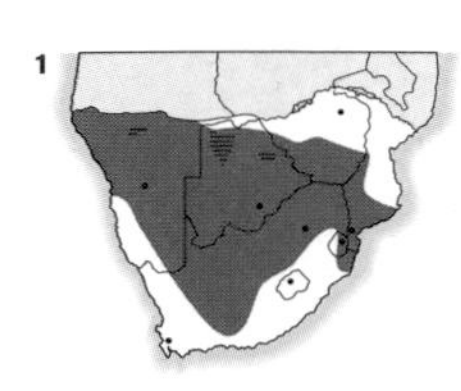

1 SABOTA LARK *Mirafra sabota*

NE

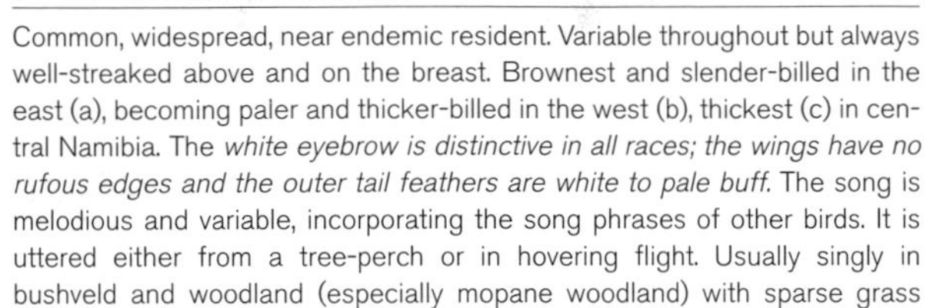

Common, widespread, near endemic resident. Variable throughout but always well-streaked above and on the breast. Brownest and slender-billed in the east (a), becoming paler and thicker-billed in the west (b), thickest (c) in central Namibia. The *white eyebrow is distinctive in all races; the wings have no rufous edges and the outer tail feathers are white to pale buff.* The song is melodious and variable, incorporating the song phrases of other birds. It is uttered either from a tree-perch or in hovering flight. Usually singly in bushveld and woodland (especially mopane woodland) with sparse grass cover or stony ground. 15 cm (Sabotalewerik)

2 DUNE LARK *Certhilauda erythrochlamys*

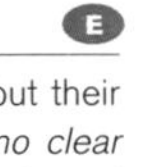

Localised and uncommon endemic resident. Closely similar to (3) but their ranges are mutually exclusive. It has *plain, dune-red upperparts, no clear facial markings and light spotting on the upper breast only;* throat, belly and flanks unmarked. The song has 2-5 'chip chip ...' lead-in notes and a long, uniform terminal trill. It occupies a *very restricted range* along the western dunes of the Namib desert between Lüderitz and Walvis Bay where it frequents sparsely vegetated Namib sand dunes plus scrub and coarse grass clumps in the dune valleys. 17 cm (Duinlewerik)

3 BARLOW'S LARK *Certhilauda barlowi*

Fairly common, endemic resident. Similar to (2) but with stronger colouring and bolder markings, these varying according to location. Birds in the north of its range resemble (2) but with *the upperparts having dark feather-centres, distinct facial markings and bolder breast-streaking.* While the song phrase follows the pattern of the other 'red-backed larks' it is variable throughout its range. It occupies a range between the Koichab River east of Lüderitz and south to Port Nolloth. In the south it overlaps with the northern race of (4). It occurs in association with *Euphorbia* scrub-vegetated dunes and sparse, succulent Karoo vegetation. 19 cm (Barlowse lewerik)

4 KAROO LARK *Certhilauda albescens*

Fairly common, endemic resident. The smallest of the 'red-backed lark' group. Distinguished by a slender bill and *breast-streaking that extends onto the belly and especially onto the flanks.* The colour of the upperparts varies from pale grey-brown on the west coast to rich rufous-brown or red in the western interior. In all colour forms the upperparts are well-streaked. The song differs from that of (5) in being higher-pitched and shorter. It occurs in dense, succulent Karoo scrub and strandveld; it does not occur in areas lacking bushes. 17 cm (Karoolewerik)

5 RED LARK *Certhilauda burra*

Fairly common, endemic resident. The largest and most distinctive of the four 'red-backed larks'; it has a comparatively long tail, *a stubby deep bill* and a heavy flight action. The colouring of its upperparts range from brick red with no dark streaking in the northern and eastern dune regions to much browner, variably streaked birds in the central and southern regions. *All are heavily blotched on the breast but with plain bellies and flanks.* The song is repeated monotonously every 2-5 seconds, a series of 'chip-chip-chip' lead-in notes followed by one or more low whistles and a slow, complex terminal trill. It occurs on well-vegetated red sand dunes in the north and east and on scrubby Karoo plains further south; seldom on stony ground. 19 cm (Rooilewerik)

a
b
c
1
2
3
4
5

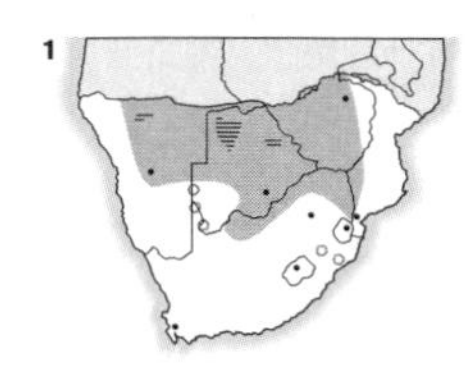

1 **DUSKY LARK** *Pinarocorys nigricans*

Uncommon, non-breeding summer visitor. Dark colouring and bold markings of face and breast resemble Groundscraper Thrush (p. 312), but upperparts darker, bill more robust and legs white. No distinctive call. Occurs in scattered flocks in low altitude bushveld and broad-leaved woodland, foraging in open patches and occasionally perching in trees. Flies with sharply dipping flight. 19 cm (Donkerlewerik)

2 **SHORT-CLAWED LARK** *Certhilauda chuana*

Uncommon endemic resident. Shape and posture like Buffy Pipit (p. 288) with longish, slender bill and tail, well-streaked upperparts with no rufous on crown or wings, but rusty colour on rump. The call is a shrill 'phew-pheeoo-pheeoo, phew-pheeoo-pheeoo, pheeeeeoo, pheeeit ...' with variations including several clear trills, usually uttered from the top of a bush. Also has a display flight in which it rises and then drops steeply calling a long, drawn-out 'foooeeee'; cf. Clapper Lark (previous page). Found in dry grassland with scattered bushes and *Acacia* savanna. 17-18 cm (Kortkloulewerik)

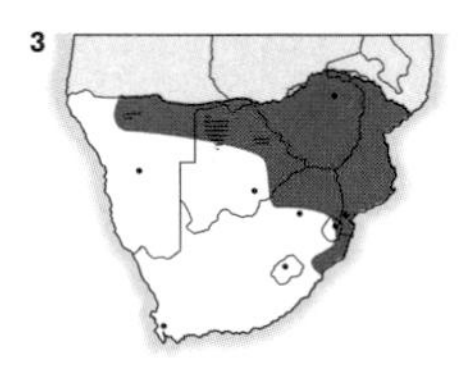

3 **FLAPPET LARK** *Mirafra rufocinnamomea*

Common resident. Similar to (4); best identified by *territorial behaviour and largely exclusive distribution.* Pallid north-western race (a) has shorter, stouter bill than rufous eastern race (b). Has a soft 'tuee-tui' call. Unobtrusive in the non-breeding season. When breeding (early to late summer according to locality) male performs a high aerial cruise, making a thin, wispy call with bursts of wing-claps, the sound a muffled 'purrit-purrit, purrit-purrit' like the ringing tone of a telephone. This is repeated after a pause; see illustration. Local variations occur in this flight pattern. May also ascend into wind to some height and then descend almost vertically before flying parallel to the ground prior to settling. Singly in hilly grassland, grassland fringing woodland and bushveld with grassy areas. 16 cm (Laeveldklappertjie)

4 **CLAPPER LARK** *Mirafra apiata*

Common, near endemic resident. A highly variable species, palest with the most robust bill (a) in the north-west, most rufous (b) in east-central areas and darkest with the sharpest bill (c) in the south. Differs from (3) mainly in territorial behaviour, habitat and distribution. May sing from the ground but more strikingly while displaying. Mostly unobtrusive but when breeding (October-February) male displays by flying upwards, hovering briefly and clapping its wings, then dropping steeply while uttering a long, drawn-out 'fooeeeeeee', see illustration. Also mimics the songs of other birds. Occurs singly or in pairs in grassland, low scrub and bushveld. 16-17 cm (Hoëveld-klappertjie)

1
2
3
a
b
c
4
a
b
wwwww
wwwww
wwwww
wwwww
wwwww
wwwww
'fooeeeeeee'

1

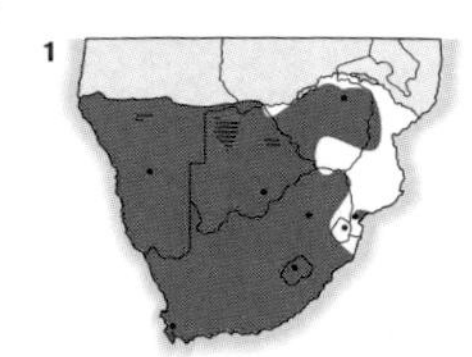

2

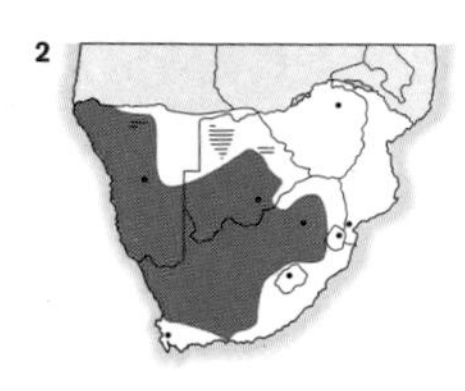

3

4

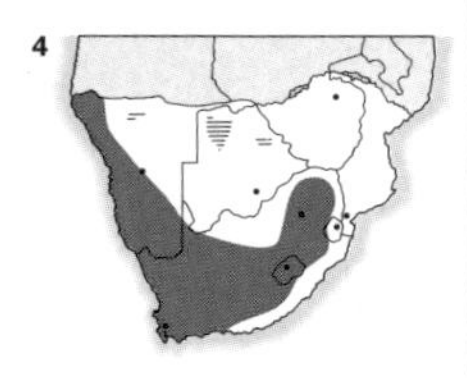

1 RED-CAPPED LARK *Calandrella cinerea*

Common resident. Orange-brown crown and *pectoral patches diagnostic.* The crest is raised only when the bird is agitated or hot. Immature is dark brown over entire upperparts, the breast well speckled blackish. The normal call is a brief 'cheep', 'chirrup' or 'cheeree'; also executes an aerial cruise early in the day while making a series of sibilant sounds terminating in a harsh 'tcheet, tcheet, tchrreet'. In pairs when breeding otherwise in small to large flocks in short grass and especially dry pans, airstrips and dirt roads, walking rapidly or running, flying short distances then dropping down again. 15 cm (Rooikoplewerik)

2 SPIKE-HEELED LARK *Chersomanes albofasciata* NE

Common, near endemic resident. Many races, the two colour extremes illustrated: north-western (a) and south-eastern (b). Characterised by erect stance, long slender bill and short tail with white terminal bar. The hind claw is long and straight. Utters a rapid mellow trill in flight. Occurs singly or in small, loose parties in a wide range of habitats from stony highveld grassland, Karoo scrublands to Kalahari dunes. Largely terrestrial in habits but flies a short distance if disturbed and perches briefly on low vegetation. 15-16 cm (Vlaktelewerik)

3 THICK-BILLED LARK *Galerida magnirostris* 

Common endemic resident. A robust, heavily marked lark with a fairly short tail; heavy bill with a yellow base and well-marked upperparts. The song is a short, musical 'chit-whitleooo-leooo', with variations and repeated at brief intervals from a low perch or while rising in a short flight. Occurs singly or in pairs in grassland, montane grassland, Karoo and wheatlands, being especially common on grassy roadside verges. 18 cm (Dikbeklewerik)

4 LONG-BILLED LARK *Certhilauda curvirostris* 

Common, near endemic resident. A large, variable species, largest, darkest and longest-billed (a) in the south-west; more rufous and with bill shorter, less decurved to the east and north-east, being darkest and dullest rufous in KwaZulu-Natal (b) and with only faint markings in the north-central area; smallest, most pallid, shortest-billed in the north-west (c). Male displays in early summer by rising steeply into the air and then plummeting down while calling a loud 'cheeeeeeeoo'; also calls 'tweer, trree-treeoo' from the ground. Singly or in pairs on rocky hills, stony ridges in grassland and Karoo shrublands. Sometimes stands on elevated ground or large rocks with erect stance from where it may call. 20-22 cm (Langbeklewerik)

283
1
a
2
b
3
a
b
c
4

1

1 RUDD'S LARK *Heteromiafra ruddi* E

Uncommon, highly localised endemic resident. Identified by long legs, short, narrow tail, bulbous head with pale eye-stripes and central head-stripe. In flight looks like a dumpy Spike-heeled Lark (previous page). Best seen in summer when the male cruises about at 15-35 m above ground alternately wing-flapping (noiselessly) and planing while calling 'pitchoo-cheree, pitchoo cheree' rising on the last syllable. Does not mimic like other aerial-singing larks. Singly in high-altitude grassland. A critically threatened species. 14-15 cm (Drakensberglewerik)

2

2 BOTHA'S LARK *Spizocorys fringillaris* E

Uncommon, localised endemic resident. Has a conspicuous eye-stripe and dark dappled upperparts, much darker than any other small lark. On take-off calls 'chuck', often repeatedly, otherwise calls 'tcheree' several times in flight or while settled. In pairs or small parties in heavily grazed flats or upper slopes of high-altitude grassland and farmlands. Often associates with (3), but is undemonstrative and inconspicuous, with no aerial displays. 12 cm (Vaalrivierlewerik)

3
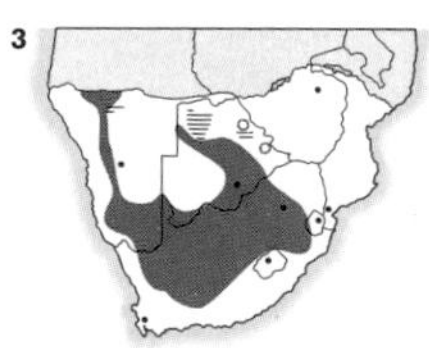

3 PINK-BILLED LARK *Spizocorys conirostris* NE

Fairly common, near endemic resident. Palest race (a) in the west, most rufous race (b) in the south and east; short, conical pink bill in all races. The call is 'chiZIC' or 'twee-twee-twee' on the ground or in flight. Usually in pairs or small parties in grassland, especially where grass is seeding; also burnt and heavily grazed ground, plus clumpy grasses on Kalahari sand. 12 cm (Pienkbeklewerik)

4

4 SCLATER'S LARK *Spizocorys sclateri* E

Uncommon, localised endemic resident. Differs from (5) in richer colouring, bold facial markings, more slender bill and lack of crest. Some races paler than illustrated. The call, while feeding, is 'proo proo, turt turt, cheer cheer ...'. Pairs, often flocks of six to 20, in arid grassland. 13 cm (Namakwalewerik)

5
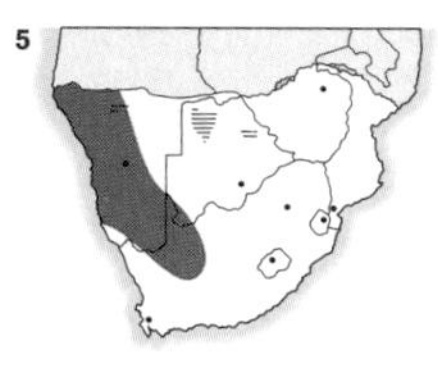

5 STARK'S LARK *Eremalauda starki* NE

Common to locally abundant, near endemic resident. A pale lark with small crest giving a peaked appearance to its head, this feature plus distinct markings on the upperparts distinguishing it from the next species. It has a melodious, rambling flight-display song 'prrt prrt troo chip chip pee-it pee-it ...'. It occurs in arid grassland, sometimes in large flocks near pans in the dry season. When disturbed, flocks take off and fly in a wide arc before resettling. 13 cm (Woestynlewerik)

6

6 GRAY'S LARK *Ammomanes grayi* NE

Locally common, near endemic resident. Palest of the small larks, appearing almost white in the field. It differs from the previous species in plainer upperparts and lack of a crest; from Tractrac Chat (p. 320) in short, *pale*, conical bill, pale legs and lack of white rump. The alarm call is 'chee chee chee', while the song, normally heard before dawn while the bird is flying, is a high-pitched 'chee chee, sweet sweet chu chu chu chu ...'. It occurs in small parties in the desert gravel plains, especially near rock outcrops. When first alarmed may remain motionless and unseen. If flushed it flies off low for a short distance; on settling may utter a double, high-pitched whistle. Nomadic within its range. 14 cm (Namiblewerik)

1
2
a
3
b
4
5
6

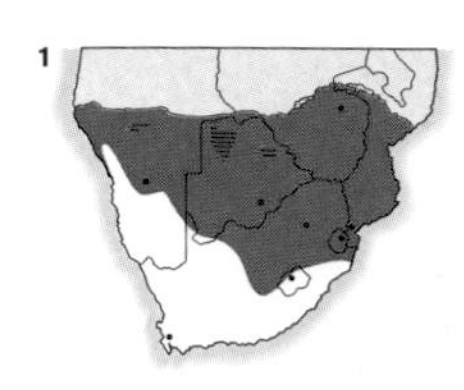

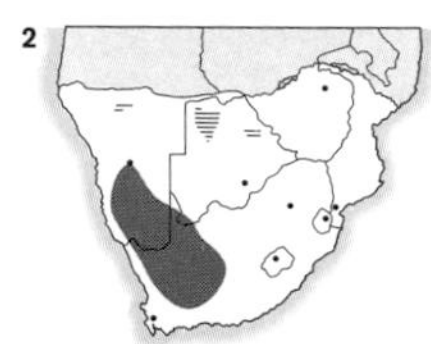

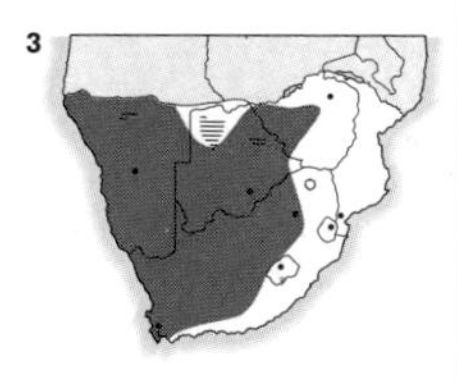

FINCHLARKS

Small, sparrow-like larks with marked sexual plumage differences. The males predominantly black. They occur in flocks, especially in the drier regions, and are highly nomadic.

1 CHESTNUT-BACKED FINCHLARK *Eremopterix leucotis*

Common to abundant resident. Both sexes differ from other finchlarks in having chestnut wing coverts and grey underwings. Has a sharp, rattling call 'chip-chwep' and pretty song in fluttering flight. Flocks occur on open flats, airfields and cultivated lands, usually with low bushes nearby. Makes off in low irregular flight when disturbed, then suddenly resettles. 12-13 cm (Rooiruglewerik)

2 BLACK-EARED FINCHLARK *Eremopterix australis*

Common endemic resident. The male has no white plumage; the upperparts of both sexes are rufous while the belly of the female lacks the black patch of other female finchlarks. It calls 'cht cht cht' in flight. It occurs in sparse, dwarf shrublands and grasslands, mostly on red sands. 12-13 cm (Swartoorlewerik)

3 GREY-BACKED FINCHLARK *Eremopterix verticalis*

Very common to abundant near endemic resident. Both sexes are distinguished by grey upperparts. Flocks make various shrill chirps while feeding. The flocks, often very large, occur in a wide variety of semi-arid to arid grasslands, gravel plains with scattered bushes or trees and dry pans. 12-13 cm (Grysruglewerik)

PIPITS, LONGCLAWS AND WAGTAILS

Family MOTACILLIDAE. Small, insectivorous terrestrial birds, water-associated in wagtails. The sexes are alike or closely similar, all with white or buff outer tail feathers. Pipits are superficially lark-like in appearance and behaviour, many so similar as to make certain field identification problematical. Most pipits utter a 'chissik' call on take-off, their flight low and dipping. Longclaws are large, colourful pipits while wagtails, also colourful or striking, are mostly well known because of their confiding and friendly behaviour. Wagtails have the habit of continually bobbing their tails up and down.

4 SHORT-TAILED PIPIT *Anthus brachyurus*

Uncommon resident. Small size, short tail, dark upperparts and well-streaked chest diagnostic. Singly or in pairs, sparsely distributed in grassland but inconspicuous and elusive. Entirely terrestrial, never perching on bushes though it may utter a short song while perched on a mound 'cheeroo, trree trree trree trreeree, trree trree ....'. When disturbed it flushes reluctantly and flies off directly showing its white outer tail feathers. 12 cm (Kortstertkoester)

♂
♀
1
♂
♀
2
♂
♀
3
4

1
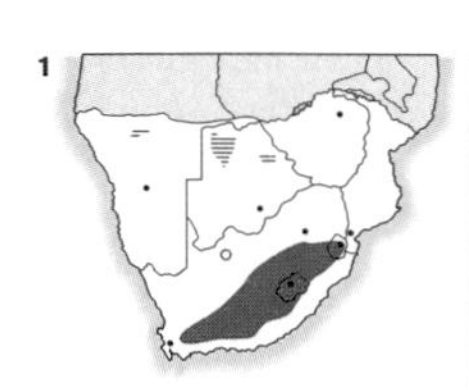

1 ROCK PIPIT *Anthus crenatus*

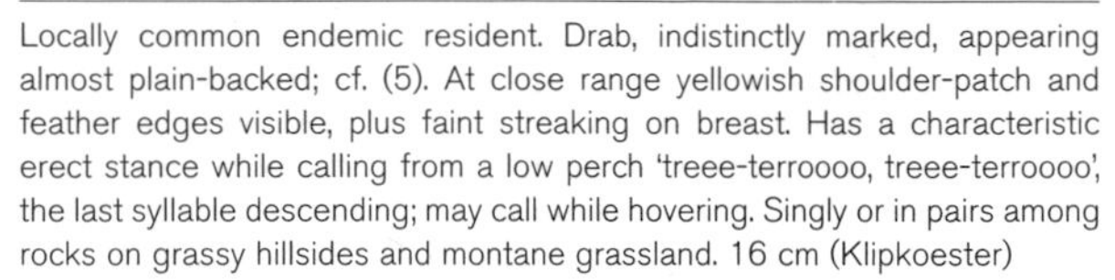

Locally common endemic resident. Drab, indistinctly marked, appearing almost plain-backed; cf. (5). At close range yellowish shoulder-patch and feather edges visible, plus faint streaking on breast. Has a characteristic erect stance while calling from a low perch 'treee-terroooo, treee-terroooo', the last syllable descending; may call while hovering. Singly or in pairs among rocks on grassy hillsides and montane grassland. 16 cm (Klipkoester)

2
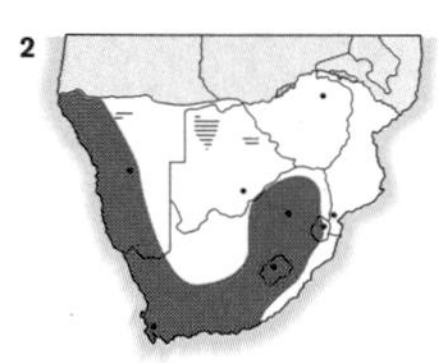

2 LONG-BILLED PIPIT *Anthus similis*

Common resident. Differs from (4) in less distinct breast-streaking and *buff* (not white) outer tail feather edges. The base of the bill is *yellow*, but the bill length is not a field feature. May call for long periods from a rock, bush or fence, a clear metallic 'kilink' or 'chip, chreep, chroop, chreep, chip ...'. Occurs singly on hillsides, especially stony regions with sparse vegetation, and in burnt areas. 18 cm (Nicholsonse koester)

3
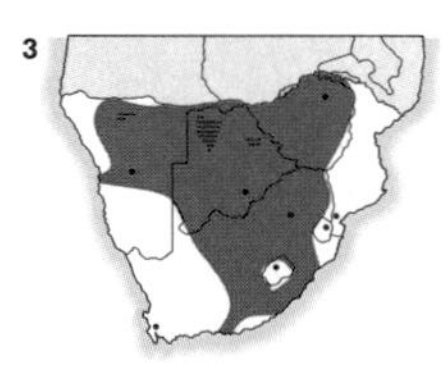

3 BUFFY PIPIT *Anthus vaalensis*

Uncommon resident. Moustacial streaks not pronounced, breast-streaking variable, often indistinct, edges of outer tail feathers *pale buff*, the base of the bill *pink*. In flight utters an occasional 'chissik' call. *Bobs its tail more frequently than most pipits*, and has the habit of running a short distance then standing erect with breast thrown out. Occurs singly in short, open grassland and on bare ground dotted with anthills and low scrub. 19 cm (Vaalkoester)

4
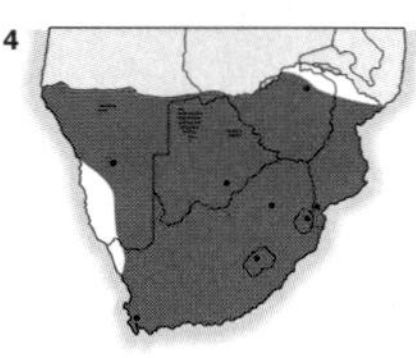

4 GRASSVELD PIPIT *Anthus cinnamomeus*

Common resident. *Yellow* base to the bill, bold facial markings, boldly marked breast and *white* (not buff) outer tail feathers distinguish this pipit. When disturbed takes off with a 'chissik' call and characteristic dipping flight; may call in flight 'chree-chree-chree-chree' during each dip. Usually singly in grassland. 16 cm (Gewone koester)

5
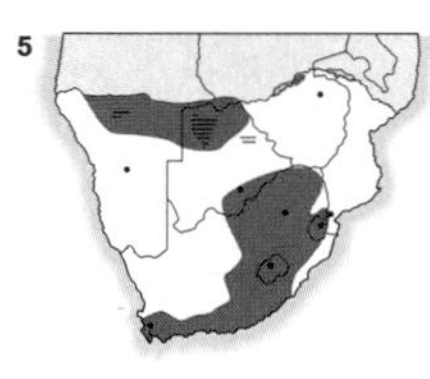

5 PLAIN-BACKED PIPIT *Anthus leucophrys*

Fairly common resident. Told by *lack of distinct markings* on the upperparts and indistinct breast markings. The edges of the outer tail feathers are *buff*, the base of the bill is *yellow*. From the ground calls a sparrow-like 'jhreet-jhroot'. Singly or in small flocks in moist grassland with short or burnt grass, also fallow lands and hilly coastal regions. 17 cm (Donkerkoester)

6

6 WOOD PIPIT *Anthus nyassae*

Fairly common, localised resident. Closely similar to (2) but bill and tail slightly shorter. Differs mainly in choice of habitat, occurring only in miombo broadleaved woodland where it readily *perches in trees* if disturbed, otherwise forages on the ground in clearings. 18 cm (Woudkoester)

7

7 MOUNTAIN PIPIT *Anthus hoeschi*

Fairly common, localised summer resident. Resembles a large version of (4) but upperparts darker, breast more boldly streaked, base of bill *pink* (not yellow), outer tail feathers *buff*. Call similar to that of (4) but deeper, slower. Occurs in montane grassland above 2 000 m in Lesotho and surroundings during summer and is believed to overwinter in eastern Angola. 18 cm (Bergkoester)

1
2
3
4
5
6
7

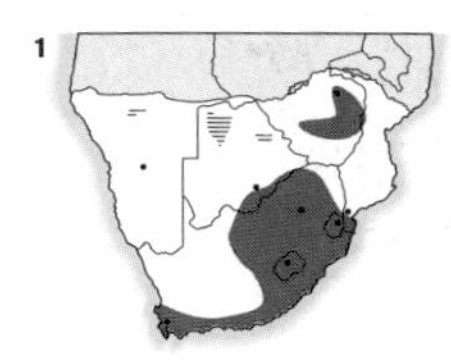

1 ORANGE-THROATED LONGCLAW *Macronyx capensis* E

Common endemic resident. Orange throat with black surround diagnostic of adult; immature may have throat same colour as underparts, then distinguished from Yellow-throated Longclaw (overleaf) by deeper yellow colouring and buff (not yellow) edges to wing feathers. Normal call is a mewing 'me-yew'; also a far-reaching whistle. Singly or in pairs in grassland. Often momentarily stands upright on grass tuft, stone or anthill. If disturbed, flies a short distance uttering its characteristic call. 20 cm (Oranjekeelkalkoentjie)

2 PINK-THROATED LONGCLAW *Macronyx ameliae*

Uncommon resident. Immature less pink, throat more buffy, black gorget vestigial. The call is a squeaky 'teee-yoo tyip-tyip-tyip-TEE YOOOO'. Singly or in pairs in marshy grassland. Less conspicuous than other longclaws; lies low when approached, then makes off in erratic flight for a short distance (when white wing-bars and dark back markings can be seen) before settling and hiding again. 20 cm (Rooskeelkalkoentjie)

3 TREE PIPIT *Anthus trivialis*

Uncommon summer visitor. Short bill, white throat and breast with tear-shaped spots useful characteristics but best identified by behaviour. Flight call 'teez'; also has a canary-like song. Singly or in pairs, but flocks when migrating, in woodland, parks and gardens, mostly in Zimbabwe. 16 cm (Boomkoester)

RED-THROATED PIPIT (Rooikeelkoester) see p. 446.

4 BUSHVELD PIPIT *Anthus caffer*

Fairly common resident. Differs from (3) in smaller size, off-white throat, breast markings less distinct but forming stripes, and more rufous colouring. From a tree-top perch calls 'skeer-trurp, skeer-trurp, skeer-trurp-skee-skee ...'; from the ground calls 'tshweep'. Usually singly but sparse in thornveld or dry bushveld. If disturbed on the ground, makes off with erratic flight, then settles on a tree from where it may call. 13,5 cm (Bosveldkoester)

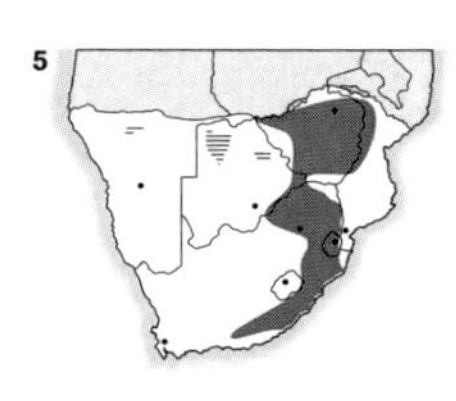

5 STRIPED PIPIT *Anthus lineiventris*

Common resident. Distinguished by clearly yellow-edged wing feathers, these more obvious than in Rock Pipit (previous page) from which it also differs in well-streaked underparts. Has a loud, whistling, thrush-like song. Singly or in pairs on stony slopes, ridges, road-cuttings and rocky banks of small rivers. When disturbed flies to a tree where it may perch lengthwise along a branch. 18 cm (Gestreepte koester)

1
2
3
4
5

1 **YELLOW-BREASTED PIPIT** *Hemimacronyx chloris* (E)

Rare, localised endemic resident. Winter plumage lacks yellow; buffy-white below with light streaking on breast. Immature has buffy flanks and breast. Male calls from grass tuft and in hovering flight, a rapid chipping like Long-tailed Widow (p. 418) 'chip chip chip chip ...'. Singly or in pairs in dense high-altitude montane grassland where it breeds in summer, moving to lower-altitude grassland in winter. Inconspicuous and secretive; lies close in the grass and flushes reluctantly, but finally flies far. 16-18 cm (Geelborskoester)

2 **YELLOW-THROATED LONGCLAW** *Macronyx croceus*

Common resident. Differs from Bokmakierie (p. 380) in brown upperparts and pink-brown legs; cf. that species. Utters a monotonous mewing from the top of a bush 'triooo, triooo, trroo-chit-chit, trroo-chit-chit-trroo-chit' and sings in flight or from a perch. A terrestrial species. Singly or in pairs in moist grassland with scattered trees. 20 cm (Geelkeelkalkoentjie)

3 **FÜLLEBORN'S LONGCLAW** *Macronyx fuelleborni*

Rare, exact status uncertain. Very similar to (2) but less bright, lacks streaking on its flanks. Makes a sparrow-like chirping 'weee', and a whistling 'jee-o-wee'. Calls from the tops of bushes. Common in Angola and has been reported from the extreme north of Namibia. Probably an occasional visitor. 21 cm (Angolakalkoentjie)

4 **GOLDEN PIPIT** *Tmetothylacus tenellus*

Very rare vagrant. Much smaller than (2), male's breast-band less extensive. Male appears rich yellow at all times; female is buffy and has no breast-band. In both sexes the visible upper leg (tibia) is unfeathered. A terrestrial species which, in its normal distribution, frequents dry bushveld, occasionally perching on bushes. 15 cm (Goudkoester)

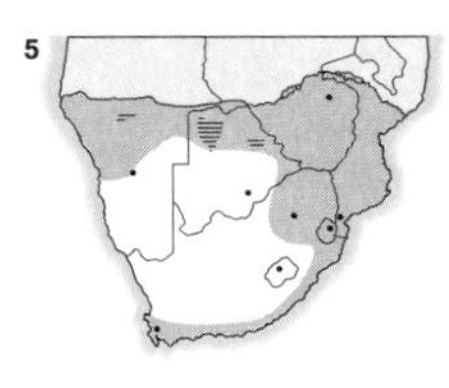

5 **YELLOW WAGTAIL** *Motacilla flava*

Locally common summer visitor. Many races with varying head patterns, (a) and (c) most common in this region but (b) and (d) also known. Race (d) has the white eyebrow bolder than the Grey Wagtail (overleaf); otherwise told by its shorter tail, green (not grey) upperparts including rump, and entirely yellow underparts. Immature in first winter plumage can also be confused with Grey Wagtail; cf. that species. The call is 'tsee-ip'. Singly in floodplains and moist grassland. 18 cm (Geelkwikkie)

1
2
3
♂
4
♀
b
a
5
c
d
J

1 GREY WAGTAIL *Motacilla cinerea*

Rare summer visitor. Distinguished from Yellow Wagtail (previous page) by grey upperparts (not green), dark shoulder-patch and white throat. Tail long, yellow at base above and below. Underparts yellow and white with faint brownish smudges; cf. Yellow Wagtail. Call is a short, metallic 'tit' or 'tidit'. Walks about bobbing its long tail constantly, usually near fast-flowing water. 18 cm (Gryskwikkie)

2 LONG-TAILED WAGTAIL *Motacilla clara*

Fairly common, localised resident. Told by very long tail and predominantly grey and white colouring, much paler than other wagtails. Calls 'chirrup' on taking flight; also sings 'ti-tuu-ui-tui-tui'. Pairs or small groups along fast-running forest rivers and streams in the eastern regions. Hops and flits from boulder to boulder with much tail-wagging. 19-20 cm (Bergkwikkie)

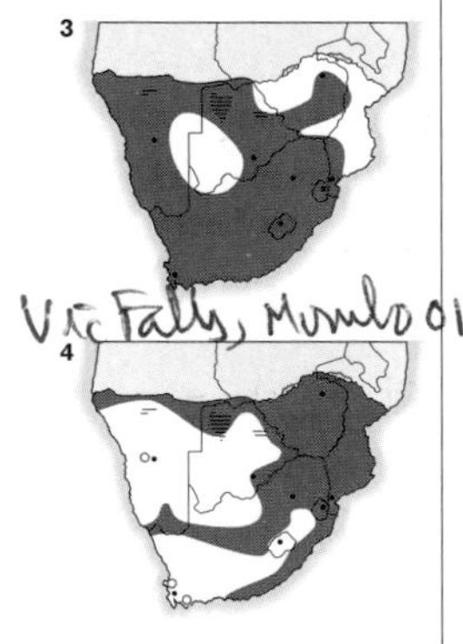

3 CAPE WAGTAIL *Motacilla capensis*

Common resident. Shorter-tailed than (1) and (2) and greyer than other wagtails. Northern races have breast-band absent or vestigial (b). Call is a loud, cheerful 'tseep-eep' or 'tseeep'. Singly or in pairs near water, in suburban gardens, cities and at sewage works. Walks about feeding on the ground, occasionally wagging its tail. If disturbed, will perch briefly on a tree, wall, fence or building. Tame and confiding. 18 cm (Gewone kwikkie)

Vic Falls, Mumbo 01

4 AFRICAN PIED WAGTAIL *Motacilla aguimp*

Common resident. Told from other wagtails by striking *black and white plumage*, tail length as in (3). Call is a loud 'tu-weee' and 'twee-twee-twee'. Singly, in pairs or family groups at lakes, dams, large rivers, sewage works, lagoons and estuaries. Habits much like (3) but enters suburbia only in the north of its distribution. 20 cm (Bontkwikkie)

Victoria Falls 6/01

♂ Br
♂ N-Br
♀ N-Br
1
2
a
3
b
4

1
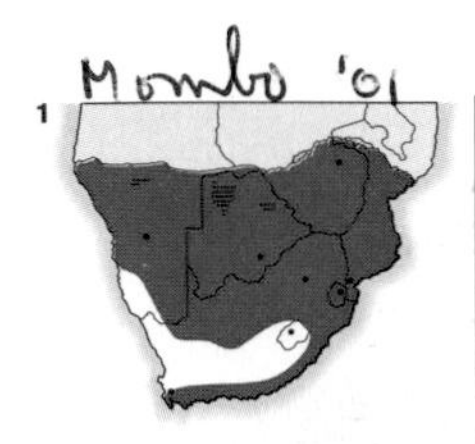

2
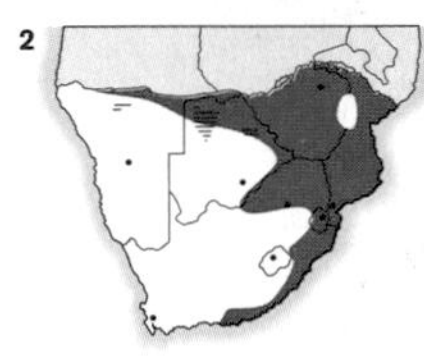

3
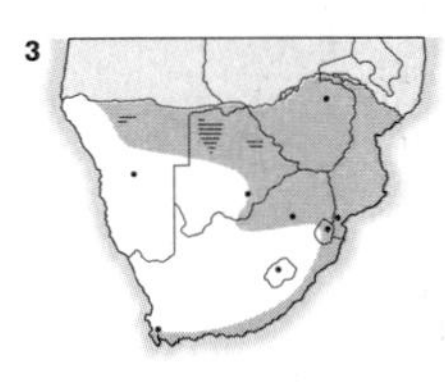

4

DRONGOS

Family DICRURIDAE. Black insectivorous birds with prominent rictal bristles. They hawk insects from a perch in woodland and bushveld and are pugnacious, habitually mobbing larger birds, even pecking the heads of eagles. Numbers (2) and (3) are included on this plate for better comparison with drongos; the Black Flycatcher belongs to the family Muscicapidae (pp. 360-65), the Black Cuckooshrike to the family Campephagidae (overleaf).

1 FORK-TAILED DRONGO *Dicrurus adsimilis*

Common resident. Differs from all similar black birds in *prominent forked tail,* the outer feathers splayed outwards: cf. (4) which has only a shallow fork in its tail. Sexes are alike; immature as illustrated. Utters a variety of unmusical twanging notes interspersed with imitations of other bird-calls, especially those of owls and other birds of prey. Singly or in pairs in almost any non-forest habitat with trees. Noisy and aggressive. 25 cm (Mikstertbyvanger)

2 BLACK FLYCATCHER *Melaenornis pammelaina*

Common resident. The tail shows a *small indentation* at the tip (not a distinct fork), the outer tail feathers being straight, not splayed. Sexes are alike; immature as illustrated. Not very vocal, uttering various low sibilant sounds 'swee' or 'swee-ur'. Singly or in pairs in any woodland, thornveld or bushveld. Catches insects on the ground, flying down from a perch in typical flycatcher fashion. Often occurs alongside (1) but, by contrast, is quiet. 19-22 cm (Swartvlieëvanger)

3 BLACK CUCKOOSHRIKE *Campephaga flava*

(See overleaf for full account.) Only the male is black, differing from similar black birds in having a *rounded tail* and prominent *orange-yellow gape;* sometimes has a yellow shoulder, see overleaf. A quiet, arboreal species. (Swartkatakoeroe)

4 SQUARE-TAILED DRONGO *Dicrurus ludwigii*

Common, localised resident. Has splayed outer tail feathers like (1) but with only a *shallow indentation;* also has *ruby-red eyes.* Calls are a loud 'cherit! cherit!' or 'cherit-wit-wit' plus other strident sounds and imitations of other bird-calls. Singly or in pairs in eastern evergreen forests, riparian forests and dense woodland where it frequents the midstratum, hawking from a perch. Active, noisy and aggressive. 19 cm (Kleinbyvanger)

J
1
J
2
♂
3
4

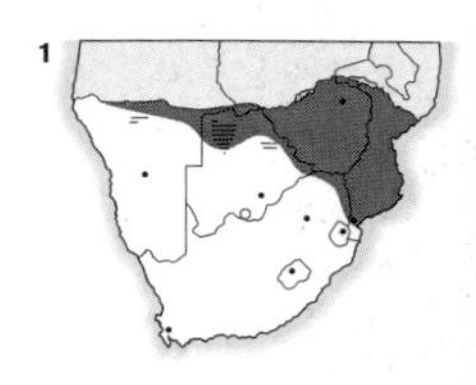

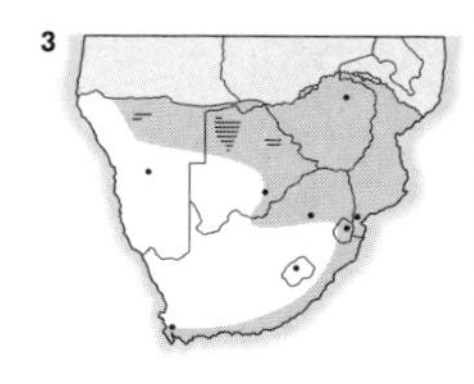

CUCKOOSHRIKES

Family CAMPEPHAGIDAE. Insectivorous, heavy-billed birds, some of cuckoo-like appearance, found in the larger trees of forest fringes, riparian forests and woodland.

1 WHITE-BREASTED CUCKOOSHRIKE *Coracina pectoralis*

Uncommon resident. Adults as illustrated; immature like female but with white barring on upperparts, grey spotting below. The call is a softly whistled 'duid duid' by the male, and a trilling 'che-e-e-e-e' by the female. Usually singly in large trees in riparian forests and broad-leaved woodland. A lethargic species, moving from branch to branch with long hops, peering closely at leaves in search of insects or making short aerial sallies. Sparsely distributed. 27 cm (Witborskatakoeroe)

2 GREY CUCKOOSHRIKE *Coracina caesia*

Uncommon, localised resident. All-grey colouring diagnostic; female lacks the black lores. Immature has white-tipped feathers, giving a freckled appearance. The call is a quiet, high-pitched 'peeeeeooooo', usually while perched; also utters a variety of chittering and trilling sounds while feeding. Singly or in pairs in eastern evergreen forests, riparian forests and forested valleys where it frequents the tree canopies. 27 cm (Bloukatakoeroe)

3 BLACK CUCKOOSHRIKE *Campephaga flava*

Uncommon summer resident. See previous page for comparison of male with other similar black birds. About half of South African male birds show the yellow shoulder (a), whereas in Zimbabwe and Botswana most males lack this (b). Female is strikingly different, cuckoo-like as illustrated; immature like female, young males with increasing areas of black as shown. The call, not often heard, is a soft, high-pitched trill 'trrrrrrrr ...'. Pairs occur sparsely in a variety of wooded habitats, thornveld, mixed bushveld, broad-leaved woodland and coastal bush. Unobtrusive unless calling, frequenting the midstratum. Often joins bird parties. 22 cm (Swartkatakoeroe)

♀
1
♂
2
3
J♂
♂
a
♂
b
3
♀

1
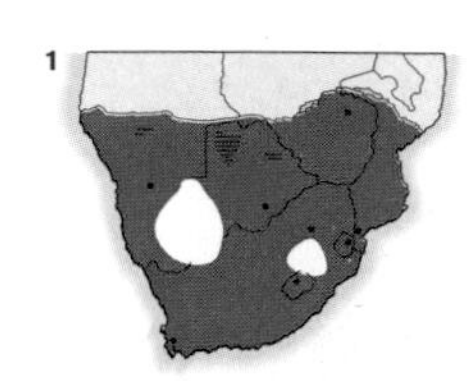

2
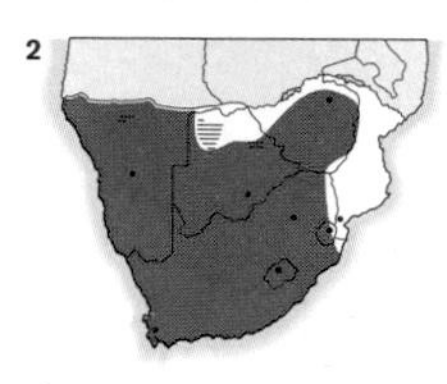

3
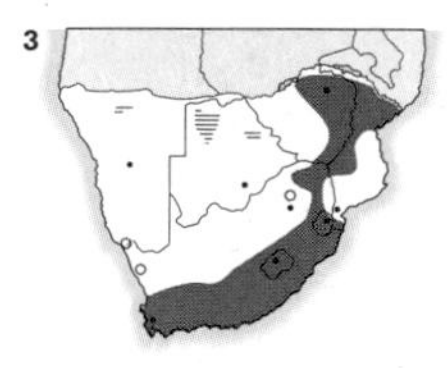

4

5

CROWS

Family CORVIDAE. Large, mainly glossy black, omnivorous birds, largest members of the passerines. Sexes are alike and immatures similar to adults. All have loud cawing calls.

1 PIED CROW *Corvus albus*

Common and widespread resident. Distinguished by white breast and collar. The call is a loud 'kwaak'. A bold species usually found in association with human settlement, where it gleans food scraps, especially haunting refuse dumps, school playing fields, highways and farmlands. Usually in loose flocks or large communal roosts. 46-52 cm (Witborskraai)

2 BLACK CROW or CAPE ROOK *Corvus capensis*

Common and widespread resident. Entirely glossy black. The call is a high-pitched 'kraaa'. Single birds, pairs or flocks frequent farmlands and open country. Generally less common than (1). Habitually perches and nests on pylons and tolerates more arid regions than the Pied Crow. 48-53 cm (Swartkraai)

3 WHITE-NECKED RAVEN *Corvus albicollis*

Common, localised resident. Has a white nape only, otherwise black with a very heavy bill. The call is a falsetto 'kraak', although deeper notes are sometimes uttered. Normally occurs in montane regions but wanders far in search of food. A bold species and a great scavenger, often feeding on carrion. Individuals usually forage alone but many may gather at food sources. 50-54 cm (Withalskraai)

4 HOUSE CROW *Corvus splendens*

Common, localised resident. An introduced species. Lacks any white plumage. Smaller than (2) and with grey nape, mantle and breast. Voice a shrill 'kwaa, kwaa'. Strictly commensal with humans, occurring in Maputo, Inhaca Island, Durban, East London and Cape Town. 43 cm (Huiskraai)

ORIOLES

Family ORIOLIDAE. Predominantly yellow, pink-billed, insectivorous and frugivorous birds with clear, liquid-sounding calls. They feed mostly in the canopies of large trees.

5 GREEN-HEADED ORIOLE *Oriolus chlorocephalus*

Rare, localised resident. Distinguished from other orioles by green upperparts including head and throat, plus yellow collar and underparts. Immature is duller yellow below, the head a paler green. Call is very similar to Black-headed Oriole (overleaf). In southern Africa occurs only in the montane forests of Mt Gorongosa in central Mozambique. 24 cm (Groenkopwielewaal)

1
2
3
4
5

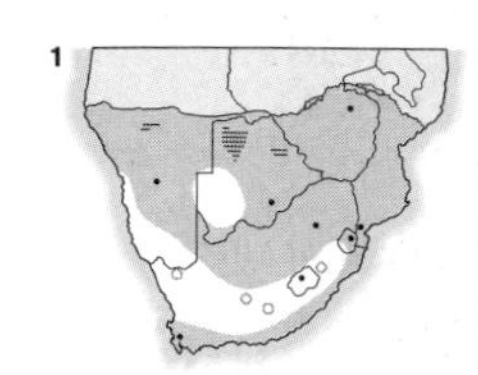

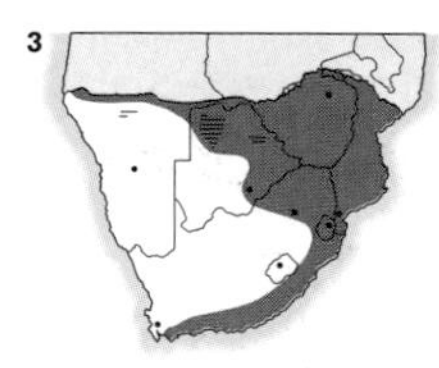

1 EUROPEAN GOLDEN ORIOLE *Oriolus oriolus*

Fairly common to uncommon summer visitor. Male differs from male of (2) in having black wings. Female resembles immature illustrated. The seldom heard call is a ringing 'weela-weeoo', plus a churring alarm note common to all orioles. Singly in broad-leaved woodland, mixed bushveld, riverine forests and various other well-wooded habitats including exotic trees. Infrequent over much of the interior, females and immatures outnumbering males at all times. 24 cm (Europese wielewaal)

2 AFRICAN GOLDEN ORIOLE *Oriolus auratus*

Uncommon summer resident. Male is the yellowest of orioles with a distinct black line through the eye to the ear coverts, this also being present in immature. Female is less bright than male, upperparts greener, underparts paler. The calls are liquid whistles 'wee-er-er-wul' or 'fee-yoo-fee-yoo-fee-yoo', longer than the calls of (3). Occurs in any well-developed woodland or riverine forests. 24 cm (Afrikaanse wielewaal)

3 BLACK-HEADED ORIOLE *Oriolus larvatus*

Common resident. Distinguished by black head and pink bill; cf. Masked Weaver (p. 412), which is smaller with a black bill. Sexes are alike; immature as illustrated. The usual call is a loud, liquid 'pheeoo' but it also utters a 'churr' alarm call. Singly or in pairs in moist, well-developed woodland or mixed bushveld, riverine forests and exotic trees. A noisy, conspicuous species. It is absent from the dry central and western regions. 25 cm (Swartkopwielewaal)

♂
J
1
♂
J
2
J
3

1

2

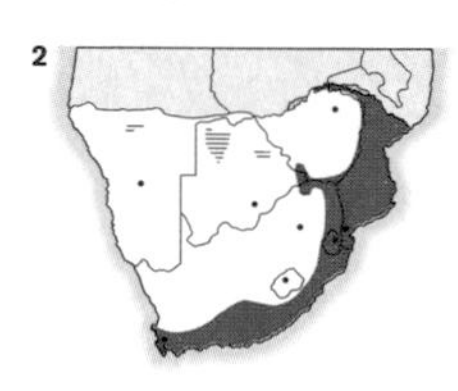

3

4

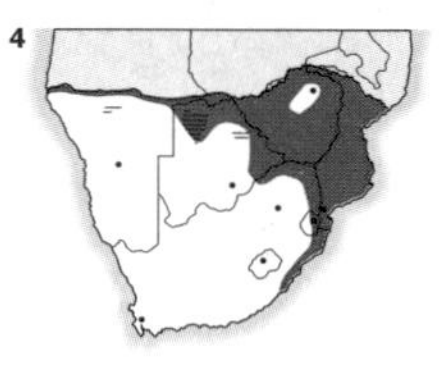

5

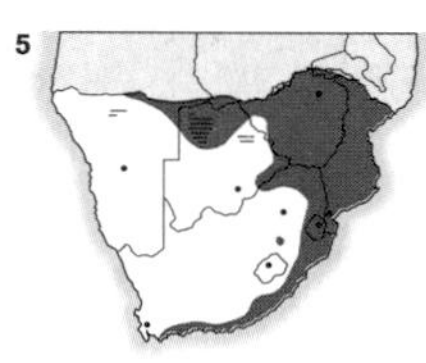

BULBULS

Family PYCNONOTIDAE. Frugivorous and insectivorous birds with clear, whistling calls. They frequent evergreen bush and forests. Sexes are alike, immatures duller.

1 BUSH BLACKCAP *Lioptilus nigricapillus* E

Family TIMALIIDAE. Uncommon endemic resident. Distinguished by black cap and pink or orange bill. The song is a lively jumble of notes similar to Black-eyed Bulbul (overleaf) but more liquid and varied. Singly or in pairs in forest-fringing scrub at high altitudes, especially on the slopes of the Drakensberg escarpment. Keeps mainly within cover and is not easily seen. 17 cm (Rooibektiptol)

2 SOMBRE BULBUL *Andropadus importunus*

Common resident. Southern form (a) is plain olive-green; northern form (b), in lower Zambezi valley and beyond, is much yellower, upperparts greener. Eye colour diagnostic: creamy-white in adults of both colour forms, greyish in immatures. Heard more often than seen. Usually calls a strident 'Willie!'; in the breeding season this is followed by a babbling trill likened to 'Willie! Come out and fight! Sca-a-ared', the final phrase barely audible. In southern coastal bush the call is often shortened to 'peeet' or 'peeeit' which is usually answered by others of the same species. When agitated this call becomes 'peeet peeet peeet ... ' in rapid succession. Usually singly in forest fringes and adjacent thickets, riverine forests and well-wooded valleys; especially common in coastal bush. Not particularly secretive but its cryptic colouring makes it difficult to see. 19-24 cm (Gewone willie)

3 YELLOW-SPOTTED NICATOR *Nicator gularis*

Uncommon resident. Identified by heavy bill and yellow-spotted wing feathers, the spots smaller in immatures. The call is a series of mellow trills and warbles. Singly in dense coastal, riverine and forest-fringe thickets or in the midstratum of riverine forests and mixed bushveld. Secretive and easily overlooked if not calling. Sparsely distributed. 23 cm (Geelvleknikator)

4 YELLOW-BELLIED BULBUL *Chlorocichla flaviventris*

Fairly common resident. Identified by olive-green upperparts and bright yellow underparts including underwings, plus reddish eyes with conspicuous *white eyelids.* Immature is similar but top of head is the same colour as back. Noisy at times, the call a loud 'pur, pur, pur, pur, peh, peh, peh, peh, peh ...', often several birds calling at once. Singly or in pairs in well-developed riverine forests, coastal and lowland forests plus thickets on moist, rocky hillsides. Spends much time foraging on the ground or in the midstratum. 20-23 cm (Geelborswillie)

5 TERRESTRIAL BULBUL *Phyllastrephus terrestris*

Common resident. A very drab brown bird apart from the white throat, the underparts barely paler than the upperparts; at close range a yellowish gape is discernible. Immature has redder wing feather edges. Feeding parties maintain a quiet chuckling or murmuring. Usually in parties of six or more in dense riverside and hillside thickets, plus dense undergrowth in forests and bushveld, scratching about in ground debris and seldom ascending above the lower stratum. Easily overlooked unless heard. 21-2 cm (Boskrapper)

1
2a
2b
3
4
5

1

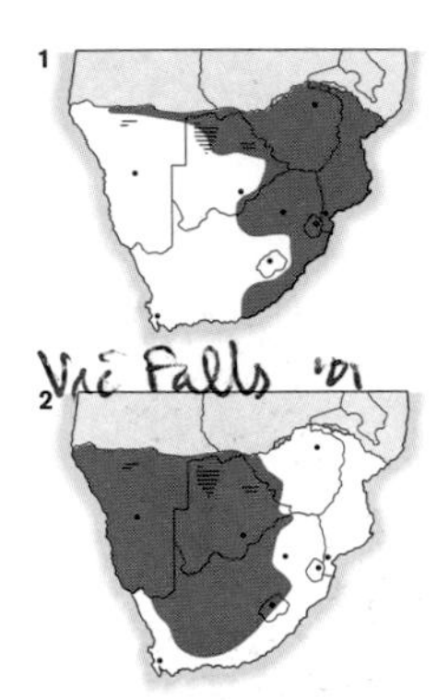

2

1 BLACK-EYED BULBUL *Pycnonotus barbatus*

Very common resident. Dark, crested head, dark eye and yellow vent identify this well-known species. Has several cheerful calls such as a short phrase sounding like 'Wake-up, Gregory' and a much repeated 'chit, chit, chit ...'. Gregarious, inhabiting most eastern and northern regions with bush and trees, especially riverine forests and suburban gardens, but not evergreen forests. 20-22 cm (Swartoogtiptol)

2 RED-EYED BULBUL *Pycnonotus nigricans*

Very common, near endemic resident. Differs from (1) mainly in red eye-wattle. Has a variety of cheerful, chattering calls similar to (1) and is very alike in most other ways. Frequents the drier western regions, usually associating with human habitation and bush along watercourses. 19-21 cm (Rooioogtiptol)

3

3 CAPE BULBUL *Pycnonotus capensis*

Common endemic resident. Differs from (1) and (2) in white eye-wattle and browner appearance of head. Has similar cheerful calls, including a liquid 'piet-piet-patata'. A lively, conspicuous species frequenting scrub, wooded watercourses and exotic coastal bush in the western and southern Cape. 19-21 cm (Kaapse tiptol)

4

4 YELLOW-STREAKED BULBUL *Phyllastrephus flavostriatus*

Fairly common, localised resident. Told from (5) by larger size, darker head, dark eye with white eyelids and prominent bill. Yellow streaks of underparts not a field feature. Has various strident call notes 'chur, chur, chi-cheee, choo-choo-choo-choo-choo, chitchitchitchit ... chee-chwer-treee-treee ...'. Small groups in the midstratum of evergreen forests and adjacent bush. Clambers about moss-covered tree trunks, branches and creepers, often hanging head downwards. *Frequently flicks open one wing at a time.* Tame and conspicuous, often in mixed bird parties. 18-21 cm (Geelstreepboskruiper)

5

5 SLENDER BULBUL *Phyllastrephus debilis*

Fairly common, localised resident. Much smaller than (4); head and eye paler, bill paler and shorter. Immature has greenish head and face. Has a loud, warbling song of explosive quality plus a sibilant, ventriloquial call on a rising scale, and a gurgling alarm note. Frequents evergreen forests and their fringing secondary growth. Warbler-like in behaviour, feeding in the upper and lower strata. 14 cm (Kleinboskruiper)

6

6 STRIPE-CHEEKED BULBUL *Andropadus milanjensis*

Fairly common, localised resident. Distinctly green with dark grey cap and white streaks on ear coverts. Underparts much greener than Yellow-bellied Bulbul (previous page). Mostly silent but has various harsh calls 'chuck, churr-rr, chuck, churr-churr-trrrr ...', made while sidling along a branch in small hops. Feeds at the edges of evergreen forests, dense lowland forest scrub, thickets and, sometimes, in broad-leaved woodland. 19-21 cm (Streepwangwillie)

1
2
3
4
5
6

TITS

Family PARIDAE. Small insectivorous, arboreal birds with short, stout bills, the nostrils obscured by bristles. Habitually forage in the tree canopies in bird parties, clambering about the branches in agile fashion and frequently feeding in inverted positions or running up tree-trunks like a woodpecker. They have rasping calls.

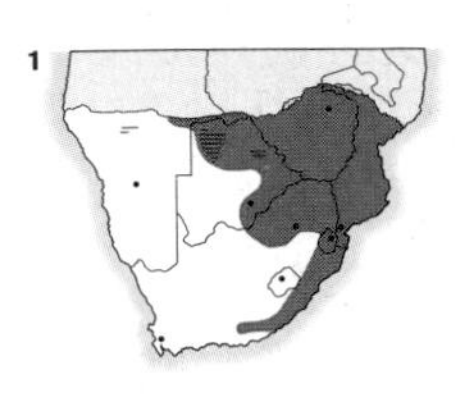

1 SOUTHERN BLACK TIT *Parus niger*

Common, near endemic resident. Male distinguished from (2) by heavier bill and more white on the vent and undertail; northern races may show more or less white on the folded wing than illustrated. Female as illustrated or darker on underparts. Immature resembles female. The calls are harsh and rasping, a rapid 'twiddy-zeet-zeet-zeet' or 'zeu-zeu-zeu-twit'. Pairs or groups occur in a wide variety of wooded habitats, including coastal forests and exotic plantations. 16 cm (Gewone swartmees)

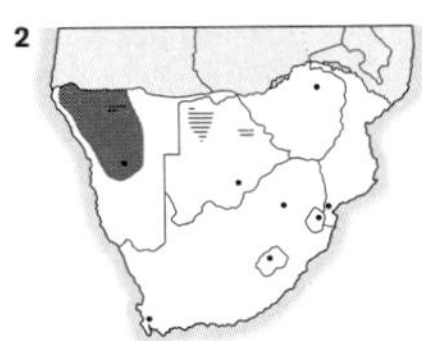

2 CARP'S BLACK TIT *Parus carpi*

Common, localised, near endemic resident. Smaller than (1), the vent and undertail with either small traces of white or none, the bill smaller. Female and immature are duller. Calls and habits like (1). Occurs in mopane and *Acacia* savanna. 14 cm (Ovamboswartmees)

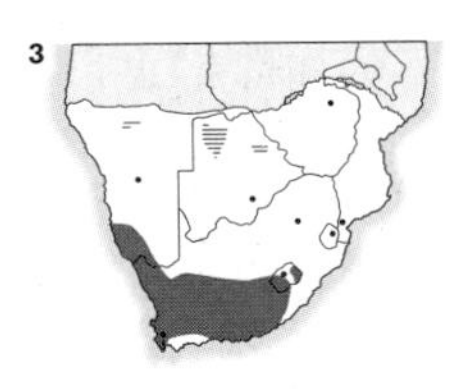

3 SOUTHERN GREY TIT *Parus afer*

Common, endemic resident. Distinguished from (4) by *grey-brown* (not blue-grey) mantle and back, more tawny appearance and shorter tail. Sexes are alike; immature similar. The call can be likened to 'Piet-jou-jou'. Pairs or small groups in Karoo scrub, dry thornveld, rocky hills and gorges. A restless species, frequenting the smaller trees and bushes. 13 cm (Piet-tjou-tjou-grysmees)

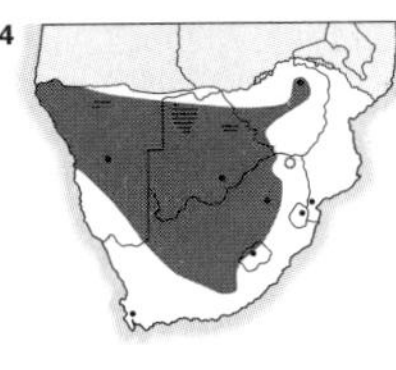

4 ASHY TIT *Parus cinerascens*

Common, near endemic resident. Identified by *blue-grey* mantle, back and underparts; of generally greyer appearance than either (3) or (5). Sexes are alike; immature duller. Singly or in pairs in thornveld and mixed bushveld, frequently in bird parties. 14 cm (Acaciagrysmees)

5 NORTHERN GREY TIT *Parus griseiventris*

Common resident. Distinguished from (4) by *white underparts* (not grey) and broader white regions on sides of head. Pairs, usually in bird parties, are found in the broad-leaved miombo woodland of Zimbabwe. 14 cm (Miombogrysmees)

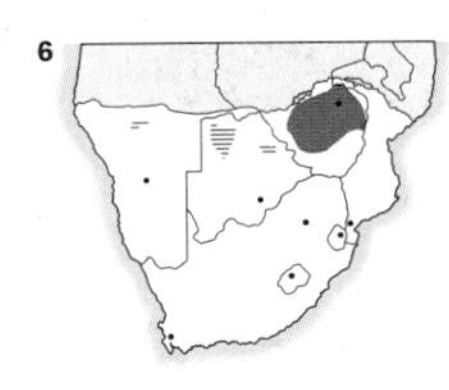

6 RUFOUS-BELLIED TIT *Parus rufiventris*

Uncommon, localised resident. The western race (a) with black head, cream-coloured eyes and rufous underparts distinctive (the underparts paler when not breeding); the pale eastern race (b) occurs only in the Zimbabwe-Mozambique border regions. Immature is duller, with brown eyes, the wing feathers edged yellowish. Calls 'chik-wee' and a rasping 'chrrr'. Pairs and small groups frequent well-developed miombo woodland, feeding mostly in bird parties in the upper stratum. 15 cm (Swartkopmees)

♂
1
♀
2
3
b
4
6
a
5

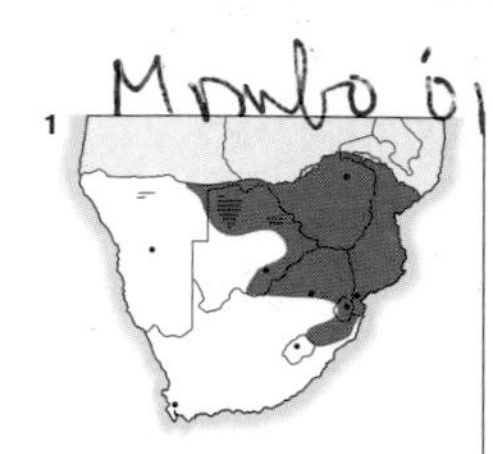

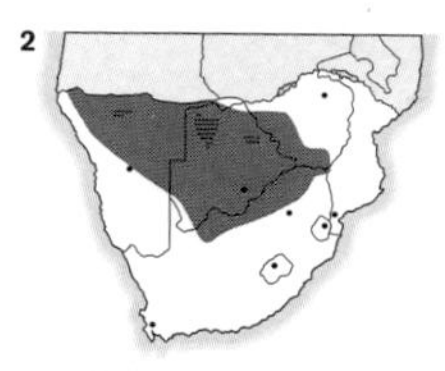

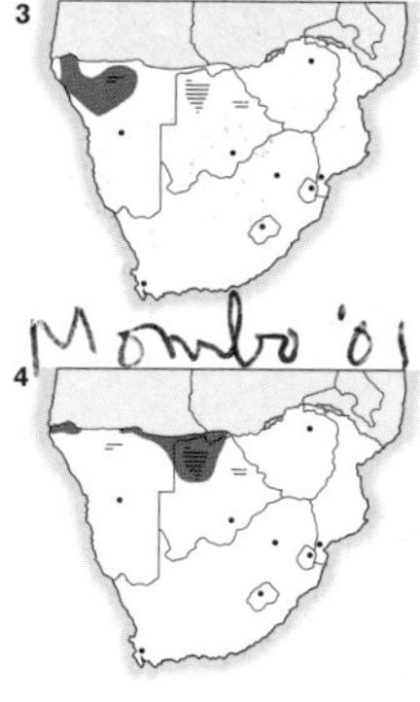

BABBLERS

Family TIMALIIDAE. Insectivorous, thrush-like terrestrial birds of gregarious habits and with distinctive babbling calls. Sexes are alike.

1 ARROW-MARKED BABBLER *Turdoides jardineii*

Common resident. Identified by call and whitish, arrow-like streaks on the underparts; cf. (4), which has scale-like breast markings and a white rump. Immature lacks the arrow marks but is usually seen with adults. The call is a noisy, excitable whirring started by one bird and taken up by all the others until it resembles hysterical giggling; the basic sound is 'scurr-scurr-scurr ...', harsher and more mechanical-sounding than the similar call of Red-billed Wood Hoopoe (p. 256). Occurs in parties of six to 10 birds within thickets in woodland, mixed bushveld, wooded hillsides, plus suburbia in Zimbabwe. Usually in the lower stratum, calling frequently. 23-5 cm (Pylvlekkatlagter)

2 PIED BABBLER *Turdoides bicolor* NE

Common, near endemic resident. Entirely white except for black wings and tail. Immature is initially olive-brown, becoming white gradually. The call is a high-pitched babbling, one bird commencing 'skerr-skerr-skerr-kikikikikiker-rkerrkerr ...' and all others joining in; shriller than (1). Parties of up to 12 birds frequent dry thornveld and woodland. 26 cm (Witkatlagter)

3 BARE-CHEEKED BABBLER *Turdoides gymnogenys* 

Fairly common, near endemic resident. Adult resembles immature of (2) except for bare black skin under eye; it differs from adult of (2) in this and in being less white, upperparts and sides of neck brown or cinnamon. Groups utter a typical babbler cackling, a high-pitched 'kurrkurrkurrkurrkurr ...'. Found in arid mopane woodland in north-western Namibia, frequenting dry watercourses and hillsides with trees. 24 cm (Kaalwangkatlagter)

4 HARTLAUB'S or WHITE-RUMPED BABBLER *Turdoides hartlaubii*

Common, localised resident. Differs from (1) mainly in white rump, the head and breast with all feathers pale-edged, giving a scaly appearance; underbelly and vent also white. Immature has a paler throat. The call is a noisy, high-pitched babbling 'kwekwekwekwekwekwekwe ...' or 'papapapapapapa ...' similar to (5). Parties occur in riverine woodland and reeds and papyrus-beds on floodplains of the Zambezi-Okavango-Cunene River system. 26 cm (Witkruiskatlagter)

5 BLACK-FACED BABBLER *Turdoides melanops*

Uncommon, localised resident. Black mask and distinctive yellow eyes diagnostic. The call is a high-pitched 'papapapapapapa ...' by several birds. Small parties occur in broad-leaved woodland and *Acacia* thickets. Shy and secretive, keeping to thick cover. 28 cm (Swartwangkatlagter)

1
2
3
4
5

1

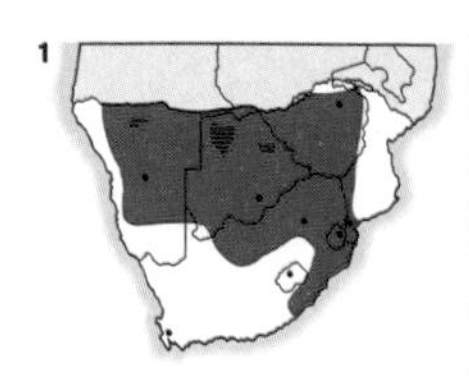

2

3

4

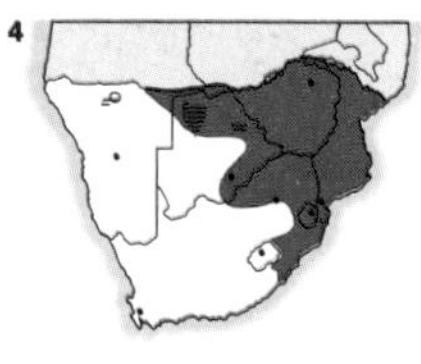

5

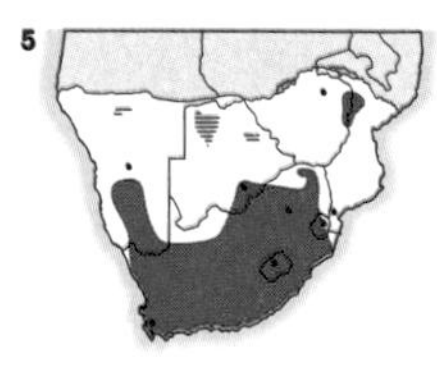

THRUSHES, CHATS AND ROBINS

Family TURDIDAE. Largely terrestrial, insectivorous or frugivorous birds which sing from trees, some robins rating as among our finest songsters. The sexes are alike unless otherwise stated, while immatures usually have the feathers of the upperparts pale-edged, the underparts spotted.

1 **GROUNDSCRAPER THRUSH** *Turdus litsitsirupa*

Common resident. Differs from (2) in erect stance, absence of white wing-spots and habitat preference; in flight shows chestnut wings. Differs from Dusky Lark (p. 280) in grey-brown (not dark brown) upperparts. Calls 'lipsit-sirupa' (hence its specific name) and sings a brisk, melodious song, the phrases continually varied. Singly in open woodland, mixed bushveld, cattle kraals and rural suburbia. 22 cm (Gevlekte lyster)

2 **SPOTTED THRUSH** *Zoothera guttata*

Fairly common, localised resident. Differs from (1) in bold white wing-spots. Has a clear, flute-like song, the accent always on the first syllable 'TCHEEooo-che-chichoo, TREEoo-tretrree ...'. Found singly or in pairs in the understorey of evergreen forests of the eastern seaboard; a winter visitor to upland Zululand forests. 23 cm (Natallyster)

3 **ORANGE THRUSH** *Zoothera gurneyi*

Uncommon, localised resident. Told by *dark bill,* rich orange throat, breast and flanks plus bold *white wing-bars.* Immature has the underparts mottled darker. Sings mostly at dawn and at last light, a variety of whistled phrases containing clear notes and complicated trills. Singly or in pairs in mist-belt evergreen forests where it is sparse and secretive. 23 cm (Oranjelyster)

4 **KURRICHANE THRUSH** *Turdus libonyana*

Common resident. Differs from (3) and (5) in distinct black and white throat markings (see enlarged head illustration) and white eyebrows (no white wing-bars); immature as illustrated. Calls a loud 'peet-peeoo' at dusk and has a mellow, complicated song with trills and warbles in short outbursts. Found mostly singly in a variety of wooded habitats including rural suburbia. 22 cm (Rooibeklyster)

5 **OLIVE THRUSH** *Turdus olivaceus*

Common resident. Duller than (4), differing in speckled throat (see head illustration) and lack of white on the belly. Birds with extensive orange underparts and whitish vent (a) most widespread, those with dull orange on the belly only and brownish vent (b) mainly in highveld regions. On the ground or in flight calls a thin 'wheet'; from a tree sings 'trootee trootee trootee, treetrrroo'. Male displays with drooped wings, splayed tail dragging on the ground. Singly or in pairs, in the north mainly in evergreen forests, elsewhere also in riverine woodland, exotic plantations and suburbia; often numerous in parks and gardens. 24 cm (Olyflyster)

313
1
2
3
4
J
5
a
b

1
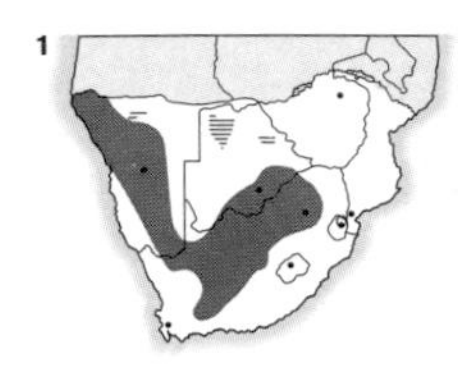

2
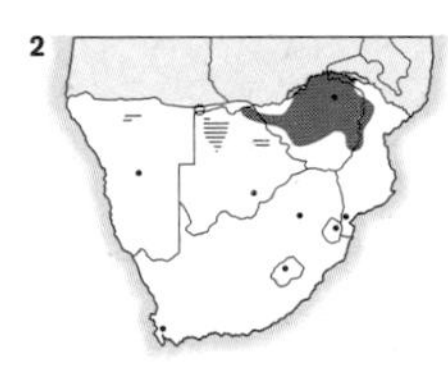

3

4
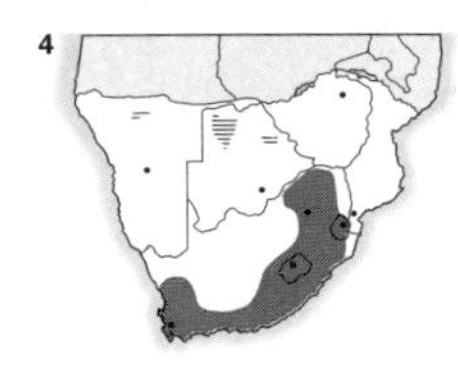

1 **SHORT-TOED ROCK THRUSH** *Monticola brevipes*

Fairly common, near endemic resident. In western regions male distinguished by whitish crown, but in its eastern distribution male *lacks the pale crown*, being of the race *M.b. pretoriae,* then difficult to distinguish from (4) except for greyer upperparts and whiter wing feather edges. Female told from female of (4) by paler upperparts and throat. Sings a sweet song phrase incorporating imitations. Singly or in pairs in arid regions, frequenting bush-covered rocky hills and rocky ridges. Often perches on roadside telephone wires in Namibia. 18 cm (Korttoonkliplyster)

2 **MIOMBO ROCK THRUSH** *Monticola angolensis*

Common, localised resident. Male distinguished by grey head with *spotted crown,* female by white throat plus moustachial streak. Immature like female but throat more speckled, only the chin white. The song is 'pe-pe-per-pee-pew, per-per, pee-pew ...'. Pairs occur in broad-leaved woodland (especially miombo) and are *not associated with rocky habitats.* 18 cm (Angolakliplyster)

3 **SENTINEL ROCK THRUSH** *Monticola explorator*

Common, localised endemic resident. Male differs from other male rock thrushes in the grey of the head extending to the mantle and onto the breast. Has a lively, melodious song beginning 'chu-chu-chu-chee-chree, chee-chroo-chi-chi-chee-troo-tree ...', followed by a sequence of warbles, trills and chattering phrases; female utters a shorter, harsher version of the initial sequence. Alarm call is a rapid, descending 'tre-e-e-e-e-e-e'. Pairs frequent rocky uplands and montane grasslands in summer; in winter they move to lower levels and then favour Karoo vegetation, fynbos and grassland. Perches prominently with erect stance. 21 cm (Langtoonkliplyster)

4 **CAPE ROCK THRUSH** *Monticola rupestris*

Common endemic resident. Larger than other rock thrushes, both sexes more richly coloured; immature more spotted than adult. The song is a soft 'checheroo' followed immediately by a loud 'cheewoo-chirri-cheewoo-tiriri' often repeated. Pairs frequent montane slopes and rocky, bush-covered hillsides at all altitudes plus rocky gorges. 21 cm (Kaapse kliplyster)

♀
1
♂
♀
2
♂
♀
3
♂
♀
4
♂

1

2

3
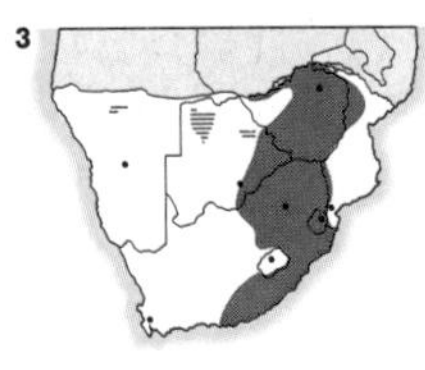

4

1 CAPE ROCKJUMPER *Chaetops frenatus* E

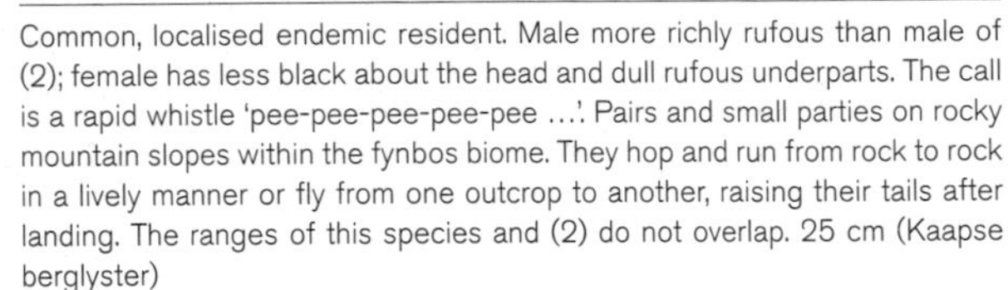

Common, localised endemic resident. Male more richly rufous than male of (2); female has less black about the head and dull rufous underparts. The call is a rapid whistle 'pee-pee-pee-pee-pee …'. Pairs and small parties on rocky mountain slopes within the fynbos biome. They hop and run from rock to rock in a lively manner or fly from one outcrop to another, raising their tails after landing. The ranges of this species and (2) do not overlap. 25 cm (Kaapse berglyster)

2 ORANGE-BREASTED ROCKJUMPER *Chaetops aurantius* E

Common, localised endemic resident. Both sexes are paler than (1) but are identical in all other ways. Pairs occur in the mountains of Lesotho and surroundings in boulder-strewn grasslands north of the previous species, mainly above 2 000 m. 21 cm (Oranjeborsberglyster)

3 MOCKING CHAT *Thamnolaea cinnamomeiventris*

Common resident. Sexes differ as illustrated; immature like female. Differs from (1) in plain upperparts, the male only with a white shoulder-bar. Has various mellow calls and an attractive song, mostly involving imitations of other birds. A cheerful, lively bird that habitually raises the rear end of its body. In pairs in various rocky habitats with bushes, especially where the fig tree *Ficus ingens* is present, and often becoming tame near country dwellings. 20-23 cm (Dassievoël)

4 BOULDER CHAT *Pinarornis plumosus*

Fairly common, localised resident. Sooty black except for white in the wings and tail; immature similar. Utters a monotonous squeaking 'ink, ink, wink, wink' like an unoiled wheel, plus a clear whistle with the bill held vertically. Lively and agile, raising its tail when landing. Pairs frequent the well-wooded lower slopes of hills with rounded, granite boulders, occasionally in similar habitat at higher levels. Is most numerous in the Matobo National Park of southern Zimbabwe. Sparsely distributed in most regions. 23-7 cm (Swartberglyster)

♂
1
♂
♀
♀
2
3
♂
♀
4

1
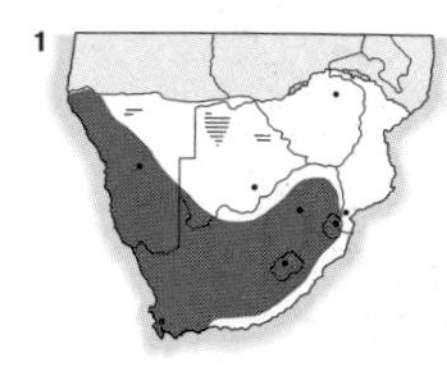

2
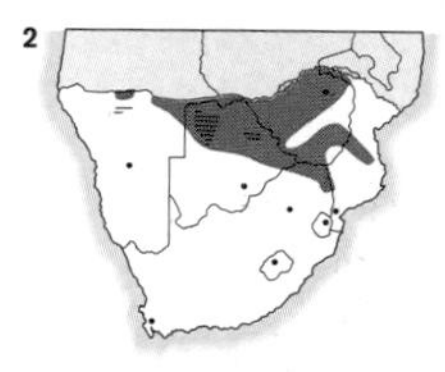

3
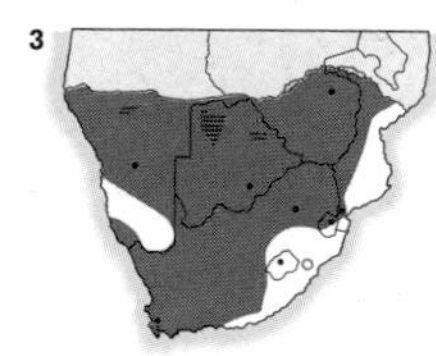

1 MOUNTAIN CHAT *Oenanthe monticola* E

Fairly common endemic resident. Male variable, usually as (a) or (b); in Namibia may have white underparts from lower breast to vent as (c). Immature resembles female. Similar to (2) but occurs in totally different habitat: boulder-strewn slopes or grassland with rocks or anthills, and in farmyards. Sings early and late in the day, mainly September-January, the song a loud jumble of fluty notes. May fly upwards a short distance, then drop down and fly low to another perch. Singly or in small groups which perch conspicuously on rocks or anthills. 17-20 cm (Bergwagter)

2 ARNOT'S CHAT *Thamnolaea arnoti*

Fairly common resident. Resembles (1) but male has a white cap (not grey), female has a white throat. Utters a shrill song containing a musical 'feeee' ascending and descending the scale. Pairs or small parties beneath trees, hopping about on the trunks and on the ground. Only in broad-leaved woodland with well-developed trees in flat country, especially mopane woodland. 18 cm (Bontpiek)

3 CAPPED WHEATEAR *Oenanthe pileata*

Common, localised resident. Immature lacks the black breast-band, eyebrow barely discernible (see illustration); told from female European Wheatear (p. 452) by paler tips to the feathers on upperparts. Sings from some low prominence or while fluttering straight up into the air, the song variable with imitations of other birds, even mechanical sounds. Walks about with much wing-flicking and tail-jerking. Loose groups on bare ground, short grassland near dams, airfields, well-grazed farmlands and burnt areas. 18 cm (Hoëveldskaapwagter)

PIED WHEATEAR (Bontskaapwagter) see p. 448.

ISABELLINE WHEATEAR (Vaalskaapwagter) see p. 448.

EUROPEAN WHEATEAR (Europese skaapwagter) see p. 452.

c
1
♀
♂ a
♂ b
3
♀
2
J
♂

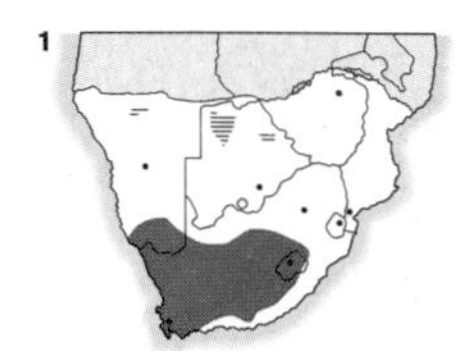

Note: The following four species are very alike in appearance and habits. All frequent open ground, perch conspicuously and ***flick their wings frequently.*** All have races showing plumage colour variations, darkest in eastern and palest in western forms with gradations between the extremes. All species call 'chak chak'. Identity best confirmed by colours of tail and upper tail coverts.

1 SICKLE-WINGED CHAT *Cercomela sinuata*

Locally common endemic resident. Most resembles (2) but is more slightly built, wing feathers more distinctly edged rufous, legs longer and eye-wattle more accentuated. Tail dark with buff outer edges; only upper tail coverts rufous. Immature spotted but tail pattern as adult. On open ground with short, scrubby vegetation, including fallow croplands and road verges. 15 cm (Vlaktespekvreter)

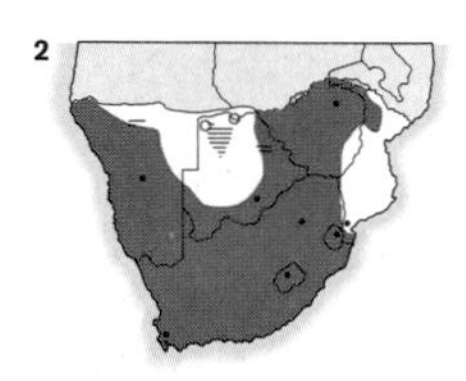

2 FAMILIAR CHAT *Cercomela familiaris*

Common resident. Very similar to (1) but appears more elongated, the edges of the wing feathers buffy and less obvious. Southern and eastern races (a) darkest and largest; Namibian race (b) palest and smallest. Tail deep rufous with dark central feathers and subterminal band. Immature told from immature of (1) only by tail pattern. Tame, frequenting rocky ground, often in hilly terrain; also walls and outbuildings on farms. 15 cm (Gewone spekvreter)

3 TRACTRAC CHAT *Cercomela tractrac*

Common, near endemic resident. Smaller and plumper than (1), (2) or (4). Dark southern race (a) has upper tail coverts very pale buff, almost white; pale Namibian race (b) has pure white on tail. Occurs in flat, arid plains, spending much time on the ground where it runs swiftly. 14-15 cm (Woestynspekvreter)

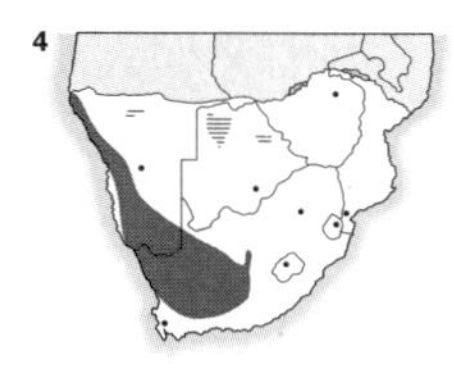

4 KAROO CHAT *Cercomela schlegelii*

Common endemic resident. Larger, more robust and elongated than (1) to (3). Southern and eastern races (a) darkest with grey rump and white on outer tail feathers; smallest, palest Namibian race (b) has white on outer tail feathers and upper tail coverts, plus beige rump. Has a rattling call 'tirr-tit-tat'. Frequents succulent Karoo scrub, perches on tall scrub, fences and telephone wires. 15-18 cm (Karoospekvreter)

J
1
a
b
2
a
b
3
a
b
4

1

1 WHINCHAT *Saxicola rubetra*

Very rare summer vagrant. Non-breeding male resembles female; this plumage most likely in southern Africa. Differs from Stonechat (overleaf) in slimmer build, bold white eyebrows and heavily streaked upperparts. Habits much like Stonechat, perching low down in open scrublands. 13-14 cm (Europese bontrokkie)

2

2 BUFF-STREAKED CHAT *Oenanthe bifasciata*

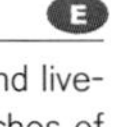

Common endemic resident. Identified by striking plumage patterns and lively, demonstrative behaviour. Has a loud and pleasant song with snatches of mimicry 'chit, chit, leleoo-chit, cherr-wee-oo, too-weelie, too-weeoo …'. Pairs inhabit rocky or stony hills and montane regions in sour grasslands. Tame, flitting from rock to rock with much flirting of tail and wings. 15-17 cm (Bergklipwagter)

3

3 HERERO CHAT *Namibornis herero*

Uncommon, near endemic resident. Unlikely to be confused with any other within its restricted distribution. Silent except when breeding, then utters a subdued 'ji-ju-jiiu' contact call, a mellow warbling song in jumbled, short phrases and a 'churrr' alarm note. Hunts from a low perch, occasionally flying down to seize insects on the ground. Found on hillsides, at the foot of hills and near dry watercourses in the arid Namib escarpment areas. Most plentiful at Groot Spitzkop, near Usakos. 17 cm (Hererospekvreter)

4

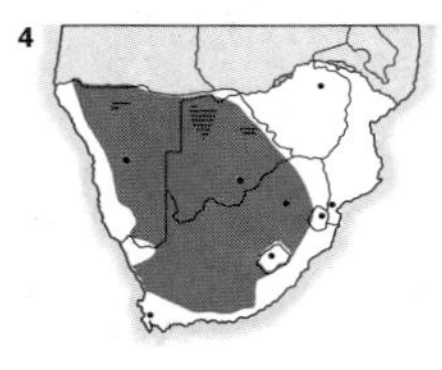

4 ANT-EATING CHAT *Myrmecocichla formicivora*

Common endemic resident. Entirely dull brown; male frequently lacks the white shoulder-patch. Pale wing feathers striking in flight. Call is a sharp 'peek'. A terrestrial species. Often perches with erect stance on termite mounds, bushes or fences in short grassland. Also makes brief fluttering flights. 18 cm (Swartpiek)

5

5 WHITE-BREASTED ALETHE *Alethe fuelleborni*

Rare, localised resident. Clear white underparts, lack of white eyebrows and robust appearance distinguish this species from robins. Sings a lively 'fweer-her-heee-her-hee-her'. A shy, retiring species. Inhabits the lower stratum of montane forests in the Dondo and Gorongosa regions of Mozambique. 18-20 cm (Witborslyster)

1
♀
♂
Br
2
♀
♂
3
4
♀
♂
5

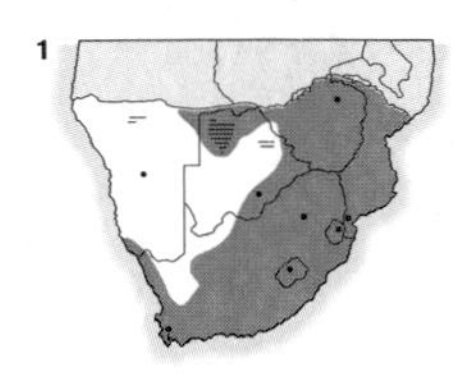

1 STONECHAT *Saxicola torquata*

Common resident. At rest the male is striking and unmistakable, in flight the female is identified by white wing-patches; both sexes identified by white rump; cf. Whinchat (previous page). Immature is like adult but more speckled. Utters a grating 'tsak, tsak'. Also has a short, shrill, warbling song. Usually in pairs in a wide variety of open grassland habitats: near marshes, vleis, dams, streams and roadsides, perching on some low shrub or fence from where it watches the ground for insects. Is seasonal in some regions, moving to lower or higher altitudes. 14 cm (Gewone bontrokkie)

(EURASIAN) REDSTART ((Eurasiese) rooistert) see p. 448.

2 CAPE ROBIN *Cossypha caffra*

Common resident. Distinguished by white eyebrows, orange upper breast and greyish underparts; in flight shows orange tail feathers and back. Immature has a pale orange breast spotted with black. Has a pleasant and continuing song, each passage starting on the same note and with the phrase 'Jan-Frederik' often repeated. Jerks its tail up when alert. Occurs in the fringes of forests at all levels (montane forests in eastern Zimbabwe), in riverine bush, patches of bush and rock on heath-covered hillsides especially at the base of cliffs and, in many regions, commonly in gardens. A winter visitor to eastern coastal districts. 18 cm (Gewone janfrederik)

3 WHITE-THROATED ROBIN *Cossypha humeralis* E

Common endemic resident. Distinguished by *white breast and wing-bar*. Immature is well spotted like all young robins. In the early morning calls repeatedly 'swee-swer, swee-swer ...'; cf. Natal Robin (p. 328). The call note is a quiet 'tseep ... tseep ... tseep ...'. Also has a beautiful song. Singly or in pairs in thickets in dry mixed bushveld, in riverine forests and at the foot of rocky, bush-covered hills and termitaria. Frequents gardens in some regions. 16-18 cm (Witkeeljanfrederik)

4 HEUGLIN'S ROBIN *Cossypha heuglini*

Common, localised resident. Identified by *entirely deep orange underparts* and black cap with prominent white eye-stripes. Immature is similar but spotted. The song consists of various melodious phrases repeated, starting quietly then working up to a crescendo, 'pip-pip-uree, pip-pip-uree ...' or 'don't-you-do-it, don't-you-do-it ...' or 'tirrootirree, tirrootirree ...' each phrase repeated up to about 16 times. Sings mostly at dawn and dusk, often two birds together from within a thicket. Inhabits dense thickets in riverine forests, at the base of densely wooded hills and termitaria. A garden bird in some Zimbabwe towns. 19-20 cm (Heuglinse janfrederik)

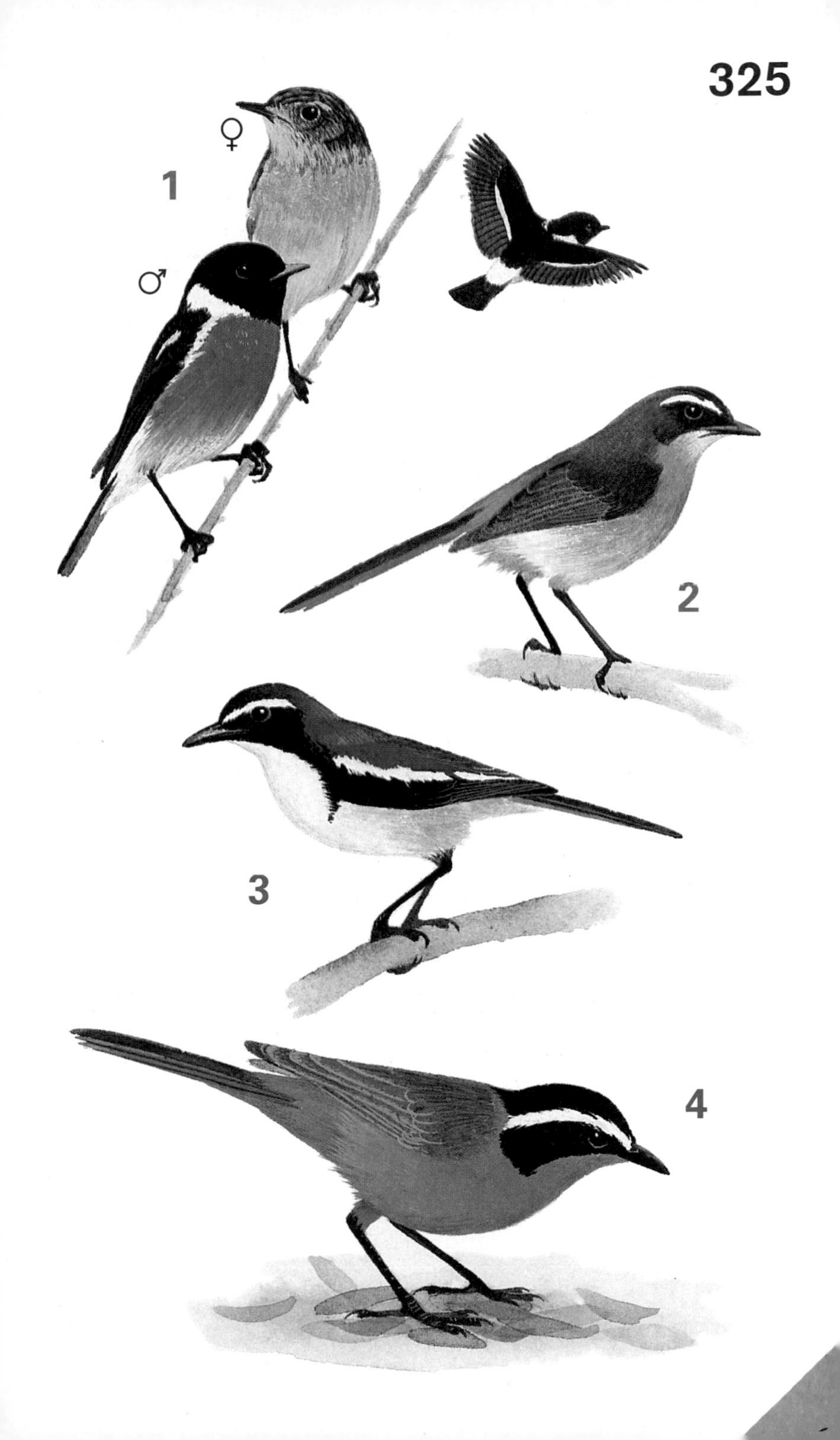

♀
1
♂
2
3
4

1

2

3
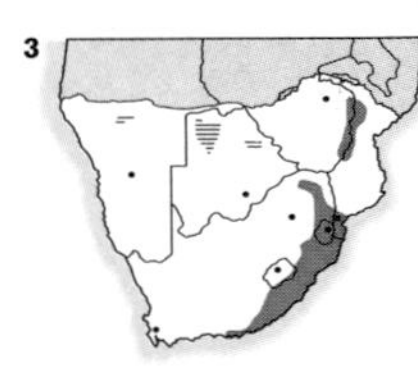

4

1 GUNNING'S ROBIN *Sheppardia gunningi*

Rare resident. Differs from other robins in entirely brown upperparts extending to below eye-level plus grey eyebrows with a small, barely visible white patch in front of the eyes. The song is loud, rapid and arresting, 'tirripeepoo-tirripeepoo-tirripeepoo, tirritee-tirritee-tirritee ...'. A small robin of Mozambique lowland forests from the Beira region northwards. Keeps mostly to the lower stratum, feeding on the ground. Shy and little known. 14 cm (Gunningse janfrederik)

2 SWYNNERTON'S ROBIN *Swynnertonia swynnertoni*

Fairly common, localised resident. Identified by white breast-band with black border. Frequently utters a quiet, sibilant 'si-see-see' and has a stuttering, drawn-out call note 'trrr-e-e-e-e-e-e-e'. A small, tame robin of montane forests in eastern Zimbabwe. Frequents the lower stratum, hopping about in a lively manner with much wing- and tail-flicking. 14 cm (Bandkeeljanfrederik)

3 STARRED ROBIN *Pogonocichla stellata*

Common resident. Told by entirely grey head, greenish upperparts and orange-yellow underparts; white 'stars' before eyes and on central breast evident only when the bird is excited or alarmed. Immature fledges with typical spotted appearance of young robins; later attains lemon-yellow underparts for one year (see illustration). The call in coastal areas is a piping 'too-twee' frequently repeated, in montane areas a repeated 'pee, du-du WHEEE ...', the accent on the last syllable which has a whip-like quality; also has a subdued, piping song. Occurs in the lower stratum of coastal and montane evergreen forests. A quiet, lively species but not secretive. 15-17 cm (Witkoljanfrederik)

4 CHORISTER ROBIN *Cossypha dichroa*

Common endemic resident. A fairly large robin with *black hood* (*no white eyebrow*) and *clear orange underparts*; immature well spotted as illustrated. The contact call is a monotonous 'toy, toy, toy ...' repeated for long periods; the song a variety of beautiful, mellow phrases incorporating imitations of other bird calls. Very vocal October-January. A montane evergreen forest species, inhabiting the midstratum. Often absent from montane forests April-September, but present in coastal forests at this time. 20 cm (Lawaaimakerjanfrederik)

1
2
3 J
3
4 J
4

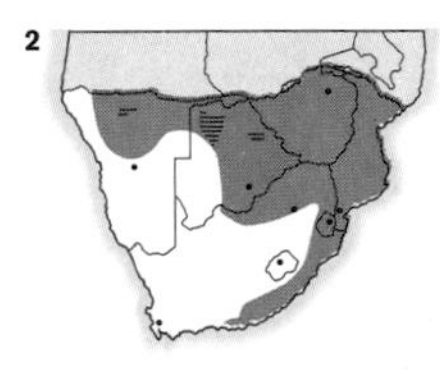

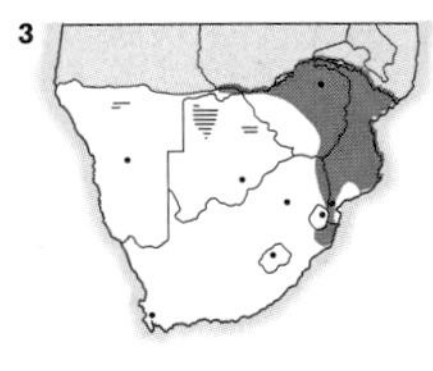

1 **NATAL ROBIN** *Cossypha natalensis*

Common resident. Entirely orange from *above the eyes* and sides of head to undertail, no white eyebrow. Immature has pale spotting on the upperparts, dark spotting below. Has a monotonous double call note 'trrree-trrirr, trrree-trrirr, trrree-trrirr ...' continued for long periods; cf. White-throated Robin (p. 324). The song is composed of various melodious phrases (remarkably similar to human whistling) and imitations of other bird calls; often imitates Chorister Robin (previous page). Singly or in pairs in thickets within coastal bush, forests, riverine forests and valley bush. Raises its tail frequently. Keeps mostly within dense cover in the lower and midstrata but feeds in the open late in the day. 18-20 cm (Nataljanfrederik)

2 **WHITE-BROWED SCRUB ROBIN** *Erythropygia leucophrys*

Common resident. A small brownish robin with white wing-markings plus a well-streaked breast (in the Okavango Delta the breast is unstreaked but has an orange wash, cf. Bearded Robin (3)); when flying it reveals an orange rump and upper tail coverts, while the fanned tail shows white tips; see illustration. Immature has mottled upperparts. Sings for long periods on warm days; various loud phrases repeated almost without pause 'pirit-pirit-tertwee-pirit-pirit-tertwee-chee-chee-chu-it-chu-it ...'. Occurs in mixed bushveld, thornveld and woodland, especially within thickets formed by low bushes and long grass. Sings from an exposed bush-top perch, but is otherwise secretive in the lower stratum. 15 cm (Gestreepte wipstert)

3 **BEARDED ROBIN** *Erythropygia quadrivirgata*

Fairly common resident. Identified by white eyebrows bordered by black lines plus white throat with black moustachial streak and dull, pale orange breast. Immature is more mottled. The song is loud and clear, a series of pleasant phrases each repeated three or four times with short pauses 'pee-pee-pee, terr-treee, chiroo-chiroo-chiroo, witchoo-witchoo-witchoo, pee-pee-pee-pee, chu-it, chu-it, chu-it ...', some phrases rising in crescendo; also imitates other bird calls. Usually singly in broad-leaved and riverine woodland. Largely terrestrial unless singing. 16-18 cm (Baardwipstert)

4 **BROWN ROBIN** *Erythropygia signata* E

Uncommon endemic resident. A brown robin with white eyebrows and wing markings plus whitish underparts. Immature is spotted and scaled, otherwise similar. The song, rendered at dawn and last light, is a high-pitched series of melancholy phrases beginning always on a single or double high note 'treetroo-tretretre ...'; the call is a sibilant 'zit-zeeeet'. Inhabits the interiors of mistbelt evergreen forests and dense riparian bush at lower altitudes, always within the lower and midstrata. Difficult to see within its habitat. 18 cm (Bruinwipstert)

1
2
3
4

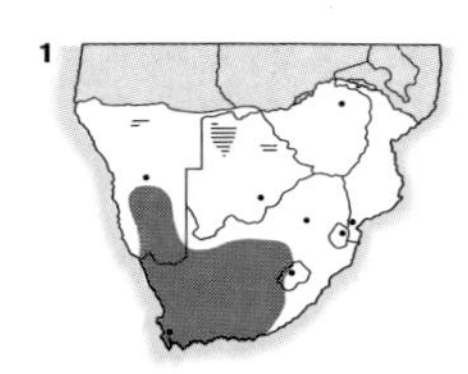

1 KAROO ROBIN *Erythropygia coryphaeus* E

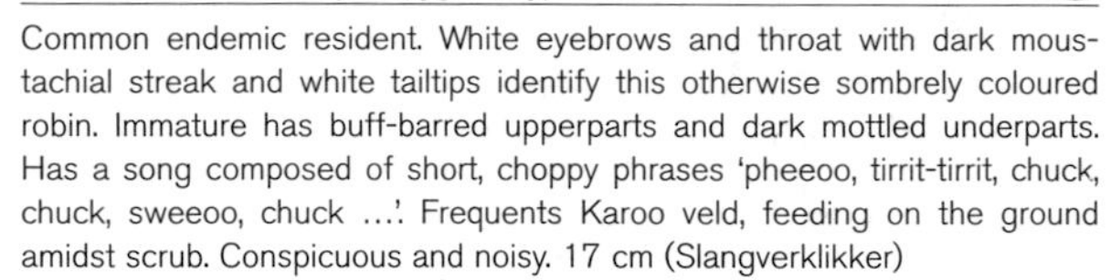

Common endemic resident. White eyebrows and throat with dark moustachial streak and white tailtips identify this otherwise sombrely coloured robin. Immature has buff-barred upperparts and dark mottled underparts. Has a song composed of short, choppy phrases 'pheeoo, tirrit-tirrit, chuck, chuck, sweeoo, chuck ...'. Frequents Karoo veld, feeding on the ground amidst scrub. Conspicuous and noisy. 17 cm (Slangverklikker)

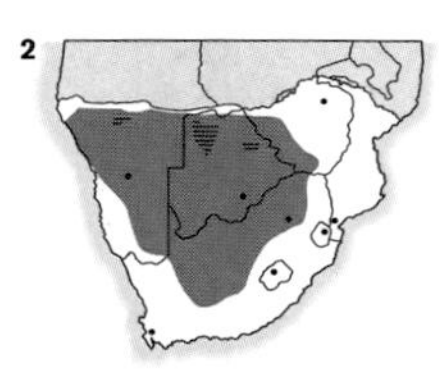

2 KALAHARI ROBIN *Erythropygia paena*

Common, near endemic resident. Much paler, sandier-looking than (1); conspicuous rufous tail has black subterminal band and white tips; see illustration. Immature has lightly spotted underparts. Often perches on a bush calling 'twee' intermittently for long periods. The song is a high-pitched sequence of repeated phrases, 'seeoo-seeoo, tweetoo-tweetoo-tweetoo, seetoo-seetoo, tritritritritri ...'. Singly or in pairs in Kalahari thornveld and old cultivations, particularly in arid western regions. Feeds on open ground and sings from a tree-top, but enters thorn thickets when alarmed. 16-17 cm (Kalahariwipstert)

3 RUFOUS-TAILED PALM THRUSH *Cichladusa ruficauda*

Uncommon, localised resident. Identified by rufous upperparts and plain buff underparts with rufous tail; (4) also has a rufous tail but their ranges are mutually exclusive. Has a rich, melodious song heard mostly at dawn and dusk, pairs often singing in duet. Occurs in association with *Borassus* and oil palms on the Cunene River and northwards. Little known in southern Africa. 17 cm (Rooistertmôrelyster)

4 COLLARED PALM THRUSH *Cichladusa arquata*

Common, localised resident. Differs from (3) mainly in black-bordered throat-patch (often broken or incomplete), grey nape, duller mantle and straw-coloured eyes, but has similar rufous tail. Immature is mottled below, black throat-border vestigial. Has a melodious, liquid song heard mostly mornings and evenings. Lively and conspicuous. Spends much time foraging on the ground. When perched on a branch droops its wings and raises and lowers its tail continuously. Pairs and small parties in palm savanna with *Borassus* and *Hyphaene* palms, being especially numerous in the Victoria Falls and Gorongosa regions. 19 cm (Palmmôrelyster)

1
2
3
4

1

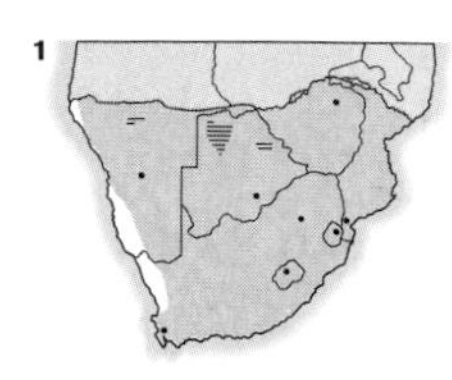

2

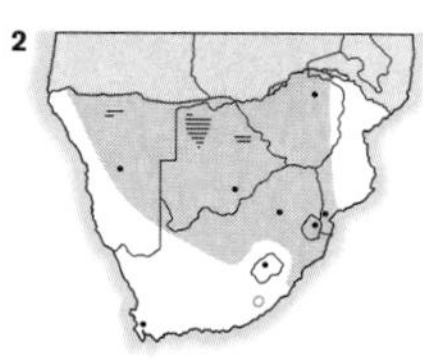

3

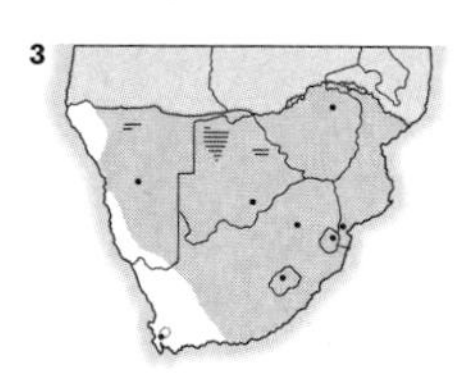

4

5

WARBLERS

Family SYLVIIDAE. Small, insectivorous birds of mostly sombre colouring. Many have attractive warbling songs which aid identification. Several species visit southern Africa from Europe during summer. Sexes are alike.

1 WILLOW WARBLER *Phylloscopus trochilus*

Common summer visitor. Also occurs in a much paler form than illustrated and also with brown upperparts and white underparts, but identified always by *distinct eyebrows and notched tailtip;* cf. (3). While feeding calls a querulous, quiet 'foo-wee'; sings, usually in the mornings, a descending jumble of notes 'tee-tee-tee-tee-tu-tu-tu-twee-twee-sweet-sweet-sweet-sweet ...'. Occurs singly in almost any bush habitat, including suburbia. An active leaf-gleaner, which works its way busily through the canopy and midstratum, occasionally darting out to hawk a flying insect. 12 cm (Hofsanger)

2 ICTERINE WARBLER *Hippolais icterina*

Fairly common summer visitor. Larger than (1), usually more yellow with clearly yellow-edged wing coverts, sharply sloping forehead, orange lower mandible and *unnotched* tailtip. Sings a repetitive, vehement jumble of warbled notes, some pleasant, others harsh. Solitary; prefers *Acacia* thornveld and hops about actively while feeding in the tree canopies, often singing. Sparsely distributed. 14-15 cm (Spotvoël)

3 GARDEN WARBLER *Sylvia borin*

Fairly common summer visitor. A plain-coloured warbler without distinctive markings. Usually located by song, a quiet warbling of rather monotonous quality uttered from the depths of a bush. Always solitary in dense bush or thickets, especially along watercourses and in parks and gardens. In some regions is not present until November. 15 cm (Tuinsanger)

(EUROPEAN) BLACKCAP ((Europese) swartkroonsanger) see p. 448.

4 THRUSH NIGHTINGALE *Luscinia luscinia*

Rare to locally common summer visitor. Tail and wing feather margins rich rufous, underparts whitish with *mottled breast.* The song is a rich melody of variable notes, some sweet, some harsh. Solitary in dense thickets, often in riverine bush, but secretive. Returns to the same thicket from mid-December to January departing March-April each year. 16-18 cm (Lysternagtegaal)

5 OLIVE-TREE WARBLER *Hippolais olivetorum*

Uncommon, localised summer visitor. A large warbler with white eyebrows, sharply sloping forehead, large two-coloured bill and pale outer edges to wing feathers and tailtip. Song louder and deeper than most warblers, a grating jumble of notes with sharp 'tch-tch' sounds interspersed; similar to that of Great Reed Warbler (p. 338). Singly in *Acacia* thornveld and riverine bush, feeding and singing from within the foliage. 16-18 cm (Olyfboomsanger)

1
2
3
4
5

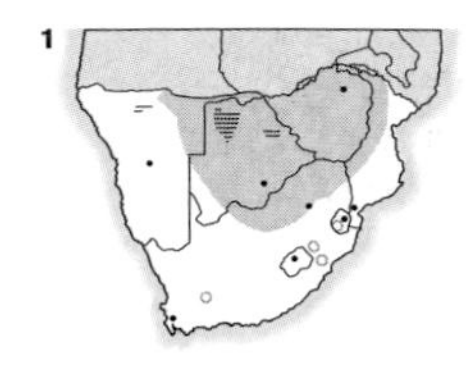

1 WHITETHROAT *Sylvia communis*

Uncommon summer visitor. Identified by white throat contrasting with pale buff breast, whitish eye-ring, *prominent rufous wing feather edges* and white outer tail feathers. The crown feathers are frequently raised, giving the head a peaked appearance. Has a sharp 'tacc-tacc' call, a conversational 'wheet, wheet, whit-whit-whit-whit' and a brisk, scratchy warble. A restless, lively species found in dry scrub thickets and thornveld. November-March. 15 cm (Witkeelsanger)

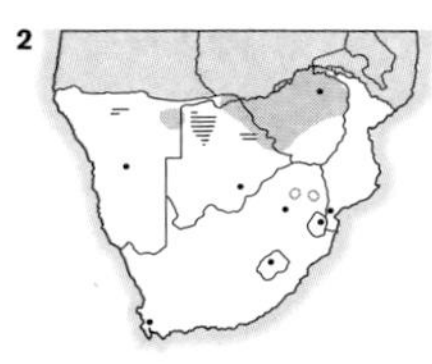

2 RIVER WARBLER *Locustella fluviatilis*

Rare midsummer visitor. Similar to (3) and (4) but broader breast markings form distinct streaks radiating from the throat; *large undertail coverts* pale-tipped, legs paler than either (3) or (4). Utters an intermittent, cricket-like 'zer zer zer zer ...'. Highly secretive in dense thickets, reed-beds and other herbage near streams, creeping about near or on the ground. When alarmed drops to the ground and *runs away.* 13 cm (Sprinkaansanger)

3 BARRATT'S WARBLER *Bradypterus barratti*

Fairly common endemic resident. Very similar to (2) except for narrower, more profuse breast markings (extending onto flanks in southern races), large *rounded tail* and darker legs. Normal call is a soft 'tuc' or 'trrr' as it creeps about or, in early summer, 'chree, chree, chooreereereereereeree'. Frequents patches of dense bush, tangled scrub and bracken in montane forest fringes. Highly secretive. 15-16 cm (Ruigtesanger)

4 KNYSNA WARBLER *Bradypterus sylvaticus*

Fairly common, localised endemic resident. Differs from (3) in duskier underparts and lack of clear breast markings. It has a high-pitched, staccato song uttered with increasing speed and ending with a trill 'tsip-tsip-tsip-tsip-tsip-tsiptsiptsiptsiptrrrrrrrrrrrrrrr'. Remains concealed in the dense foliage of forest fringes and wooded kloofs but lively and active, feeding in both the mid- and lower strata. 14-15 cm (Knysnaruigtesanger)

5 VICTORIN'S WARBLER *Bradypterus victorini*

Common, localised endemic resident. Best identified by *orange-yellow eyes.* In the brief song the notes go up and down with increasing rapidity 'missis-sippippippippi'. Occurs in dense montane scrub on rain-exposed slopes, in rocky kloofs and alongside mountain streams. Emerges from cover to sing from a low bush. 16 cm (Rooiborsruigtesanger)

6 BROAD-TAILED WARBLER *Schoenicola brevirostris*

Uncommon resident. Recognised by *voluminous black tail* with buff-tipped feathers. Male utters a weak metallic 'trreep, trreep, trreep' call; female a harsh 'chick' and 'zink, zink, zink' repeated rapidly and regularly. Frequents tall grass, reeds and tangled vegetation near streams and vleis. Remains mostly within the vegetation, but sometimes perches conspicuously in a *vertical position.* If flushed makes off with conspicuous bobbing flight, then drops down and runs off; seldom flushes a second time. 17 cm (Breëstertsanger)

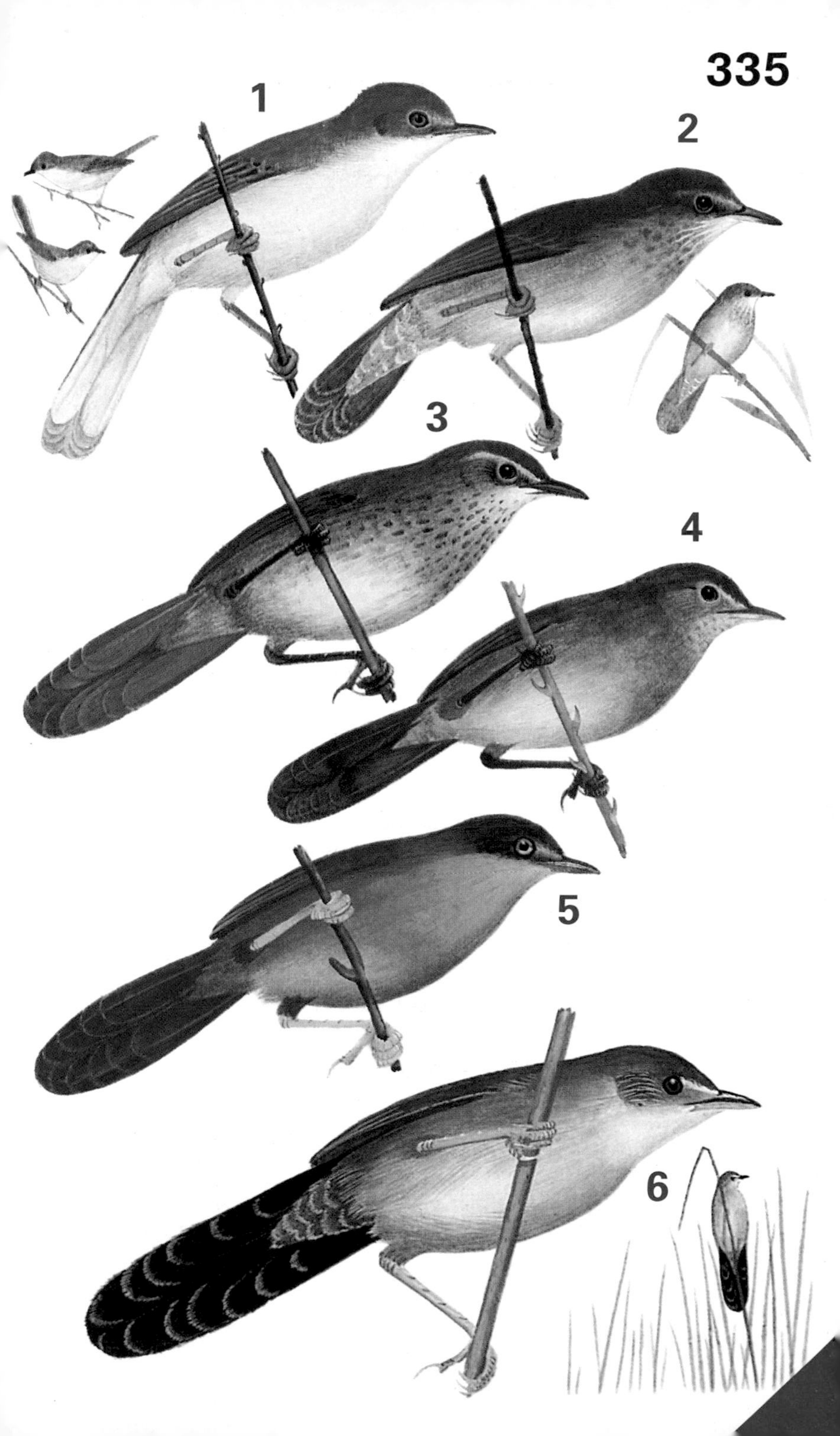
1
2
3
4
5
6

1
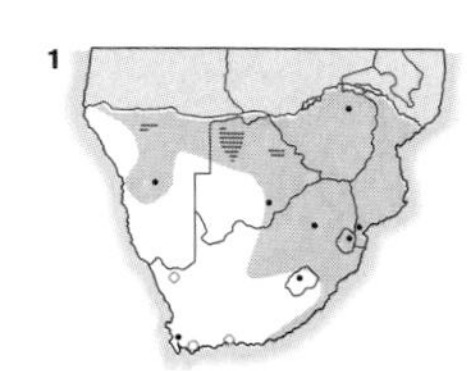

2
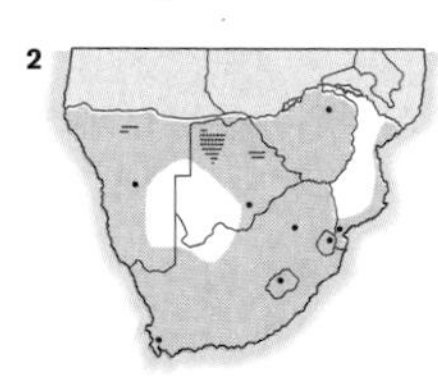

3
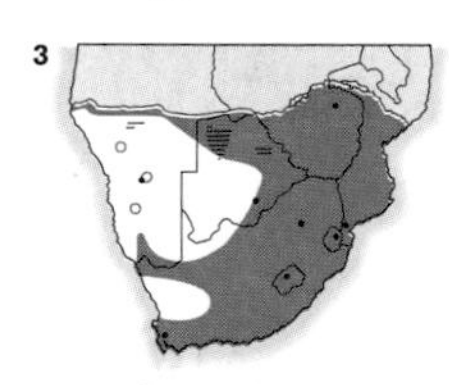

4
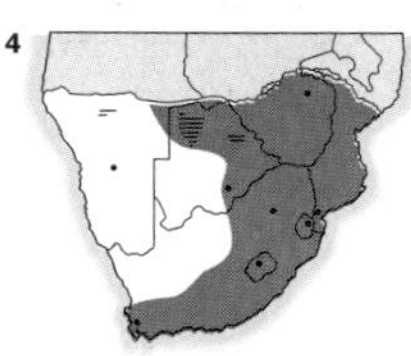

5

6
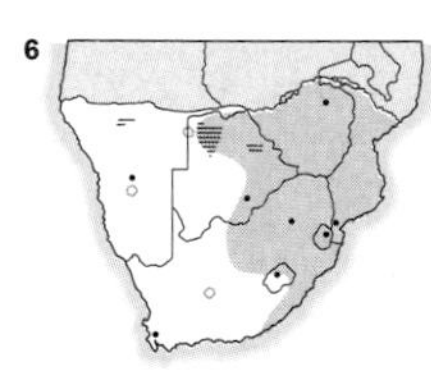

7

1 EUROPEAN SEDGE WARBLER *Acrocephalus schoenobaenus*

Fairly common summer visitor. Recognised by boldly marked upperparts, especially eye-stripes, streaked crown and faintly blotched breast. Feeding call is a quiet 'tick, tick ...', alarm call a harsh, rasping 'churrr'. Has a loud, hurried song with little repetition, chattering and sweet passages mixed with imitations of other birds. Solitary in dense riverside vegetation, marsh fringes and sewage settlement pans. Creeps about at low level. 13 cm (Europese vleisanger)

2 AFRICAN MARSH WARBLER *Acrocephalus baeticatus*

Common summer resident; occasional in winter. No distinctive eyebrow. Underparts predominantly white, legs purple-brown. Utters a sharp 'tik' while creeping about in thick cover, plus a harsh, racket-like 'churrr' when alarmed. Song is a slow, monotonous warbling 'chuck-chuck-weee-chirruc-churr-werr-weee-weee-chirruc ...' for long periods when breeding; cf. (6). In reeds or other dense herbage near swamps or away from water in tall grass, bushes and suburbia. Remains well hidden but moves about constantly. 13 cm (Kleinrietsanger)

3 CAPE REED WARBLER *Acrocephalus gracilirostris*

Common resident. Has a distinct white eyebrow and dark brown legs. The rich, melodious song is 'chiroo-chrooo, tiririririririri', slowly at first, then fast. Always found *near fresh water* in reeds, bulrushes or other waterside herbage. Bold and inquisitive. 15-17 cm (Kaapse rietsanger)

4 AFRICAN SEDGE WARBLER *Bradypterus baboecala*

Common resident. Upperparts dark, *tail broad and rounded,* definite eye-stripe plus faint markings on the upper breast. Call is a loud, distinctive 'cruk, cruk, cruk, crukcrukcrukcrukcrukcrukcruk' like a stick drawn across a railing, followed by wing-snapping. Singly or in pairs in dense vegetation *over water.* Secretive, mostly in the lower stratum. 17 cm (Kaapse vleisanger)

5 CINNAMON REED WARBLER *Acrocephalus cinnamomeus*

Rare vagrant. A single specimen from Umvoti on the east coast. Possibly regular in the Zambezi Valley. Similar to (6) and (7) but smaller, upperparts washed cinnamon. May be a race of (2). 10,5 cm (Kaneelrietsanger)

6 EUROPEAN MARSH WARBLER *Acrocephalus palustris*

Common, widespread summer visitor. Eyebrows indistinct, underparts (except throat) lightly washed yellow-buff, upperparts including rump uniformly olive-brown; cf. (7) from which it cannot be distinguished in the field except by habitat. Utters a frequent 'tuc' while creeping about in cover, and has a pleasant, varied warbling song which includes mimicry. Is found *away from water* in dense bracken-brier patches, riparian thickets, parks and gardens from where it sings almost continuously December-March. Highly secretive. 12 cm (Europese rietsanger)

7 EUROPEAN REED WARBLER *Acrocephalus scirpaceus*

Rare summer visitor. Very few records for southern Africa. In the field indistinguishable from (6) except by habitat. Found in waterside vegetation. 13 cm (Hermanse rietsanger)

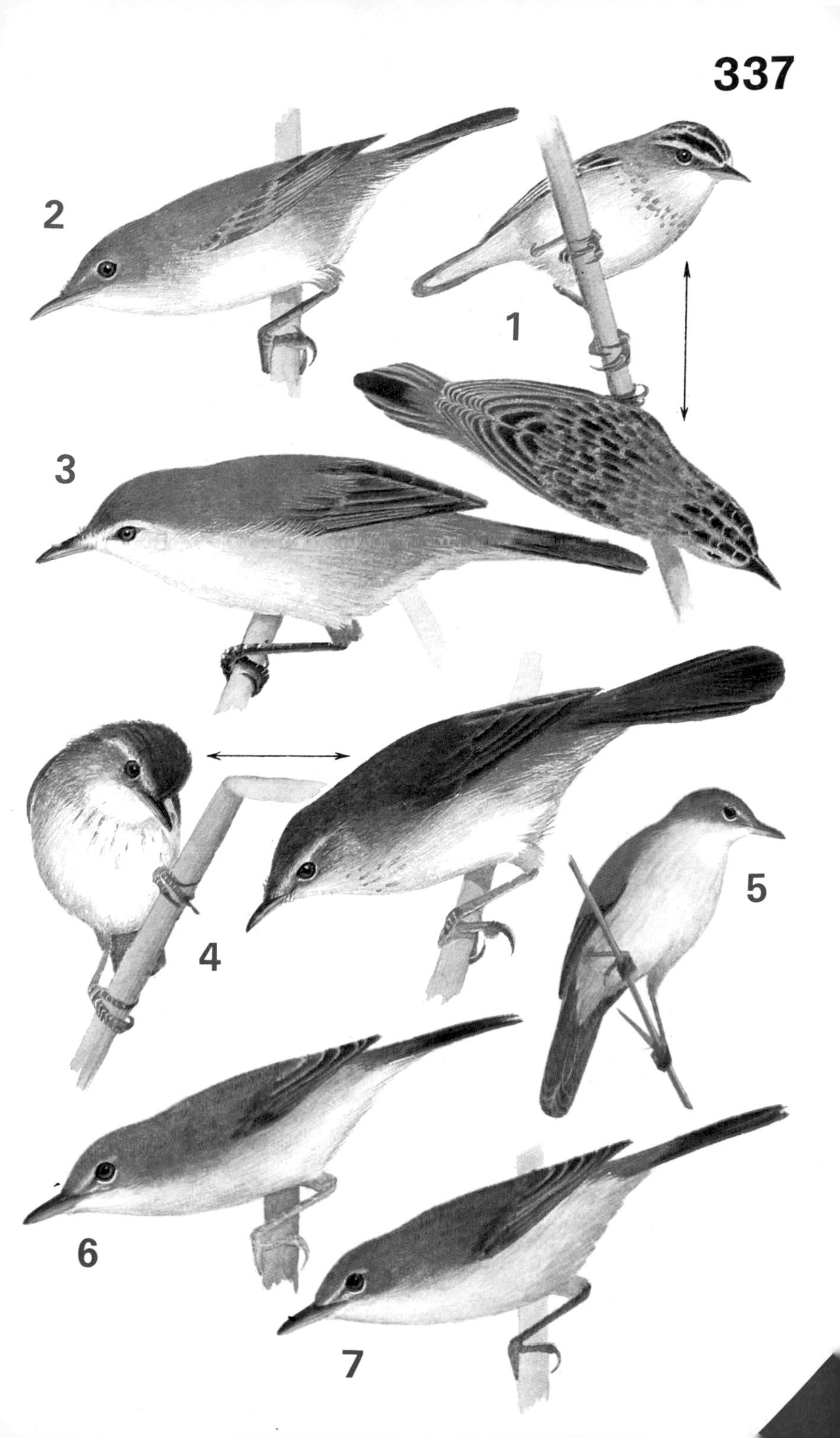
2
1
3
4
5
6
7

1 **GREATER SWAMP WARBLER** *Acrocephalus rufescens*

Fairly common, highly localised resident. A large, dark warbler with prominent slender bill and dark legs; no eyebrow. Has a rich, short song with guttural notes 'cheruckle, truptruptruptruptrup, weeweeweewee'. Heard more often than seen. Secretive in permanent papyrus and reed-beds of the Okavango-'Linyanti'-Chobe region of northern Botswana. 18 cm (Rooibruinrietsanger)

2 **BASRA REED WARBLER** *Acrocephalus griseldis*

Rare summer visitor. Sometimes regarded as a race of (3) but is smaller, the legs grey-brown. Little known, the voice not recorded in southern Africa. A few records for eastern coastal regions. 15 cm (Basrarietsanger)

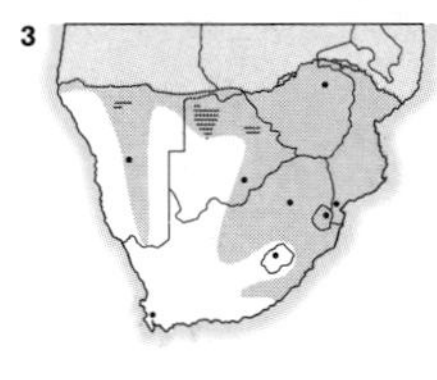

3 **GREAT REED WARBLER** *Acrocephalus arundinaceus*

Fairly common summer visitor. Best told by very large size (for a warbler) and characteristic song: a slow, harsh warble 'gurk-gurk, twee-twee, gurk-gurk, trrit-trrit, gackle, kurra-kurra ...'. Solitary in reed-beds, thickets or dense bush in suburbia. Less secretive, more inquisitive than most reed warblers, occasionally perching conspicuously, its movements heavy. 19 cm (Grootrietsanger)

4 **YELLOW WARBLER** *Chloropeta natalensis*

Fairly common resident. Differs from the yellow weavers in more slender bill. Female is duller yellow; immature orange-yellow, the wing edges, rump and tail more buff. The song is 'trrp-trrp-chirichirichirichiri', rendered quickly and frequently repeated. Singly or in pairs near water in reeds or other tall, rank cover, or away from water in bracken-brier patches of highveld valleys and forest fringes. Its habits are typical of the reed warbler group: secretive but ascends some vertical stem occasionally to perch conspicuously. 14-15 cm (Geelsanger)

1
2
3
4

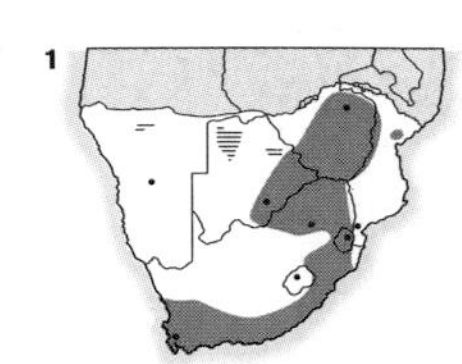

1 BAR-THROATED APALIS *Apalis thoracica*

Common resident. Highly variable; basic forms illustrated, all males. Most yellow form (a) in northern South Africa; brown-capped form (b) in Zimbabwe; with grey upperparts (c) in the south-west. More subtle variations also occur. In female the black throat-band is usually narrower, sometimes entirely lacking. Told from (2) by *pale yellow eye, white* outer tail feathers plus darker upperparts. Has a loud, distinctive call, 'pilly-pilly-pilly ...'; pairs also sing in duet, the female's call being much faster than the male's. In pairs, frequently in bird parties, in heavily wooded kloofs, streams, hillsides and forests. 12-13 cm (Bandkeelkleinjantjie)

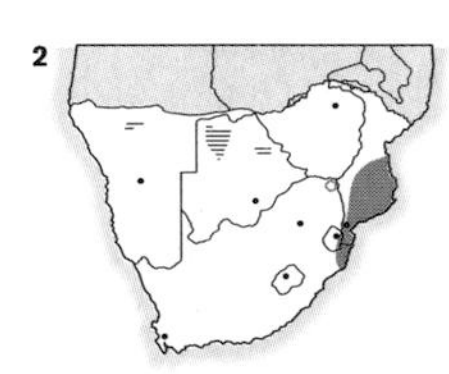

2 RUDD'S APALIS *Apalis ruddi*

Common, near endemic resident. Differs from (1) in *dark eye, yellowish* undertail with white spots at the tips of the outer feathers, more yellow-green upperparts and buff wash to underparts, especially throat. The call is a fast, loud 'tritritritritritritrit ...' by one bird, the other calling at the same time (but out of phase) 'punk-punk-punk ...'. Usually seen in pairs in coastal bush and dune forests, especially in dense thickets overgrown with creepers, though not secretive. 10,5-12 cm (Ruddse kleinjantjie)

3 CHIRINDA APALIS *Apalis chirindensis*

Uncommon, localised endemic resident. More uniformly grey than (4). The call is a rapid series of notes. Occurs in highland forests and dense woodland where it frequents open, sunny patches rather than the gloomy interior. Often joins mixed bird parties. 13,5 cm (Gryskleinjantjie)

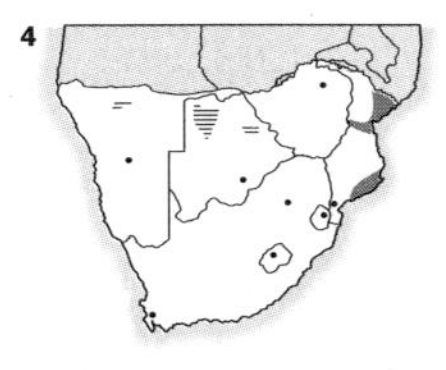

4 BLACK-HEADED APALIS *Apalis melanocephala*

Common, localised resident. Distinguished from (3) by contrasting dark upperparts and whitish underparts. The call is a fast trilling 'pee-pee-pee-pee ...' repeated 20-30 times, often answered by another. Occurs in lowland forests, dense woodland, thick riverine bush and coastal scrub, often in the tree canopies. 14 cm (Swartkopkleinjantjie)

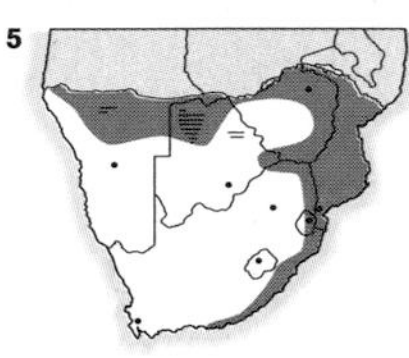

5 YELLOW-BREASTED APALIS *Apalis flavida*

Common resident. Amount of grey on head varies; most extensive (a) in northern Namibia and northern Botswana; least extensive (b) in Mozambique, elsewhere variable between these extremes. Tail length also varies. In all races black central breast-bar may be absent or vestigial. The normal call is 'skee-skee-skee-chizZICK-chizZICK', to which the mate replies 'krik-krik-krik'. Usually in pairs in a variety of bushveld habitats, riverine bush and forest fringes. 10-12,5 cm (Geelborskleinjantjie)

a
b
1
c
♂
♀
2
3
a
5
b
4

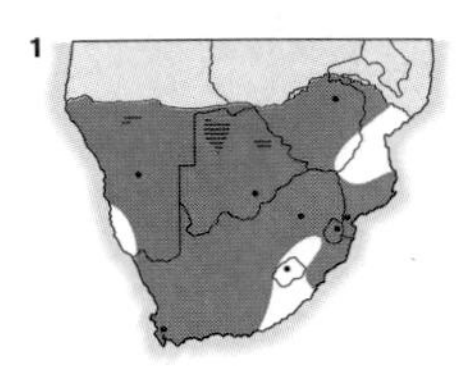

1 LONG-BILLED CROMBEC *Sylvietta rufescens*

Common resident. Tailless appearance makes confusion possible only with (2) and (3). Most similar to (3) but has distinct eyebrow, dusky eye-stripe, paler colouring about face and ear coverts and more prominent bill. Age differences negligible. The call is a loud, urgent-sounding 'tree-cheer, tree-cheer, tree-cheer ...'. Usually in pairs in bushveld and woodland, often in bird parties. Feeds on branches and tree trunks. 10-12 cm (Bosveldstompstert)

2 RED-FACED CROMBEC *Sylvietta whytii*

Fairly common resident. Differs from (1) in lack of distinct eye-stripe; has a more rufous face and ear coverts and shorter bill. The call is a twittering 'si-si-si-see'; alarm call a sharp 'tip', uttered so frequently as to become a rattling trill. Occurs in broad-leaved woodland, feeding mainly among the small branches and outer twigs of trees. 10-11 cm (Rooiwangstompstert)

3 RED-CAPPED CROMBEC *Sylvietta ruficapilla*

Very rare, exact status uncertain. Identified by chestnut ear coverts and upper breast (crown may lack chestnut entirely); upperparts and underparts washed pale lemon. Immature undescribed. The call is a loud 'richi-chichi-chichir' repeated about six times. Behaviour similar to other crombecs but feeds in the tree canopies. One record west of Victoria Falls. 11 cm (Rooikroonstompstert)

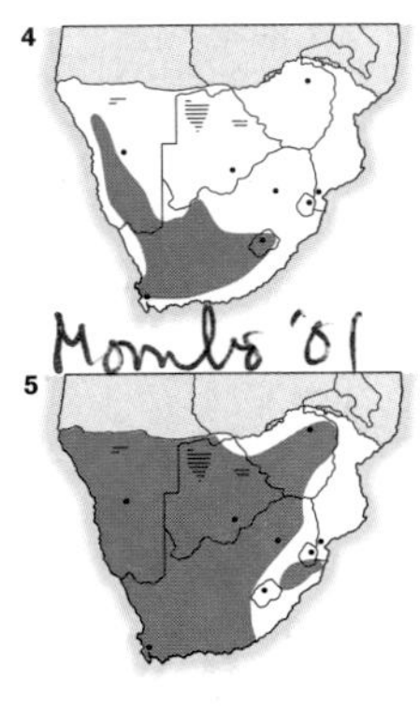

4 LAYARD'S TITBABBLER *Parisoma layardi* E

Uncommon endemic resident. Told from (5) by *white undertail coverts*; otherwise distinguished by pale yellow eye and spotted throat. Immature has brownish upperparts; throat less clearly spotted. Utters several clear song phrases, each interspersed with rattling notes, 'chiroo-chirroo-chirroo, trrrrr, chirree-chirree-chirree, trrrrr ...'. Creeps about actively within dense cover, then darts to the next bush in quick, jerky flight. Occurs in fynbos and in both desert and mountain scrub. 15 cm (Grystjeriktik)

5 TITBABBLER *Parisoma subcaeruleum* NE

Common, near endemic resident. Told from (4) by *chestnut* vent. Immature resembles adult. Calls frequently, a variety of clear, ringing, quickly rendered notes, typically 'cheriktiktik' or 'chuu-ti chuu-ti chuu-chuu'. Occurs in thickets in any woodland, mixed bushveld or thornveld. Habits very similar to previous species. 15 cm (Bosveldtjeriktik)

1
2
3
4
5

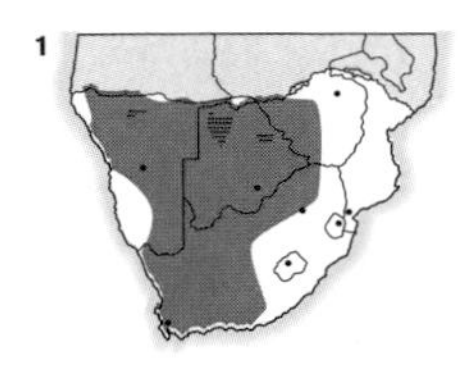

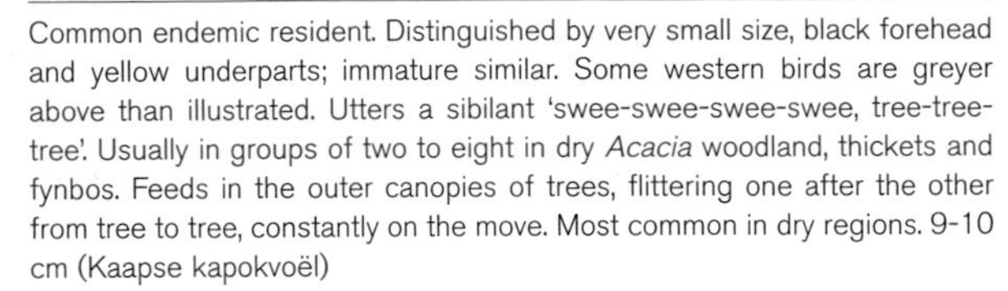

1 CAPE PENDULINE TIT *Anthoscopus minutus* E

Common endemic resident. Distinguished by very small size, black forehead and yellow underparts; immature similar. Some western birds are greyer above than illustrated. Utters a sibilant 'swee-swee-swee-swee, tree-tree-tree'. Usually in groups of two to eight in dry *Acacia* woodland, thickets and fynbos. Feeds in the outer canopies of trees, flittering one after the other from tree to tree, constantly on the move. Most common in dry regions. 9-10 cm (Kaapse kapokvoël)

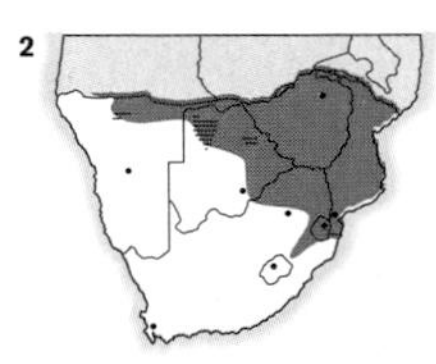

2 GREY PENDULINE TIT *Anthoscopus caroli*

Common resident. Underparts more buff than (1), throat and breast pale grey; immature similar. Western and some northern races are olive-green or yellow-green above, more yellowish on belly. The call is 'chikchikZEE, chikchikZEE, chikchikZEE ...'. Occurs in small groups in moist broad-leaved woodland where it feeds mainly in the tree-tops. 8-9 cm (Gryskapokvoël)

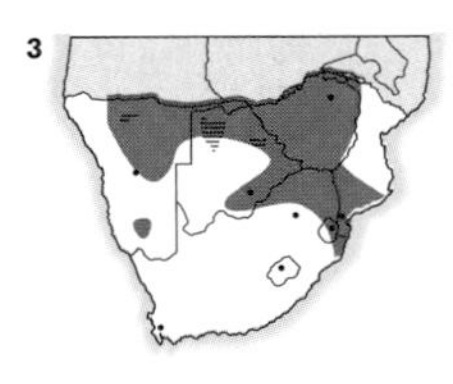

3 BURNT-NECKED EREMOMELA *Eremomela usticollis*

Common resident. Distinguished by brown throat-bar when this is present, otherwise best told from other small warblers by pale yellow-buff underparts and pale eye with brown surround. The call is a rapid, high-pitched 'teeup-ti-ti-ti-ti-ti-ti ...', followed by a short trill. In groups of two to five in *Acacia* woodland, feeding in the tree canopies. 12 cm (Bruinkeelbossanger)

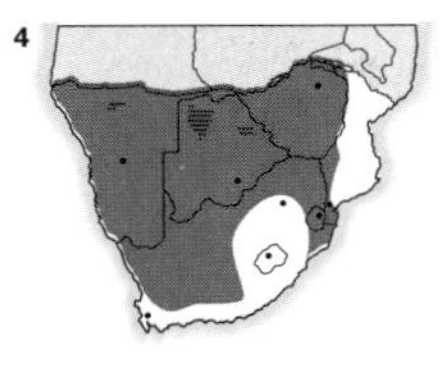

4 YELLOW-BELLIED EREMOMELA *Eremomela icteropygialis*

Common resident. Differs from white-eyes (p. 402) lacking a white eye-ring, grey (not green) upperparts plus a dark eye-stripe. Western birds generally paler, central birds with a fulvous wash to the breast. Has a lively song 'chirri-chee-chee-choo' or 'How are you two'. In pairs in mixed bushveld or, in arid regions, scrub, feeding in the outer and lower branches of bushes. 9-10 cm (Geelpensbossanger)

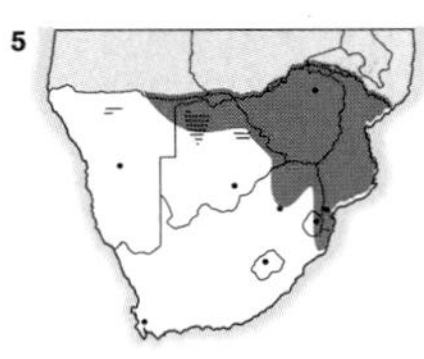

5 GREEN-CAPPED EREMOMELA *Eremomela scotops*

Uncommon resident. Identified by greyish lores and yellow eye surrounded by a red ring. North-western birds are whiter on lower abdomen and vent. Has various calls, a twittering 'nyum-nyum-nyum' or a repeated, monotonous 'tip-tip-tip ...', plus a liquid song. Found in the leafy canopies of woodland and riverine forests, often in small groups which chase about restlessly in the upper branches while feeding. In bird parties in winter. 12 cm (Donkerwang-bossanger)

6 YELLOW-THROATED WARBLER *Phylloscopus ruficapillus*

Common resident. Differs from other yellow warblers in brown cap and habitat preference. In southern birds yellow extends onto flanks and belly; in northern birds yellow confined mainly to throat. Immature has a greenish wash to the breast. Has a plaintive 'tieuu' call repeated for long periods, plus a high-pitched song 'tirritee tirritee tirritee' or 'sip sip sip sip pilly pilly pilly'. It also repeats 'chirreee chirreee ...'; cf. Collared Sunbird (p. 394). A bird of evergreen forests and forested kloofs where it forages in the canopy and midstratum. 11 cm (Geelkeelsanger)

1
2
3
4
5
6

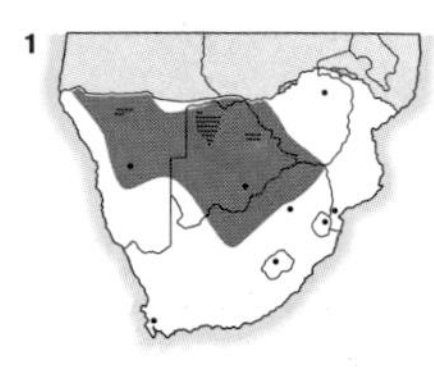

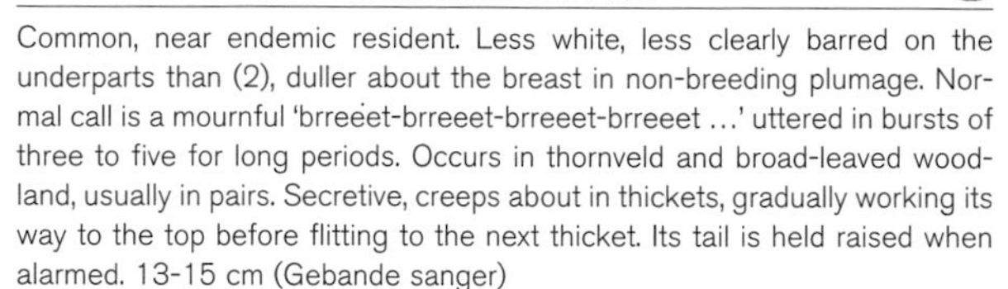

1 BARRED WARBLER *Calamonastes fasciolatus* NE

Common, near endemic resident. Less white, less clearly barred on the underparts than (2), duller about the breast in non-breeding plumage. Normal call is a mournful 'brreeet-brreeet-brreeet-brreeet …' uttered in bursts of three to five for long periods. Occurs in thornveld and broad-leaved woodland, usually in pairs. Secretive, creeps about in thickets, gradually working its way to the top before flitting to the next thicket. Its tail is held raised when alarmed. 13-15 cm (Gebande sanger)

2 STIERLING'S BARRED WARBLER *Calamonastes stierlingi*

Common resident. Whiter, more boldly barred below than (1), tail shorter, bill blacker. Has a far-carrying, much-repeated call 'birribit-birribit-birribit-birribit'. Found within thickets in mixed bushveld and broad-leaved woodland but may ascend to the tree canopy if disturbed. Very secretive, often creeping about with tail raised. 11,5-13 cm (Stierlingse sanger)

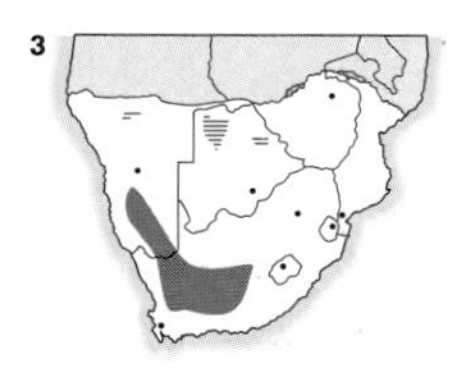

3 CINNAMON-BREASTED WARBLER *Euryptila subcinnamomea* 

Fairly common, localised endemic resident. Blackish tail and cinnamon forehead, breast and tail coverts diagnostic. The call is a plaintive whistle 'eeeeeeee …', lasting about one and a half seconds. Found on rock- and bush-strewn hills in arid regions. Hops about rocks with great agility, tail usually raised. 13-14 cm (Kaneelborssanger)

BLEATING WARBLERS

The two forms are treated by some as full species, by others as races of the same species. The Green-backed occurs in moist, lowland habitats and has no distinct non-breeding plumage; the Grey-backed frequents drier regions and has distinctly different breeding and non-breeding plumages, however hybridisation between the two is known. Sexes are alike.

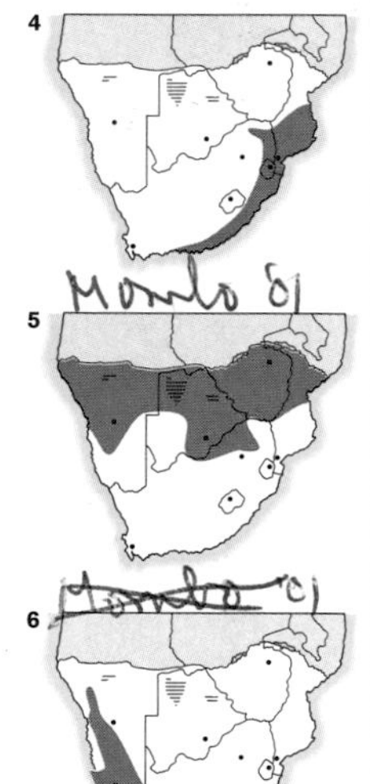

4 GREEN-BACKED BLEATING WARBLER *Camaroptera brachyura*

Common resident. Upperparts entirely dark olive-green (has grey crown in central and southern Mozambique); closely similar to (5). Utters a kid-like bleating 'bzeeeb' and, in the breeding season, a loud territorial call 'chirrup, chirrup, chirrup …' continued for long periods. Singly or in pairs in evergreen forest fringes, moist, well-wooded lowland valleys, riverine and coastal bush. Mostly secretive in the lower stratum except when male ascends to a higher level to call. 12 cm (Groenrugkwêkwêvoël)

5 GREY-BACKED BLEATING WARBLER *Camaroptera brevicaudata*

Common resident. Breeding and non-breeding plumages illustrated; in non-breeding plumage some races have a white to deep cream-buff upper breast, not grey. Differs from (4) in grey (not green) upperparts, except immature which *does* have green upperparts. Voice as (4). Singly or in pairs in dry thickets in thornveld, woodland and especially bush-covered termitaria. 12 cm (Grysrugkwêkwêvoël) Mombo 6/01

6 KAROO EREMOMELA *Eremomela gregalis* 

Uncommon, localised endemic resident. Distribution does not overlap with (5); differs in having *pale yellow eyes*, a smaller bill and pale yellow undertail coverts. Calls a continuous, high-pitched 'peewip peewip peewip …'. Contact call a sharp 'twink'. Feeding groups call continuously 'ti-ti-ti-ti …'. Small groups in Karoo scrub. 12 cm (Groenbossanger)

1
Br
N-Br
2
3
4
N-Br
5
Br
6

1

2

3
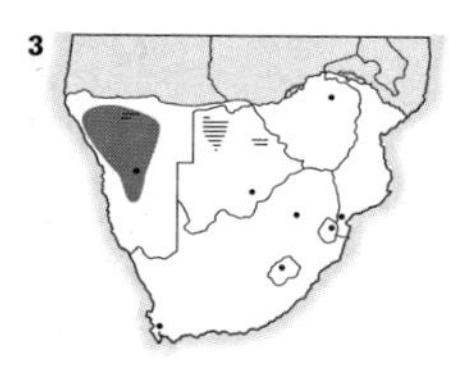

4
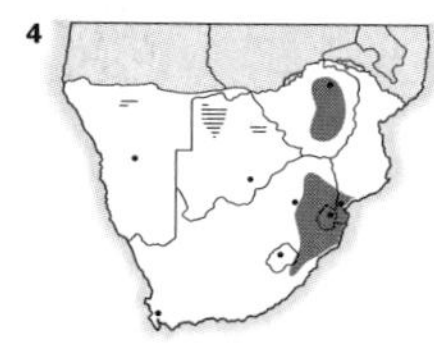

1 MOUSTACHED WARBLER *Melocichla mentalis*

Uncommon, localised resident. Told from (2) by plain upperparts and underparts, rounded tail and rufous forehead, *not* crown. The song is 'tip, tip, twiddle-iddle-see', the first two sounds slow, the rest fast. Occurs in short rank grass, bracken and scattered bushes in marshy ground near streams. Very similar in behaviour to (2). Remains mostly concealed within vegetation. 19 cm (Breëstertgrasvoël)

2 GRASSBIRD *Sphenoeacus afer*

Common endemic resident. Differs from (1) in heavily marked upperparts, streaked underparts (except race (b) of eastern regions) and generally rusty colouring; from cisticolas in larger size, moustachial streaks and tapering tail feathers. Has a distinctive burst of song 'chirp-chirp-chirp does it tickle yoooou', plus a cat-like mewing. Frequents the long grass and bracken of hillsides and open streams away from hills. Occasionally perches prominently on some tall grass or weed, otherwise skulks within the vegetation. 19-23 cm (Grasvoël)

3 ROCKRUNNER *Achaetops pycnopygius*

Common, localised near endemic resident. Differs from any other grass warbler within its limited distribution in heavily streaked head and mantle, bold facial markings and habit of keeping its tail raised high. The song is a warbling 'tip-tip-tootle-titootle-tootle-too' heard early mornings and evenings. A shy but lively bird of grassy rock- and bush-strewn hillsides and dry watercourses in Namibia. 17 cm (Rotsvoël)

CISTICOLAS

Small, closely similar, brown grass warblers. Breeding and non-breeding plumages often differ markedly as do tail lengths and the sexes. Best identified by song, habitat preference and behaviour. Territorial behaviour common to the very small 'cloud' cisticolas (this page and overleaf) is an aerial cruise by the males. They rise high into the air with rapidly whirring wings, often out of sight, and then cruise about singing, while some species make audible wing-snaps. The descent is a near vertical plunge, but they check just above the grass and fly level briefly before dropping down. In some species the descent is accompanied by wing-snaps.

4 PALE-CROWNED CISTICOLA *Cisticola brunnescens*

Uncommon, localised resident. Male in summer identified by pale crown, both sexes otherwise indistinguishable from Cloud and Ayres' Cisticolas (overleaf). Immature has brightly sulphured underparts. The song in flight is a quiet, continually repeated 'siep-siep-siep ...', sometimes varied every few seconds by scarcely audible notes 'twee-twee-twee-ti-ti-ti-ti-ti-ti-ti-tsee-tsee ...'; this may be repeated rapidly during the descent which is without wing-snaps. Occurs in grassland in damp localities. 9-11 cm (Bleekkopklopkloppie)

1
a
2
b
3
♂Br
♀Br
4

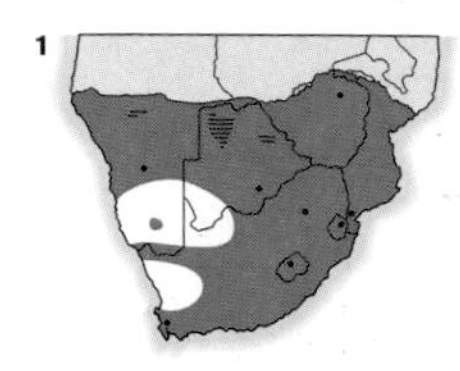

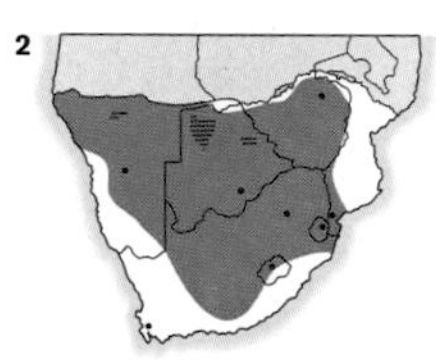

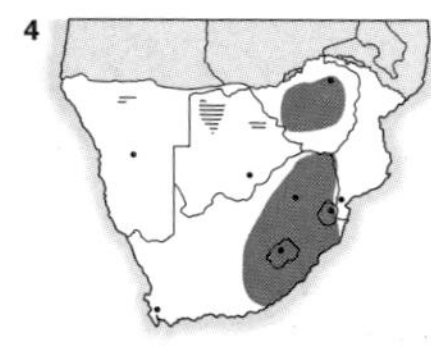

Note: The cisticolas on this plate are all so similar that accurate field identification based on plumage alone is almost impossible, but the main breeding and non-breeding differences are illustrated. They all indulge in aerial cruises combined with characteristic calls and behaviour during summer and this must be considered the most reliable guide.

1 FAN-TAILED CISTICOLA *Cisticola juncidis*

Common resident. Female resembles non-breeding male. Conspicuous only in summer when male cruises at a height of about 50 m with dipping flight, calling 'zit zit zit zit ...' at each dip at about half-second intervals. The call may also be made while perched on a grass stem. Does *not* snap its wings. Found in grassland, often near marshes or vleis, also fallow lands and waste ground. 10-12 cm (Landeryklopkloppie)

2 DESERT CISTICOLA *Cisticola aridula*

Common resident. Sexes closely similar. In summer male utters a repetitive, high-pitched 'zink zink zink zink ...' while cruising *low* over grassland, climbing and dropping with *wing-snaps* and irregular dashes; also calls 'tuc tuc tuc tuc weee'. Occurs in more arid grassland than (1), especially short grass, old burnt areas and fallow lands, never in moist regions. 10-12 cm (Woestynklopkloppie)

3 CLOUD CISTICOLA *Cisticola textrix* 

Common, near endemic resident. Female resembles male. In the south either sex may have clear or heavily spotted underparts. In summer male rises high into the air, usually being invisible to the naked eye, and cruises about, uttering a wispy 'see-see-see-see-chick-chick-chick' repeated at two- or three-second intervals. When descending makes an almost vertical plunge, calling a rapid 'chick-chick-chick-chick ...'. Does *not* snap its wings when descending. Occurs in short grassland at most levels but not montane grassland. 10 cm (Gevlekte klopkloppie)

4 AYRES' CISTICOLA *Cisticola ayresii*

Common resident. In summer male cruises high in the sky, usually out of sight, calling a wispy, high-pitched 'soo-see-see-see ...' at about three-second intervals while flying into wind. This is followed by 10 or more volleys of wing-snaps while flying downwind before plummeting to earth while calling a rapid 'ticka-ticka-ticka ...' with violent wing-snapping and terminal swooping and swerving. Occurs in high-altitude short, dry grassland and near vleis; does not perch conspicuously. 9-11 cm (Kleinste klopkloppie)

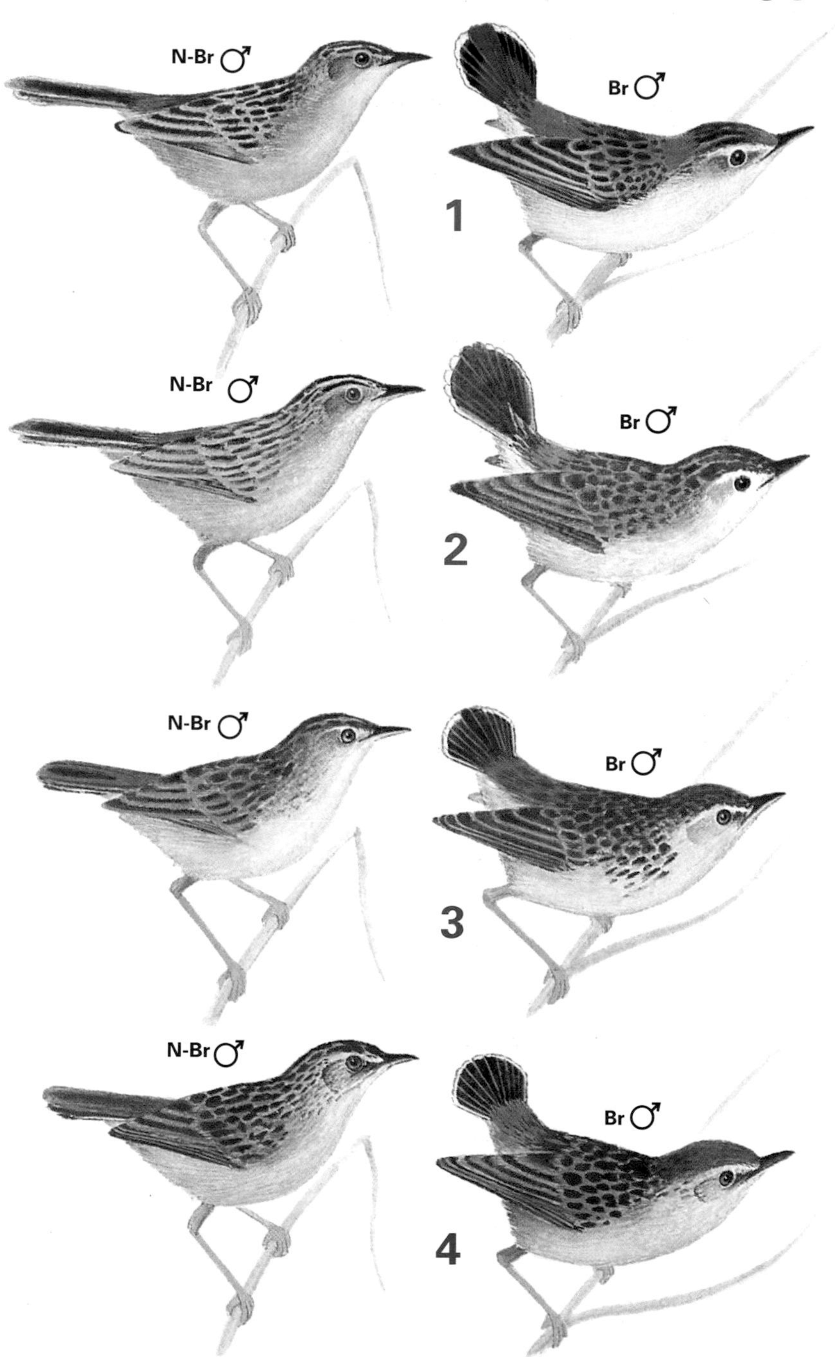

N-Br ♂
Br ♂
1
N-Br ♂
Br ♂
2
N-Br ♂
Br ♂
3
N-Br ♂
Br ♂
4

1

1 **SHORT-WINGED CISTICOLA** *Cisticola brachyptera*

Uncommon, localised resident. *Dark brown cap* the same colour as rest of the *unmarked* upperparts; sexes are alike. Immature is more yellow-washed, eyes grey. In the breeding season male sings from the top of a dead tree, a wispy, descending series of notes 'seee see-see-see ...'. Also has a high aerial display and plunge-dives like Cloud Cisticola (previous page). Occurs in broad-leaved woodland where it forages below the canopy or in the grass. Occurs mostly in palm savanna in Mozambique, just entering eastern Zimbabwe. 10-11 cm (Kortvlerktinktinkie)

2
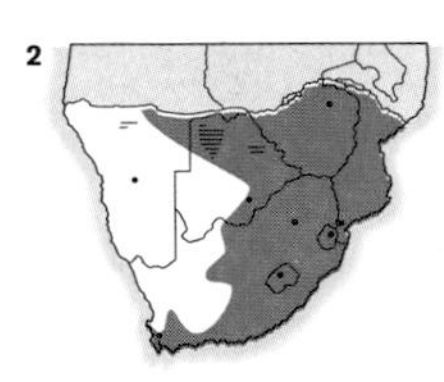

2 **NEDDICKY** *Cisticola fulvicapilla*

Common resident. Plain-backed like (1) but larger, longer-tailed, the *cap rufous*. Southern and eastern races (a) have blue-grey underparts, elsewhere as (b). Sexes are alike; immature dull. In the rainy season sings for long periods 'chirri-chirri-chirri ...'. The alarm call is a rapid tinkling by several birds 'ticki-ticki-ticki-ticki-ticki' while flitting from bush to bush. In pairs and family parties, frequenting the lower stratum: (a) in montane regions, (b) in grassy woodlands and thornveld thickets. 10-11 cm (Neddikkie)

3

3 **CHIRPING CISTICOLA** *Cisticola pipiens*

Fairly common, localised resident. Non-breeding plumage illustrated; breeding plumage less rufous about the face, lores and underparts, the tail shorter; cf. Black-backed Cisticola (overleaf). The song, in late summer, is four twanging notes repeated 'trrrit-trrrit-trree-trreeeeee ...'. Occurs in the northern Botswana wetlands, inhabiting reeds and papyrus in water, or shoreline bushes and grass. In flight the tail is fanned and flirted from side to side as though loose. 12,5-15 cm (Piepende tinktinkie)

4

4 **SINGING CISTICOLA** *Cisticola cantans*

Uncommon, localised resident. The only plain-backed cisticola with *conspicuous reddish primary feathers*, these and the crown contrasting with grey-brown upperparts when breeding (summer). Brighter in winter, upperparts washed rufous with faint, darker blotches, eyebrow then distinct, tail longer. Immature is duller, *sulphured on the breast and belly*. The call is a loud 'jhu-jee'or 'wheech-oo'; also 'cheer cheer cheer' reminiscent of Rattling Cisticola (overleaf). Secretive in rank undergrowth and bracken-brier patches near forest fringes in eastern Zimbabwe. 12-14 cm (Singende tinktinkie)

5
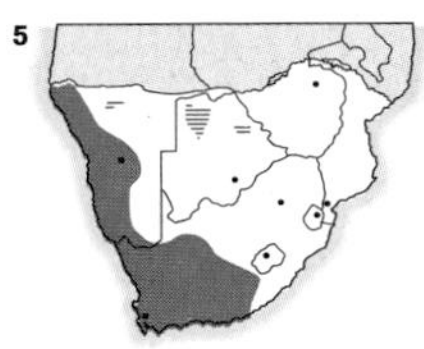

5 **GREY-BACKED CISTICOLA** *Cisticola subruficapilla* 

Common, near endemic resident. Southern race (a) has grey back with black streaking extending to forehead, ear coverts and upper breast; north-western race (b) has upperparts less obviously grey, streaks finer, fainter, sub-loral spot absent. Immature is rustier, ochreous about the face, eyes grey, bill yellower, legs paler. The breeding song is a hurried, high-pitched jumble of descending notes 'weesisee-chizzarizzaree-chichioo ...'; at other times calls 'prouee, tweep, tweep'. Alarm note is a piping 'tee-tee-tee ...'. A lively species found in coastal fynbos, scrub and grass on estuarine flats, montane foothills, Karoo and semi-desert western regions. 12-13 cm (Grysrugtinktinkie)

1
Br
a
2
b
N-Br
3
N-Br
a
Br
5
4
b

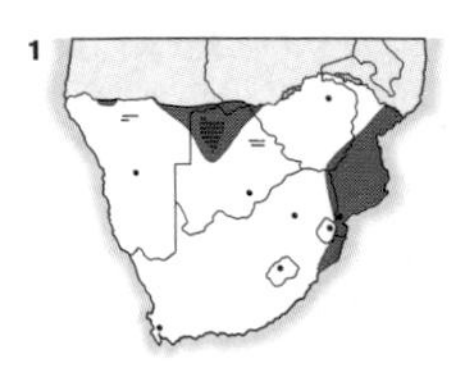

1 BLACK-BACKED CISTICOLA *Cisticola galactotes*

Common resident. Similar to (2), the back even blacker when breeding, but their ranges overlap only slightly. Best identified by habitat, behaviour and call. Associated mostly with *large waterways*, marshes and swamps; also cane fields near water along the east coast. Frequents reed-beds, sedges and grasses. Usually secretive; conspicuous only when breeding, at which time male calls from an exposed perch a loud, rasping 'zreeee' or 'rraaare' often interspersed with various chirps or 'chit-chit-chit …' or 'trrrp-trrrp-trrrp …'. When alarmed calls a loud, deliberate 'prrrit-prrrit-prrrit'. 12-13 cm (Swartrugtinktinkie)

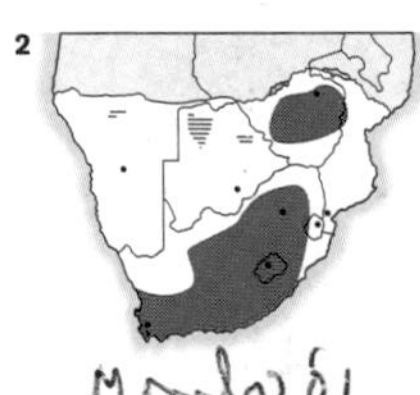

2 LEVAILLANT'S CISTICOLA *Cisticola tinniens*

Common resident. Superficially similar to (1) in having a black back, but confusion is unlikely since there is *very little overlap* in the ranges of the two species. Best told by habitat, behaviour and call. Levaillant's is the common pond and streamside cisticola frequenting waterside sedges and the edges of reed-beds (which it does not enter). It is not secretive, but perches conspicuously and sings 'chi-chi-chirrrueee', the first two notes almost inaudible, the final phrase loud; also has a plaintive 'dzwee, dzwee, dzwee' alarm call. 12,5 cm (Vleitinktinkie)

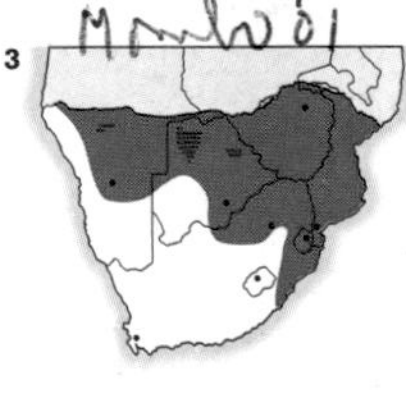

3 RATTLING CISTICOLA *Cisticola chiniana*

Very common resident. A robust cisticola with few distinguishing features; seasonal differences slight. Best told by habitat, behaviour and song. The characteristic song of the male, with slight locality differences, is 'chi chi chi ch-r-r-r-r-r', the last syllable with a distinct rattle. When alarmed calls a continuing 'cheer, cheer, cheer …'. When singing the black interior of the mouth is visible. This is the common bushveld cisticola that can be heard, and seen, singing for much of the year from the top of a bush. Also occurs in thornveld and coastal bush. Forages low down in tangled grass and bush. 14-16 cm (Bosveldtinktinkie)

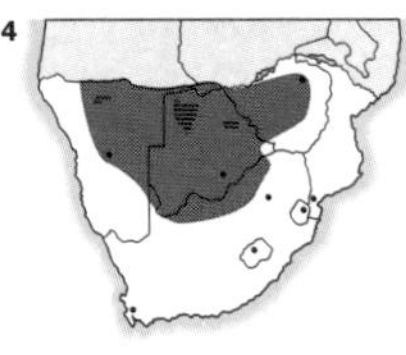

4 TINKLING CISTICOLA *Cisticola rufilata*

Fairly common, localised resident. Has distinctly reddish head markings, white eyebrow and orange-brown tail. The male's song is a leisurely series of high, bell-like notes 'to-wee, to-wee, to-wee …' repeated six to eight times; alarm call a high-pitched series of 'dididididi' notes. Occurs in dry, small-tree savanna with rank grass and scrub. Shy and retiring. 13-14 cm (Rooitinktinkie)

5 WAILING CISTICOLA *Cisticola lais*

Common resident. The head is well marked at all times, lores and ear coverts dusky; plumage redder and tail longer when not breeding. Immature has strongly sulphured underparts. Characteristic call is a wailing 'hweeeeeet' or 'to-weee-yeh' increasing in volume. Calls repeatedly when disturbed. Occurs on well-grassed hillsides and mountain slopes, often in patches of scrub. 13-14 cm (Huiltinktinkie)

N-Br
1
2
Br
3
1
J
N-Br
N-Br
Br
5
Br
4

1
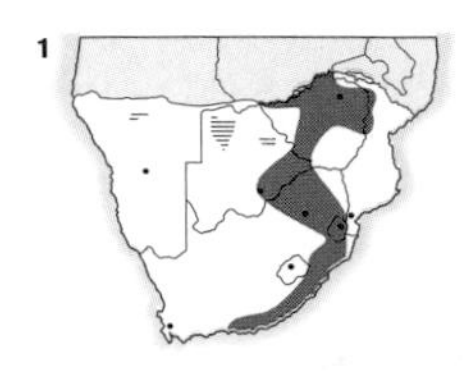

2
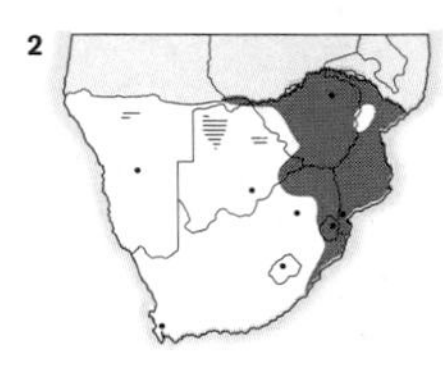

3
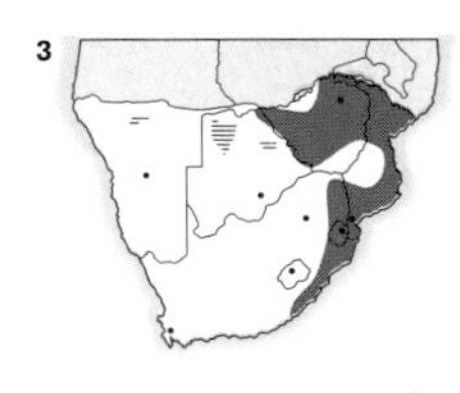

1 **LAZY CISTICOLA** *Cisticola aberrans*

Common, localised resident. Appears plain-backed; non-breeding plumage (April-October) generally warmer rufous on upperparts, underparts more strongly suffused with ochre, tail length constant. Immature is more rusty-coloured. The song is a series of fairly loud metallic notes 'tu-hwee-tu-hwee-tu-hwee ...' reaching a crescendo; alarm call a loud 'breeerp' or 'tu-hweeee', usually uttered with the longish tail cocked vertically. Frequents hillsides with bushes, rocks and long grass, often in the dense vegetation near the foot of a hill close to a stream; also forest-fringe scrub. Hops about on rocks and flirts its tail upwards like a prinia. 14-16 cm (Luitinktinkie)

2 **RED-FACED CISTICOLA** *Cisticola erythrops*

Common resident. A plain-backed cisticola, crown the same colour as rest of upperparts in all seasons, greyish when breeding (December-March), more rufous at other times; lores, eyebrows and ear coverts washed reddish, most strongly when not breeding. The call, loud and arresting, is 'wink-wink-WINK' getting louder with successive notes, or a series of eight to 10 notes, 'weep, weep, weep ...' rising to a crescendo. Inhabits waterside vegetation near rivers, dams and swamps, or away from water in damp situations. Secretive but calls frequently. 12-13 cm (Rooiwangtinktinkie)

3 **CROAKING CISTICOLA** *Cisticola natalensis*

Common resident. A large, heavy-bodied, thick-billed cisticola with well-streaked upperparts and *without rufous crown*. Seasonal differences as illustrated. Female smaller than male; immature like non-breeding adult but bright sulphur below. Breeding male cruises a few metres above the ground with a loose wing action, uttering a harsh 'cru-cru-cru-cru ...'; also calls from a low bush, a harsh 'chee-fro' or 'chip-MUNK'; alarm call is a frog-like 'tee-YRRR'. Frequents rank grassland with scattered bushes, or grassy clearings in bushveld. Very active and conspicuous when breeding (November-March), unobtrusive at other times. Often feeds on the ground. 13-17 cm (Groottinktinkie)

1
Br
2
J
N-Br
2
N - Br
3
Br
♀

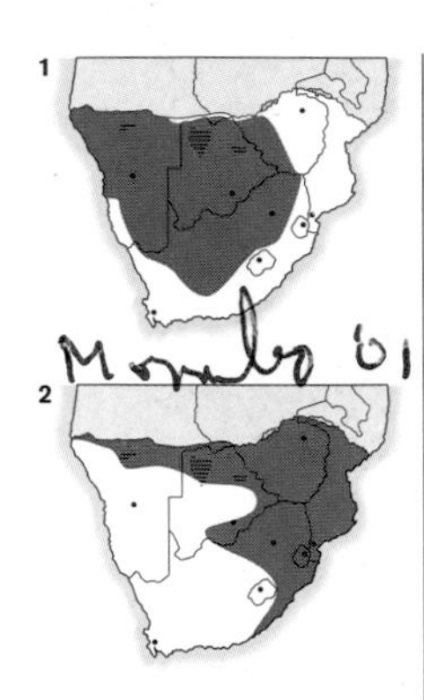

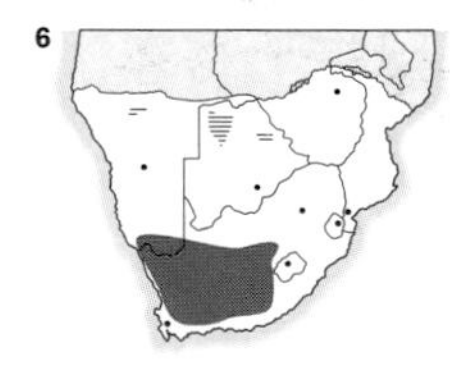

PRINIAS

Small warblers characterised by long tails frequently held in near vertical position. Sexes are alike. Calls consist of a single repetitive note and are often closely similar.

1 BLACK-CHESTED PRINIA *Prinia flavicans* NE

Common, near endemic resident. Distinctive in breeding plumage (summer), at other times the black breast-band is either absent or vestigial, the underparts more sulphurous-yellow. The call is a loud, much-repeated 'chip-chip chip ...'; also an occasional 'zrrrrt-zrrrrt-zrrrrt'. Pairs and small family parties occur in dry thornveld, scrub, rank grass and suburbia. 13-15 cm (Swartbandlangstertjie)

2 TAWNY-FLANKED PRINIA *Prinia subflava*

Common resident. Told by clear white underparts, rufous flanks and red-brown wing edges. When disturbed utters a characteristic weeping sound 'sbeeeee-sbeeeee ...'; the normal call is a loud, continuous 'przzt-ptzzt-przzt ...' or 'trit-trit-trit ...'; the actual sound variable. Noisy and conspicuous, usually in parties of four to six in riverine vegetation and suburban gardens, preferring moister situations than (1). 10-15 cm (Bruinsylangstertjie)

3 BRIER WARBLER *Oreophilais robertsi* E

Uncommon, localised endemic resident. A dusky, prinia-like bird lacking any distinctive markings. Utters occasional outbursts of noisy chattering 'cha cha cha cha ...'. Usually in small groups in dense scrub and bracken-brier patches, or in bush among rocks and near forests in the eastern highlands of Zimbabwe. 14 cm (Woudlangstertjie)

4 KAROO PRINIA *Prinia maculosa* E

Very common endemic resident. This prinia is told by its *well-spotted breast and flanks* on *pale yellow underparts plus pale brown eyes*. The voice is a chirping 'tweet-tweet-tweet' and a churring alarm call: cf (5). Its general actions and behaviour much like other prinias. It occurs in small family parties in dense, matted scrub and fynbos within the Karoo from the southern Drakensberg west and north to southern Namibia. Easily located by its call from within dense habitat. 14 cm (Karoolangstertjie)

5 SAFFRON or SPOTTED PRINIA *Prinia hypoxantha* E

Fairly common endemic resident. Closely similar to (4) in all ways except coloration, its underparts being a *rich saffron-yellow* while its upper breast is *only lightly spotted*. Its call is identical to that of (4). It occurs in small family groups in rank growth in vleis, matted river scrub and forest-edge thickets northwards along the Drakensberg escarpment from about East London to the Soutpansberg. It shares its habitat with (2). 14 cm (Gevlekte langstertjie)

6 NAMAQUA WARBLER *Phragmacia substriata* E

Fairly common endemic resident. Differs from (4) in white underparts with more rufous flanks and vent plus more rufous upperparts. The call is an explosive 'chit-churrr'; also calls 'che-kee-kee', the song a rapid series of 'tik-tik-tik-tik ...' notes. Often in small family groups; secretive and rapid in movements, occurring in *Acacia* scrub in dry Karoo river gullies and in reed-beds along watercourses and near dams. 14 cm (Namakwalangstertjie)

N-Br
1
Br
1
2
3
4
5
6

1
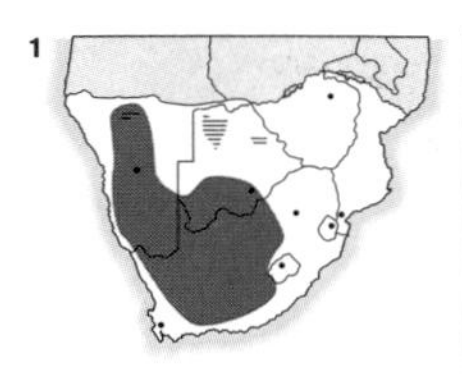

1 RUFOUS-EARED WARBLER *Malcorus pectoralis* E

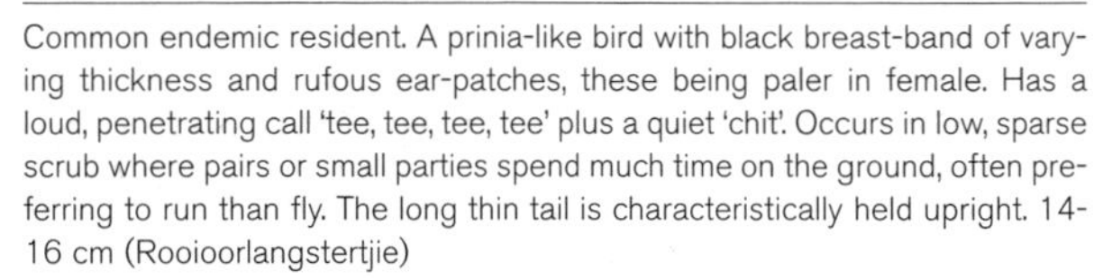

Common endemic resident. A prinia-like bird with black breast-band of varying thickness and rufous ear-patches, these being paler in female. Has a loud, penetrating call 'tee, tee, tee, tee' plus a quiet 'chit'. Occurs in low, sparse scrub where pairs or small parties spend much time on the ground, often preferring to run than fly. The long thin tail is characteristically held upright. 14-16 cm (Rooioorlangstertjie)

2

2 RED-WINGED WARBLER *Heliolais erythroptera*

Uncommon resident. Seasonal plumage differences as illustrated. At all times the red-brown wings and yellow-brown eyes are conspicuous and distinguish this species from other small warblers. Calls frequently, a squeaky 'pseep-pseep-pseep'; also utters a high-pitched 'chirrr'. An active, restless bird that occurs in well-grassed woodland, especially where long grass touches low branches. 13,5 cm (Rooivlerksanger)

3

3 MASHONA HYLIOTA *Hyliota australis*

Uncommon resident. Male told from (4) by dull, purple-black upperparts and limited white wing markings, these not extending onto the secondaries; underparts marginally paler; female by dark brownish upperparts, *not* grey. Immature resembles female but is lighter brown. Has a two-syllabled chippering whistle and a trilling warble. A highly mobile, active leaf-gleaner found mostly in the upper canopy of broad-leaved woodland, often in bird parties. 14 cm (Mashonahyliota)

4

4 YELLOW-BREASTED HYLIOTA *Hyliota flavigaster*

Rare resident. Male differs from (3) in glossy blue-black upperparts and white wing feather edges extending to the secondaries; female in dark grey above (not brown). Immature has finely barred upperparts and pale feather edges. Calls and habits are very similar to those of (3). Occurs in miombo woodland in Mozambique. 14 cm (Geelborshyliota)

5

FLYCATCHERS

Family MUSCICAPIDAE. Small, insectivorous birds with prominent bristles protruding from the base of their bills. Many of the soberly coloured species catch insects on the ground or in flight after watching from a low perch; others, especially the colourful and ornate species, are leaf-gleaners in addition to hawking insects in short aerial sallies.

5 COLLARED FLYCATCHER *Ficedula albicollis*

Very rare summer visitor. Male told from other pied flycatchers, especially Fiscal Flycatcher (p. 364) by smaller size, *white forehead and collar* and small bill (non-breeding male, normally seen in southern Africa, resembles female and *lacks the collar*); female by more extensive white on wings, duskier breast and small bill. The call is a sharp 'whit-whit'. Perches on some low branch from where it hunts insects; usually solitary. 13 cm (Withalsvlieëvanger)

1
♂
N·Br
Br
2
♀
3
♂
♀
4
♂
♂
♀
5

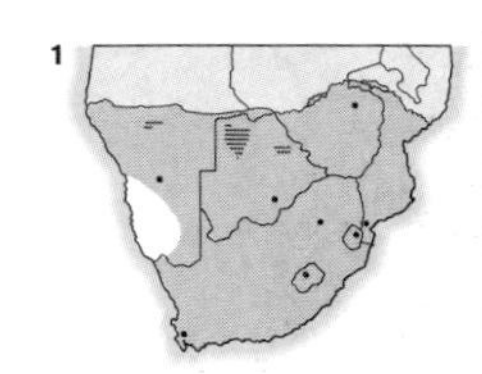

1 SPOTTED FLYCATCHER *Muscicapa striata*

Common summer visitor. Distinguished from (2) by slimmer, less dumpy shape plus *streaked crown* and underparts. Sometimes utters a thin, sibilant, two-syllabled 'tze-ee' while flicking its wings. Solitary in any open woodland or mixed bushveld plus well-wooded suburbia. Perches on a low branch beneath a tree from where it hawks insects or catches them on the ground, frequently returning to the same perch. 14-15 cm (Europese vlieëvanger)

2 DUSKY FLYCATCHER *Muscicapa adusta*

Common, localised resident. More dumpy than (1), the underparts duskier with faint smudges (not streaks). Immature is like adult. Utters a thin, sibilant 'zeeet'. Singly or in pairs in forest fringes, riverine forests and broad-leaved woodland in moister regions. Behaviour much like (1) but frequents the more lush coastal and montane mist-belt regions. 12-13 cm (Donkervlieëvanger)

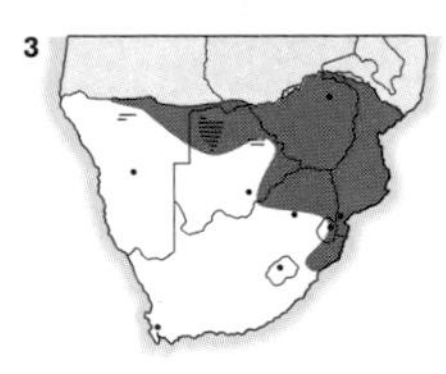

3 PALLID FLYCATCHER *Melaenornis pallidus*

Uncommon resident. A dull, featureless bird, the underparts scarcely paler than the upperparts; cf. Marico and Chat Flycatchers (overleaf). Immature has upperparts with buff-edged feathers; streaked below. Mostly silent. Usually in pairs in *broad-leaved woodland* or mixed bushveld (not thornveld). Perches on a low branch from where it watches the ground for insects. Sparsely distributed throughout its range. 15-17 cm (Muiskleurvlieëvanger)

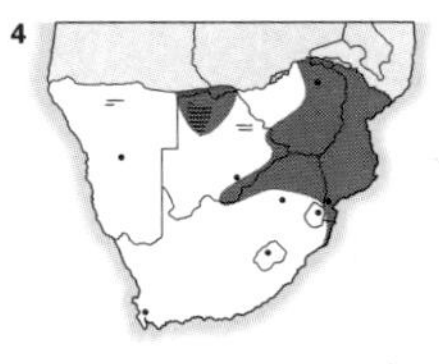

4 FAN-TAILED FLYCATCHER *Myioparus plumbeus*

Uncommon resident. Differs from (5) mainly in behaviour and *white outer tail feathers*. Immature is like adult. The call is a loud, cheerful 'teee-reee', the second syllable lower than the first. Singly or in pairs in broad-leaved woodland, mixed bushveld and riverine forests. Calls frequently and *fans its tail while raising and lowering it*, constantly moving through the midstratum; cf. habits of (5). Often joins bird parties. 14 cm (Waaierstertvlieëvanger)

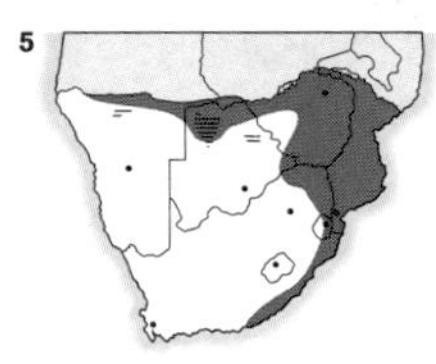

5 BLUE-GREY FLYCATCHER *Muscicapa caerulescens*

Fairly common resident. Differs from (4) in behaviour and lack of any white in the tail. Immature has spotted upperparts and mottled underparts. Calls 'tsip-tsip-tsip-tsip-tse-tslipip' but is mostly silent. Usually solitary in coastal bush, riverine forests, forest fringes and broad-leaved woodland. Perches in the midstratum and watches the ground for insects or catches them in mid-air, often returning to the same perch. A quiet, inconspicuous species. 14-15 cm (Blougrysvlieëvanger)

BLACK FLYCATCHER (Swartvlieëvanger) see p. 296.

1
2
3
J
4
5

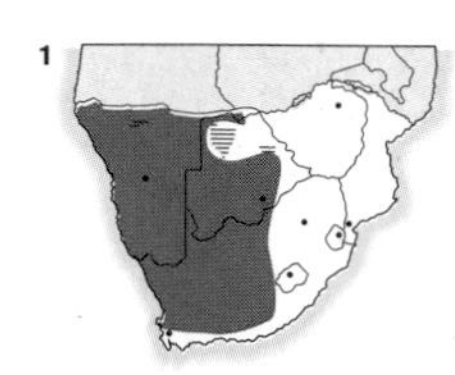

1 CHAT FLYCATCHER *Melaenornis infuscatus*

Common, near endemic resident. Very similar to Pallid Flycatcher (previous page) but larger, pale wing edges more prominent. Their ranges are mutually exclusive. Immature heavily speckled as illustrated. The song is a warbled 'cher cher chirrup' with some hissing notes. Perches prominently on a bush, post or wire from where it flies to the ground to seize insects. A bird of the Kalahari and Karoo, common on roadside telephone wires. 20 cm (Grootvlieëvanger)

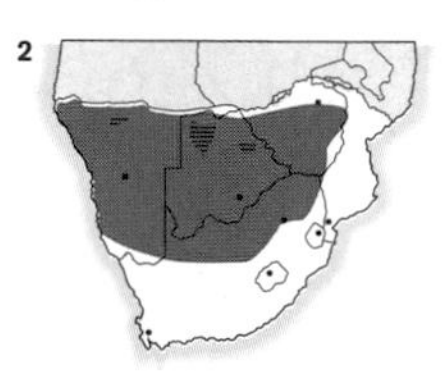

2 MARICO FLYCATCHER *Melaenornis mariquensis*

Common, near endemic resident. Differs from similar flycatchers in white underparts contrasting strongly with brown upperparts. Immature is spotted whitish above, streaked dark on white below as illustrated, this streaking heavier than in immature of (1). Call is a soft 'chew-week'. Frequents *Acacia* thornveld. Perches prominently on the outer branch of a bush from where it watches the ground for insects, occasionally hawking them in the air. 18 cm (Maricovlieëvanger)

3 VANGA FLYCATCHER *Bias musicus*

Rare; probably resident. Sexes markedly different as illustrated; both have crested heads, heavy bills, prominent rictal bristles, yellow eyes and short, yellow legs. Utters sharp whistling notes 'tchi-kik-you' or 'we-chip! we-chip!' and sings 'wit-tu-wit-tu-tu-tu', the notes first ascending then descending the scale. Pairs or parties occur in the tops of tall trees in forest fringes and bushveld in central Mozambique. Has the habit of circling around a tree in slow flight with rapid wing beats. 16 cm (Witpensvlieëvanger)

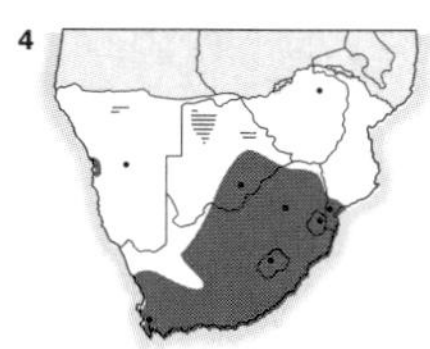

4 FISCAL FLYCATCHER *Sigelus silens*

Common endemic resident. Differs from Fiscal Shrike (p. 372) in less robust bill and white 'windows' in the tail; the white wing-bar extends only halfway along the folded wing, *not* to the shoulder. Has a sibilant, rather weak song 'swee-swee-ur' and other similar sounds, often in prolonged sequence. Usually in pairs in bush country, grassy Karoo, fynbos and suburbia. Perches prominently on a branch or post and flies to the ground to seize insects. 17-20 cm (Fiskaalvlieëvanger)

1
J
2
J
3
♂
♀
4
♂
♀
J

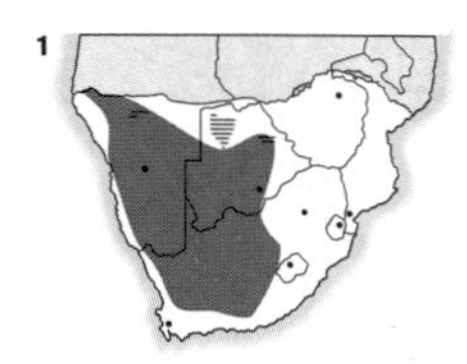

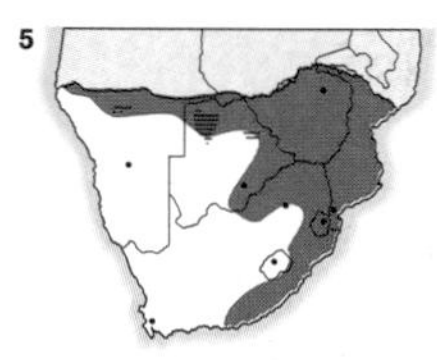

BATISES

Small leaf-gleaning flycatchers of similar appearance, characterised by grey caps and upperparts, black masks, black or rufous breast-bands and varying amounts of rufous colouring elsewhere. Immatures are dull versions of the adults. Often found in bird parties. When alarmed they fly about with whirring wings.

1 PRIRIT BATIS *Batis pririt*

Common, near endemic resident. Most resembles (5), but their ranges are mutually exclusive. The males are difficult to tell apart; the female has a much paler buff throat and breast than that of (5). The call is a long, descending sequence of notes 'peep-peep-peep-peep ... choo-choo-choo-choo ...' up to about 100 times. Pairs occur in dry western thornveld, often along watercourses. 12 cm (Priritbosbontrokkie)

2 WOODWARDS' BATIS *Batis fratrum*

Fairly common, near endemic resident. Male lacks black breast-band and resembles female; confusion with (1) is unlikely as their distributions are widely separated. The contact call by either sex is 'phoee-phoee-phoee'; male also calls 'chuririri, chuririri, chuririri ...'. A species of coastal bush, forests and riverine forests, preferring dense undergrowth and usually remaining in the lower stratum. 11-12 cm (Woodwardse bosbontrokkie)

3 MOZAMBIQUE BATIS *Batis soror*

Common resident. Like a very small version of (5), and sometimes regarded as a race of that species, but in both sexes the markings of the underparts are less clearly defined, the male generally more speckled on the back and flanks. The call is 'tiroo, tiroo, tiroo, whit, whit, whit, phep, phep ...'. Habits like (5), but occurs only in Mozambique from Inhambane northwards, and in extreme eastern Zimbabwe. 10 cm (Mosambiekbosbontrokkie)

4 CAPE BATIS *Batis capensis*

Common endemic resident. The most heavily marked batis; male has a very broad black breast-band and rufous flanks, female rich rufous breast-band, throat and flanks; both have rufous on wing coverts; eyes yellow when not breeding. Has a grinding 'prrritt, prrritt, prrritt' alarm note; other calls variable, a monotonous 'keep, keep, keep ...', a grating 'WEE-warrawarra' and a soft 'foo-foo-foo-foo ...'. In pairs and small parties in forests, forested kloofs, fynbos, succulent scrub and well-wooded suburban gardens; in the north confined to montane forests. 12-13 cm (Kaapse bosbontrokkie)

5 CHIN-SPOT BATIS *Batis molitor*

Very common resident. Male lacks any rufous colouring; very similar to (1) and (2) but their ranges do not overlap. Female has a clearly defined, rich rufous chin-spot and breast-band but *white* flanks. Has several calls, the most characteristic a descending series of three notes 'choi-choi-choi', sounding like 'three blind mice'. Also calls 'chi-chirr' or 'chee-chir-chir'; one of the first species to be heard at dawn. In pairs in mixed bushveld and woodland, always in drier country than (4). Frequently joins bird parties, feeding in the mid- and lower strata. 12-13 cm (Witliesbosbontrokkie)

♀
1
♂
♀
2
♂
♀
3
♂
♀
4
♂
♀
5
♂

1

1 BLUE-MANTLED FLYCATCHER *Trochocercus cyanomelas*

Fairly common resident. Both sexes differ from (5) in white wing-bars and whiter underparts. Usually first detected by call, a rasping 'zwee-zwer' uttered frequently, identical to (2). Male also sings a high-pitched 'kwew-ew-ew-ew' followed by four clicks. A lively, active little bird, usually in pairs in the mid- and higher strata of dense coastal bush, coastal forests and montane forests near streams. 17-18 cm (Bloukuifvlieëvanger)

2
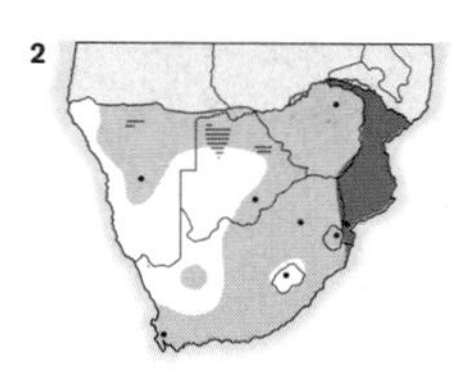

2 PARADISE FLYCATCHER *Terpsiphone viridis*

Common summer resident, present all year in the east and north-east. The only small flycatcher with orange-brown upperparts and blue-grey underparts; some females have slightly elongated tails. The call, a sharp 'zwee-zwer', is identical to that of (1); the song is a lively trill 'wee-te-tiddly, wit-wit'. A highly active and vociferous little bird found among large trees along rivers, forest fringes, well-wooded hills and suburbia. MM 41 cm; FF 23 cm (Paradysvlieëvanger)

3

3 LIVINGSTONE'S FLYCATCHER *Erythrocercus livingstonei*

Uncommon, localised resident. Colour combination distinctive. Immatures and adults of northern races have the head the same colour as the back. Has a sharp 'chip-chip' or 'zert' call, plus a sunbird-like 'tweet' in flight. Also gives an occasional outburst of warbling song and makes snapping sounds with its bill. Found in bird parties in thickets and large trees in riverine forests, also the edges of woodland clearings. A highly agile, restless little bird, constantly flitting from branch to branch or sidling down branches with fanned tail moving. 12 cm (Rooistertvlieëvanger)

4

4 WATTLE-EYED FLYCATCHER *Platysteira peltata*

Uncommon resident. Female has all-black breast, male has narrow breast-band only, both have red eye-wattles. Immature male lacks breast-band. Has a guttural 'chak-chak' call, a weak, tinkling song 'er-er-fea-er-er-fee-fea' and a louder 'tree-tree-tree, che-chreet-che-chreet-che-chreet ...'. Pairs live in the lower stratum of riverine and coastal thickets. 18 cm (Beloogbosbontrokkie)

5

5 WHITE-TAILED FLYCATCHER *Trochocercus albonotatus*

Fairly common, localised resident. Most resembles (1) but is smaller, greyer, with duskier underparts and no white wing-bar or crest. The call is a rapid 'chrrit-tit-tit'. Highly active and agile in forest canopies and trees bordering forests. Fans its tail frequently (thus revealing the white outer tail feathers) while working its way up and down branches. 14-15 cm (Witstertvlieëvanger)

6
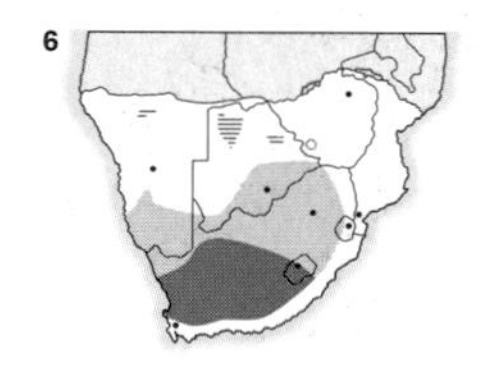

6 FAIRY FLYCATCHER *Stenostira scita* E

Common endemic resident. Very small grey and black bird with conspicuous white wing-bar and outer tail feathers; the pink central belly is inconspicuous in the field. Immature has brownish rather than grey plumage. The call is a short, sibilant trill 'kisskisskisskiss'. Flits about actively feeding within bushes or the outer canopy of trees within the Karoo biome, frequently bobbing and fanning its tail. In the south often occurs near rivers; moves north in winter where it frequents woodland, montane scrub, plantations and suburbia. 12 cm (Feevlieëvanger)

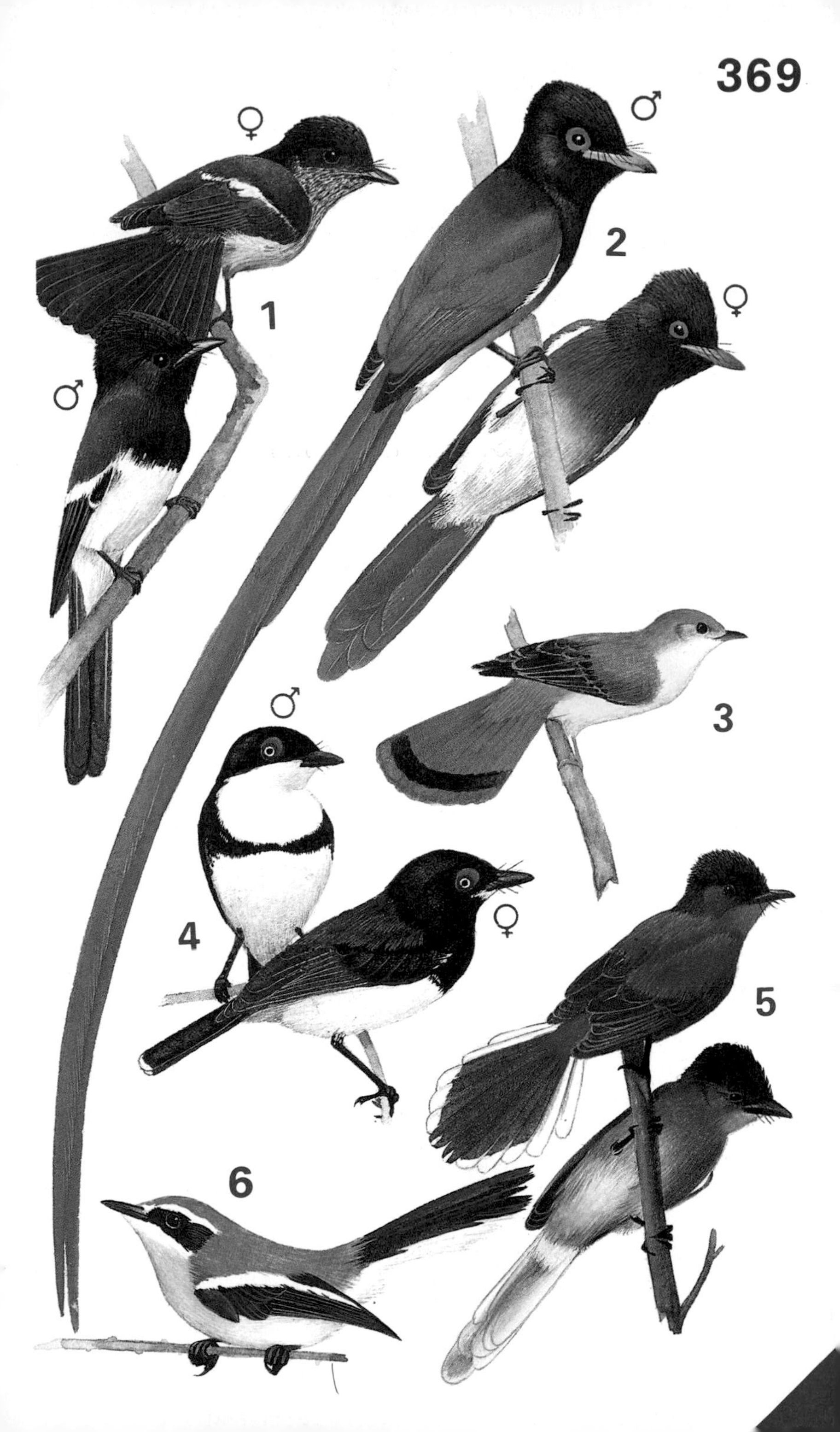
♀
♂
1
2
♀
♂
3
♂
4
♀
5
6

1
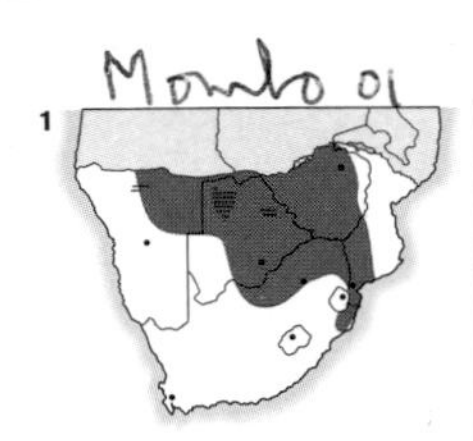

2
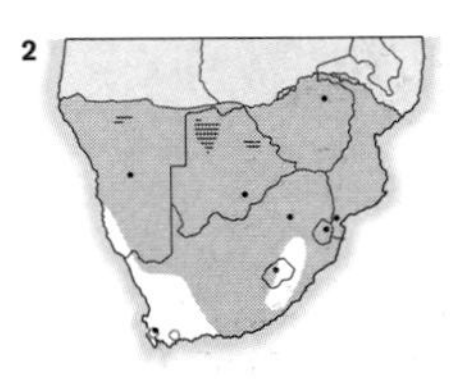

3
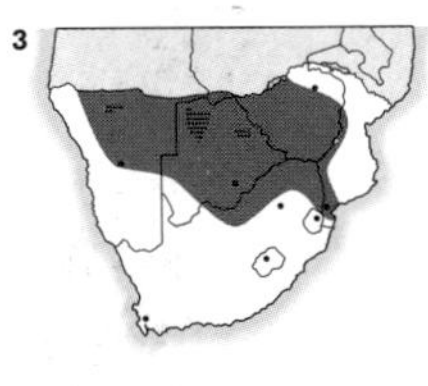

4
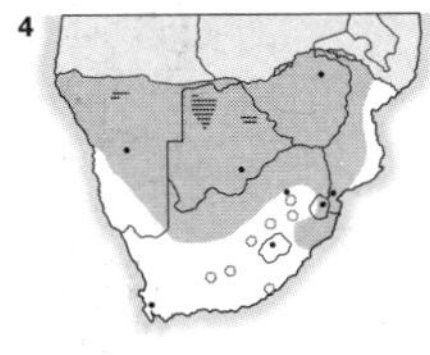

TRUE SHRIKES

Family LANIIDAE and allies. Insectivorous or partially carnivorous birds with stout, hooked or slightly hooked bills. Members of the various genera are illustrated according to plumage similarity.

1 LONG-TAILED SHRIKE *Corvinella melanoleuca*

Common resident. A distinctive, long-tailed, pied bird. Female may show white on the flanks and have a shorter tail. Immature is bronze-brown with a grey rump. The call is 'prooit-preeoo, prooit-preeoo-preeoo' the first sound descending, the second ascending. Small groups of three to 10 birds occur in thornveld and mixed bushveld, preferring lightly wooded, well-grassed regions where they hunt from a perch on a bush. 40-50 cm (Langstertlaksman)

2 RED-BACKED SHRIKE *Lanius collurio*

Common summer visitor. Sexes differ as illustrated. Female differs from immature Fiscal Shrike (overleaf) in more rufous upperparts and lack of white wing-bars. Rarely, male occurs with white wing-bars, then resembles Sousa's Shrike (p. 374), but differs in more rufous unbarred mantle and clearer grey cap. Mostly silent; sometimes utters a harsh 'chak, chak'. Solitary in a variety of wooded habitats, preferring mixed bushveld and thornveld, being most common in the central Kalahari. Perches conspicuously on a low branch and still-hunts. Arrives late October-November, departs early April. 18 cm (Rooiruglaksman)

3 WHITE-CROWNED SHRIKE *Eurocephalus anguitimens* NE

Common, near endemic resident. Distinguished by white crown and black mask. Sexes are alike. Utters a curious 'kwep, kwep' sound. Singly or in small, scattered groups in mixed bushveld, thornveld and broad-leaved woodland. Perches conspicuously on a branch or roadside telephone wire from where it still-hunts. 23-5 cm (Kremetartlaksman)

4 LESSER GREY SHRIKE *Lanius minor*

Fairly common summer visitor. The full black mask (a) is often absent from November to early January, then appears as (b). Sexes are alike. Normally silent. Solitary in thornveld and mixed bushveld. Still-hunts from a branch. Arrives late October-November, departs early April. 20-2 cm (Gryslaksman)

1
2
♀
♂
3
a
4
b

1
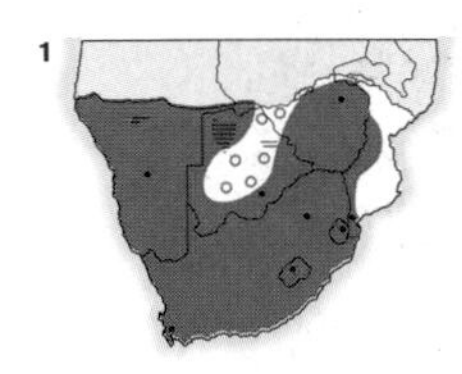

2
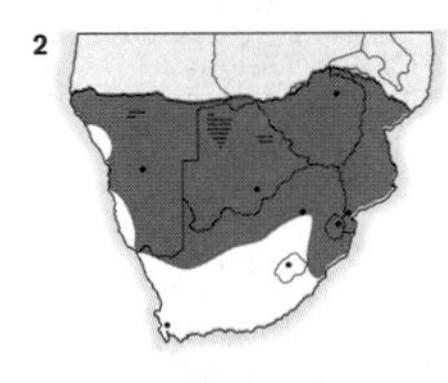

3
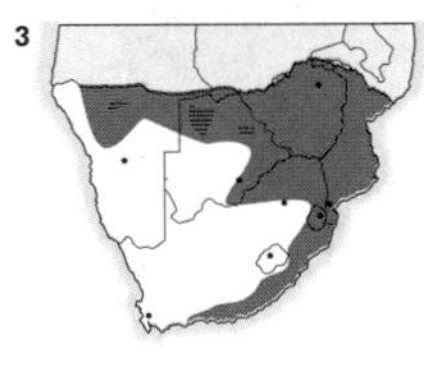

4

1 FISCAL SHRIKE *Lanius collaris*

Very common resident. A pied, heavy-bodied, heavy-billed bird with white wing-bar *extending to the shoulder.* Female has rufous flanks. (Fiscal Flycatcher (p. 364) has thinner bill and wing-bar that does *not* reach the shoulder.) Western race (a) has a white eyebrow. Immature is ash-brown above, greyish-brown below with fine barring. Call is a harsh 'gercha, gercha …' or 'skiza, skiza …'; also a rambling song incorporating sweet notes and the characteristic 'gercha' sound. Perches conspicuously on a branch, post or wire, flying to the ground occasionally to seize insects and other small prey. Singly or in pairs in lightly wooded country and suburbia. 23 cm (Fiskaallaksman)

2 BRUBRU *Nilaus afer*

Fairly common resident. Small pied bird with rich rufous flanks in both sexes. Female is dark brown above. Immature is similar but has streaked breast. Male utters a drawn-out, far-carrying whistle 'trrioooo' like a telephone, the female replying with a softer, wheezy 'wheee'. An active, restless species of open woodland. Usually in pairs, which call continuously while working their way through the midstratum. 15 cm (Bontroklaksman)

3 PUFFBACK *Dryoscopus cubla*

Common resident. Small pied bird with crimson eyes. Female has a white forehead and eyebrow, both have distinctive wing-barring. When excited male erects its back feathers to form a puff (see illustration); may fly from tree to tree like this while calling sharply 'chick-weeu, chick-weeu …'; this is also uttered less frequently while feeding. Flies in a heavy manner, the wings making a distinct purring sound. Pairs, often in bird parties, in woodland, riverine bush and evergreen forests, favouring the canopies of large trees. 18 cm (Sneeubal)

4 WHITE-TAILED SHRIKE *Lanioturdus torquatus* NE

Fairly common, localised, near endemic resident. Small black, white and grey bird with a very short tail and long legs. Has a loud, clear 'huo-huo-huo' call similar to Black-headed Oriole (p. 302) plus various querulous churrs, croaks and scolding notes. An active, restless species of striking appearance. In pairs or small groups (flocks of up to 20 in winter) in thornveld and mixed woodland, spending much time hopping about on the ground with characteristic bouncing gait. 15 cm (Kortstertlaksman)

1
♂
♀
♀
♂
2
♀
♂
3
♂
a
4

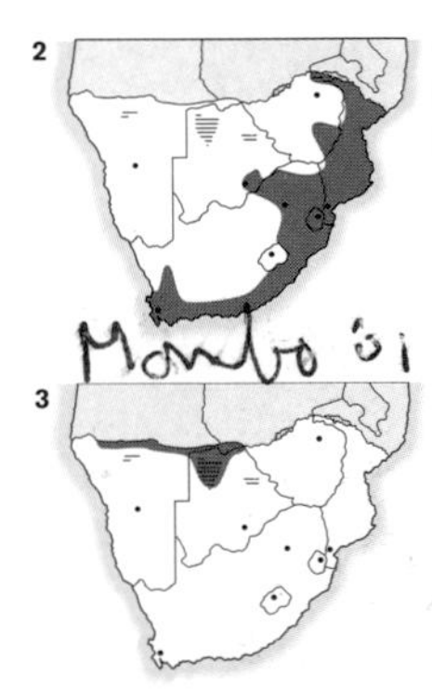

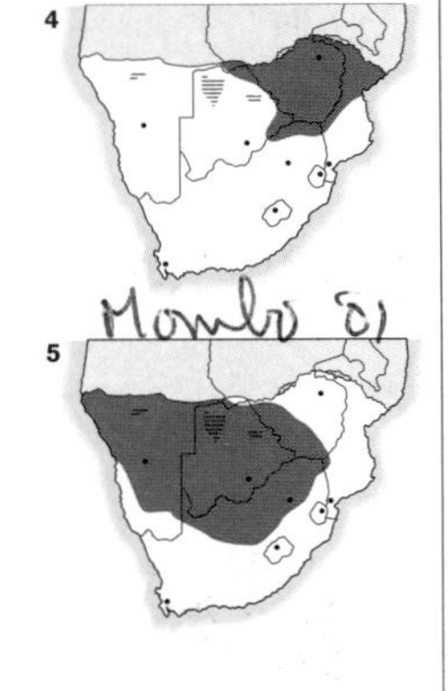

1 SOUSA'S SHRIKE *Lanius souzae*

Rare resident. Told from Red-backed Shrike (p. 370) by *dull* brown wings and tail, bold white wing-bar reaching the shoulder and dusky underparts, only the throat being white. Tail feathers very narrow. Female has tawny flanks and immature is narrowly barred blackish on underparts. Has a low, scraping call note. Perches on some low branch from where it flies down occasionally to seize insects on the ground. Singly or in pairs in broad-leaved woodland and Kalahari sand. 17-18 cm (Sousase laksman)

2 SOUTHERN BOUBOU *Laniarius ferrugineus* 

Common endemic resident. Cinnamon colouring of belly sometimes extends in pale wash to throat, but is always richer towards belly and vent. White wing-bar appears narrow or wide depending on feather arrangement. South-eastern females are dark brown above, not black. Calls in duet: first bird utters 'ko-ko' replied to by 'kweet', or 'boo-boo' replied to by 'whee-oo', or a liquid-sounding 'phooweeol' replied to by 'hueee' or 'churrr'. Many variations of these basic calls occur. Fairly secretive, pairs remaining concealed in dense bush, usually in the lower stratum. 23 cm (Suidelike waterfiskaal)

3 SWAMP BOUBOU *Laniarius bicolor*

Fairly common resident. Differs from (2) and (4) in underparts being white, no pinkish tinge even to feather bases. Call is less musical than other boubous, a short whistle replied to by a harsh 'kick-ick'. Also less secretive than other boubous; will perch openly while calling. Pairs occur in papyrus, riverine woodland and thickets in the Okavango-Linyanti-Chobe region of northern Botswana. 22-3 cm (Moeraswaterfiskaal)

4 TROPICAL BOUBOU *Laniarius aethiopicus*

Fairly common resident. Differs from other boubous in entire underparts being lightly washed pinkish, less cinnamon on flanks and vent. Calls a remarkable series of duets, the two calls uttered so simultaneously they sound like one; normally three liquid, bell-like notes answered by 'hueee', but variations occur. Pairs frequent dense vegetation in broad-leaved woodland, dense lowveld bushveld and riverine thickets. 21 cm (Tropiese waterfiskaal)

5 CRIMSON-BREASTED BOUBOU or SHRIKE *Laniarius atrococcineus* 

Common, near endemic resident. Distinctive because of entirely scarlet underparts; rarely occurs with yellow underparts. Otherwise identical to other boubous. Very young birds are ash-grey below, finely barred black. Calls in duet, both birds often calling almost simultaneously, a sharply delivered 'qui-quip-chiri'. Pairs occur mostly in thornveld, frequenting the lower stratum. Most common in arid western regions. 22-3 cm (Rooiborslaksman)

1
2
3
4
5

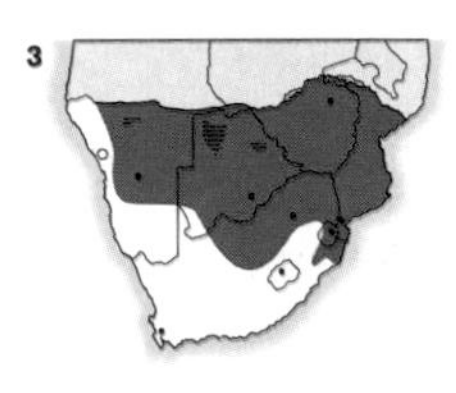

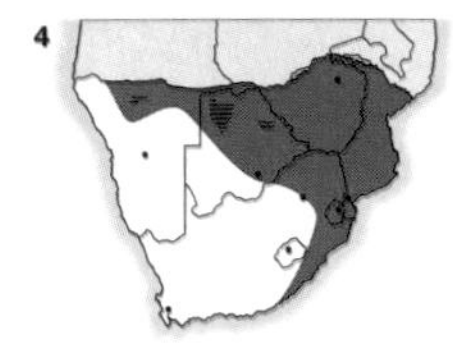

TCHAGRA SHRIKES

Heavy-billed, similarly coloured shrikes which feed on or near the ground, creeping about in the lower stratum of their preferred habitat and moving from bush to bush in low, rather heavy flight. Often reveal their presence by distinctive calls.

1 MARSH TCHAGRA *Tchagra minuta*

Uncommon, localised resident. Told from other tchagras by black cap extending to below eyes and very rufous body; female has a small white eyebrow forward of the eye. Immature has a brownish cap and horn-coloured bill. The call resembles the words 'today or tomorrow' uttered slowly. In courtship sings a shrill song while mounting steeply upwards on rapidly fluttering wings. Frequents tall grass and reeds in swamps or low bushes adjacent to damp regions. Restricted to low-lying eastern Zimbabwe and Mozambique. 18 cm (Vleitjagra)

2 SOUTHERN TCHAGRA *Tchagra tchagra* E

Common to fairly common endemic resident. Larger than (3), differing from it and (4) in reddish-brown crown grading into olive-brown mantle, back and central tail feathers. Immature is duller with buffy wing coverts and fulvous-grey underparts. The call is a loud rattling sound followed by a rapid 'chchchch ...', ending with 'tew-a-tew'. Also has a loud whistle. Singly or in pairs in dense thickets in coastal bush, thornveld and valley bush; less common in the north. A reluctant flier but performs an aerial display like (3). 21 cm (Grysborstjagra)

3 THREE-STREAKED TCHAGRA *Tchagra australis*

Common resident. Smaller than (2) and (4), less rufous, more buff-brown. The flight pattern is very similar to that of (4). Immature is like adult but duller. The alarm note is a guttural 'churr'; in summer male displays by flying steeply upwards to above tree height, then planing down with quivering wings while calling 'tui-tui-tui-tui-tui ...' in a descending cadence. A thornveld species which spends much time in thickets or on the ground under bushes. If disturbed, hops onto some low branch before hopping or flying into cover. Usually seen singly. 19 cm (Rooivlerktjagra)

4 BLACK-CROWNED TCHAGRA *Tchagra senegala*

Common resident. Told from (2) and (3) by *black* crown. Immature has a blackish-brown crown and horn-coloured bill. Has a 'krok-krok-krokrakror' alarm note and a loud, ponderous and rather flat-sounding call 'CHEER-tcharee, trichi CHEER-tcharoo, cheeroo, cheeroo'. Pairs also duet with a variety of grating, churring and whistling calls. Singly or in pairs in thornveld, woodland, coastal bush and plantations, frequenting the lower stratum. 21-3 cm (Swartkroontjagra)

1
2
3
4

1

2

3

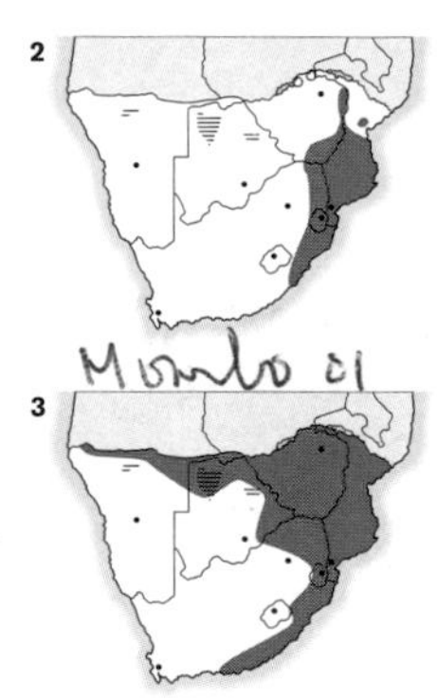

4

BUSH SHRIKES

Colourful shrikes with olive-green and grey upperparts and yellow or orange-yellow underparts. Most inhabit dense bush and all have distinctive calls.

1 OLIVE BUSH SHRIKE *Telophorus olivaceus* 

Common, near endemic resident. Two forms: (a) with cinnamon breast (intensity variable), male with white eyebrow; (b) with entirely green upperparts and yellow underparts in both sexes; cf. (3) and (4). Immature as illustrated. Calls include about six notes of varying pitch, sometimes preceded by a single higher note, 'phwee-phwee-phwee-phwee-phwee-phwee' or 'tew-tew-tew-tew-tew' or 'tee-toy-toy-toy-toy'; also a descending cadence 'CHE-che-che-che-che-che' and a warbling trill. Pairs in coastal and montane forest thickets, montane scrub, dense bush and plantations. In bush habitats it feeds in the lower stratum, in forests in the mid- and lower strata. Secretive at all times. 17 cm (Olyfboslaksman)

2 GORGEOUS BUSH SHRIKE *Telophorus quadricolor*

Fairly common resident. Male distinguished by scarlet throat and black gorget; female similar but black gorget much reduced. Immature shown in first plumage. The call is a liquid, ventriloquial and rapidly delivered 'kong-kong-koit'. Pairs in dense coastal and valley bush, lowland forest fringes, riverine forests and mixed bushveld. Secretive, frequenting the lower stratum. 20 cm (Konkoit)

3 ORANGE-BREASTED BUSH SHRIKE *Telophorus sulfureopectus*

Common resident. Male distinguished by yellow forehead and eyebrow plus yellow underparts with only the *breast* orange, this much reduced in female. Immature shown in first plumage. Calls a musical, much-repeated 'poo-poo-poo-pooooo' or 'pipit-eeez, pipit-eeez ...'. In pairs in mixed bushveld, thornveld and valley bush, plus riverine and coastal thickets, usually in the midstratum. Not secretive but often difficult to locate. 18-19 cm (Oranjeborsboslaksman)

4 BLACK-FRONTED BUSH SHRIKE *Telophorus nigrifrons*

Uncommon, localised resident. Male identified by black forehead and facial mask (no eyebrow) plus extensive orange wash from throat to belly; female's underparts less orange than male's, distinguished from female of (1b) by *grey head and mantle*. Normal call is a repetitive 'oo-poo', sounding like 'doh-me' in the tonic sol-fa scale. Pairs mainly in montane forests in the eastern regions, but also lowland forests in Mozambique. Feeds in the upper and mid-strata and joins bird parties in winter. 19 cm (Swartoogboslaksman)

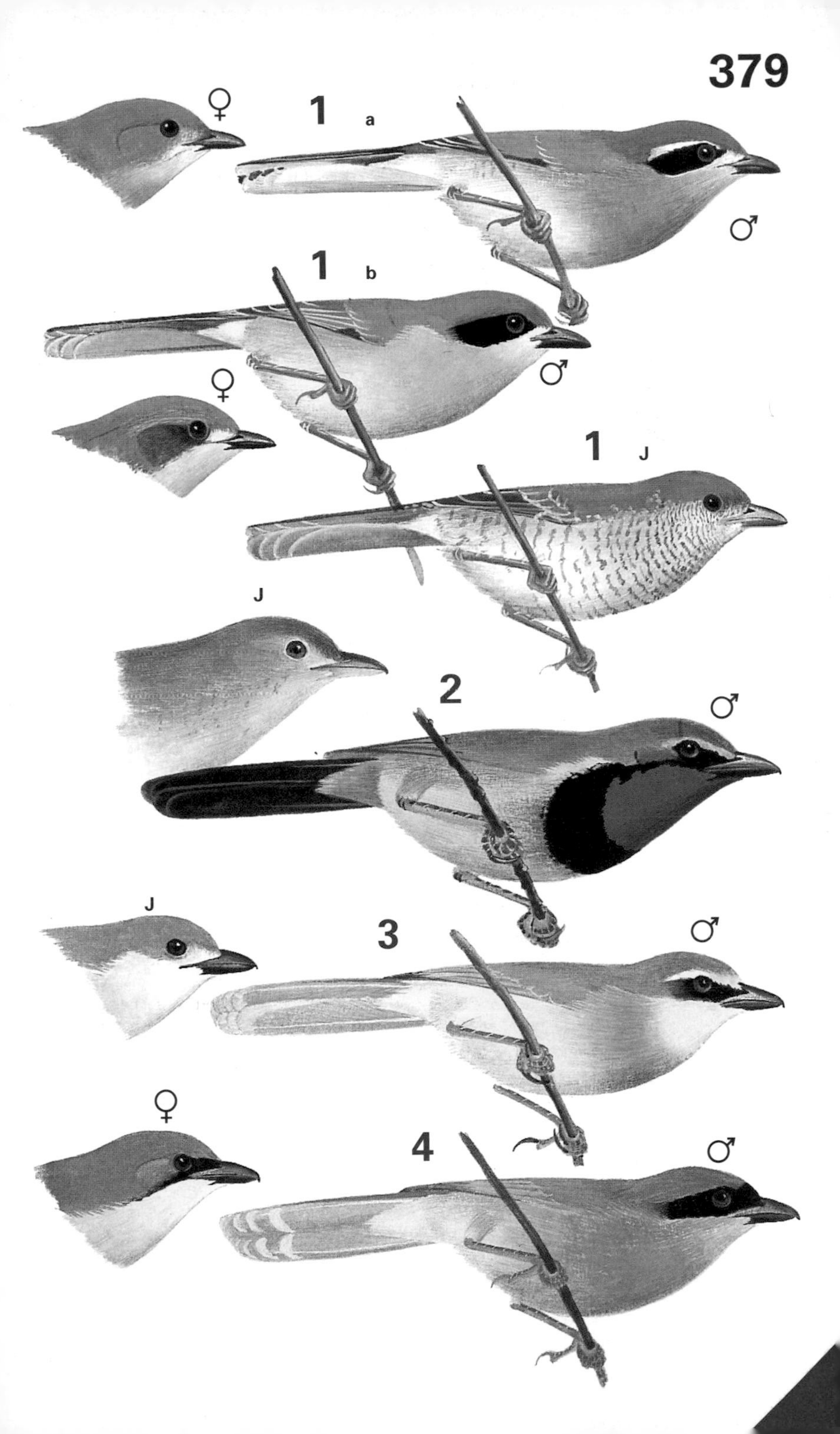
1 a
♀
♂
1 b
♂
♀
1 J
J
2
♂
J
3
♂
♀
4
♂

1

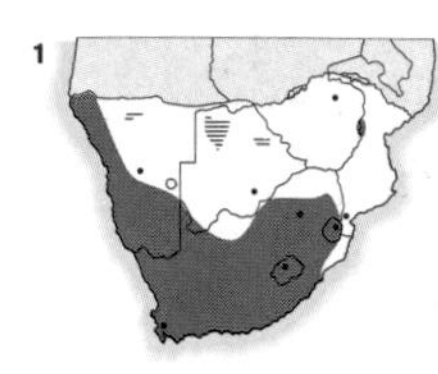

2

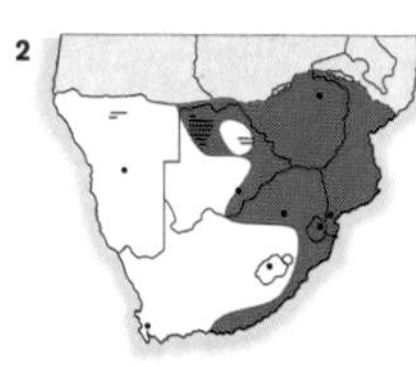

3 4 5

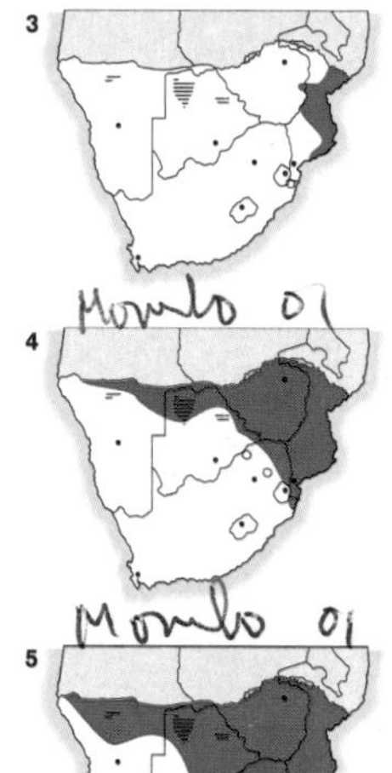

1 BOKMAKIERIE *Telophorus zeylonus* NE

Common, near endemic resident. Distinguished from Yellow-throated Long-claw (p. 292) by grey and green upperparts. Immature lacks the black gorget. The calls are duets and are variable, e.g. 'bok-makiri', 'kok-o-vik', 'bok-bok-chit', 'wit, wit-wit' or 'pirrapee-pirrapoo', each sequence repeated at about three-second intervals. Pairs occur in a wide range of habitats from montane foothills to the coast, in bush patches in grassland or on rocky hillsides and in semi-arid regions in the west; common in suburbia in most regions. Feeds on the ground. 23 cm (Bokmakierie)

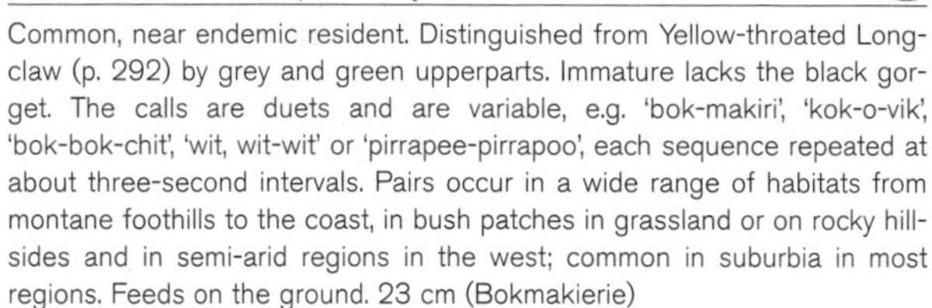

2 GREY-HEADED BUSH SHRIKE *Malaconotus blanchoti*

Fairly common resident. Identified by large size, *very heavy bill* and white patch before a yellow eye. Immature has a horn-coloured bill. The most characteristic call is a haunting, drawn-out 'hoooooooooooop'; also utters a 'clip-clip ....' sound. Singly or in pairs in coastal and lowland forests, riverine forests, mixed bushveld and thornveld. Usually feeds in the mid- and lower strata. (Spookvoël) 25-7 cm

HELMET SHRIKES

Characterised by intense sociability; usually groups of six to 12 birds of all ages feed and roost together, share nest-building and chick-feeding. Nomadic unless breeding. They move from tree to tree continuously and maintain a noisy chattering comprised of harsh whirring and grating sounds plus bill snapping. Sexes are alike.

3 CHESTNUT-FRONTED HELMET SHRIKE *Prionops scopifrons*

Rare resident. Distinguished by grey underparts and chestnut forehead plus white lores and chin. Immature has dusky forehead. Occurs in dense lowland forests and adjacent woodland of the Rusitu-Haroni region of Zimbabwe and in Mozambique, where it frequents the tree canopies. 19 cm (Stekelkophelmlaksman)

4 RED-BILLED HELMET SHRIKE *Prionops retzii*

Fairly common resident. Entirely black except for white vent and tailtips. Immature is browner. Parties in broad-leaved woodland or well-developed riverine forests where they frequent the tree canopies, sometimes in company with the White Helmet Shrike (5). 22 cm (Swarthelmlaksman)

5 WHITE HELMET SHRIKE *Prionops plumatus*

Common resident. Identified by pied plumage and butterfly-like flight. Immature has a browner crown. Parties in broad-leaved and mixed woodland, frequenting the mid- and lower strata. 20 cm (Withelmlaksman)

381
J
1
2
3
4
5

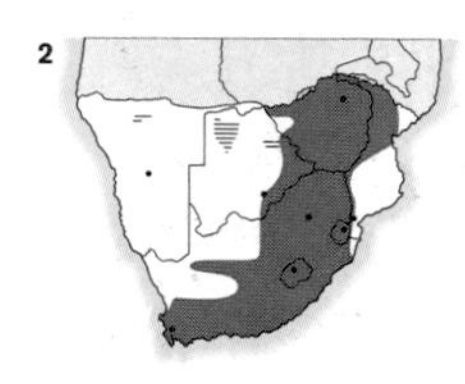

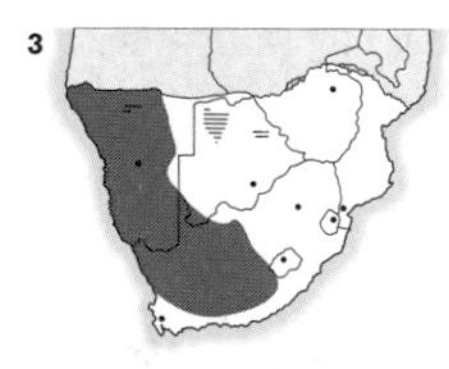

STARLINGS

Family STURNIDAE. A well-known family of frugivorous and insectivorous birds with strong, slightly decurved bills and strong legs. Many species form flocks, especially when roosting. Their calls are mainly various unmusical squeaks and squawks. Several species have adapted to town life and two have been introduced from other countries. Unless otherwise stated the immatures resemble adults.

1 WATTLED STARLING *Creatophora cinerea*

Common resident. A pale starling, male particularly so when breeding, at which time the head may be ornamented with yellow and black skin plus wattles as illustrated (b), or have only the wattles (c). Female and non-breeding male (a) appear drab, but can be told by diagnostic white rump in flight. The call is a rasping, squeaky sound. Highly gregarious in dry grassland or open bushveld, often associating with cattle. Flocks feed on the ground. When breeding they build hundreds of nests colonially in thorn bushes; highly nomadic when not breeding. 21 cm (Lelspreeu)

2 RED-WINGED STARLING *Onychognathus morio*

Common resident. Told from (3) by larger size, entirely red-brown flight feathers and sexual plumage differences as illustrated. The eye is dark. Has a variety of pleasant, loud whistles, the most frequent being a drawn-out 'spreeooo'. Pairs and flocks (large at communal roosts) frequent cliffs, caves or buildings where they roost and breed, dispersing daily to seek fruits and berries. 27-8 cm (Rooivlerkspreeu)

3 PALE-WINGED STARLING *Onychognathus nabouroup* 

Common, near endemic resident. Told from (2) by orange eyes and whitish wing feathers tinged orange only on the leading edge; the outer half of the wings appears entirely pale in flight; cf. Red-billed Buffalo Weaver (p. 404). Has similar melodious whistles to (2). Flocks occur in rocky localities in arid regions in the west and south-west. 26 cm (Bleekvlerkspreeu)

4 PIED STARLING *Spreo bicolor* E

Common endemic resident. A long-legged, dark brown starling with purple-green iridescence to the plumage and white vent and belly; the pale yellow eye and prominent orange gape are good field features. Call is a soft 'squeer' and similar melancholy whistles. Occurs in flocks in grassveld, open Karoo, dry dongas and riverbeds; a common roadside bird in many regions. 25-7 cm (Witgatspreeu)

♀
♂
N-Br
1
b
♂ Br
a
2
c
♂
Br
3
4

1

2

3
4
5
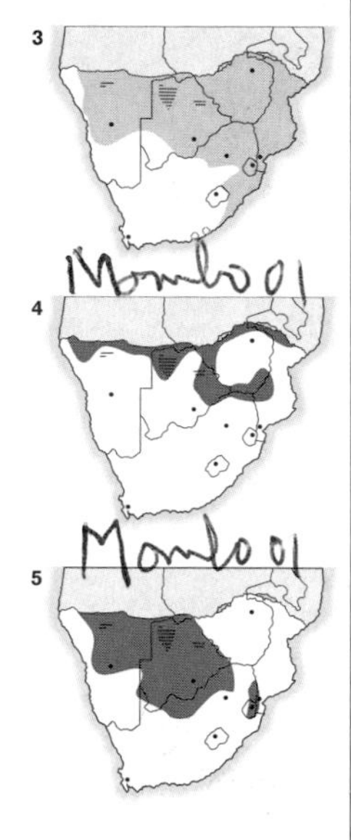

1 EUROPEAN STARLING *Sturnus vulgaris* (I)

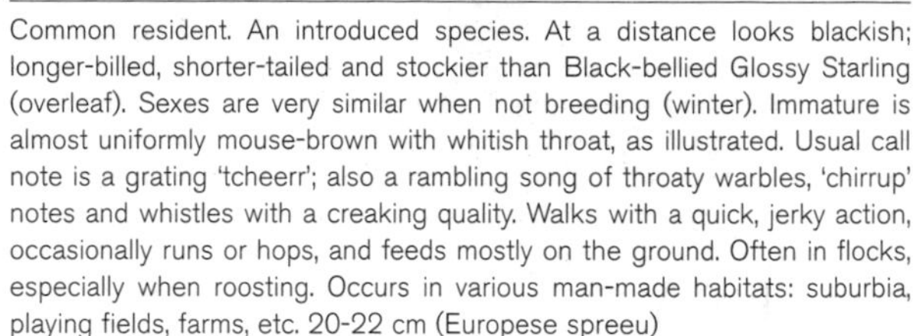

Common resident. An introduced species. At a distance looks blackish; longer-billed, shorter-tailed and stockier than Black-bellied Glossy Starling (overleaf). Sexes are very similar when not breeding (winter). Immature is almost uniformly mouse-brown with whitish throat, as illustrated. Usual call note is a grating 'tcheerr'; also a rambling song of throaty warbles, 'chirrup' notes and whistles with a creaking quality. Walks with a quick, jerky action, occasionally runs or hops, and feeds mostly on the ground. Often in flocks, especially when roosting. Occurs in various man-made habitats: suburbia, playing fields, farms, etc. 20-22 cm (Europese spreeu)

2 INDIAN MYNA *Acridotheres tristis* (I)

Very common or abundant resident. An introduced species. In flight large white wing-patches conspicuous. Immature has duller facial skin. Has a variety of chattering calls, clucking sounds, squeaks and some melodious phrases. Struts about with a swaggering gait, in pairs or small flocks, gathering in large flocks to roost. Commensal with humans, scavenging in urban habitats. 25 cm (Indiese spreeu)

3 PLUM-COLOURED STARLING *Cinnyricinclus leucogaster*

Fairly common summer resident. Female differs from spotted thrushes (p. 312) in stockier build, shorter bill with yellow gape, yellow eyes and lack of black markings on ear coverts. Immature is like female, eyes darker. The call is a short series of pleasant, slurred notes. An arboreal, frugivorous species of mixed broad-leaved woodland. In pairs when breeding, otherwise in nomadic flocks of mostly one sex. Resident in the extreme north-west; a few present all year elsewhere. 18-19 cm (Witborsspreeu)

4 LONG-TAILED GLOSSY STARLING *Lamprotornis mevesii* (NE)

Common, near endemic resident. Differs from other glossy starlings in combination of *dark eyes* and long *graduated* tail; the folded wings shorter than in (5). Immature is similar, duller. Groups utter a chattering 'trrreer-eeear ...'. Usually in small flocks in well-developed woodland (especially mopane) with open ground. 30-34 cm (Langstertglansspreeu)

5 BURCHELL'S GLOSSY STARLING *Lamprotornis australis* (NE)

Common, near endemic resident. The largest glossy starling, differing from most others in dark eyes, from (4) in dark ear-patch, lanky appearance and shorter, ungraduated tail. The folded wings reach halfway down the tail. Immature is duller, brownish below. The call is a squeaky 'churrik-urr, churrick-urrik-kerr ...'. In pairs, small parties or large flocks in savanna woodland. Feeds on the ground, preferring heavily grazed areas. 30-34 cm (Grootglansspreeu)

♂ Br
J
N-Br
1
2
♂
3
♀
4
5

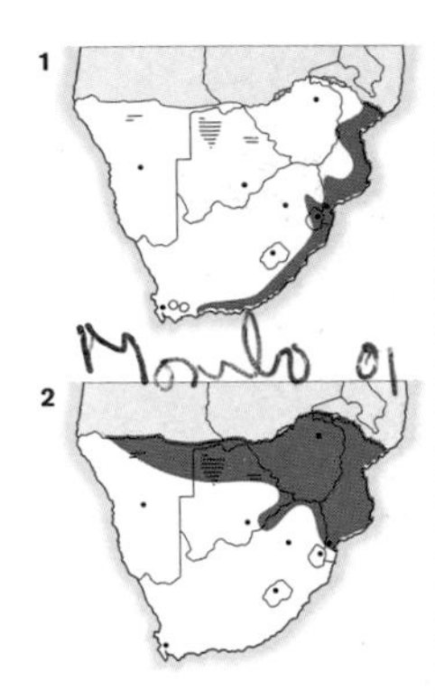

1 BLACK-BELLIED GLOSSY STARLING *Lamprotornis corruscus*

Common resident. Dullest of the glossy starlings, appearing black at a distance; female and immature dullest. Eye colour orange-yellow to red in adult, dark grey in immature. Flocks utter various pleasant warbling notes while feeding. Breeding pairs make a garbled series of mellow trills interspersed with harsher notes. Nomadic when not breeding. Occurs in coastal towns, forests and bush, extending inland to riparian and lowland woodland in the north. In Zimbabwe occurs in summer only in the Rusitu-Haroni region. 20-21 cm (Swartpensglansspreeu)

2 GREATER BLUE-EARED GLOSSY STARLING *Lamprotornis chalybaeus*

Common resident. One of three short-tailed and closely similar glossy starlings; cf. (3) and (5). Differs from (5) in blackish ear-patch and royal blue belly and flanks, from (3) in larger size, blue (not magenta) flanks and two distinct rows of black spots on the wing coverts. Immature is duller, underparts sooty, eye grey. The call is 'sque-eear, sque-eear-eeear'. In pairs when breeding, otherwise in large flocks in woodland and bushveld; in the Kruger National Park lives commensally with humans at rest camps during winter. 21-3 cm (Groot-blouoorglansspreeu)

3 LESSER BLUE-EARED GLOSSY STARLING *Lamprotornis chloropterus*

Common resident. Smaller than (2), flanks more magenta, the upper row of wing covert spots usually obscured, otherwise closely similar. Immature as illustrated, frequently flocking with adults. The song is a variety of pleasant notes 'chirp-chirrup-treerroo-chirp-trooo'; on take-off and in flight calls 'wirri-girri'. Occurs in broad-leaved woodland (especially miombo woodland) and bushveld, usually in flocks when not breeding. 20 cm (Klein-blouoorglansspreeu)

4 SHARP-TAILED GLOSSY STARLING *Lamprotornis acuticaudus*

Fairly common, localised resident. Identified by wedge-shaped tail. General colouring like (5) but has black ear-patch, blue flanks and red (male) or orange (female) eyes. Immature has grey underparts, the feathers tipped buff. Calls 'wirri wirri' in flight. Occurs in deciduous woodland of the north-east. 26 cm (Spitsstertglansspreeu)

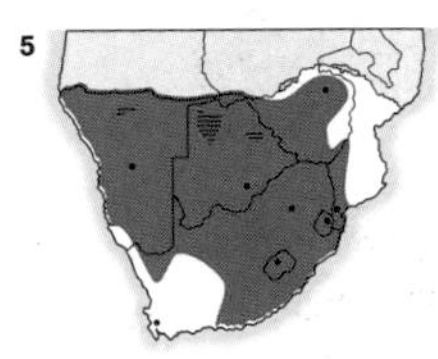

5 CAPE GLOSSY STARLING *Lamprotornis nitens* NE

Common, near endemic resident. Differs from (2) and (3) in *lack of dark ear-patch*, underparts uniformly blue-green. In poor light appears blue overall, even blackish; in good light is peacock-blue or green. Immature is drabber with much dull, blackish feathering. Song is a pleasant 'trrr-treer-treer-cheer ...'. Pairs or flocks in thornveld, mixed woodland and suburbia. Particularly common at camps in the southern Kruger National Park in winter. Also in arid western regions, extending into the Namib Desert within riverine bush. 23-5 cm (Kleinglansspreeu)

1
2
J
3
4
5

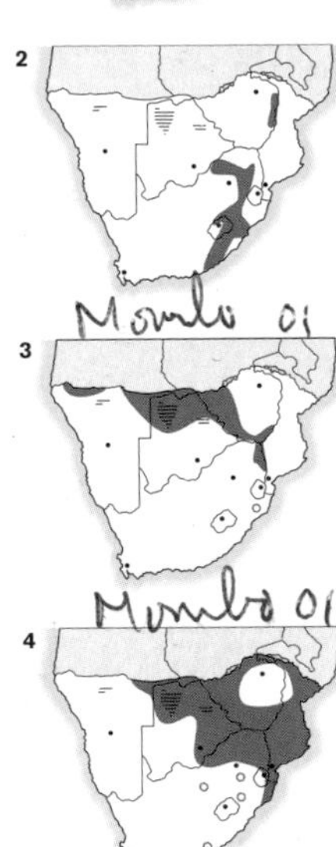

SUGARBIRDS

Family PROMEROPIDAE. Related to starlings and characterised by long, graduated tails, decurved bills and brown plumage with yellow vents. They feed on insects and nectar.

1 CAPE SUGARBIRD *Promerops cafer*

Very common endemic resident. Female told from (2) by shorter tail, pronounced moustachial streak, less rufous breast and lack of rufous cap. The song is a series of jumbled metallic, grating and churring notes. When breeding (winter) male calls conspicuously from a perch or flies about in undulating flight, wing-clapping with tail held high. Pairs occur where proteas are flowering on coastal mountain slopes and flats, moving about between seasons. MM 37-44 cm; FF 24-9 cm (Kaapse suikervoël)

2 GURNEY'S SUGARBIRD *Promerops gurneyi*

Common endemic resident. Told from (1) by more rufous breast and rufous cap. The call is three or four ascending notes, the last one repeated several times. Occurs on eastern mountain slopes where proteas or aloes are flowering; unless breeding (summer), somewhat nomadic. 25-9 cm (Rooiborssuikervoël)

OXPECKERS

Family BUPHAGIDAE. Related to starlings, but with very sharp claws for clinging to large mammals. Their bills are used to comb the animal's fur for ticks and bloodsucking flies. Their tails are used as props in woodpecker fashion as they clamber all over their hosts.

3 YELLOW-BILLED OXPECKER *Buphagus africanus*

Fairly common, localised resident. Differs from (4) in heavy yellow bill with red tip, *pale rump and upper tail coverts* and longer tail. Immature has a dusky brown bill, is generally duller. Utters a hissing 'kuss, kuss' sound. Flocks are normally seen in association with buffalo, rhinoceros and domestic cattle. 22 cm (Geelbekrenostervoël)

4 RED-BILLED OXPECKER *Buphagus erythrorhynchus*

Common resident. Differs from (3) in entirely red bill and *larger yellow eye-wattle*; does *not* have a pale rump. Immature has blackish bill and yellow gape; general appearance duller. Utters a hissing 'churr' and a 'tzik, tzik' sound; most noisy when flying. Normally seen in association with giraffe or antelope in game reserves; in remote rural areas on domestic cattle. In the evenings flocks gather to roost in dead trees standing in water. 20-22 cm (Rooibekrenostervoël)

♀
♂
1
2
3
4
J
3
4

1

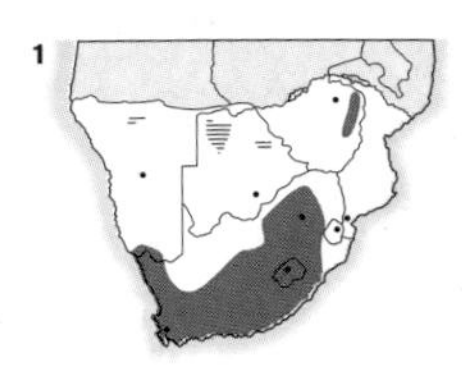

2

3

SUNBIRDS

Family NECTARINIIDAE. Small, insectivorous and nectar-eating birds with decurved bills adapted to flower-probing. Males have iridescent plumage and yellow, orange or red tufts on the sides of the breast (pectoral tufts) which are displayed in excitement. Some males undergo an annual eclipse when they adopt drab, non-breeding plumage resembling the normal plumage of the female. Immatures are like females, often with a dark throat. Their flight is swift and erratic, males spending much time chasing females and other males. Often gather in numbers when favoured nectar-rich plants are in blossom.

1 MALACHITE SUNBIRD *Nectarinia famosa*

Common resident. Breeding male is entirely iridescent green except for blue-black wings and tail; non-breeding male is yellow below, variably speckled overall with green feathers as illustrated; female told by large size and long bill. The call is 'chew-chew-chew, chi-chi-chi-chiew … chit-chit-chit …' with variations in speed and sequence; also a rapid warbling song. Usually found in groups on fynbos-covered hillsides (including suburbia in coastal regions), Karoo hills and montane foothills. Male frequently calls from a high vantage point and is aggressive towards other males. MM 25 cm; FF 15 cm (Jangroentjie)

2 COPPERY SUNBIRD *Nectarinia cuprea*

Uncommon, localised resident. Male differs from (3) in lack of long tail; female in clear, pale yellow underparts except for some speckling on the throat and upper breast. Has a harsh 'chit-chat' call and a high-pitched 'cher, cher, cher …' alarm note, plus a soft warbling song. Pairs occur in a variety of habitats including woodland fringes, montane forest fringes, the edges of marshlands and suburbia. Sometimes roosts in large groups. 12 cm (Kopersuikerbekkie)

3 BRONZE SUNBIRD *Nectarinia kilimensis*

Common, localised resident. Male differs from male of (2) in long tail-shafts; female in streaked underparts. Call is a shrill 'chee-oo, chee-oo' or 'pee-view, pee-view'. Pairs occur in montane grassland, montane forest fringes and woodland in eastern Zimbabwe. MM 21 cm; FF 14 cm (Bronssuikerbekkie)

♂
N-Br
♂
2
♀
1
♂
Br
♀
♂
♀
3

1 NEERGAARD'S SUNBIRD *Nectarinia neergaardi*

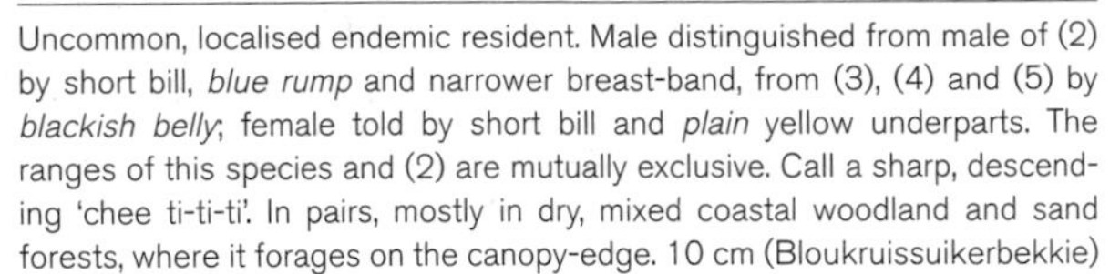

Uncommon, localised endemic resident. Male distinguished from male of (2) by short bill, *blue rump* and narrower breast-band, from (3), (4) and (5) by *blackish belly*; female told by short bill and *plain* yellow underparts. The ranges of this species and (2) are mutually exclusive. Call a sharp, descending 'chee ti-ti-ti'. In pairs, mostly in dry, mixed coastal woodland and sand forests, where it forages on the canopy-edge. 10 cm (Bloukruissuikerbekkie)

2 SHELLEY'S SUNBIRD *Nectarinia shelleyi*

Rare, strictly localised resident. Male distinguished from male of (1) by longer bill, green rump and wider breast-band, from (3), (4) and (5) by *blackish* belly; female by pale yellow underparts and streaked breast. The ranges of this species and (1) are mutually exclusive. The call is a rapidly repeated 'didi-didi', the song a nasal 'chibbee-cheeu-cheeu'. Individuals occur sparsely in the Mana Pools region of the Zambezi River and also upriver from Victoria Falls at Kazungula. 12,5 cm (Swartpenssuikerbekkie)

3 LESSER DOUBLE-COLLARED SUNBIRD *Nectarinia chalybea*

Common endemic resident. Male distinguished from male of (1) and (2) by longer bill and *greyish* (not black) belly, from (4) by *blue* rump and from (5) by shorter bill and narrower breast-band; female differs from (1) and (2) in greyer, less yellow underparts, but distinguishable from (4) and (5) by bill length only. Calls a harsh 'zzik-zzik' and a soft, abrupt 'swik, swik'; also has a high-pitched, swizzling song. Pairs in a variety of habitats from forest fringes to Karoo; a common garden species in many regions where suitable flowering plants are present. 12,5 cm (Kleinrooibandsuikerbekkie)

4 MIOMBO DOUBLE-COLLARED SUNBIRD *Nectarinia manoensis*

Common resident of the Zimbabwean plateau. Male differs from male of (3) only in grey rump (upper tail coverts only blue) and paler belly; females indistinguishable. Voice and behaviour like (3). Pairs in miombo and other broad-leaved woodland, montane forest fringes and suburbia. 13 cm (Miombo-rooibandsuikerbekkie)

5 GREATER DOUBLE-COLLARED SUNBIRD *Nectarinia afra*

Common endemic resident. Distinguished from (3) and (4) by larger size and longer bill; male by *broad* red breast-band. Song is a loud, scratchy jumble of rapidly warbled notes frequently repeated. Pairs and small groups in coastal and montane forests plus coastal and valley bush, frequenting the fringes and canopies depending on the availability of nectar-bearing flowers. 14 cm (Grootrooibandsuikerbekkie)

♀
1
♂
♀
♂
2
♀
♂
3
♂
4
♂
5
♀

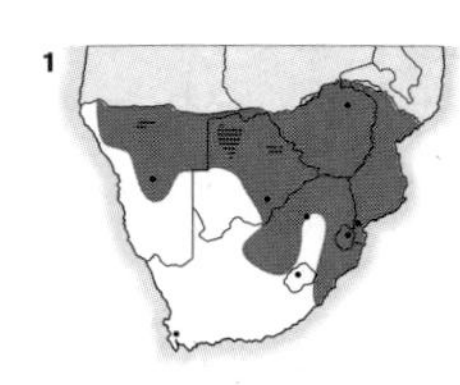

1 WHITE-BELLIED SUNBIRD *Nectarinia talatala*

Common resident. Male unique in having a bright iridescent *blue-green* head, mantle, throat and breast plus white underparts; cf. Dusky Sunbird (p. 400). Female very similar to female Dusky Sunbird but underparts less clear white. Immature male may have *pale yellow underparts and blue throat-patch*; can then be mistaken for the smaller Blue-throated Sunbird (p. 400) in eastern regions where their ranges overlap. The male has a loud, distinctive song, 'chu-ee, chu-ee, chuee-trrrrrr' repeated frequently. Pairs in mixed bushveld, any woodland and suburbia. Male is conspicuous by its habit of singing for long periods from a prominent perch. 11,5 cm (Witpenssuikerbekkie)

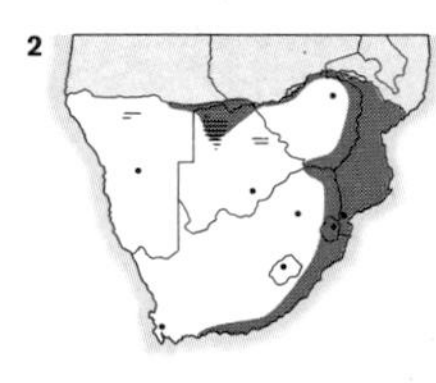

2 COLLARED SUNBIRD *Anthreptes collaris*

Common resident. Both sexes told from Blue-throated Sunbird (p. 400) by *bright iridescent* green upperparts and rich yellow underparts, male by all-green head and throat with blue and purple collar; from (3) by short bill and narrow collar. Song is a weak, cricket-like 'chirrreee, chirreee, chirreee' or a brisk 'tseep, t-t-t-t-t'. Pairs frequent the fringes of forests, riverine forests, coastal and valley bush, especially where there are flowering creepers. Often joins bird parties. 10 cm (Kortbeksuikerbekkie)

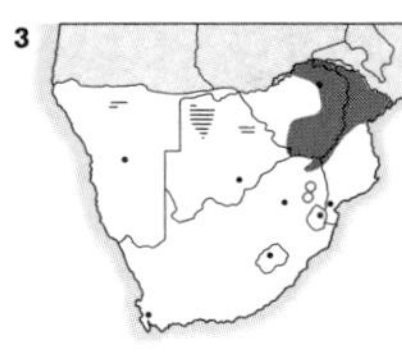

3 YELLOW-BELLIED SUNBIRD *Nectarinia venusta*

Fairly common resident. Larger and longer-billed than (2), male more blue-green on the upperparts and with a *broad* purple breast-band; female differs from double-collared sunbird females (previous page) in whiter breast and throat. Calls are 'tsiu-tse-tse' and an occasional trill, the song a rippling burst of twittering notes. Occurs on the fringes of forests, in riverine forests and patches of hillside bush, always preferring the lower scrubby vegetation and bracken-brier patches. 11 cm (Geelpenssuikerbekkie)

♀
♂
1
J
♂
♀
2
♂
3
♀

1

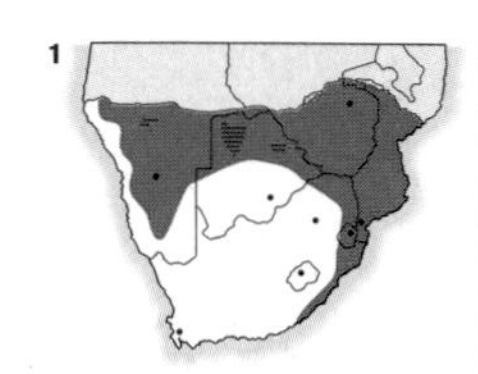

2

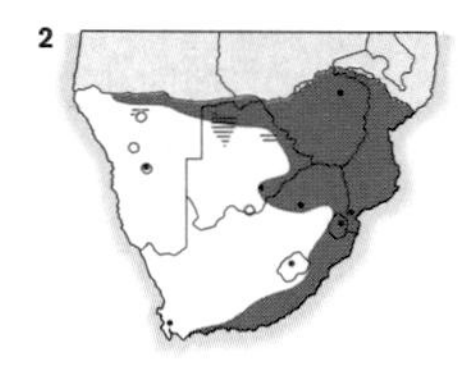

1 SCARLET-CHESTED SUNBIRD *Nectarinia senegalensis*

Common resident. Male resembles only the male of (2) but the large red breast-patch is diagnostic; female told by the heavy dark markings of the underparts. Utters a high-pitched chattering sound and a much-repeated 'cheep, chip, chop' from a prominent perch. Pairs occur in a variety of habitats including bushveld, woodland, riverine forests and suburbia where they are attracted to flowering creepers. A noisy, conspicuous species. 13-15 cm (Rooikeelsuikerbekkie)

2 BLACK SUNBIRD *Nectarinia amethystina*

Common resident. Male lacks the scarlet breast of (1), appearing all-black; female identified by creamy underparts and dusky throat with *pale yellow moustachial streak.* The call, often given in flight, is 'tschiek' or 'zit'; also utters a stuttering 'chichichichi' and a pleasant, subdued warbling song for long periods while concealed in foliage. Singly or in pairs in woodland, forest and riverine forest fringes, less often in bushveld, frequently in suburbia. Lively and conspicuous. 15 cm (Swartsuikerbekkie)

♂ J
♀
1
♂
2
♀
♂

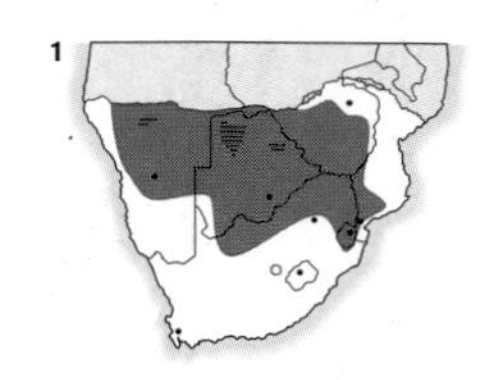

1 MARICO SUNBIRD *Nectarinia mariquensis*

Common resident. Male distinguished from male of (2) by larger size and longer, more decurved bill; from Neergaard's Sunbird (p. 392) also by these features plus *deep claret-red* (not bright red) breast-band; from the double-collared sunbirds (p. 392) by black belly. Female told by long bill, dusky throat and orange-yellow breast. Immature starts with yellow underparts and black bib (see illustration); as the yellow fades with ageing the plumage can resemble female Black Sunbird (previous page). The call is a brisk 'chip-chip' or a husky 'schitz-schitz' often given as a stuttering series; the song is a rapid warbling. Usually in pairs in *Acacia* thornveld. 13-14 cm (Maricosuikerbekkie)

2 PURPLE-BANDED SUNBIRD *Nectarinia bifasciata*

Fairly common resident. Similar colouring to (1) but much smaller, the bill short and only slightly decurved; male differs from male of Neergaard's Sunbird (p. 392) in *deep claret-red* (not bright red) breast-band. Call is a distinctive 'tsikit-y-dik' plus a trill, often by two birds in unison; the song is a high-pitched, descending trill. Pairs occur in riverine forests, the fringes of coastal evergreen forests, woodland, coastal bush and occasionally mangroves, preferring dense thickets in all habitats. A restless, nomadic species. 10-11,5 cm (Purperbandsuikerbekkie)

3 VIOLET-BACKED SUNBIRD *Anthreptes longuemarei*

Fairly common resident. The violet upperparts and white underparts of male and violet tail of female unmistakable. The call is a sharp 'chit' or 'skee'; the song a series of chittering sounds. Pairs occur in broad-leaved woodland where they frequent the tree canopies, feeding in the foliage and probing beneath loose bark; sometimes in groups on flowering trees It especially favours *Erythrina* and *Faurea* tree blossoms. 12,5-14 cm (Blousuikerbekkie)

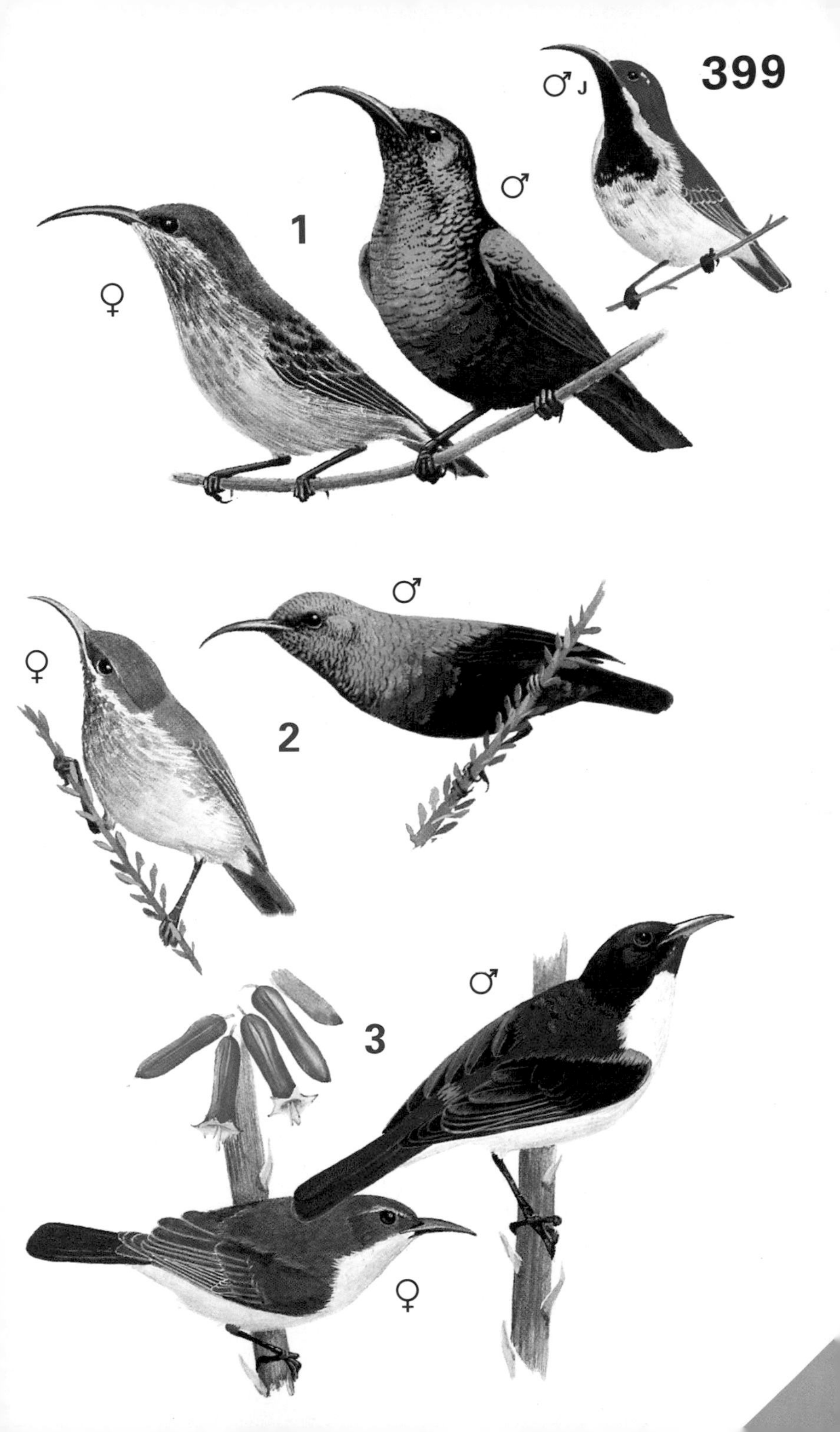

♂ J
♂
1
♀
♂
♀
2
♂
3
♀

1 BLUE-THROATED SUNBIRD *Anthreptes reichenowi*

Rare, localised resident. Male identified by dark blue throat and forehead. Female resembles a white-eye (overleaf), but has a slightly longer, slightly decurved bill and no white eye-rings; both sexes have *dull olive-green* upperparts, not iridescent green like Collared Sunbird (p. 394). Call is 'tik-tik'. Pairs frequent coastal, montane and riverine forests, feeding unobtrusively in both the upper and lower strata. 10 cm (Bloukeelsuikerbekkie)

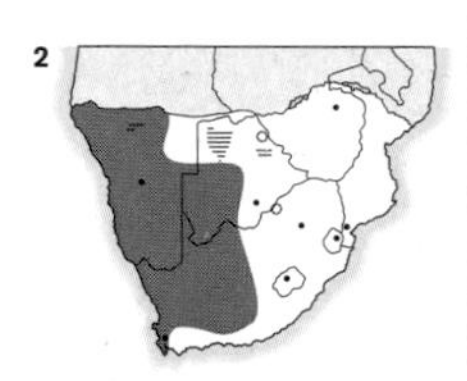

2 DUSKY SUNBIRD *Nectarinia fusca*

Common, near endemic resident. Breeding male is blackish with white belly, the breast with a coppery iridescence, pectoral tufts bright orange. Non-breeding male has dull brown upperparts, the underparts with an irregular blackish patch from chin to breast (see small illustration). Female is smaller, underparts white; cf. female White-bellied Sunbird (p. 394). Has a loud warbling song reminiscent of White-bellied Sunbird 'chuee-chuee-trrrrr' and 'tiroo tiroo tiroo sweet sweet sweet' with variations. In pairs in Karoo and Kalahari scrub, the riverine growth of dry river courses and even on rocky outcrops almost devoid of vegetation. 10-12 cm (Namakwasuikerbekkie)

3 ORANGE-BREASTED SUNBIRD *Nectarinia violacea*

Common endemic resident. Female differs from female Lesser Double-collared Sunbird (p. 392) in yellower underparts. Call is 'sshraynk' uttered one or more times; the song a subdued, high-pitched warbling. Pairs or loose parties on fynbos-covered coastal hillsides. Male indulges in much chasing with conspicuous aerial manoeuvres. MM 15 cm; FF 12 cm (Oranjeborssuikerbekkie)

4 GREY SUNBIRD *Nectarinia veroxii*

Common resident. Sexes are alike. Southern race (a) has pink-grey underparts, northern race (b) has pale green-grey underparts. Calls are a husky 'zzip' or 'tsit-tswaysit' and similar brisk notes; the song is loud, starting with single slow syllables and speeding up to a stuttering finish 'styeep-styip-styip-styip, yip, yip, yip, yip, yipyipyip ...'. Pairs occur in coastal forests, riverine forests and valley bush, feeding in both upper and lower strata. When singing often flicks its wings and displays its pectoral tufts. 14 cm (Gryssuikerbekkie)

5 OLIVE SUNBIRD *Nectarinia olivacea*

Common resident. A large, dull sunbird. Sexes are alike. Southern race (a) has orange on throat and upper breast, northern race (b) is smaller, much paler on underparts, no orange on throat. Calls a sharp 'tuk, tuk, tuk', sings a reedy 'tsee-tsee-tsee-tsee, tseedlee, eedlee-id-id-id-seedle ...'. Singly or in pairs in coastal and montane forests, mixed woodland, valley bush, riverine forests and suburban gardens. 13-15 cm (Olyfsuikerbekkie)

1
♀
♂
2
♀
♂
♂J
3
♀
♂
4
a
b
5
a
b

1
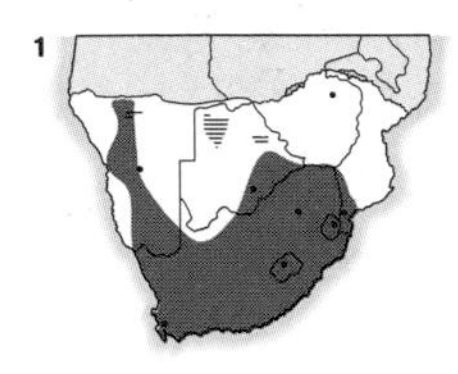

2
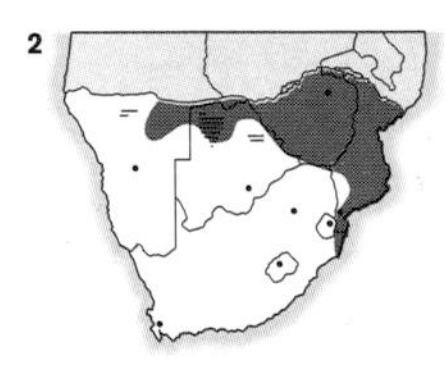

3

4

WHITE-EYES

Family ZOSTEROPIDAE. Very small, yellow-green birds which glean insects from leaves and probe flowers for nectar. Unless breeding, they occur in flocks which go from tree to tree where they search the foliage closely, frequently in the inverted position. Immatures are duller and lack white eye-wattles initially.

1 CAPE WHITE-EYE *Zosterops pallidus*

Very common endemic resident. Three basic colour forms occur as illustrated, with intergradings between them: (a) in the south with grey underparts; (b) in eastern regions and highveld with greener underparts; (c) from Orange River to western regions with paler underparts and flanks washed cinnamon. Normal call is a continual melancholy 'phe' by several in a party; also sings a loud rambling song from tree-tops in summer, plus a subdued warbling song from the depths of bushes. Gregarious, flocks occurring in almost any well-wooded habitat, including gardens. 12 cm (Kaapse glasogie)

2 YELLOW WHITE-EYE *Zosterops senegalensis*

Common resident. Distinguished from all forms of (1) by clear yellow underparts and more yellow-green upperparts. Calls like (1). Occurs in riverine forests, broad-leaved woodland (miombo), forests, exotic plantations and suburbia. Behaviour and habits like (1). 10,5 cm (Geelglasogie)

WEAVERS, SPARROWS AND ALLIES

Family PLOCEIDAE. A very large group of conical-billed, mainly seed-eating birds. Many breed colonially and weave complicated nests which help in identification. See nest drawings on pp. 414-15.

3 RED-HEADED QUELEA *Quelea erythrops*

Uncommon resident. Both sexes differ from Red-billed Quelea (overleaf) in brownish-horn bill; male in entirely red head; female in more ochreous colouring. Male distinguished from male Red-headed Finch (p. 428) by very small size and lack of scaly appearance on underparts. Immature resembles female. No distinctive call; flocks utter a twittering sound. In flocks, often with other small seed-eaters, in damp grassland, marshes and woodland where they feed on grass seeds. Irregular and nomadic. 11,5 cm (Rooikopkwelea)

4 CARDINAL QUELEA *Quelea cardinalis*

Rare vagrant. Its presence in southern Africa only recently confirmed with sightings in Zimbabwe and the Caprivi region. Similar to (3) but the red head of the male extends to the breast while the bill is blackish; in the female the bill is horn-coloured. It has been seen among Red-headed Queleas. 10-11 cm (Kardinaalkwelea)

a
b
1
1
c
2
♀
♂
♂
3
4

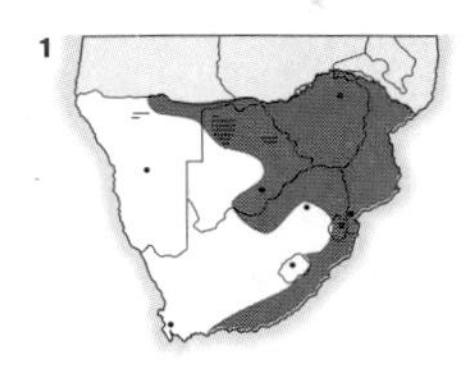

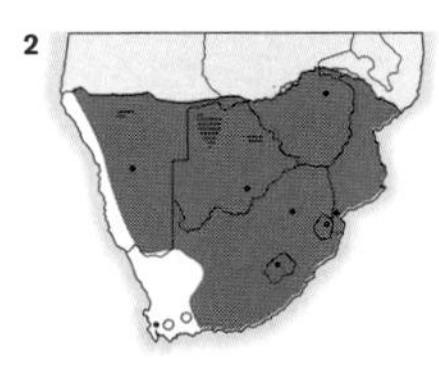

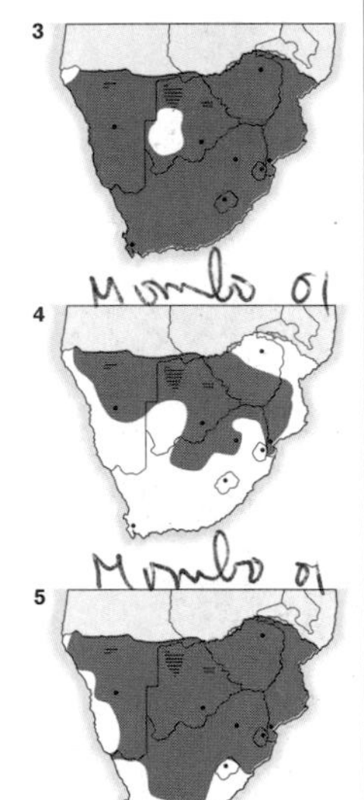

1 YELLOW-THROATED SPARROW *Petronia superciliaris*

Fairly common resident. Yellow throat-spot *not* a field character. Best identified by *broad white eyebrows*; cf. Streaky-headed Canary (p. 438) which also has broad white eyebrows but lacks the white wing-bars of this sparrow. Usual call is a rapid 'chree-chree-chree-chree'. Usually in pairs, frequenting tall woodland, thornveld and mixed bushveld. Often common around villages and camps. On the ground it walks, does not hop like other sparrows. 15-16 cm (Geelvlekmossie)

2 SOUTHERN GREY-HEADED SPARROW *Passer diffusus*

Common resident. Identified by entirely grey head and single white wing-bar; bill black when breeding, otherwise horn-coloured. Sexes are alike. Immature has streaked mantle. Utters a repetitive 'cheep-chirp', the first note descending, the second ascending, plus an occasional trill. Pairs in summer, small flocks in winter, in various wooded habitats including thornveld and mixed bushveld but not forests; common in many towns. Generally frequents large trees but feeds on the ground. 15-16 cm (Gryskopmossie)

3 HOUSE SPARROW *Passer domesticus*

Very common resident. An introduced species. Male distinguished by grey cap and black bib; cf. larger, brighter Great Sparrow (overleaf). Female and immature differ from (2) in having white eyebrows and much paler colouring. The call is 'chissip' or 'chee-ip'. Pairs and small parties occur in association with human habitation, breeding under the eaves of houses. Found in most towns and small settlements, even isolated permanent camps. Distribution patchy but widespread. 14-15 cm (Huismossie)

4 RED-BILLED BUFFALO WEAVER *Bubalornis niger*

Fairly common resident. A distinctive blackish bird with red bill and white feathers on the flanks and shoulders. Immature is greyish with much mottling on sides of head and underparts, the bill initially horn-coloured, then dull yellow, then orange. Utters chattering sounds at the nest plus a mellow trill, 'tridlyoo-triddlyoo-triddlyoo-triddlyoo'. Pairs and small flocks in thornveld and mixed bushveld, especially in dry regions, in association with baobab trees and large *Acacia* trees in which they build their communal nests (see illustration on p. 414). Patchily distributed and nomadic when not breeding. 24 cm (Buffelwewer)

5 RED-BILLED QUELEA *Quelea quelea*

Common to locally abundant resident. Breeding male variable as illustrated; breeding female has yellow bill. Non-breeding birds all have red bills. Occurs in flocks and is nomadic when not breeding, mainly in dry thornveld and mixed bushveld. Flocks utter a twittering when flying and nesting. Breeding colonies may be huge, involving tens of thousands, and cover many hectares of bush. Flying flocks resemble columns of smoke. 13 cm (Rooibekkwelea)

1
2
Br
3
♂
♀
4
♀
♂
5
N-Br
♂
♀
♂

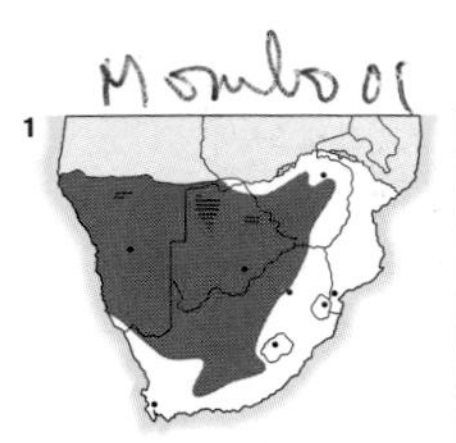

1 SCALY-FEATHERED FINCH *Sporopipes squamifrons* NE

Common, near endemic resident. Identified by very small size, *pink bill*, 'bearded' appearance and black wing feathers boldly edged with white. Sexes are alike; immature much duller, bill horn-coloured. When disturbed, flies off making a chattering sound. Small parties in dry thornveld regions, often around human settlements, frequenting fowl-runs, gardens and camps. 10 cm (Baardmannetjie)

2 SOCIABLE WEAVER *Philetairus socius* E

Common endemic resident. Pale bill offset by black face and throat diagnostic; a small, pallid, highly gregarious weaver. Sexes are alike; immature similar. Groups utter an excitable twittering at the nest. Flocks occur in the vicinity of their communal nests in dry western regions. The huge nests are placed in a large tree, frequently a thorn, and accommodate many pairs of birds for both breeding and roosting. 14 cm (Versamelvoël)

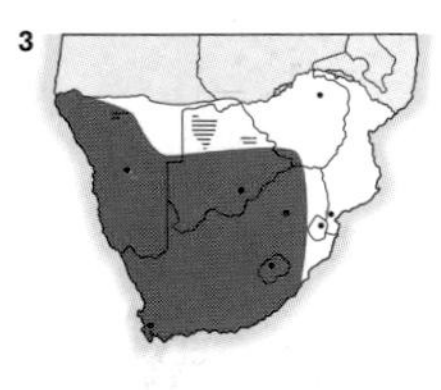

3 CAPE SPARROW *Passer melanurus* NE

Very common, near endemic resident. Black and white head and breast pattern of male distinctive; female told from female House Sparrow (previous page) by richer colouring, greyer head and *black bill*. Immature resembles female. Normal call is 'chirrup' or 'chissik'. Usually seen near human habitation. When not breeding, flocks occur in farmlands and cattle kraals. Tame and confiding. 15 cm (Gewone mossie)

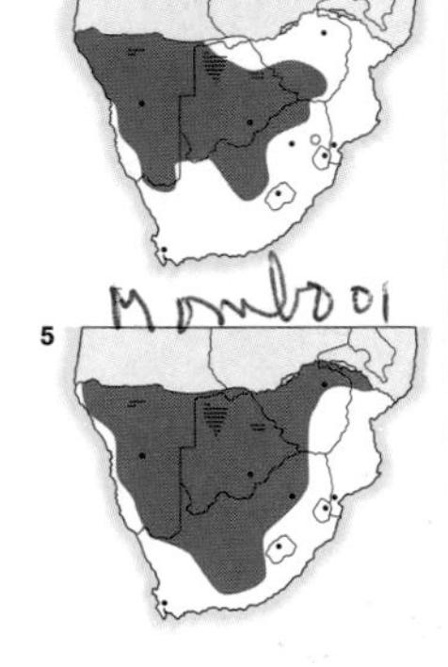

4 GREAT SPARROW *Passer motitensis*

Uncommon resident. Most resembles House Sparrow (previous page) but is larger, more brightly coloured. The call is typically sparrow-like: 'chirrup, chirroo, t-t-t-t-t'. Pairs occur in dry thornveld regions, *seldom near human settlements*, differing in this respect from House Sparrow and (3). 15-16 cm (Grootmossie)

5 WHITE-BROWED SPARROW-WEAVER *Plocepasser mahali*

Common resident. Distinguished by bold white eyebrow and, in flight, white rump and upper tail coverts; also occurs with pure white underparts. Sexes are alike; immature has a horn-coloured bill. Call is a harsh 'chick-chick'; also a loud, rambling song of liquid notes 'cheeoo-preeoo-chop-chop, cheeoo-trroo-cheeoo-preeoo-chop-chip ...'. Pairs and loose flocks in dry thornveld, usually near the trees containing their nests. Conspicuous and active, nest-building at all times of year. 18 cm (Koringvoël)

2
1
♂
♀
3
♂
4
♀
5

Weaver nests are illustrated on pp. 414-15.

1
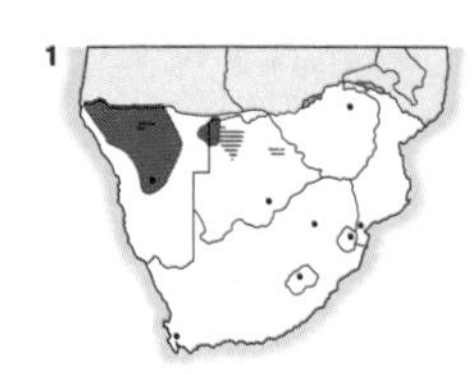

1 CHESTNUT WEAVER *Ploceus rubiginosus*

Uncommon, localised summer resident. Female and non-breeding male best identified by *grey bill* and brownish (not greenish) colouring. Call is a swizzling sound like (3). Usually in flocks, females outnumbering males while breeding, frequenting thornveld in the arid north-western regions of Namibia. 14-15 cm (Bruinwewer)

2

2 FOREST WEAVER *Ploceus bicolor*

Common, localised resident. Adults identical, maintaining the same plumage all year. Race (a) typical of southern birds, race (b) in coastal southern Mozambique, northern Mozambique and north-eastern Zimbabwe. Immatures are similar, the flanks with an olive wash. The song is a duet by both sexes, the most common phrase a high-pitched series of pleasant notes 'fweeee, foo-fwee foo-fwee ...', repeated with variations plus some soft rattling sounds. A non-gregarious, insectivorous weaver usually occurring in pairs in the midstratum of coastal and inland forests, dense riverine forests and valley bush. A quiet species which creeps about branches and probes for its food beneath bark and into *Usnea* lichen ('old man's beard'). 16 cm (Bosmusikant)

3
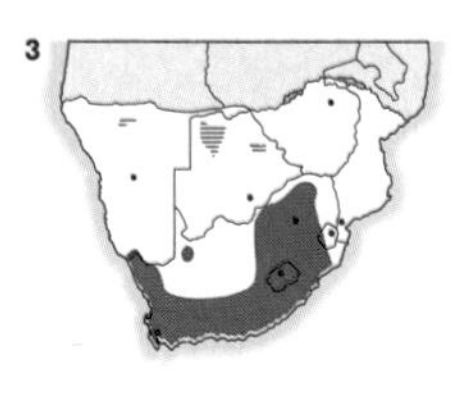

3 CAPE WEAVER *Ploceus capensis* E

Common endemic resident. Breeding male distinguished from female Spectacled Weaver (overleaf) by large size and black eye-line not extending behind the eye; non-breeding male like female but yellower on underparts and with pale eye. Female distinguished from female Masked or Lesser Masked Weavers (p. 412) by larger size and heavier, more sharply pointed bill. The normal sound in the vicinity of nests when breeding is a rapidly repeated swizzling 'a-zwit, a-zwit, zweeeeee-zt-zt-zt-zt ...' similar to that of Masked and Spotted-backed Weavers but harsher. Singly, in pairs or flocks almost anywhere where there are trees, especially near water and in suburbia where exotic trees are used for nesting. 16-18 cm (Kaapse wewer)

4

4 OLIVE-HEADED WEAVER *Ploceus olivaceiceps*

Uncommon, localised resident. Unmistakable within its restricted range and preferred habitat; female has the entire head olive. The song is 'tzee-twa-twa-twa-twa'. Usually in pairs in broad-leaved (miombo) woodland in Mozambique where it feeds on insects in the tree canopies, often in bird parties. 14,5 cm (Olyfkopwewer)

1
♂
♀
2
a
b
3
♂
♀
4
♂
♀

1

2
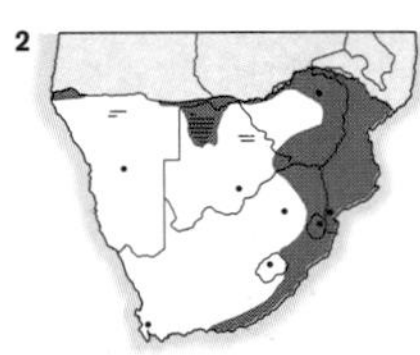
3

4
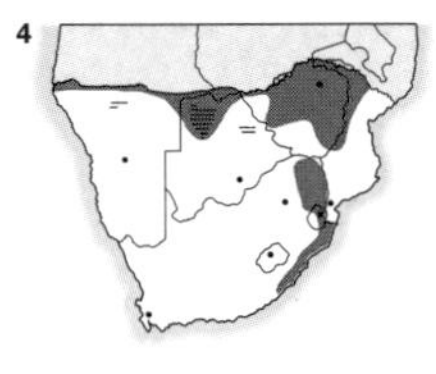
5
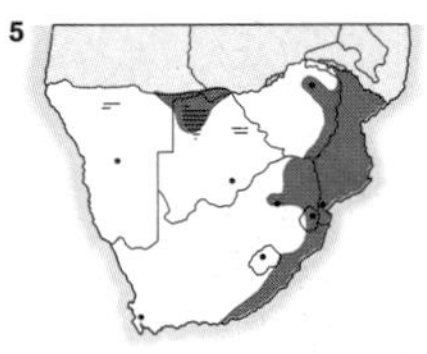

Weaver nests are illustrated on pp. 414-15.

1 YELLOW WEAVER *Ploceus subaureus*

Common resident. Palest yellow of the yellow weavers, upperparts slightly greener when not breeding. Immature resembles female. Utters a harsh 'zik' and a soft swizzling sound. Pairs and flocks in the eastern coastal and littoral zones, moving inland along rivers. Breeds in reed-beds and trees on rivers and lagoons; when not breeding occurs in riverine bush and adjacent woodland. 16 cm (Geelwewer)

2 SPECTACLED WEAVER *Ploceus ocularis*

Common resident. An insectivorous weaver distinguished by pale eyes and black streak through eye to ear coverts, male also by black bib; cf. Cape Weaver (previous page). Immature has a horn-coloured bill. Call is a good identification character, a descending 'tee-tee-tee-tee-tee-tee-tee'. Pairs occur in riverine forests, fringes of lowland and coastal forests, thornveld around pans and vleis, around farmsteads and in suburbia. Not a social weaver. 15-16 cm (Brilwewer)

3 BROWN-THROATED WEAVER *Ploceus xanthopterus*

Uncommon to locally common resident. A small, short-tailed weaver. Male has a *distinct brown patch* on throat and lores, female has a pale bill. *Both sexes have brown eyes and cinnamon rumps.* Pairs and small flocks occur in large reed-beds over water when breeding, in adjacent riverine forests and thickets when not breeding. Mostly on the east coast and littoral, the Zambezi River and extreme northern Botswana. Seldom far from water or swamps. 15 cm (Bruinkeelwewer)

4 GOLDEN WEAVER *Ploceus xanthops*

Uncommon to locally common resident. A large golden-yellow weaver with heavy black bill and pale yellow eyes. In the Okavango region and western Zimbabwe the male has an *orange wash over the throat*, this not present in southern birds; cf. (3) which has a *brown throat-patch.* The immature resembles the female but is greener and more streaked above. Utters a harsh chirp and a prolonged swizzling. In pairs or small flocks in reeds and thickets on rivers, marshes and gardens. Sparse in the south. 18 cm (Goudwewer)

5 THICK-BILLED WEAVER *Amblyospiza albifrons*

Common resident. Heavy bill diagnostic; the male's white frontal patches are present in the breeding season only. The immature resembles the female but the bill is yellower. Nesting birds (summer) utter a monotonous chattering; male occasionally sings an almost musical song. Pairs and small parties occur in reed-beds and the bush adjacent to rivers, pans and swamps when breeding; at other times coastal bush, riverine forests and wooded valleys. 18 cm (Dikbekwewer)

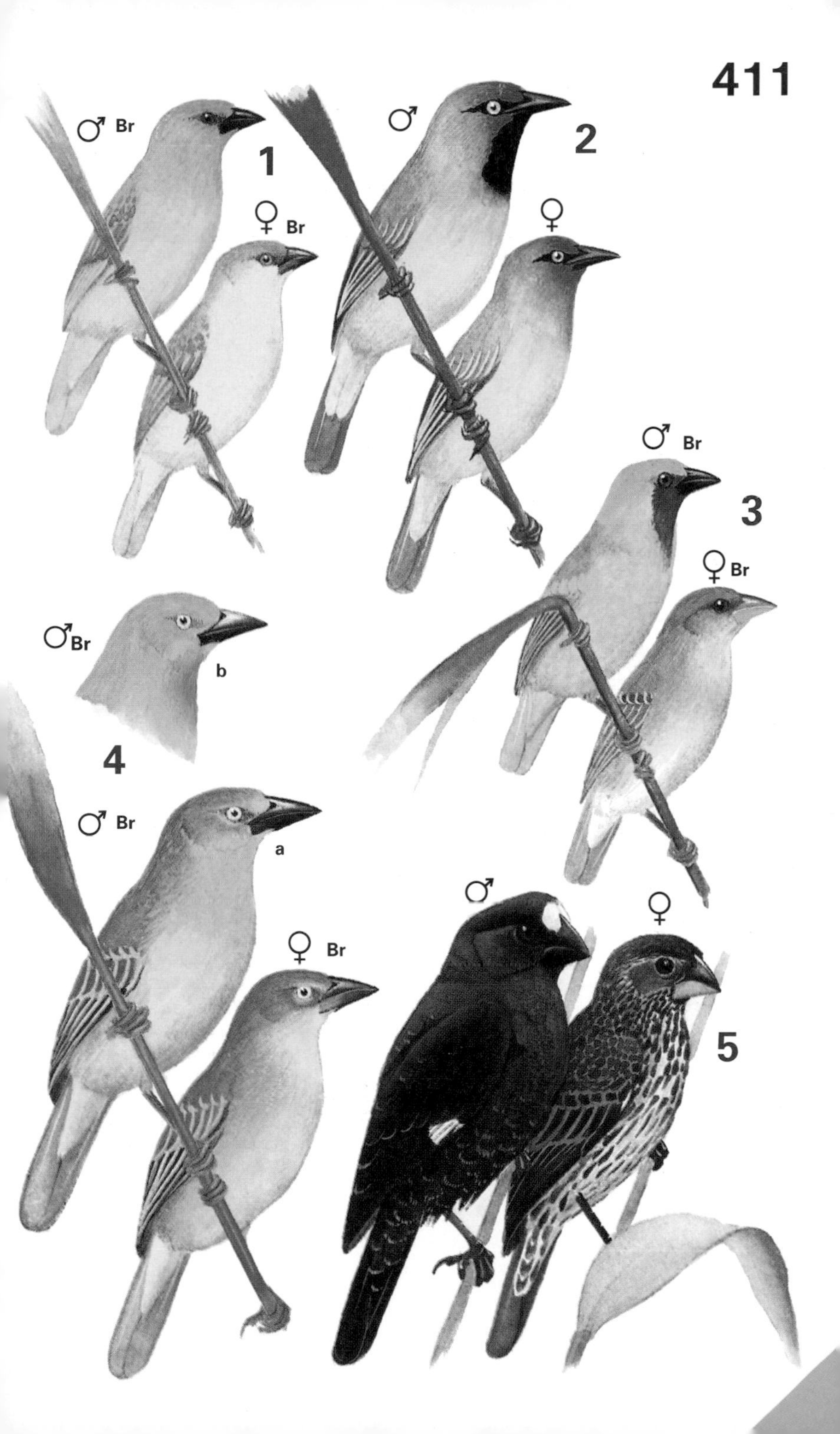
♂ Br
1
♀ Br
♂
2
♀
♂ Br
3
♀ Br
♂Br
b
4
♂ Br
a
♀ Br
♂
♀
5

1
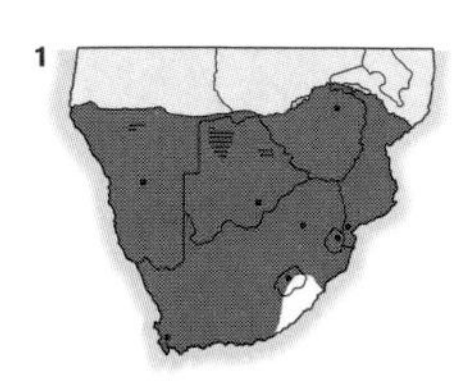

2
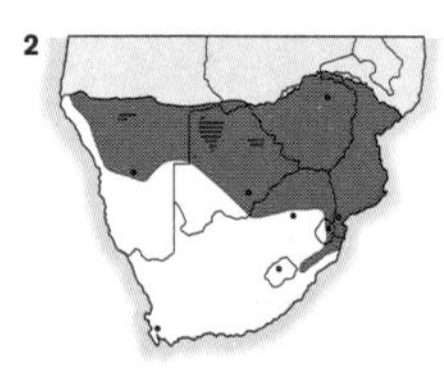

3
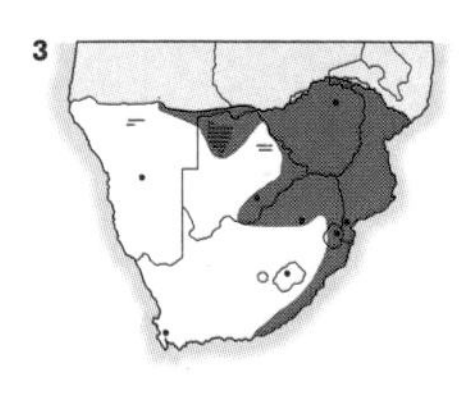

4
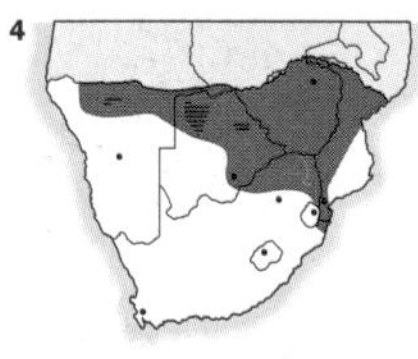

5
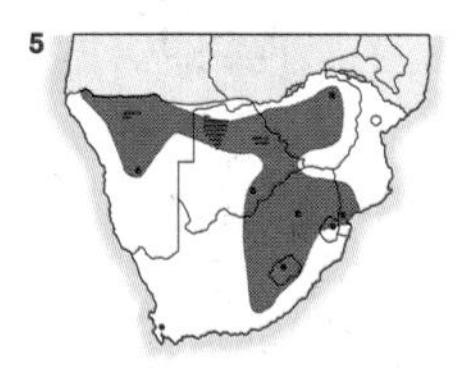

Weaver nests are illustrated on pp. 414-15.

1 MASKED WEAVER *Ploceus velatus*

Very common resident. Breeding male distinguished from (2) by *red eyes* and more yellow crown (*black mask extends across forehead only*), from (3) by plain back and black forehead. Non-breeding male resembles female. Breeding female has slightly more yellow underparts and redder eyes. Immature is duller, greyer on underparts. Utters prolonged swizzling sounds when breeding plus a sharp 'zik'. Gregarious at all times, small parties and flocks in thornveld, riverine bush, exotic trees around homesteads and farms. Breeds in small colonies in trees away from water, commonly in suburbia, or in large colonies in waterside bushes and reeds. Nomadic when not breeding, often in farmlands. 15 cm (Swartkeelgeelvink)

2 LESSER MASKED WEAVER *Ploceus intermedius*

Fairly common, localised resident. Breeding male differs from male of (1) and (3) in *pale yellow eyes* and black mask *extending over the top of the head*; female more yellow at all times. Immature is like female but whitish on belly. Utters swizzling sounds typical of most weavers, especially when nesting. Occurs in thornveld, mixed bushveld and riverine forests, being attracted to *Acacia* trees or reeds when breeding; colonies often large and sometimes with (1) or (3). 14 cm (Kleingeelvink)

3 SPOTTED-BACKED WEAVER *Ploceus cucullatus*

Common resident. Breeding male identified by spotted back and, in the northern race (a), by entirely black head; in the southern race (b) by the *clear yellow crown* with black only on face and throat; eyes red. Female has yellow breast and white underparts plus brown eyes. Non-breeding male like female but retains the red eyes. Breeds in colonies, often large, in thorn trees overhanging water, sometimes in reeds or away from water in exotic trees at farms and in suburbia. Male displays by hanging beneath the nest, swinging from side to side with quivering wings while making husky swizzling sounds. Nomadic in flocks when not breeding. 17 cm (Bontrugwewer)

4 RED-HEADED WEAVER *Anaplectes rubriceps*

Fairly common resident. Breeding male has red head and mantle; non-breeding male and immature like female. Normally silent but utters a squeaky chattering at the nest. Pairs or males with several females occur in broad-leaved woodland, breeding in isolation. Nomadic when not breeding. 15 cm (Rooikopwewer)

5 GOLDEN BISHOP *Euplectes afer*

Common resident. Breeding male conspicuous, displaying by flying about puffed up with rapidly whirring wings while making various buzzing sounds. Found in vleis, near dams, in grassland and cultivations when breeding, otherwise in nomadic flocks which wander widely, often with other weavers. 12 cm (Goudgeelvink)

♂ Br
♀ N-Br
1
♂ Br
♀
2
a
b
♀ N-Br
3
♂ Br
5
♂
4
♀
♂ Br
♀

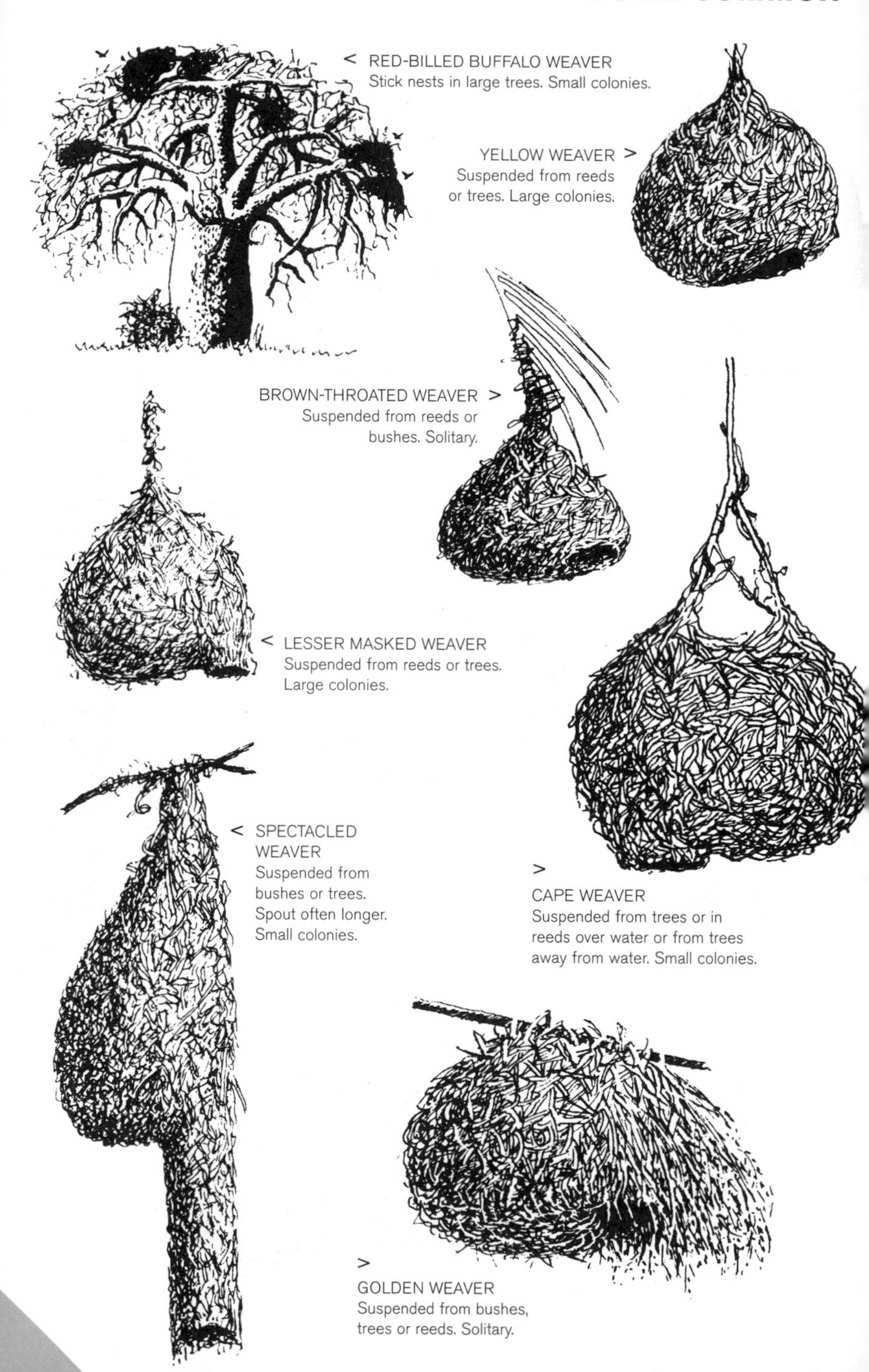

< RED-BILLED BUFFALO WEAVER
Stick nests in large trees. Small colonies.
YELLOW WEAVER >
Suspended from reeds or trees. Large colonies.
BROWN-THROATED WEAVER >
Suspended from reeds or bushes. Solitary.
< LESSER MASKED WEAVER
Suspended from reeds or trees. Large colonies.
< SPECTACLED WEAVER
Suspended from bushes or trees. Spout often longer. Small colonies.
>
CAPE WEAVER
Suspended from trees or in reeds over water or from trees away from water. Small colonies.
>
GOLDEN WEAVER
Suspended from bushes, trees or reeds. Solitary.

WEAVER NESTS

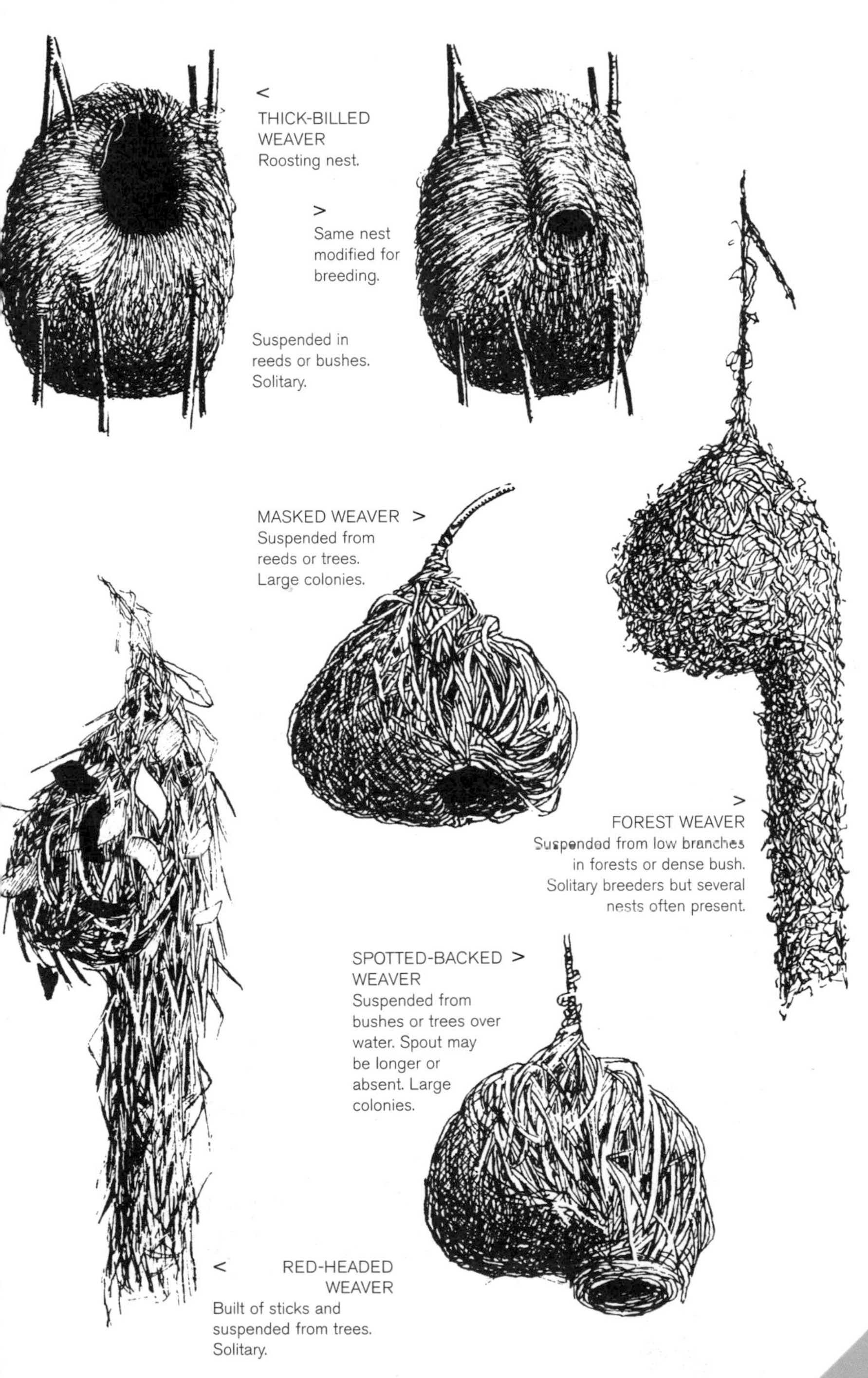

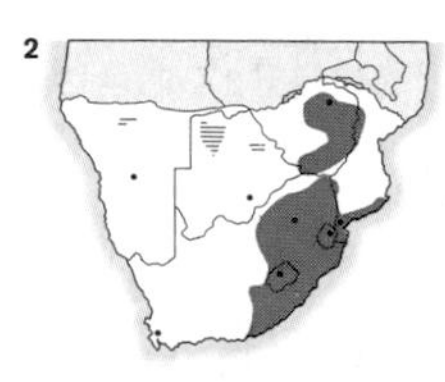

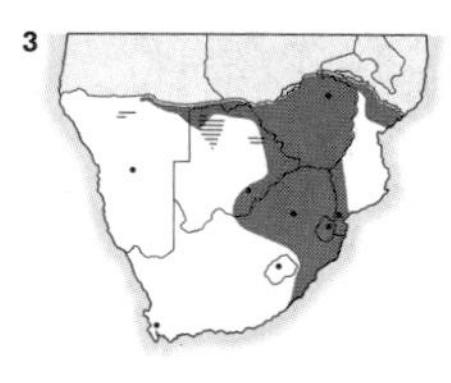

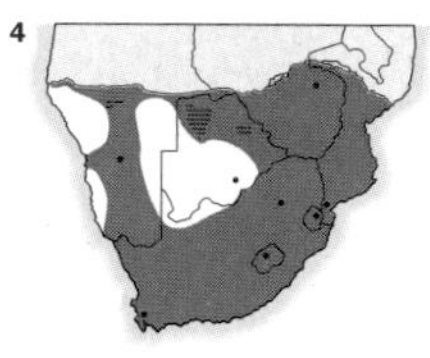

WIDOWBIRDS AND BISHOPBIRDS

Reed- and grass-loving weavers, differing from other Ploceidae in that males are predominantly black when breeding, some with long tails, and habitually puff out their plumage in display. Non-breeding males resemble females, as do immatures. Thin, ball-type nests are placed in grass or reeds.

1 RED-SHOULDERED WIDOW *Euplectes axillaris*

Common resident. Breeding male identified by short tail and red shoulders. Male utters a husky 'tseek, wirra, wirra, wirra, wirra' when displaying. Occurs in grass and coarse vegetation fringing marshes, riverine reed-beds and papyrus, cultivated fields, fallow lands and even canefields. In summer male flies about conspicuously over its territory, otherwise inconspicuous and in flocks. 19 cm (Kortstertflap)

2 RED-COLLARED WIDOW *Euplectes ardens*

Common, localised resident. Breeding male has only a narrow red collar and is much smaller than Long-tailed Widow (overleaf), tail thinner. When displaying, male utters a weak 'kizz-zizz-zizz-zizz'. In well-grassed bushveld, vleis, streams, rank grass in old cultivations and on hillsides. In summer male flies about with spread tail or perches conspicuously on bushes. 15-40 cm (Rooikeelflap)

3 WHITE-WINGED WIDOW *Euplectes albonotatus*

Common resident. Breeding male is recognised by yellow and white wings, bluish bill and broad tail frequently fanned. Utters a twittering sound when displaying. Frequents marshes or damp vleis in otherwise dry thornveld and mixed bushveld, also rank vegetation bordering cultivations. Male displays and perches conspicuously during summer. 15-19 cm (Witvlerkflap)

4 RED BISHOP *Euplectes orix*

Common resident. Breeding male could be mistaken in north-eastern regions for the next species, which however has an entirely red crown. In summer male calls a wheezy, spluttering 'zik-zik-zik ... zayzayzayzayzay'. In flocks in association with reeds, rank grassland and cultivations; common in vleis. In summer male displays by puffing out its plumage while perched or flying over its territory (see illustration), usually several are visible at a time. In winter forms flocks and is nomadic. 14 cm (Rooivink)

5 FIRE-CROWNED BISHOP *Euplectes hordeaceus*

Uncommon localised resident. Breeding male differs from (4) in having an *entirely red crown, black flight feathers and upper tail* plus a *whitish vent*. When not breeding the black wing feathers and central upper tail feathers remain. Female more yellowish than female Golden Bishop (p. 412), distinguished at all times by black central upper tail feathers. Usually in pairs, behaviour and habitat otherwise very similar to (4), both species often nesting in close proximity. Found in Eastern Zimbabwe and Mozambique. 13-15 cm (Vuurkopvink)

1
2
3
4
5

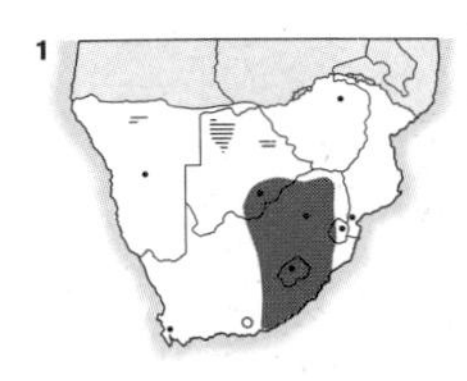

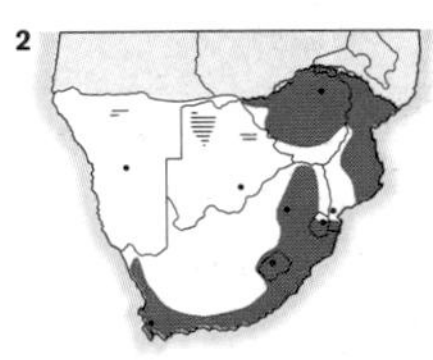

1 LONG-TAILED WIDOW *Euplectes progne*

Common resident. Breeding male has longer and fuller tail than Red-collared Widow (previous page), red shoulder-patch and pale bill good field features. Non-breeding male has same wing pattern, is much larger than female and all others in this group. Female and immature normally seen in a flock with male. Normal call is a repeated 'chip ... chip ... chip ...'; while breeding male utters a subdued, swizzling song. A grassland species, especially in vleis and valleys with rich growth. When breeding (summer) females are inconspicuous but male perches prominently on a tall weed near the nest, or patrols its territory in low flight, wings flapping slowly and deliberately. When not breeding these widows form flocks, often mixing with other grassland seed-eaters. MM 19-60 cm; FF 15 cm (Langstertflap)

2 YELLOW-RUMPED WIDOW *Euplectes capensis*

Common resident. Non-breeding male resembles female but *retains the yellow rump and shoulders*. Female and immature have a dull yellow rump. Breeding male calls 'skeet' from the top of a tree. Family groups or flocks (when not breeding) in vleis and marshy regions near streams in foothills and bracken slopes near montane forests and plantations. Displaying male makes audible wing-flutters both at rest and in flight. At these times the plumage is puffed out, the yellow rump conspicuous. 15 cm (Kaapse flap)

3 YELLOW-BACKED WIDOW *Euplectes macrourus*

Locally common resident. Breeding male has *yellow shoulders and back*; cf. (2) from which it is also identified by longer tail. Non-breeding male resembles female but retains yellow shoulders, distinguished from White-winged Widow (previous page) by lack of white in wings. Immature resembles female. Call is a thin buzzing sound. Occurs in grassland near water. Breeding male displays with a jerky flight, the tail jerking up and down. When not breeding these widows form flocks, often with other grassland species. 14-22 cm (Geelrugflap)

419
♂Br
1
♂Br
2
♀
♂N-Br
♂Br
♀
♀
3

FINCHES, WAXBILLS, TWINSPOTS, MANNIKINS, etc.

Family ESTRILDIDAE. Small, conical-billed, ground- or grass-feeding seed-eaters. Mostly colourful; gregarious when not breeding.

1

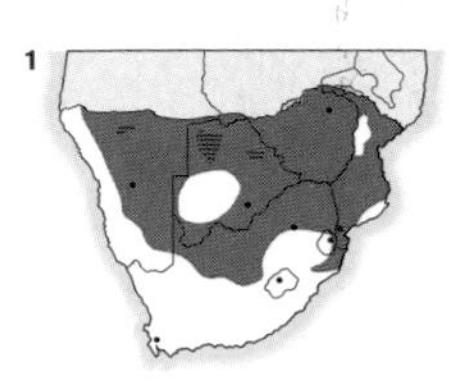

1 MELBA FINCH *Pytilia melba*

Common resident. Both sexes differ from (2) in black and white barred underparts, all-green wings and longer, predominantly red bill. Usual call is a single, low 'wick'; also utters a plaintive whistle and has an attractive short song. Pairs frequent thorny thickets, often near water, and associate with other waxbills and firefinches, feeding on open ground. 12-13 cm (Gewone melba)

2

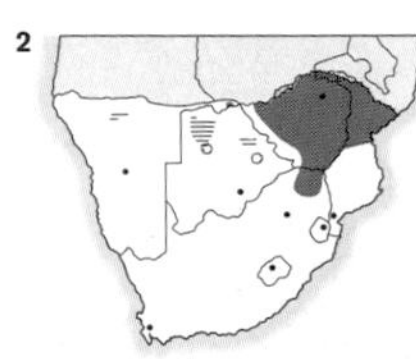

2 GOLDEN-BACKED PYTILIA *Pytilia afra*

Locally common resident. Differs from (1) mainly in the underparts being barred green (not black) and in having orange-edged wing feathers, which appear as an *orange patch on the folded wing*; the bill is shorter and mostly brown on the upper mandible. Call is a single, flat 'seee' and a two-note, piping whistle. Behaviour and habitat preferences very similar to (1). 11 cm (Geelrugmelba)

3

3 RED-FACED CRIMSON-WING *Cryptospiza reichenovii*

Uncommon, localised resident. A distinctive dark green bird with deep crimson wings and back, thus differing from (4) which is predominantly brown; only the male has a red mask. The call is a high-pitched 'zeet'; also utters a descending song of four notes followed by a chirp. A very shy, mostly silent species of forests. Small parties feed on the ground in dense shade by forest streams and at forest fringes, seldom flying more than a few metres when disturbed. 12 cm (Rooirugsaadvretertjie)

4

4 NYASA SEEDCRACKER *Pyrenestes minor*

Uncommon, localised resident. Male has a larger area of red than the female; it extends to the breast. Differs from (3) in being generally earth-brown (not green) and lacking red wings. Call is 'tzeet', plus a sharp clicking when alarmed. Pairs frequent thick woodland along streams or forest fringes, preferring hilly regions with high rainfall. Stays low down in the vegetation but not in dense cover. 13 cm (Rooistertsaadvretertjie)

♀
1
♂
♂
♀
2
♂
♀
3
♂
♀
4

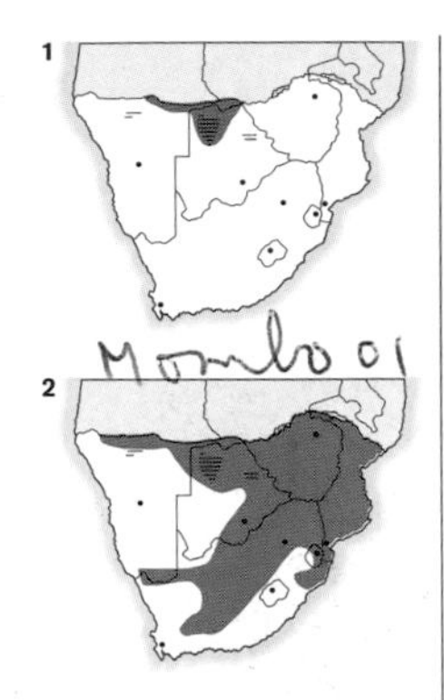

1 BROWN FIREFINCH *Lagonosticta nitidula*

Fairly common, localised resident. Might be confused with (2), but the red is confined to the face, throat and upper breast; *the rump has no red.* Sexes are alike. The call is a flat, unmusical 'tsiep, tsiep' or 'chick, chick'. Occurs in thickets and reeds near water in the extreme north of the region, but groups feed in open ground, often on termite hills. 10 cm (Bruinvuurvinkie)

2 RED-BILLED FIREFINCH *Lagonosticta senegala*

Common resident. Both sexes have the red rump; cf. (1). Male has more extensive red on head and underparts. Distinguished from other firefinches by reddish bill or, in mixed parties, by the grey-brown females. The call is a nasal 'fweet, fweet'. Occurs in pairs or small parties in mixed bushveld, especially near watercourses and, in the north, in suburbia. Is host to Steel-blue Widowfinch (p. 434). 10 cm (Rooibekvuurvinkie)

3 BLUE-BILLED FIREFINCH *Lagonosticta rubricata*

Common resident. The bill appears black in the field. Identified by *grey crown and nape* plus blackish belly in the male; in Zimbabwe the grey crown and nape are *washed with pink*; then differs from (4) in distinctly browner wings and mantle. Has a trilling, bell-like call involving 'chit-chit-chit' sounds and ending with 'wink-wink-wink'; also a stuttering alarm call. Pairs and small parties in dense bushveld, forest fringes and in thorn and grass tangles. Is host to Black Widowfinch (p. 434). 11 cm (Kaapse vuurvinkie)

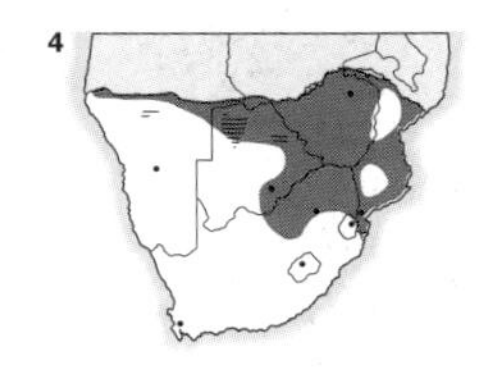

4 JAMESON'S FIREFINCH *Lagonosticta rhodopareia*

Common resident. The reddest firefinch; bill blackish in both sexes. Male has the crown, nape and mantle washed pink, rest of upperparts less dark than (3), underparts rose-pink. Female more orange-pink on underparts. Immature male (see illustration) more uniformly brown above, below rose-pink with a brownish wash on lateral breast. Has a tinkling 'trrr-trrr' alarm note plus various musical calls 'tewee-tewee ...' or 'fweeee' or 'zik, zik'. Frequents thickets and rank grass in thornveld, and riparian and secondary growth around cultivated lands. Is host to Purple Widowfinch (p. 434). 11 cm (Jamesonse vuurvinkie)

1
2
♂
♀
3
♂
♀
4
♂
♀
J

1 LOCUST FINCH *Ortygospiza locustella*

Uncommon, localised resident and visitor. A very small, ground-feeding bird. Female has much darker upperparts than (2), and orange edges to wing feathers. Call is a querulous 'pink-pink'. Frequents wet grassland in dense flocks except when breeding (late summer). Flocks usually fly only a short distance before resettling, but flight fast and dipping. 9 cm (Rooivlerkkwartelvinkie)

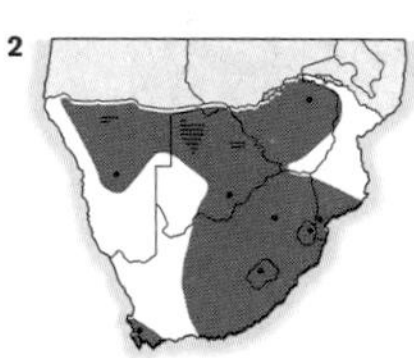

2 QUAIL FINCH *Ortygospiza atricollis*

Common resident. Differs from (1) in paler, less striking colouring, well-banded breast and flanks plus white facial markings. Call is a querulous, metallic 'tirrilink', given in flight and often the only clue to the species' presence. Pairs or small parties frequent short grassland, especially overgrazed regions, pan fringes and other damp localities. Occasionally takes off in brief flight, suddenly descending again. In courtship the male towers to a great height and then descends like a falling object while making a clicking sound; cf. 'cloud' cisticolas (pp. 348-50). 9,5 cm (Gewone kwartelvinkie)

3 GREEN TWINSPOT *Mandingoa nitidula*

Uncommon resident. Mature adult differs from other small green birds in having white-spotted underparts, but immature has plain green underparts. Call is a chirping 'tzeet'; also has a subdued song. An elusive, shy species which frequents the fringes of forests and coastal bush, feeding in areas of open ground, but darting into thick cover if disturbed. 10 cm (Groenkolpensie)

4 PINK-THROATED TWINSPOT *Hypargos margaritatus*

Common, localised endemic resident. Most resembles (5), but red colouring of male is *dull rose pink*, not deep crimson; female has only the rump and tail pink. Call is a trilling 'tit-it-it-it-it-it-it' or 'trrr-it'. Pairs or small groups frequent dense, tangled scrub in patches of open ground and forest fringes, darting into cover when alarmed. 12 cm (Rooskeelkopensie)

5 RED-THROATED TWINSPOT *Hypargos niveoguttatus*

Common, localised resident. Male differs from (4) in *deep crimson* colouring; female in more rusty breast. Call is a stuttering, grasshopper-like trill 'trree-rree'. Pairs and small parties on open ground near forests, dense bush and streams or in dry, open country. 12,5 cm (Rooikeelkolpensie)

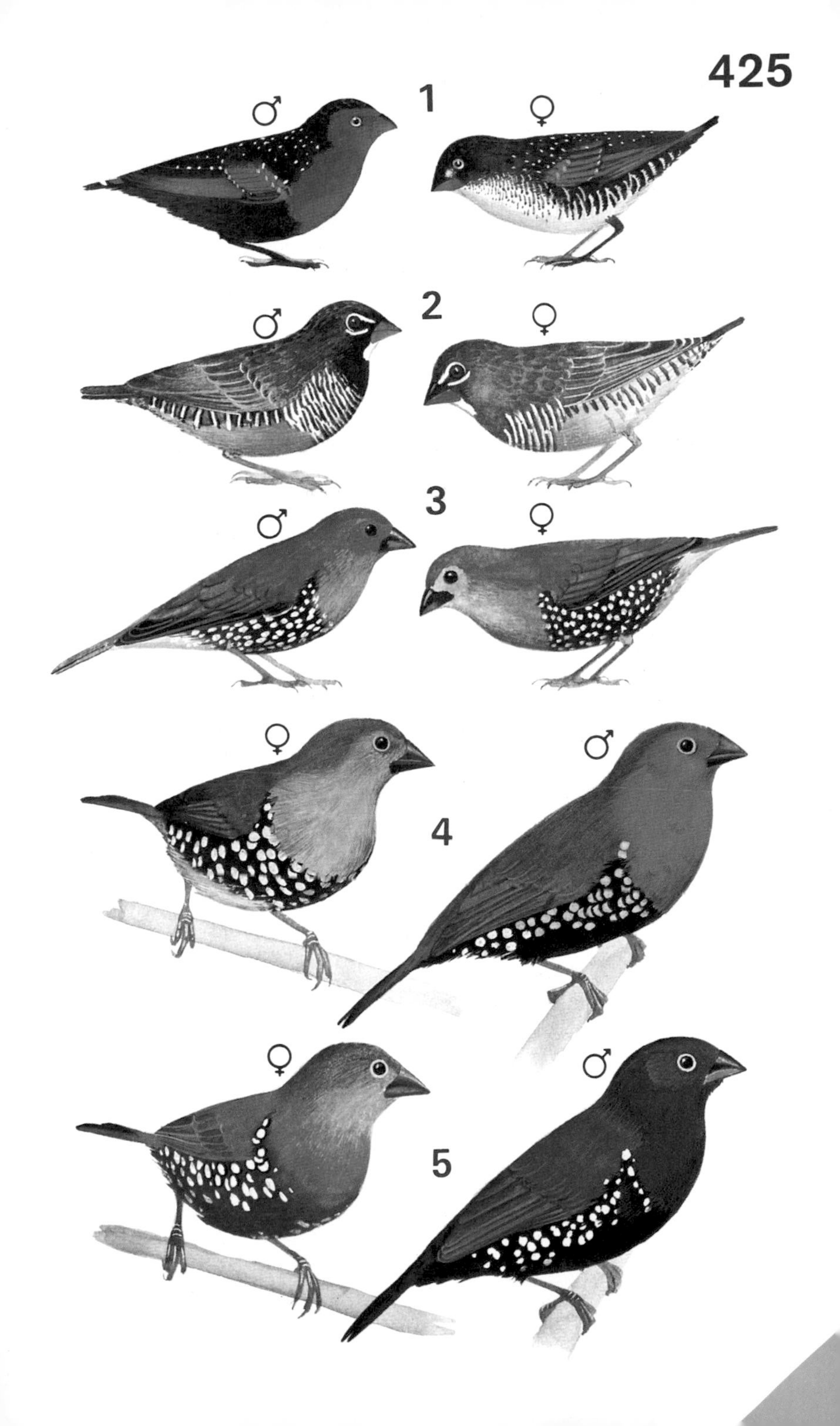
425
1
♂
♀
2
♂
♀
3
♂
♀
4
♀
♂
5
♀
♂

1

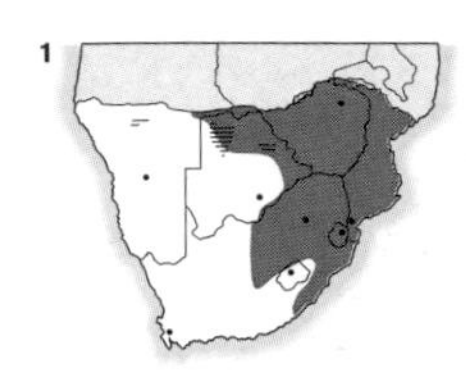

1 ORANGE-BREASTED WAXBILL *Sporaeginthus subflavus*

Common resident. The male's orange breast is variable in extent, sometimes absent. Immature is like female but has black bill. Call is a quiet, metallic tinkling often made in flight. Pairs and small flocks occur in waterside grass and reeds, especially in vleis and other marshy regions plus cultivated fields. Very active, mobile little birds which make off in straggling sequence at low height, then suddenly drop down again. 8,5-9 cm (Rooiassie)

2

3

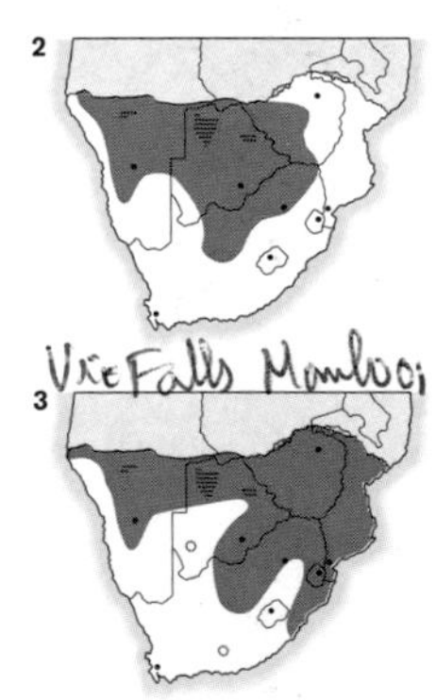

2 BLACK-CHEEKED WAXBILL *Estrilda erythronotos*

Fairly common resident. Female is slightly duller, less red. Immature is like female. Call is an ascending 'fwooee'. In pairs; flocks occur when not breeding. In dry thornveld and on the slopes of the north-eastern escarpment in misty conditions. Feeds mainly on the ground but flies into trees if disturbed. Seldom plentiful and probably nomadic much of the year. 12-13 cm (Swartwangsysie)

3 BLUE WAXBILL *Uraeginthus angolensis*

Very common resident. Immature paler than female, bill black. Calls frequently on the ground and in flight, a high-pitched 'weet-weet'. Pairs and small parties, frequently with other small seed-eaters, in dry thornveld, often in dry watercourses, bare patches of ground under bushes and in kraals, flying into bushes when disturbed. Never far from water. 12-14 cm (Gewone blousysie)

4

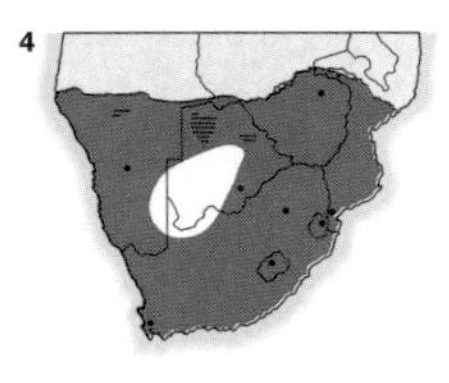

4 COMMON WAXBILL *Estrilda astrild*

Very common resident. Red bill, facial skin and underbelly distinctive; immature has blackish bill. The call is 'chik-chik-ZEEE, chik-chik-ZEEE', descending on the third syllable. Small or large flocks in grassy riverbanks, reed-beds, vleis and rank vegetation bordering cultivated lands. Very active birds, flocks always flying off in straggling procession from place to place. Feeds on the ground and on seeding grasses. 13 cm (Rooibeksysie)

5

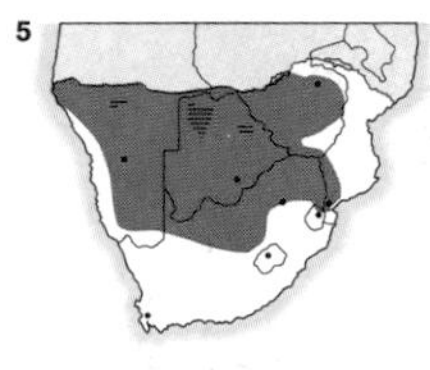

5 VIOLET-EARED WAXBILL *Uraeginthus granatinus* NE

Common, near endemic resident. A long-tailed species. In flight the tail appears broad. Immature is duller than female. The often-repeated call is 'tiuwoowee'. Pairs, often in company with (3), in dry thornveld, especially sandveld. Feeds on the ground, flying into thickets when disturbed. 13-15 cm (Koningblousysie)

♂
♀
1
2
3 ♂
♀
4
♂ 5
♀

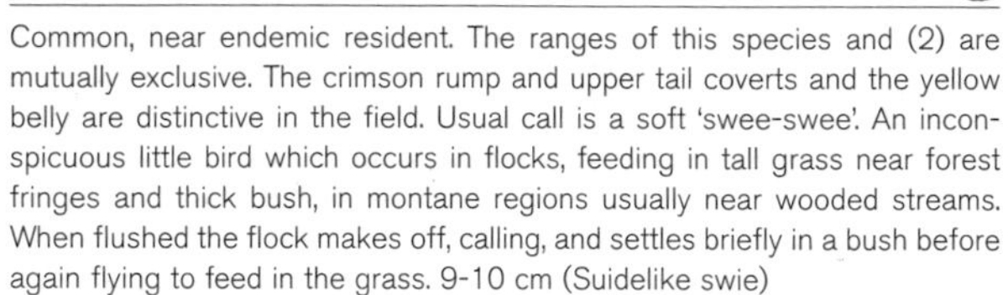

1 SWEE WAXBILL *Estrilda melanotis* NE

Common, near endemic resident. The ranges of this species and (2) are mutually exclusive. The crimson rump and upper tail coverts and the yellow belly are distinctive in the field. Usual call is a soft 'swee-swee'. An inconspicuous little bird which occurs in flocks, feeding in tall grass near forest fringes and thick bush, in montane regions usually near wooded streams. When flushed the flock makes off, calling, and settles briefly in a bush before again flying to feed in the grass. 9-10 cm (Suidelike swie)

2 EAST AFRICAN SWEE *Estrilda quartinia*

Uncommon, localised resident. Both sexes are identical to the female of (1); often regarded as a race of that species. Habits, habitat and voice identical. Occurs only on the eastern Zimbabwe-Mozambique border. 10 cm (Tropiese swie)

3 GREY WAXBILL *Estrilda perreini*

Uncommon resident. Similar to (4) but darker grey with a black bill, no red on the flanks. The only grey waxbill likely to be seen in southern Africa, becoming darker grey in northern races. Call is a thin 'pseeu, pseeu'. An inconspicuous species of woodland and forest edges where thick bush tangles with tall grass. Usually in pairs, which seldom venture far from dense cover. 11 cm (Gryssysie)

4 CINDERELLA WAXBILL *Estrilda thomensis*

Fairly common, localised resident. Superficially resembles (3), but the grey is paler with a rosy flush on the upperparts and belly; the bill is red with a black tip; the flanks are red and black. Small parties occur in low bushes along the Cunene River in northern Namibia. The call is 'seee' or 'see-eh see-eh sueee'. 11 cm (Swartoogsysie)

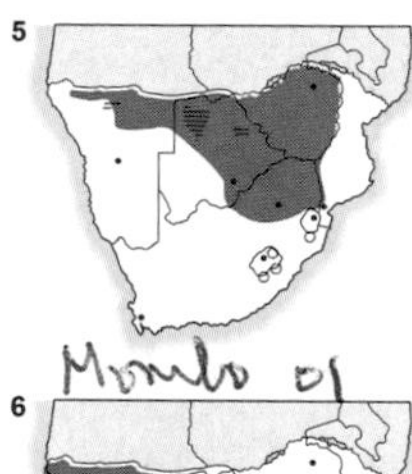

5 CUT-THROAT FINCH *Amadina fasciata*

Common resident. Female has a generally scaly appearance with a pale bill; smaller and darker than female of (6). A thin 'eee-eee-eee' call is uttered in flight. In pairs when nesting, otherwise in flocks in dry broad-leaved woodland, often near villages and cultivations. 12 cm (Bandkeelvink)

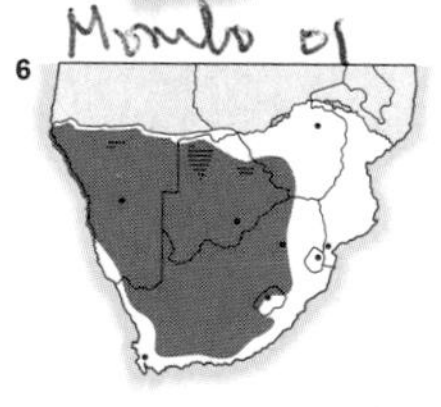

6 RED-HEADED FINCH *Amadina erythrocephala*

Common, near endemic resident. Larger than (5), male with an entirely red head, female paler, plainer on the upperparts, lightly barred below, bill dark horn. Call is a distinctive double note 'chuck-chuck'. Mostly seen in small flocks in dry thornveld or grassland, feeding on the ground, often with other species. A frequent visitor to waterholes. 12-13 cm (Rooikopvink)

2
♂
1
♀
3
4
♂
♀
5
♂
♀
6

1

2
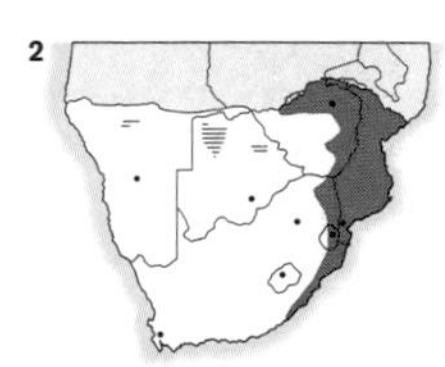

3

4
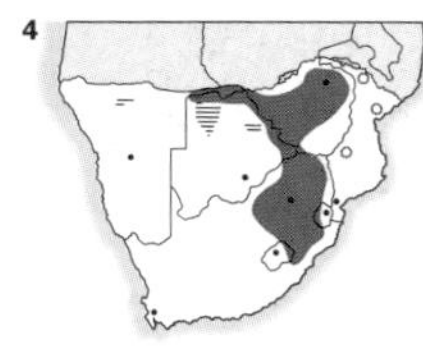

1 BRONZE MANNIKIN *Spermestes cucullatus*

Very common resident. Adult differs from (2) in earth-brown upperparts grading to blackish over the head, face, throat and upper breast, all blackish areas washed with bottle-green or bronze, some bottle-green feathers present on the mantle, the bill with dark upper mandible. Immature as illustrated, upperparts less rufous than immature of (2), bill all-dark. Call is a wheezy 'chik, chik, chikka'. Found in a wide variety of mixed grass and bushveld, forest fringes, coastal scrub and old cultivated lands. A very small, highly gregarious bird. Feeds in flocks, clambering about grass stems to obtain the seeds; when flushed all fly into a bush, eventually returning to feed in ones and twos. 9 cm (Gewone fret)

2 RED-BACKED MANNIKIN *Spermestes bicolor*

Fairly common resident. Differs from (1) in red-brown upperparts and more extensive area of black over the sides of head and breast; bill uniformly blue-grey. Immature is duller. Utters a clear whistling note in flight. Small flocks occur in open bushveld and coastal dune forests, feeding on the seeds of grasses. 9,5-10 cm (Rooirugfret)

3 PIED MANNIKIN *Spermestes fringilloides*

Rare, localised resident. Much larger than (1) and (2), with distinctly pied appearance and heavy black bill. Immature also told by robust build and black bill. Utters a chirruping 'pee-oo-pee-oo'. Small flocks in clearings in coastal bush and riverine woodland, usually near bamboo thickets. 12-13 cm (Dikbekfret)

CUCKOO FINCH

Family PLOCEIDAE. See also pp. 402-13.

4 CUCKOO FINCH *Anomalospiza imberbis*

Fairly common resident. Adult most resembles one of the yellow weavers (pp. 408-13), but the black bill is shorter and stouter. Juvenile (a) and immature (b) have a two-coloured bill and more orange-brown appearance. Male calls 'tsileu, tsileu, tsileu' or, in display, utters a weaver-like swizzling. Usually in small flocks in well-vegetated vleis, grassland or grassland with scattered bushes. Unlike other weavers this bird is a brood parasite of cisticolas and prinias. It is migratory in certain regions. 12-13 cm (Koekoekvink)

J
1
J
2
J
3
J b
J a
4

1
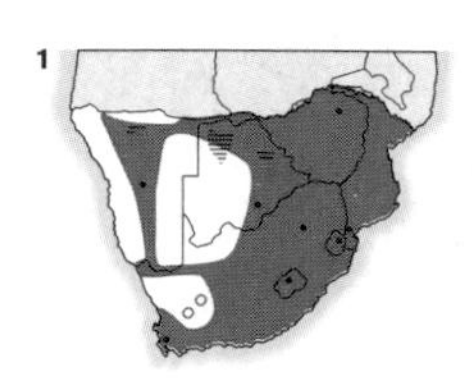

2
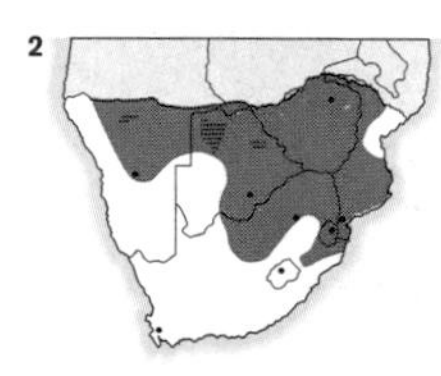

3
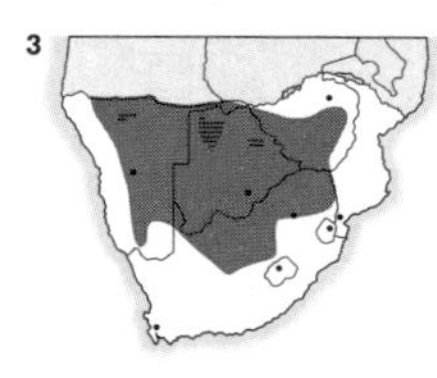

WHYDAHS AND WIDOWFINCHES

Family VIDUIDAE. Small, ground-feeding, seed-eating finches that are brood parasites, laying their eggs in the nests of waxbills. Male whydahs in breeding plumage have very long tails, different in all species, but when not breeding they resemble the confusingly similar females. At times males may be seen in transient plumage with traces of the breeding colours visible. Immatures are very plainly coloured and are probably indistinguishable. See overleaf for description of widowfinches.

1 PIN-TAILED WHYDAH *Vidua macroura*

Common resident. Breeding male distinctive; the red bill is retained in non-breeding plumage. Courting male hovers over the females, describing a circle in the vertical plane, while calling a continuous wispy 'peetzy-peetzy-peetzy ...'. In normal flight calls 'tseet-tseet-tseet'. Male is pugnacious, chasing other small birds and dominating at food sources. Usually in parties, one male and several females, which frequent a wide variety of habitats including suburbia. Parasitises Common Waxbill (p. 426). 12-34 cm (Koningrooibekkie)

2 PARADISE WHYDAH *Vidua paradisaea*

Common resident. Distinctive plumage of breeding male (a) similar only to Broad-tailed Paradise Whydah (overleaf), but differs in *tapering* tail feathers; transitional plumage (b) frequently seen. Female and non-breeding male have whiter head-stripes than (1). Has a short, sparrow-like song and utters an occasional 'chit'. Small flocks mainly in thornveld. Breeding male has a display flight in which the two short tail feathers are held erect; see illustration overleaf. Also hovers over females in slow, bobbing flight causing the tail to undulate. Parasitises Melba Finch (p. 420). 12-38 cm (Gewone paradysvink)

3 SHAFT-TAILED WHYDAH *Vidua regia* NE

Common, near endemic resident. Breeding male distinguished by colour of underparts plus tail-shafts with *bulbous ends*. Female and non-breeding male have less distinctive head markings than other whydahs. The voice is 'chit-chit-chit ...'. Singly or in small flocks, females predominating, in dry thornveld, sandveld with sparse vegetation and grassland with scattered thorn bushes. Male chases other small birds at feeding assemblies. Parasitises Violet-eared Waxbill (p. 426). 12-34 cm (Pylstertrooibekkie)

1 BROAD-TAILED PARADISE WHYDAH *Vidua obtusa*

Common resident. Male differs from Paradise Whydah (previous page) only in the *wide tail feathers*, not tapering as in that species. Females and immatures of the two species are indistinguishable. Male, like Paradise Whydah, has a display flight as in (b); also identical in other respects. Its distribution is linked to that of its hosts, the *Pytilia* group (p. 420). 12-38 cm (Breëstertparadysvink)

WIDOW FINCHES

Brood parasites of the firefinches (p. 422) and, in one instance, the Red-throated Twinspot (p. 424). They appear to be so strictly host-specific that their presence in a region is an indication of the presence of the species they parasitise. Breeding males are black with a blue, green or mauve iridescence. Non-breeding males resemble females, illustration (2). Immatures are more russet-brown, especially on the underparts; crowns unstreaked. Males are identified by bill and leg colouring plus song, which mimics that of the host.

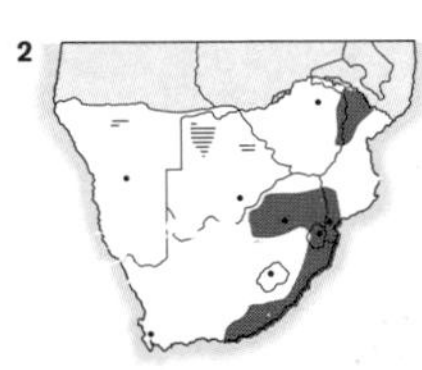

2 BLACK WIDOW FINCH *Vidua funerea*

Common resident. Has *whitish* bill and *reddish* legs. Male has a grating song interspersed with the notes of Blue-billed Firefinch (p. 422), which the female parasitises; may bob up and down in front of the female calling a harsh 'cha, cha'. Occurs in thornveld and forest fringes. 11 cm (Gewone blouvinkie)

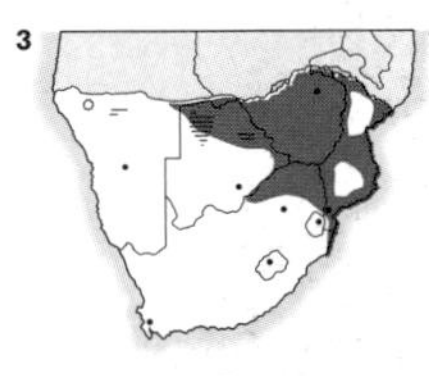

3 PURPLE WIDOW FINCH *Vidua purpurascens*

Fairly common resident. Male told by *whitish bill and legs*, female by *whitish bill and pink legs*. Parasitises Jameson's Firefinch (p. 422) and mimics the bell-like call-note of that species. Habits as for other widow finches. It frequents thickets and rank grass in thornveld plus riparian and old cultivated lands like its host. 11 cm (Witpootblouvinkie)

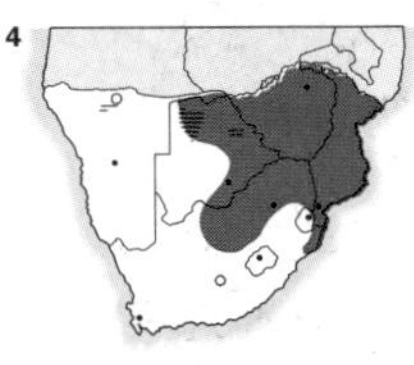

4 STEEL-BLUE WIDOW FINCH *Vidua chalybeata*

Common resident. Male told by *red bill and legs*; in the female the *bill is pink, legs red*. (In Botswana the male's bill is white in local birds.) It parasitises the Red-billed Firefinch (p. 422) and mimics the call of that species. Occurs in the same habitat as its host; mixed bushveld near watercourses, and in suburbia. 11 cm (Staalblouvinkie)

5 GREEN WIDOW FINCH *Vidua codringtoni*

Fairly common resident. Has a whitish bill and orange legs and feet, the black body plumage showing a green gloss in good light, otherwise appears all-black. The female is similar to other female widow finches. This species occurs in the eastern regions of Zimbabwe and is unusual in that it parasitises the Red-throated Twinspot (p. 424). Its call imitates the call of the twinspot. 11 cm (Groenblouvinkie)

b
♂
1
♀
2
♂
3
♂
4
♂
5
♂

CANARIES, SISKINS AND BUNTINGS

Family FRINGILLIDAE. Sparrow-sized songbirds; canaries and siskins have strong conical bills, usually notched tails and undulating flight; buntings are strongly terrestrial and have weaker, narrower bills. Many species are nomadic.

1
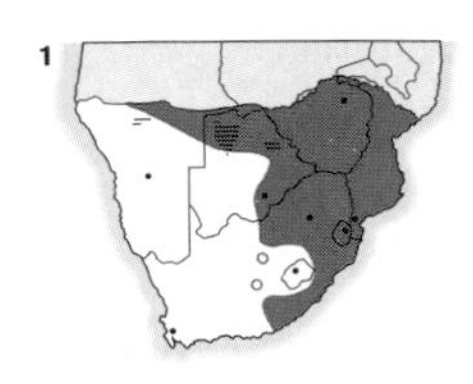

1 YELLOW-EYED CANARY *Serinus mozambicus*

Common resident. A small canary with bold facial markings, greyish crown and nape, plus yellow rump; the eyes are brown. Sexes are alike. Immature is duller. Has a lively song delivered in short bursts. Occurs in small parties and flocks in all types of woodland, bushveld, forest and plantation fringes and suburbia. Feeds both in the grass and in trees. 12 cm (Geeloogkanarie)

2

2 FOREST CANARY *Serinus scotops*

Common endemic resident. Heavily streaked appearance diagnostic, boldest in northern birds. Immature resembles adult. Normal call is a thin, plaintive 'tweetoo, twee-ee' given frequently and often the first clue to its presence; also has a brisk warbling song of sibilant quality. Pairs and small parties frequent the tree canopies in forests at all altitudes, as well as adjacent forested kloofs and plantation fringes. 13 cm (Gestreepte kanarie)

3
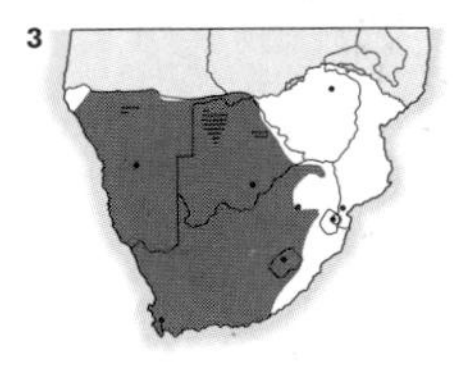

3 YELLOW CANARY *Serinus flaviventris*

Common, near endemic resident. Palest, yellowest males with bright yellow rumps (a) occur in the north-west; cf. Bully Canary (5b); darkest males with greenish rumps (b) in the south-east, with degrees of intergrading elsewhere. Females of (b) duskier about the breast, streaking less obvious than in females of (a). Immatures are like females, upperparts greener. Males sing well and vigorously from tree-tops. Small parties and flocks in semi-arid regions, frequenting low-growing bushes of mountain sides, Karoo and coastal scrub, especially along watercourses; they also enter small towns. Nomadic in some regions. 13-14 cm (Geelkanarie)

4

4 CAPE CANARY *Serinus canicollis*

Common resident. Identified by grey nape, ear coverts and sides of neck. Female and immature are duller than male. Song is a series of loud, rolling warbles and trills. Singly or in flocks in a wide variety of habitats from coastal scrub to montane grassland and protea-covered slopes, plantations and farmlands. Feeds mostly on the ground. 13-14 cm (Kaapse kanarie)

5

5 BULLY CANARY *Serinus sulphuratus*

Common resident. A thickset, heavy-billed species. Southern birds (a) mainly dull olive-green with dark-streaked upperparts; northern birds (b) much paler, more yellow and smaller; other races between these extremes. Race (b) differs from (3a) in lack of white edges to wing coverts, plus dark crown extending to base of bill. Immature is duller than adult. Song slower, huskier, less tuneful than other canaries. Singly, in pairs or small flocks in various bushy habitats: hillsides, kloofs, forest fringes, bracken-brier patches and riverside thickets. 14-15 cm (Dikbekkanarie)

1
2
♂a
3
♀
♂b
4
a
5
b

1

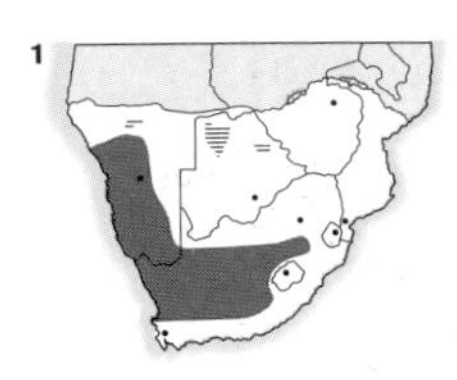

1 BLACK-HEADED CANARY *Serinus alario*

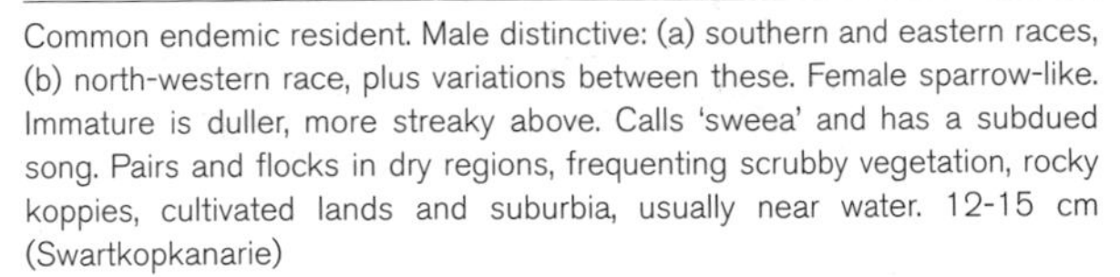

Common endemic resident. Male distinctive: (a) southern and eastern races, (b) north-western race, plus variations between these. Female sparrow-like. Immature is duller, more streaky above. Calls 'sweea' and has a subdued song. Pairs and flocks in dry regions, frequenting scrubby vegetation, rocky koppies, cultivated lands and suburbia, usually near water. 12-15 cm (Swartkopkanarie)

2

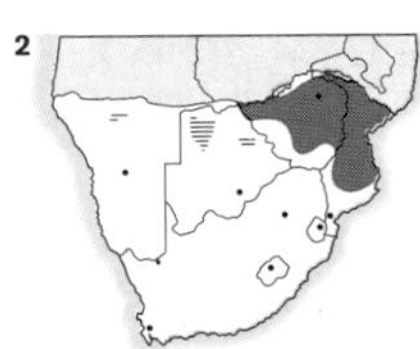

2 BLACK-EARED CANARY *Serinus mennelli*

E

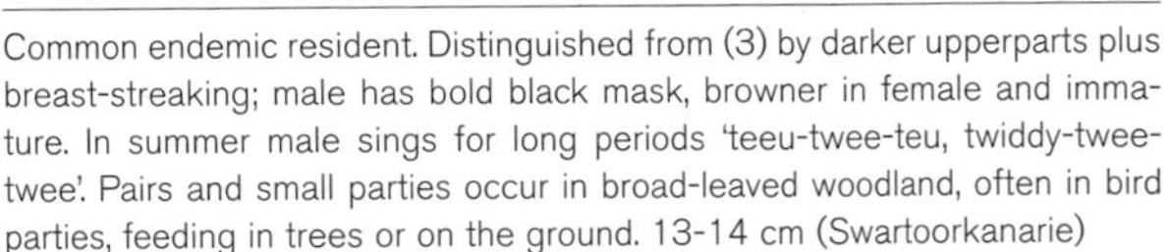

Common endemic resident. Distinguished from (3) by darker upperparts plus breast-streaking; male has bold black mask, browner in female and immature. In summer male sings for long periods 'teeu-twee-teu, twiddy-tweetwee'. Pairs and small parties occur in broad-leaved woodland, often in bird parties, feeding in trees or on the ground. 13-14 cm (Swartoorkanarie)

3

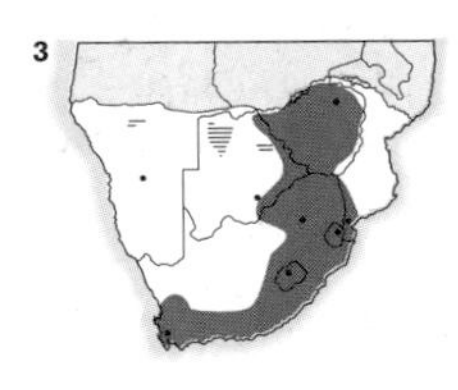

3 STREAKY-HEADED CANARY *Serinus gularis*

Common resident. Identified by *very bold white eyebrows* and streaked crown; from (2) by lack of a distinct mask or any breast-streaking; cf. Yellow-throated Sparrow (p. 404) which has similar bold eyebrows. Has a pleasant song, rendered in short bursts 'wit-chee-chee-chee-cha, cha, cha, cha, cha, chip', rising to a crescendo; when nest-building utters a repetitive 'tweu, tweu, tirrirrit-tirik'. Singly, in pairs or small parties in woodland, fallow farmlands and suburbia. Inconspicuous and seldom numerous. 16 cm (Streepkopkanarie)

4

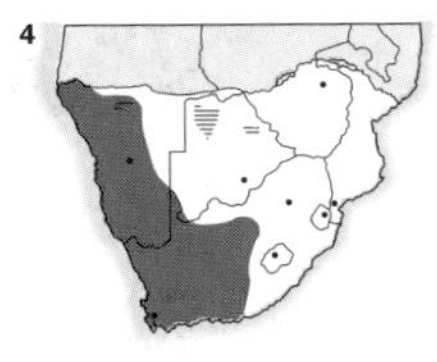

4 WHITE-THROATED CANARY *Serinus albogularis*

Common, near endemic resident. Distinguished from all other brown canaries except (6) by yellow rump; palest birds with brightest rump in Namibia (b), darkest with greenish-yellow rump in south (a), with intergrading elsewhere. Distinguished from (6) by white throat. Has a strong, tuneful song 'weetle, weetle, frrra, weetle, frree, tee, chipchipchipchip …'. Singly or in small flocks in dry thornveld, Karoo, desert and coastal dunes, generally not far from water. 14-15 cm (Witkeelkanarie)

5

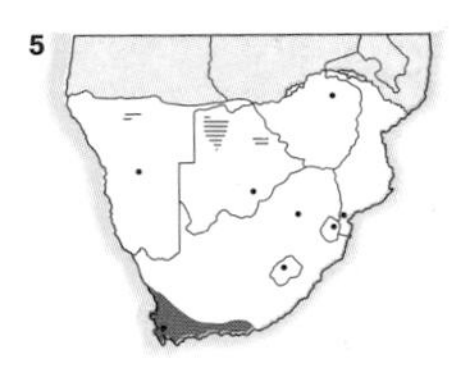

5 PROTEA CANARY *Serinus leucopterus*

Fairly common, localised endemic resident. A large, drab canary with a pale bill and two distinct light wing-bars on the folded wing; cf. (3). Distinctive call is 'tree-lee-loo', the song soft, sweet and varied; an excellent mimic. Small, scattered parties occur in protea bush on southern mountains, occasionally in wooded kloofs and forest fringes. Shy and retiring, the flight swift and direct. 16 cm (Witvlerkkanarie)

6

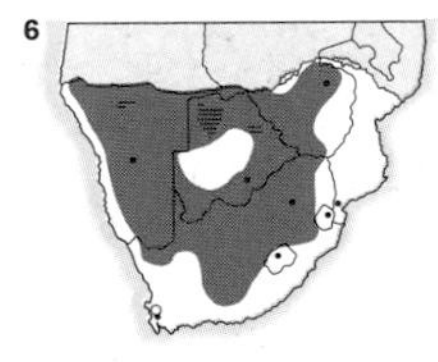

6 BLACK-THROATED CANARY *Serinus atrogularis*

Common resident. A small canary with yellow rump; black throat diagnostic when present but *may be absent* or vestigial. Gives a strong and sustained, rambling song from a tree-top. Small flocks feed on grass and weed seeds in woodland, fallow farmlands, waste ground and on roadside verges. 11-12 cm (Bergkanarie)

1
♂
a
♀
♂
b
2
a
3
4
b
5
6

1

1 CAPE SISKIN *Pseudochloroptila totta*

E

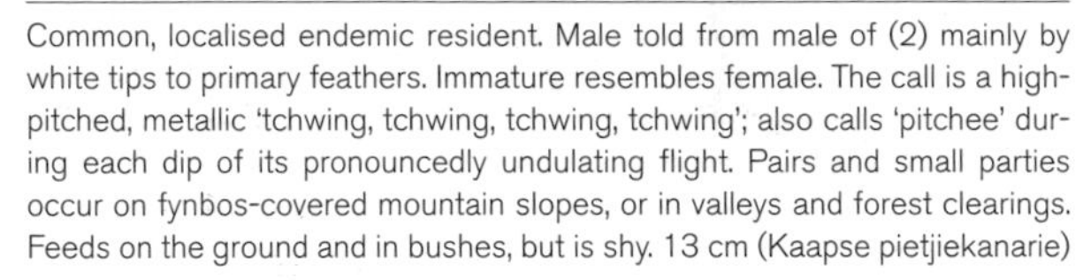

Common, localised endemic resident. Male told from male of (2) mainly by white tips to primary feathers. Immature resembles female. The call is a high-pitched, metallic 'tchwing, tchwing, tchwing, tchwing'; also calls 'pitchee' during each dip of its pronouncedly undulating flight. Pairs and small parties occur on fynbos-covered mountain slopes, or in valleys and forest clearings. Feeds on the ground and in bushes, but is shy. 13 cm (Kaapse pietjiekanarie)

2

2 DRAKENSBERG SISKIN *Pseudochloroptila symonsi*

Common, localised endemic resident. Male lacks any white in the wings. Female is much browner than female of (1). Sings well. Pairs and small parties occur on high grassy slopes of the Drakensberg, moving to lower levels in winter. Habits much like (1). 13 cm (Bergpietjiekanarie)

3

3 LEMON-BREASTED CANARY *Serinus citrinipectus*

Fairly common, localised, near endemic resident. Told by very small size, male with buffy flanks and belly; cf. Yellow-eyed Canary (p. 436). Female has buffy underparts and yellow rump. Has a pretty song of sparrow-like quality. Flocks, often with Yellow-eyed Canaries, occur in dry woodland, cultivated lands and coastal grassland. Like Yellow-eyed Canary is attracted to seeding grasses. Somewhat nomadic when not breeding. 9,5-10 cm (Geelborskanarie)

4

4 CHAFFINCH *Fringilla coelebs*

Uncommon, localised resident. An introduced species. Calls 'chink, chink' and has a distinctive, frequently repeated song 'chip-chip-chip-tell-tell-tell-cherry-erry-erry-tissi-cheweeoo'. Singly or in pairs in suburban gardens, parks and pine plantations around Cape Town. 15 cm (Gryskoppie)

♀
1
♂
♀
2
♂
♀
3
♂
♀
4
♂

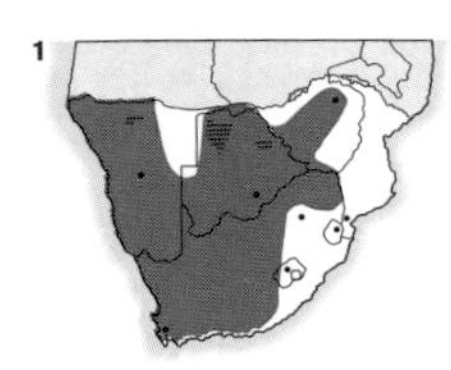

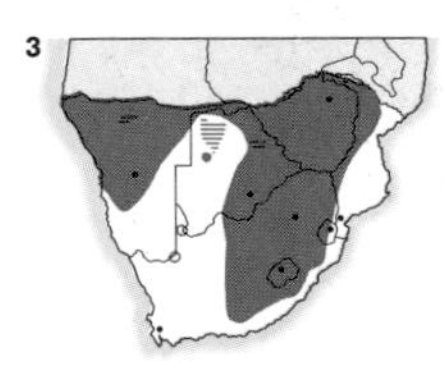

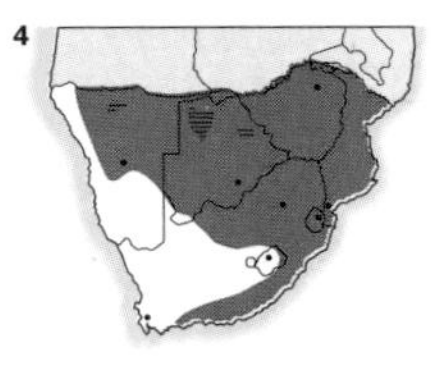

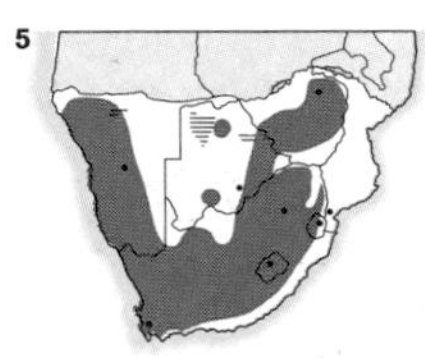

1 LARK-LIKE BUNTING *Emberiza impetuani* NE

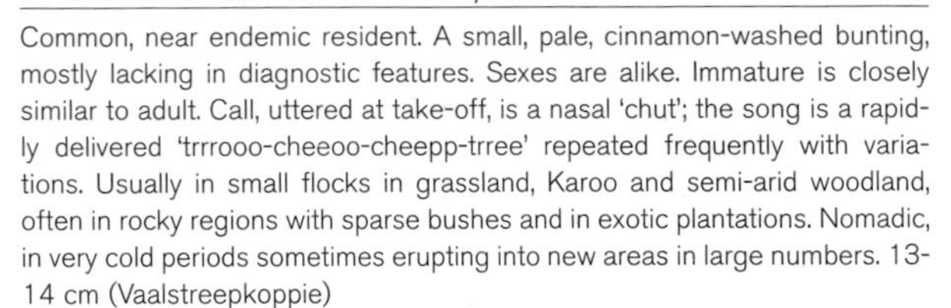
Common, near endemic resident. A small, pale, cinnamon-washed bunting, mostly lacking in diagnostic features. Sexes are alike. Immature is closely similar to adult. Call, uttered at take-off, is a nasal 'chut'; the song is a rapidly delivered 'trrrooo-cheeoo-cheepp-trree' repeated frequently with variations. Usually in small flocks in grassland, Karoo and semi-arid woodland, often in rocky regions with sparse bushes and in exotic plantations. Nomadic, in very cold periods sometimes erupting into new areas in large numbers. 13-14 cm (Vaalstreepkoppie)

2 CABANIS'S BUNTING *Emberiza cabanisi*

Uncommon, localised resident. Distinguished from (4) by black face and ear coverts, no white line below eyes, plus greyer mantle. Female is like male but head markings are more brown than black. Immature has brownish (not white) head streaks and browner flanks. Has a soft 'tureee' call and a sweet but variable song 'wee-chidderchidder, chidder-wee' or 'her-ip-ip-ip ... her-hee'. Usually singly or in pairs in miombo woodland. 15 cm (Geelstreepkoppie)

3 ROCK BUNTING *Emberiza tahapisi*

Common resident. Distinguished by cinnamon colouring of body with black, white-streaked head. Immature resembles female. The short, distinctive song is repeated at frequent intervals, 'tee-trrr, chirri-chee' or 'swiddle-swiddle-saaa'. In pairs, occasionally flocks, on rocky or stony ground with or without bushes, often on soil-eroded ground or in broad-leaved woodland and mixed bushveld. 13-14 cm (Klipstreepkoppie)

4 GOLDEN-BREASTED BUNTING *Emberiza flaviventris*

Common resident. Distinguished from (2) by white stripe *below* eyes plus browner mantle and more orange breast. Female has yellowish head-streaks, immature brown ones. The normal call is 'pret-ty-boyeee', sometimes answered by the mate 'sitee'; the song is a frequently repeated 'chipchipchipchipchip-teee, teeu-teeu-teeu-teeu'. Pairs occur in mixed bushveld, thornveld, broad-leaved woodland and exotic plantations. 16 cm (Rooirugstreepkoppie)

5 CAPE BUNTING *Emberiza capensis* NE

Common, near endemic resident. Sexes are alike. Immature is duller. Call is 'cheriowee', the song, uttered from a rock or bush-top, is 'cheep, cheep, tip, cheeucheeu, tip-cheeu-tip-cheeu'. Singly, in pairs or flocks in a variety of semi-arid, coastal montane regions, coastal sand dunes with sparse scrub, rocky hillsides in the Karoo and Zimbabwe, broad-leaved woodland in Zimbabwe plus suburbia in many regions. 16 cm (Rooivlerkstreepkoppie)

1
♂
2
3
♀
♂
4
♂
5

1

2

3

4

5

RECENT VAGRANTS TO SOUTHERN AFRICA

(Recorded after the original publication of this fieldguide)

1 SNOWY SHEATHBILL *Chionis alba*

Differs from the Lesser Sheathbill (p. 24) in pink cere, yellow bill with black tip and grey legs. A conspicuous terrestrial scavenger from the Antarctic from where it migrates northwards to the southern tip of South America; unafraid of humans. Birds recorded in our region have been ship-assisted. 40 cm (Amerikaanse peddie)

2 LAYSAN ALBATROSS *Diomedea immutabilis*

Cf. similar dark-backed albatrosses on pp. 30 and 32. Underwing pattern not unlike that of Grey-headed, Black-browed and Yellow-nosed Albatrosses but blackish marks on underwing coverts usually present, though variable; dark eye-patch visible only at close range. Bill dull yellow with dark tip; pinkish feet protrude beyond tail. A wanderer from the north Pacific Ocean. 80 cm (Laysanmalmok)

3 BROWN BOOBY *Sula leucogaster*

Very rare vagrant. Brown with pale bill, white underbody separated from brown neck by sharp demarcation on upper breast and clear white central underwing; cf. immature Cape Gannet (p. 48). Occurs rarely in east coast waters. 78 cm (Bruinmalgas)

4 MATSUDAIRA'S STORM PETREL *Oceanodroma matsudairae*

A dark brown storm petrel, slightly larger than others in our waters (cf. p. 46). Upperwings show small but clear white patch at base of primaries and distinct crescent shape formed by pale wing covert edges. Flight mostly leisurely with frequent gliding action. A wanderer from islands near Japan. 25 cm (Matsudairase stormswael)

5 HERRING GULL *Larus argentatus*

Adults differ from gulls on p. 54 in having *pale grey* upperwings with black tips (not black upperwings as in the Kelp Gull or dark grey as in the Lesser Black-backed). Underparts white, legs and feet either pink or grey. A wanderer from the northern hemisphere. 56-65 cm (Haringmeeu)

Illustrations not to scale.

1
2
3
4
5

1 GREATER YELLOWLEGS *Tringa melanoleuca*

Occurs in non-breeding plumage. Larger than the Lesser Yellowlegs (p. 116) with longer, Greenshank-like bill and orange-yellow (not lemon-yellow) legs. Compared to the Greenshank (p. 108), the bill is straighter with greenish or yellowish base, while the breast has greyish streaking. In flight the very long wings and square, white tail-patch are diagnostic. A wanderer from North and South America. 29-33 cm (Grootgeelpootruiter)

2 HUDSONIAN GODWIT *Limosa haemastica*

Occurs in non-breeding plumage, when similar to the Black-tailed and Bar-tailed Godwits (p. 118). Most diagnostic features are seen in flight when *black underwing coverts* are apparent; rest of underwing grey except for narrow white region at base of secondaries and inner primaries (the other godwits have mostly white underwings, dark edged in the Black-tailed). May mix with other godwits. Breeds in northern Canada. The few South African records may refer to the same individual. 37-42 cm (Amerikaanse griet)

3 KENTISH PLOVER *Charadrius alexandrinus*

In non-breeding plumage easily confused with the White-fronted Plover (p. 108) (to which it is closely related) or immature Chestnut-banded Plover (p. 106) but best told by clear white hindcollar and lateral breast-patches which, however, never form a complete breast-band. In breeding plumage upperparts are darker, the male with forecrown, eye-stripe and breast-patches black. Frequents sandy beaches or shorelines of brackish pans. Breeds throughout the tropics. 15-17,5 cm (Bleekstrandkiewiet)

4 EURASIAN TURTLE DOVE *Streptopelia turtur*

About the size of a Cape Turtle Dove (p. 196). Folded wings dark chestnut mottled black, crown and nape grey; no black collar but black and white patches on either side of neck, breast pinkish, underbelly white. From below shows dark underwings and black tail fringed white. Breeds in Europe and North Africa, winters in the Sahelian zone. 27 cm ((Europese) tortelduif)

5 RED-THROATED PIPIT *Anthus cervinus*

In breeding plumage has variable amount of brick-red on its throat, even on the breast and eyebrow, traces of which may be visible in non-breeding plumage. Otherwise differs from the similar Tree Pipit (p. 290) in smaller size, heavier breast-streaking and a streaked rump; outer tail feathers appear very white in flight. Frequents marshes, estuaries, vleis, wet fields. Breeds in the Arctic, normally winters in East Africa. 14,5 cm (Rooikeelkoester)

Illustrations not to scale.

1
2
3
4
5

1

1 **PIED WHEATEAR** *Oenanthe pleschanka*

Whereas the male in breeding plumage is distinctive, it is most likely to be seen in southern Africa in non-breeding plumage, which often retains some vestige of the dark head pattern. Female (larger illustration) can be confused with a chat (p. 320) or female European Wheatear (p. 318) and is probably indistinguishable except for the upper tail pattern. Has a 'zack' call note. Prefers stony scrublands, cultivated and fallow lands. One record from KwaZulu-Natal. 15 cm (Bontskaapwagter)

2

2 **ISABELLINE WHEATEAR** *Oenanthe isabellina*

A rare, non-breeding wheatear from the north, told from a non-breeding European Wheatear (p. 318) and female Pied Wheatear (1) only with difficulty unless the diagnostic upper tail pattern can be seen. The Isabelline has the terminal half of the tail black, and less extensive white on the rump; other pointers are longish legs, the black alula and an erect posture. Only one record from Botswana. 16,5 cm (Vaalskaapwagter)

3

3 **EURASIAN REDSTART** *Phoenicurus phoenicurus*

A robin-like bird with rufous tail in both sexes. Male in breeding plumage (recorded in southern Africa) is distinctive with grey upperparts, white eyebrow, black mask and throat and rufous breast; female much duller; except for rufous tail has pale sandy-grey upperparts and whitish underparts. Calls 'hwee-tuc-tuc' and frequents a range of lightly wooded habitats. Breeds in Europe, winters in Africa. One record from North West Province. 14 cm (Europese rooistert)

4

4 **EUROPEAN BLACKCAP** *Sylvia atricapilla*

A small warbler easily identified by the black cap of the male and rusty cap of the female. Calls 'tuc-tuc' or 'churr' and has a subdued warbling song. Frequents mixed woodland and gardens. Breeds in Europe, winters in Africa. 14 cm (Swartkroonsanger)

Illustrations not to scale.

♂
N-Br
Br
♂
1
♂
N-Br
2
♀
♂
3
♂
4
♀

1 WHITE-THROATED BEE-EATER *Merops albicollis*

A greenish bee-eater told by its prominent black and white head pattern; the tail streamers are longer than in any local bee-eater. Flocks behave much as other colonial bee-eaters. Normally occurs in Central and West Africa, extending southwards occasionally to northern Angola and eastern Tanzania. Vagrants to southern Africa are likely to be single birds. See also pp. 244-7. 20-32 cm (Witkeelbyvreter)

2 ANGOLA SWALLOW *Hirundo angolensis*

Rare vagrant to the extreme northern Caprivi region. Closely similar to European Swallow (p. 232) but chestnut chin colour extends to breast, the blackish breast-band is narrow, broken or indistinct, rest of underparts dull ash-brown, outer tail feathers only slightly elongated. May utter a warbling song in flight with wings depressed and quivering. Habits otherwise much the same as European Swallow. *This swallow was not recorded in the southern African sub-region during the 1987-92 bird atlasing period.* 15 cm (Angolaswael)

3 WHITE-HEADED SAW-WING SWALLOW *Psalidoprocne albiceps*

A blackish swallow, like the Black Saw-wing Swallow (p. 234), but the male is distinctive with its white head and black eye-stripe, the female with white throat only. Frequents broad-leaved woodland. Its home range is Angola and East Africa. Recorded near Victoria Falls. 15 cm (Witkopsaagvlerkswael)

4 SPUR-WINGED PLOVER *Vanellus spinosus*

Differs from the superficially similar Blacksmith Plover (p. 122) in lacking any grey plumage, having the entire cap black; upper breast to neck white with an expanding black stripe from chin to black lower breast; upperparts dull brown. When alarmed calls a sharp, metallic 'pick' repeated. One record from northern Botswana. Could occur on any wetland, especially shorelines of large rivers. 25-8 cm (Spoorvlerkkiewiet)

5 LITTLE BLUE HERON *Ardea caerulea*

A slate-blue heron, head and neck washed maroon-red, the bill grey with a black tip, legs and feet greenish-grey. Frequents rivers, lagoons and marshlands where it stalks its aquatic prey while walking slowly. A wanderer from the Americas. One record from the Berg River estuary. 64-74 cm (Kleinbloureier)

Illustrations not to scale.

1

2

3

4

5

1 **GREATER FRIGATEBIRD** *Fregata minor*

Male told by large, angled wings and all-dark appearance; female similar but for white throat and breast. Immature has head and neck buffy. A straggler to eastern shorelines, especially Mozambique, where occasionally in small numbers after cyclones. Soars effortlessly and pursues other seabirds for food, causing them to disgorge, or snatches fishing bait. Roosts in trees at night. 100 cm (Grootfregatvoël)

2 **LESSER FRIGATEBIRD** *Fregata ariel*

Smaller than the Greater Frigatebird (1), male told by white 'armpits'; female by less extensive white on the breast. Like (1) a straggler to the Mozambique and KwaZulu-Natal coasts; behaviour identical. 76 cm (Kleinfregatvoël)

3 **ELEONORA'S FALCON** *Falco eleonorae*

In size between the Peregrine and Hobby Falcons (p. 188). Colouring highly variable between pale morph (illustrated) and dark morph, which has blackish underparts. In flight both morphs have sooty-brown underwings and appear *much darker* (almost black) than the Hobby Falcon; light morph only with chin and throat-patch paler. Has a unique flight action with soft, slow wing beats, but capable of fast, dashing flight when hunting. Breeds in the Mediterranean and migrates to Madagascar; occasional sightings in Zimbabwe and Mozambique. 38 cm (Eleonoravalk)

4 **EUROPEAN WHEATEAR** *Oenanthe oenanthe*

Very rare summer vagrant. Occurs in non-breeding plumage as shown. Has a characteristic wheatear bowing action with tail raised high, at which time the T-shaped tail pattern can be seen; cf. immature Capped Wheatear (p. 318) and others on p. 448 from which it can only be distinguished with difficulty. The common call is 'chack-chack', similar to Stonechat (p. 324). Singly in Kalahari grassland and similar dry terrain with sparse grass cover. 16 cm (Europese skaapwagter)

5 **PINTAIL** *Anas acuta*

Very rare visitor. Male most likely to occur in non-breeding plumage, resembling female. Told by slender proportions, dull grey bill and pale, grey-brown plumage; long tail may not be present. In flight appears pointed-winged; underbody, wing linings and trailing edge of secondaries white, upperwing with green speculum. May occur singly or in small groups on any inland waters. Recorded Zimbabwe and north-western South Africa in November-February. 51-66 cm (Pylsterteend)

Illustrations not to scale.

♀
1
♂
♀
J
2
♂
♀
3
♂
N-Br
4
♂
N-Br
5
♂Br
♀

1 LONG-LEGGED BUZZARD *Buteo rufinus*

The presence of this buzzard in southern Africa is controversial. It is a European species that normally migrates only as far as North Africa. It is variable in colour and larger, more bulky-bodied than either Steppe Buzzard (p. 170) or Forest Buzzard (p. 170), with a pale head. The normal morph in flight shows dark underbelly and vent, broader, paler wings with dark carpal patches, white outer panels and a plain tail. A rare dark morph occurs. 51-66 cm (Langbeenjakkalsvoël)

2 RÜPPELL'S GRIFFON VULTURE *Gyps rueppellii*

The adult is similar to the Cape Griffon Vulture (p. 152) but has more white in the plumage which gives it a scaly appearance; the eye is dark, the bill yellowish. The immature (not recorded in the subregion) is all dark and probably difficult to tell from the young Cape Griffon Vulture. Adults have been seen in very small numbers at Blouberg in the Northern Province. A common East African cliff-nesting vulture. 95-107 cm (Rüppelse aasvoël)

3 CITRINE WAGTAIL *Motacilla citreola*

A central European species not normally recorded in southern Africa. A single bird was present in the Eastern Cape during the winter of 1998. Thought to be the result of a 'reverse migration'. 16,5 cm (Sitroengeelkwikkie)

The following ocean wanderers have been sighted within the 200 nautical mile territorial limits:

Buller's Albatross *Diomedea bulleri*
Mascarene Shearwater *Puffinus atrodorsalis*
Short-tailed Shearwater *Puffinus tenuirostris*
Yelkouan Shearwater *Puffinus p. yelkouan*
Streaked Shearwater *Calonectris leucomelas*
Red-footed Booby *Sula sula*

Illustrations not to scale.

1
a
b
2
3

Glossary of terms

Acacia deciduous trees of the genus *Acacia*. In Africa these are thorny, with bipinnately compound leaves (each leaf is again divided into small leaflets) and small, powderpuff-like or elongated flowers.

Accipiter sparrowhawks and goshawks. Long-tailed, short-winged raptors with long, unfeathered legs and long toes. They specialise in catching small birds (or small mammals in the larger species) in swift pursuit from a standing start.

Afrotropical Region Africa south of the Palaearctic Region, the Tropic of Cancer roughly forming its northern limit. Formerly called the Ethiopian region.

Aggregation a gathering (of birds) brought about by some common interest such as a temporary food availability, after which individuals disperse separately.

Albinistic white or partially white plumage resulting from a lack of normal colour pigmentation.

Altitudinal migrant a bird which moves seasonally from one altitude to another.

Brood parasite a bird which deposits its eggs in the nest of another species; e.g. cuckoos, honeyguides, whydahs.

Broad-leaved woodland woodland comprising trees with broad leaves as opposed to thornveld where trees of the genus *Acacia* are dominant.

Bush refers to any terrain with trees of moderate height as opposed to the taller, more luxuriant growth of woodland or riparian forest; see Bushveld.

Bushveld a terrain with mixed trees of moderate height (5-10 m) where the trees frequently touch each other below canopy height; sometimes in dense thickets and usually with a grassy groundcover.

Coastal bush dense, humid, evergreen bush found on coastal dunes; mainly along the east coast.

Coastal forest larger trees than in coastal bush and frequently extending inland in dense patches with grassland in between.

Conspecific being of the same species.

Crepuscular active at dusk. When applied to birds, it usually infers that they are active in the half-light hours, *dawn* and *dusk*.

Dam an artificial water impoundment, usually with a retaining wall at the end opposite the inflow.

Damaraland Plateau the inland plateau region of north-central Namibia, the home of many endemic bird species. The habitat varies from semi-desert transition in the south to thornveld in the north-east and mopane and teak woodland in the north.

Delta a river mouth with several diverging branches forming a triangle. In the context of this fieldguide, usually refers to the inland delta of the Okavango River drainage system (also known as the Okavango Swamps) in northern Botswana.

Desert a region of extremely low rainfall, usually less than 25 mm. In southern Africa the driest desert is the Namib, comprising sand dunes in the southern and coastal regions and stony plains elsewhere, with isolated patches of thornbush in some lower-lying areas or on hillsides. The Kalahari Desert in central Botswana consists of dunes in the south and sandy or stony plains, with sparse thorn scrub elsewhere, merging into Kalahari thornveld further north.

Dispersal a more or less random centrifugal movement away from a locality.

Display actions that have become specialised in the course of evolution: threat display, courtship display, social displays, etc.

Donga a gully caused by erosion.

Egg-dumping the habit among secondary females in such social species as the Ostrich and guineafowls, of laying their eggs in the nest of another female of the same species, usually the dominant female in a flock. Also refers to random egg-laying in places other than nests by immature or unmated hens of any species.

Endemic a species found only in a specific region or country.

Estuary	the tidal mouth of a large river, an important feeding area for many water-associated birds because of its food-rich mud flats and floodplains.
Escarpment	the long steep face of a plateau. In southern Africa usually refers to the eastern escarpment which forms the edge of the inland plateau or highveld.
Ethiopian Region	old name for Africa south of the Palaearctic Region, now replaced by the term Afrotropical Region.
Falcon	small, swift-flying raptor with pointed wings; specialises in catching flying birds by means of a rapid descent from above, known as a 'stoop'.
FF	females.
Flats	level grassland.
Fledgling	a young bird that has recently acquired its first feathers.
Flock	a group of birds that moves as a more or less cohesive unit.
Floodplain	grassland, especially that adjacent to estuaries, which becomes inundated by river spillage.
Forest	a tract of land covered by tall evergreen trees with interlocking canopies.
Fynbos	a natural habitat occurring in the south-eastern and south-western coastal regions of South Africa; a Mediterranean-type scrub composed of proteas, ericas and legumes among other plants.
Gamebird	an outdated term used by hunters. Refers to ducks, geese, pheasants, partridges, guineafowls and others. In the past bustards were included in this category.
Graduated tail	a tail in which the central feathers are longest and all others progressively shorter, the outermost being shortest.
Grassland	any region with extensive grass coverage, especially the plateau or highveld regions of southern Africa, but can also refer to grass-covered foothills or montane grassland.
Gregarious	living in flocks or communities.
Highveld	the plateau region of inland southern Africa; consists mainly of grassland above *c.* 1 500 m.
Immature	in the context of this fieldguide, refers to any bird beyond the nestling stage.
Intra-Africa migrant	a bird that migrates regularly within the African continent.
Irruption	an irregular migration into a new area, often brought about by unfavourable conditions in the normal range of a species, and usually of a temporary nature.
Juvenile	a young bird below sub-adult stage.
Kalahari thornveld	thornveld with stunted, scattered or more or less continuous *Acacia* or *Dichrostachys* tree species on Kalahari sand and calcareous soil with tufty grasses.
Karoo veld	stony plains with little soil, dotted with dwarf trees and succulent plants, or undulating stony plains with numerous grasses and shrubs but few succulents and trees, or rocky hills with scrub. Annual rainfall 150-300 mm. The driest region is known as the arid Karoo, where desert grasses predominate. Annual rainfall 50-200 mm.
Kloof	a cleft or valley, usually with steeply inclined or rocky sides, often well-wooded.
Koppie	a small hill, often with a rocky summit.
Lagoon	a stretch of salt water separated from the sea by a low sandbank.
Leaf-gleaner	a bird that seeks insects from the leaves of the tree canopy.
Littoral	the region of land lying along the sea shore.
Local movement	a mass movement, not necessarily regular, within a comparatively small area.
Lowland	those regions lying below *c.* 900 m. Mixed bush and grassland.

Lowveld the eastern part of southern Africa, which lies between *c.* 100 m and 900 m and comprises bushveld.

Mangrove a forest, comprising mainly trees of the family Rhizophoraceae, which grows in tidal estuaries. The trees produce air roots, which protrude upwards from the mud.

Melanistic darkness of plumage colour resulting from abnormal development of black pigmentation.

Migration a regular movement of birds (or other animals) between two alternative regions inhabited by them at different times of the year, one region in which they breed and the other region used by them when not breeding.

Miombo broad-leaved woodland in which trees of the genus *Brachystegia* dominate; common in Zimbabwe.

Mist-belt the eastern region of southern Africa at 900-1 350 m above sea level (otherwise known as the escarpment) where the rainfall is between 900 mm and 1 150 mm per annum and the conditions are frequently misty during easterly maritime winds: of mostly hilly or montane grassland with isolated forest patches and, these days, with exotic plantations.

Mixed bushveld a region of mixed tree types, including both broad-leaved and thorny species, growing more or less continually or in clumps, to an average height of about 7-10 m. This form of bush covers much of the eastern lowveld of South Africa and Mozambique plus the northern lowlands of Mozambique where various palms become dominant. Soils may be sandy or stony, with good grass cover.

MM males.

Monoculture regions extensively planted with one crop, e.g. sugarcane.

Montane mountainous country.

Mopane a broad-leaved, deciduous tree, *Colophospermum mopane*. In some regions remains a smallish bush, in others grows to a height of *c.* 12 m. Leaves are rounded, heart-shaped and reddish when young.

Morph an alternative but permanent plumage colour.

Nomad a species with no fixed territory when not breeding.

Palaearctic Region the northern hemisphere, incorporating North Africa, Europe, Scandinavia and Asia.

Pan (or floodpan) a natural depression which fills with water as the result of rainfall or river spillage.

Parkland regions of woodland with well-spaced trees, little secondary growth and a grassy groundcover.

Passerine a bird that habitually sings or calls and that has 'normal' feet, with three toes facing forward and one facing backward; excludes birds with webbed, lobbed or zygodactylous feet.

Pectoral the breast region; in birds especially the lateral breast regions.

Pelagic seabird a bird of the open seas as opposed to one which roosts or breeds on mainland shores.

Plantation trees, usually exotic species (gums, wattles or pines) planted for timber; closely planted and devoid of groundcover, their interiors unattractive to most birds.

Range expansion the process in which a species increases its breeding range; a spread into regions not previously occupied.

Raptor a bird of prey; one that hunts and kills other animals for food.

Retrices the main tail feathers of a bird (rectrix in the singular).

Recurved bill a bill that bends upwards, e.g. Avocet.

Remiges the primary and secondary wing feathers of a bird (remex in the singular).

Riparian of or on riverbanks.

Riverine forest the trees fringing a river, usually evergreen and more luxuriant than trees of the surrounding country and often with an understorey of dense thickets and secondary growth. In the more arid regions growth is less well developed, then often referred to as riverine bush.

Scrub brushwood or stunted bushes.

Sexual dimorphism difference in appearance between male and female of a species.

Soft parts a bird's bill, legs and feet, eye-surround and bare facial skin if present.

Speculum a patch of iridescent colour on the wings of some birds, notably ducks.

Still-hunt watching for prey (usually on the ground) while perched.

Subantarctic the southern oceans between 45 °S and the Antarctic Circle.

Sub-song a birdsong of lower than normal pitch, sometimes of longer than normal duration.

Tail streamer elongated tail feathers, often the central or outer feathers.

Teak the tree *Baikiaea plurijuga* (Rhodesian teak) which grows extensively in the northern parts of southern Africa.

Thicket a number of shrubs or trees growing very close together.

Thornveld a bush habitat or woodland comprising *Acacia*, *Albizia* or *Dichrostachys* trees, all of which are thorny.

Understorey the lowest stratum in (usually) forest or woodland; secondary growth consisting of young trees, small bushes and annual plants.

Upland high-altitude regions, but below montane.

Valley bush narrow belts of dense bush, often thorny and with succulent plant species, found in hot river valleys which drain into the Indian Ocean. Rainfall 500-900 mm per annum.

Veld a term used loosely in reference to various types of terrain, thus grassveld, bushveld, etc.

Vlei a marshy area, usually in grassland.

Watercourse the dry course of a river that flows only during good rains.

Waterhole any natural or artificial water-point used by animals for drinking.

Woodland regions with trees of moderate height and well-developed canopies which are so spaced as not to interlock; may cover flat ground or hillside, with or without well-developed secondary growth or groundcover.

Zygodactyl feet which, in certain non-passerine birds, have two toes directed forward and two backward: cuckoos, barbets, woodpeckers, honeyguides and others.

References

Brown, L.H., Urban, E.K. & Newman, K. *Birds of Africa*, vol 1. Academic Press, London, 1982.

Clancey, P.A. *A Handlist of the Birds of Southern Mozambique.* Instituto de Investigação Cientifica de Moçambique, Lourenço Marques, 1971.

Clancey, P.A. (ed.) *SAOS Check List of Southern African Birds.* Southern African Ornithological Society, Johannesburg, 1980.

Clinning, C.F. & Jensen, R.A.C. *Birds of the Daan Viljoen Game Park.* Division of Nature Conservation and Tourism, Windhoek, 1973.

Cyrus, Digby & Robson, Nigel. *Bird Atlas of Natal.* University of Natal Press, Pietermaritzburg, 1980.

Harrison, J.A., Allan, D.G., Underhill, L.G., Herremans, M., Tree, A.J., Parker, V. & Brown, C.J. (eds) *The Atlas of Southern African Birds,* vols 1 & 2. BirdLife South Africa, Johannesburg, 1997.

Irwin, M.P.S. *The Birds of Zimbabwe.* Quest Publishing, Harare, 1981.

Jensen, R.A.C & Clinning, C.F. *Birds of the Etosha National Park.* Division of Nature Conservation and Tourism, Windhoek, 1976.

Johnsgard, Paul A. *The Plovers, Sandpipers and Snipes of the World.* University of Nebraska Press, Lincoln & London, 1981.

Mackworth-Praed, C.W. & Grant, C.H.B. *Birds of the Southern Third of Africa*, vols 1 & 2. Longman Green, London, 1963.

Maclean, Gordon Lindsay (ed.) *Roberts' Birds of Southern Africa.* John Voelcker Bird Book Fund, Cape Town, 1985.

Newman, K. *Birds of the Kruger National Park.* Macmillan South Africa, Johannesburg, 1980.

Newman, K. (ed.) *Birdlife in Southern Africa.* Macmillan South Africa, Johannesburg, 1980.

Smithers, Reay H.N. *A Check List of the Birds of the Bechuanaland Protectorate and the Caprivi Strip.* Trustees of the National Museums, Southern Rhodesia, 1964.

Steyn, Peter. *Birds of Prey of Southern Africa.* David Philip, South Africa, 1982.

Tarboton, W.R. *Check List of Birds of the Southern Central Transvaal.* Witwatersrand Bird Club, Johannesburg, 1968.

Watson, George W. *Birds of the Antarctic and Sub-Antarctic.* American Geophysical Union, Washington D.C., 1975.

Index to scientific names

Index to Afrikaans names

Index to German names

The German bird names and spellings are those recommended by the Ornithology Working Group of the Namibian Scientific Society, as prepared by Hermann Kolberg. Subantarctic birds are excluded.

Index to English names and life list

Place | Date

		Place	Date
Batis, Cape/*Kaapse bosbontrokkie* Kapschnäpper	366		
Batis, Chin-spot/*witliesbosbontrokkie* Weißflankenschnäpper	366		
Batis, Mozambique/*Mosambiekbosbontrokkie* Sansibarschnäpper	366		
Batis, Pririt/*priritbosbontrokkie* Priritschnäpper	366		
Batis, Woodwards'/*Woodwardse bosbontrokkie* Woodwardschnäpper	366		
Bee-eater, Blue-cheeked/*blouwangbyvreter* Blauwangenspint	246		
Bee-eater, Böhm's/*roeskopbyvreter* Böhmspint	244		
Bee-eater, Carmine/*rooiborsbyvreter* Scharlachspint	246		
Bee-eater, European/*Europese byvreter* (Europäischer) Bienenfresser	246		
Bee-eater, Golden-backed *see* European Bee-eater	246		
Bee-eater, Little/*kleinbyvreter* Zwergbienenfresser (-Spint)	246		
Bee-eater, Olive/*olyfbyvreter* Madagaskar-Bienenfresser	246		
Bee-eater, Swallow-tailed/*swaelstertbyvreter* Schwalbenschwanz-Bienenfresser (-Spint)	244		
Bee-eater, White-fronted/*rooikeelbyvreter* Weißstirnbienenfresser	246		
Bee-eater, White-throated/*witkeelbyvreter* Weißkehlspint	450		
Bishop, Fire-crowned/*vuurkopvink* Feuerweber (Flammenweber)	416		
Bishop, Golden/*goudgeelvink* Tahaweber (Napoleonweber)	412		
Bishop, Red/*rooivink* Oryxweber	416		
Bittern/*grootrietreier* Große Rohrdommel	70		
Bittern, Dwarf/*dwergrietreier* Sturms Zwergrohrdommel (Graurückendommel)	66		
Bittern, Little/*woudapie* Zwergrohrdrommel	66		
Blackcap, Bush/*rooibektiptol* Buschschwarzkäppchen	304		
Blackcap, European/*swartkroonsanger* Mönchsgrasmücke	448		
Bokmakierie/*Bokmakierie* Bokmakiri	380		
Booby, Brown/*bruinmalgas* Brauntölpel	444		
Boubou, Crimson-breasted/*rooiborslaksman* Rotbauchwürger (Reichsvogel)	374		
Boubou, Southern/*suidelike waterfiskaal* Flötenwürger	374		
Boubou, Swamp/*moeraswaterfiskaal* Zweifarbenwürger	374		
Boubou, Tropical/*tropiese waterfiskaal* Flötenwürger	374		
Broadbill, African/*breëbek* Kap-Breitrachen	274		
Brubru/*bontroklaksman* Brubru (-würger)	372		
Bulbul, Black-eyed/*swartoogtiptol* Graubülbül	306		
Bulbul, Cape/*Kaapse tiptol* Kapbülbül	306		
Bulbul, Red-eyed/*rooioogtiptol* Maskenbülbül	306	Vic Falls	6-17-01

Species	Page	Place	Date
Bulbul, Slender/*kleinboskruiper* Kleiner Gelbstreifen-Laubbülbül	306		
Bulbul, Sombre/*gewone willie* Kap-Grünbülbül	304		
Bulbul, Stripe-cheeked/*streepwangwillie* Strichel-Grünbülbül	306		
Bulbul, Terrestrial/*boskrapper* Laubbülbül	304		
Bulbul, Yellow-bellied/*geelborswillie* Gelbbrustbülbül	304		
Bulbul, Yellow-streaked/*geelstreepboskruiper* Gelbstreifen-Laubbülbül	306		
Bunting, Cabanis's/*geelstreepkoppie* Cabanisammer	442		
Bunting, Cape/*rooivlerkstreepkoppie* Kapammer	442		
Bunting, Golden-breasted/*rooirugstreepkoppie* Gelbbauchammer	442		
Bunting, Gough/*Gough-streepkoppie*	26		
Bunting, Lark-like/*vaalstreepkoppie* Lerchenammer	442		
Bunting, Rock/*klipstreepkoppie* Bergammer	442		
Bunting, Tristan/*Tristanstreepkoppie*	26		
Bunting, Wilkins'/*dikbekstreepkoppie*	26		
Bustard, Kori/*gompou* Riesentrappe	136		
Bustard, Ludwig's/*Ludwigse pou* Ludwigstrappe	134		
Bustard, Stanley's/*veldpou* Stanleytrappe	134		
Button Quail, Black-rumped/*Kaapse kwarteltjie* Hottentotten-Laufhühnchen	148		
Button Quail, Kurrichane/*bosveldkwarteltjie* Laufhühnchen	148		
Buzzard, Augur/*witborsjakkalsvoël* Augurbussard	172		
Buzzard, Forest/*bosjakkalsvoël* Bergbussard	170		
Buzzard, Honey/*wespedief* Wespenbussard	172		
Buzzard, Jackal/*rooiborsjakkalsvoël* Felsenbussard	172		
Buzzard, Lizard/*akkedisvalk* Sperberbussard	174		
Buzzard, Long-legged/*langbeenjakkalsvoël* Adlerbussard	454		
Buzzard, Steppe/*bruinjakkalsvoël* Mäusebussard	170		
Canary, Black-eared/*swartoorkanarie* Schwarzwangengirlitz	438		
Canary, Black-headed/*swartkopkanarie* Alariogirlitz	438		
Canary, Black-throated/*bergkanarie* Angolagirlitz	438		
Canary, Bully/*dikbekkanarie* Schwefelgirlitz	436		
Canary, Cape/*Kaapse kanarie* Gelbscheitelgirlitz	436		
Canary, Forest/*gestreepte kanarie* Schwarzkinngirlitz	436		
Canary, Lemon-breasted/*geelborskanarie* Gelbbrustgirlitz	440		
Canary, Protea/*witvlerkkanarie* Proteagirlitz	438		

		Place	Date
Canary, Streaky-headed/*streepkopkanarie* Brauengirlitz	438		
Canary, White-throated/*witkeelkanarie* Weißkehlgirlitz	438		
Canary, Yellow/*geelkanarie* Gelbbauchgirlitz	436		
Canary, Yellow-eyed/*geeloogkanarie* Mossambikgirlitz	436		
Chaffinch/*gryskoppie* Buchfink	440		
Chat, Ant-eating/*swartpiek* Termitenschmätzer (Ameisenschmätzer)	322		
Chat, Arnot's/*bontpiek* Arnotschmätzer	318		
Chat, Boulder/*swartberglyster* Steindrossling	316		
Chat, Buff-streaked/*bergklipwagter* Fahlschulterschmätzer	322		
Chat, Familiar/*gewone spekvreter* Rostschwanzschmätzer	320		
Chat, Herero/*Hererospekvreter* Namibschnäpper	322		
Chat, Karoo/*Karoospekvreter* Bleichschmätzer (Wüstenschmätzer)	320		
Chat, Mocking/*dassievoël* Rotbauchschmätzer	316		
Chat, Mountain/*bergwagter* Bergschmätzer	318		
Chat, Sickle-winged/*vlaktespekvreter* Namibschmätzer	320		
Chat, Tractrac/*woestynspekvreter* Oranjeschmätzer	320		
Cisticola, Ayres'/*kleinste klopkloppie* Zwergpinkpink	350		
Cisticola, Black-backed/*swartrugtinktinkie* Schwarzrückenzistensänger	354		
Cisticola, Chirping/*piepende tinktinkie* Sumpfzistensänger	352		
Cisticola, Cloud/*gevlekte klopkloppie* Pinkpink	350		
Cisticola, Croaking/*groottinktinkie* Strichelzistensänger	356		
Cisticola, Desert/*woestynklopkloppie* Kalahari-Zistensänger	350		
Cisticola, Fan-tailed/*landeryklopkloppie* Zistensänger	350		
Cisticola, Grey-backed/*grysrugtinktinkie* Bergzistensänger	352		
Cisticola, Lazy/*luitinktinkie* Smiths Zistensänger	356		
Cisticola, Levaillant's/*vleitinktinkie* Uferzistensänger	354		
Cisticola, Pale-crowned/*bleekkopklopkloppie* Blaßkopfpinkpink	348		
Cisticola, Rattling/*bosveldtinktinkie* Rotscheitelzistensänger	354		
Cisticola, Red-faced/*rooiwangtinktinkie* Rotgesichtzistensänger	356		
Cisticola, Short-winged/*kortvlerktinktinkie* Kurzflügel-Zistensänger	352		
Cisticola, Singing/*singende tinktinkie* Grauer Zistensänger	352		
Cisticola, Tinkling/*rooitinktinkie* Rotschwanzzistensänger	354		
Cisticola, Wailing/*huiltinktinkie* Trauerzistensänger	354		
Coot, Red-knobbed/*bleshoender* Kammblesshuhn	96		

		Place	Date
Cormorant, Bank/*bankduiker* Küstenscharbe	64		
Cormorant, Cape/*trekduiker* Kapkormoran	64		
Cormorant, Crowned/*kuifkopduiker* Wahlbergscharbe	64		
Cormorant, Imperial/*keiserduiker*	20		
Cormorant, Reed/*rietduiker* Riedscharbe	64		
Cormorant, White-breasted/*witborsduiker* Weißbrustkormoran	64		
Corncrake/*kwartelkoning* Wachtelkönig	102		
Coucal, Black/*swartvleiloerie* Grillkuckuck	212		
Coucal, Burchell's/*gewone vleiloerie* Tiputip	214		
Coucal, Coppery-tailed/*grootvleiloerie* Angola-Mönchkuckuck	214		
Coucal, Green/*groenvleiloerie* Erzkuckuck	212		
Coucal, Senegal/*Senegalvleiloerie* Senegal-Spornkuckuck	214		
Coucal, White-browed/*witbrouvleiloerie* Weißbrauen-Spornkuckuck	214		
Courser, Bronze-winged/*bronsvlerkdrawwertjie* Bronzeflügel Rennvogel	130		
Courser, Burchell's/*bloukopdrawwertjie* Rostrennvogel	130		
Courser, Double-banded/*dubbelbanddrawwertjie* Doppelbandrennvogel	130		
Courser, Temminck's/*trekdrawwertjie* Temminckrennvogel	130		
Courser, Three-banded/*driebanddrawwertjie* Bindenrennvogel	130		
Crake, African/*Afrikaanse riethaan* Steppenralle	102		
Crake, Baillon's/*kleinriethaan* Zwergsumpfhuhn	102		
Crake, Black/*swartriethaan* Neger- (Mohren-)ralle	102		
Crake, Spotted/*gevlekte riethaan* Tüpfelsumpfhuhn	100		
Crake, Striped/*gestreepte riethaan* Graukehlsumpfhuhn	100		
Crane, Blue/*bloukraanvoël* Paradieskranich	138		
Crane, Crowned/*mahem* Kronenkranich	138		
Crane, Wattled/*lelkraanvoël* Klunkerkranich	138		
Creeper, Spotted/*boomkruiper* Fleckenbaumläufer	274		
Crimson-wing, Red-faced/*rooirugsaadvretertjie* Reichenows Bergastrild	420		
Crombec, Long-billed/*bosveldstompstert* Langschnabel- (Kurzschwanz-) Sylvietta	342		
Crombec, Red-capped/*rooikroonstompstert* Rotohrsylvietta	342		
Crombec, Red-faced/*rooiwangstompstert* Whytes Sylvietta	342		
Crow, Black/*swartkraai* Kapkrähe	300		
Crow, House/*huiskraai* Glanzkrähe (Hauskrähe)	300		
Crow, Pied/*witborskraai* Schildrabe	300		

Species	Page	Place	Date
Cuckoo, African/*Afrikaanse koekoek* Afrikanischer Kuckuck	210		
Cuckoo, Barred/*langstertkoekoek* Bergkuckuck	210		
Cuckoo, Black/*swartkoekoek* Schwarzkuckuck	212		
Cuckoo, Diederik/*diederikkie* Diderikkuckuck (Goldkuckuck)	208		
Cuckoo, Emerald/*mooimeisie* Smaragdkuckuck	208		
Cuckoo, European/*Europese koekoek* Kuckuck	210		
Cuckoo, Great Spotted/*gevlekte koekoek* Häherkuckuck	212		
Cuckoo, Jacobin/*bontnuwejaarsvoël* Jakobinerkuckuck	208		
Cuckoo, Klaas's/*meitjie* Klaaskuckuck	208		
Cuckoo, Lesser/*kleinkoekoek* Gackelkuckuck	210		
Cuckoo, Madagascar Lesser/*Madagaskarkoekoek* Madagaskarkuckuck	210		
Cuckoo, Red-chested/*piet-my-vrou* Einsiedlerkuckuck	210		
Cuckoo, Striped/*gestreepte nuwejaarsvoël* Kapkuckuck	208		
Cuckoo, Thick-billed/*dikbekkoekoek* Dickschnabelkuckuck	212		
Cuckooshrike, Black/*swartkatakoeroe* Kuckuckswürger	296, 298		
Cuckooshrike, Grey/*bloukatakoeroe* Grauer Raupenfänger	298		
Cuckooshrike, White-breasted/*witborskatakoeroe* Wießbrustraupenfänger	298		
Curlew/*grootwulp* Großer Brachvogel	124		
Dabchick/*kleindobbertjie* Zwergtaucher	96		
Darter/*slanghalsvoël* Schlangenhalsvogel	64	Vic Falls	6/01
Dikkop, Spotted/*dikkop* Kaptriel	128		
Dikkop, Water/*waterdikkop* Wassertriel	128		
Dove, African Mourning/*rooiooglorteIduif* Angolaturteltaube (Angolalach-/Brillentaube)	196		
Dove, Blue-spotted/*blouvlekduifie* Stahlflecktaube	200		
Dove, Cinnamon/*kaneelduifie* Zimttaube	198		
Dove, Emerald-spotted/*groenvlekduifie* Bronzeflecktaube	200		
Dove, Laughing/*rooiborsduifie* Senegal- (Palmen-)taube	196		
Dove, Namaqua/*Namakwaduifie* Kaptäubchen	196		
Dove, Red-eyed/*grootringduif* Halbmondtaube	196		
Dove, Tambourine/*witborsduifie* Tamburintaube	198		
Dove, Turtle, Cape/*gewone tortelduif* Kapturteltaube	196		
Dove, Turtle, Eurasian/*(Europese) tortelduif* Turteltaube	446		
Drongo, Fork-tailed/*mikstertbyvanger* Trauerdrongo	296		
Drongo, Square-tailed/*kleinbyvanger* Geradschwanzdrongo	296		

		Place	Date
Eremomela, Yellow-bellied/*geelpensbossanger* Gelbbaucheremomela	344		
Falcon, Eleonora's/*Eleonoravalk* Eleonorenfalke	452		
Falcon, Hobby/*Europese boomvalk* Baumfalke	188		
Falcon, Hobby, African/*Afrikaanse boomvalk* Afrikanischer Baumfalke	190		
Falcon, Lanner/*edelvalk* Lannerfalke	188		
Falcon, Peregrine/*swerfvalk* Wanderfalke	188		
Falcon, Pygmy/*dwergvalk* Zwergfalke	186		
Falcon, Red-necked/*rooinekvalk* Rothalsfalke	186		
Falcon, Sooty/*roetvalk* Schieferfalke (Blaufalke)	186		
Falcon, Taita/*Taitavalk* Kurzchwanz (Taita-)falke	186		
Finch, Cuckoo/*koekoekvink* Kuckucksweber	430		
Finch, Cut-throat/*bandkeelvink* Bandfink	428		
Finch, Locust/*rooivlerkkwartelvinkie* Heuschreckenastrild	424		
Finch, Melba/*gewone melba* Buntastrild	420		
Finch, Quail/*gewone kwartelvinkie* Wachtelastrild	424		
Finch, Red-headed/*rooikopvink* Rotkopfamadine	428		
Finch, Scaly-feathered/*baardmannetjie* Schnurrbärtchen	406		
Finchlark, Black-eared/*swartoorlewerik* Schwarzwangenlerche	286		
Finchlark, Chestnut-backed/*rooiruglewerik* Weißwangenlerche	286		
Finchlark, Grey-backed/*grysruglewerik* Nonnenlerche	286		
Finfoot, African/*watertrapper* Afrikanische Binsenralle	84		
Firefinch, Blue-billed/*Kaapse vuurvinkie* Dunkelroter Amarant	422		
Firefinch, Brown/*bruinvuurvinkie* Großer Pünktchenamarant	422		
Firefinch, Jameson's/*Jamesonse vuurvinkie* Jamesons Amarant	422		
Firefinch, Red-billed/*rooibekvuurvinkie* (Kleiner) Amarant	422		
Flamingo, Greater/*grootflamink* Flamingo	82		
Flamingo, Lesser/*kleinflamink* Zwergflamingo	82		
Flufftail, Buff-spotted/*gevlekte vleikuiken* Schmuckzwergralle	102		
Flufftail, Red-chested/*rooiborsvleikuiken* Rotbrustzwergralle	102		
Flufftail, Streaky-breasted/*streepborsvleikuiken* Böhms Zwergralle	100		
Flufftail, Striped/*gestreepte vleikuiken* Streifenzwergralle	100		
Flufftail, White-winged/*witvlerkvleikuiken* Weißflügelzwergralle	100		
Flycatcher, Black/*swartvlieëvanger* Drongoschnäpper	296		
Flycatcher, Blue-grey/*blougrysvlieëvanger* Schieferschnäpper	362		

		Place	Date
Flycatcher, Blue-mantled/*bloukuifvlieëvanger* Blaumantel-Schopfschnäpper	368		
Flycatcher, Chat/*grootvlieëvanger* Drosselschnäpper	364		
Flycatcher, Collared/*withalsvlieëvanger* Halsbandschnäpper	360		
Flycatcher, Dusky/*donkervlieëvanger* Dunkelschnäpper	362		
Flycatcher, Fairy/*feevlieëvanger* Elfenschnäpper	368		
Flycatcher, Fan-tailed/*waaierstertvlieëvanger* Meisenschnäpper	362		
Flycatcher, Fiscal/*fiskaalvlieëvanger* Würgerschnäpper	364		
Flycatcher, Lead-coloured *see* Fan-tailed Flycatcher	362		
Flycatcher, Livingstone's/*rooistertvlieëvanger* Livingstones Rotschwanzschnäpper	368		
Flycatcher, Marico/*Maricovlieëvanger* Maricoschnäpper	364		
Flycatcher, Pallid/*muiskleurvlieëvanger* Fahlschnäpper	362		
Flycatcher, Paradise/*paradysvlieëvanger* Paradiesschnäpper	368		
Flycatcher, Spotted/*Europese vlieëvanger* Grauschnäpper	362		
Flycatcher, Vanga/*witpensvlieëvanger* Vangaschnäpper	364		
Flycatcher, Wattle-eyed/*beloogbosbontrokkie* Schwarzkehl-Lappenschnäpper	368		
Flycatcher, White-tailed/*witstertvlieëvanger* Weißschwanz-Schopfschnäpper	368		
Francolin, Cape/*Kaapse fisant* Kapfrankolin	142		
Francolin, Coqui/*swempie* Coquifrankolin	142		
Francolin, Crested/*bospatrys* Schopffrankolin	142		
Francolin, Grey-wing/*bergpatrys* Grauflügelfrankolin	144		
Francolin, Hartlaub's/*klipfisant* Hartlaubfrankolin	144		
Francolin, Natal/*Natalse fisant* Natalfrankolin	146		
Francolin, Orange River/*Kalaharipatrys* Rebhuhnfrankolin	146		
Francolin, Red-billed/*rooibekfisant* Rotschnabel Frankolin (Sandhuhn)	142		
Francolin, Red-necked/*rooikeelfisant* Nacktkehl- (Rotkehl-)frankolin	144		
Francolin, Red-wing/*rooivlerkpatrys* Rotflügelfrankolin	146		
Francolin, Shelley's/*laeveldpatrys* Shelleyfrankolin	146		
Francolin, Swainson's/*bosveldfisant* Swainsonfrankolin	144		
Frigatebird, Greater/*grootfregatvoël* Binden-Fregattvogel	452		
Frigatebird, Lesser/*kleinfregatvoël* Zwerg-Fregattvogel	452		
Fulmar, Antarctic/*silwerstormvoël* Silbermöwensturmvogel	36		
Gallinule, Lesser/*kleinkoningriethaan* Afrikanisches Sultanshuhn	98		
Gallinule, Purple/*grootkoningriethaan* Purpurhuhn	98		
Gallinule, Purple, American/*Amerikaanse koningriethaan* Amerikanisches Sultanshuhn	98		

		Place	Date
Harrier, Pallid/*witborsvleivalk* Steppenweihe	182		
Hawk, Bat/*vlermuisvalk* Fledermausaar	184		
Hawk, Cuckoo/*koekoekvalk* Kuckucksweih	186		
Hawk-harrier, African *see* Gymnogene	184		
Helmet Shrike, Chestnut-fronted/*stekelkophelmlaksman* Braunstirnwürger	380		
Helmet Shrike, Red-billed/*swarthelmlaksman* Dreifarbenwürger	380		
Helmet Shrike, White/*withelmlaksman* Brillenwürger	380		
Heron, Black-headed/*swartkopreier* Schwarzkopf- (Schwarzhals-)reiher	74		
Heron, Goliath/*reusereier* Goliathreiher	74		
Heron, Great White/*grootwitreier* Silberreiher	72		
Heron, Green-backed/*groenrugreier* Mangrovereiher	66		
Heron, Grey/*bloureier* Graureiher	74		
Heron, Little Blue/*kleinbloureier* Kleiner Blaureiher	450		
Heron, Night, Black-crowned/*gewone nagreier* Nachtreiher	70		
Heron, Night, White-backed/*witrugnagreier* Weißrückennachtreiher	70		
Heron, Purple/*rooireier* Purpurreiher	74		
Heron, Rufous-bellied/*rooipensreier* Rotbauchreiher	66		
Heron, Squacco/*ralreier* Rallenreiher	68		
Heron, Squacco, Madagascar/*Malgassiese ralreier* Madagaskar-Rallenreiher	68		
Honeyguide, Eastern/*oostelike heuningwyser* Olivmantel-Honiganzeiger	272		
Honeyguide, Greater/*grootheuningwyser* Großer Honiganzeiger	272		
Honeyguide, Lesser/*kleinheuningwyser* Kleiner Honiganzeiger	272		
Honeyguide, Scaly-throated/*gevlekte heuningwyser* Gefleckter Honiganzeiger	272		
Honeyguide, Sharp-billed/*skerpbekheuningvoël* Schmalschnabel-Honiganzeiger	274		
Honeyguide, Slender-billed/*dunbekheuningvoël* Zwerghoniganzeiger	274		
Hoopoe/*hoephoep* Wiedehopf	256		
Hornbill, Bradfield's/*Bradfieldse neushoringvoël* Bradfieldtoko	260		
Hornbill, Crowned/*gekroonde neushoringvoël* Kronentoko	258		
Hornbill, Grey/*grysneushoringvoël* Grautoko	258	Vic Falls	6/01
Hornbill, Ground/*bromvoël* Hornrabe	262		
Hornbill, Monteiro's/*Monteirose neushoringvoël* Monteirotoko	260		
Hornbill, Red-billed/*rooibekneushoringvoël* Rotschnabeltoko	258		
Hornbill, Silvery-cheeked/*kuifkopboskraai* Schopfhornvogel	260		
Hornbill, Southern Yellow-billed/*geelbekneushoringvoël* Gelbschnabeltoko	260		

		Place	Date
Hornbill, Trumpeter/*gewone boskraai* Trompeterhornvogel	260		
Hyliota, Mashona/*Mashonahyliota* Maschona-Hyliota	360		
Hyliota, Yellow-breasted/*Geelborshyliota* Gelbbauch-Hyliota	360		
Ibis, Bald/*kalkoenibis* Glattnacken- (Kahlkopf-)rapp	84		
Ibis, Glossy/*glansibis* Brauner Sichler	84		
Ibis, Hadeda/*hadeda* Hagedasch-Ibis	84		
Ibis, Sacred/*skoorsteenveër* Heiliger Ibis	84		
Jacana, African/*grootlangtoon* Blaustirn-Blatthühnchen (Jacana)	118		
Jacana, Lesser/*dwerglangtoon* Zwergblatthühnchen	118		
Kestrel, Amur *see* Eastern Red-footed Kestrel	192		
Kestrel, Common *see* Rock Kestrel	192		
Kestrel, Dickinson's/*Dickinsonse grysvalk* Schwarzrückenfalke	190		
Kestrel, Greater/*grootrooivalk* Steppenfalke	190		
Kestrel, Grey/*donkergrysvalk* Graufalke	190		
Kestrel, Lesser/*kleinrooivalk* Rötelfalke	192		
Kestrel, Red-footed, Eastern/*oostelike rooipootvalk* Amur- (Rotfuß-)falke	192		
Kestrel, Red-footed, Western/*westelike rooipootvalk* Rotfußfalke	192		
Kestrel, Rock/*rooivalk* Turmfalke	192		
Kingfisher, Brown-hooded/*bruinkopvisvanger* Braunkopfliest	252	Vic Falls	6/01
Kingfisher, Chestnut-bellied *see* Grey-hooded Kingfisher	250		
Kingfisher, Giant/*reusevisvanger* Riesenfischer	248		
Kingfisher, Grey-hooded/*gryskopvisvanger* Graukopfliest	250		
Kingfisher, Half-collared/*blouvisvanger* Kobalteisvogel	252		
Kingfisher, Malachite/*kuifkopvisvanger* Malachiteisvogel (Haubenzwergfischer)	252		
Kingfisher, Mangrove/*manglietvisvanger* Mangroveliest	250		
Kingfisher, Pied/*bontvisvanger* Graufischer	248		
Kingfisher, Pygmy/*dwergvisvanger* (Natal-) Zwergfischer (Zwergeisvogel)	252		
Kingfisher, Striped/*gestreepte visvanger* Streifenliest	252		
Kingfisher, Woodland/*bosveldvisvanger* Senegalliest	250		
Kite, Black/*swartwou* Schwarzer Milan	158		
Kite, Black-shouldered/*blouvalk* Gleitaar	174		
Kite, Yellow-billed/*geelbekwou* Schmarotzermilan	158		
Kittiwake, Black-legged/*swartpootbrandervoël* Dreizehenmöwe	52		
Knot/*knoet* Knutt	114		

		Place	Date
Korhaan, Black/*swartkorhaan* Gackeltrappe	132		
Korhaan, Black, White-winged/*witvlerkkorhaan* Gackeltrappe	132		
Korhaan, Black-bellied/*langbeenkorhaan* Schwarzbauchtrappe	136		
Korhaan, Blue/*bloukorhaan* Blautrappe	132		
Korhaan, Karoo/*vaalkorhaan* Nama- (Knarr-)trappe	134		
Korhaan, Red-crested/*boskorhaan* Rotschopftrappe	132		
Korhaan, Rüppell's/*woestynkorhaan* Rüppelltrappe	134		
Korhaan, White-bellied/*witpenskorhaan* Weißbauchtrappe	132		
Lammergeier *see* Bearded Vulture	152		
Lark, Barlow's/*Barlowse lewerik* Barlows Lerche	278		
Lark, Botha's/*Vaalrivierlewerik* Finkenlerche	284		
Lark, Clapper/*hoëveldklappertjie* Grasklapperlerche	280		
Lark, Dune/*duinlewerik* Dünenlerche	278		
Lark, Dusky/*donkerlewerik* Drossellerche	280		
Lark, Fawn-coloured/*vaalbruinlewerik* Steppenlerche	276		
Lark, Flappet/*laeveldklappertjie* Baumklapperlerche	280		
Lark, Gray's/*Namiblewerik* Namiblerche	284		
Lark, Karoo/*Karoolewerik* Karrulerche	278		
Lark, Long-billed/*langbeklewerik* Langschnabellerche	282		
Lark, Melodious/*spotlewerik* Spottlerche	276		
Lark, Monotonous/*bosveldlewerik* Sperlingslerche	276		
Lark, Pink-billed/*pienkbeklewerik* Rotschnabellerche	284		
Lark, Red/*rooilewerik* Oranjelerche	278		
Lark, Red-capped/*rooikoplewerik* Rotscheitellerche	282		
Lark, Rudd's/*Drakensberglewerik* Spornlerche	284		
Lark, Rufous-naped/*rooineklewerik* Rotnackenlerche	276		
Lark, Sabota/*sabotalewerik* Sabotalerche	278		
Lark, Sclater's/*Namakwalewerik* Sclaters Kurzhaubenlerche	284		
Lark, Short-clawed/*kortkloulewerik* Betschuanenlerche	280		
Lark, Spike-heeled/*vlaktelewerik* Zirp- (Langsporn-)lerche	282		
Lark, Stark's/*woestynlewerik* Starks Kurzhaubenlerche	284		
Lark, Thick-billed/*dikbeklewerik* Dickschnabellerche	282		
Longclaw, Fülleborn's/*Angolakalkoentjie* Füllebornpieper	292		
Longclaw, Orange-throated/*oranjekeelkalkoentjie* Kapgroßsporn	290		

Species	Page	Place	Date
Longclaw, Pink-throated/*rooskeelkalkoentjie* Rotkehlgroßsporn	290		
Longclaw, Yellow-throated/*geelkeelkalkoentjie* Gelbkehl- (Safran-)großsporn (Gelbkehlpieper)	292		
Lourie, Grey/*kwêvoël* Graulärmvogel	206	Vic Falls	6/01
Lourie, Knysna/*Knysnaloerie* Helmturako	206	〃	〃
Lourie, Purple-crested/*bloukuifloerie* Glanzhaubenturako	206		
Lourie, Ross's/*rooikuifloerie* Rossturako	206		
Lovebird, Black-cheeked/*swartwangparkiet* Rußköpfchen	204		
Lovebird, Lilian's/*Niassaparkiet* Erdbeerköpfchen	204		
Lovebird, Rosy-faced/*rooiwangparkiet* Rosenpapagei	204		
Mannikin, Bronze/*gewone fret* Kleinelsterchen	430	Vic F	6/16/01
Mannikin, Pied/*dikbekfret* Riesenelsterchen	430		
Mannikin, Red-backed/*rooirugfret* Glanzelsterchen	430		
Martin, Banded/*gebande oewerswael* Gebänderte Uferschwalbe	236		
Martin, Brown-throated/*Afrikaanse oewerswael* Afrikanische Uferschwalbe	236		
Martin, House/*huisswael* Mehlschwalbe	236		
Martin, Mascarene/*gestreepte kransswael* Maskarenenschwalbe	234		
Martin, Rock/*kransswael* Felsenschwalbe	236		
Martin, Sand, (European)/*Europese oewerswael* (Europäische) Uferschwalbe	234		
Moorhen/*waterhoender* Teichhuhn	98		
Moorhen, Gough/*Gough-eilandwaterhoender*	24		
Moorhen, Lesser/*kleinwaterhoender* Zwergteichhuhn	98		
Mousebird, Red-faced/*rooiwangmuisvoël* Rotzügelmausvogel	244		
Mousebird, Speckled/*gevlekte muisvoël* Braunflügelmausvogel	244		
Mousebird, White-backed/*witkruismuisvoël* Weißrückenmausvogel	244		
Myna, Indian/*Indiese spreeu* Hirtenmaina	384		
Neddicky/*neddikkie* Brauner Zistensänger	352		
Nicator, Yellow-spotted/*geelvleknikator* Bülbülwürger	304		
Nightingale, Thrush/*lysternagtegaal* Sprosser	332		
Nightjar, European/*Europese naguil* Ziegenmelker (Nachtschwalbe)	224		
Nightjar, Fiery-necked/*Afrikaanse naguil* Rotnacken-Nachtschwalbe	224		
Nightjar, Freckled/*donkernaguil* Fleckennachtschwalbe	224		
Nightjar, Mozambique/*laeveldnaguil* Gabunnachtschwalbe	224		
Nightjar, Natal/*Natalse naguil* Natal-Nachtschwalbe	222		
Nightjar, Pennant-winged/*wimpelvlerknaguil* Ruderflügel	224		

		Place	Date
Nightjar, Rufous-cheeked/*rooiwangnaguil* Rostwangen-Nachtschwalbe	224		
Noddy, Common/*grootbruinsterretjie* Noddi (-seeschwalbe)	60		
Noddy, Lesser/*kleinbruinsterretjie* Schlankschnabelnoddi	60		
Oriole, Black-headed/*swartkopwielewaal* Maskenpirol	302		
Oriole, Golden, African/*Afrikaanse wielewaal* Schwarzohrpirol	302		
Oriole, Golden, European/*Europese wielewaal* Pirol	302		
Oriole, Green-headed/*groenkopwielewaal* Grünkopfpirol	300		
Osprey/*visvalk* Fischadler	184		
Ostrich/*volstruis* Strauß	150		
Owl, African Scops/*skopsuil* Zwergohreule	218		
Owl, Barn/*nonnetjie-uil* Schleiereule	216		
Owl, Barred/*gebande uil* Kapkauz	218		
Owl, Eagle, Cape/*Kaapse ooruil* Kapuhu	220		
Owl, Eagle, Giant/*reuse-ooruil* Milchuhu	220		
Owl, Eagle, Spotted/*gevlekte ooruil* Fleckenuhu (Berguhu)	220		
Owl, Grass/*grasuil* Graseule	216		
Owl, Marsh/*vlei-uil* Kapohreule	216		
Owl, Pearl-spotted/*witkoluil* Perlkauz	218		
Owl, Pel's Fishing/*visuil* Fischeule	222		
Owl, White-faced/*witwanguil* Weißgesichtohreule	218		
Owl, Wood/*bosuil* Woodfordkauz	216		
Oxpecker, Red-billed/*rooibekrenostervoël* Rotschnabelmadenhacker	388		
Oxpecker, Yellow-billed/*geelbekrenostervoël* Gelbschnabelmadenhacker	388		
Oystercatcher, African Black/*swarttobie* Schwarzer Austernfischer	124		
Oystercatcher, European/*bonttobie* Austernfischer	124		
Parakeet, Rose-ringed/*ringnekpapegaai* Halsbandsittich	202		
Parrot, Brown-headed/*bruinkoppapegaai* Braunkopfpapagei	202		
Parrot, Cape/*grootpapegaai* Kappapagei	202		
Parrot, Meyer's/*bosveldpapegaai* Goldbugpapagei	202		
Parrot, Rüppell's/*bloupenspapegaai* Rüppellpapagei	202		
Partridge, Chukar/*Asiatiese patrys* Chukarsteinhuhn	146		
Pelican, Eastern White/*witpelikaan* Rosapelikan	62		
Pelican, Pink-backed/*kleinpelikaan* Rötelpelikan	62		
Penguin, Adelie/*Adeliepikkewyn* Adeliepinguin	20		

Species	Page	Place	Date
Penguin, Chin-strap/*bandkeelpikkewyn* Kehlstreif- (Zügel-)pinguin	20		
Penguin, Emperor/*keiserpikkewyn* Kaiserpinguin	20		
Penguin, Gentoo/*witoorpikkewyn* Eselspinguin	20		
Penguin, Jackass/*brilpikkewyn* Brillenpinguin	28		
Penguin, King/*koningpikkewyn* Königspinguin	28		
Penguin, Macaroni/*macaronipikkewyn* Goldschopfpinguin	28		
Penguin, Rockhopper/*geelkuifpikkewyn* Felsenpinguin	28		
Petrel, Antarctic/*Antarktiese stormvoël* Grauweißer (Antarktik-/Weißflügel-) Sturmvogel	36		
Petrel, Atlantic/*bruinvlerkstormvoël* Schlegels Sturmvogel	36		
Petrel, Blue/*bloustormvoël* Blausturmvogel	40		
Petrel, Bulwer's/*Bulwerse stormvoël* Bulwersturmvogel	38		
Petrel, Diving, Common/*gewone duikstormvoël* Lummensturmvogel	22		
Petrel, Diving, South Georgian/*kleinduikstormvoël*	22		
Petrel, Giant, Northern/*grootnellie* Nördlicher Riesensturmvogel (Hallsturmvogel)	34		
Petrel, Giant, Southern/*reusenellie* Riesensturmvogel	34		
Petrel, Great-winged/*langvlerkstormvoël* Langflügelsturmvogel	34		
Petrel, Grey/*pediunker* Grausturmvogel	42		
Petrel, Kerguelen/*Kerguelense stormvoël* Kerguelensturmvogel	38		
Petrel, Pintado/*seeduifstormvoël* Kapsturmvogel	38		
Petrel, Snow/*witstormvoël* Schneesturmvogel	24		
Petrel, Soft-plumaged/*donsveerstormvoël* Weichfedersturmvogel	38		
Petrel, Spectacled/*brilstormvoël* Brillensturmvogel	34		
Petrel, Storm, Black-bellied/*swartpensstormswael* Schwarzbauchmeerläufer (-sturmschwalbe)	46		
Petrel, Storm, European/*swartpootstormswael* Sturmschwalbe	46		
Petrel, Storm, Grey-backed/*grysrugstormswael* Graurückensturmschwalbe	22		
Petrel, Storm, Leach's/*swaelstertstormswael* Wellenläufer	46		
Petrel, Storm, Matsudaira's/*Matsudairase stormswael* Matsudaira-Wellenläufer	444		
Petrel, Storm, White-bellied/*witpensstormswael* Weißbauchmeerläufer (-sturmschwalbe)	46		
Petrel, Storm, White-faced/*witwangstormswael*	22		
Petrel, Storm, Wilson's/*geelpootstormswael* Buntfußsturmschwalbe	46		
Petrel, White-chinned/*bassiaan* Weißkinnsturmvogel	34		
Petrel, White-headed/*witkopstormvoël* Weißkopfsturmvogel	36		
Phalarope, Grey/*grysfraiingpoot* Thorshühnchen	110		
Phalarope, Red-necked/*rooihalsfraiingpoot* Odinshühnchen	110		

Species	Page	Place	Date
Phalarope, Wilson's/*bontfraiingpoot* Wilsons Wassertreter (Amerikanisches Odinshühnchen)	110		
Pigeon, Delegorgue's/*withalsbosduif* Bronzehalstaube	198		
Pigeon, Domestic *see* Feral Pigeon	200		
Pigeon, Feral/*tuinduif* Haustaube	200		
Pigeon, Green/*papegaaiduif* Grüne Fruchttaube	198		
Pigeon, Rameron/*geelbekbosduif* Oliventaube	200		
Pigeon, Rock/*kransduif* Guineataube	198		
Pigeon, Town *see* Feral Pigeon	200		
Pintail/*pylsterteend* Spießente	452		
Pipit, Buffy/*vaalkoester* Vaalpieper	288		
Pipit, Bushveld/*bosveldkoester* Buschpieper	290		
Pipit, Golden/*goudkoester* Goldpieper	292		
Pipit, Grassveld/*gewone koester* Spornpieper	288		
Pipit, Long-billed/*Nicholsonse koester* Langschnabelpieper	288		
Pipit, Mountain/*bergkoester* Hochlandpieper	288		
Pipit, Plain-backed/*donkerkoester* Braunrückenpieper	288		
Pipit, Red-throated/*rooikeelkoester* Rotkehlpieper	446		
Pipit, Rock/*klipkoester* Klippenpieper	288		
Pipit, Short-tailed/*kortstertkoester* Kurzschwanzpieper	286		
Pipit, Striped/*gestreepte koester* Streifenpieper	290		
Pipit, Tree/*boomkoester* Baumpieper	290		
Pipit, Wood/*woudkoester* Miombopieper	288		
Pipit, Yellow-breasted/*geelborskoester* Gelbbrustpieper	292		
Pitta, Angola/*Angolapitta* Angolapitta	274		
Plover, Black-winged/*grootswartvlerkkiewiet* Schwarzflügelkiebitz	120		
Plover, Black-winged, Lesser/*kleinswartvlerkkiewiet* Trauerkiebitz	120		
Plover, Blacksmith/*bontkiewiet* Waffenkiebitz	122		
Plover, Caspian/*Asiatiese strandkiewiet* Wermutregenpfeifer	104		
Plover, Chestnut-banded/*rooibandstrandkiewiet* Fahlregenpfeifer	106		
Plover, Crab/*krapvreter* Reiherläufer	126		
Plover, Crowned/*kroonkiewiet* Kronenkiebitz	122		
Plover, Golden, American/*Amerikaanse goue strandkiewiet* Wanderregenpfeifer	120		
Plover, Golden, Pacific/*oosterse goue strandkiewiet* Wanderregenpfeifer	120		
Plover, Grey/*grysstrandkiewiet* Kiebitzregenpfeifer	120		

		Place	Date
Plover, Kentish/*bleekstrandkiewiet* Seeregenpfeifer	446		
Plover, Kittlitz's/*geelborsstrandkiewiet* Hirtenregenpfeifer	106		
Plover, Long-toed/*witvlerkkiewiet* Langzehenkiebitz	122		
Plover, Mongolian/*Mongoolse strandkiewiet* Mongolenregenpfeifer	106		
Plover, Ringed/*ringnekstrandkiewiet* Sandregenpfeifer	106		
Plover, Sand/*grootstrandkiewiet* Wüstenregenpfeifer	106		
Plover, Spur-winged/*spoorvlerkkiewiet* Spornkiebitz	450		
Plover, Three-banded/*driebandstrandkiewiet* Dreibandregenpfeifer	106		
Plover, Wattled/*lelkiewiet* Senegalkiebitz	122		
Plover, White-crowned/*witkopkiewiet* Langspornkiebitz	122		
Plover, White-fronted/*vaalstrandkiewiet* Weißstirnregenpfeifer	108		
Pochard, Southern/*bruineend* Rotaugenente	90		
Pratincole, Black-winged/*swartvlerksprinkaanvoël* Schwarzflügelige Brachschwalbe	128		
Pratincole, Red-winged/*rooivlerksprinkaanvoël* Brachschwalbe	128		
Pratincole, Rock/*withalssprinkaanvoël* Weißnackenbrachschwalbe	128		
Prinia, Black-chested/*swartbandlangstertjie* Brustbandprinie	358		
Prinia, Karoo/*Karoolangstertjie* Fleckenprinie	358		
Prinia, Saffron/*gevlekte langstertjie* Fleckenprinie	358		
Prinia, Spotted *see* Saffron Prinia	358		
Prinia, Tawny-flanked/*bruinsylangstertjie* Rahmbrustprinie	358		
Prion, Antarctic/*Antarktiese walvisvoël* Taubensturmvogel	40		
Prion, Broad-billed/*breëbekwalvisvoël* Entensturmvogel	40		
Prion, Fairy/*swartstertwalvisvoël* Feensturmvogel	40		
Prion, Fulmar/*fulmarwalvisvoël* Feensturmvogel	40		
Prion, Medium-billed *see* Salvin's Prion	40		
Prion, Salvin's/*Salvinse walvisvoël* Kleiner Entensturmvogel	40		
Prion, Slender-billed/*dunbekwalvisvoël* Dünnschnabelsturmvogel	40		
Puffback/*sneeubal* Schneeballwürger	372		
Pytilia, Golden-backed/*geelrugmelba* Wiener Astrild	420		
Quail, Blue/*bloukwartel* Afrikanische Zwerg- (Adonson-)wachtel	140		
Quail, Common/*Afrikaanse kwartel* Wachtel	140		
Quail, Harlequin/*bontkwartel* Harlekinwachtel	140		
Quelea, Cardinal/*kardinaalkwelea* Kardinalweber	402		
Quelea, Red-billed/*rooibekkwelea* Blutschnabelweber	404		

Species	Page	Place	Date
Sandgrouse, Namaqua/*kelkiewyn* Namaflughuhn	194		
Sandgrouse, Yellow-throated/*geelkeelsandpatrys* Gelbkehlflughuhn	194		
Sandpiper, Baird's/*Bairdse strandloper* Bairds Strandläufer	116		
Sandpiper, Broad-billed/*breëbekstrandloper* Sumpfläufer	110		
Sandpiper, Buff-breasted/*taanborsstrandloper* Grasläufer	116		
Sandpiper, Common/*gewone ruiter* Flußuferläufer	112		
Sandpiper, Curlew/*krombekstrandloper* Sichelstrandläufer	112		
Sandpiper, Green/*witgatruiter* Waldwasserläufer	112		
Sandpiper, Marsh/*moerasruiter* Teichwasserläufer	108		
Sandpiper, Pectoral/*geelpootstrandloper* Graubruststrandläufer	114		
Sandpiper, Terek/*Terekruiter* Terekwasserläufer	114		
Sandpiper, White-rumped/*witrugstrandloper* Weißbürzel-Strandläufer	116		
Sandpiper, Wood/*bosruiter* Bruchwasserläufer	112		
Secretarybird/*sekretarisvoël* Sekretär	150		
Seedcracker, Nyasa/*rooistertsaadvretertjie* Kleiner Purpurastrild	420		
Shearwater, Audubon's/*swartkroonpylstormvoël* Audubonsturmtaucher	44		
Shearwater, Cory's/*geelbekpylstormvoël* Gelbschnabel-Sturmtaucher	42		
Shearwater, Flesh-footed/*bruinpylstormvoël* Blaßfuß-Sturmtaucher	44		
Shearwater, Great/*grootpylstormvoël* Großer Sturmtaucher	42		
Shearwater, Little/*kleinpylstormvoël* Kleiner Sturmtaucher	44		
Shearwater, Manx/*swartbekpylstormvoël* Schwarzschnabel-Sturmtaucher	42		
Shearwater, Sooty/*malbaatjie* Dunkler Sturmtaucher	44		
Shearwater, Wedge-tailed/*keilstertpylstormvoël* Keilschwanzsturmtaucher	44		
Sheathbill, Lesser/*kleinpeddie*	24		
Sheathbill, Snowy/*Amerikaanse peddie* Weißgesicht-Scheidenschnabel	444		
Shelduck, South African/*kopereend* Graukopfrostgans (-kasarka)	88		
Shikra *see* Little Banded Goshawk	176		
Shoveller, Cape/*Kaapse slopeend* Kaplöffelente	92		
Shoveller, Northern/*Europese slopeend* Löffelente	92		
Shrike, Bush, Black-fronted/*swartoogboslaksman* Schwarzstirn-Buschwürger	378		
Shrike, Bush, Gorgeous/*konkoit* Vierfarbenwürger	378		
Shrike, Bush, Grey-headed/*spookvoël* Graukopfwürger	380		
Shrike, Bush, Olive/*olyfboslaksman* Olivwürger	378		
Shrike, Bush, Orange-breasted/*oranjeborsboslaksman* Orangewürger (Orangebrustwürger)	378		

	Place	Date
Starling, Glossy, Black-bellied/*swartpensglansspreeu* Schwarzbauchglanzstar 386		
Starling, Glossy, Blue-eared, Greater/*groot-blouoorglansspreeu* Grünschwanzglanzstar 386		
Starling, Glossy, Blue-eared, Lesser/*klein-blouoorglansspreeu* Messingglanzstar 386		
Starling, Glossy, Burchell's/*grootglansspreeu* Riesenglanzstar (Glanzelster) 384		
Starling, Glossy, Cape/*kleinglansspreeu* Rotschulterglanzstar 386		
Starling, Glossy, Long-tailed/*langstertglansspreeu* Meves-Glanzstar 384		
Starling, Glossy, Sharp-tailed/*spitsstertglansspreeu* Keilschwanzglanzstar 386		
Starling, Pale-winged/*bleekvlerkspreeu* Bergstar 382		
Starling, Pied/*witgatspreeu* Zweifarbenstar 382		
Starling, Plum-coloured/*witborsspreeu* Amethystglanzstar 384		
Starling, Red-winged/*rooivlerkspreeu* Rotschwingenstar 382		
Starling, Wattled/*lelspreeu* Lappenstar 382		
Stilt, Black-winged/*rooipootelsie* Stelzenläufer 126		
Stint, Little/*kleinstrandloper* Zwergstrandläufer 110		
Stint, Long-toed/*langtoonstrandloper* Langzehen-Strandläufer 116		
Stint, Red-necked/*rooinekstrandloper* Rotkehl-Strandläufer 110		
Stint, Temminck's/*Temminckse strandloper* Temminckstrandläufer 116		
Stonechat/*gewone bontrokkie* Schwarzkehlchen 324		
Stork, Abdim's/*kleinswartooievaar* Abdimsstorch 78		
Stork, Black/*grootswartooievaar* Schwarzstorch 78		
Stork, Marabou/*maraboe* Marabu 76		
Stork, Open-billed/*oopbekooievaar* Klaffschnabel 80		
Stork, Saddle-billed/*saalbekooievaar* Sattelstorch 76		
Stork, White/*witooievaar* Weißstorch 78		
Stork, Woolly-necked/*wolnekooievaar* Wollhalsstorch 80		
Stork, Yellow-billed/*nimmersat* Nimmersatt 80		
Sugarbird, Cape/*Kaapse suikervoël* Kap-Honigfresser 388		
Sugarbird, Gurney's/*rooiborssuikervoël* Gurneys Honigfresser 388		
Sunbird, Black/*swartsuikerbekkie* Amethystglanzköpfchen 396		
Sunbird, Blue-throated/*bloukeelsuikerbekkie* Blaukehlnektarvogel 400		
Sunbird, Bronze/*bronssuikerbekkie* Bronzenektarvogel 390		
Sunbird, Collared/*kortbeksuikerbekkie* Wald-(Stahl-)nektarvogel 394		
Sunbird, Coppery/*kopersuikerbekkie* Kupfernektarvogel 390		
Sunbird, Double-collared, Greater/*grootrooibandsuikerbekkie* Großer Halsbandnektarvogel 392		

	Place	Date
Sunbird, Double-collared, Lesser/*kleinrooibandsuikerbekkie* Halsbandnektarvogel 392		
Sunbird, Double-collared, Miombo/*miombo-rooibandsuikerbekkie* Miombonektarvogel 392		
Sunbird, Dusky/*Namakwasuikerbekkie* Rußnektarvogel 400		
Sunbird, Grey/*gryssuikerbekkie* Graunektarvogel 400		
Sunbird, Malachite/*jangroentjie* Malachitnektarvogel 390		
Sunbird, Marico/*Maricosuikerbekkie* Bindennektarvogel 398		
Sunbird, Neergaard's/*bloukruissuikerbekkie* Neergaards Nektarvogel 392		
Sunbird, Olive/*olyfsuikerbekkie* Olivnektarvogel 400		
Sunbird, Orange-breasted/*oranjeborssuikerbekkie* Goldbrustnektarvogel 400		
Sunbird, Purple-banded/*purperbandsuikerbekkie* Kleiner Bindennektarvogel 398		
Sunbird, Scarlet-chested/*rooikeelsuikerbekkie* Rotbrustnektarvogel 396		
Sunbird, Shelley's/*swartpenssuikerbekkie* Shelleys Nektarvogel 392		
Sunbird, Violet-backed/*blousuikerbekkie* Violettmantel-Nektarvogel 398		
Sunbird, White-bellied/*witpenssuikerbekkie* Weißbauchnektarvogel 394		
Sunbird, Yellow-bellied/*geelpenssuikerbekkie* Gelbbauchnektarvogel 394		
Swallow, Angola/*Angolaswael* Angolaschwalbe 450		
Swallow, Blue/*blouswael* Stahlschwalbe 230		
Swallow, European/*Europese swael* Rauchschwalbe 232		
Swallow, Grey-rumped/*gryskruisswael* Graubürzelschwalbe 232		
Swallow, Mosque/*moskeeswael* Senegalschwalbe 228		
Swallow, Pearl-breasted/*pêrelborsswael* Perlbrustschwalbe 232		
Swallow, Red-breasted/*rooiborsswael* Rotbauchschwalbe 228		
Swallow, Red-rumped/*rooinekswael* Rötelschwalbe 230		
Swallow, Saw-wing, Black/*swartsaagvlerkswael* Sundevalls Sägeflügelschwalbe 234		
Swallow, Saw-wing, Eastern/*tropiese saagvlerkswael* Reichenows Sägeflügelschwalbe 234		
Swallow, Saw-wing, White-headed/*witkopsaagvlerkswael* Weißkopf-Sägeflügelschwalbe 450		
Swallow, South African Cliff/*familieswael* Klippenschwalbe 230		
Swallow, Striped, Greater/*grootstreepswael* Streifenschwalbe 228		
Swallow, Striped, Lesser/*kleinstreepswael* Kleine Streifenschwalbe 228		
Swallow, White-throated/*witkeelswael* Weißkehlschwalbe 230		
Swallow, Wire-tailed/*draadstertswael* Rotkappenschwalbe 232		
Swee, East African/*tropiese swie* Grünastrild 428		
Swift, Alpine/*witpenswindswael* Alpensegler 240		
Swift, Black/*swartwindswael* Kapsegler 242		

Species	Page	Place	Date
Swift, Bradfield's/*muiskleurwindswael* Damarasegler	240		
Swift, Eurasian/*Europese windswael* Mauersegler	242		
Swift, European *see* Eurasian Swift	242		
Swift, Horus/*horuswindswael* Horussegler	240		
Swift, Little/*kleinwindswael* Haussegler	240		
Swift, Mottled/*bontwindswael* Schuppensegler	242		
Swift, Pallid/*bruinwindswael* Fahlsegler	242		
Swift, Palm/*palmwindswael* Palmensegler	240		
Swift, Scarce/*skaarswindswael* Maussegler	242		
Swift, White-rumped/*witkruiswindswael* Weißbürzelsegler (Kaffernsegler)	240		
Tchagra, Black-crowned/*swartkroontjagra* Senegaltschagra	376		
Tchagra, Marsh/*vleitjagra* Sumpftschagra	376		
Tchagra, Southern/*grysborstjagra* Kaptschagra	376		
Tchagra, Three-streaked/*rooivlerktjagra* Damaratschagra	376		
Teal, Cape/*teeleend* Kapente	92		
Teal, Hottentot/*gevlekte eend* Hottentottenente	90		
Teal, Red-billed/*rooibekeend* Rotschnabelente	90		
Tern, Antarctic/*grysborssterretjie* Gabelschwanzseeschwalbe	58		
Tern, Arctic/*Arktiese sterretjie* Küstenseeschwalbe	58		
Tern, Black/*swartsterretjie* Trauerseeschwalbe	60		
Tern, Black-naped/*swartkroonsterretjie* Schwarznackenseeschwalbe	56		
Tern, Bridled/*brilsterretjie* Zügelseeschwalbe	60		
Tern, Caspian/*reusesterretjie* Raubseeschwalbe	54		
Tern, Common/*gewone sterretjie* Flußseeschwalbe	58		
Tern, Crested, Lesser/*kuifkopsterretjie* Rüppellsche Seeschwalbe	56		
Tern, Damara/*Damarasterretjie* Damaraseeschwalbe	58		
Tern, Gull-billed/*oostelike sterretjie* Lachseeschwalbe	56		
Tern, Kerguelen/*Kerguelensterretjie*	24		
Tern, Little/*kleinsterretjie* Zwergseeschwalbe	56		
Tern, Roseate/*rooiborssterretjie* Rosenseeschwalbe	58		
Tern, Royal/*koningsterretjie* Königsseeschwalbe	54		
Tern, Sandwich/*grootsterretjie* Brandseeschwalbe	56		
Tern, Sooty/*roetsterretjie* Rußseeschwalbe	60		
Tern, Swift/*geelbeksterretjie* Eilseeschwalbe	56		

		Place	Date
Tern, Whiskered/*witbaardsterretjie* Weißbartseeschwalbe	60		
Tern, White-cheeked/*witwangsterretjie* Weißwangenseeschwalbe	58		
Tern, White-winged/*witvlerksterretjie* Weißflügelseeschwalbe	60		
Thrush, Groundscraper/*gevlekte lyster* Akaziendrossel	312		
Thrush, Kurrichane/*rooibeklyster* Rotschnabeldrossel	312		
Thrush, Olive/*olyflyster* Kap- (Oliv-)drossel	312		
Thrush, Orange/*oranjelyster* Gurneys Grunddrossel	312		
Thrush, Palm, Collared/*palmmôrelyster* Morgenrötel	330		
Thrush, Palm, Rufous-tailed/*rooistertmôrelyster* Graubruströtel	330		
Thrush, Rock, Cape/*Kaapse kliplyster* Klippenrötel	314		
Thrush, Rock, Miombo/*Angolakliplyster* Großes Waldrötel (Angola-/Miomborötel)	314		
Thrush, Rock, Sentinel/*langtoonkliplyster* Langzehenrötel	314		
Thrush, Rock, Short-toed/*korttoonkliplyster* Kurzzehenrötel	314		
Thrush, Spotted/*Natallyster* Fleckengrunddrossel	312		
Thrush, Tristan/*Tristanlyster*	26		
Tit, Black, Carp's/*Ovamboswartmees* Rüppellmeise	308		
Tit, Black, Southern/*gewone swartmees* Mohrenmeise	308		
Tit, Grey/*Acaciagrysmees* Aschenmeise	308		
Tit, Grey, Northern/*miombogrysmees* Miombomeise	308		
Tit, Grey, Southern/*piet-tjou-tjougrysmees* Kapmeise	308		
Tit, Penduline, Cape/*Kaapse kapokvoël* Kapbeutelmeise	344		
Tit, Penduline, Grey/*gryskapokvoël* Weißstirnbeutelmeise	344		
Tit, Rufous-bellied/*swartkopmees* Rotbauchmeise	308		
Titbabbler/*bosveldtjeriktik* Meisensänger	342		
Titbabbler, Layard's/*grystjeriktik* Layards Meisensänger	342		
Trogon, Narina/*bosloerie* Narina-Trogon	204		
Tropicbird, Red-billed/*rooibekpylstert* Rotschnabel-Tropikvogel	48		
Tropicbird, Red-tailed/*rooipylstert* Rotschwanz-Tropikvogel	48		
Tropicbird, White-tailed/*witpylstert* Weißschwanz-Tropikvogel	48		
Turnstone, Ruddy/*steenloper* Steinwälzer	114		
Twinspot, Green/*groenkolpensie* Grüner Tropfenastrild	424		
Twinspot, Pink-throated/*rooskeelkolpensie* Perlastrild	424		
Twinspot, Red-throated/*rooikeelkolpensie* Rotkehl Tropfenastrild	424		
Vulture, Bearded/*baardaasvoël* Bartgeier	152		

Species	Page	Place	Date
Warbler, Reed, European/*Hermanse rietsanger* Teichrohrsänger	336		
Warbler, Reed, Great/*grootrietsanger* Drosselrohrsänger	338		
Warbler, River/*sprinkaansanger* Schlagschwirl	334		
Warbler, Rufous-eared/*rooioorlangstertjie* Rotbackensänger	360		
Warbler, Sedge, African/*Kaapse vleisanger* Sumpfbuschsänger	336		
Warbler, Sedge, European/*Europese vleisanger* Schilfrohrsänger	336		
Warbler, Swamp, Greater/*rooibruinrietsanger* Papyrusrohrsänger	338		
Warbler, Victorin's/*rooiborsruigtesanger* Rostbrustbuschsänger	334		
Warbler, Willow/*hofsanger* Fitis	332		
Warbler, Yellow/*geelsanger* Schnäpperrohrsänger	338		
Warbler, Yellow-throated/*geelkeelsanger* Rotkopflaubsänger	344		
Waxbill, Black-cheeked/*swartwangsysie* Elfenastrild	426		
Waxbill, Blue/*gewone blousysie* Angola Schmetterlingsfink	426	Vic Falls	6/01
Waxbill, Cinderella/*swartoogsysie* Cinderella-Schönbürzel	428		
Waxbill, Common/*rooibeksysie* Wellenastrild	426		
Waxbill, Grey/*gryssysie* Schwarzschwanzschönbürzel	428		
Waxbill, Orange-breasted/*rooiassie* Goldbrüstchen	426		
Waxbill, Swee/*suidelike swie* Gelbbauchastrild	428		
Waxbill, Violet-eared/*koningblousysie* Granatastrild (Blaubäckchen)	426		
Weaver, Brown-throated/*bruinkeelwewer* Braunkehlweber	410		
Weaver, Cape/*Kaapse wewer* Kapweber	408		
Weaver, Chestnut/*bruinwewer* Rotbrauner Weber	408		
Weaver, Forest/*bosmusikant* Waldweber	408		
Weaver, Golden/*goudwewer* Großer Goldweber	410		
Weaver, Masked/*swartkeelgeelvink* Maskenweber	412		
Weaver, Masked, Lesser/*kleingeelvink* Cabanisweber	412		
Weaver, Olive-headed/*olyfkopwewer* Olivenkopfweber	408		
Weaver, Red-billed Buffalo/*buffelwewer* Büffelweber	404		
Weaver, Red-headed/*rooikopwewer* Scharlachweber	412		
Weaver, Scaly *see* Scaly-feathered Finch	406		
Weaver, Sociable/*versamelvoël* Siedelweber	406		
Weaver, Spectacled/*brilwewer* Brillenweber	410		
Weaver, Spotted-backed/*bontrugwewer* Textor	412		
Weaver, Thick-billed/*dikbekwewer* Weißstirnweber	410		

	Place	Date
Woodpecker, Olive/*gryskopspeg* Goldrückenspecht 266		
Woodpecker, Speckle-throated/*Tanzaniese speg* Schriftschwanzspecht 270		
Wryneck, Red-throated/*draaihals* Braunkehl-Wendehals 270		
Yellowlegs, Greater/*grootgeelpootruiter* Großer Gelbschenkel 446		
Yellowlegs, Lesser/*kleingeelpootruiter* Gelbschenkel 116		

Popular bird names in general use

American Sheathbill	Snowy Sheathbill
Anhinga	Darter
Banded Harrier Hawk	Gymnogene
Blackcap Tchagra	Marsh Tchagra
Black-throated Wattle-eye	Wattle-eyed Flycatcher
Black-winged Bishop	Fire-crowned Bishop
Blue Jay	Erroneous name for Lilac-breasted Roller
Bosunbird	Any tropicbird
Bronze-naped Pigeon	Delegorgue's Pigeon
Butcherbird	Fiscal Shrike
Cape Bishop	Yellow-rumped Widow
Cape Dikkop	Spotted Dikkop
Cape Hen	White-chinned Petrel
Cape Pigeon	Pintado Petrel
Cape Rook	Black Crow
Cape Thrush	Olive Thrush
Cloud Scraper	Fan-tailed, Cloud, Ayres' or Pale-winged Cisticola (any small cisticola with high territorial display flight)
Collared Pratincole	Red-winged Pratincole
Comic tern	Either a Common or Arctic Tern in non-breeding plumage
Crimson-breasted Shrike	Crimson-breasted Boubou
Denham's Bustard	Stanley's Bustard
Duiker	Any cormorant
Flop	Long-tailed Widow
Fret	Bronze Mannikin
Fruit Pigeon	Green Pigeon
Gadfly Petrel	Any petrel of the genus *Pterodroma* or *Bulweria*
Glossy Starling	Cape Glossy Starling
Go-away Bird	Grey Lourie
Great Sand Plover	Sand Plover
Greater Crested Tern	Swift Tern
Green-spotted Dove	Emerald-spotted Dove
Griffon	Any vulture of the genus *Gyps*
Gurney's Thrush	Orange Thrush
Honeysucker	Any sunbird
Hottentot Button Quail	Black-rumped Button Quail
Indigobird	Any widow finch
Jacky Hangman or Hanger	Fiscal Shrike
Jeager	Any skua
Kaffervink	Any widowbird
Kakelaar	Red-billed Wood Hoopoe
Kiewietjie	Crowned Plover
King of Six	Pin-tailed Whydah
Konkoit	Gorgeous Bush Shrike
Lady Ross's Tauraco	Ross's Lourie
LBJ	A general name for any small, brownish bird
Lesser Sand Plover	Mongolian Plover
Lesser Swamp Warbler	Cape Reed Warbler
Lily-trotter	African Jacana
Little Grebe	Dabchick
Little Rush Warbler	African Sedge Warbler
Long-legged Korhaan	Black-bellied Korhaan
Magpie Shrike	Long-tailed Shrike
Malgas	Any gannet
Mollymawk	Any albatross with black upperwings and mantle
Mossie	Any sparrow
Mother Cary's Chicken	Any storm petrel
Mountain Buzzard	Forest Buzzard
Mouse-coloured Flycatcher	Pallid Flycatcher
Muttonbird	Any shearwater
Namaqua Prinia	Namaqua Warbler
Natal Thrush	Spotted Thrush
Nellie	Giant Petrel
Nicholson's Pipit	Long-billed Pipit
Peach Canary	Black-throated Canary
Piet-my-vrou	Red-chested Cuckoo
Rail Heron	Dwarf Bittern
Rainbird	Burchell's, White-browed or Senegal Coucal
Reeve	Female Ruff

Richard's Pipit	Grassveld Pipit
Ring Dove	Cape or Red-eyed Turtle Dove
Roberts's Prinia	Brier Warbler
Rufous-tailed Morning Warbler	Rufous-tailed Palm Thrush
Rough-wing Swallow	Saw-wing Swallow
Rufous Reed Warbler	Greater Swamp Warbler
Sakabula	Any long-tailed widow
Sea swallow	Any tern
Short-toed Lark	Red-capped Lark
Singing Bush Lark	Melodious Lark
Snakebird	Darter
Spotted Sandgrouse	Burchell's Sandgrouse
Spreeu	Any starling
Sugarbird	Erroneous name for any sunbird, correctly refers to the family Promeropidae
Thick Knees	Spotted Dikkop
Tickbird	Erroneous name for Cattle Egret
Tinkerbird	Any tinker barbet
Tinktinkie	A general name for a small, brownish bird, especially a cisticola
Toppie	Black-eyed or Cape Bulbul
Violet-backed Starling	Plum-coloured Starling
Vlei Lourie	Burchell's Coucal
White-collared Pratincole	Rock Pratincole
Willie Wagtail	Cape Wagtail
Willie	Sombre Bulbul
Wood Ibis	Yellow-billed Stork
Yellow Finch	Any yellow weaver
Yellow Weaver	Masked or Lesser Masked Weaver

BIRDLIFE SOUTH AFRICA

For details of membership contact your nearest branch:

Cape Bird Club: PO Box 5022, Cape Town 8000
Eastern Cape Wild Bird Society: PO Box 27454, Port Elizabeth 6057
Free State Bird Club: PO Box 6614, Bloemfontein 9300
Lowveld Bird Club: PO Box 2600, White River 1240
Natal Bird Club: PO Box 1218, Durban 4000
Natal Midlands Bird Club: PO Box 2772, Pietermaritzburg 3200
Pretoria Bird Club: PO Box 12563, Hatfield 0028
Rand Barbets Bird Club: PO Box 130355, Bryanston 2021
Sandton Bird Club: PO Box 650890, Benmore 2010
Wesvaal Bird Club: PO Box 2413, Potchefstroom 2520
Witwatersrand Bird Club: PO Box 72091, Parkview, Johannesburg 2122

or

BIRDLIFE SOUTH AFRICA
P O Box 515, Randburg 2125
Tel: (011) 789-1122
Fax: (011) 789-5188
e-mail: info@birdlife.org.za
www.birdlife.org.za